D0723356

The J. Hillis Miller Reader

Edited by

JULIAN WOLFREYS

Stanford University Press
Stanford, California   2005

Stanford University Press
Stanford, California

Editorial arrangement and Introduction © Julian Wolfreys, 2005.
Responses © the individual authors, 2005.

Originating publisher: Edinburgh University Press Ltd

A CIP record for this book is available from the Library of Congress

ISBN 0-8047-5055-6 (hardback)
ISBN 0-8047-5056-4 (paperback)

Typeset in Bembo
by Hewer Text Ltd, Edinburgh, and
printed and bound in Great Britain by
The Cromwell Press, Trowbridge

Contents

To Jacques Derrida,
Friend to so many . . .

Preface
J. Hillis Miller and Julian Wolfreys

Tell you my author
I knew his hand
Susan Howe

The J. Hillis Miller Reader gathers edited essays from fifty years of a remarkable career. From 1955 to the present, as many facets of J. Hillis Miller's critical interests as it is possible to represent in one volume are offered here: essays on Victorian literature; on modernism and twentieth-century British, North American and European writers; on philosophers, poets, and novelists; on ethics, poetics, politics, and aesthetics, on the disruption within writing that is the performative speech act, and on the demands of the act of criticism and what Miller calls good reading. There is, there can be, no introduction to such a diverse and heterogeneous body of work that is justified, so it is enough to say read J. Hillis Miller, but first understand what Miller means by reading before you attempt to read him.

The choice of pieces for the reader was by no means easy, and a balance, doubtless precarious, has been sought between providing a comprehensive view (one among many others) and offering the reader of this volume a detailed sense of the subtleties of Miller's thought and the close, careful scrutiny that he gives to the texts of others, whether Kant or Kafka, Derrida or de Man, the university today or the work of trope in linguistic and literary structures. In most cases, the essays have been edited from their original length, in order to be able to include twenty-two chapters. At the same time, responses have been included, commissioned from a number of leading critical voices, in order that the reader might find illuminated the profound, wide-reaching effect of Miller's reading and writing in so many ways and in so many areas, in what we call literary studies, the humanities, literary theory, the university. This effect is without parallel, and has both touched and called so many of us, who read, who write, and who teach, not merely as a profession, but from a sense of calling and in response to that calling issued from every page, in the turn of every phrase, and across the years.

Where essays have been edited, I have sought to maintain the contours of an argument, even though, inevitably, details have been sacrificed. On several, though not all, occasions, I have supplied a brief footnote to indicate in paraphrase the focus of the excised material; though doubtless there can be no justification for such a procedure, I have offered paraphrase where the elided passage can be read as offering a significant transformation of the argument rather than functioning in a purely illustrative manner of an argument in which it is embedded. (However, I would, in any case, urge the reader to locate the original versions in every case; even supposing my paraphrase to be more or less in keeping with what has been removed, it is in the very nature of language that, in my effort at fidelity, I will have betrayed the other to which I am responding.) This occurs usually when a paragraph or more than a paragraph has been deleted. Because the motion of Miller's analyses is so densely enfolded at every point, in every line, it has often been the case that I have removed only a line or two, often merely a phrase. Where this has happened, no ellipsis has been included so that the page not look untidy and the eye distracted. As a rule of thumb, an ellipsis is included only when three or more lines of text have been removed. The ellipsis fills the place of the missing lines within paragraphs. When a paragraph or more has been cut, then the ellipsis appears in square brackets in the place of the missing paragraphs.

Julian Wolfreys
April 2004

It is a great honor to have a J. Hillis Miller Reader, especially one gathered and edited by so distinguished a scholar, critic, and theorist, my friend Julian Wolfreys. Except for one or two suggestions I made, the selections in this reader have all been made by Julian Wolfreys. I have found it extremely interesting to see the implicit portrait of myself generated by the choices made in this reader. As I say in the interview that completes this volume, my interest in literature over the years has been primarily focused not on the generation of theoretical paradigms but on the act of reading specific works and attempting to account for their singularity, peculiarity, or strangeness. That remains, even now, what most interests me about literature.

J. Hillis Miller
April 2004

Acknowledgements

Any book incurs a number of debts of gratitude, none of which are ever truly repaid. I would like, however, to acknowledge at least my debts and my inability to honor those.

Doris Bremm's editorial assistance went above and beyond any reasonable expectation, and she was a model of celerity and attention to detail.

I would like to thank Thomas Docherty, Jean-Michel Rabaté, and Henry Sussman for their suggestions regarding the project, its shape, scope, and possibilities.

Thank you also, to each of the contributors – Derek Attridge, Mieke Bal, Juliet Flower MacCannell, Pamela Gilbert, James Kincaid, Arkady Plotnitsky, Tom Albrecht, Nicholas Royle, Tom Cohen, Rachel Bowlby, Megan Becker-Leckrone, John Leavey, and Barbara Cohen – who have, each in their own singular fashion, introduced and 'invented' J. Hillis Miller much more appropriately than I would ever have been able.

At Edinburgh University Press and Stanford University Press, I would like to thank, respectively, Jackie Jones and Norris Pope.

Finally, the person to whom I owe that which is the most impossible debt is J. Hillis Miller. His support for this project has been unqualified, and this is only the smallest measure of his generosity, his patience, and his encouragement, from all of which I have benefited in ways beyond the possibility of words to express. The limit of words is perhaps the most appropriate indication, the indirect trace of that which is without limits in Hillis. Even though it may not be apparent in my own work, there can be no doubt that I feel I have learnt much from his writing, his acts of good reading, and I have gained immeasurably from his friendship.

I gratefully acknowledge permission to reprint Derek Attridge's essay, 'Miller's Tale,' which has been published in a different form in *Journal for Cultural Research*, 8:1 (April 2004): 115–21.

Chapters 3, 5, 6, 8, 9, 12, 13, 14, 17, 18, 19, 20, 21 J. Hillis Miller. The Editor and Publishers would like to thank J. Hillis Miller for permission to reprint this material, and gratefully acknowledge the following for permission to reprint the material in this volume: Chapter 1, 'The Critic as Host', by J. Hillis Miller, from

Introduction: responsibilities of J
or, aphorism's other
Julian Wolfreys

Our main business in the coming years will be to teach people to read – to read all the signs, including those of the newspaper and of the mass culture surrounding us, as well as those signs inscribed on the pages of the old canonical books. In the coming years an informed citizenry in our democracy will be one that can read and think clearly about all the signs that at every moment bombard us through eye and ear. Figuring out the best ways to ensure the existence of this citizenry will be a great responsibility but also an exhilarating opportunity.

J. Hillis Miller

My selfbeing, my consciousness and feeling of myself, that taste of myself, of *I* and *me* above and in all things . . . is incommunicable by any means to another man.

Gerard Manley Hopkins

and what if, resonance in this other language still leading you astray, I liked words *in order to be-tray* (to treat, triturate, trice, in-trigue, trace, track).

Jacques Derrida

✍ You start with the event of reading, which is neither illusory nor arbitrary, but is something that occurs when you read, and you go on from there.

You can learn quite a lot about reading from J. Hillis Miller. Among so many things into which you might gain insight, if you attend with patience, diligence, care, and responsibility to only one or two threads drawn from the vast weave of fifty years of publication, of reading and writing, of response and responsibility, is that, in the act of reading, there is always the singular encounter with the other, with others. Or, perhaps more accurately, there is always the chance of that encounter. One can never be certain, ahead of the event. As Miller's lucid, eloquent, engaged prose makes plain, if otherness is missed in what to all intents and purposes looks like an act of reading, no amount of elucidation after the fact will ever explain it to the reader who has missed that momentary passage. This is true whether one is speaking of a novel, of poetry, of 'deconstruction,' so-called, or criticism in general. Each of J. Hillis Miller's texts are comprised of so many singular encounters with or experiences of the other in their acts of reading, but they also comprise, equally, so many articulations of the other, of innumerable others, for which each and every good reader of Miller is responsible. Yet nothing can be more certain than the fact that, in the effort to be responsible, the reader of Miller may, to speak in litotes, have got it wrong.

This is not to impugn the intelligence of the reader; it is though to suggest a certain deceptive and therefore disabling force that underlies the apparent calm of any text by Miller. Perhaps this can best be explained, in the manner of an introduction, through illustration as analogy. Were I to seek the appropriate metaphor or image for Miller's texts, it might be that of a still, shimmering surface of a lake. The tranquillity and composure of that lake remains for the most part undisturbed, offering to those who contemplate it an apparently unruffled play of light and shade, mediating rather than merely reflecting the composition, the structure and form of whatever is glimpsed on or across the surface. Something emerges without warning, however, from the darkness that the surface calm belies, disturbing irrevocably the illusion of placidity and liquid unity. Or, to continue this metaphor, there is that other effect. You are out on the lake, moving across its surface or remaining relatively still at one point (the point is illusory; you only imagine a point in the otherwise unbroken surface). An agitation begins, imperceptibly at first, gradually building to a swell of irresistible proportions, in the midst of which you find yourself thrown around, disoriented, capsized even. To bear witness to this is – hopefully – to become an approximation of the reader Miller desires, to be translated by one's having been touched by the aphoristic pulsing of the other (and this *is* aphoristic, as I shall show). However, supposing one (believes that one) has read aright, even to the smallest degree, this is not to say that reading has come to an end or that the responsibilities entailed in any act of reading have been fulfilled. In recognition of these, I hope my reader will allow me what might appear a brief, perhaps somewhat elliptical reflection. These will take place through a consideration of what the title of this introduction – *responsibilities of J or, aphorism's other* – puts to work as a means of opening oneself to a dialogue with the others in the text of J. Hillis Miller.

A question arises from the title. I can imagine it: why speak of aphorism at all, let alone address it through this strange phrase, *aphorism's other*, which appears to have imposed itself on me, when writing an introduction to a collection of essays by J. Hillis Miller? What is it about aphorism that appears an appropriate figure for addressing Miller's criticism? The second part of my title involves a double genitive. On the one hand, it announces that other, that singular example without example and experience of the other, which we call aphorism. In this sense, the aphorism, every aphorism, is other because it arrives, it *calls* (I will return to the call, below); but the supposed or hypothetical place from which it arrives, the guise, persona, in which it comes to call, that which we might want to identify as the 'style,' 'tone', or 'voice' of the aphorism's origin (supposing there were such a thing) in order to give location or identity – these are unlocatable, unidentifiable, perhaps even radically undecidable. Every aphorism, it might be said, is different from every other aphorism; every aphorism is wholly aphoristic and therefore singular. It departs from an unlocatable horizon, being other than that, even as it gestures towards the illusion of a horizon, which its inscription inscribes rather than merely describes. Aphorism is thus always already double, and in being double, opens abyssally. It doubles itself for, arriving under cover as elliptical or occluded knowledge, aphorism 'does' something with words, it is performative within and other than its glacial, yet provocative placidity.

On the other hand – there will, by the way, be more than two hands; and these will have been multiple, diverse, heterogeneous –, there is remarked the other that the performative we call aphorism gives place to, that which, in the place of the aphorism, takes place. This place, however, is strange, a place, if it is one, concerning the very ground of which one cannot have knowledge, let alone be certain concerning its existence. The aphorism is thus a singular manifestation of the *atopical*, and 'this strange locus is another name for the ground of things . . . *something other* to any activity of mapping' (Miller 1995, 7; emphasis added); neither absolutely groundless nor firmly grounded, but *something other*, a ghostly passage or, for want of a better phrase, a 'tropological entity' (Hamacher 2004, 178). What might be considered the appropriate ground then? From which location do I begin, if mapping is impossible? What is the ground on which I build or embellish, in order to produce either structure or counterpoint? And what is it in Miller's work as so many singular attestations of the other that calls to me, to us, to so many readers over the years? What is it that comes, returns, continues to come unceasingly, and promises to come? What is it within the act of reading in Miller's writing that, as the encounter with an other, signals the promise of the to-come? What is that arrives, often with the lightning flash of aphorism or insight, or what Jacques Derrida has called, with regard to aphorism, the *trait d'esprit* (1989, 123)[1] in a manner that, in being just this compulsive call, is both command and gift?

✍ Each form of repetition calls up the other, by an incalculable compulsion.

It is not for me to answer these questions definitively, at least not here, not with the patience they demand, in the space and time of an introduction. Indeed, this inaugural proliferation of queries[2] and interrogations will have been only the first in a series. Such inquiries are part of a structure that informs and disorders the place of the introduction; the ineluctable, iterable arrival and gesture of adumbrated semaphore in the guise of questioning signals the absence of any justifiable introduction, which absence comes to be filled by the endless demands for (and of) response. What might be suggested in the face of such activity, and as one response to the other's impossible demand, is that the *trait d'esprit* is, it can be imagined, the trace of the wholly other, that which is not only singularly atopical, involved with an undermining of topographical certainties, but also temporally disruptive from within any supposed present, and having to do with the unbearable time of reading: 'in one way or another the wholly other is ghostly and takes the form of an apparitional promise. The *tout autre* is something already there, a revenant from some immemorial past, and yet heralds or invokes or demands a future . . .' (Miller 2001a, 2) What comes to me from some unmappable locus as the aphoristic remains remains to be answered. In the face of the other's arrival or return, if such a thing takes place, there is no proper time. It may be that the *trait d'esprit* which countersigns aphorism gives rise to 'a consciousness of temporality,' and this consciousness gives us to reflect that there is no proper time, even though we remain attentive to its possibility.[3]

Let me, therefore, as a bare acknowledgement to the glimpse of what I will call provisionally J. Hillis Miller's *trait d'esprit*,[4] single out three words as traces of that which arrives aphoristically, and which calls. These traces set up a particular resonance, and find themselves insistently reiterated in the work of the subject of this volume, while also, already, circulating in this introduction: *other, performative, topos*. As with the question or, more properly, the admission of a difficulty in the face of the demand of the question, it is not my intention here to analyse these words, to give them much space beyond their having been remarked. That they arrive and return insistently must be enough. But what is remarked here is the recognition that I am called upon by the other. I am addressed by each and every other, in each of these figures, and find myself repeating these figures, a few among many. In repeating, I am obliged to respond, if not to them (for, once again, there is not the space to do them justice), then to what is announced in their arrival. The other(s) arrive(s)[5] to call me by some 'incalculable compulsion' (Miller 1982, 9) to responsibility. Whatever this responsibility is, it is without doubt more than one, even if, at the same time, it is less than this. It is, furthermore, endless, 'forever impossible' (Miller 2001b, 214). Such inescapable impossibility may well reside in the fact that, even in the sketched gesture that is reiteration, there is still to be read a 'search for grounds', which nonetheless 'finds its groundless ground, its *abgründlichen Grund* . . . That thought was there waiting for me (but where is "there"?)' (Miller 1985, 433). Where is *there* indeed, when there is no there *there* as such. I am not sure therefore that I can even begin to identify correctly where precisely the responsibilities lie. So, for now at least, it is enough – and also never enough – to locate responsibility in a graphic mark, a sign or trace, as encrypted as it is readable, which, on the one hand, offers a name for responsibility, while, on the other hand, offers to stand in for the impossibility of either of limiting responsibility or speaking of a limited responsibility. In this, to hazard a performative gesture (and to risk also the chance that the performativity of the inscription will have been missed), it has to be said that '[t]he moment is, so to speak, its own image. It is haunted by itself as if it were its own uncanny *revenant*. The moment is single, and yet it is imperceptibly doubled within itself' (Miller 1985, 432). Another way to remark what takes place here is to suggest that the critical repetition involves an action whereby the 'second [act of writing] is . . . [the] "counterpart" [or counterpoint of the first writing] in a strange relation whereby the second is the subversive ghost of the first, always already present within it as a possibility which hollows it out' (Miller 1982, 9). Acknowledging this, and thereby conceding that which is also, already, admitted – and therefore doubled, divided –, I will turn back to my title even as it returns to me, in order to move on, by taking responsibility for *responsibilities of J*.

What exactly is being articulated in this phrase, *responsibilities of J*? Who, or what, is *J*, supposing even that this single letter stands (in) for an identity, that it is the sign of an identity, however encrypted or however transparent? What are *J's responsibilities*? Does this mark, this *trait*, sign or assign responsibility, does it stand in for the promise to be responsible? Or does it in some manner dictate or demand responsibility? Certainly, this merest figure, at once both readable and enigmatic, invites as much as it resists reading, and '[t]he reader can never know any of these secrets' (Miller 2003, 30). As I have just rewritten the phrase, wherein there appears the *turn* of phrase (and which thereby turns the screw on translation's responsibilities), *responsibilities of J* is translated, not quite symmetrically, as *J's responsibilities*. So, another double genitive appears, one that is, of course, already in place in the former version through the articulating fulcrum of *of*. On the one hand, as you can no doubt read, this expression, which perhaps aspires if not to being an aphorism then at least to some axiomatic status, announces itself in different hands; to the ghost of one hand in the hand of the other we might say, in which there is that visible-invisible touch of discontinuous relation without relation, 'a complex tissue of repetitions and of repetitions within repetitions, or of repetitions linked in chain fashion to other repetitions' (Miller 1982, 2–3). The phrase with all its possible repetitions announces therefore the responsibilities that are *J's* – who, or whatever, *J* might be. On the other hand, it also gives us to understand those undeniably inscrutable responsibilities traced in the very letter *J*, which, in seeking to read them, I will have *be-trayed*. And this, it might be said, is the double bind of writing and reading, the double bind that finds itself re-marked, traced, and treated in *J*, from one *J* to another, between the *J*s. Or, in another language, recalling another *J's* remark,[6] in the *jeu* between that *J* (hear this in French) which is an other and the *Je*, which, touched by an other, that other *J* that, aphoristically calls on and in me/*Je*, inscribing me every time I write and read and every time *I* is written with that gift which is also the call to responsibility. (Just because you can no longer hear the other *J*, that *J* which is the multiply other in and of the Greco-Latinate-English *I*, as you can in a certain fashion in French, does not mean to say that *I* is not haunted by *J* for all that.) For, if the question of *J* is indeed one of the *trait d'esprit*, it is also one of the *jeu d'esprit*, wherein '[t]he act of trying to understand repeats the enigmatic, unknowable event that is the object of anxious interrogation'. An act such as this is 'a way of doing things with words rather than the constative expression of achieved knowledge' (2001b, 214). The critic's act of response in its responsibility seeks to personify, if only through the inscription of *I* and at least in part, as a means of economizing on the abyss (Derrida 1987b, 37)[7] of *J*, as it were, as a way of opening the encryption that is *J*. And, to re-cite in other words the assertion just cited in a gesture of haunting citation concerning performativity, such personifications or 'prosopopoeias . . . are potent speech acts. They have to do with doing rather than knowing' (Miller 1995, 8).

✍ Yet another mode of character reading is displayed, with an explicit reference to hieroglyphs.

Yet where am *I*? Where is *I* to be found, on what ground, as you open this volume to this page? Or, to put this another way, what are the grounds for saying, writing I, except that call of *J*? Do *I* accept the call of *J*, and how do I know it is meant for me? *I am* is, in Miller's own words, 'suspended always on a vibrating tightrope over the abyss of its own impossibility' (1998, 157). Moreover, in having to acknowledge seriously, in the face of my subject's writing, the 'impossibility of criticism in the sense of [the impossibility of criticism's ability to effect] a demonstrable decoding of meaning' (1998, 157), I have to take responsibility and admit that I am faced with an impossible task. But the very fact that it is impossible in no way alleviates the responsibility I have in attempting this commission. The assignment (admittedly self-imposed or at least seemingly so) is multiple. It is not simply one. It is not only, merely, the question of writing, or attempting to write this introduction, though, it has to be said, there can be no doubt that this, in itself, is great enough. No. The task involves a series of obligations and responsibilities, all having to do in some manner, more or less directly, with the fraught question of reading, along with a number of related matters. And all of this is written – take it as read – in the letter *J*. *J* calls and thus names me, *J* taking place every time I respond, I is written. To call, as we know, is to name, and naming, as *J* has occasion to remind us, 'is an initiatory performative utterance, a "calling."' I find myself called, but '[t]hat calling is based or *grounded* on nothing but the call from the other that impassions me' (emphasis added), hence the very nature of what you are reading, because '[t]his call I respond to in another calling, for example in writing an essay or a book'; or, indeed, what is called an introduction. This act of writing, which is also one of reading, in turn 'constitutes another demand for response. It is a demand for which I, as the one who has first responded, must, and hereby do, take responsibility' (2001b, 215). Yet this can always be missed. Even my attempted maneuver, my opening strategy if you will, of announcing my obligation, itself intended to be both a response to and a reading of what is at stake in the writings of J. Hillis Miller, runs a risk here: the chance of its being read (misread, not read at all), as being merely a formula, just a gambit and not the necessary admission of what takes place in a place such as an introduction when one is seeking, without totalizing summary or synthesis, to respond to the other, to the wholly other and to every other.

Yet, despite – indeed, because of – this, in being faced; *no*, more accurately, in attempting (impossible scenario) to come face to face with every other and the wholly other that is the text, and signed in the name, of *J. Hillis Miller*, what can be said in the face of every other and the wholly other, which is every text, every inscription of a critical singularity? It has to be admitted that the 'wholly other otherness of the other' arrives 'as a perturbation . . . in language' (2001b, 269), and, moreover, 'individual works, even those by the same author, must be read as a unique testimony to otherness' (2001a, 3). Thus I read as a short-hand encryption for this perturbation, this singularity and otherness, the figure or siglum J^8 that appears to say everything and all the rest; and all the while this being, I would like to imagine, a figure for a particular, singular revenance, an arrival that is a return, as well as a disclosure that nonetheless retains its secrets. What is it about *J* that authorizes me to say this? What takes place in the passage between *I* and the other, between *J* and *I*, between *J* and *J*? It is of course the case that 'argument cannot pass from here to there [or from there to here, even though, you will recall, we cannot say where *there* is or, for that matter, if it is possible to speak, ontologically as it were, of a *there is*, an *il y a*, which is not, first and foremost, the deconstruction of ontology, through the spectral passage of the other haunting the phrase *es gibt*] without the help of . . . quotations. This happens according to the law of each text's dependence on other texts' (1998, 161). Every time I write – and all the more so, whenever I write *I – J* haunts and disables, even as it makes possible, authorizes, and demands my response. Thus *I* – as the column of a haunted house, an architecture in ruins. Reading, responding to, accepting the *responsibilities of J* discloses the necessary 'substitution of language for consciousness, figural for literal, interliterary for mimetic generation of meaning' (2000a, xviii), so that consciousness – that false consciousness at least to which I ascribe through certain assumptions concerning *I* – 'may be a function of language, a fictive appearance generated by language, rather than something language describes or reflects' (2000a, xv). So reading gets going by opening itself to that somewhat 'mazy' motion always already underway, and it is this motion that is caught for me in the singularity, and in the singular call, of the letter *J*. *J* gives; it gives (to) *I*; *J* lends *I* a hand, as it were, even though this hand has long since become invisible, a ghost writer causing *I* to appear, in part at least by disappearing under the sign of the phallic illusion of the Greco-Latinate-English column, and recognizable as that phantasm named by Miller 'the "consciousness of the author"' (2000a, xv). Thus *I* is doubled and divided from within. At most, 'a sequence of disconnected evanescent persons' (as Miller has it in the essay on Thomas Hardy in the section on nineteenth-century literature), the surety of *I*'s ground is disrupted from within itself, from within the 'iteslf', 'haunted by itself,' to recall and be disturbed by an earlier citation, 'as if it were its own uncanny *revenant.*' In responding to the aphoristic call of *J*, then, I am taking responsibility for this revenant that divides me from and within myself, that divides *I* and, in doing so, exceeds it.

Such an act of reading is only ever a 'hypothetical fiction' of course, an act that seeks to take possession of the other and so to 'build its structure of interpretation on that heterogeneous base, partly its own and partly' the other's (2000a, xv). As images in fiction are understood to give the self material form, so might citations be said to function, at least analogously, in criticism, but in a manner that doubles: on the one hand, *I* cites for the purpose of taking partial possession of the work; on the other citation haunts the self as so many aphoristic resonances of the other, an identity in ruins. The responsibility of reading and writing chances everything in its attempt to map the unmappable 'domain where the reality *beyond* or *within* may be momentarily apprehended' (Miller 1958, 329). But how will I know whether my reading gets anything right? 'The consequences,' Miller reminds us, 'of taking seriously the otherness and singularity of the other are by no means trivial' (2001a, 268). So, *once again*, what can one do except to write, to respond, in obligation to the singularity of *le tout autre*, a phrase which, though not Miller's, has taken possession of his writing on a number of occasions in recent years as the gift of the other, as he admits in 'A Profession of Faith'? What can one do, indeed, except write and read, hoping all the while to figure oneself as the merest approximation of the good reader that Miller desires, even though 'the consequences may be intolerable, the intolerable as such, something that no one can bear to see face to face' (2001a, 268)? Faced with *le tout autre*, one might answer the previous question in French by saying: *Bon qu'a ça*. It's all I can do, it's all I'm fit for, what else can I do?

✍ These are ungrounded doublings which arise from differential interrelations among elements which are all on the same plane.

Perhaps at the most fundamental level, the problem of the task of producing a *J. Hillis Miller Reader* (or, by extension, any reader) must begin with unreasonable, and doubtless violent, acts of selection. How to select from so huge a body of works a collection of essays, the assumption behind which selection being that these are, in some manner, representative of my subject, or, more strictly, if not of him exactly, then, at the very least, of his published works? Given all that Miller has written concerning acts of good reading, of ethical commitment, and the responsibility of the good reader to bear witness faithfully and with necessary patience, diligence, and rigor to the singularity of a given text or subject, how is it even thinkable – I will not presume to say possible – that one could ignore such singularity at each and every turn of the page, and pretend to produce a volume (even at the generous length of some 400 pages or 200,000 words provided by my publishers) that is in some manner representative, and which, by implication, elides all difference between each singular text in some double act of violence and betrayal in the name – or, indeed, semblance – of resemblance? Doubtless, it is patently clear by now that this is, according to my reading of Miller's ethical standards, just not possible, to stress the point once more. More than that, it is unthinkable, it is 'the intolerable as such,' as you have just read. Yet, I have to try; it is necessary that I do, this is unavoidable. So, to reiterate, this is the irresolvable impossibility with which I find myself faced, with which I have repeatedly found myself faced, moving within and across – and as a result of – a series of doublings which it would be a mistake to regard as merely rhetorical – with which I have come face to face, again and again, in the process of arriving at the point at which you are now reading.

Inescapably, I am faced with the fact that I have committed already, in so many ways, the unthinkable; there is no justification for acts of cutting, editing, or putting in place what might be called translations of the essays that you find herein, in what is called a *reader*. To paraphrase Miller on the reading of Thomas Hardy's poetry (Ch. 7), it would be hard to imagine a book that gathered together all of Miller's publications, while all attempts to reduce that work to a manageable size by selection will be unsuccessful. Writing an introduction only focuses the problem ever more acutely. Conventionally, one might proceed by producing a précis of each chapter, as though each of the chapters were somehow insufficient and the editor was, in some manner a more careful reader than any other, including the original author. So what exactly does one do in this place? Does one provide those individual sketches – let's not say readings – of each essay chosen? Or does one seek to provide a survey of the whole 'and organize it thematically . . . by noting similarities and generalizing on that basis'? This is Miller, again on Hardy. As he concludes, both procedures are unsatisfactory. Yet despite such difficulties – and they are as real as they are insurmountable if we are faithful to Miller's own thought – another procedure might be to pull at one of those strands already alluded to from among what Miller calls, with reference to Gerard Manley Hopkins' writing (see Ch. 6), this 'heterogeneous collection of documents,' as was suggested at the beginning of the introduction. In doing this, another question arises, one in which I find myself anticipated by Miller, yet again: might it be possible, or at least permissible, to proceed (quoting the essay on Hopkins, again) to take, as a limited objective the attempt to 'reveal [a] pervasive imaginative structure,' a structure that stands provisionally, as the approximation of the 'substance of thought,' for the 'very substance' of Miller himself? This last question should not be misread. The very last thing I wish to imply here is that what the reader will find (and, doubtless, there will be some 'readers' who will find what they want despite all the precautions I take) is an image or representation of J. Hillis Miller. Rather, let us say that *J. Hillis Miller* becomes the signature for which I take responsibility. This involves and invokes not some essence or presence, not some essence within presence; instead a structure of what Miller has called 'related minds' or, to use the phrase in the essay on Hardy, 'a sequence of disconnected evanescent persons' comes to be embodied by the words, and this pattern 'exists as a temporal structure' (1968, 29), the temporality of which is that improper time of reading and citation, 'according to the law [let us remind ourselves of this] of each text's dependence on other texts' (1998, 161) – therefore, not *J. Hillis Miller*, but *J* as the mark of relation without relation.

One manner in which the structures and patterns come to appear is through the work of the question. The iteration of questions allows for a certain structure of responsibilities to be constructed, however precarious this might be. Clearly, asking myself such questions, I recognize that I am faced not simply with editorial responsibilities, even though these are daunting, as I have already indicated. More significantly, more urgently and more immediately, I am forced to acknowledge, if not address, once again, those ethical responsibilities in response to the other, to so many others, in pursuing various acts of reading that, at every stage of a project such as this, from selection, to editing and organizing, to writing an introduction, is *always already* a matter of translation, wherein one is always caught in the snares of both fidelity and betrayal. I must, and do, take responsibility, here, and every time a reader opens this reader, for the choices I have made, the words I have excised, the outlines of readings that I have in effect shaped, and those I have invited to contribute to this volume.

Now, it may well be that the ' "consciousness of the author" ' or, in this case, the editor is an 'illusion or phantasm generated by the words on the page' and that 'this phantasm may have nothing necessarily to do with the actual mind of the person who put those words down on paper' (2000a, xv); *I* may well be, moreover, 'a linguistic function in a process that occurs of its own accord and is authorized by no independent witnessing "I," ' but this does not let me off the hook from ethical responsibility, as Miller makes unequivocally clear. Of *I*, he remarks:

> It is not an 'I' who speaks or writes . . . It is an impersonal possibility of thinking, speaking, and writing, there already within language, that takes possession of the 'I' to think itself, speak itself, or write itself, and thereby enter into history . . . The ethics of reading, 'I' have once more discovered, is this impersonal response to an implacable and impersonal demand . . . At the same time, however, by an equally inescapable necessity . . . that 'I' must in its own proper name take responsibility for the results of its acts of reading, writing, or speaking. (1991, 126–7)

So, this is where we begin; it is the point to which we must return even as it returns insistently to us. The ethical moment 'in the act of reading . . . if there is one . . . is a response to something, responsible for it, responsive to it, respectful of it' (Miller 1987, 4). Of course, otherness and the ethical response is not simply a matter of literature, even if it is *always* a question of reading and even though the strangeness of literature gives place to the other's most enigmatic and aphoristic apparitions. Here is Miller in the final essay of this collection, 'Literary

Study in the Transnational University': 'the radical otherness of another culture or its artifacts, . . . the radical otherness of another person, possibly the result of a different gender or sexual orientation, but possibly also an otherness in other persons, of whatever gender or sexual orientation, [there is a] relay for an absolute otherness that speaks through them and makes demands on me for ethical commitment, decision, and action.' This demand is where this *reader* begins, with the commitment to raising the question of such ethical issues and acts, and acting upon them. And this will be found to be the case in every essay in this collection, from the earliest, 'The Creation of the Self in Gerard Manley Hopkins' (Ch. 6), the first version of which was published in 1955, to one of the most recent (as I write), 'A Profession of Faith' (2004, Ch. 17). Indeed, the very questions by which I find myself suspended are announced, as I have already shown in passing, in those citations and paraphrases from the essays on Hopkins and Hardy where one encounters from the outset the inescapable awareness that reading is difficult, impossible, always fallible, *but necessary*. Even as both these (and every other one of the) essays announces in its own singular fashion the inescapable responsibilities of reading, of responding to the other, to each and every other, so too does this responsibility come to be received in, through, and from, each and every singular analysis by J. Hillis Miller, whether one refers immediately to the essays gathered here, or to any, and every, other essay, review, or book that is signed by him, that bears his name, and which arrives to call us to bear witness. These are the *responsibilities of J*. Beginning to recognize this, the good reader might desire the appropriate aphorism, as the call, the act of naming, the demand and gift of the other. To risk a location after all that has been said about the impossibility of locating the ground, I would like to suggest that such an aphorism is given here in this collection in Chapter 20, 'The Imperative to Teach,' which opens appropriately with the question of the call: 'who or what (today) calls on us to teach?' The aphorism is not Miller's but arrives from Franz Kafka:

✍ There is a goal but no way. What we call the way is only wandering.

Notes

1. The phrase, which remains in French in the translation, as if it were some ghostly remainder, some aphoristic other returning, arriving, retreating, and yet all the while remaining to be read, comes from the following remark: 'Under the brilliant singularity of Valéry's aphorism or *trait d'esprit*, one recognizes those profound invariables, those repetitions which their author opposes, precisely, as nature to spirit.' Appropriately – more or less – at least with regard to that which I wish to situate or, at least, acknowledge as that which arrives from the texts of J. Hillis

Miller, Derrida is writing of the certain movement of the *revenant*, the ghost, and spirit of a particular identity (in his case, European), as this comes to be articulated through a series of articles by Paul Valéry. In the same footnote as I have just quoted, Derrida has occasion to cite Valéry's definition of spirit as 'very simply a *power of transformation* . . .' It is precisely this power of transformation that arrives in Miller's writing, often with an aphoristic force, with the force of an undeniable command and an excessive gift for which there can never be any adequate acknowledgement or recompense, except the acknowledgement of response and the responsibility which that entails, as I go on to discuss in the introduction. Miller's writing, it has to be said, is always marked by this ghostly trace, this *trait d'esprit*. The other arrives, aphoristically, from within the calm, considered, measured and rigorous place of exegesis (which is there to be read in every essay in this collection, at the turn of every page), as that which is given us to read.

2. While there is no collective noun for questions, at least not one of which I am aware, I like to imagine that *proliferation* might serve as that noun, thus: a proliferation of questions.

3. I am paraphrasing, and partially citing, Diane Elam's essay, 'Waiting in the Wings' (2003, 46). Elam is addressing waiting and its relation to temporality in Henry James's *The Wings of the Dove* and Maurice Blanchot's *The Writing of the Disaster*. Waiting *qua* reading and the question of the impossible temporality of reading is most acutely brought to consciousness through the problematic of aphorism.

4. Another double genitive, and one which, properly addressed, would exceed the capabilities of both this introduction and its author.

5. How exactly is one to read or receive these opening words of the sentence? The other arrives? The others arrive? Both and yet neither, solely? There is a troubling and, doubtless, to some, irritating undecidability in the graphic suspension of readily identifiable meaning or access to that meaning. Writing betrays voice here, the *gramme* announcing, without voice, an otherness that is irreducible to any mastery.

6. The comments, and the play between *Je, Jeu,* and *J* are Jacques Derrida's, from his essay ' "Justices" ' (2005). The collection, drawn from a conference, ' "J": Around the work of J. Hillis Miller' (18–19 April 2003), celebrating the work of Miller (from which comes James R. Kincaid's essay to be found in the present volume), also has several articles which consider the letter *J*, and what is written in this letter, with regard to the text of J. Hillis Miller.

7. Jacques Derrida: 'economize on the abyss: not only to save oneself from falling into the bottomless depths by weaving and folding back the cloth to infinity, textual art of the reprise, multiplication of patches within patches, but also establish the laws of reappropriation, formalize the rules which constrain the logic of the abyss and which shuttle between the economic *and* the aneconomic . . . the abyssal operation which can only work toward the *relève and* that in it which regularly reproduces collapse' (1987b, 37). See also Derrida on that which gets reading underway: 'every thesis (bands erect) a prosthesis; what affords reading affords reading by citations (necessarily truncated, clippings, repetitions, suctions, sections, suspensions, selections, stitchings, scarrings, grafts . . .). Thus does a text become infatuated. With another' (1986a, 168). Both citations, which might best be described as two *J* columns, are readable as hypothetical commentaries on what takes place in this introduction.

8. Which among the histories or genealogies of *J* might be told? *J* might be said to be the singular manifestation of James Joyce's (*JJ's*) assertion that 'Jewgreek is greekjew' (1986, 411). First appearing or first returning in the middle ages as the excess of *I* and difference that had previously haunted *I*, *J*'s parentage, so to speak, is Greek and Semitic, a vowel and consonant, *iota* and *yod*. *Yod*, itself having descended from the Phoenician symbol for hand (a wholly fanciful and hopefully inventive hypothesis, hypothesis as prosthesis at this juncture: it is *as if* by some prescience the Phoenician 'hand'/*J* were, prosthetically, proleptically, and in disembodied uncanniness, gesturing towards Miller's commentary on 'the hand of Mr. Mould' from *Martin Chuzzlewit* (Miller 1958, 100); see James R. Kincaid's 'Hillis among the Victorians' in this reader), and which is taken to be a precursor to *J*, is, in Hebrew, the letter used in prefixes for future conjugations and tenses. There is thus no proper time for *J*; arriving from a past which has never been present, as an encrypted, hieratic figure, it figures its own non-presence through its gesture towards an arrival to come that writing remarks. The work of the prefix in Hebrew thus uncannily prosthetizes in a performative manner the letter's *revenance* as the other within, and in excess of, the hegemonic Greco–Latinate–English *I*. *I* is therefore never simply *I*. Indeed, *I* is an other / *Je est un autre*. In French, *J* is already the graphic return of the other in *Je*, the play of *différance* by which *I/Je* comes to speak, but never as itself.

The Ethics of Reading

The Critic as Host

'*Je meurs où je m'attache*', Mr. Holt said with a polite grin. 'The ivy says so in the picture, and clings to the oak like a fond parasite as it is'.
    'Parricide, sir!' cries Mrs. Tusher.

Henry Esmond, Bk. I, ch. 3

I

At one point in 'Rationality and Imagination in Cultural History' M. H. Abrams cites Wayne Booth's assertion that the 'deconstructionist' reading of a given work 'is plainly and simply parasitical' on 'the obvious or univocal reading' (1976, 457–8). The latter is Abrams' phrase, the former Booth's. My citation of a citation is an example of a kind of chain which it will be part of my intention here to interrogate. What happens when a critical essay extracts a 'passage' and 'cites' it? Is this different from a citation, echo, or allusion within a poem? Is a citation an alien parasite within the body of the main text, or is the interpretive text the parasite which surrounds and strangles the citation which is its host? The host feeds the parasite and makes its life possible, but at the same time is killed by it, as criticism is often said to kill literature. Or can host and parasite live happily together, in the domicile of the same text, feeding each other or sharing the food?

Abrams, in any case, goes on to add 'a more radical reply.' If 'deconstructionist principles' are taken seriously, he says, 'any history which relies on written texts becomes an impossibility' (458). So be it. That's not much of an argument. A certain notion of history or of literary history, like a certain notion of determinable reading, might indeed be an impossibility, and if so, it might be better to know that. That something in the realm of interpretation is a demonstrable impossibility does not, however, prevent it from being 'done', as the abundance of histories, literary histories, and readings demonstrate. On the other hand, I should agree that the impossibility of reading should not be taken too lightly. It has consequences, for life and death, since it is incorporated in the bodies of individual human beings and in the body politic of our cultural life and death together.

'Parasitical' . . . no doubt describes well enough the way some people feel about the relation of a 'deconstructive' interpretation to 'the obvious or univocal reading.' The parasite is destroying the host. Is the 'obvious' reading, though, so 'obvious' or even so 'univocal'? May it not itself be the uncanny alien which is so close that it cannot be seen as strange, host in the sense of enemy rather than host in the sense of open-handed dispenser of hospitality? Is not the obvious reading perhaps equivocal rather than univocal, most equivocal in its intimate familiarity and in its ability to have got itself taken for granted as 'obvious' and single-voiced?

'Parasite' is one of those words which calls up its apparent opposite. It has no meaning without that counterpart. There is no parasite without its host. At the same time both word and counterword subdivide. Each reveals itself to be fissured already within itself, to be, like *Unheimlich, unheimlich*. Words in 'para,' like words in 'ana,' have this as an intrinsic property. 'Para' as a prefix in English (sometimes 'par') indicates alongside, near or beside, beyond, incorrectly, resembling or similar to, subsidiary to, isomeric or polymeric to. In borrowed Greek compounds 'para' indicates beside, to the side of, alongside, beyond, wrongfully, harmfully, unfavorably, and among. Words in 'para' form one branch of the tangled labyrinth of words using some form of the Indo-European root *per*. This root is the 'base of prepositions and preverbs with the basic meaning of "forward", "through", and a wide range of extended senses such as "in front of", "before", "early", "first", "chief", "toward", "against", "near", "at", "around".'[1]

If words in 'para' are one branch of the labyrinth of words in 'per', the branch is itself a miniature labyrinth. 'Para' is a double antithetical prefix signifying at once proximity and distance, similarity and difference, interiority and exteriority, something inside a domestic economy and at the same time outside it, something simultaneously this side of a boundary line, threshold, or margin, and also beyond it, equivalent in status and also secondary or subsidiary, submissive, as of guest to host, slave to master. A thing in 'para,' moreover, is not only simultaneously on both sides of the boundary line between inside and out. It is also the boundary itself, the screen which is a permeable membrane connecting inside and outside. It confuses them with one another, allowing the outside in, making the inside out, dividing them and joining them. It also forms an ambiguous transition between one and the other. Though a given word in 'para' may seem to choose univocally one of these possibilities, the other meanings are always there as a shimmering in the word which makes it refuse to stay still in a sentence. The word is like a slightly alien guest within the syntactical closure where all the words are family friends together. Words in 'para' include: parachute, paradigm, parasol, the French *paravent* (windscreen), and *parapluie* (umbrella), paragon, paradox, parapet, parataxis, parapraxis, parabasis, paraphrase, paragraph, paraph, paralysis, paranoia, paraphernalia, parallel, parallax, parameter, parable, paresthesia, paramnesia, paramorph, paramecium, Paraclete, paramedical, paralegal − and parasite.

'Parasite' comes from the Greek *parasitos*, 'beside the grain,' *para*, beside (in this case) plus *sitos*, grain, food. 'Sitology' is the science of foods, nutrition, and diet. A parasite was originally something positive, a fellow guest, someone sharing the food with you, there with you beside the grain. Later on, 'parasite' came to mean a professional dinner guest, someone expert at cadging invitations without ever giving dinners in return. From this developed the two main modern meanings in English, the biological and the social. A parasite is 'Any organism that grows, feeds, and is sheltered on or in a different organism while contributing nothing to the survival of its host'; or 'A person who habitually takes advantage of the generosity of others without making any useful return.' To call a kind of criticism 'parasitical' is, in either case, strong language.

A curious system of thought, or of language, or of social organization (in fact all three at once) is implicit in the word parasite. There is no parasite without a host. The host and the somewhat sinister or subversive parasite are fellow guests beside the food, sharing it. On the other hand, the host is himself the food, his substance consumed without recompense, as when one says, 'He is eating me out of house and home'. The host may then become host in another sense, not etymologically connected. The word 'host' is of course the name for the consecrated bread or wafer of the Eucharist, from Middle English *oste*, from Latin *hostia*, sacrifice, victim.

If the host is both eater and eaten, he also contains in himself the double antithetical relation of host and guest, guest in the bifold sense of friendly presence and alien invader. The words 'host' and 'guest' go back in fact to the same etymological root: *ghos-ti*, stranger, guest, host, properly 'someone with whom one has reciprocal duties of hospitality.' The modern English word 'host' in this alternative sense comes from the Middle English (*h*)*oste*, from Old French, host, guest, from Latin *hospes* (stem *hospit-*), guest, host, stranger. The 'pes' or 'pit' in the Latin words and in such modern English words as 'hospital' and 'hospitality' is from another root, *pot*, meaning 'master.' The compound or bifurcated root *ghos-pot* meant 'master of guests,' 'one who symbolizes the relationship of reciprocal hospitality', as in the Slavic *gospodi*, Lord, sir, master. 'Guest,' on the other hand, is from Middle English *gest*, from Old Norse *gestr*, from *ghos-ti*, the same root as for 'host.' A host is a guest, and a guest is a host. A host is a host. The relation of household master offering hospitality to a guest and the guest receiving it, of host and parasite in the original sense of 'fellow guest,' is inclosed within the word 'host' itself.

A host in the sense of a guest, moreover, is both a friendly visitor in the house and at the same time an alien presence who turns the home into a hotel, a neutral territory. Perhaps he or she is the first emissary of a host of enemies (from Latin *hostis* 'stranger, enemy'), the first foot in the door, followed by a swarm of hostile strangers, to be met only by our own host, as the Christian deity is the Lord God of Hosts. The uncanny antithetical relation exists not only between pairs of words in this system, host and parasite, host and guest, but within each word in itself. It reforms itself in each polar opposite when that opposite is separated out. This subverts or nullifies the apparently unequivocal relation of polarity which seems the conceptual scheme appropriate for thinking through the system. Each word in itself becomes divided by the strange logic of the 'para,' a membrane which divides inside from outside and yet joins them in a hymeneal bond, or which allows an osmotic mixing, making the stranger friend, the distant near, the *Unheimlich heimlich*, the unhomely homey, without, for all its closeness and similarity, ceasing to be strange, distant, and dissimilar.

One of the most frightening versions of the parasite as invading host is the virus. In this case, the parasite is an alien who has not simply the ability to invade a domestic enclosure, consume the food of the family, and kill the host, but the strange capacity, in doing all that, to turn the host into multitudinous pro-liferating replications of itself. The virus is at the uneasy border between life and death. It challenges that opposition, since, for example, it does not 'eat,' but only reproduces. It is as much a crystal or a component in a crystal as it is an organism. The genetic pattern of the virus is so coded that it can enter a host cell and violently reprogram all the genetic material in that cell, turning the cell into a little factory for manufacturing copies of itself, so destroying it.

Is this an allegory, and if so, of what? The use by modern geneticists of an 'analogy' (but what is the ontological status of this analogy?) between genetic reproduction and the social interchanges carried by language or other sign systems may justify a transfer back in the other direction. Is 'deconstructive criticism' like a virus which invades the host of an innocently metaphysical text, a text with an 'obvious or univocal meaning,' carried by a single referential grammar? Does such criticism ferociously reprogram the *gramme* of the host text to make it utter its own message, the 'uncanny,' the 'aporia,' 'la différance,' or what have you? Some people have said so. Could it, on the other hand, be the other way around? Could it be that metaphysics, the obvious or univocal meaning, is the parasitical virus which has for millennia been passed from generation to generation in Western culture in its languages and in the privileged texts of those languages? Does metaphysics enter the language-learning apparatus of each new baby born into that culture and shape the apparatus after its own patterns? The difference might be that this apparatus, unlike the host cell for a virus, does not have its own pre-existing inbuilt genetic code.

Is that so certain, however? Is the system of metaphysics 'natural' to man, as it is natural for a cuckoo to sing 'cuckoo' or for a bee to build its comb in hexagonal cells? If so, the parasitical virus would be a friendly presence carrying the same message already genetically programmed within its host. The message would predispose all European babies or perhaps all earth babies to read Plato and become Platonists, so that anything else would require some unimaginable mutation of the species man. Is the prison house of language an exterior constraint or is it part of the blood, bones, nerves, and brain of the prisoner?

Could that incessant murmuring voice that speaks always within me or constantly weaves the web of language there, even in my dreams, be an uncanny guest, a parasitical virus, and not a member of the family? How could one even ask that question, since it must be asked in words provided by the murmuring voice? Is it not that voice speaking here and now? Perhaps, after all, the analogy with viruses is 'only an analogy,' a 'figure of speech,' and need not be taken seriously.

What does this have to do with poems and with the reading of poems? It is meant as an 'example' of the deconstructive strategy of interpretation. The procedure is applied, in this case, not to the text of a poem but to the cited fragment of a critical essay containing within itself a citation from another essay, like a parasite within its host. The 'example' is a fragment like those miniscule bits of some substance which are put into a tiny test tube and explored by certain techniques of analytical chemistry. To get so far or so much out of a little piece of language, context after context widening out from these few phrases to include as their necessary milieux all the family of Indo-European languages, all the literature and conceptual thought within those languages, and all the permutations of our social structures of household economy, gift-giving and gift-receiving – this is an argument for the value of recognizing the equivocal richness of apparently obvious or univocal language, even of the language of criticism. Criticism is in this respect, if in no other, continuous with the language of literature. This equivocal richness, my discussion of 'parasite' implies, resides in part in the fact that there is no conceptual expression without figure, and no intertwining of concept and figure without an implied narrative, in this case the story of the alien guest in the home. Deconstruction is an investigation of what is implied by this inherence in one another of figure, concept, and narrative.

My example presents a model for the relation of critic to critic, for the incoherence within a single critic's language, for the asymmetrical relation of critical text to poem, for the incoherence within any single literary text, and for the skewed relation of a poem to its predecessors. To speak of the 'deconstructive' reading of a poem as 'parasitical' on the 'obvious or univocal reading' is to enter willynilly into the strange logic of the parasite, to make the univocal equivocal in spite of oneself, according to the law that language is not an instrument or tool in human hands, a submissive means of thinking. Language rather thinks man and woman and his or her 'world,' including poems, if he or she will allow it to do so.

The system of figurative thought (but what thought is not figurative?) inscribed within the word parasite and its associates, host and guest, invites us to recognize that the 'obvious or univocal reading' of a poem is not identical to the poem itself. Both readings, the 'univocal' one and the 'deconstructive' one, are fellow guests 'beside the grain,' host and guest, host and host, host and parasite, parasite and parasite. The relation is a triangle, not a polar opposition. There is always a third to whom the two are related, something before them or between them, which they divide, consume, or exchange, across which they meet. The relation in question is always in fact a chain. It is a strange sort of chain without beginning or end, a chain in which no commanding element (origin, goal, or underlying principle) may be identified. In such a chain there is always something earlier or something later to which any link on which one focuses refers and which keeps the series open. The relation between any two contiguous elements in this chain is a strange opposition which is of intimate kinship and at the same time of enmity. It cannot be encompassed by the ordinary logic of polar opposition. It is not open to dialectical synthesis. Each 'single element,' moreover, far from being unequivocally what it is, subdivides within itself to recapitulate the relation of parasite and host of which, on the larger scale, it appears to be one or the other pole. On the one hand, the 'obvious or univocal reading' always contains the 'deconstructive reading' as a parasite encrypted within itself as part of itself. On the other hand, the 'deconstructive' reading can by no means free itself from the metaphysical reading it means to contest. The poem in itself, then, is neither the host nor the parasite but the food they both need, host in another sense, the third element in this particular triangle. Both readings are at the same table together, bound by a strange relation of reciprocal obligation, of gift or food-giving and gift or food-receiving.

The poem, in my figure, is that ambiguous gift, food, host in the sense of victim, sacrifice. It is broken, divided, passed around, consumed by the critics canny and uncanny who are in that odd relation to one another of host and parasite. Any poem, however, is parasitical in its turn on earlier poems, or it contains earlier poems within itself as enclosed parasites, in another version of the perpetual reversal of parasite and host. If the poem is food and poison for the critics, it must in its turn have eaten. It must have been a cannibal consumer of earlier poems.

Take, for example, Shelley's *The Triumph of Life*. It is inhabited, as its critics have shown, by a long chain of parasitical presences – echoes, allusions, guests, ghosts of previous texts. These are present within the domicile of the poem in that curious phantasmal way, affirmed, negated, sublimated, twisted, straightened out, travestied, which Harold Bloom has begun to study and which it is one major task of literary interpretation today to investigate further and to define. The previous text is both the ground of the new one and something the new poem must annihilate by incorporating it, turning it into ghostly insubstantiality, so that the new poem may perform its possible-impossible task of becoming its own ground. The new poem both needs the old texts and must destroy them. It is both parasitical on them, feeding ungraciously on their substance, and at the same time it is the sinister host which unmans them by inviting them into its home, as the Green Knight invites Gawain. Each previous link in the chain, in its turn, played the same role, as host and parasite, in relation to its predecessors. From the Old to the New Testaments, from Ezekiel to

Revelation, to Dante, to Ariosto, to Spenser, to Milton, to Rousseau, to Wordsworth and Coleridge, the chain leads ultimately to *The Triumph of Life*. That poem, in its turn, or Shelley's work generally, is present within the work of Hardy or Yeats or Stevens and forms part of a sequence in the major texts of Romantic 'nihilism' including Nietzsche, Freud, Heidegger, and Blanchot. This perpetual re-expression of the relation of host and parasite forms itself again today in current criticism. It is present, for example, in the relation between 'univocal' and 'deconstructionist' readings of *The Triumph of Life*, between the reading of Meyer Abrams and that of Harold Bloom, or between Abrams' reading of Shelley and the one I am proposing here, or within the work of each one of these critics taken separately. The inexorable law which makes the 'alogical' relation of host and parasite re-form itself within each separate entity which had seemed, on the larger scale, to be one or the other, applies as much to critical essays as to the texts they treat. *The Triumph of Life* contains within itself, jostling irreconcilably with one another, both logocentric metaphysics and nihilism. It is no accident that critics have disagreed about it. The meaning of *The Triumph of Life* can never be reduced to any 'univocal' reading, neither the 'obvious' one nor a single-minded deconstructionist one, if there could be such a thing, which there cannot. The poem, like all texts, is 'unreadable', if by 'readable' one means a single, definitive interpretation. In fact, neither the 'obvious' reading not the 'deconstructionist' reading is 'univocal.' Each contains, necessarily, its enemy within itself, is itself both host and parasite. The deconstructionist reading contains the obvious one and vice versa. Nihilism is an inalienable alien presence within Occidental metaphysics, both in poems and in the criticism of poems.

II

[. . .] Nihilism is somehow inherent in the relation of parasite and host. Inherent also is the imagery of sickness and health. Health for the parasite, food and the right environment, may be illness, even mortal illness, for the host. On the other hand, there are innumerable cases, in the proliferation of life forms, where the presence of a parasite is absolutely necessary to the health of its host. [. . .]★ Nihilism is the latent ghost encrypted within any expression of a logocentric system, for example in Shelley's *The Triumph of Life*, or in any interpretation of such a text, for example in Meyer Abrams' reading of *The Triumph of Life* or in reversed form in Harold Bloom's reading. The two, logocentrism and nihilism, are related to one another in a way which is not antithesis and which may not be

---

★ The two passages elided address specific discussions of nihilism in Nietzsche's *The Will to Power*, and Heidegger's *The Question of Being*. [Ed.]

synthesized in any dialectical *Aufhebung*. Each defines and is hospitable to the other, host to it as parasite. Yet each is the mortal enemy of the other, invisible to the other, as its phantom unconscious, that is, as something of which it cannot by definition be aware.

If nihilism is the parasitical stranger within the house of metaphysics, 'nihilism,' as the name for the devaluation or reduction to nothingness of all values, is not the name nihilism has 'in itself'. It is the name given to it by metaphysics, as the term 'unconscious' is given by consciousness to that part of itself which it cannot face directly. In attempting to expel that other than itself contained within itself, logocentric metaphysics deconstitutes itself, according to a regular law which can be demonstrated in the self-subversion of all the great texts of Western metaphysics from Plato onward. Metaphysics contains its parasite within itself, as the 'unhealable' which it tries, unsuccessfully, to cure. It attempts to cover over the unhealable by annihilating the nothingness hidden within itself.

Is there any way to break this law, to turn the system around? Would it be possible to approach metaphysics from the stand-point of 'nihilism'? Could one make nihilism the host of which metaphysics is the alien guest, so giving new names to both? Nihilism would then not be nihilism but something else, something without a melodramatic aura, perhaps something so innocent-sounding as 'rhetoric,' or 'philology,' or 'the study of tropes,' or even 'the trivium.' Metaphysics might then be redefined, from the point of view of this trivium, as an inevitable rhetorical or tropological effect. It would not be a cause but a phantom generated within the house of language by the play of language. 'Deconstruction' is one current name for this reversal.

[. . .]*

Deconstruction does not provide an escape from nihilism, nor from meta-physics, nor from their uncanny inherence in one another. There is no escape. It does, however, move back and forth within this inherence. It makes the inherence oscillate in such a way that one enters a strange borderland, a frontier region which seems to give the widest glimpse into the other land ('beyond metaphysics'), though this land may not by any means be entered and does not in fact exist for Western man. By this form of interpretation, however, the border zone itself may be made sensible, as quattrocento painting makes the Tuscan air visible in its invisibility. The zone may be appropriated in the torsion of the mind's expropriation, its experience of an inability to comprehend logically. This procedure is an attempt to reach clarity in a region where clarity is not possible. In the failure of that attempt, however, something moves, a limit is encountered. This encounter may be compared to the uncanny experience of reaching a frontier where there is no visible barrier, as when Wordsworth found

---

* A 'history' of deconstruction is traced from the Greek Sophists to Derrida, via a return to *The Will to Power*, in order to demonstrate how deconstruction is not a nihilism. [Ed.]

he had crossed the Alps without knowing he was doing so. It is as if the 'prisonhouse of language' were like that universe finite but unbounded which some modern cosmologies posit. One may move everywhere freely within this enclosure without ever encountering a wall, and yet it is limited. It is a prison, a milieu without origin or edge. Such a place is therefore all frontier zone without either peaceful homeland, in one direction, land of hosts and domesticity, nor, in the other direction, any alien land of hostile strangers, 'beyond the line.'

The place we inhabit, wherever we are, is always this in-between zone, place of host and parasite, neither inside nor outside. It is a region of the *Unheimlich*, beyond any formalism, which reforms itself wherever we are, if we know where we are. This 'place' is where we are, in whatever text, in the most inclusive sense of that word, we happen to be living. This may be made to appear, however, only by an extreme interpretation of that text, going as far as one can with the terms the work provides. To this form of interpretation, which is interpretation as such, one name given at the moment is 'deconstruction.'

III

As an 'example' of the word 'parasite' functioning parasitically within the 'body' of work by one author, I turn now to an analysis of the word in Shelley.

The word 'parasite' does not appear in *The Triumph of Life*. That poem, however, is structured throughout around the parasitical relationship. *The Triumph of Life* may be defined as an exploration of various forms of the parasitical relation. The poem is governed by the imagery of light and shadow, or of light differentiated within itself. The poem is a series of personifications and scenes each of which gives a figurative 'shape' (Shelley's word) to a light which remains the 'same' in all its personifications. The figurative shape makes the light a shadow. Any reading of the poem must thread its way through repeated configurations of the polarity of light and shadow. It must also identify the relation of one scene to the next which replaces it as sunlight puts out the morning star, and the star again the sun . . . These repetitions make the poem a *mise en abîme* of reflections within reflections or a nest of Chinese boxes. This relation exists within the poem, for example, in the juxtaposition of the poet's vision and the prior vision which is narrated by Rousseau within the poet's vision. Rousseau's vision comes later in the linear sequence of the poem but earlier in 'chronological' time. It puts early late, metaleptically, as late's explanatory predecessor. The relation in question also exists in the encapsulation in the poem of echoes and references to a long chain of previous texts in which the emblematic chariot or other figures of the poem have appeared: Ezekiel, Revelation, Virgil, Dante, Spenser, Milton, Rousseau, Wordsworth. Shelley's poem in its turn is echoed by Hardy, by Yeats, and by many others.

This relation inside the poem between one part of it and another, or the relation of the poem to previous and later texts, is a version of the relation of parasite to host. It exemplifies the undecidable oscillation of that relation. It is impossible to decide which element is parasite, which host, which commands or encloses the other. It is impossible to decide whether the series should be thought of as a sequence of elements each external to the next or according to some model of enclosure like that of the Chinese boxes. When the latter model is applied it is impossible to decide which element of any pair is outside, which is inside. In short, the distinction between inside and outside cannot be held to across that strange membrane, wall at once and copulating hymen, which stands between host and parasite. Each element is both exterior to the adjacent one and at the same time encloses and is enclosed by it.

One of the most striking 'episodes' of *The Triumph of Life* is the scene of self-destructive erotic love. This scene matches a series of scenes elsewhere in Shelley's poetry in which the word 'parasite' is present. The scene shows sexual attraction as one of the most deadly forms of the triumph of life. The triumph of life is in fact the triumph of language. For Shelley this takes the form of the subjection of each man or woman to illusory figures projected by his or her desire. Each of these figures is made of another substitutive shape of light which fades as it is grasped. It fades because it exists only as a transitory metaphor of light. It is a momentary lightbearer. Venus, star of evening, as the poem says, is only another disguise of Lucifer, fallen star of the morning. Vesper becomes Hesper by a change of initial consonant, masculine H for feminine V.

When the infatuated lovers of *The Triumph of Life* rush together, they annihilate one another, like particle and antiparticle, or, in the metaphors Shelley uses, like two thunderclouds colliding in a narrow valley, or like a great wave crashing on the shore. This annihilation, nevertheless, is not complete, since the violent collision leaves always a trace, a remnant, foam on the shore. This is Aphrodite's foam, seed or sperm which starts the cycle all over again in Shelley's drama of endless repetition. The darkest feature of the triumph of life, for Shelley, is that it may not even be ended by death. Life, for him, though it is a living death, may not die. It regenerates itself interminably in ever-new figures of light:

> . . . in their dance round her who dims the Sun
> Maidens & youths fling their wild arms in air
> As their feet twinkle; they recede, and now
> Bending within each other's atmosphere
>
> Kindle invisibly; and as they glow
> Like moths by light attracted & repelled,
> Oft to new bright destruction come & go.

Till like two clouds into one vale impelled
That shake the mountains when their lightnings mingle
And die in rain, – the fiery band which held

Their natures, snaps . . . ere the shock cease to tingle
One falls and then another in the path
Senseless, nor is the desolation single,

Yet ere I can say *where* the chariot hath
Past over them; nor other trace I find
But as of foam after the Ocean's wrath
Is spent upon the desert shore.

(ll. 148–64)[2]

This magnificent passage is the culmination of a series of passages writing and rewriting the same materials in a chain of repetitions beginning with *Queen Mab*. In the earlier versions the word 'parasite' characteristically appears, like a discreet identifying mark woven into the texture of the verbal fabric. The word appears in *Queen Mab* and in the version of one episode of *Queen Mab* called *The Daemon of the World*. It appears then in *Alastor*, in *Laon and Cythna*, in *The Revolt of Islam*, in *Epipsychidion*, and in *The Sensitive Plant*, always with the same surrounding context of motifs and themes. These include narcissism and incest, the conflict of generations, struggles for political power, the motifs of the sun and the moon, the fountain, the brook, the caverned enclosure, ruined tower, or woodland dell, the dilapidation of man's constructions by nature, and the failure of the poetic quest.

[. . .]*

Shelley's poetry is the record of a perpetually renewed failure. It is a failure ever to get the right formula and so end the separate incomplete self, end love-making, end politics, and end poetry, all at once, in a performative apocalypse in which words will become the fire they have ignited and so vanish as words, in a universal light. The words, however, always remain, there on the page, as the unconsumed traces of each unsuccessful attempt to use words to end words. The attempt must therefore be repeated. The same scene, with the same elements in a slightly different arrangement, is written by Shelley over and over again from *Queen Mab* to *The Triumph of Life*, in a repetition ended only with his death. This repetition mimes the poet's failure ever to get it right and so end the necessity of trying once more with what remains.

The word 'parasite,' for Shelley, names the bridge, wall, or connecting membrane which at once makes this apocalyptic union possible, abolishing difference, and at the same time always remains as a barrier forbidding it. Like the thin line of Aphrodite's foam on the shore, this remnant starts the process all

---

* There follow sketched readings of the parasitic trope in *Queen Mab, Alastor, Laon and Cythna, The Revolt of Islam*, and *Epipsychidion*. [Ed.]

over again after the vanishing of the previous couple in their violent attempt to end the interminable chain. The parasite is, on the one hand, the barrier and marriage hymen between the horizontal elements which make some binary opposition. This opposition generates forms and generates also a narrative of their interaction. At the same time the parasite is the barrier and connecting screen between elements on different planes vertically, Earth and Heaven, this world and a spiritual one above it. The world above is the white radiance of eternity. This world's opposing pairs, male, for example, against female, both figure forth and hide that white fire.

Parasites for Shelley are always parasite *flowers*. They are vines which twine themselves around the trees of a forest to climb to light and air, or they grow on a ruined palace to cover its stone and make fragrant bowers there. Parasitical flowering vines feed on air and on what they can take from their hosts. Those hosts they join with their stems. Shelley's parasites flower abundantly, making a screen between sky and earth. This screen remains even in winter as a lattice of dried vines.

A final ambiguity of Shelley's version of the system of parasite and host is the impossibility of deciding whether the sister-beloved in these poems is on the same plane as the desiring poet or a transcendent spirit infinitely above him. She is both at once. She is a sister to whom the protagonist might make love, incestuously. At the same time she is an unattainable muse or mother who governs all, as the spirit eyes Alastor pursues are those of no earthly sister, or as the poet's love for Emily in *Epipsychidion* is also an attempt, like that of Prometheus, to steal heavenly fire, or as the scene of erotic love in *The Triumph of Life* is presided over by the devouring female goddess, riding in her triumph, Life, or as, in the first version of this pattern, the earthly Ianthe beloved by Henry is doubled by the female Daemon of the World who presides over their relation and who is present at the end of the poem as the star repeating the heroine's eyes. These star-like eyes are a constant symbol in Shelley of the unattainable transcendent power in its relation to the earthly signs of it, but at the same time they are no more than the beloved's eyes, and also, at the same time, the protagonist's own eyes reflected back to him.

IV

The motif of a relation between the generations in which one generation is related parasitically to another, with the full ambiguity of that relation, appears in *Epipsychidion* in its most complete form. This version makes clearest the relation of this theme to the system of parasite and host, to the theme in Shelley of a repetition generated always by what is left over after an earlier cataclysmic self-destruction, to the political theme which is always present in these passages, to the relation of man's works to nature, and to the dramatization of the power of poetry which is always one of Shelley's themes.

The ruined tower in the Sporades to which the poet will take his Emily in *Epipsychidion* is said, in one of the drafts of the preface, somewhat prosaically, to be 'a Saracenic castle which accident had preserved in some repair'. In the poem itself this tower is a strange structure which has grown naturally, almost like a flower or stone, saxifrage and saxiform. At the same time it is almost supernatural. It is a house for a god and a goddess, or at any rate for a semi-divine Ocean-King and his sister-spouse. The building brackets the human level. It is above and below that level at once:

> But the chief marvel of the wilderness
> Is a lone dwelling, built by whom or how
> None of the rustic island-people know:
> 'Tis not a tower of strength, though with its height
> It overtops the woods; but, for delight,
> Some wise and tender Ocean-King, ere crime
> Had been invented, in the world's young prime,
> Reared it, a wonder of that simple time,
> An envy of the isles, a pleasure-house
> Made sacred to his sister and his spouse.
> It scarce seems now a wreck of human art,
> But, as it were Titanic; in the heart
> Of Earth having assumed its form, then grown
> Out of the mountains, from the living stone,
> Lifting itself in caverns light and high:
> For all the antique and learned imagery
> Has been erased, and in the place of it
> The ivy and the wild-vine interknit
> The volumes of their many-twining stems;
> Parasite flowers illume with dewy gems
> The lampless halls, and when they fade, the sky
> Peeps through their winter-woof of tracery
> With moonlight patches, or star atoms keen,
> Or fragments of the day's intense serene; −
> Working mosaic on their Parian floors.
>
> (ll. 483–507)

An 'Ocean-King' is, possibly, a human king of this ocean isle and at the same time, possibly, a King of the Ocean, an Olympian or a Titan. In any case, this dwelling was built 'in the world's young prime.' It was built near the time of origin, when the opposites were confounded or nearly confounded and when incest was not a crime, as it was not for those Egyptian pharaohs who always mated with their sisters, only fit spouses for their earthly divinity. In the same way, in that young time, nature and culture were not opposed. The palace seems at once 'Titanic,' the work of a superhuman strength, and at the same time human, since it is, after all, 'a wreck of human art,' though it scarcely seems so. At the same time it is natural, as though it had grown from the rock, not been built by human art at all. Though the building was once adorned with elaborate carved inscriptions and images, those have been effaced by time. Its towers and facades now seem once more natural rock, grown out of the mountains, living stone. The natural, the supernatural, and the human were reconciled in a union whose symbol was brother-sister incest, the same mating with the same, so short-circuiting normal human love with its production of new genetic lines. The prohibition against incest, as Lévi-Strauss has argued, is both human and natural at once. It therefore breaks down the barrier between the two. This breaking was doubly broken by the Ocean-King and his sister. Their copulation kept crime from being invented. It held nature, the supernatural, and the human together – mimicking and maintaining that vision of unity which can be seen from the palace. This seascape-landscape, two in one, makes the particulars of nature seem the ideal dream of a fulfilled sexuality between two great gods, Earth and Ocean:

> And, day and night, aloof, from the high towers
> And terraces, the Earth and Ocean seem
> To sleep in one another's arms, and dream
> Of waves, flowers, clouds, woods, rocks, and all that we
> Read in their smiles, and call reality.
>
> (ll. 508–12)

To this place the poet plans to bring his Emily, promising a renewal of that ideal sexual union of the prime time. This renewal will magically renew the time itself. It will take them back to a time prior to the invention of crime and reconcile once more, in a performative embrace, nature, supernature, and man.

This performance, however, can never be performed. It remains at the end of *Epipsychidion* a proleptic hope which is forbidden by the words which express it. It can never be performed because in fact this union never existed in the past. It is only a projection backward from the present. It is a 'seeming' created by reading the signs or remnants still present in the present. The Ocean-King, wise and tender though he may have been, was human after all. The prohibition against incest precedes the committing of incest. It precedes the division between natural and human while at the same time creating that division. The lovemaking of the Ocean-King and his spouse was itself the act which 'invented crime.' Though it was a mating of the same with the same, it did not put a stop to the difference of sexes, families, and generations, as the peopling of the earth, the presence of political and paternal tyranny, the existence of the poet with his unassuaged desire for Emily all demonstrate.

Moreover, the building only seemed to be natural, divine, and human at once. Though its stone is natural enough, its shape was in fact a product of human art, as is demonstrated by the presence on it once of 'antique and learnèd imagery.' This imagery was learned because it pointed back still further to a human tradition already immemorial. The 'volumes' of the ivy and the wild vine, that screen of parasite flowers, the former making a hieroglyphic pattern on the stone, the latter casting mosaic patterns in tracery on the marble floors, are substitutes for that effaced writing. The purely natural vines and parasites here paradoxically become a kind of writing. They stand for the erased pattern of learned imagery carved in the stone by the Ocean-King's builders. They stand also by implication for writing in general, the writing for example of the poem itself which the reader is at that moment retracing. Yet the pattern of parasite vines is no legible language. It remains 'in place of' the erased human language. In this 'in place of' all the imaginary unity of 'the world's young prime' breaks down. It is dispersed back into irreconcilable compartments separated by the dividing textured membrane which tries to bring them together. Male and female; divine, human, supernatural − all become separate realms. They are realms separated by language itself and by the dependence of language on figure, on the 'in place of' of metaphor or allegorical substitution. Any attempt to cross the barrier and unify what have from all time been separated by the language which brings them together (that antique and learned imagery which was already there even for the wise and tender Ocean-King and his sister-spouse), leads only to an exacerbation of the distance. It becomes a transgression which creates the barrier it attempts to efface or ignore. Incest cannot exist without kinship names and is 'invented' as a crime not so much in sexual acts between brother and sister as in any imagery for them. This imagery, however, is always there, of immemorial antiquity. It joins nature and culture in what divides them, as the living stone is covered with carved images making it humanly significant, and as the parasite vines or rather the filigrees of their shadows are taken as signs.

In the same way the poet's attempt to repeat with Emily the pleasure of the Ocean-King and his sister only repeats the crime of illicit sexual relations, always at least implicitly incest for Shelley. 'Would we two had been twins of the same mother!' (l. 45) says the protagonist to his Emily. The speaker's love only prolongs the divisions. His union with Emily remains always in the future, as is Henry's love in *The Daemon of the World*, or as is the hero's love in *Alastor*, and as the union of Laon and Cythna is paid for when they are burned at the stake. The lovemaking of Laon and Cythna does not in any case produce the political liberation of Islam. In the same way, the poet's attempt in *Epipsychidion* to express in words this union becomes itself the barrier forbidding it. It forbids also the poet's Promethean attempt to scale heaven and seize its fire through language and through erotic love. The passage is one of Shelley's grandest symphonic climaxes, but what it expresses is the failure of poetry and the failure of love. It expresses the destruction of the poet-lover in his attempt to escape his boundaries, the chains at once of selfhood and of language. This failure is Shelley's version of the parasite structure.

Who, however, is 'Shelley'? To what does this word refer if any work signed with this name has no identifiable borders, and no interior walls either? It has no edges because it has been invaded from all sides as well as from within by other 'names', other powers of writing – Rousseau, Dante, Ezekiel, and the whole host of others, phantom strangers who have crossed the thresholds of the poems, erasing their margins. Though the word 'Shelley' may be printed on the cover of a book entitled *Poetical Works*, it must name something without identifiable bounds, since the book incorporates so much outside within its inside. The parasite structure obliterates the frontiers of the texts it enters. For 'Shelley,' then, the parasite is a communicating screen of figurative language which permanently divides what it would unify in a perpetual 'in place of' forbidding union. This screen creates the shadow of that union as an effect of figure, a phantasmal 'once was' and 'might yet be,' never 'now' and 'here':

> Our breath shall intermix, our bosoms bound,
> And our veins beat together; and our lips
> With other eloquence than words, eclipse
> The soul that burns between them, and the wells
> Which boil under our being's inmost cells,
> The fountains of our deepest life, shall be
> Confused in Passion's golden purity,
> As mountain-springs under the morning sun.
> We shall become the same, we shall be one
> Spirit within two frames, oh! wherefore two?
> One passion in twin-hearts, which grows and grew,
> Till like two meteors of expanding flame,
> Those spheres instinct with it become the same,
> Touch, mingle, are transfigured; ever still
> Burning, yet ever inconsumable:
> In one another's substance finding food,
> Like flames too pure and light and unimbued
> To nourish their bright lives with baser prey,
> Which point to Heaven and cannot pass away:
> One hope within two wills, one will beneath
> Two overshadowing minds, one life, one death,
> One Heaven, one Hell, one immortality,
> And one annihilation. Woe is me!
> The wingèd words on which my soul would pierce
> Into the height of Love's rare Universe,
> Are chains of lead around its flight of fire –
> I pant, I sink, I tremble, I expire!

(ll. 565–91)

No reader of these extraordinary lines can fail to feel that the poet here protests too much. Every repetition of the word 'one' only adds another layer to the barrier forbidding oneness. The poet protests too much not only in the attempt in words to produce a union which these words themselves keep from happening, but even in the concluding outcry of woe. Not only does the poet not achieve union through words with his Emily and so climb to Love's fiery heights. He does not even 'expire' through the failure of these magic performatives. Words do not make anything happen, nor does their failure to make anything happen either. Though the 'Advertisement' to *Epipsychidion* tells the reader the poet died in Florence without ever reaching that isle, 'one of wildest of the Sporades,' the reader knows that words did not kill him, for 'I pant, I sink, I tremble, I expire!' is followed by the relatively calm post-climax dedicatory lines beginning: 'Weak Verses, go, kneel at your Sovereign's feet' (l. 591).

The grand climactic passage itself is made of variations on the paradoxical parasite structure. The verbal signs for union necessarily rebuild the barrier they would obliterate. The more the poet says they will be one the more he makes them two by reaffirming the ways they are separated. The lips that speak with an eloquence other than words are doors which are also a liminal barrier between person and person. Those lips may eclipse the soul that burns between them, but they remain as a communicating medium which also is a barrier to union. The lips are the parasite structure once more. Moreover, the voice that speaks of an eloquence beyond words uses eloquent words to speak of this transverbal speech. By naming such speech it keeps the soul from being eclipsed. In the same way, the image of the deep wells reaffirms the notion of cellular enclosure, just as the clash of fire and water in the figure of the mountain-springs being 'confused' under the morning sun tells the reader that only by evaporating as entities can lovers become one. The images of two frames with one spirit, the double meteors becoming one floating sphere, the pair each both eater and eaten ('in one another's substance finding food'), are the parasitical relation again. All play variations on 'Shelley's' version of the parasite structure, the notion of a unity which yet remains double but in the figurative expression of that unity reveals the impossibility of two becoming one across a parasitic wall and yet remaining two.

This impossibility is mimed in the final *mise en abîme*. This is a cascade of expressions describing a twoness resting on the ground of a oneness which then subdivides once more to rest on a still deeper ground which ultimately reveals itself to be, if it exists at all, the abyss of 'annihilation.' The vertical wall between cell and cell, lover and beloved, is doubled by a horizontal veil between levels of being. Each veil when removed only reveals another veil, ad infinitum, unless the last veil exposes an emptiness. This would be the emptiness of that oneness which is implored into existence in the reiteration of 'one,' 'one,' 'one,' 'one': 'One hope within two wills, one will beneath / Two overshadowing minds, one life, one death / One Heaven, one Hell, one immortality, / And one annihilation. Woe is me!' The language which tries to efface itself as language to give way to an unmediated union beyond language is itself the barrier which always remains as the woe of an ineffaceable trace. Words are always there as remnant, 'chains of lead' which forbid the flight to fiery union they invoke.

This does not mean that lovemaking and poetry-making are the 'same thing' or subject to the same impasses determining their failure as performatives magically transforming the world. In a sense they are antagonists, since love-making attempts to do wordlessly what poetry attempts to do with words. No one can doubt that Shelley believed sexual experience 'occurs' or that he 'describes' it in his poetry, for example in *Laon and Cythna* and in the great passage on erotic love in *The Triumph of Life*. Love-making and poetry-making are not, however, stark opposites in Shelley either. Each is, so to speak, the dramatization of the other or the figure of it. This is an elliptical relation in which whichever of the two the reader focuses on reveals itself to be the metaphorical substitution for the other. The other, however, when the reader moves to it, is not the 'original' but a figure of what at first seemed a figure for it. Lovemaking, as *The Triumph of Life* shows, is a way to 'experience,' as incarnate suffering, the self-destructive effects of sign-making, sign-projecting, and sign-interpretation. The wordlessness of lovemaking is only another way of dwelling within signs after all, as is shown in *The Triumph of Life* by the affirmed identity between Venus, evening star of love, and Lucifer, star of morning, 'light-bearer,' personification of personification and of all the other tropes, all the forms of the 'in place of.'

Poetry-making, on the other hand, is for Shelley always a figure of, as well as figured by, the various forms of life – political, religious, familial, and erotic. It does not have priority as an origin but can exist only embodied in one or another of the forms of life it figures. There is, for Shelley, no 'sign' without its material carrier, and so the play of substitutions in language can never be a purely ideal interchange. This interchange is always contaminated by its necessary incarnation, the most dramatic form of which is the bodies of lovers. On the other hand, lovemaking is never a purely wordless communion or intercourse. It is in its turn contaminated by language. Lovemaking is a way of living, in the flesh, the aporias of figure. It is also a way of experiencing the way language functions to forbid the perfect union of lovers. Language always remains, after they have exhausted or even annihilated themselves in an attempt to get it right, as the genetic trace starting the cycle all over again.

V

Five times, or seven times if one counts *The Daemon of the World* and *The Revolt of Islam* as separate texts, seven times, or even more than seven if one includes other passages with the same elements where the word 'parasite' does not appear – more than seven times, then, throughout his work, Shelley casts himself against the lips of the parasitical gate. Each time he falls back, having failed to make two into one without annihilating both. He falls back as himself the remainder, the power of language able to say 'Woe is me!' and forced to try again to break the barrier only to fail once more, in repetitions which are terminated only by his death.

The critic, in his turn, like those poets, Browning, Hardy, Yeats, or Stevens who have been decisively 'influenced' by Shelley, is a follower who repeats the pattern once again and once again fails to 'get it right,' just as Shelley repeats himself and repeats his precursors, and just as the poet and Emily follow the Ocean-King and his sister-spouse.

The critic's version of the pattern proliferated in this chain of repetitions is as follows. The critic's attempt to untwist the elements in the texts he or she interprets only twists them up again in another place and leaves always a remnant of opacity, or an added opacity, as yet unraveled. The critic is caught in his or her own version of the interminable repetitions which determine the poet's career. The critic experiences this as his or her failure to get the poet right in a final decisive formulation which will allow the critic to have done with that poet, once and for all. Though each poet is different, each contains his own form of undecidability. This might be defined by saying that the critic can never show decisively whether or not the work of the writer is 'decidable,' whether or not it is capable of being definitively interpreted. The critic cannot unscramble the tangle of lines of meaning, comb its threads out so they shine clearly side by side. He or she can only retrace the text, set its elements in motion once more, in that experience of the failure of determinable reading which is decisive here.

The blank wall beyond which rational analysis cannot go arises from the copresence in any text in Western literature, inextricably intertwined, as host and parasite, of some version of logocentric metaphysics and its subversive counterpart. In Shelley's case these are, on the one hand, the 'idealism' always present as one possible reading of his poems, even of *The Triumph of Life*, and on the other hand, the putting in question of this in Shelley's 'scepticism' by a recognition of the role of projections in human life.

[. . .]*

The dismantling of the linguistic assumptions necessary to dismantle Shelley's idealism must occur, not by a return to idealism, and not by the appeal to some 'metalanguage' which will encompass both, but by a movement through rhetorical analysis, the analysis of tropes, and the appeal to etymologies, to something 'beyond' language which can yet only be reached by recognition of the linguistic moment in its counter-momentum against idealism or against logocentric metaphysics. By 'linguistic moment' I mean the moment in a work of literature when its own medium is put in question. This moment allows the critic to take what remains from the clashing of scepticism and idealism as a new

---

* Consideration is given to the limit of analysis imposed by the deconstruction that takes place in Shelley's text between idealism and scepticism, which the critic can only redouble. [Ed.]

starting place, for example by the recognition of a performative function of language which has entered into my discussion of Shelley. This again, in its reinstating of a new form of referentiality and in its formation of a new clashing, this time between rhetoric as tropes and rhetoric as performative words, must be interrogated in its turn, in a ceaseless movement of interpretation which Shelley himself has mimed in the sequence of episodes in *The Triumph of Life*.

This movement is not subject to dialectical synthesis, nor to any other closure. The undecidable, nevertheless, always has an impetus back into some covert form of dialectical movement, as in my terminology here of the 'chain' and the 'going beyond.' This is constantly countered, however, by the experience of movement in place. The momentary always tends to generate a narrative, even if it is the narrative of the impossibility of narrative, the impossibility of getting from here to there by means of language. The tension between dialectic and undecidability is another way in which this form of criticism remains open, in the ceaseless movement of an 'in place of' without resting place.

The word 'deconstruction' is in one way a good one to name this movement. The word, like other words in 'de,' 'decrepitude,' for example, or 'denotation,' describes a paradoxical action which is negative and positive at once. In this it is like all words with a double antithetical prefix, words in 'ana,' like 'analysis,' or words in 'para,' like 'parasite.' These words tend to come in pairs which are not opposites, positive against negative. They are related in a systematic differentiation which requires a different analysis or untying in each case, but which in each case leads, in a different way each time, to the tying up of a double bind. This tying up is at the same time a loosening. It is a paralysis of thought in the face of what cannot be thought rationally: analysis, paralysis; solution, dissolution; composition, decomposition; construction, deconstruction; mantling, dismantling; canny, uncanny; competence, incompetence; apocalyptic, anacalyptic; constituting, deconstituting. Deconstructive criticism moves back and forth between the poles of these pairs, proving in its own activity, for example, that there is no deconstruction which is not at the same time constructive, affirmative. The word says this in juxtaposing 'de' and 'con.'

[. . .]*

Insofar as 'deconstruction' names the use of rhetorical, etymological, or figurative analysis to demystify the mystifications of literary and philosophical language, this form of criticism is not outside but within. It is of the same nature as what it works against. Far from reducing the text back to detached fragments, it inevitably constructs again in a different form what it deconstructs. It does again as it undoes. It recrosses in one place what it uncrosses in another. Rather than surveying the text with sovereign command from outside, it remains caught within the activity in the text it retraces.

To the action of deconstruction with its implication of an irresistible power of

---

* Miller offers a *caveat* against considering deconstruction as an extrinsic critical method. [Ed.]

the critic over the text must always be added, as a description of what happens in interpretation, the experience of the impossibility of exercising that power. The dismantler dismantles himself. Far from being a chain which moves deeper and deeper into the text, closer and closer to a definitive interpretation of it, the mode of criticism sometimes now called 'deconstruction,' which is analytic criticism as such, encounters always, if it is carried far enough, some mode of oscillation. In this oscillation two genuine insights into literature in general and into a given text in particular inhibit, subvert, and undercut one another. This inhibition makes it impossible for either insight to function as a firm resting place, the end point of analysis. My example here has been the co-presence in the parasite structure in Shelley of idealism and scepticism, of referentiality which only proleptically refers, in figure, therefore does not refer at all, and of performatives which do not perform. Analysis becomes paralysis, according to the strange necessity which makes these words, or the 'experience,' or the 'procedure,' they describe, turn into one another. Each crosses over into its apparent negation or opposite. If the word 'deconstruction' names the procedure of criticism, and 'oscillation' the impasse reached through that procedure, 'undecidability' names the experience of a ceaseless dissatisfied movement in the relation of the critic to the text.

The ultimate justification for this mode of criticism, as of any conceivable mode, is that it works. It reveals hitherto unidentified meanings and ways of having meaning in major literary texts. The hypothesis of a possible hetero-geneity in literary texts is more flexible, more open to a given work, than the assumption that a good work of literature is necessarily going to be 'organically unified.' The latter presupposition is one of the major factors inhibiting recognition of the possibly self-subversive complexity of meanings in a given work. Moreover, 'deconstruction' finds in the text it interprets the double antithetical patterns it identifies, for example the relation of parasite and host. It does not claim them as universal explanatory structures, neither for the text in question nor for literature in general. Deconstruction attempts to resist the totalizing and totalitarian tendencies of criticism. It attempts to resist its own tendencies to come to rest in some sense of mastery over the work. It resists these in the name of an uneasy joy of interpretation, beyond nihilism, always in movement, a going beyond which remains in place, as the parasite is outside the door but also always already within, uncanniest of guests.

Notes

1. All definitions and etymologies in this essay are taken from *The American Heritage Dictionary of the English Language* (1969).
2. *The Triumph of Life* is cited from the text established by Reiman (1965). All other citations from Shelley are taken from *Poetical Works*, ed. Hutchinson (1973).

2.

The Ethics of Narration

[. . .]

In addressing the ethics of reading, I give special attention to prosopopoeia as the fundamental generative linguistic act making a given story possible. If there is no ethics without story and no story without prosopopoeia, then understanding that figure of speech is essential to an understanding of ethics and especially of the ethics of reading.

My inaugural or constitutive questions are: Is there an ethical dimension to the act of reading as such (as opposed to the expression of ethical themes in the text read)? Does some moral good come to me out of the solitary act of reading? How would one measure that good accurately, and what kind of good, exactly, would it be? Reinforcement and creation of my values, my further incorporation into the values of my society?

A. Bartlett Giamatti seemed to be affirming something like the latter in a vigorous attack on literary theory written while he was still president of Yale University. He was of course implicitly criticizing some influential colleagues at Yale. The address was delivered, of all places, before the Signet Society at Harvard. It was reported in some detail in the *Boston Globe* for Wednesday, 17 April 1985. The function of the mass media in sustaining the attack on literary theory or the resistance to it deserves analysis. It has received some discussion since then. Literary study, Giamatti reportedly said, 'is meant to be a means to clarify the values and strengthen the lessons that make life bearable or even joyful . . . language shapes and transmits values, creates the environment for a rational, decent and civilized life.' This seems so reasonable and plausible a claim that one would hesitate to quarrel with it, beyond asking for some demonstration of just how this happens in a given case and perhaps asking what the difference is between 'shaping' and 'transmitting' values. Just how much autonomous power was Giamatti willing to allow in that word 'shapes'? In any event, if the study of literature does so much good and demonstrates that language has this humane value as creator and sustainer of civilization, does my reading diffuse that good to others, to my students if I am a teacher, to my readers if I am a critic? What good is reading?

Reading would seem to be initially and perhaps primarily a matter of getting the meaning of what is read right, that is, a cognitive or epistemological matter, not an ethical matter having to do with conduct and responsibility. Nevertheless, just as Henry James in the eloquent paragraph ending the preface to *The Golden Bowl* claims that the act of writing is a privileged part of what he calls 'the conduct of life' (1971, xxiv), so I claim that the act of reading is also part of the conduct of life. [. . .]

My questions are the following: In the pragmatic, 'real-life' situation of reading a work of literature, or teaching it to a class, or writing an essay about it, what exactly are the ethical responsibilities of the reader, teacher, or critic? To what or to whom are we obligated, and what, exactly, does that obligation require us to do? Are we primarily responsible to society in general or to our particular local community or, if one is a teacher, to the institution that hires and pays us, or are teachers primarily responsible to their students? Must not the work of reading, on the other hand, all grow out of what is traditionally called 'respect for the text'? How can the reader fulfill all those perhaps conflicting obligations at once? What power adjudicates in case of a conflict among these responsibilities? The 'conscience' of the reader? Some external authority? If respect for the text takes priority, exactly to what or to whom are we responsible when we have 'respect for the text'? At exactly what point, in relation to the total transaction with a text, including cognitive responsibility to 'get the text right,' does a properly ethical moment intervene for the reader, teacher, or critic of literature?

But, first, what do I mean by 'ethics' in the phrase 'the ethics of reading'? I mean more or less what Henry James means in that preface to *The Golden Bowl*, when he says that 'the whole conduct of life consists of things done, which do other things in their turn' (1971, xxiv). If James is correct to say that writing, say writing *The Golden Bowl*, is a thing done that does other things in its turn, my question is concrete and specific. In what sense is reading novels, poems, or philosophical texts, teaching them, or writing about them a thing done that does other things in its turn? Does reading have a proper and unavoidable ethical dimension, along with its cognitive or epistemological one, and, if so, what is it? How does reading differ from other ethical acts, such as making promises and keeping them, proferring a true report, giving and receiving gifts, or greeting my neighbor?

But I mean by an ethical act not only a doing that does other things in its turn. An ethical act must also be free, free in the sense that I must be free to do it or not to do it, therefore taking responsibility for it. How can I be held responsible for something I cannot *not* do? At the same time, in any act properly to be called ethical, I must be directed by some imperative 'I must; I cannot do otherwise'. Some such demand or exigence is an essential feature of ethical acts, including acts of reading insofar as they are ethical. Examples of ethical acts represented *in* works of literature (which is by no means the same thing as the ethical moment involved in reading those works) are Nora Rowley's decision to refuse Mr. Glascock's offer of marriage because she does not love him, in Anthony Trollope's *He Knew He Was Right:* 'She must refuse the offer that was so brilliant, and give up the idea of reigning as queen at Monkhams' (1983, I.104); or Maisie's offer, at the end of James's *What Maisie Knew*, to give up Mrs. Wix if Sir Claude will give up Mrs. Beale. Maisie's 'I must', James's narrator says, is based on 'something still deeper than a moral sense' (James, II.354). What is the source of this 'I must,' and is it analogous to the demand James responded to when he wrote the novel, the demand we respond to when we read it, teach it, write about it?

It will be seen from my use of examples that I think my topic is one that cannot be adequately discussed in the abstract. It *must* be analyzed and demonstrated in terms of specific cases. The relation between examples and conceptual generalizations is one of the problematic areas in any theory of the ethics of reading. It is easy to see that no selection of an example is innocent. Each is a somewhat arbitrary choice for which the chooser must take responsibility. On the other hand, there is no doing, in this region of the conduct of life, without examples. This is as true of philosophical treatises on ethics as it is in literary study. Narratives, examples, stories, such as Kant's little story in the *Grundlegung zur Metaphysik der Sitten* of the man who makes a promise intending not to keep it, are indispensable to thinking about ethics. An understanding of ethics as a region of philosophical or conceptual investigation depends, perhaps surprisingly, on a mastery of the ability to interpret written stories, that is, on a kind of mastery usually thought to be the province of the literary critic. If this is true, it has important implications for my claim that the rhetorical study of literature has crucial practical implications for our moral, social, and political life. Narrative examples are especially appropriate for an investigation of the ethics of reading. But it is not because stories contain the thematic dramatization of ethical situations, choices, and judgments that makes them especially appropriate for my topic; it is, on the contrary, because ethics itself has a peculiar relation to that form of language we call narrative. The thematic dramatizations of ethical topics in narratives are the oblique allegorization of this linguistic necessity.

Some theories of ethics would contest my claim that an ethical act must be both free and at the same time a response to a categorical imperative. The history of speculation about ethics since Kant is the story of attempts to deal with this apparent contradiction. It is possible to argue, for example, that one is as ethically responsible for acts done inadvertently or automatically as for those that are done by free choice. Not only is ignorance of the law no excuse – ignorance of what I have done unintentionally, as when I was sleepwalking, is no excuse either. Being able to say 'I did not mean to do it' does not free me of ethical responsibility. This issue is precisely one of those ethical themes often dramatized within works of literature, as in the opening sentence and all the ensuing action of Kafka's *The Trial*: 'Someone must have been telling lies about Joseph K., for without having done anything wrong he was arrested one fine morning' (1953b, 7). The novel turns on the question of whether Joseph K. has done anything wrong, whether it is just that he should be condemned to death for the infraction of a law of which he is not only initially ignorant but which he has no possibility of ever confronting face to face or reading as an ascertainable written law. The parable within the text of *The Trial*, 'Before the Law,' dramatizes this situation as subjection to a law that is invisible but sovereign.

A different result is obtained when one shifts, as I am trying to do, from the thematic representation within a work of ethical issues to the ethical issues involved in the act of reading itself. It is easy to see that the act of reading is in a curious way both free and not free. Surely I am relatively free to read or not to read a given book, to teach it, or to write about it. Or am I? If my department or institution has charged me with teaching a certain course, or if I am a student forced to take a required course within a certain curriculum, then I can hardly be said to be free not to read the books on the curriculum of that course. This freedom would be even more radically curtailed if the current movement back to the establishment of a basic canon of works of literature that all American schoolchildren *must* read were successful.

Let me try to clarify this curious constraint on my freedom to read or not to read. Imagine a situation in which by accident I take a certain book down from the shelf or spot an open book on someone's desk. If I know the language, I may be said to read it whether or not I want to do so. And I must take responsibility for the consequences of that act. Reading is in a certain sense automatic, involuntary. I just happen to have read a certain book, say one I find in a hotel room or in a rented summer house. This accidental encounter may have the most extensive ethical consequences in my own life, and in those of others, as my act of reading causes other things to be done in their turn. My own reading of the criticism of Georges Poulet, for example, occurred in just this fortuitous way. It was nevertheless decisive for my professional career as teacher and critic, even for my personal life.

It is an intrinsic feature of written pieces of language that they demand to be read, even though they may never find their readers. All those books lining the shelves of all the libraries do not just passively sit there. They cry out to be read. They do not cease day and night to clamor for readers, just as, according to Walter Benjamin in 'The Task of the Translator,' each text demands to be translated, even though it may never find its translator. This demand will be met only when the text is turned into another language, perhaps into all other languages. The ethics of reading begins with the reader's response to a parallel demand that each text be read, and even read again and again.

This response begins and remains in a painful double bind. Each book, text, essay, scrap of written language, even those in languages I do not know, asks to be read. The call is directed to me personally and with equal force by each text. I *must* read them all. There is no initial way or principle, other than arbitrary or contingent ones, by which I can decide an order of priority among all the books. I must get on with it and begin where I can. But in choosing to respond to the demand made by the book that has fallen by accident into my hands, I am betraying my responsibility to all the other books. This is a responsibility I can never fulfill. So I live in a perpetual condition of guilty arrears, which is my fate as soon as I have learned to read. I shall go to my grave still in debt and unable by the most heroic efforts to pay off my obligation. Thomas Wolfe reports how as a student at Harvard he was tormented not only by the impossibility of ever reading through all the books in Widener Library, but also by learning that there were a hundred thousand new books in German published each year, that is, in a language he did not even know. His ignorance did not lessen one whit the obligation he felt to read all the books in German as well.

The situation is made even worse by the fact that my decision to read means a suspension of other responsibilities and contractual obligations, to my family, to my institution, to my students and colleagues, whose 'secondary' texts I have a perpetually mounting obligation to assess, to all those committees and advisory boards on which I serve. Proust, in his description of the youthful reading of Marcel, has dramatized what is furtive, guilty, private about reading, the way someone, the reader's grandmother for example, is always trying to get him to do something else, to get out in the sunlight and take part in the world of action. There are many other representations *in* novels of what the reader of the novel is at that moment doing. Examples are George Eliot's description of Maggie Tulliver's childhood readings, the decisive effect on Conrad's Jim of his reading of adventure stories, or the effects of reading novels on Don Quixote and Emma Bovary. These novels warn against what the reader must do in order to understand the warning. It might be better not to read. Nor does this manifold pressure not to read disappear as you get older. By a familiar paradox of the teaching profession, the older and more established you get, the less and less time you are allowed for what was your vocation in the first place, that is, a calling to read works of literature, as many as possible in all the languages, and a commitment to talking and writing about what you have read.

Nor is this initial demand, command, or exigency that I read all the books a fantasy or mere theoretical concept. It is a concrete and real experience, the experience of an implacable and at the same time entirely unfulfillable obligation. Any reader who takes reading at all seriously will have felt the force of this responsibility, however successfully one may have suppressed it as an absurdity. Who or what says I must read all the books? My situation as reader is a little as if I had signed an impossible contract without having in fact signed it, as if I were born into the world encumbered with a debt I have no chance of ever paying off. It is as if someone or something else had signed in my stead. As soon as I learn to read I am already bound by an obligation I had no idea I was taking on. I am in this like Joseph K. arrested one fine day without having done anything wrong.

In this ethical emergency, as in other unbreakable double binds, the only way to live with it in the most responsible way is to do something. A parallel may be made with that irreconcilability between spiritual love and bodily love demonstrated so irrefutably in Shakespeare's *As You Like It*. Both the verbal texture and the dramatic action of this play demonstrate that you cannot, logically, love in both ways at once. Nevertheless, the denouement of *As You Like It* is the celebration of four marriages. These marriages do not break the knot of the double bind by tying new bonds within which lust is lawful and compatible with spiritual love. Instead they put all the protagonists, high and low, in the situation of dwelling with the greatest tension within that double bind, as anyone who has been married will know.

In the case of the double bind of reading, the analogous leap in the dark is clear. In all desperation I must take up the first book that falls into my hands and begin reading. *Tolle, lege* is the first law of reading. In order to fulfill the obligations involved in the ethics of reading, I must first read something, some one book, poem, novel, or essay, in spite of the fact that to single out one over all the others is not only an arbitrary and unjustified choice, but also a betrayal of my obligation to all the other books. They call out with equal peremptoriness to be read. To read one book is therefore to get even further behind in fulfilling my duty to read all those other books. Still I must read.

What happens when I read, when I *really* read, which does not happen all that often? What happens is something always fortuitous and unpredictable, something surprising, however many times the book in question has been read before, even by me. One way to define this unexpected quality of true acts of reading is to say that they never correspond exactly to what other readers tell me I am going to find when I read that book, however learned, expert, and authoritative those previous readers have been. Another way to describe what is unpredictable about a genuine act of reading is to say that reading is always the disconfirmation or modification of presupposed literary theory rather than its confirmation. What happens when I read a particular book never quite fits my theory (or anyone else's) of what is going to happen. You can never be sure what is going to happen when someone in a particular situation reads a particular book. Rather than thinking of all those books on the shelf as the sure and safe repository of the values of Western culture, the army of unalterable law ranged in rows, it might be better to think of them as so many unexploded bombs that may have who knows what result when they get read by the right (or the wrong) person at the right (or the wrong) place or time. A book is a dangerous object, and perhaps all books should have warning labels. Strange things happen when someone reads a book.

A theory of the ethics of reading that takes seriously the possibility that reading might lead to other morally good or valuable actions would also have to allow for the possibility that the reading even of a morally exemplary book might cause something morally deplorable to occur. This has in fact happened more than once. Paul de Man is right in his shrewd adaptation of Hölderlin's 'Es ereignet aber das Wahre' into a formula for what happens in reading. Hölderlin's phrase, says de Man, 'can be freely translated, 'What is true is what is bound to take place.' And, in the case of the reading of a text, what takes place is a necessary understanding. What marks the truth of such an understanding is not some abstract universal but the fact that 'it has to occur regardless of other considerations' (de Man 1978, xi).

De Man's formulation must not be understood as meaning that exactly the same thing occurs each time a given text is read. 'Ereignen' means 'happen, come to pass, occur.' An act of reading takes place as an event. It is something that happens, with the same inaugural violence, breaking any predictable concatenation, as other events in the real world like birth, copulation, death, or declarations of independence. That such events, including reading, may be in one way or another a repetition by no means disables their disruptive force, as Kierkegaard recognized in his concept of repetition, described as follows by Sylviane Agacinski: repetition 'is like a tear or rip that blows or blows up, pops, pierces, opens and shows up. There it was, and now here it is. It happens' (1988, 3). The event of reading, like the writing of that text in the first place, 'takes place,' with all the enigmatic force in this notion of an event as something that comes out of nowhere, so to speak, occupies space, and makes that space into a place, with orienting coordinates. Reading occurs in a certain spot to a certain person in a certain historical, personal, institutional, and political situation, but it always exceeds what was predictable from those circumstances. It makes something happen that is a deviation from its context, and what happens demands a new definition each time. The record of those deviations includes the further language written or spoken in response to the act of reading, such as critical essays or acts of teaching, but of course reading may lead to many other kinds of acts. Another way to put this is to say that reading always has a performative as well as a cognitive dimension. It follows that the historical and practical, as well as the theoretical, study of literature should include attention to the performative force in reading.

3

The Ethics of Reading:
Vast Gaps and Parting Hours

> A wicked book they seized; the very Turk
> Could not have read a more pernicious work . . .
> George Crabbe,
> 'The Parting Hour' (ll. 355–6)

A distinctive feature of literary study in America at the present time is its internationalization. The result has been a fissuring of what not too long ago seemed perhaps about to become a seamless whole, whether under the aegis of literary history and the history of ideas, or under the aegis of the New Criticism, or under the aegis of the archetypal criticism of Northrop Frye. The diffusion in America of new linguistic theories of various sorts, of Slavic formalism, of phenomenology, of structuralism, of continental Marxism and Freudianism, and of so-called 'deconstruction' has put an end, for the moment at least, to any dreams of unification. Nor can the various invading theories be reconciled among themselves. This penetration, fracturing, or 'crazing' has made the institution of literary studies in America a house divided against itself, its domestic economy invaded by alien hosts or guests from abroad. These foreign imports have been around long enough now for their disruptive implications to be at least partly understood, and we are in the midst of the predictable negative reaction against them.

My purpose here is to investigate the question of the ethics of reading in the context of this situation. The phrase 'the ethics of reading' might seem to be an oxymoron. The obligation of the reader, the teacher, and the critic would seem to be exclusively epistemological. The reader must see clearly what the work in question says and repeat that meaning in his commentary or teaching. He functions thereby, modestly, as an intermediary, as a midwife or catalyst. He transmits meanings which are objectively there but which might not otherwise have reached readers or students. He brings the meaning to birth again as illumination and insight in their minds, making the interaction take place without himself entering into it or altering it. It would seem that the field covered by reading involves exclusively the epistemological categories of truth and falsehood, insight and blindness. The teacher is a revealer, not a creator.

Nevertheless, ethical issues arise in all sorts of ways, both practical and theoretical, in the act of reading. Men and women have given up their lives over questions of interpretation, the reading of a phrase of scripture, for example. One expects reading in one way or another to have moral effects, for good or for ill. To the couplets, truth and falsehood, insight and blindness, themselves not quite congruent, must be added the pair good and bad, both in the sense of aesthetic judgement and in the sense of ethical judgement, and the pair speech and silence. These pairs cross the others widdershins, and no one of them may be easily twisted to superimpose exactly on the others in a single act of critical judgement. It is impossible to divide, discriminate, sift, or winnow the wheat from the chaff, true from false, good from bad, in a single moment of parting.

As a result, difficult questions arise in the attempt to adjudicate between epistemological and ethical responsibilities. Does a teacher or critic have an obligation to choose only certain works to teach or write about? Who has the right to set the canon and to establish the Index? Should 'the state see to it,' as Matthew Arnold thought? Is a good work always moral? Should a teacher or a critic keep silent if he is led, perhaps unexpectedly, to ethically negative conclusions about a given work? Should certain aspects of a given work be suppressed at a preliminary level of teaching, or should there perhaps be a hierarchy of works of increasing ethical complexity in a given curriculum? How is the need for a firm ethical commitment in the teacher-critic compatible with that openness or 'pluralism' often said to be necessary to the sympathetic understanding of works from different periods and cultures? The commitment of both the scientific and religious strands of our American heritage to seeing and saying the truth fearlessly can easily, in a given teaching or writing situation, come to collide with concrete ethical responsibilities towards students and colleagues, no less a part of our heritage. Nor is this conflict external, between one critic and another, one teacher and another, one mode of criticism and another. The most intense conflict is likely to take place within the mind and feelings of a single person, in his or her attempt to fulfill incompatible responsibilities.

[. . .] The concrete situation of teachers of the humanities is changing at the moment with unusual rapidity. More even than usual it seems as if we stand within the instant of a crisis, a dividing point, a 'parting hour'. Aspects of the change include the increasing emphasis on the teaching of writing (which may be all to the good if it does not involve the imposition of narrow notions of clarity and logic), the decline of enrollments in traditional courses in literature and other humanities, the catastrophic reduction of the number of positions open to younger humanists, and a conservative reaction in the universities. This tends to declare certain kinds of speculative questioning anathema. Perhaps this reaction is confined within the universities and colleges, a response in the seventies to the sixties. Perhaps it is part of much larger political shifts in our society as a whole.

One form of the closing of ranks is a return to basics in the name of a reaffirmation of traditional humanistic values, perhaps in the name of a reaffirmation of the faith in reason of the enlightenment. This tends to be accompanied by a rejection of 'theory' as such and in particular by a strong hostility to certain fairly recent methodological developments in Europe and America. The latter have converged to put in question the most cherished stabilities of traditional humanistic studies in the United States: the stability of the self, the coherence of story-telling, the possibility of straightforward referential language, the possibility of a definitive, unified reading of a given work, the traditional schemas of history and of literary history which have formed the bases for the structuring of curricula in the humanities, for example the objective and definable existence of literary 'periods.'

Some of the methodological innovations which have challenged the traditional bases of literary study in America are scientific or claim to be part of the so-called 'human sciences.' These would include insights about the way language works from modern linguistics, from psychology, from psychoanalysis, from anthropology, from semiotics, and from common language philosophy, Wittgenstein and his progeny. Some of these methodological innovations are ideological or have developed from recent historical pressures. An example would be the newer forms of Marxist literary criticism which are beginning to be institutionalized in America and to exert force, particularly over younger teachers. A curious and I think important fact should be noted, however. Marxist literary criticism, both in its somewhat more naïve traditional American forms and in the more sophisticated (sophisticated perhaps in the sense of 'adulterated' as well as 'wiser') newer forms influenced by semiotics, structuralism, Lacanian psychoanalysis, and so on, tends, strangely enough, to join forces with that conservative reaction to affirm more or less traditional notions of history, of selfhood, of the moral function of literature, and, most of all, of its mimetic or referential status. For Marxism, literature cannot help but reflect social and historical conditions and the superstructure of ideology these have created. Marxism here joins forces with the most traditional 'humanism' against those methodological innovations I am describing.

Many of these have been imported from abroad, for example, phenomenology, structuralism, semiotics, and so-called 'deconstruction.' This is often held against them on the argument that methods brought in from old Europe cannot thrive in New World soil. Nevertheless, an internationalization in literary study is one of its most obvious features today, and this has concrete effects, for example in a tendency to weaken the departmental boundaries of the curricula devoted to national literatures. The transnational diffusion of literary theory and literary methodology occurs now more rapidly than ever before, in part because of technological developments, the rapidity of global transportation which can bring people together from all over the world for a conference anywhere in the world, electronic communication, the increased speed of translation, publication, and distribution, the improved teaching of foreign languages, at least in some schools and programs,[1] the development of international journals in the various branches of humanistic study.

The internationalization of literary study has, as I have said, generated attacks from various directions in defense of those stabilities which seem endangered. These attacks are more or less reasoned or cogent, but their existence is itself an important symptom of our current version of the problem of the ethics of reading. Whether a given anathematizing of these new developments as immoral, nihilistic, or un-American is based on an understanding of them and is a genuine going beyond the challenges they offer, or is only a coverup, a repression, can only be told by a careful study of each case. It can be said, however, that the excommunications, extraditions, or convictions of heresy seem often to take place without a careful reading of the documents involved. At least so it seems on the evidence of the inadequacy of what is often said of them: 'A wicked book they seized.' The texts of the new methodologies must be mastered before they can be discussed, no easy task, since in part they have to do with the impossibility of mastery. Most of all, the readings of particular works which are derived from these theories or from which the theories derive need to be confronted in detail. The efficacy of a theory is to be measured by its results in interpretations. A theory as such cannot be confuted in isolation, for example by deploring its presumed destructive consequences, but only by showing in detail that the readings to which it leads are inadequate or wrong, untrue to the texts. It can also be supposed that young teachers and critics are more likely to have taken genuine stock of the new methodological developments before trying to go beyond them or to return in a new way to the old verities of literary study. For better or for worse literary study in America can never be quite the same again. A difference, perhaps even a 'vast gap' has been introduced.

I propose to investigate the problem of ethics of reading in this moment of our history a little more closely. I shall do so by way of an example, though with an awareness that my example, like any other, raises the question of exemplarity or of synecdoche. Is this part an adequate sample of such a vast whole? That issue is in fact exemplified and thematized within the poem I shall discuss as well as in my use of it.

Suppose there should fall into my hands 'The Parting Hour,' a poem by George Crabbe (1754–1832) published in *Tales* (1812). Should I teach it or write about it? What will happen when I do so?

It might be said that this poem is a marginal part of the canon of English literature, even more marginal a part of Western literature as a whole. No one and no institution or curriculum force me to teach or to write about this particular poem. There may be something willful or perverse in my choice of this example. This is to some degree true of any choice of an item for a syllabus, however, and this particular poem may in fact be a good choice. If even Crabbe offers support to those who challenge the assumptions of traditional humanistic study in America, then there may be some force in the challenges.

Crabbe's place in English literary history is an honorable but relatively small one. He is seen as a writer of narratives in verse of idiosyncratic distinction. His work moves across the transition in modes from eighteenth-century styles to verse stories by Wordsworth such as 'The Ruined Cottage.' There is a general sense that Crabbe's poems are of great interest and that he has perhaps not yet received his due. The debt of criticism to Crabbe will soon be at least partially paid off by Gavin Edwards of Saint Davids College, University of Wales. Edwards has a book on Crabbe in preparation, and my obligation to him is considerable. 'The Parting Hour,' in any case, is an admirable poem. It raises just those questions about the ethics of reading which are most my interest here and which, as I hope to indicate, are always present in literature and literary criticism in the West, for example in Aristotle's *Poetics* and Sophocles' *Oedipus the King.* Crabbe's poem is a good example of the way an apparently peripheral and unproblematic example in literary studies, taken more or less at random, always turns out to raise again all the most difficult questions about literature and about literary criticism.

'The Parting Hour' opens with no less than five epigraphs from Shakespeare, about each of which there would be much to say, as well as about the fact itself of the multiplication of epigraphs. It is as though Crabbe must try over and over to find a precursor fragment which will be a solid foundation allowing him to begin telling the story he has to tell. The text proper begins with a double claim: the claim that any human life, however strange, hangs together, and the claim that any human life is therefore narratable. It can be retraced later on as a continuous story which makes sense, has a beginning, middle, and end:

> Minutely traces man's life; year after year,
> Through all his days let all his deeds appear,
> And then, though some may in that life be strange.
> Yet there appears no vast nor sudden change;
> The links that bind those various deeds are seen.
> And no mysterious void is left between.
>
> (ll. 1–6)

The opposition here is between strangeness and mystery; minutely traced causal continuity on the one hand, and sudden discontinuous change on the other, across the 'void' or 'vast gap.' Though a given life may in one way or another be odd, if it is narrated with an absolute fidelity to detail it will hang together like the unbroken links of a chain. 'Minutely traced': the figure is of one image superimposed on an earlier image and following it over again, like marked tracing paper over a previously made design, tracking it again with the utmost care as one follows the spoor of a beast. This is the image latently present in the Greek word for narrative or history: *diegesis.* On the other hand, if there is any failure at all in this tracing, the life will appear not strange but utterly mysterious, unfathomable. It will be broken by the abyss of a blank. Crabbe's image for this is what happens if one juxtaposes a vignette from the early life of a person with one from his old age without tracing minutely every event between. The opposition is between a continuous temporal line and the placing side by side of two spatial images separated by an unfilled temporal gap, like two portraits beside one another, in a diptych of 'before' and 'after'. This graphic figure of the picture or of two pictures side by side Crabbe himself uses more than once during the course of the poem:

> But let these binding links be all destroy'd,
> All that through years he suffer'd or enjoy'd;
> Let that vast gap be made, and then behold –
> This was the youth, and he is thus when old;
> Then we at once the work of Time survey,
> And in an instant see a life's decay;
> Pain mix'd with pity in our bosoms rise.
> And sorrow takes new sadness from surprise.
>
> (ll. 7–14)

This passage is curious in a number of ways. It opposes the line of the temporal continuity, within which binding links may be minutely traced, to the spatial juxtaposition, within a single instant, of two images from different times of a man's life. The two are separated by the blank of the temporal gap. The continuous narrative is by implication appeasing to the mind. It gives calm understanding, since the rationale of the movement of the person from here to there, from youth to old age, is all exposed. No gap for surprise and shock is left. On the other hand, the sudden exposure, across the gap, of the difference between youth and old age produces pain, pity, sorrow, a sadness generated by surprise. The terminology closely approximates that of Aristotle in the *Poetics* if we can understand 'pain' to involve some fear for ourselves as well as pity for the degradation exposed in the juxtaposition of the two pictures: 'This was the youth, and he is thus when old.' The same elements as those in Aristotle are present but apparently in a crisscross relationship, a chiasmus. In Aristotle's theory of tragedy it is the blinding revelation, the recognition (*anagnorisis*) of the links of connection binding apparently dispersed data together which produces the pity and fear appropriate to tragedy, for example in Oedipus' discovery that he has fulfilled the oracles, killed his father, and married his mother. For Crabbe, it is the vision of a non-connection, the confrontation of an unbridgeable gap, which produces these emotions, while the demonstration, by a careful retracing, of all the links of connection is appeasing. It abolishes mystery and satisfies the mind's need for rational understanding.

The chiasmus, however, is only apparent. After all, the Aristotelean recognition and reversal, showing how everything fatally hangs together and bringing the tragic hero down, not only produces pity and fear but also effects the catharsis of these emotions. This catharsis is a transformation or transport turning the painful emotions of pity and fear into the pleasure appropriate to a successful *mimesis*. This transport, as S. H. Butcher long ago recognized in his brilliant essay on the *Poetics* (1951, 113–407; see especially 'The Function of Tragedy,' 240–73), is in effect a metaphor turning this into that or carrying this over to that, renaming pain as pleasure. The image of the ship is of course one of Aristotle's basic metaphors in the *Poetics*. It serves not only as an example of metaphor but implicitly as a metaphor of metaphor. The same metaphor is woven into the text of his prime example of tragedy, *Oedipus the King*. It appears in the recurrent image of all the citizens of Thebes as frightened passengers on a ship steered, for better or for worse, by Oedipus. The chorus of Theban priests and citizens, all the citizens of Thebes, the actual audience in Athens watching Sophocles' play, all those who have read it or seen it or tried to translate it, down through Hölderlin and Freud to readers and interpreters of today, are carried by the ship, the vehicle Oedipus steers. We are taken where he takes us, in the tragic transport of our witness of the self-blinded hero at the end. We are, strangely, the tenor of that vehicle, the subject of the metaphor. We are what is carried over by it.

Where we are carried we know: 'How can we ever find the track of ancient guilt now hard to read?' (*Oedipus the King*, ll. 108–9; trans. Gould 1970, 29). Oedipus is the type of the successful interpreter. He reads the various riddles and oracles right, puts two and two together to make a coherent story, the continuous track of a *diegesis*. He is so strongly motivated to obtain at any expense a rational understanding, an absolutely perspicuous vision of the whole line from here to there, that he is willing (or forced by his interpreter's zeal) to convict himself of the most terrible of crimes, parricide and incest, in order to preserve the values of clear and complete seeing through. These are just the values Aristotle says a good tragedy offers its spectators. The beast whose spoor he follows is himself, but only if he follows the track wherever it leads can full enlightenment take place, the audience be purged of pity and fear, the land of Thebes be freed from Apollo's plague.

In Aristotle's theory of tragedy, in *Oedipus the King* itself, and in the narrative theory proposed by Crabbe at the beginning of 'The Parting Hour,' the unbroken causal continuity of the plot is the necessary means of a transport which transforms pain into pleasure by giving full knowledge. The pleasure of *mimesis*, or what Crabbe calls minute tracing, is both for Aristotle and for Crabbe the pleasure of learning the truth about what is imitated. It is also the pleasure of rhythm or of the harmonious hanging together of the elements of the work. Crabbe in the opening lines of 'The Parting Hour' implicitly affirms all Aristotle says in Section VII of the *Poetics* (1450 b 22–1451 a 15) about the primacy of plot. Plot is the soul of the work. For both, a good work should be like a living organism, with no discontinuities and nothing present which does not form part of an unbroken whole. It should have a beginning, a causally linked middle, an end, and an underlying ground or unifying soul binding all together and making it live. It should have a sufficient magnitude, 'a length,' as Aristotle says, 'which can be easily embraced by the memory,' so that it is 'perspicuous' (Butcher

1951, 33). The efficacy of a *mimesis* depends on our being able to see through it, to hold it all in our memory, or to 'embrace [it] in one view' (33): 'the beginning and the end must be capable of being brought within a single view' (91). This is just what Crabbe says in his emphasis on the need to see all the links that bind the various deeds of a man's life.

Crabbe's poem, Aristotle's *Poetics*, and Sophocles' *Oedipus the King* as interpreted by Aristotle are all versions of a certain system of concepts, figures, and narratives which have recurred in different ways throughout our history. That system includes just those assumptions about the continuity of selfhood, determinate univocal meaning in literary works, the sovereignty of reason, and the coherence of the march of history which, as I began by saying, seem most endangered by those methodologies imported from abroad. Crabbe's 'The Parting Hour' states those assumptions with elegant economy in its opening lines. It presents itself as a promise to fulfill once more these millennial claims for the possibility of a narrative coherence. These are based on the necessary though sometimes hidden coherence of each man's or woman's life from one end of it to the other.

Are the claims paid off, the promise fulfilled, the debt discharged, by the story Crabbe then tells? By no means. What happens, rather, is that the more the story-teller or his protagonist try to fill in all the gaps by a careful retracing, the more they discover that inexplicable gaps remain. The continuity of the story line and of the life is suspended, the line pulverized into static moments which do not hang together, like a rope of sand. Once the apparently innocent fissure of a parting hour has been inserted, the continuity can never be reestablished.

About the details of Crabbe's poem there would be much to say. Only an opening toward a full interpretation can be made here. Like others of Crabbe's narratives, 'The Parting Hour' is a poem about thwarted or inhibited sexual desire. It is almost, one might say, the Oedipus story in reverse. It is the story of a man who does not marry the woman he loves because of a bar which is, metaphorically at least, that of consanguinity. Though Allen Booth and Judith Flemming are of different families in their village, they have loved one another almost like brother and sister as children and, as Gavin Edwards says, there is some vaguely Oedipal taboo opposed by the parents on either side against their marriage. In their old age they live together in a relation shown as entirely innocent sexually. She cherishes him in his feeble state as mother, sister, wife, though she is none of these. She is connected even more closely to him, in a nameless proximity or alliance, across the gap of their permanent difference and distance from one another: 'No wife, nor sister she, nor is the name / Nor kindred of this friendly pair the same; / Yet so allied are they, that few can feel / Her constant, warm, unwearied, anxious zeal' (ll. 18–21). 'Few can feel her . . . zeal' – this seems to mean both that few people can experience anything like the strength of her feelings for him and that few people are so lucky as he in being the recipient of such zealous care.

'The Parting Hour' begins its narration proper with a reverse diptych. Not 'This was the youth, and he is thus when old', but first Allen Booth in old age, cared for by Judith ('Beneath you tree, observe an ancient pair –' [l. 15]), and then, in abrupt juxtaposition, Allen Booth as a child ('To David Booth, his fourth and last-born boy, / Allen his name, was more than common joy' [ll. 32–3]). The rest of the poem then attempts to fill in the void between the two pictures by showing the binding links joining the deeds between.

This attempt conspicuously fails. The way it fails turns on just that opposition, so important already in Aristotle, between what is conspicuous or perspicuous, what is theatrical, what can be seen or seen through, so that time becomes space, the diachronic synchronic, and, on the other hand, what can be told or narrated in a minute tracing which retains its diachronic sequentiality, like the links of a chain, one following another. Such a claim may be seen or seen through only metaphorically, as when one says. 'I see it all now.' The words 'prospect,' 'prospects,' 'picture,' 'feature,' and 'scene' echo through the poem. These words keep before the reader the visual image for understanding. To understand is to read a picture. The poem demonstrates, however, that all the attempts by the poet-narrator and by the hero to bring into the light of clear-seeing the continuity of his life only makes more evident the gaps within it. These make his life not like a picture but like a sentence of faulty grammar, an anacoluthon beginning with one person or tense and shifting suddenly and unaccountably to another. The hour during which Allen Booth parts from his beloved on the beach and fares forth by ship to seek his fortune so that he may marry her inserts a void between them and within his life which can never be filled by any retrospective narration. His subsequent betrayal of Judith and of his community by marrying a Spanish Catholic maiden, fathering Catholic children, and converting to Catholicism only reaffirms the betrayal which occurred when he parted from Judith in the first place. Once he has left her he can never return to her and never return to himself, nor can he explain how he came to differ from himself, how he came to betray both Judith and himself;

> They parted, thus by hope and fortune led,
> And Judith's hours in pensive pleasure fled;
> But when return'd the youth? – the youth no more
> Return'd exulting to his native shore;
> But forty years were past, and then there came
> A worn-out man with wither'd limbs and lame . . .
>
>   (ll. 181–6)

Two of Crabbe's four epigraphs from Shakespeare, chosen with admirable insight, provide models for this discontinuity. The first is from Imogen's speech in *Cymbeline*, I: 3. It opposes a 'parting kiss' as the jointure between two words to the abrupt intervention of her father: 'ere I could / Give him that parting kiss, which I had set / Betwixt two charming words – comes in my father.' A 'parting kiss' is an oxymoron combining joining and separation. The entrance of the father only anticipates the separation the kiss would have signalled, just as the loving separation of Allen and Judith is imposed by their parents' disapproval. They cannot marry until he has a fortune. Once something which does not fit the sequence has been inserted between two words, even a parting kiss, the grammar of the sentence of which they are part can never be satisfactorily completed. The sentence becomes a failure in following, which is the etymo-logical meaning of the word anacoluthon.

In the second epigraph, from *Comedy of Errors*, V: 1, Aegeon tells how 'careful hours with Time's deformed hand / Have written strange defeatures in my face,' just as time changes Allen Booth from hopeful youth of fair prospects into an old man in no recognizable way like his former self. Far from being that principle of irresistible force making for form, for continuity, and guaranteeing them, as Crabbe's opening lines promise, time is for Crabbe, as for Shakespeare, a deforming power making things differ from themselves. The figure for this is the changes in a face, its 'defeaturing,' in Shakespeare's use of a word of which this is the first example in the *OED*. The word shifts the understanding of a face from a visual image to an image of reading. This parallels the clash between picture and story, scene and narrative, theater and discourse, in Crabbe's poem. The face is not an image to see but a set of signs or features, a written text to decipher. The distinctive feature of the text written by time on a face is its unreadability, its disconnection from itself, its discontinuity with itself, its defeaturing. Allen Booth tries in vain, when he returns to his native shore after forty years' exile, 'to trace / Some youthful features in some aged face' (ll. 221–2).

Time for man is not a natural or organic continuity, nor is it ever a picture which can be seen at a single glance. Time for man is always experienced as some kind of sign, as a track to be followed, a line to be retraced, a face with features to be read. This means that time is always experienced as an incon-gruous repetition. It is experienced as a picture with gaps or as two pictures side by side which cannot be reconciled. This means also, as Crabbe's story-teller and his protagonist find out, discovering those gaps, discontinuities, incongruities, and incoherences which are intrinsic to any repetitive structure of signs. When one tries to retrace the line it never can be made to hang together. Far from doing what he promises at the beginning, showing the continuity of a life, all Crabbe's story-teller's efforts only make the 'mysterious void[s] . . . between' more evident. His narration presents discontinuous vignettes rather than a continuous chain of events. There is no way to explain how or why Allen Booth came to differ from himself, why he married someone else, abjured his faith, failed to come back sooner, postponing from day to day and year to year the reunion that would heal the gap opened by the parting hour.

The temporal structure of 'The Parting Hour' is strange enough. First the narrator presents the 'ancient pair' beneath the tree. Next he leaps back to Allen Booth's childhood and the events leading up to his parting from Judith

Flemming. Then he leaps forward forty years to Allen's return and to his attempt to pick up again the continuity of his life by returning to Judith. This he can do only if he can satisfactorily account for the intervening years and bring the past up to the present.

The narrative responsibility at this point shifts to Allen himself. He is shown compulsively telling his story over and over to Judith, 'running it through' in the phrase from Othello's narration of his life to Desdemona Crabbe uses as his fourth epigraph (*Othello*, I: 3). Allen tells his story repeatedly in a hopeless attempt to get it right, to justify himself in his eyes and hers. The key term for this narration is the word 'relate'. It is a word for connection, for telling, and for family tie. The signal of the temporal incoherence of his 'relation' is the shift back and forth between the past tense and the historical present. Only if his narrative can turn the past sequence of events into a present simultaneous possession can the relation succeed, but this can never happen, and so his relation vibrates between the two tenses, and must be repeated over and over without any hope of ever succeeding: 'To her, to her alone, his various fate, / At various times, 'tis comfort to relate' (ll. 309–10); 'First he related . . .' (l. 313); 'He next related . . .' (l. 372); 'Here his relation closes . . .' (l. 434). Far from connecting the past to the present by a minute tracing of the intervening events, Allen only succeeds in bringing himself back to a present in which he is two persons, the faithful husband of his Spanish wife Isabel, father of her children, and at the same time the faithful fiancé of Judith. Whichever way he turns he must betray one or the other of them. Each is the dream which makes the other impossible as waking reality, and so his selfhood, his 'life,' is irrevocably divided, parted from itself. With that parting goes any hope of a coherent narrative with beginning, middle, and end:

> . . . how confused and troubled all appear'd;
> His thoughts in past and present scenes employ'd,
> All views in future blighted and destroy'd:
> His were a medley of bewild'ring themes,
> Sad as realities, and wild as dreams.

(ll. 429–33)

Separated from his origin by his betrayal of his childhood love, Allen has no certain prospects or views toward the future. He can only hope for the 'little earth' Cardinal Wolsey asks for in the passage from *Henry VIII* (IV: 2) Crabbe uses as his fifth epigraph to the poem. Allen Booth returns to 'his native bay / Willing his breathless form should blend with kindred clay' (ll. 189–90). The old folk of his native village say, 'The man is Allen Booth, and it appears / He dwelt among us in his early years; / We see the name engraved upon the stones, / Where this poor wanderer means to lay his bones' (ll. 279–82). Only when Allen Booth is a dead body buried in a little plot of earth, a tombstone over his head with a single name engraved on it joining him to his family already buried there, can he be related enough to himself to be joined to anything or to anyone else without danger of parting from it or from her. He can be indissolubly wedded only to the 'kindred clay.'

'The Parting Hour' ends where it began, with the aged Allen Booth sleeping under a tree watched over by the unwearied care of his beloved Judith. Far from being an unequivocal ending tying Allen Booth's life together, this picture, the reader now knows, is the image of Allen Booth's disconnection from himself, as he dreams of his Spanish wife and children in the presence of the loving Judith whom he cannot help but betray as long as he is still alive. The poem ends with his waking from his dreams of Isabel to face Judith and cry, 'My God! 'twas but a dream' (l. 473).

'The Parting Hour' provides one striking image for this failure of narrative continuity. Allen is exiled for heresy from the Spanish colony where he has married and prospered. While he is poor no one pays any attention to him, but when he is wealthy they notice him and single him out for punishment:

> Alas! poor Allen, through his wealth was seen
> Crimes that by poverty conceal'd had been;
> Faults that in dusty pictures rest unknown
> Are in an instant through the varnish shown.
>
> (ll. 361–4)

It was lack of money which drove Allen away from England in the first place. If he had had enough of it he could have married Judith and maintained his continuity with himself and with his sworn fidelity to Judith. Money in the first life of Allen Booth stands for the missing principle of coherence. In his second life, however, when money is obtained it becomes the instrument of discontinuity, separating him forever from Isabel, from his children, and from his second self. The figure Crabbe uses seems an especially striking one when the use of the image of the 'picture' elsewhere in the poem as a metaphor of a given state of a man's life is remembered. The attempt to varnish over a dirty picture only brings out its 'faults.' 'Faults' – the word recalls 'gaps' and 'void' in the opening of the poem. Varnish may be taken as a figure for narrative, for the attempt to relate one thing to another in a sequential discourse. This attempt at varnishing over only brings out its impossibility. It reveals unbridgeable gaps, like geological faults in a terrain. Crabbe's 'The Parting Hour,' in its attempt to fulfill its promise of being able to show how a life hangs together, reveals the impossibility of fulfilling this promise. Any attempt to do so is a coverup, a varnishing over. This infallibly betrays the hiatuses it tries to obscure.

'The Parting Hour,' almost in spite of itself, deconstructs two of those cherished certainties of humanist literary study, the continuity of the self and the organic continuity of narrative from beginning to middle to end. It might be claimed that the poem is an aberration among those by its author or among those of its period, but this could be shown not to be the case. One need only think of the doubts raised about the unity of the self and about the cohesion of time by Locke, Diderot, or Hume, or in their different ways, by Rousseau and Wordsworth, to recognize that Crabbe's poem is a miniature version of one of the distinctive features of Pre-romanticism and Romanticism. This feature is the copresence of a powerful affirmation of the system of metaphysical assumptions of which Greek thought was one version, along with an equally powerful disarticulation of that system. This double affirmation and denial, tying and untying, in fact characterizes our own moment as I began by describing it. Without denying that there have been vast gaps and new beginnings both in linguistic history and in cultural history, this affirmation and denial may by hypothesis be said to form the unity in disunity of any 'period' in Western intellectual and literary history, even that of the Greeks. The distinctiveness of any historical period, 'the Renaissance,' 'Romanticism,' 'Modernism,' or whatever, lies in its special combination of certain recurring elements rather than in its introduction of anything unheard of before. The gaps and disconti- nuities making linguistic and cultural history a vast anacoluthon are within each synchronic expression, making it heterogeneous, as well as in the diachronic movement from one expression to another.

[. . .]

Beginning with an apparently marginal or innocuous example, Crabbe's 'The Parting Hour,' I have been led to recognize that in this poem the system of assumptions about selfhood, history, and literary form I began by describing is both affirmed and dismantled. If one should dare to extrapolate from this example, one might formulate this hypothetically as a general law for all texts in our tradition. If this law holds, then the conflict at this moment in American literary study between conservatives and deconstructers is only the latest example of a recurrent pattern in Western literature and literary criticism. If this should be the case, what then follows for 'the ethics of reading'?

Two related provisional hypotheses about this may be briefly made in conclusion. The first is that neither the challenges to traditional humanistic certainties in contemporary American criticism nor the defensively aggressive reaffirmation of those certainties is willful, malicious, or blindly ignorant, nor is either something unique to our epoch, some unheard of nihilism, the 'end of man,' in one case, or a 'new humanism' special to these far Western shores, in the other. Each position repeats operations of writing and reading which have recurred throughout our history. The perhaps necessary error or blindness of either is not to recognize the necessity of the other.

The second conclusion is embodied in that word 'necessity.' Both sorts of reading are necessitated by the words of the texts they treat. This means that reading is always an epistemological necessity before it is a matter of ethical choice or evaluation. More radically, it means that the ethics of reading is subject to a categorical imperative which is linguistic rather than transcendent or a matter of subjective will. Epistemology must take precedence over ethics in reading. One cannot make ethical judgments, perform ethical actions, such as teaching a poem, without first subjecting oneself to the words on the page, but once that has happened, the ethical operation will already necessarily have taken place. As Hölderlin says, in a phrase quoted by Paul de Man in a recent essay, *Es ereignet sich aber das Wahre*. As de Man says, this can be freely translated, 'What is true is what is bound to take place,' which means that 'reading . . . has to go against the grain of what one would want to happen in the name of what has to happen' (de Man 1978, xi). A reading is true as an acute angle is true to its model, or as one voice or word is true to another voice or word. The ethics of reading is not some act of the human will to interpretation which extracts moral themes from a work, or uses it to reaffirm what the reader already knows, or imposes a meaning freely in some process of reader response or perspectivist criticism, seeing the text in a certain way. The ethics of reading is the power of the words of the text over the mind and words of the reader. This is an irresistible coercion which shapes what the reader or teacher says about the text, even when what he says is most reductive or evasive. *Es ereignet sich aber das Wahre*. The ethics of reading is the moral necessity to submit in one way or another, whatever one says, to the truth of this linguistic imperative.

Note

1. The recent statistics are appalling enough. In 1964 only one high school student in four studied a foreign language. Now the ratio has dropped to one in seven. In 1966, thirty-four percent of American colleges required a foreign language for admission. Now only eight percent do. (*The New York Times*, Saturday, 10 November 1979.) Nevertheless, the techniques of teaching foreign languages have greatly improved in America, and some students, in public as well as in private high schools, are given excellent foreign language training.

4

Reading Telling: Kant

'No,' said the priest, 'it is not necessary to accept everything as true, one must only accept it as necessary.' 'A melancholy conclusion', said K. 'It turns lying into a necessary principle.'

K said that with finality, but it was not his final judgment. He was too tired to survey all the conclusions arising from the story, and the trains of thought into which it was leading him were unfamiliar, dealing with impalpabilities . . .

Franz Kafka, *The Trial*[1]

My example is from Immanuel Kant's *Grundlegung zur Metaphysik der Sitten (Foundations of the Metaphysics of Morals)* (1785). Already that choice involves a complex set of moves or placements, even 'political' commitments, if not ethical choices, in the sense that we speak of 'academic politics.' [. . .]

To choose Kant, so it seems, is to commit oneself to a certain theory of ethics among others, one that is voluntarist and subjectivistic, but at the same time reaffirms the category of duty and those highest values of renunciation and disinterested service which are inherited from Stoicism, on the one hand, but are on the other hand inseparable from Christianity and especially important in Protestantism. In spite of Kant's pretense of magisterial objectivity and universality he ends up reaffirming just the morality of his country, class, religion, and time. This comedy is nowhere more likely to be played out than in ethical theory. Under the guise of universal truth, it can be argued, Kant is doing no more than reaffirming the presuppositions, the ideology, of a certain class, religion, time in history, and place in Europe. To invoke Kant today, it might appear, is to beg all the questions that ought to remain questions.
[. . .]

To choose Kant is to place oneself, willynilly, within a complex history of the reception of Kant. This history has for an American student of literature writing today at least a double line. On the one hand there is the immense diffuse importance Kant has had, partly by way of his misinterpretation by Schiller, on the development of theories of literature and on the creation of the institutionalized study of literature and the humanities generally in England and the United States. An American writing today writes from within that heritage, whether he knows it or not, as witness, for example, the invocation of Kant at crucial moments in the polemics of both René Wellek and Walter Jackson Bate

against 'deconstruction' for 'destroying literary studies' and helping to pre-
cipitate and greatly exacerbate a 'crisis in English studies.'[2] On the other hand,
Kant enters in a complex way into the history since Kant's time of European
philosophy. This includes of course all three of his main topics, epistemology
and aesthetics as well as ethics.

The names of Nietzsche, Heidegger, and Freud will schematize three main
moments in the response to Kant as a theorist of ethics. Each of these has in a
different way fundamentally challenged Kant's claim to have established universal foundations of the metaphysics of morals, foundations valid for all times
and places. It would be exceedingly naive to write about Kant without
awareness of this after-history, which is our own history, for example without
taking into account the challenge posed to Kant's theories of freedom and
subjectivity by Freud's concept of the unconscious, or by Nietzsche's constant
polemic against Kant, for example in *The Genealogy of Morals* (though Nietzsche
is more dependent on Kant than he is willing to admit), or by Heidegger's
situating of the definition of man as subjectivity and will as a climactic moment
in the history of metaphysics, that is, the history in some sense of an error
induced by the occultation of Being. All this extremely dense, complex, and
thick history stands between us and Kant like an opaque mist or like an
impenetrable thicket of thorns around the sleeping beauty, forbidding direct
access to Kant. Nevertheless, let us look at a crucial passage in Kant's
Grundlegung, to try to see just what it says and what is problematic about what
it says, keeping in mind that my interest is not in ethics as such but in the ethics
of reading and in the relation of the ethical moment in reading to relation in the
sense of giving an account, telling a story, narrating.

The passage is a footnote in which Kant defends his use of the term 'respect'
(Achtung). Footnotes, as any astute reader will know, are often places where an
author gives him or herself away in one way or another in the act of fabricating a
protective cover. A footnote often reveals an uneasiness, identifies a fissure or
seam in an author's thought by saying it is not there. Kant's footnote is no
exception. This footnote says a mouthful, as they say. Moreover, it is an
example of that sort of passage where an author reads him or herself. In such
passages the ethics of reading is manifested in one of its most revealing versions,
that is, in places where the author and the reader are the same. At such moments
an author turns back on him- or herself, so to speak, turns back on a text he or
she has written, re-reads it, and, it may be, performs an act which can be called
an example of the ethics of reading. A footnote, as in this case, is often a
commentary on the main text, a reading of it, with all the possibilities of
alteration, suppression, inadvertent revelation, or irrelevance which characterize
'readings' by a third party, you or I, for example, as readers of Kant.

Kant has been explaining that 'Duty is the necessity of an action executed
from respect for law' (Pflicht ist die Notwendigkeit einer Handlung aus
Achtung fürs Gesetz) (1982, 7: 26; 1978, 19).[3] This means that a moral action

must not be performed either from 'inclination' (Neigung), that is, because I want to do it, am attracted by something outside myself, nor from calculation of its results, even good ones for myself or for others. When these private and social motives are removed, 'nothing remains which can determine the will objectively except the law [das Gesetz], and nothing subjectively except pure respect [reine Achtung] for this practical law'. Readers of Kant will know the importance of this notion of purity. It means the removal of everything contingent, empirical, local, such as the moral codes of a particular time, place, class, country, or culture, in order to leave the absolutely universal, abstracted from all particularity. What Kant calls 'the highest and unconditional good' can only be found in the pure will of a rational being directed out of respect toward what he calls the 'law in itself' (Gesetz an sich selbst) (E, 20; G, 27), the 'law as such' (Gesetzmäßigkeit) (E, 21; G, 28), whatever *that* means. This is just what is most in question here and for the ethics of reading 'in general.'

At this point Kant draws himself up and inserts a footnote attempting to clarify what he means by *Achtung* and distinguishing it from any sort of subjective feeling. Though *Achtung* would have been the ordinary eighteenth-century German word for 'respect,' and though the word did not apparently carry the military connotations it has today, nevertheless its nuances were not quite the same as the English word *respect*. *Achtung* means 'attention, heed,' as well as 'esteem, respect, regard.' It suggests a coerced or alarmed taking notice of something possibly dangerous. The verb *achten* with 'auf' means 'pay attention or regard or heed to' as well as (without 'auf') 'esteem, respect, value, set store by, have regard for, have a high opinion of.' *Achtung!*, now at least, means 'look out! take care! beware!' In his footnote Kant wants to say that *Achtung* in the sense he is using it to mean respect for the moral law as such is a feeling which is not a feeling, or not in the usual sense a feeling. It is easy to see that much hangs on persuading the reader to accept this distinction, since otherwise he or she might be led to believe that ethics is in one way or another the product of mere subjective feeling. Here is the entire footnote. If we can read it accurately in the context of its surrounding paragraphs in the main text we shall have at least a preliminary grasp of Kant's theory of ethics as well as of what is most problematic about that theory, what is unspoken or implicit in it. Whether my reading of this passage by Kant about respect is properly respectful, or does violence to the text, and whether my reading of Kant or my reader's reading of what I say are in any sense ethical acts I must leave it to the reader to judge:

> It might be objected that I take refuge in an obscure feeling [in einem dunkelen Gefühle] behind the word 'respect', instead of clearly resolving the question with a concept of reason. But though respect is a feeling, it is not one received through any [outer] influence [kein durch Einfluß empfangenes] but is self-wrought by a rational concept [einen Vernunftbegriff selbstgewirktes Gefühl]: thus it differs specifically

from all feelings of the former kind which may be referred to inclination or fear [Neigung oder Furcht]. What I recognize directly as a law for myself [als Gesetz für mich] I recognize with respect, which means merely the consciousness of the submission of my will to a law without the intervention of other influences on my mind. The direct determination of the will by the law and the consciousness of this determination is respect: thus respect can be regarded as the effect of the law on the subject and not as the cause of the law [nicht als Ursache desselben]. Respect is properly the conception of a worth which thwarts my self-love. Thus it is regarded as an object neither of inclination nor of fear, though it has something analogous to both [obgleich es mit beiden zugleich etwas Analogisches hat: the translation omits 'zugleich,' which means 'at the same time, simultaneously,' and hence hides the play on two words ending in 'gleich,' which means 'like, analogous to,' as a 'Gleichnis' is a likeness; 'obgleich,' 'zugleich,' 'Analogisches,' words for likeness echo through the phrase as a kind of underthought or ground bass emphasizing the problem Kant is raising]. The only object of respect is the law, and indeed only the law which we impose on ourselves and yet recognize as necessary in itself [das wir uns selbst und doch als an sich notwendig auferlegen]. As a law, we are subject to it without consulting self-love; as imposed on us by ourselves, it is a consequence of our will. In the former respect it is analogous to fear and in the latter to inclination. All respect for a person is only respect for the law [Alle Achtung für eine Person ist eigentlich nur Achtung fürs Gesetz] (of righteousness, etc.) of which the person provides an example [das Beispiel]. Because we see the improvement of our talents as a duty, we think of a person of talents as the example of a law, as it were [auch gleichsam das Beispiel eines Gesetzes vor] (the law that we should by practice become like him in his talents), and that constitutes our respect. All so-called moral interest consists solely in respect for the law. (E, 20–1; G, 27–8)

Is it possible, I ask first, to add another analogy to those Kant proposes and to say that our respect for a text is like our respect for a person, that is, it is respect not for the text in itself but respect for a law which the text exemplifies? Which would be the literal ground of this analogy, a text or a person, which the metaphor? What would it mean to say in this case that a text is like a person? My claim that reading this footnote by Kant will help understand the ethics of reading depends on presuming the validity of this analogy. Kant shows what it might mean to say that our response to a person is ethical, in the sense that we see him or her as an example of a transcendent and universal moral law. Is there any possibility that the law exemplified by a text might also be properly ethical, or have an ethical moment, as opposed to grammatical, syntactic, or tropological dimensions? I mean by an ethical moment not the thematic statement or dramatization of some ethical law ('Thou shalt not commit adultery,' for example, surely a staple ethical theme of novels), but the effective and functional embodiment of some ethical law in action. If that were the case, the effect on the reader of the text would be like the effect on him of the moral law, that is, a categorical imperative, necessarily binding his will or leading him willingly to bind his own will. The act of reading would lead the reader voluntarily to impose the necessary ethical law embodied in that text on himself.

Accepting for the moment the possibility that respect for a text may be somehow analogous to respect for a person who is an example of the moral law, let me return to Kant's words, out of respect for the text of his footnote. The careful reader will have noted that Kant somewhat uneasily evades several dangers simultaneously with his carefully circumscribed definition of 'respect.' He does this, however, only to be vulnerable to another danger which remains at the end of the footnote still only implicit in what he says, as if it were generated by the act of protective circumscription. This danger becomes more explicit in the following paragraphs of the main text. If respect, as Kant affirms, is a feeling, it lacks one of the main characteristics of feelings for Kant, namely that feelings are generated as 'inclination' or 'fear,' a tendency to approach or flee, in response to something external to the self. A feeling is a response to an 'influence' (Einfluß) which flows into the mind from without, coercing it and generating its affects. Respect, however, is not a feeling in this sense. It is a feeling which is not a feeling. It is self-wrought rather than being a response to something external. It is not a movement toward or away from something desired or feared. On the other hand, respect is a response to something that preexists it and exists outside the mind, not the creation of that something. If Kant must avoid at all costs (at the cost of logical coherence) the possibility that *Achtung* is mere reflex reaction of desire or fear, in the other direction he must avoid at all costs the possibility that since respect is 'self-wrought' it creates or projects its object, the moral law as such. Kant is like a man walking a knife-edge on a mountaintop, with an abyss on either side, the abyss of a productive spontaneity on the one side, the abyss of a passive receptivity on the other. The knife-edge, however, itself turns into an abyss.

If respect neither spontaneously creates its own object nor is a passive response to something outside itself that exists as a manifest objective power, what then is respect respect for or respectful of? What, exactly, is the law? How can I confront it, or define it, or have access to it? The reader would like to know, just as Kafka's man from the country, in the parable 'Before the Law,' respectfully requests a face-to-face confrontation with the law. Kant gives, and can give, only negative or indirect definitions of the moral law. The law is not, for example, any particular moral law that can be formulated as a maxim: 'Don't tell lies'; 'Thou shalt not steal'; 'Thou shalt not commit adultery,' etc. The law in question is the law as such. This means that the relation of any particular moral law that can be formulated in so many words to the law as such is something like, or is analogous to, the relation between a person we respect because he or she embodies the moral law and the law itself. 'Mere conformity to the law as such,' says Kant in the paragraph in the main text following the footnote, '(without assuming any particular law applicable to certain actions) serves as the principle of the will' (Hier ist nun die bloße Gesetzmäßigkeit überhaupt (ohne irgend ein auf gewisse Handlungen bestimmtes Gesetz zum Grunde zu legen) das, was dem Willen zum Prinzip dient) (E, 21; G, 28); the translation misses the metaphor of grounding or establishing a solid base in the German phrase 'zum Grunde zu legen,' 'to lay down as a ground.'

What, then, is the law as such? The reader would like to know. He or she would like to have access to it, to confront it face to face, to see it written down somewhere, so he or she can know whether or not he or she is obeying it. Well, Kant cannot tell you exactly what the law as such is, in so many words, nor can he tell you exactly where it is, or where it comes from. The law, as Jacques Derrida puts it, gives itself without giving itself.[4] It may only be confronted in its delegates or representatives or by its effects on us or on others. It is those effects that generate respect for the law. But if Kant cannot tell you exactly what the law is, where it is, or where it comes from, he can nevertheless tell you to what it is analogous. Into the vacant place where there is no direct access to the law as such, but where we stand respectfully, like the countryman in Kafka's parable, 'before the law,' is displaced by metaphor or some other form of analogy two forms of feeling that *can* be grasped and named directly. Respect for the law is said to be analogous to just those two feelings which it has been said not to be: inclination and fear. The name for this procedure of naming by figures of speech what cannot be named literally because it cannot be faced directly is catachresis or, as Kant calls it in paragraph fifty-nine of the *Critique of Judgment*, 'hypo-typosis' (Hypotypose). Kant's linguistic procedure in this footnote is an example of the forced or abusive transfer of terms from an alien realm to name something which has no proper name in itself since it is not an object which can be directly confronted by the senses. That is what the word *catachresis* means; etymologically: 'against usage.' What is 'forced or abusive' in this case is clear enough. Kant has said that respect for the law is not based on fear or inclination, but since there is no proper word for what it is based on, he is forced to say it is like just those two feelings, fear and inclination, he has said it is not like.

Respect for the law, says Kant, is like fear in that we recognize the law as necessary, unavoidable. In this the law is like, say, some natural catastrophe that we fear. The law is something we are subject to whether we like it or not. We accept the law, necessarily, without consulting that most basic of motives, self-love. Respect for the law, on the other hand, is also analogous to inclination in that we impose the law freely on ourselves. We really want to obey the law. In this sense respect for the law is like the inclination that leads us to desire something desirable. Not only do we really want to respect the law, but since the law is a law for ourselves, it is something we impose freely on ourselves as reasonable beings. In that sense respect for the law is respect for ourselves as being worthy of the law or worthy of having a law for ourselves, worthy of having a categorical imperative imposed on us. Or rather, since each act of respect for the law is unique and individual, a moment within historical time, so to speak, even though the law as such is universal and transhistorical, it would be better to stick to the first person singular and say, 'I freely impose the moral law on myself, though at the same time I respect its absolute necessity. I freely impose the moral law on myself, as a law for myself, out of respect for the law, and in respecting the law I respect myself as a free rational self able to have respect for the law and able to act ethically on the basis of the law.' In doing all this, if I can do it, in one complex single momentary movement of my will, I myself become an example of the moral law, an embodiment of it. As such I become worthy of the respect of others.

If I remember at this point the additional analogy I added to Kant's analogies and say that respect for a text is like respect for a person, can I say that this is because the creation of the text by the author is a response to the law, not in answer to any particular, specifiable moral law, such as the prohibition against adultery, but a response to the moral law as such? [. . .] If a philosophical, literary, or critical text is worthy of our respect it can only be because it has been created out of respect for the law, just as my respect is not for a person as such but for the person as an example of the law. Which way does this analogy go? Is the concept of a person perhaps covertly modeled on the concept of a text, or is a text worthy of our respect because it is like a person, or are both like one another because each is analogous to that third thing, spring and generative source of both, the law as such? It is easy to assume that the concept of the freely willing subjectivity, the self, ego, or 'Ich,' takes precedence here and is the fundamental presupposition of all Kant's thinking about ethics or the practical reason, but analogies have a way of working both ways. It may be that the concept of a person is to some degree or in some way modeled on that for which it is the model. Novels may be a place to see how this question of priority remains a question. The question is experienced concretely by the reader of a novel in the analogy he recognizes between the character in the novel as an example of the moral law and the text itself as an example of the moral law. My act of reading the character, understanding him, an act articulated in the novel by the narrator, is an allegory of my act of reading the text, figuring it out, as they say.

But is this analogy really justified in the case of Kant? Am I not doing disrespectful violence to the passage in Kant I claim to be reading by arguing that it can be used as the basis of a theory of the ethics of reading novels? What does Kant's theory of ethics have to do with narrative, with storytelling, or even with history as the story we tell about the changes of society through the centuries? The moral law as such is above and beyond all that. It remains absolutely the same at all times and places and for all persons. No person can be more than a contingent example of it. No story, it would seem, can do other than falsify it by entangling the law in the meshes of the extrinsic particulars of a time and place, imaginary or real. In spite of that, and as if to give it the lie, the reader can watch a shadowy narrative and the inadvertent demonstration of the necessity of narrative in any account of ethics slowly emerge as Kant develops his concept of respect. Even when it is defined as pure practical reason, ethics involves narrative, as its subversive accomplice. Storytelling is the impurity which is necessary in any discourse about the moral law as such, in spite of the law's austere indifference to persons, stories, and history. There is no theory of ethics, no theory of the moral law and of its irresistible, stringent imperative, its 'Thou shalt' and 'Thou shalt not,' without storytelling and the temporalization (in several senses of the word) which is an intrinsic feature of all narrative. This justifies, I claim, my choice of novels and stories to illustrate the ethics of reading.

The reader has already encountered in the footnote itself one narrative element. I have respect not for a person but for a person as an example of some ethical value which is in turn an example of the law as such. If I cannot confront the law directly, stand face to face with it, so to speak (for reasons which are not yet clear, perhaps will never be wholly clear), I can, on the other hand, confront face to face a person who is an example of the law. There is already a latent story in that confrontation. It implies the story of their interaction or mutual influence or growing knowledge of one another. If I know the person well enough to know that he is an example of the law, there must be a story to tell about our relation. It might be the basic story, for example, so fundamental to the novel as a genre, of the relation between the narrator and the protagonist whose story he tells as an example for himself and for the reader. The narrator can only know what the character knows. The narrator therefore, it may be, has access to the moral law only through the protagonist and can experience the law only through the protagonist's experience of it. An example would be the dependence of Henry James' narrator on the limits of Maisie's knowledge in *What Maisie Knew*. Or the confrontation of the person as example may be that of one character by another within the tale, as, to stick with Henry James, Strether's confrontation of Chad in *The Ambassadors* generates all the story in that novel. Strether learns by way of what Chad learns, since he does not himself have Chad's transformative 'learning experience.'

One glimpses here a curious relation between the necessity of narrative in any discourse about ethics and the necessity of using analogies or figures of speech in place of an unavailable literal or conceptual language. Narrative, like analogy, is inserted into that blank place where the presumed purely conceptual language of philosophy fails or is missing. The relation of the character who is an example of the law to the law as such is figurative. The person is a synecdoche, part for whole and affirmed to be like the whole, as a sample of cloth is said to be like the whole cloth. This relation of person to law is a form of analogy or likeness, since the example is said to be like that of which it is an example. In being an analogy, the person who is an example of the law and thereby worthy of our respect is related to the law in a way analogous to the way fear and inclination are related to respect for the law. The exemplary person is not the law. He is in a certain sense not even like the law. How can a particular person be said to be like a universal law? But he is in another sense like the law. If we can never confront the law as such, we *can* confront the person who is an example of the law, just as fear and inclination are feelings we can understand and define and which we move into the place of respect which cannot be understood and defined in so many literal words. Confrontation with a person who is an example of the law stands in the place of, substitutes for, is a figure of, the law which is in no place we can reach and enter. The law is always somewhere else or at some other time, back there when the law was first imposed or off to the future when I may at last confront it directly, in unmediated vision. Within that space, between here and that unattainable there of the law as such, between now and the beginning or the end, narrative enters as the relation of the search for a perhaps impossible proximity to the law. If the authority of narrative, its coherence and force as a story, depends on that proximity to the law which would be defined by saying that the narration, like a person, is worthy of our respect because it is an example of the moral law as such, a clear manifestation of its productive force, then insofar as narrative takes place within the space of a perpetual deferral of direct confrontation with the law, it can be said that narrative is the narration of the impossibility of narrative in the sense of a coherent, logical, perspicuous story with beginning, middle, end, and paraphrasable meaning. The function of narrative, for those who have eyes to see and ears to hear with and understand, is to keep this out in the open.

Kant's obscure, evasive, and carefully concealed recognition both of the necessity of narrative in any account of the moral law as such and of the necessary failure of any narration to take the reader where he wants to be, face to face with the law, is expressed in the paragraphs in the main text of the *Grundlegung zur Metaphysik der Sitten* which follow just after the paragraph to which the footnote is appended. In the first of these following paragraphs the entanglement of narration and ethics is obliquely revealed in Kant's insertion, just at this place in his argument, of his celebrated formulation that I should act, if I wish to act ethically, at all times and places as if the private maxim according to which I choose to do or not to do were to be made the universal law for all mankind. How do I know I am acting ethically? I must ask myself what would happen if a law were made commanding everyone, everywhere at all times, to act also in just that way in such a situation. I must act in such a way (als so) that it is as if I were assuming that to be the case. In that 'as if' a whole fictive narrative is implicit. Here are Kant's words, or rather the words of his translator, with some of Kant's own words inserted parenthetically:

> 'But what kind of law can that be, the conception of which must determine the will without reference to the expected result? Under this condition alone the will can be called absolutely good without qualification. Since I have robbed the will of all impulses which could come to it from obedience to any law [die ihm aus der Befolgung irgend eines Gesetzes entspringen könnten], nothing remains to serve as a

principle of the will except universal conformity of its action to law as such. That is, I should never act in such a way that I could not also will that my maxim should be a universal law [d. i. ich soll niemals anders verfahren, als so, *daß ich auch wollen könne, meine Maxime solle ein allgemeines Gesetz werden*: A more literal translation would be: 'That is, I should never act in any other way than in such a manner that I could also will that my maxim should be a universal law'.] Mere conformity to law as such (without assuming any particular law applicable to certain actions) serves as the principle of the will, and it must serve as such if duty is not to be a vain delusion and chimerical concept [ein leerer Wahn und chimärischer Begriff]. (E, 21; G, 28)

Kant's tone here is so reasonable, so blandly affirmative and apodictic, that what is extraordinary about his theory of ethics may slip by the reader. A truly moral act, he says, the act of a will absolutely good without qualification (ohne Einschränkung) must not only be performed without consideration of the expected result. It also must not be based on 'obedience to any law' (aus der Befolgung irgend eines Gesetzes). Obedience to the law must not be based on obedience to any law. It is all very well to say that Kant means on the one hand any particular law, the law against adultery or the law against lying, for example, and on the other hand the 'law as such,' the fundamental principle of lawfulness, free of any particularity or delimitation. To say that only brings the paradox (if that is the word for it) more fully into the open in revealing the apparently uncrossable abyss between the law as such and any particular moral law which we might be able to use as a standard of judgement and obey or not obey. What kind of code of ethics or table of 'Thou shalts' and 'Thou shalt nots' is it which is wholly detached, apparently irrevocably detached, from any ascertainable connection to the principle of law as such on which it should be grounded? On the other hand, what can one say of a law as such, presumed foundation or *Grundlegung* of all morals, that is detached from all embodiment in any particular code of ethics and seems to give me no directions about how to act in a particular case, or at best directions which seem to be exceedingly evasive and indirect? In order to act morally I must act with complete indifference to any expected results of my actions, good, bad, or indifferent, for others or for myself, and I must act in abstraction from any impulse of obedience to any particular moral law. In order to act morally I must act immorally, or amorally, out of pure self-wrought universal conformity of my action to the law as such (die allgemeine Gesetzmäßigkeit der Handlungen). But how in the world am I going to make my actions conform to (in the sense of fit, be suitably measured by) a law which is without law, so purified of any identifiable content that it seems utterly useless as a standard of action in any practical sense? The law seems to impose on me a double interdict. On the one hand, it exists as an interdict against approaching it, confronting it directly, taking possession of it, giving it any specific content, for example in the verbal enunciation of the law as such. On the other hand, the law is an interdict against crossing over the gulf between the law as such and any particular maxim I might formulate on the basis of which I might decide how to act in a given case. If I am to act morally I must not act out of calculation of consequences, nor out of obedience to any particular law. I seem to be caught in an impossible double bind. Either way I have had it. And yet I must act. I must choose. Not to act is an act, not to choose a choice, and I want with all my heart to act morally, to be able to say that what I do I do out of absolute duty, do because I must do it. Unless I can find some way to ground my decision, my choice, my action on the law as such, duty will be no more than another name for doing what one likes, groundless and insubstantial, 'a vain delusion and chimerical concept,' a will-o'-the-wisp.

Kant's solution to this apparently insoluble knot in thinking is just the place where the necessity of narrative enters into his theory of ethics. We must, he says, perform a little experiment, enter in imagination into a little fiction, an 'in such a way' or 'als so.' I must pretend that my maxim, that is the particular ethical rule by which this particular action is guided, were to be a universal legislation for all mankind. It is an act of imagination, like writing a novel. When I enter in imagination into the miniature novel I have created for myself, then I shall be able to tell in a moment whether or not my action is moral. Narrative as a fundamental activity of the human mind, the power to make fictions, to tell stories to oneself or to others, serves for Kant as the absolutely necessary bridge without which there would be no connection between the law as such and any particular ethical rule of behavior. Just as the blank place where respect is indefinable, can be given no predicate, is filled by the figurative analogy with fear and inclination, two things respect is not, and just as art or the work of art is defined in Kant's third critique, the *Critique of Judgment*, as the only possible bridge between epistemology, on the one hand, the work of pure reason, and ethics, the work of practical reason, on the other (which would otherwise be separated by the great gulf, *die grosse Kluft*, between them),[5] so here within the theory of the practical reason itself another chasm opens up. This chasm too can only be bridged by a species of artwork, though one not openly defined as such by Kant. Across the gap between the law as such and the immediate work in the real world of the practical reason must be cast a little fictional narrative. This narrative must be on both sides of the gulf at once, or lead from the one to the other. It must be within the law as such, and it must at the same time give practical advice for the choices of the pure will in a particular case in the real work of history, society, and my immediate obligations to those around me. If the story I tell myself is a fictional narrative, it must be at the same time firmly implanted, like a bridge's abutments, on both sides of the chasm, in the law as such, which is no chimera, and in the real world where my choices and actions have real effects.

But the story I must tell myself is not just any anecdote involving the ethical choice which is in question for me. Such an imaginary anecdote would return me to the calculation of expected results or to the action out of fear or inclination which Kant has firmly rejected as offering no valid grounds for choice. The story I must tell myself is a miniature version of the inaugural act which creates a nation, a people, a community. I must act as though my private maxim were to be universal legislation for all mankind. In the fiction of this 'in such a way' universal and particular, public and private, the law as such and a particular code of behavior, are bridged, and I become myself an example of the moral law, worthy of respect. The implied story in such an 'als so' is the grand historical story of the divinely sanctioned law-giver or establisher of the social contract, Moses, Lycurgus, or the framers of the Declaration of Independence or of the Rights of Man. In every moral act I must behave as if I were like someone or a small group who make a definitive and revolutionary break in history, ending one era and starting another, as Moses came down from Sinai with the tablets of the law, handing down that law, or laying it down in an act that was radically inaugural, a new beginning for his people. Such an act creates the social order. It establishes the code of law which makes a people a community, not just a lawless conglomeration in which each man's hand is against his neighbor. This inaugural act, moreover, has an implicit teleology. It creates history. It is the prolepsis of a story not only with a beginning but with a middle and an end. Like all founding legislation or drawing up of a social contract it makes a promise: if you follow this law you will be happy and prosperous; if you do not, disaster will follow. My act is not ethical unless I act in such a way that what I do implies a miniature version of this initiating act of lawgiving, and has implicit within it a miniature version of a universal historical narrative. It is the story of a people who are paradigmatic for all mankind, a story moreover which goes from the first beginning of that people to its promised millennial end in a universal reign of justice and peace. Only if I act according to the fiction of this particular 'in such a way' can I be an example of the law and worthy of the respect of others.

In the two paragraphs just after the one which I have been reading, Kant follows up his universal prescription (always to act as if my maxim were to be legislation for all mankind) by giving a little example of the making of a private act a universal example. He makes up a little story or fiction, an 'als so' of the 'als so', so we can see in imagination the sort of thing he means. His procedure is not too different from the use of novels as what George Eliot calls 'experiments in life.' We read novels to see in a safe area of fiction or imagination what would happen if we lived our lives according to a certain principle of moral choice. We take the novel as potentially an example of the moral law as such and as the basis of a legislation for all mankind. All mankind ought to act as Maisie does in *What Maisie Knew* or as Strether does in *The Ambassadors* or as Maggie does in *The Golden Bowl*. The exact terms of the example Kant proposes are an example of a particular form of philosophical genius about which there would be much to say. This is a choice of examples in the course of an argument which are not only not innocent (no example is innocent) but which in open or covert ways pose a fundamental challenge to just the conceptual formulations the examples are apparently meant to exemplify and support. The example undermines that of which it is posed as an example.

'Let the question, for example [zum Beispiel], be:' proposes Kant, 'May I, when in distress, make a promise [ein Versprechen tun] with the intention not to keep it?' (E, 21; G, 29). He then goes on to distinguish two ways of thinking about this. On the one hand I may make calculations of a prudential sort about whether lying in this way will get me out of my fix, whether I am likely to get away with it, whether I shall get in even more trouble later on when it is discovered that I have lied in this way, and so on. Such calculations, for example that of the man who promises the cannibals a better meal later on if they do not eat him now, have nothing whatsoever of the moral about them. Even if I decide to make it my habitual maxim not to make a promise I do not intend to keep because I may get in even more trouble later on, 'such a maxim is based only on an apprehensive concern with consequences' (nur die besorglichen Folgen zum Grunde habe) (E, 22; G, 29). It is not moral because it is based on fear rather than on respect for the law. It is based on prudent calculation of results, not on duty. It is easy to see that there might indeed be cases in which it would be prudent to lie in this way. My real duty reveals itself when I ask myself whether I would be content that my maxim about making false promises should be the basis of a universal legislation. Here is Kant's formulation of what happens when I tell this little story to myself, create a private 'in such a way' or fiction:

> The shortest but most infallible way to find the answer to the question as to whether a deceitful promise is consistent with duty is to ask myself: Would I be content that my maxim (of extricating myself from difficulty by a false promise) should hold as a universal law for myself as well as for others? And could I say to myself that everyone may make a false promise when he is in difficulty from which he cannot otherwise escape? I immediately see that I could will the lie but not a universal law to lie. For with such a law there would be no promises at all, inasmuch as it would be futile to make a pretense of my intention in regard to future actions to those who would not believe this pretense or – if they overhastily did so – who would pay me back in my own coin. Thus my maxim would necessarily destroy itself as soon as it was made a universal law. (E, 22–3; G, 29–30)

As I have said, the motif of making promises is already implicit in the formulation about acting as if my maxim were to be universal legislation for all mankind, so this little narrative of the man making a false promise is already latent in the law of which making false promises is given as merely one example among many. In fact the example is not random but essential. It is implicit as a fundamental aspect of the concept of which it is an exemplification. It is therefore not really an example but a bringing to the surface of the narrative implicit in the concept.

Making promises, moreover, is in two ways subversive of the apparent meaning of the concept of moral action. Making promises, first, is not just any act. It is a specifically linguistic act. It is, in addition, an example of that particular kind of linguistic event called a performative. Making a promise, like betting, excusing, and the like, is a way of doing things with words. The fact that the example Kant chooses is linguistic opens the possibility that the moral law is not just named in words but is brought into existence in words. The fact that the example is not just any form of language but a form which is performative doubles this possibility with a further possibility inherent in all performatives, namely the possibility that it will be impossible ever to confirm with certainty whether the form of language in the performative makes happen what it promises will happen. A performative makes something happen, but, it may be, whether or not it makes happen what it says will happen or intends will happen can never be known for certain. In one direction, then, a promise is 'undecidable' because its authority is uncertain. It cannot be known whether it is based on something outside itself or whether it creates its own autonomous authority in the act of being made. In the other direction its teleology is uncertain. The keeping of a promise is a matter of time or of temporality, the matching of one time, the time of the promising, with another time, the time of the keeping of the promise. That second time may be indefinitely deferred or postponed. But these are just the two things Kant wants the example to exemplify: on the one hand the way a truly moral act is at once autonomous, free, self-wrought, and at the same time based on respect for a universal moral law which precedes it and gives it the law, so to speak, and on the other hand the way such an action can be made the basis of a universal legislation for all mankind, promising them happiness, social stability, and prosperity.

The example Kant chooses is therefore not innocent. It goes against the grain of the argument Kant seems to want above all to secure. He wants to persuade his readers that respect for the law is self-wrought but at the same time determined by a law which precedes it and is external to it. This law exercises over me an implacable necessity, a categorical imperative. I may discover this irresistible coercion, for example, by trying to act contrary to it. The example Kant gives, however, is of a special kind of performative language, the promise. A promise creates its own conditions of obedience in a temporalization requiring a comparison of before and after. Today I make a promise which later on I shall keep or not keep. The validity of the promise does not lie in itself but in its future fulfillment. It may be argued that this future fulfillment is never certainly confirmed, which is to say that it can never be confirmed that a promise has been kept, since something might always be done later on to invalidate my apparent fulfillment of my promise. A promise intrinsically demands an indefinite postponement of its fulfillment. For example, if I promise to be faithful to the woman I marry, it is always possible that after a lifetime of faithfulness I shall at the last minute betray her. [. . .]

This differential, deferential, or, as Jacques Derrida would say, 'differantial,' feature of the law, the way it both is divided within itself and at the same time defers, postpones, its validation, is the place where narrative and the law come together. Narrative can be defined as the indefinite postponement of that ultimate direct confrontation of the law which narrative is nevertheless instituted to make happen in an example worthy of respect. In the space between the promise and the perpetually deferred fulfillment of the promise the story takes place. The law itself, it would seem, is differentiated within itself, inaccessible because of that, and the story is divided against itself in response to that differentiation, out of respect for the division of the law within itself. Such a narrative leaves its readers at the end as dissatisfied as ever, still in expectation of the fulfillment of the promise which was the whole reason for being of the story. What the good reader confronts in the end is not the moral law brought into the open at last in a clear example, but the unreadability of the text. This unreadability is to be defined as the fact that the text commits again the error it denounces, namely, in this case, the error of claiming to be able to speak directly for the law and with the direct authority of the law. [. . .]

As a conclusion to this section of my argument, I turn back to the little hypothetical story Kant proposes as an example of reading, so to speak, his formulation about making my maxim the basis of a universal legislation. [. . .]*

In the case of Kant's little textual allegory in the paragraphs with their footnote I have been trying to read, Kant promises that an example involving promises will make clear the relation of the universal law to the particular case. The example, he assures us, will serve as the safe bridge between the one and the other. Instead of that, the example divides itself within itself between two possible but incompatible readings and so becomes unreadable. The bridge which was to vault over the abyss between universal and particular law opens another chasm within itself. In this case it is the impossibility of deciding whether the immorality of making a promise I do not intend to keep is really an example of a maxim founded on the law as such or whether it is only an example of the way civil order is a fact of language. In the latter case, society would be seen as depending altogether on conventions of language whereby words must go on meaning the same if men and women are to live together in society. An agreement to keep the rules of language the same would then be the foundation of civil order, not the law as such. One might see this as a version of utilitarianism. Who cares whether the state rests 'on the basis of' anything, has any 'ground' or *Grundlegung*, so long as its laws work and lead to the greatest happiness of the greatest number? In this version of utilitarianism, however, society would rest on the extremely precarious ground of a linguistic contract. Such a contract is liable to be broken at any moment. Indeed it necessarily breaks itself all the time. If the possibility of making a lying promise were made a universal law, says Kant, 'there would be no promises at all, inasmuch as it would be futile to make a pretense of my intention in regard to future actions to those who would not believe this pretense or – if they overhastily did so – who would pay me back in my own coin. Thus my maxim would necessarily destroy

---

* There follows a consideration of Paul de Man's reading of the act of legislation in his essay on Rousseau's *Social Contract*. [Ed.]

itself as soon as it was made a universal law.' It is impossible to tell whether this means society depends on a purely human and linguistic contract, or whether it means that there is somewhere an implacable transcendent law against making false promises. Moreover, Kant's formulation does not even give the reader any directions for how one might go about distinguishing between those two possibilities, even though everything hangs on being able to decide which is the correct hypothesis.[6]

Kant's example therefore does not exemplify that of which it is meant to be an example. *Versprechen* as promise here becomes a *Versprechen* in its secondary meaning of 'slip of the tongue'. When that happens *versprechen* as 'to promise' becomes *widersprechen*, 'to contradict,' and the discourse as a whole becomes a *Widersprechung*, a contradiction, something that contradicts itself. There is always a latent contradiction in that German prefix *ver*, which may be either an intensive or, conversely, a privative, a negation. Kant says something other than what he means to say. This something betrays a hidden flaw in his argument and makes that argument a non sequitur or an anacoluthon, a failure in following. The example of the man who makes a promise intending not to keep it is like a bridge that does not meet in the middle, but starts off from either bank and remains incomplete, with a gap where the joining ought to be. What Kant promises to show is that the law as such grounds a particular law against making lying promises. What he actually shows by his little imaginary story is that the social order depends on a precarious intralinguistic and interpersonal agreement to go on meaning the same thing by words. A lying promise is like a private language in that it is impossible with either to count on the internal rules and conventions governing language to remain stable or consistent. If, however, it is an intrinsic feature of language, and especially of that kind of performative called a promise, for example Kant's promise that his example will conclusively demonstrate the categorical necessity of the law, that it makes promises it cannot keep, so that the facts of language exceed the intentions of its users, then that autodestruction Kant describes ('Thus my maxim would necessarily destroy itself as soon as it was made a universal law') will occur whatever my intention. It is an intrinsic feature of promises as a mode of language use that they destroy themselves in this way.

To put this more precisely, intending is another kind of performative, like promising itself. Kant's example contains in fact a double use of performative language. First I promise so and so, to give the cannibals a better meal later if they do not eat me, to be faithful to my wife. Then, or at the same time, I intend or do not intend to keep the promise. The first performative is ratified by the second performative, as though the first were not enough in itself. It is not enough to enunciate a promise. I must also enact a second performative, the intention to keep the promise. The problem is that an intention may be, and in this case clearly is, enunciated only privately. I say to myself that I intend to keep the promise that I have made, or I say to myself that I do not intend to keep it.

The intention not to keep it is what makes it a lying promise. A private intention, however, is like a private language, that is, it is vulnerable to the argument Wittgenstein makes against its possibility. Like a private game, a private language has no independent measure by which it is possible to be sure that its rules remain the same from moment to moment. A private language is therefore no language, or there is no such thing as a private language. The same thing may be said of that special kind of performative called a private intention. The unsettling or even terrifying implication latent in Kant's example is therefore the possibility that in the end it may not be possible to distinguish between a promise made with the intention to keep it and one made with the intention not to keep it. This is so because neither form of intention is open to objective measurement of its consistency and validity. Such enclosure cuts the promise off from its intention and makes it another example of that disjunction between necessity and truth which Joseph K., in my epigraph from Kafka, says is a 'melancholy conclusion.' It is more than simply melancholy. It is in fact an unmitigated disaster, since 'it turns lying into a universal principle.' Whether I intend to lie or do not intend to lie I lie in any case, by an intrinsic necessity of language.

The endpoint of my reading of the ethics of reading in action has led to the encounter with the unreadability of the example. On the one hand Kant asserts the rules whereby one can be certain to act ethically. He demonstrates the function of narrative as an essential part of that assertion, namely as the bridge between the law as such and any particular law applied in a specific familial, social, and historical situation. On the other hand, the story Kant tells, the story of the man who makes promises intending not to keep them, is undecidable in meaning. It therefore leaves the question open. The reader cannot decide whether the morality of promising is grounded in the law as such or whether it is an example of an ungrounded act which would define morality as a linguistic performative to be judged only by an internal temporal consistency which the example shows, as by a slip of the tongue, can never be attained. The unreadability of the text is to be defined as the text's inability to read itself, not as some failure on my part to read it. Having argued that a duty which is cut off from clear grounding in the law as such is no duty but a vain delusion and chimerical concept, Kant goes on in his example to show that it is never possible to be sure that duty is not a fiction in the bad sense of an ungrounded act of self-sustaining language, that is, precisely a vain delusion and chimerical concept, a kind of ghost generated by a sad linguistic necessity.

[. . .]

The reader of these paragraphs in Kant, with their appended footnote, is left, then, hovering in uncertainty, betrayed by the text. The text has not given him what it seemed to promise, a clear understanding of the ethics of reading. To appropriate Kant's own metaphor, I have been paid in counterfeit coin and have been forced to pay back bad treatment in its own coin, by a failure to find a certain ground for the ethics of reading in Kant's theory of ethics. I have been obliged by an inevitable necessity which may be the true ethics of reading (a strange truth in which lying becomes a universal principle), to pass this counterfeit coin on to my readers, just as those good citizens in Kant's little parable pay back the one who has made lying promises in his own coin. [. . .]

Notes

1. The epigraph from Kafka does not appear at the beginning of this essay as it appeared in *The Ethics of Reading*, but rather as an epigraph (one of two, the other being from Yeats, 'The Man and the Echo') to the book in its entirety. The citation from Kafka has been reproduced here however, as it is made reference to in the essay, its transposition dictated by an internal necessity. [Ed.]
2. A full bibliography would be extensive. As the tips of various icebergs, one might cite the invocation of Kant at crucial places in their polemics against literary theory by W. J. Bate and R. Wellek. On the other side, there are the essays by Paul de Man on Kant written in his last years and collected in *Aesthetic Ideology* (1996). Within American academic philosophy John Rawls' *A Theory of Justice* (1971) is as much a response to Kant's ethical theory as it is an attempted refutation of utilitarianism. For an authoritative recent analysis of Kant's ethics see Onora Nell, *Acting on Principle: An Essay on Kantian Ethics* (1975). Nell discusses Kant's example of the man who makes a lying promise. On the continent, there is the work of Jacques Derrida on Kant, for which see especially 'Parergon,' *La vérité in peinture* (1978a, 21–168). For French work responding more particularly to Kant's ethical theory see Jean-François Lyotard and Jean-Loup Thébaud. *Au juste* (1979) and the book of essays by various scholars growing out of a conference at Cerisy-la-Salle on Lyotard, *La faculté de juger* (1985).
3. In parenthetical citations, the German edition is referred to henceforth as G, the English translation E. [Ed.]
4. In an unpublished seminar on Kant's second critique, the *Kritik der praktischen Vernunft*, but for an oblique distillation of the reflection on Kant's ethical theory in that seminar see Derrida's admirable essay on Kafka's parable, *Vor dem Gesetz*: 'Préjugés, *devant la loi*,' *La faculté de juger* (1985b, 87–139).
5. See my discussion of this image in 'The Search for Grounds in Literary Study,' *Rhetoric and Form: Deconstruction at Yale* (1985, 30).
6. Friedrich Nietzsche, good if ungrateful reader of Kant, in *Zur Genealogie der Moral* makes the ability to make promises and keep them the very foundation of human (as opposed to animal) nature and of civilized society. In the second section of the second essay of *On the Genealogy of Morals* he distinguishes, however, between those men who have been coerced into being 'necessary, uniform, like among like, regular, and consequently calculable' [notwendig, einförmig, gleich unter Gleichen, regelmäßig und folglich berechenbar], hence able to make promises and keep them

and, on the other hand, the '*sovereign individual*' [*souveräne Individuum*] who can make and keep promises because he is a law unto himself and imposes on himself his own consistency through time, sustained by nothing but his own independent will: 'the *sovereign individual* [is] like only to himself [nur sich selbst gleiche], liberated from morality of custom [Sittlichkeit der Sitte], autonomous and supramoral (for 'autonomous' and 'moral' are mutually exclusive), in short, the man who has his own independent, protracted will and the *right to make promises*.' Friedrich Nietzsche, *Werke in Drei Bänden*, Karl Schlecia, ed. (1966, 2: 800–1; 1967, 59). One might express the difference between Kant and Nietzsche here by saying that it is as if Nietzsche had not only understood clearly the subversive implications of Kant's example of the man who makes a lying promise, that is, the way it goes against the concept Kant means it to exemplify, but had also gone beyond that understanding to propose a mode of making and keeping promises which would see the fulfilled promise as depending on the precarious balancing act of a willed linguistic consistency held together through time.

Responses I

Miller's Tale
Derek Attridge

'The critic keeps wanting to add just one more word, in the futile hope of making it all clear.' Thus Hillis Miller, in an essay entitled 'Zero.' Miller is talking about the effect, and the effectiveness, of Henry James's story 'The Altar of the Dead,' but might he not, also, be talking about the impulse that has kept him producing literary criticism over so many decades, discussing author after author, text after text, passage after passage? For even though he has often engaged with the most recalcitrant and elusive of writers and writings – Kleist, James, Nietzsche, Derrida, de Man, and many more – and even though his topic is very often the inexpressible or the inherently ambiguous, there is always that perceptible drive, one might even call it a compulsion, to explain, to make clear, to render as perspicuous as the intractability of the material will allow. Knowing that a hope is futile does not diminish its force and productivity, of course, and, like James's story, Miller's extraordinary career provides ample evidence of this truth.

It's not surprising, therefore, that the statement in 'Zero' that I began with is followed by an assurance which is offered as a reassurance to the reader: 'This impossibility of clear understanding or expression is, on the terms of the story, a lucky thing, since to understand fully, to fill the gap, would be to be dead.' Miller's drive for clarity is founded on a paradoxical acknowledgement of the impossibility of clarity, or at least of the kind of clarity which would mean that that text or that topic need not be revisited, that the work of understanding and responding is over. All his careful analyses pronounce, at some level, their own failure; yet it is failure that guarantees success, since it enacts, performatively, the central point – that the literary cannot be exhausted by analysis.[1]

Why not simply announce this fact, and spare readers the details of the many analyses? Because, I am guessing Miller would tell us, it is not quite a fact, or is more than a fact. Without the specific engagements with texts, the assertion that 'the literary cannot be exhausted by analysis' amounts to something like a tautology, a purely analytic statement that tells us nothing we did not know already. For the point is not so much that the literary *resists* analysis, but rather that it *invites* it, endlessly and inexhaustibly (and rewardingly). And only by pursuing the analysis, with as much rigor and precision as possible, in a wide range of examples, only by developing a vocabulary that will resituate the problematic of literature's inexhaustibility in a shared present, can the assertion be given content and purchase.

Inexhaustibility is not a synonym for richness or complexity, however. *Finnegans Wake* is inexhaustible, certainly, but so is a six-line poem by Celan. And although the *Wake* may have enough accumulated meanings and allusions to keep the professors busy for several hundred years, its inexhaustibility as literature lies not in this sheer mass of interpretable signification, but in the undecidabilities produced by its remarkable dealings with language. When Miller sets out to clarify a literary work, or to demonstrate the constitutive impossibility of clarity by being as clear as he can, it is the moments of undecidability he focuses on, the moments where one thing is said but another is done, where language refers to itself as well as to the world and thus complicates the very process of referentiality, where meaning appears and disappears in the same gesture. Mere difficulty or density in a work requires only the following through of the work's own logic and the conventions of reading to reach understanding. The target of clarification, as Miller practises it, is the unclarifiable.

The master of this kind of thinking was, of course, Paul de Man, and I'm sure Miller would be the first to agree that de Man's distinctive operation of the logical double-bind, the machine that never lets you off the hook no matter which way you twist, is something whose influence he has never shaken off, and probably has no desire to shake off. When Miller tells us that there is an implacable law of this or that aspect of language or literature – and he often does – we hear de Man turning the handle in the background. There are laws, it seems, and there are implacable laws. One might even say that Miller is fascinated by the stony gaze of implacability, but it is no Medusa for him, since it has given rise to some of his most creative work.[2]

To see this creative fascination in operation, I want to turn to what I think is one of Miller's most important books, although one of his shortest: *The Ethics of Reading*, from which I've already quoted, and whose contents were first given as the Wellek Library Lectures in 1985. We have all become so used to the debate about ethics that it's hard to recall the time when it was a word little used and much suspected in literary studies, especially on the left (including the deconstructive left). But de Man had used it in *Allegories of Reading* in 1979 – no doubt at the time sending his political stocks even lower than they had been – and this interest in ethics and ethicity was one of Miller's starting points for the Wellek Lectures a few years later. Miller's argument in the book, it will be recalled, is that 'there is a necessary ethical moment in [the] act of reading as such, a moment neither cognitive, nor political, nor social, nor interpersonal, but properly and independently ethical' (1987, 1). By the 'ethics of reading,' Miller tells us, 'I mean that aspect of the act of reading in which there is a response to the text that is both necessitated, in the sense that it is a response to an irresistible demand, and free, in the sense that I must take responsibility for my response and for the further effects, "interpersonal," institutional, social, political, or historical, of my act of reading' (43). And 'Each reading is, strictly speaking, ethical, in the sense that it *has* to take place, by an implacable necessity [you can hear the screw turning], as the response to a categorical demand, and in the sense that the reader *must* take responsibility for it and for its consequences in the personal, social, and political worlds' (59).

Let me take the second of Miller's two senses of 'the ethics of reading' first: the fact that I *must* take responsibility for my reading and for its consequences. At first sight, this obligation seems no different from my obligation to take responsibility for all my actions and their consequences, unless I can claim to have been under duress or walking in my sleep or otherwise incapable of exercising my will. I don't even have to *take* responsibility: I *am* responsible – that is, I can be called to account, made to answer for, what I have done, as long as it is the case that I chose to do it. Responsibility thus entails freedom of choice. Accepting responsibility means accepting that one was a free agent in doing what one did.

But Miller's account of the 'implacable necessity' that governs the response to the text, his first sense of 'the ethics of reading,' denies the possibility of responsible action in this sense. Reading, in his description, sounds much more like a matter of acting under duress than of freely choosing – and if that is the case, how can I, as reader, be held responsible for what I do? In order to make sense of this, we have to have recourse to a different understanding of responsibility, and therefore a different sense of ethics, one not tied to freedom of choice. One such under-standing would be Levinas's sense of the ethical demand of the other, a demand we cannot escape by saying 'I didn't *choose* to come face to face with this person or this situation.' For Levinas, ethics lies not in the responsibility implicit in my freely chosen acts but in the responsibility I find myself gripped by, 'taken hostage' by, as he puts it in language close to de Man's.[3]

Yet Miller says that the act of taking responsibility for my reading and for its effects is 'free' (in contrast to the determined character of the reading process itself). To ask a favorite question of Miller's, what can this mean? If it can't mean that I accept the responsibility implicit in my free act of responding to the text, it must mean a more difficult action: I have to accept that, although I had no choice in the way I responded, I am responsible for my response. (For Levinas, if I am free, it is a freedom only to acknowledge or deny the ethical force that already binds me.)

And one can go further: I am responsible for the *ir*responsibility of my response: for in doing justice to the singularity of the text I have to do justice to my own situation as I engage with it in a particular time and place (this is perhaps one aspect of the implacable law to which I am subject as reader), and to do this I have to make the text anew, as it has never been before (and never will be again). As Miller puts it towards the end of *The Ethics of Reading*, the reader is forced 'to betray the text or deviate from it in the act of reading it, in the name of a higher demand that can yet be reached only by way of the text' (120).

I, as responsible reader, am not, in other words, seeking to reveal an unchanging core of meaning, the text's 'secret' in the conventional sense of an unrecoverable interior, but rather attempting to perform, here and now, an affirmation of its singularity and alterity – a different kind of secret that cannot simply be revealed. If this performative response is to do justice to the singularity of the text, to countersign its signature, to use Derrida's terms (see 1992a, 66– 67), it must itself be singular and inventive – not merely an act of obedience to a law. It must, that is, be irresponsible as well as responsible, or, more accurately, must deconstruct the opposition between these concepts.

It may sound now as if I am disagreeing with Miller on the question of the text's implacable demand: I am suggesting that irresponsibility is as important as responsibility in the face of that demand, which implies that there is a certain freedom involved, that my response is not entirely determined by the text. To clarify this apparent disagreement, let us remind ourselves of the reason why reading is not, for Miller, a question of choosing whether to obey or disobey the demand being made by the text. It is that it is not possible to know this demand *in itself*: we cannot state it as a law, and it does not present itself to us as an injunction we might decide to disregard. All we can do is tell stories about our experience of it, stories which inevitably translate into an ontological register the linguistic necessity that reading, and the text being read, have to obey. All our critical commentaries, that is to say, are *tales*, no matter how logical and precise and clear we try to be. Indeed, as I've suggested, the more logical and precise and clear we succeed in being – and Miller's tales aim always at logic and precision and clarity – the more evident it will be that we have not escaped storytelling.

So in exercising our freedom to tell stories about the text – to performatively countersign its singular signature, in our best attempt to do justice to it for our place and time – we are obeying the text's injunction: be responsible in your irresponsibility, tell my secrets with as much care and respect as you can even though you know they will remain secret, let my inventiveness be validated in your inventiveness. This, at least, is what good reading would be, if there is such a thing – and Hillis Miller's readings come closer than most to this ideal.

Notes

1. When Miller says that Derrida's 'intuition (though that is not quite the right word) of a certain unsayable or something unavailable to cognition is . . . the motivation of all his work' (2001c, 76), he could be speaking of his own work. The passage

continues, quoting an unidentified text of Derrida's: ' "The inaccessible incites from its place of hiding." It incites speech or writing in an interminable, never successful, never satisfactory, never complete, attempt to "get it right," or "do it right." '

2. Although de Man is the writer in whose work a sense of implacable laws is strongest, Derrida has commented, in the course of an interview, on the importance of the term in his own thinking: 'All of a sudden, the word *implacable* comes to me. That cannot be appeased, assuaged, quenched [*désaltérer*] (and with good reason), but, for the same reason (following the drift of the derivation) that one can in no sense abandon or give up [*plaquer*]. The trace of the implacable: that is what I am following and what leads me by the nose to write' (1995a, 47–48).

3. See, for example, Levinas (1981, 99–129).

4. I develop this account of the responsible response to literary works in Attridge (2004).

To Read a Picture
Mieke Bal

'. . . language is not an instrument or tool in man's hands, a submissive means of thinking. Language rather thinks man and his "world," including poems, if he will allow it to do so.' In this statement, one of many statements with this level of lucidity that Hillis Miller has forged in his long career, I find enough ideas to fill a two-hour class, for freshmen, masters students, or PhD candidates alike. It is a statement that works, in the way Miller's many works work, as do the literary and philosophical texts he puts to work in his commentaries. Always both lucid and open, clear and endlessly dialogic, his prose is, in the true sense of the word, ethical. For if, to recycle another of his key statements, a conduct of life is ethical, if it consists of things done that do other things in turn ('The Critic as Host'), then this body of literary criticism is ethical, because it works. This ethical conduct of life gets things done in its turn, things that are not necessarily in agreement or obedience to it – criticism may be ethical, precisely, because it is *not* the law – but that pay homage to the text in that they bring it to an unforeseeable next step, perhaps fruition.

The statement thrives on personification: language thinks. Saying that as if he is speaking literally is an act of disavowing the possibility to distinguish literal from figurative language. It is, moreover, a way of yielding power to language outside of the individualist self that is so central to Western thought. It is the building of a bridge between 'man' and 'the world' that makes communication possible. It is precluding a predetermined restriction of who it is that can do this thinking. It is, in other words, stating a program without turning that program into a prison. It is taking a position that harbors quite a few assumptions while enabling those assumptions to be perceived, understood, and hence, contradicted.

Like this statement, all of Miller's work is eminently teachable, not because it is simple, for it is not, but because it is colored with the effort to communicate. The imperative to clarity common to both teaching and criticism is in my view one of those commandments that are ethical: both freely endorsed and inevitably given. In concrete situations, clarity, I submit, is a political imperative as much as an ethical one. Clarity fights intimidation, obfuscation, and the formation of authoritarian personalities that obscurity encourages. Clarity is, thus, also a tool for an inclusive and thoughtful democracy. It serves the shaping of critical thinking and creative engaging texts that refuse to be imprisoned in obvious and unified meanings. It sponsors a thinking, that is, that enables resistance against rhetorical manipulation while also facilitating enjoyment of rhetorical pleasure. Only if we heed Miller's injunction to allow language to 'think man and his world' will we, students and teachers alike, ever be able to learn from teaching and come closer to that strangely persistent ideal of a free spirit.

Like many of us, in the years after the rule of New Criticism, that most precious of formative schools, Miller has encountered the turn to politics, which he contributed to inflecting into ethics. If I have my ambivalence about that turn to ethics insofar as it threatens to take the concrete, combative sting out of political reading, this ambivalence is not due to a lack of persuasiveness in writings such as Miller's, so keen to make that distinction and to return us relentlessly to the ethical imperative to read 'well' – even regardless of how exactly that would take place. On the contrary: it is because that imperative does carry persuasion that, I feel, it opens reading up to a politics of culture that is not bound to be partisan, partial to factions or special interest. Instead, a politics of reading as I see it is only feasible – teachable, that is – within the framework of an ethics of reading. Only then can it frame any special interests in need of addressing in such a way that they become accessible as well as urgent for all those involved in cultural activity. This framing connects an ethics of reading to cultural politics, whether it is in the sense of affirmative action or of translation, in the thick sense Spivak has given to that notion (2003).

For having formulated the grounding of such an ethics I will always be grateful to Miller. And for laying out such grounding in terms that are as open to contradiction as they are to adhesion, but especially to extension and specification, this work will always be on the top of my list of works that *work*. The reason ethics is an indispensable grounding for a politics of reading is what Miller mentions in 'The Ethics of Narration' as its 'peculiar relation to that form of language we call narrative.' True to his deconstructive bent, he proceeds to unpack that word, 'relation,' and to show how it connects ideas of connection, storytelling, and family. The peculiarity consists of the irresolvable problematic of the relation between conceptual generalizations and examples. In his analysis of Kant's struggle with the ethical imperative of respect in 'Reading Telling: Kant' he turns to the promise and its failure as a paradigmatic speech act because it entails a secondary speech act which is the intention to keep the given promise. This example is a good instance of how and why Miller's work works so well.

Overdetermined by Derrida's critical engagement with Austin's theory of performative speech acts, in which promising is such a crucial example that it could almost stand as the only true case – if it weren't for the fact that its problematic aspects lead Austin's critics to declare all utterances performative! – Miller's discussion of Kant lends itself to filling up an entire course on language and the way it 'thinks man and his "world." ' 'Including poems,' he adds, and that, of course, says it all: literature, often considered a parallel world separate from the real one, is just part of it. So, of course, are stories, including those stories Miller has been analyzing as if they were poems, or philosophical essays.

While offering important insights into both the useful ambiguities of 'relation' and the multi-layeredness of promising, these essays leave more implicit the reasons why narrative as a semiotic or linguistic mode is so crucial to ethics and hence to politics. This is one of many instances where Miller's prose, in its exemplary clarity, invites the kind of insertions that make it so fruitful for an open, teacherly communication. To be sure, pointing out how Kant's example works is already engaging narrativity. I read Miller's title to suggest that the use of examples in Kant is 'telling,' as is invariably the case in philosophy. This tellingness is inherent in all telling, all narrative. Hence, the peculiar relation of ethics to narrative. Precisely because stories focus our attention to the particular, they harbor food for thought of a more general kind. This is why, I submit, both narrative and politics are crucial to an ethics of reading along the lines of Miller's argument.

In a congenial context, Gayatri Spivak has also demonstrated Kant's examples to be far from arbitrary. Let me return briefly to a passage in which she makes this case, as a way into the issue of narrative's centrality for philosophy – for a philosophy that keep ethics and aesthetics in relation, so to speak, by way of politics. In a move comparable to Miller's elaboration on a Kantian footnote in 'Reading Telling,' Spivak willfully 'mistakes' as seriously consequential Kant's casual and bracketed example of the *Neuholländer* and the *Feuerländer*, alleged by him apropos of man's free will, as the limit of humanity – 'raw man'.[1] Spivak takes this example as if it belonged to the 'pure' text of reasoning, infusing both the example and Kant's text with literariness.[2] The philosophical question implied in this move concerns the status of the marginal, the literary-aesthetic one concerns the status of the detail. Thus the elaborate analysis of an ostensively marginal example demonstrates, in Miller's as well as Spivak's case, the philosophical relevance of literary aesthetic. In this relevance lies the fascination of, for example, Miller's close reading of Shelley's *Triumph of Life* in 'The Critic as Host,' a reading entirely based on the symptoms of the absent, or foreclosed, word 'parasite' (including the resonance with 'parricide').

This reading for the absent key word in Miller's engagement with Shelley is quite similar, in spite of the profound differences in both intellectual commitment and style, to Spivak's search for her own, subversive version of the 'native informant' in Kant. Invoking psychoanalysis as a speculative theory whose use is an ethical responsibility, as well as a technique that helps her read the *pre-emergent* (4), Spivak is able to notice a symptom of foreclosure which is also a symptom of 'not-pure' reasoning in Kant.[3] The relation to Kant's aesthetics is, therefore, as central to Spivak's book as it is to Miller's discussion of Kantian ethics, and this on many different levels. It is a *critical intimacy*, performed so that an ethical relation, foreclosed by the 'pure' reasoning, can become possible.

I am trying to establish the kind of critical intimacy between Miller and Spivak that I myself harbor towards both. They both struggle with the relation – in the multiple sense of that word Miller expounds – between ethics and politics, and both engage aesthetics in that attempt. Miller remains on the side of ethics, Spivak privileges politics. That they both need aesthetics, and that they both establish a critical intimacy with Kant, goes to show the family relationship between the three domains, a relationship that needs relating to become visible. In a different context I have argued that what I call an 'ethical non-indifference' that constitutes literature's basic relevance, is artistically motivated, just as the artistic quality of such a literary work is ethically non-indifferent. Although I would need to write far more to substantiate this claim, each of the three stories I discuss in that essay, if framed within their own aesthetics, has literary brilliance. And in each case, the literary quality involves ethical issues. Because the means of literature, especially narrative literature, touches upon the intricate connections between private and public aspects of subjectivity, all attempts to pass off objectionable ethics under the cover of literary brilliance are doomed. So is any attempt to separate the two – that is, to condemn a work on ethical grounds while continuing to read it canonically on aesthetic premises – through ethical indifference (Bal 2000).

But such an ethical non-indifference entails that level of specificity that inevitably leads to political considerations. The kind of engagement with detail (aesthetics) and foreclosure (ethics) both Miller and Spivak practise cannot be maintained in a political vacuum. For example, Spivak reads Kant's aesthetics but only unearths the native informant in a space beyond it, where the philosopher expands in order to tie up the aesthetics' loose ends. Miller invokes the cannibal's postponed meal as the ultimate (im)possibility to perform a promise that is not (one). Both figures are staples of Western thought, and neither can be invoked without entailing the entire 'thick description' of two things: of our classics on the one hand, and of the 'humanistic unconscious' that keeps returning to them on the other. Such baring of foreclosed 'details' necessitates that description.[4]

For Spivak, the foreclosed native informant comes (im)possibly in sight at the end of the first part of Kant's two-part book, when aesthetic judgement is left in need of a subject.[5] 'He' becomes visible in the second part, but only in the corner of one's eye. The division of Kant's book into two – aesthetic and teleological judgment – is a cut that covers over a problem, much like the discontinuity in George Crabbe's narrative that Miller evokes as a key to the problem of the ethics of reading. In both cases, in order to reach the knot where ethics, aesthetics, and politics meet, we need to see narrative as occasions to, as Miller phrases it, 'read a picture.'

Miller's reading of Crabbe's poem points to an opposition between a continuous temporal line and the placing side by side of two spatial images separated by an unfilled temporal gap, like two portraits beside one another, in a diptych of 'before' and 'after.' Given my own joint interests in narrative and visual art, I found this display of visuality at the heart of narrative quite exhilarating, indeed, as a demonstration of the impossibility of narrative as it is commonly conceived. It becomes even more so once I put it in conjunction – perhaps I should say, in critical intimacy – with Spivak's alerting us to that gap in Kant, which occurs not within the text but within the reading, between the two wings of the diptych that the text constitutes. The aesthetic part of Kant's diptych is fundamentally incomplete. For the subject there still lacks the subjectivity required for the jubilant outcome of the sublime experience, later explained as the free will to reason. The second part supplements the first in the truly Rousseauist-Derridean-Spivakian sense (Derrida 1976).[6] According to Spivak's reasoning, then, it makes the first part fundamentally 'impure,' quite similarly to the way Crabbe's poem makes narrative 'impure.'

To unearth the ethical *and* political centrality of narrative from Miller's ethics the appeal to the inherent narrativity of examples as such may not be enough. Paradoxically for a discussion of ethics, it is in Kant's aesthetics, rather than his ethics, that I would contend narrativity to show its imperative hand. Kant's aesthetics comprises two key terms that have aroused a lot of commentary: 'disinterestedness' – for aesthetic experience to be possible, the subject must cut himself off from his earthly interests – and 'the sublime' – which has definitively, albeit ambivalently, shifted aesthetics from beautiful objects to the subject's experience.[7] Most contemporary commentaries focus on the sublime, and often try to save that concept for an aesthetics that is not based on disinterestedness, so that sublimity can function in the social world.[8] Even regardless of Kant's exclusive focus on nature, not art, in his discussion of the sublime, contemporary misreadings turn the experience into a feature of the object. They also tend to follow Schiller in his psychologizing of the narrative implied in Kant's description (see de Man 1996). Spivak's discussion of Kant's text entails a powerful refocusing of the entire aesthetics, by way of negotiating the transition between the two parts. And just as the sublime, then, is of the order of the performative, just so the inscription of the 'native informant' is performatively accomplished. As is, in Miller's essay, that of the cannibal.

Helpfully for my attempt, here, to bring Miller's work within the orbit of politics, Spivak straddles the gap by reverting to narrativity. This is an imperative move according to Miller's ethics. For, in Miller's terms, 'narrative, like analogy, is inserted into that blank place where the presumed purely conceptual language of philosophy fails or is missing.' Spivak's mini-narrative is the following: 'In the moment of the Sublime the subject accedes to the rational will' (Critique 10). But here is the point of the sublime, as Spivak elaborates: 'It has often been noted that the rational will intervene to cover over a moment of deprivation' (ibid.). The aporia Miller points out in Kant's ethics – the need to analyze the insincere promise into a double speech act, one of which is out of reach – shows its hand here in the middle of the aesthetics. The structure of Kant's work – its divisions – is an icon of that deprivation and its repression.[9] Spivak writes: 'The feeling of the sublime is . . . a feeling of pain arising from the want of accordance between the aesthetical estimation . . . formed by the imagination and the same formed by reason.' Here is the rift within Kant's rationality. In this rift, narrativity takes hold, in the shape of a readable picture.[10]

What Miller writes about examples in literary studies turns out just as true, then, for philosophy: 'an apparently peripheral and unproblematic example in literary studies, taken more or less at random, always turns out to raise again all the most difficult questions about literature and about literary criticism.' This is equally true for philosophy, in spite of that discipline's commitment to the continuity of its own tradition, and its blindness to the manner in which, sometimes, reasoning produces what Miller calls so beautifully 'a rope of sand.' As Miller writes, 'to understand is to read a picture.' This doesn't mean that he endorses a kind of visual essentialism, for nothing is further from the truth, in the work of this scholar so consistently committed to literature. It means, instead, that the kind of clarity that makes us 'see,' that is, understand in a flash and in depth, beyond the heaviness of reasoning through rationality-alone, can emerge more easily if we abandon the cramped attachment to, or imprisonment in, 'obvious or univocal meaning.' Whether what we then get to see takes the form of portraits or of stories, in both cases, as Miller wrote while connecting Aristotle's theory of tragedy, Sophocles' Oedipus, and Crabbe's belated home-comer, it 'transforms pain into pleasure by giving full knowledge.' It does that by compelling us, belated homecomers to what we encounter in our culture, to read a picture.[11]

Notes

1. New Hollanders, aboriginal population of Australia, and Firelanders, of the southern part of present-day Argentina (Kant 1951; Spivak 1999).
2. In one of those substantial footnotes that make her book rhizomatic, Spivak speculates on the *poetic* reasons for Kant's choice of ex-centric, sub-human examples. Here, the sound of the German names is relevant (27). This footnote

forecasts her next chapter, 'Literature,' where she expands on a 'touristic' and silencing use of exotic names, while also enacting loyalty to the object under scrutiny (by responding to Kant's aesthetics aesthetically). The other programmatic 'detail' in this context is Spivak's search for the real existence of the two peoples, which is an act of what I have called elsewhere 'archival ardor.' For a more extensive response to Spivak's book, see the last chapter of my *Travelling Concepts in the Humanities: A Rough Guide* (2002).

3. The term 'pre-emergence' is taken from Raymond Williams (1980, 40–2). I use the term 'symptom' on my own account, but not in the psychoanalytic sense. 'Symptom' in Peircean semiotics is a sign that is involuntarily produced as sign. In fact, in the anti-intentionalist perspective that deconstruction entails – and which I fully share – symptoms are everything. But I use the term in the more limited cases of small details with unprogrammed significance.

4. 'Thick description' was introduced in anthropology by Clifford Geertz (1983). I am developing a notion of a 'humanistic unconscious' in work in preparation, provisionally titled 'The Anthropomorphic Imagination.' The graphism 'that is not (one)' alludes to Luce Irigaray (1977).

5. The graphism (im)possible is explained in Spivak (1987, 263).

6. *Of Grammatology* is profoundly present in both Miller's and Spivak's writing.

7. The German word *Interesse* is strongly bound up with partiality and partisanship, rather than with what we consider 'interesting.' Thinking of Habermas's famous book helps keep this difference in mind (1972 [1968]).

8. A feminist attempt can be found in Battersby (1998, 167).

9. I use the term 'icon' here in the strictly Peircean sense (most accessible in Peirce 1984, 4–23). Miller uses the term 'mise en abyme' in this sense.

10. Spivak argues that since this 'judgment of the inadequacy of our greatest faculty of sense' is reasonable and correct, 'a pleasure [is] excited.' The superiority of the rational over the sensible 'arouses in us the feeling of our supersensible determination [*Bestimmung*]' (Kant, 96–7).

11. For the concept of 'visual essentialism' see my essay 'Visual essentialism and the object of visual culture' (2003, 5–32).

J. Hillis Miller: Miller's ~~Crossing~~ (under erasure)
Juliet Flower MacCannell

It is a measure of J. Hillis Miller's singular vigilance that well over four years before the fall of the Berlin Wall he had already grasped that *ethics* would presently come to dominate all discourses of moral reflection. Miller, it seems, had once again showed himself uncannily prescient about things to come where critical alterations in subjective life are concerned. Indeed, now that transnationalism has swept aside local laws and customs and economic liberalism has breached all geographic limits[1] – such as that Wall – *ethics* has come to prominence as the necessary supplement to a fading moral security.[2]

Miller proposed an *Ethics of Reading* in 1987, which he began by entering into a dialogue with Kant (and the Paul de Man who inspired Kant's rereading). Later he would bring similar concerns to the widely different thinkers Derrida, Austin, and Proust in *Speech Acts in Literature* (2001b). But from first to last, Hillis's ethical speculation is marked by two things: one, a sustained reading of texts focused on their unique access to the moral law, through what Miller calls 'the ethical moment of reading'. And, secondly, a post-Kantian appreciation for 'the moral law' as experienced both as universal and as utterly unintelligible, exceeding yet inhabiting positive law and understanding as we know it.

The 'ethical moment' about which Miller will have so much to say and yet which is unsayable, is one where a fissure in our symbolic contexts is fathomed *and* where the unfathomable moral command that issues from that faultline is somehow responded to:[3] 'The wholly other enters through these gaps into any given context and makes an unconditional demand on the one who dwells within the context to intervene in a certain way in it' (2001b, 129). The response to this 'wholly other' establishes that an *event* (a moral injunction) has undeniably been experienced – but also that its articulation is disturbingly disarticulated from direct relatability. For Miller, the ethical moment is the heeding of a call that cannot quite be heard, but which is somehow indisputably 'right' (or for Kant, rational). And for Miller, this ethical response is strangely best exemplified by *writing*: 'the creation of a text by the author is a response to the law . . . a response to the moral law itself' (1987, 22).[4] This writing is, however, no simple narration of the 'event.' Rereading Kant's several texts on the moral law, Miller argues that the reason the act of writing and those who respect the moral law (in the absence of all direct experience of it) are 'like one another' is 'because each is analogous to that third thing, spring and generative source of both, the law as such' (1987, 22).

Miller thus declines any conception of 'ethics in literature' as a comfortable (and comforting) modeling of difficult moral choices and exemplary moral acts. He chooses, that is, not to second the view that literature is one bridge over the yawning chasm between 'the law as such and the application of that law to a particular case of moral decision [such as] Kant suggests narration or storytelling should be' (1987, 97). Rather, Miller proposes that if anything, literature makes us more intensely aware of the chasm ('the uncrossable abyss' (1987, 26)) than whatever might traverse it.[5] I would even suggest that an undeniable urge to confront what haunts the vacancy between law and experience sustains much of Miller's own writing.[6]

His focus on the missing limit and the gap (rather than what spans the 'between') clarifies that Miller's interest is not in 'ethics as such' but 'in the ethics of reading' and in '*the relation of the ethical moment in reading to relation* in the sense of giving an account, telling a story, narrating' (1987, 15; my italics). For Miller, the essential ethical moment *in* reading, that is, is not the illustrating of moral choices but the urgent, exemplary suffering of a law that 'gives itself without giving itself,' (Derrida) in a profoundly 'vacant place where there is no direct access to the law as such, but where we stand respectfully, like the countryman in Kafka's parable, "before the law" ' (1987, 20).

The moral law as such, divided from us by an absolute abyss, nonetheless moves us in some way (moves us to respect, for example) – a peculiar experience that Kant's language both acknowledges and tries to explain away. This 'moving' us (by unknown means) is the mysterious heart of the moral law itself: a peremptory summoning to act in the absence of all knowable co-ordinates. Hillis's fidelity is to the opaque 'ethical moments *in* reading' that accept this permanence of a gap and generate this active respect: these are the linguistic creations and ethical acts that inspire him in authors from Trollope to James. But how they actually 'work' precisely is what Miller proposes to wring from Kant's moral texts. To grasp the complexity of the question, Miller will wrangle from Kant's texts an admission of their own 'obscure, evasive, and carefully concealed recognition both of the necessity of narrative in any account of the moral law as such and of the necessary failure of any narration to take the reader where he wants to be, face to face with the law' (1987, 25).

Thus Miller's ethical point of departure is hardly reassuring: the sensing of 'some anarchic power that is felt in [literature] and that one would like to tame, control or repress' (1987, 5). And yet Miller's exposition of our abyssal moral situation and Kant's own denial/revelation of that impossible abyss is executed entirely without the tragic, apocalyptic tone usually reserved to that experience. For if Miller's straight-ahead confrontation with the empty space between the moral law and the relating of it has foreshadowed our current sense of an acute global deficit in legal order (e.g. terrorism and the collapse of organized international agreements and alliances), his geniality in the face of it constitutes a most unusual response to that situation. The 'principle' that urges itself upon you despite your rational, economic, social, and political control, has also been described and analyzed by philosophers, students of religion like Max Weber's studies of 'calling' in *Protestantism and Capitalism*, and Freud's psychoanalytic unconscious *Drives* or Lacan's *superego voice*.[7] The outcomes in these are rather different from what Miller derives from his rereading of Kant, even or especially where Kant insufficiently characterizes its dangerous, overwhelming power. This is, after all, a power that resists rational explication. What permits Miller to look steadily at something potentially terrifying, out of control, and which nonetheless increasingly fuels our acts, small and great, is precisely the model he finds in *writing* – which if nothing else is always a confrontation with a blank, coupled with the urge to write and write and write, and that comes both from without and within, constituting thereby its own point of departure. Where Miller's work supplements, in an exemplary way, what is missing in accounts of the ethical urge that first emerged in Kant's writing, is the calm courage with which he faces the implications of so radical a removal of 'political, social, and historical contexts' for one's acts (1987, 5) as, read closely, all theories of this 'categorical imperative' necessarily imply. His is a courage gained, one might say, from a Pascalian act of *reading* in which all bets are off and one is always confronted with 'some anarchic power that is felt in it and that one would like to tame, control, or even repress' (1987, 5) in the 'real situation of a man or woman reading a book . . .' (1987, 4).

To focus on figurative language is, of course, a logical consequence of Miller's lifelong concern for literature's unique, compelling power. But its significance escalates enormously in *The Ethics of Reading*. Figurative language (particularly the catachretic instance of facing the void) becomes paradigmatic of, or better yet, parallels (is perhaps even the very same as) the response to the over-whelming pressure that the unfathomable moral law exerts on any and every particular moral decision and act. This is a figurative language not necessarily bound to 'what is' in human affairs, and which has the extraordinary power to deny, imagine, reframe, restate or reinvent those affairs, imaginatively.

Yet how, one has to ask, are we to decide (after the Fall of so many of our Walls) on the authentically ethical side of the call? Miller cautions strongly against seemingly 'moral' decisions that are in actuality 'fully determined by political considerations' (1987, 4 [I couldn't help thinking of Eichmann's self-deceiving urge to obey a call to conscience that he conflated with his Führer's voice]). Well, one must recognize the necessary paradox of the moral law in Kant (which Miller so brilliantly draws our attention to): Kant tells us that 'obedience to the law must not be based on obedience to any law' (1987, 26–8). This is an impossible double bind, resolved only by recourse to narrative – telling the story of the dilemma.

But even here things are not so easy as might appear at first blush – it is not simply a matter of denying the double bind's reality, lying about it elegantly, or making up something compensatory. For Miller details how in Kant's accounts, fictional narrative first seems to play a 'bridging' role, but that this first effort finally goes awry:

> Across the gap between the law as such and the immediate work in the real world of the practical reason must be cast a little fictional narrative. This narrative must be on both sides of the gulf at once, or lead from the one to the other . . . The story I tell myself is not just any anecdote involving the ethical choice which is in question for me . . . [T]he story I must tell myself is a miniature version of the inaugural act which creates a nation, a people, a community. I must act as though my private maxim were to be universal legislation for all mankind . . . In the fiction of this 'as if' universal and particular, public and private, the law as such and a particular code of behavior, are bridged and I become myself an example of the moral law, worthy of respect. (1987, 28)

Miller then says '[Kant] wants to persuade his readers that respect for the law is self-wrought but at the same time determined by a law which precedes it and is external to it' (1987, 32) but that this does not really work:

> The example Kant gives, however, is of a special kind of performative language, the promise. A promise creates its own conditions of obedience in a temporalization requiring a comparison of before and after . . . (1987, 33)

Instead, Miller concludes, the bridging intention of the 'as if' fiction does not and cannot belie the actual form in which it is proposed. In Kant's case, the *promise* is a form that quintessentially exemplifies the moral law's double binding, its permanent gapping, and the 'anarchic' power it exerts:

> This differential . . . feature of the law, the way it both is divided within itself and at the same defers, postpones, its validation, is the place where narrative and the law come together. Narrative can be defined as the indefinite postponement of that ultimate direct confrontation with the law which narrative is nevertheless instituted to make happen in an example worthy of respect. (1987, 33)

'Reading Telling: Kant' becomes itself an instance, however much it denies it, of an 'ethical moment' in literature.

Notes

1. It also preceded by a little bit the self-examination Europe would begin as silenced memories of wartime acts began to be voiced.
2. Those who have followed Miller into the ethical arena include such different voices from his as Alain Badiou, Slavoj Žižek, and Alenka Zupancic.
3. See his strong reading in *Speech Acts in Literature* (2001b, 130–1), of Jacques Derrida's reflections on resistance to apartheid as an 'unconditional demand':
   > Neither human beings nor objects can exist without a context, nor, Derrida is saying, can an unconditional ethical or political demand exist without a context. Nevertheless, such a demand arises from what might be called the outside of the inside. It depends on the fact that no context is closed or bounded, but has at its limit or boundary what Derrida . . . calls 'a clause of nonclosure' . . . That nonclosure offers the chance for an ethical or political intervention that is justified by an unconditional injunction.

   The 'outside of the inside' Lacan calls '*extimité*' in his *Ethics of Psychoanalysis* (1992).
4. Miller shows that Kant's moral law (stringent in its universality and its refusal to be founded in subjective feeling) and its relation to effective action do require, despite Kant's disclaimers, something *like* a feeling: the respect for moral law (*Achtung*) generated by its own unfathomability.
5. As his Heidegger chapter in *Topographies* also suggests: he considered giving this chapter the alternative title of 'Double Crossing Heidegger' (1995, 216).
6. He is still writing about this, for example, when he speaks of Derrida (2001b, 129–31). The concern for the disappearing God that stands at the origin of Miller's own *oeuvre* has, it seems, endured.
7. It is what the Freudians would call '*Trieben*' and theologians would call 'divine or satanic power': and it requires more courage to face it than Miller's verbal demeanor ever betrays.

II

Victorian Interests

5

Emily Brontë

When Emily Brontë began to write *Wuthering Heights* she did not leave the world of the Gondal poems. She transposed into fictional form the vision of things which her poems express. Just as there is no real distinction between the Gondal poems and those which are direct expressions of Emily Brontë's own inner experience, so the same moral and metaphysical laws prevail in the novel as in the poems.

Poems and novel share a quality which identifies them as belonging to the romantic tradition. Like the prophetic books of Blake they employ privately created personages and events to speak of things usually expressed in terms of collective religious myths. Heathcliff and Catherine Earnshaw in *Wuthering Heights*, Augusta Geraldine Almeda, Julius Brenzaida, and the other shadowy figures of the Gondal poems (see 'Dramatis Personae,' Ratchford 1955, 43, 44) derive from no recognizable religious archetypes. They are creations of Emily Brontë's imagination, just as Urizen and Enitharmon are creations of the imagination of Blake, even though they may reembody figures or concepts from various traditions. Yet Emily Brontë's characters, like the personages of Blake, are used to express general notions about the relations of God, man, and the universe.

[. . .]*

Both poems and novel express themselves in hyperbole. They dramatize the clash of figures who embody elemental energies, and the special value of Emily Brontë's work lies in the way it explores the ultimate implications of certain traditional ideas and themes.

> All creation is equally insane. There are those flies playing above the stream, swallows and fish diminishing their number each minute: these will become in their turn, the prey of some tyrant of air or water; and man for his amusement or for his needs will kill their murderers. Nature is an inexplicable puzzle, life exists on a principle of destruction; every creature must be the relentless instrument of death to the others, or himself cease to live. (Brontë 1948, 17)[1]

For Emily Brontë, created beings can only be related to one another destructively. The strongest and most implacable beings live the longest, for

---

* Brontë's writing, it is argued, whether in *Wuthering Heights* or the Gondal poems, is essentially visionary, expressing an irreconcilable struggle between spiritual submission and defiance. [Ed.]

the life of each depends on the death of others, and if it does not relentlessly kill it will be killed, or die of inanition. The model of this relation is the consumption of one being by another. Nature is like a patternless maze created by a madman. Its insanity lies in the fact that the good of one part is the evil of another part. Therefore no coherent moral judgment can be made of any action or event. What is the worst evil for the flies, being eaten by the fish and swallows, is the highest good for the fish and swallows, since it is necessary to their life. Any attempt to make sense of life leads to inextricable confusion, and the creation can only be described, not understood. Viewed as a totality, nature is engaged in a constant act of suicide, tearing itself to pieces in the very effort to prolong its own life. Murder is the sole law of life, that is to say, life paradoxically depends upon death, and is impossible without it.

[. . .]*

The darkest meaning of Emily Brontë's assertion that 'all creation is equally insane' is the fact that no man can understand why a good God should have chosen to create such a world at all. Each man's life, like that of any other creature of nature, is merely a sequence of violent acts done or suffered, and it ends in death. '. . . why was man created?' asks Emily Brontë. 'He torments, he kills, he devours; he suffers, dies, is devoured – that's his whole story' (1948, 17, 18).

[. . .] The opening chapters of *Wuthering Heights* introduce the reader, through the intermediary of the narrator, to a set of people living in the state of nature as it is defined in 'The Butterfly.' This state also matches that of the Gondal poems, with their wars and rebellions and sadistic cruelties. In Gondal, as in the country of *Wuthering Heights*, every man's hand is against his neighbor.

Lockwood's discovery of the nature of life at Wuthering Heights coincides with his step-by-step progress into the house itself. On his two visits he crosses various thresholds: the outer gate, the door of the house, the door into the kitchen, the stairs and halls leading to an upstairs room. Finally he enters the interior of the interior, the oaken closet with a bed in it which stands in a corner of this inner room. Wuthering Heights is presented as a kind of Chinese box of enclosures within enclosures. The house is like the novel itself, with its intricate structure of flashbacks, time shifts, multiple perspectives, and narrators within narrators. However far we penetrate toward the center of Wuthering Heights there are still further recesses within. When Lockwood finally gets inside the family sitting-room he can hear 'a chatter of tongues, and a clatter of culinary utensils, deep within' (1931, 3), and Joseph can be heard mumbling indistinctly in the 'depths of the cellar' (5). This domestic interior is, by subtle linguistic touches, identified with the interior of a human body, and therefore with another human spirit. Lockwood's progress toward the interior of Wuthering Heights matches his unwitting progress toward the spiritual secrets it hides. Just

---

* Miller offers a comparison between Brontë's vision of creation and that of John Wesley. [Ed.]

as the 'narrow windows' of Wuthering Heights are 'deeply set in the wall' (2), so Heathcliff's 'black eyes withdraw . . . suspiciously under their brows' (1), and Lockwood's entrance into the house is his inspection of its 'anatomy' (3).

The nature of human life within this 'penetralium' (3) is precisely defined by the animals Lockwood finds there. The shadowy recesses of these strange rooms are alive with ferocious dogs: 'In an arch, under the dresser, reposed a huge, liver-coloured bitch pointer surrounded by a swarm of squealing puppies; and other dogs, haunted other recesses' (3). Lockwood tries to pet this liver-colored bitch, but her lip is 'curled up, and her white teeth watering for a snatch' (5), and later when, left alone, he makes faces at the dogs, they leap from their various biding places and attack him in a pack. In a moment the hearth is 'an absolute tempest of worrying and yelping' (6). The storm which blows at the exterior of the house and gives it its name (2) is echoed by the storm within the house, a tempest whose ultimate source, it may be, is the people living there. Lockwood's encounter with Heathcliff's dogs is really his first encounter with the true nature of their owner, as Heathcliff himself suggests when he says: 'Guests are so exceedingly rare in this house that I and my dogs, I am willing to own, hardly know how to receive them' (6).

The animal imagery used throughout *Wuthering Heights* is one of the chief ways in which the spiritual strength of the characters is measured. Heathcliff is 'a fierce, pitiless, wolfish man' (117), while Edgar Linton is a 'sucking leveret' (131), and Linton Heathcliff is a 'puling chicken' (237). Such figures are more than simple metaphors. They tell us that man in *Wuthering Heights*, as in the essay on the butterfly, is part of nature, and no different from other animals. Critics have commented on the prevalence of verbs of violent action in *Wuthering Heights*, verbs like 'writhe, drag, crush, grind, struggle, yield, sink, recoil, outstrip, tear, drive asunder' (Schorer 1950, xv). No other Victorian novel contains such scenes of inhuman brutality. No other novel so completely defines its characters in terms of the violence of their wills. In *Wuthering Heights* people go on living only if their wills remain powerful and direct, capable of action so immediate and unthinking that it can hardly be called the result of choice, but is a permanent and unceasing attitude of aggression. Continuation of life for such people depends on their continuing to will, for in this world destruction is the law of life. If such characters cease to will, or if their wills weaken, motion slows, things coagulate, time almost stops, and their lives begin to weaken and fade away. Unless they can find some way to recuperate their wills, their lives will cease altogether, or tend slowly in the direction of death. So Lockwood, after his terrifying dreams, says, as the hours crawl toward morning, '. . . time stagnates here' (30). So the second Catherine, at the low point of her life, when only her own action will save her, says, 'Oh! I'm tired – I'm *stalled* . . .' (342). And so Isabella, one of the weak people in the novel, can only escape from the tyranny of Heathcliff by precipitating herself into the realm of violence inhabited by the other characters who survive. The description of her escape from Wuthering Heights is a condensed distillation of the quality of life in the novel: 'In my flight through the kitchen I bid Joseph speed to his master; I knocked over Hareton, who was hanging a litter of puppies from a chairback in the doorway; and, blest as a soul escaped from purgatory, I bounded, leaped, and flew down the steep road: then, quitting its windings, shot direct across the moor, rolling over banks, and wading through marshes; precipitating myself, in fact, towards the beacon light of the Grange' (208).

Lockwood learns when he makes his second visit to Wuthering Heights what it means to say that the people there live like ferocious dogs, and can survive only through the strength of their wills. He finds that everyone at the Heights hates everyone else with a violence of unrestrained rage which is like that of wild animals. Anarchy prevails. [. . .]

This animality of the people at the Heights is caused by the loss of an earlier state of civilized restraint. For a human being to act like an animal means something very different from a similar action performed by the animal itself. There are no laws for an animal to break, and there is nothing immoral in the slaughter of one animal by another. The characters in *Wuthering Heights* have *returned* to an animal state. Such a return is reached only through the transgression of all human law. The inmates of Wuthering Heights have destroyed the meaning of the word 'moral,' so that it can be used, as Heathcliff uses it, to define the most in-human acts of cruelty (174).

In civilized society man's needs are not satisfied immediately and selfishly, but are mediated by a complex system of cooperative action. Most social actions are for others, or for the sake of a future satisfaction. As a result, there is in civilized society little direct contact between men. Emily Brontë's example of civilized man is Lockwood, the foppish representative of fashionable society. Lockwood is mortally afraid of any close relation with another human being He is bored and weak, and has no idea what to do with himself. Ennui has brought him to Thrushcross Grange, and his attitude toward the country people is that of a condescending sophisticate who goes slumming in search of excitement.

Wuthering Heights is the opposite of this. There, people are open to one another. Nothing stands between them, and no law restrains them. Though this savagery puts people in extreme danger, it is, for Emily Brontë, better than Lockwood's artificiality and insincerity. Lockwood himself comes eventually to recognize this. 'I perceive,' he says, 'that people in these regions acquire over people in towns the value that a spider in a dungeon does over a spider in a cottage, to their various occupants; and yet the deepened attraction is not entirely owing to the situation of the looker-on. They *do* live more in earnest, more in themselves, and less in surface change, and frivolous external things. I could fancy a love for life here almost possible; and I was a fixed unbeliever in any love of a year's standing . . .' (70). Unmediated relations to others may be a mortal danger to the self, but such relations are also a way of living a deeper and more authentic life. Lockwood has been a fixed unbeliever in any love of a year's standing. At Wuthering Heights he witnesses a love which has lasted beyond the grave.

There is one further reality to which Lockwood is introduced at the Heights. If civilized society keeps out the savagery of wild animals and northern tempests, it also keeps out the irrational tumult of supernatural forces. The latter, like the former, can never be reduced to man's measure. When Lockwood slides back the panels of the oaken bed and encloses himself in the innermost chamber of all he feels 'secure against the vigilance of Heathcliff, and every one else' (20). But just here he is most in danger, not from human or natural violence, but from supernatural energies. This innermost room has a window to the outdoors, and through that window, in Lockwood's dream, the ghost of Catherine Earnshaw tries to come. The otherness of nature is replaced by the more frightening otherness of a ghost, and the stormy moors are established as the expressions of a supernatural as well as a natural violence. These spiritual powers are immanent in nature, and identified with its secret life. The expression of this double life in *Wuthering Heights*, as in Emily Brontë's poems, is an ancient and primitive symbol: the wind. There is a great storm on the night Mr. Earnshaw dies; another tempest when Heathcliff leaves the Heights splits a tree whose bough falls on the house; and there is a rainstorm on the night Heathcliff dies beside the very same window where Lockwood has seen Catherine's ghost. The immeasurable violence of occult forces matches the unrestrained violence of wild animals and of storms. In his dream the effete cosmopolitan Lockwood is brought, in spite of himself, to participate in the turbulence of Wuthering Heights. In a paroxysm of fear he rubs the wrist of the ghost-child to and fro on the broken pane until the blood runs down and soaks the bedclothes.

[. . .]

[. . .]*

For Emily Brontë no human being is self-sufficient, and all suffering derives ultimately from isolation. A person is most him- or herself when he or she participates most completely in the life of something outside him- or herself. The self outside the self is the substance of a man's being, in both the literal and etymological senses of the word (Burke 1945, 21–3). It is the intimate stuff of the self, and it is also that which 'stands beneath' the self as its foundation and support. A person's real being is outside him- or herself. Emily Brontë's writings are an exploration of the consequences of this strange situation.

[. . .]†

In *Wuthering Heights* Cathy asserts exactly this of Heathcliff. Her relation to Heathcliff gives her possession not merely of Heathcliff, but of the entire

---

* In what follows, Miller explores how violence in Brontë is a reaction to loss or a fall from some happier state. [Ed.]

† The poems and the relationship between Cathy and Heathcliff give expression to the human desire to connect to another (whether God, nature, or a human other), in order to fulfill a sense of self, and thereby alleviate a sense of suffering occasioned by loss. [Ed.]

universe through him, in an intimacy of possession which obliterates the boundaries of the self and makes it an integral part of the whole creation. 'If all else perished,' says Cathy, 'and *he* remained, I should still continue to be; and if all else remained, and he were annihilated, the Universe would turn to a mighty stranger. I should not seem a part of it' (93). [. . .] What Heathcliff is for Cathy, Cathy is also for Heathcliff. He speaks in exactly the same way about her as she speaks about him, and exactly the same relation is being dramatized, whether we see their love from the point of view of Cathy or from the point of view of Heathcliff. 'Two words,' cries Heathcliff, 'would comprehend my future – *death* and *hell* – existence, after losing her, would be hell' (170). And in another place: '– oh God! would *you* like to live with your soul in the grave?' (185). If Heathcliff is the ground of Cathy's being, Cathy is the ground of Heathcliff's, whereas, though God's creatures could not exist without God, God is defined by His absolute self-sufficiency.

Cathy and Heathcliff are as inseparably joined as trunk and root of the living tree. Their relation to one another excludes or absorbs their relation to everything else. Each is related to the rest of the universe only through the other. Through Heathcliff, Cathy possesses all of nature. Through Cathy, Heathcliff possesses it. As in Donne's 'The Sun Rising,' the whole creation has organized itself around their relation, as around its center or source, and God in his heaven is ignored or dismissed. If the mystic says: 'I am because I am God,' or if Descartes says he is because he thinks, Cathy must say: 'I am Heathcliff, therefore I exist.' Her hyperbole is the climax and endpoint of the long tradition making love a private religion in which the loved one is God and there is a single worshipper and devotee. Emily Brontë, here as elsewhere, dramatizes in extremes, and carries the tradition of romantic love as far as it can go.

To remain happy Cathy need only maintain her identification with Heathcliff. That identification seems invulnerable, for, as Cathy affirms, it will survive every vicissitude of her relations to others. Her love guarantees its own permanence. If the lovers endure, their love will endure untouched. If either is annihilated, then the other will also disappear. The existence of each is altogether determined by the other.
[. . .]*

> I dreamt, once, that I was there . . . [H]eaven did not seem to be my home; and I broke my heart with weeping to come back to earth; and the angels were so angry that they flung me out, into the middle of the heath on the top of Wuthering Heights; where I woke sobbing for joy.
>
> (91)

Cathy's love for Heathcliff and existence in heaven seem to her mutually exclusive. To fulfill the former is to exclude herself from the latter. To be in

---

* The deleted section of the essay explores the complexities of the relation between Heathcliff and Cathy, in relation to other modes of relation, particularly those concerning destruction and loss. [Ed.]

heaven would be exile for her because it would separate her from Heathcliff. Either one goal may be reached or the other, not both. Cathy's love for Heathcliff is defiance of God and transgression of His law.

This opposition between love and religious duty has existed from the beginning of her relation to Heathcliff. The reader's first glimpse of this relation shows that their love exists as the repudiation of religious and moral obligation. 'H. and I,' writes Cathy in her diary, 'are going to rebel' (21). They rebel against the coercion of religious and family authority. They rebel in the name of the anarchic freedom of their love. The diary entry describes events taking place on 'an awful Sunday' after the death of Cathy's father, when her brother Hindley has become the tyrannical head of the household. Though the weather has been too bad to go to church, Joseph has conducted, for Cathy, Heathcliff, and the plowboy, a three-hour service in the garret. The tyranny of the foster-father (' "You forget you have a master here," says the tyrant. "I'll demolish the first who puts me out of temper! I insist on perfect sobriety and silence" ' (22) is equated with the tyranny of a religion which requires that all pleasure be banished and every thought and act be directed to its service.

The symbol of this tyranny is books, the codified expression of an authority which demands to be obeyed. When Cathy and Heathcliff seek to escape from Sunday by hiding behind their pinafores in the arch of the dresser, Joseph sends them back to the good old Protestant Sunday occupation of reading pious tracts: 'T' maister nobbut just buried, and Sabbath nut oe'red, und t' sahnd uh't gospel still i' yer lugs, and yah darr be laiking! shame on ye! sit ye dahn, ill childer! they's good books eneugh if ye'll read 'em; sit ye dahn, and think uh yer sowls!' (22). Reading is here opposed to 'laiking.' The former is directed to salvation, the latter is a vicious turning away from God for the sake of selfish pleasure. The Christian 'either/or' is reaffirmed in the titles of the two tracts which Cathy and Heathcliff throw into the dog-kennel: 'The Helmet of Salvation' and 'The Broad Way to Destruction.' There are only two possibilities open to these children: they may encase themselves within the rigid bounds of the helmet of salvation, or they may break through all barriers and go the broad way to destruction.

Joseph is of great importance in *Wuthering Heights*. He is 'the wearisomest, self-righteous pharisee that ever ransacked a bible to rake the promises to himself, and fling the curses on his neighbours' (46). It is 'his vocation to be where he [has] plenty of wickedness to reprove' (74). For Joseph the world divides itself into two kinds of people, those who are, by God's grace, saved, and the much larger number who are irrevocably damned. Joseph considers himself one of the elect. As he says, in distorted echo of St. Paul (Rom. 8: 28): 'All warks togither for gooid tuh them as is chozzen, and piked aht froo' th' rubbidge!' (97). God, in Joseph's view of him, has established things for most people so that whatever they do they will be damned. Hence Joseph feels it his duty to serve as an avenue through which God's curses can be directed at the wicked, and through which information about the wickedness of mankind can be reported back to God: 'O, Lord,' he cries, 'judge 'em, fur they's norther law nur justice amang wer rullers!' (352). Joseph's God is a God of wrath, a God who, like Joseph himself, judges everybody but himself as 'nowt,' to use one of Joseph's favorite words (see 15, 45, 99, 164, 352). Such a God is a sadist who takes pleasure in the suffering of his creatures, and joys in excluding them forever from joy.

Joseph's religion might seem of marginal interest in *Wuthering Heights*, a kind of foil for the gentler Christianity of Nelly Dean, if it were not for the fact that the central drama of the novel derives from the children's acceptance of Joseph's judgement of them. Though they 'rebel' against it, they nowhere deny its validity. Their sense of their lives has been determined by the influence of Joseph in the Earnshaw family. 'By his knack of sermonizing and pious discoursing,' says Nelly Dean, '[Joseph] contrived to make a great impression on Mr. Earnshaw, and, the more feeble the master became, the more influence he gained. He was relentless in worrying him about his soul's concerns, and about ruling his children rigidly. He encouraged him to regard Hindley as a reprobate; and, night after night, he regularly grumbled out a long string of tales against Heathcliff and Catherine; always minding to flatter Earnshaw's weakness by heaping the heaviest blame on the last' (46).

Joseph makes articulate the view of the situation of man which underlies *Wuthering Heights*. This view is a certain version of Protestant Christianity. As is well known, Emily Brontë was influenced by two forms of Protestantism, the Evangelicalism of her father, who was an Anglican clergyman, and the Methodism of her Aunt Branwell and their servant Tabby. Mrs. Gaskell's biography of Charlotte Brontë gives one glimpse of these influences at work. She shows the Reverend Brontë asking one of his daughters (Maria, the eldest, who died at eleven) 'what was the best mode of spending time,' and being answered, 'By laying it out in preparation for a happy eternity' (Gaskell 1879, 42). The rejection of all pleasure now for the sake of eternal pleasure in heaven, the image of the docile and submissive child, even the use of commercial language to describe the bargain of salvation – all these elements of Protestant-ism are present in this vignette. It was perhaps Aunt Branwell who most directly imposed on the Brontë children notions which might have been held at that time either by a Methodist or by an Anglican influenced by Evangelicalism: the concept of the natural depravity of man, the need for a saving relation to God, the relative unimportance of systematic theology, and the insistence on a few simple ideas, such as the view that all pleasure is evil, the notion that all life here must be directed to the ultimate end of salvation, and the idea that only a life of restraint, abnegation, and submission to duty will have any chance of reaching that end. The theory of child-raising shared by Methodism and Evangelicalism, and enshrined in the children's books of the period, presupposes an absolute opposition between those thoughts and actions which are instinctive or natural, and those which can be approved. The former are all bad, for is not the child guilty of original sin, and therefore hellbent down the broad way to destruction? The only good acts are those done under coercion, whether that coercion is imposed from without or voluntarily imposed from within. The moral life is a strenuous battle between the forces of good and the forces of evil, and if there is a moment of relaxation the forces of evil will win. So John Wesley, in his sermon 'On the Education of Children,' says: 'To humour children is, as far as in us lies, to make their disease incurable. A wise parent, on the other hand, should begin to break their will, the first moment it appears . . . [N]ever, on any account, give a child any thing that it cries for . . . [T]each your children, as soon as possibly you can, that they are fallen spirits . . . Show them that, in pride, passion, and revenge, they are now like the Devil. And that in foolish desires and grovelling appetites, they are like the beasts of the field . . . [A] wise and truly kind parent will take the utmost care, not to cherish in her children the desire of the flesh, their natural propensity to seek happiness in gratifying the outward senses' (*Works*, VII, 126–9).[2]

It is easy to see how a sensitive child subjected to these religious teachings might conclude that the battle is already lost before it begins, that the natural instincts for evil are too strong to be defeated by any natural means, and that the terms of the conflict are established in such a way that victory is impossible. Just such a view of the relations between God and man is given in *Wuthering Heights* and in Emily Brontë's poems. The situation in which Cathy, Heathcliff, and the characters of the Gondal poems find themselves is simple, unequivocal, and altogether reasonable. They have been taught that only two kinds of action exist. Those acts are good which are not an end in themselves, but are a means to the only good end: obeying God and getting to heaven. Bad acts are defined as all those which are pleasurable, a present good in themselves. This present life is to be defined as exile from heaven, an exile imposed by God, and any attempt to transcend it is disobedience of God's law.

For this reason the Methodists were opposed to mysticism, the most obvious expedient for crossing the empty space between a fallen world and God. If I can break through the heavy barriers of sinful flesh and enjoy here and now the measureless pleasure of union with God, then the irreconcilable opposition between the need to reach God and the impossibility of reaching him in this life will be broken. But the Methodists, like many other Christian sects, felt that union with God in mystic ecstasy is, even if authentic, only momentary, therefore simply a distraction from the main business of life.

Emily Brontë also recognized the insufficiency of mysticism. [. . .] Brontë shared with the Methodists a recognition that every joy attained in this life, even the pleasure of mystic union with God, is temporary and fleeting, a pale image of the eternal joy of heaven. Only after death can man hope to attain everlasting and immeasurable joy: 'A thoughtful Spirit taught me soon / That we must long till life be done . . .' (232). As long as we are alive our separation from God will persist. Therefore any experience in this world which is like union with God is another step down the broad way to destruction. It is to take an image of the only good end in place of that end itself. This is to commit the sin of idolatry, to put God's creature in the place of God, as when Heathcliff says of his imminent reunion with Cathy: 'I tell you, I have nearly attained *my* heaven; and that of others is altogether unvalued, and uncoveted by me!' (381), or as when Emily Brontë writes of one of the Gondal characters: 'His soul is glad to cast for her / Virtue and faith and Heaven away' (140), or has another say to his lady: 'For thee, through never-ending years, / I'd suffer endless pain . . .' (152).

In order to be saved Heathcliff and Cathy apparently have only to choose the helmet of salvation rather than the broad way to destruction. There is only one difficulty: without God's grace, all human acts whatsoever, for Emily Brontë, are evil; they are all steps in the direction of hell. It is impossible to 'lay out time in preparation for a happy eternity,' for there is nothing a man can do with his time which will in any way bring him closer to God or ensure his being received in heaven after death. Whether he goes toward God, which means to seek here and now the pleasure of union with the deity, or whether he accepts his separation from God, all his acts increase the already infinite distance between his soul and God. Emily Brontë's world, like those of Kafka or Matthew Arnold, is a realm of the unavailability of God. For Emily Brontë, as for Kafka, man is doomed to commit one of two sins, the sin of impatience or the sin of laziness, the sin of trying to reach here and now, against God's interdict, union with Him, or the sin of accepting separation from God and seeking to establish a satisfactory world without Him. Emily Brontë would agree with Kafka that the sin most natural to man is not laziness but impatience. The difference is that Kafka's characters (K. in *The Castle* is a good example) always retain enough innocence to believe that they are just about to reach the goal of union with God, whereas Emily Brontë's characters do not hope to escape their situation in this life. In Emily Brontë's writings, all men are worthy of damnation, and there is no way to *choose* salvation. If it is attained it will come as a free gift from God to sinful man. As other critics have suggested, it may be that the Gondal poems in this owe something to Byron, as well as to the traditional doctrine of original sin. Augusta is a kind of female Manfred. She too is haunted by an inexpiable guilt, and whatever she does she is doomed. For Emily Brontë, as for Byron, all men are cursed, and no man deserves salvation, though all long to be virtuous: 'All [are] doomed alike to sin and mourn / Yet all [live] with long gaze fixed afar, / Adoring virtue's distant star' (122).

In this doctrine of the inevitability of sin Emily Brontë is more like the Calvinistic Methodist, George Whitefield, than like the Arminian Wesley. Wesley holds that God's grace is freely given to all; all men can be saved if they will accept this grace. But for Whitefield grace is offered only to the chosen few: '. . . God intends to give saving grace, through Jesus Christ, only to a certain number; and . . . the rest of mankind, after the fall of Adam, being justly left of

God to continue in sin, will at last suffer that eternal death which is its proper wages.'[3] Whitefield accepts the doctrines of election and reprobation. The free will of the individual has no real effect on his destiny, for a man's will is in the hands of God. Few are called and few are chosen, and some men, perhaps *most* men, are predestined to damnation, whatever they do. Emily Brontë, like Whitefield, emphasizes man's penchant for sin, and the seemingly Godforsaken situation of many men.

In the strange situation God has imposed on man, there are only two possible acts which man can perform, both of them evil, neither of them obedience to God's law. A man may go directly, in the present, toward the lost fusion with God, break down the walls cutting him off from what is around him, and seek to regain the boundless joy of heaven. To do this is to reach only a false and damnable image of communion. Taking the other course, a man may accentuate the gap separating him from nature, from other people, and from God. The expression of this choice is the ordinary moral expediency of civilized society, represented in *Wuthering Heights* by the Lintons. This selfish calculation is obedience to God in one way at least: it makes the present moment not an end in itself, but only the means to some future end, the conservation of one's property or the acquisition of more. But though worldly prudence begins as fulfillment of God's law, it ends as the establishment of a city of the world cut off from God, dedicated to its own ends, and based on the calculating cooperation of individuals, each intent on the perpetuation of his own good. Historically the expression of this city of the world is the commercial society of getting and spending which grew up within Christendom, as if called into being by a profound contradiction at the heart of its doctrine.[4]

Whether he seeks idolatrous fusion with some other person or thing, in place of the impossible fusion with God, or whether he seeks to perpetuate his own separateness, a man is, for Emily Brontë, equally guilty. In her world the universal state of fallen man is that described at the beginning of her last poem:

> Why ask to know the date – the clime?
> More than mere words they cannot be:
> Men knelt to God and worshipped crime,
> And crushed the helpless, even as we.
>
> (244)

The condition of man in Emily Brontë's world is at once reasonable and unreasonable, and this contradiction derives from a contradiction in the nature of God himself. It seems perfectly reasonable that we should be required to obey God's law against actions which do not have union with Him as their goal, but since no action here can have God as its goal, man's situation is unreasonable. God is at once the ordainer of separateness and the promise of the ultimate joy of fusion with Him. The divine realm is universal intimacy, the copresence of all things and persons in perfect possession of one another. The God of this heaven establishes reason, morality, and the isolation of objects and people in a spatialized world. To obey God in one way is to disobey him in another, and either way to merit damnation.

The fine line dividing a just and yet merciful God from an irrational tyrant is perfectly dramatized in the sermon Lockwood hears in his strange dream near the beginning of *Wuthering Heights*. Lockwood's dream suggests that Emily Brontë's God is at once a God of mercy, a God who will forgive man's sins, though they should number seventy times seven, and at the same time a God who dooms man to commit not only seventy times seven sins but also the unforgivable first of the seventy-first, 'the sin that no Christian need pardon' (25).

The text of Jabes's sermon is Mat. 18: 21, 22:[5] 'Then came Peter to him, and said, Lord, how oft shall my brother sin against me, and I forgive him? till seven times? Jesus saith unto him, I say not unto thee, Until seven times: but, Until seventy times seven.' The text bears first on the relations between neighbors, and expresses in striking form the Christian virtue of turning the other cheek. In the context of Christ's teaching the 'seventy times seven' seems to suggest that we should go on forgiving our neighbor as often as he sins against us, even though he does so an outrageous number of times. But Jabes and his congregation are literalists, and read the text to mean that we should wait patiently through four hundred and ninety sins and then rise up and smite our neighbor down. So the congregation rushes on poor Lockwood at the end of the sermon, and so Lockwood demands the destruction of Jabes for having preached such an interminable sermon: 'Fellow martyrs, have at him! Drag him down, and crush him to atoms, that the place which knows him may know him no more!' (26). This sounds not like the New Testament but like the Old Testament attitude echoed by Isabella later when she demands 'an eye for an eye, a tooth for a tooth' (206) in her revenge on Heathcliff. Or we are reminded of Hindley's formulation of the moral law of the Heights: 'Treachery and violence are a just return for treachery and violence!' (201). Jabes, Lockwood, and the congregation are interested not in the way Jesus' words are an admonishment to forgiveness, but in the way, to their perverted interpretation, they seem to justify, after a certain point, condign vengeance. The text is reversed in the same way that the pilgrim staves of the congregation are transformed into 'heavy-headed cudgels.'

The Reverend Jabes Branderham should have read further in his Bible, for in the verses following his text Jesus tells a parable which establishes a connection between the relations of man and man and the relations of man and God (Mat. 18: 23–35). The parable is the familiar one of the Lord who forgives his servant a debt until he discovers that the servant has dealt without compassion with a fellow servant who owes him money. The Lord then turns the first servant over to the 'tormentors,' saying: 'Shouldest not thou also have had compassion on thy fellow servant, even as I had pity on thee?' The verses assert that God will forgive us our sins if we forgive our neighbors' sins, but that he will punish us according to our deserts if we act without pity toward our neighbors. The God of *Wuthering Heights* is justified in treating his creatures cruelly. They are, for the most part, without pity or forgiveness for one another, and their conscious defiance of the law by which God reserves vengeance to himself echoes through the novel (see 69, 205, 206). Emily Brontë was fascinated by the moment when God, having forgiven man four hundred and ninety times, should be justified in replacing mercy with the most ferocious justice. Emily Brontë's God gives himself as unreservedly to vengeance as do Heathcliff, Hindley, or Isabella:

> The time of grace is past
> And mercy scorned and tired
> Forsakes to utter wrath at last
> The soul so steeled by pride.
>
> That wrath will never spare,
> Will never pity know,
> Will mock its victim's maddened prayer,
> Will triumph in his woe.
>
> Shut from his Maker's smile
> The accursed man shall be:
> Compassion reigns a little while,
> Revenge eternally.

(121)

In Jabes' sermon, as elsewhere in Emily Brontë's writings, both God and man are represented as waiting, with ill-concealed impatience, through the legally required time of mercy and forgiveness, until they can get down to the pleasant business of doing justified violence on one another to the limit of their powers. God is different only in that his power is infinite.

The sermon of the Reverend Jabes Branderham is a striking dramatization of the way Protestantism, in its attempt to recognize the uniqueness of each person and remove all intermediaries between the soul and God, can end by putting each man at an infinite distance from his neighbors and from God. Enmity and hatred are the only relations between man and man or between man and God which Jabes' sermon seems to allow. In the Christian society of *Wuthering Heights*, as in the state of nature in Emily Brontë's essay, destruction is the law of life, and God has condemned man to separateness. Never in this world will a man be able to enjoy with impunity anything which is like 'the endless and shadowless hereafter,' the eternity of Heaven where life is boundless in its duration, and love in its sympathy, and joy in its fulness.

Even more is implied by Jabes' sermon. Though the God of the sermon seems to be a deity whose ways can be understood by man, the mind overreaches itself in the attempt to comprehend him and attains at last the exasperation of a confrontation with infinite mystery. The Protestant tradition of 'dividing' a text, in order to make more comprehensible to human reason the revelation of God to man, becomes, when it produces a sermon 'divided into *four hundred and ninety* parts – each fully equal to an ordinary address from the pulpit' (25), an absurdity exceeding the patience and comprehension of man. If each of these four hundred and ninety parts must discuss 'a separate sin,' sins, as Lockwood says, 'of the most curious character – odd transgressions that I never imagined previously' (25), another absurdity in the situation of man is revealed. Sinning can no longer be neatly compartmentalized into seven groups, easy to understand and remember. There are so many sins that their number seems to be infinite. The number of sins exceeds the grasp of reason, and each time a man sins he is doomed to commit a new and different sin: '. . . it seemed necessary the brother should sin different sins on every occasion' (25). Another corollary follows from this. Since there are so many different sins, it is unlikely that any two persons should commit the same sin. Though all men are sinners, each person is cut off from his fellows by his sins, just as the various moments of a man's life are divided from one another, since each new act is a new and different sin. The human condition imposed by the God of wrath leads to hatred, misunderstanding, and separation among people, for each man is isolated in the prison of his own odd transgressions, and cannot be measured by the standards which apply to others. It is no wonder that Jabes' sermon ends with a free-for-all among the members of the congregation, for if each man is unique it is natural that every man's hand should be against his neighbor.

In such a world the separation of Cathy and Heathcliff is inevitable, and their scamper on the moors leads them fatefully to the adventure which leaves Heathcliff outside the window of Thrushcross Grange looking in at a Cathy almost instantaneously changed, a Cathy with whom he is no longer consubstantial. Sooner or later, in their case as in all others, the isolation and discontinuity natural to human existence will be established. The separation of Cathy and Heathcliff happens as naturally and inevitably as growing up. Though Heathcliff can with some justice accuse Cathy of reaffirming their separation by marrying Edgar Linton, she is not the cause of its original occurrence. Its ultimate cause is the nature of human existence as God has established it.

The divine law making isolation follow escape from separateness operates repeatedly in Emily Brontë's poems. The characteristic dramatic sequence of the poems is the seizing of illicit sexual pleasure, followed by the inevitable sequel of separation, exile, imprisonment, and, eventually, death. The immediate causes of these sufferings are various, but their ultimate cause is always the same. The poems several times formulate this universal law of human existence. Gondal is a world where 'future grief' is 'entailed on present joy' (187), a world where 'Pleasure still will lead to wrong, / . . . And Joy [is] the shortest path to Pain . . . !' (185), a world where 'bliss' is 'bought by years / Dark with torment and with tears' (121). Gondal is, finally, a world in which there are: 'Relentless laws that disallow / True virtue and true joy below' (122). No passage in Emily Brontë more perfectly expresses her grim view of the human condition. Both virtue and joy on earth are against God's law, and will inevitably be punished by the stern ruler who has established his irrevocable decree, as the childhood love of Heathcliff and Cathy is necessarily followed by their separation.

Once Cathy and Heathcliff are separated, what are they to do? What action is possible when the relentless laws have been enforced? Neither obedience of God nor defiance of him seem possible, for neither virtue nor joy is allowed in this lower world. In the reactions of Cathy and Heathcliff to their separation we can watch their apparently hopeless struggles against a God who seems, like his creation, to live on a principle of destruction.

[. . .]*

Cathy does not reach happiness in death. She reaches only the condition of absolute division from the being who is more herself than she is. During her death agony she expresses her desire to be in heaven: '. . . the thing that irks me most is this shattered prison, after all. I'm tired, tired of being enclosed here. I'm wearying to escape into that glorious world, and to be always there; not seeing it dimly through tears, and yearning for it through the walls of an aching heart; but really with it, and in it' (183). Cathy makes it clear that she will not be happy in heaven unless Heathcliff is there too. Heathcliff remains alive, on this side of the barrier separating all earthly creatures from the boundless realm of sympathy and joy which is heaven, so she deludes herself with the notion that the Heathcliff of flesh and blood is not the real Heathcliff. She will take the real Heathcliff with her, the Heathcliff who is her own being: 'That is not *my* Heathcliff. I shall love mine yet; and take him with me – he's in my soul' (183). The division between them is so complete that she sees two Heathcliffs, one an objective being separate from herself, the other existing in the depths of her own soul. She knows, nevertheless, that to be dead, and even in heaven, while Heathcliff is still alive, will only more irrevocably confirm her division from him. As she twice tells Heathcliff, she will not rest in the grave while he lives: 'I'll not lie there by myself: they may bury me twelve feet deep, and throw the church down over me; but I won't rest till you are with me . . . I never will!' (144); 'I shall not be at peace' (182).

By willing her own death Cathy retains control of her fate, but she does not transcend her separation from Heathcliff. Her way of dealing with her life leads to a more irrevocably confirmed isolation. Whether one waits passively for God to impose separateness, or whether one despairingly causes separation, whether one causes the death of others, or anticipates inevitable separation by choosing

---

* Virtue and joy are opposites in Brontë's universe, and this is seen both through Cathy and, analogously, in Augusta, the heroine of the Gondal poems. [Ed.]

death for oneself, the result is the same – the 'hopeless, endless mourning' of division from all that might bring joy.

Heathcliff's situation after Cathy's death is different from hers while she lived, and his reaction to that situation is not the despairing acceptance of separateness, but the attempt to regain his lost fullness of being. The universal human desire is for union with something outside oneself. People differ from one another only in the intensity of their desire, and in the diversity of the ways they seek to assuage it.

After Cathy's death Heathcliff's whole life is concentrated on the suffering caused by his loss, and on the violence of his desire to get her back, for she is his soul, and without her he grovels in an abyss of nothingness. Why does Heathcliff spend so much of his time in an elaborate attempt to destroy Thrushcross Grange and Wuthering Heights, with all their inhabitants? Why does he take delight in torturing Hindley, Isabella, Hareton, the second Cathy, his son Linton? Why does he, both before Cathy's death and after, enter on a violent career of sadistic destruction? Is it because he is, as Cathy says, a 'fierce, pitiless, wolfish man,' or does his sadism have some further meaning?

During the violent scene of mutual recrimination between Heathcliff and Cathy which ends in the fight between Heathcliff and Edgar, Heathcliff tells Cathy that she has treated him 'infernally' by betraying him and marrying Edgar. He will not, he says, 'suffer unrevenged' (128). But, says Heathcliff, 'I seek no revenge on you . . . The tyrant grinds down his slaves and they don't turn against him, they crush those beneath them – You are welcome to torture me to death for your amusement, only, allow me to amuse myself a little in the same style . . .' (128). Heathcliff's cruelty toward others is a mode of relation to Cathy. Though his appearance at Wuthering Heights in itself disrupts the Earnshaw family, Heathcliff's relation to Cathy forms the basis of his defiance of everyone else, and his destructive hatred attains its full development only after he is separated from her. His sadistic treatment of others is the only kind of revenge against Cathy he can take, for the person who most controls events in *Wuthering Heights* is not Heathcliff. It is Cathy herself.

Heathcliff's sadism is more than an attempt to take revenge indirectly on Cathy. It is also a strange and paradoxical attempt to regain his lost intimacy with her. If Cathy can say, 'I *am* Heathcliff,' Heathcliff could equally well say, 'I *am* Cathy,' for she is, as he says, his 'soul.' Possession of Heathcliff gives Cathy possession of the entire universe. If she were to lose Heathcliff, 'the universe would turn to a mighty stranger,' just as Heathcliff becomes an alien and outcast from all the world after he loses Cathy. If his childhood relation to Cathy gave him possession of the whole world through her, perhaps now that Cathy is lost he can get her back by appropriating the world. The sadistic infliction of pain on other people, like the destruction of inanimate objects, is a way of breaking down the barriers between oneself and the world. Now that he has lost Cathy, the only thing remaining to Heathcliff which is like the lost fusion with her is the destructive assimilation of other people or things. So he turns sadist, just as, in the Gondal poems, Julius Brenzaida turns on the world in war when he has been betrayed by Augusta. Heathcliff's violence against everyone but Cathy plays the same role in *Wuthering Heights* as does the theme of war in the poems. In both cases there is an implicit recognition that war or sadism is like love because love too is destructive, since it must break down the separateness of the loved one. Augusta too is a sadist. She moves quickly from inspiring her lovers to abandon honor for her sake to betraying them and causing them to suffer. Like love, sadism is a moment of communion, a moment when the barriers between person and person are broken down. The climax of sadistic joy is loss of the sense of separateness. It is as though the person who is forced to suffer had lost his limits and had melted into the whole universe. At the same moment the self of the sadist dissolves too, and self and universe become one. Heathcliff's relation to Cathy has been fusion with the whole world through her. He feels that he can reverse the process and regain her by assimilating the world, for his sole aim is to 'dissolve with' Cathy and be happy at last (329). Now he proposes to do this by getting control of Wuthering Heights and Thrushcross Grange in order to destroy them both. 'I wish,' says Heathcliff of his property, 'I could annihilate it from the face of the earth' (380). So he gives himself whole-heartedly to acts of sadistic destruction. No other figure in English literature takes so much pleasure in causing pain to others: 'I have no pity! I have no pity!' he cries. 'The more the worms writhe, the more I yearn to crush out their entrails! It is a moral teething, and I grind with greater energy, in proportion to the increase of pain' (174). In another place he tells Nelly his feelings about his son and the second Cathy: 'It's odd what a savage feeling I have to anything that seems afraid of me! Had I been born where laws are less strict, and tastes less dainty, I should treat myself to a slow vivisection of those two, as an evening's amusement' (308).

Heathcliff's effort to regain Cathy through sadistic destruction fails, just as does Augusta's attempt to achieve through sadistic love a fusion with something outside herself, and just as does Cathy's decision to will her own death. Heathcliff's sadism fails because, as things or people are annihilated under the blows of the sadist, he is left with nothing. He reaches only an exacerbated sense of the absence of the longed-for intimacy rather than the intimacy itself. Augusta goes from lover to lover, destroying them one by one because she cannot reach what she wants through them. And Heathcliff finds that his career of sadistic revenge is a way of suffering the loss of Cathy more painfully rather than a way of reaching her again. 'It is a poor conclusion, is it not,' he asks. 'An absurd termination to my violent exertions? I get levers, and mattocks to demolish the two houses, and train myself to be capable of working like Hercules, and when everything is ready, and in my power, I find the will to lift a slate off either roof has vanished! . . . I have lost the faculty of enjoying their destruction . . .' (369).

The reason Heathcliff gives for having lost the will to demolish the two houses is a confirmation of the fact that his relation to everything in the world is a relation to Cathy, and an admission of the defeat of his attempt to regain her by destroying the Grange and the Heights. He says that everything in the universe is a reminder that Cathy has existed and that he does not possess her. Through his destruction of others he has reached, in the wreckage left after his violence, the full realization of her absence: '. . . what is not connected with her to me?' he asks, 'and what does not recall her? I cannot look down to this floor, but her features are shaped in the flags! In every cloud, in every tree – filling the air at night, and caught by glimpses in every object, by day I am surrounded with her image! The most ordinary faces of men, and women – my own features mock me with a resemblance. The entire world is a dreadful collection of memoranda that she did exist, and that I have lost her!' (370). The universe is identified not with Cathy, but with the absence of Cathy, and to possess the world through its destructive appropriation is not to possess Cathy, but to confront once more the vacant place where she is not. This is the hell in which Heathcliff lives after her death: 'I could *almost* see her, and yet I *could not*! I ought to have sweat blood then, from the anguish of my yearning, from the fervour of my supplications to have but one glimpse! I had not one. She showed herself, as she often was in life, a devil to me! And, since then, sometimes more, and sometimes less, I've been the sport of that intolerable torture!' (331). Heathcliff's sadistic tormenting of others only leads him to be the more tormented, tormented by a Cathy whose strongest weapon is her invisibility.

There is no escape in this world from the suffering of isolation. Neither by passivity nor by willful action, neither by obeying God's law nor by transgressing it, will any living man or woman, for more than a delusory minute, cease to be bound by the suffocating walls of his own identity. The law dooming man to sin and suffer for his sins is irrevocably established. All creatures of God, both human and animal, are like the ugly caterpillar who hides in the flower and secretly destroys it, and it seems as if the whole creation were a mistake, a machine for creating evil, something which God should have annihilated the moment after the fall of man. Emily Brontë's vision of things leads her to reject and condemn the whole fabric of creation:

> I picked a flower at my side. It was pretty and newly opened, but an ugly caterpillar had hidden himself among the petals and already they were drawing up and withering. 'Sad image of the earth and its inhabitants!' I exclaimed, 'This worm lives only by destroying the plant which protects him; why was he created and why was man created?' . . . I threw the flower to the ground; at that moment the universe appeared to me a vast machine constructed only to bring forth evil: I almost doubted the goodness of God for not annihilating man on the day of his first sin. 'The world should have been destroyed,' I said, 'crushed, just as I crush this reptile, which has done nothing during his life but make everything he touches as disgusting as himself'. (1948, 17, 18)

If the whole world is accursed, then man must seek death, not the death of others, but his own death. Much of Emily Brontë's work is an exploration of the various ways in which it seems man might attain, here in this world, something like the boundless sympathy and joy which are remembered from childhood or from some prenatal paradise. All the ways fail. Each leads only to a confirmation of the sin and suffering to which man is doomed. As a result, many of Emily Brontë's characters are led to the moment when, all else having failed, they expend their vitality to reach, as quickly as possible, the realm of death. Only in death can they find 'endless bliss through endless years' (185), the interpenetration of all things with one another which is heaven.

Her characters do not seek death passively, through a relaxation of the life force which will let death flow in as life slowly evaporates. They are cursed with too much vitality for that. 'So much the worse for me, that I am strong,' cries Heathcliff. 'Do I want to live?' (185). Death is the most violent act of will. It is the will destroying itself by destroying the inner strength of the self, for only when that strength is exhausted can death be reached.

What experience awaits man beyond the gates of death?

> Shall these long, agonising years
> Be punished by eternal tears?
> No; *that* I feel can never be;
> A God of *hate* could hardly bear
> To watch through all eternity
> His own creations dread despair!
>   (138)

For Emily Brontë, if it is true to say that all men are worthy of damnation, it is equally true to say that all men may be saved, without exception. She does truly hold that doctrine of 'universal redemption' which Whitefield accuses Wesley of preaching (1834, 629, 634, 636). Or in any case she believes that all men have a chance to be saved. If some men are to be saved, then all men may be saved, since no man is any more worthy of salvation than his neighbor. It is as though Emily Brontë had moved to the moment of death or to the moment of the Last Judgment the time of the descent of God's saving grace. She agrees with John Wesley that 'God justifieth not the godly, but the ungodly; not those that are holy already, but the unholy' (*Works,* V, 50). For Wesley, God's grace operates on man in this world and its acceptance is confirmed afterward in good works. By these works a man will be assessed at the Last Judgment, for good works are the sign of faith and of its supervening sanctification. Hence Wesley's opposition to antinomianism. Emily Brontë, however, believes that some men can receive God's saving grace at the moment of death.

This reversal of the law which seems to destine all men to damnation is affirmed repeatedly in the poems. One Gondal character says: 'If I have sinned, long, long ago / That sin was purified by woe' (138). Augusta tells one of her lovers to 'Call Death – yes, Death, he is thine own!' for though he has sinned in loving Augusta and is being punished for it by death, that death will be a liberation into eternal bliss. The dust of earthly sin never makes the soul impure:

> If thou hast sinned in this world of care,
> 'T was but the dust of thy drear abode –
> Thy soul was pure when it entered here,
> And pure it will go again to God.
>
> (71)

The most paradoxical consequence of Emily Brontë's view of the human condition is her belief that the suffering sin brings will be sufficient expiation for that sin. Each person is fated to commit a certain number of sins and to suffer a certain amount of pain before he can escape to heaven. The passive, obedient people, the Edgar Lintons of this world, do not really act within the law. They eke out over a longer period the necessary allotment of sin. Furthermore, the transfiguration of the world at the Last Judgment will be postponed until 'Sin [has] spent its last drop of poison, [and] death [has] thrown its last dart.' A certain number of sins are necessary to complete the great work of the exhaustion of evil which will make possible resurrection into the new life. The climax of Emily Brontë's drama of history is a universal holocaust in which all the sin and suffering of man and the animal world, through being endured and worked out to their bitter end, will be transfigured into the happiness of heaven: 'God is the God of justice and mercy; then, assuredly, each pain that he inflicts on his creatures, be they human or animal, rational or irrational, each suffering of our unhappy nature is only a seed for that divine harvest which will be gathered when sin having spent its last drop of poison, death having thrown its last dart, both will expire on the funeral pyre of a universe in flame, and will leave their former victims to an eternal realm of happiness and glory.' (1948, 18, 19).

Since all are doomed alike to sin and mourn, all men quite properly should long for death, and the luckiest reach it soonest. In the same way the goal of the whole creation is its final flaming death, when all sin shall have been exhausted at last. One of the Gondal characters can cry, with perfect justification:

> Yet I would lose no sting, would wish no torture less;
> The more that anguish racks the earlier it will bless;
> And robed in fires of Hell, or bright with heavenly shine,
> If it but herald Death, the vision is divine.
>
> (239)

In the same way King Harold, in Emily's essay 'King Harold on the Eve of the Battle of Hastings,' is free from the smothering pleasures and intrigues of his court only when he faces death on the battlefield. Here, as in the Gondal poems, war leads to death, and the most heroic warrior is not the victor but the one who is killed in the fight. King Harold on the eve of the battle of Hastings is transfigured, sovereign, and free not only because he can now unleash all his instincts for cruelty and unrestrained violence (all good warriors are sadists), but because he is about to experience the truly liberating event of his life, his own death: 'A soul divine, visible to his fellow men as to his Creator, gleams in his eyes; at the same time a multitude of human emotions awaken in him, but they are exalted, sanctified, made almost divine. His courage is not temerity, nor is his pride arrogance. His anger is justified, his assurance is free from presumption. He has an inner conviction that by no mortal power will he be defeated. Death alone can gain victory over his arms. To her he is ready to yield, for Death's touch is to the hero what the striking off his chains is to the slave' (1948, 12).[7]

Anything which leads to death is divine, for death is an absolute transformation of our earthly state. The image which dominates Emily Brontë's description of this change is the transmutation of the ugly caterpillar into a beautiful butterfly, traditional image for the liberation of the soul. Between this life and the world to come there is no likeness, even though this life with all its horror and discord is a necessary prelude to the harmony of heaven. For this reason Emily Brontë, after describing the creation as 'insane,' can say, without irony: 'Nevertheless, we celebrate the day of our birth, and we praise God that we entered such a world' (1948, 17). The signs that the sufferings of Cathy and Heathcliff have been transformed into the boundless peace of heaven are the 'moths fluttering among the heath, and hare-bells' which Lockwood sees at the very end of the novel (385). In the same way, in the essay on the butterfly, the speaker has no sooner crushed the caterpillar (thus participating in the universal destruction of nature), than a beautiful butterfly springs forth and disappears into the sky (1948, 18).

The fact that the caterpillar must be crushed in order to make possible the butterfly shows that even the most extreme example of radical change in nature is not adequate for Emily Brontë. The caterpillar has to die not 'naturally' but violently, which is according to nature as Emily Brontë sees it. Life does not grow out of life, as butterfly from caterpillar, but only from death, as the butterfly rises from the crushed caterpillar. It is not a question of a flowing, however sudden the change of pace, but of an absolute break: life out of death, heavenly bliss out of earthly torment.

The image of the caterpillar transformed into a butterfly is not solely an expression of the change of sinful man into a blessed soul after death. It is also the proper image for the transformation of the whole world, at the last trump, into 'a new heaven and a new earth.' A recognition that this transformation is inevitable will answer all our presumptuous questions about the wisdom of God in permitting the creation to endure. Just as there can be no butterfly without a caterpillar, so there can be no 'eternal realm of happiness and glory' without this insane world and its gradual exhaustion of the allotted measure of evil – down to the last drop. In the essay on the butterfly the speaker is moved by his vision of the miraculous change taking place before his eyes to exclaim: 'Let not the creature judge his creator, here is a symbol of the world to come – just as the ugly caterpillar is the beginning of the splendid butterfly, this globe is the embryo of a new heaven and of a new earth whose meagerest beauty infinitely surpasses mortal imagination. When you see the glorious outcome of what now seems to you so mean, how you will despise your blind presumption in blaming Omniscience for not having destroyed nature in its infancy' (1948, 18).

In several of the poems the same double vision of the world appears. The world is at once the ugly sight it appears to mortal eyes, and at the same time those same elements glorified and transformed into their opposites. Every bit of suffering, violence, and sin is necessary and good, for all are required by the ultimate transfiguration. In one poem this transformation appears in the change of an 'inky sea' to a brilliant ocean, 'sparkl[ing] wide and bright,' 'white as the sun' (221), and in another the speaker laments the inevitable destruction of the beautiful landscape of summer by the cold of winter. But suddenly the air seems kindled with 'a thousand thousand glancing fires,' and these 'little glittering spirits' tell the visionary that the death of plants and animals in winter is necessary, like the evil of mankind, for it brings more quickly the 'everlasting day.' The song of the little glittering spirits is another expression of the idea that suffering is good, for the more intensely we suffer the sooner we shall reach death, and death is the one goal of life:

> O mortal, mortal, let them die;
> Let Time and Tears destroy,
> That we may overflow the sky
> With universal joy.
>
> Let Grief distract the sufferer's breast,
> And Night obscure his way;
> They hasten him to endless rest,
> And everlasting day.
>
> To Thee the World is like a tomb,
> A desert's naked shore;
> To us, in unimagined bloom,
> It brightens more and more.
>
> And could we lift the veil and give
> One brief glimpse to thine eye
> Thou would'st rejoice for those that live,
> Because they live to die.
>
> (200)

If life is good only because it makes death possible, then Heathcliff is perfectly justified in calling his career of sadism a 'moral teething,' and there is no doubt that he and Cathy reach again the joy of possessing one another only when they are 'restored into the Deity' (211), in spite of Heathcliff's defiant claim that he seeks only his own heaven. Death is the true goal of life, and death is most quickly reached by those who exhaust themselves in the futile attempt to deny the law of separateness imposed by God. In the poems and in the novel the two kinds of action which lead most directly to death are illicit love and physical violence. Though sadistic cruelty or illicit union with another person are not the same as death and the union with God which follows death, they are more like them than patient endurance of separateness. They break down the tough envelope of the self and prepare it for its dissolution into the boundless sympathy and love of heaven.

Cathy and Heathcliff reach in death what they possessed in this world when they were unself-conscious children, and did not know of their separateness. They reach peace not through obedient acceptance of isolation, but through the final exhaustion of all their forces in the attempt to reach union in this life. Their heroism is, in Georges Bataille's phrase, an 'approbation of life to the point of death' (1957, 12).[8] Cathy's death is caused by their embrace: 'An instant they held asunder; and then how they met I hardly saw, but Catherine made a spring, and he caught her, and they were locked in an embrace from which I thought my mistress would never be released alive. In fact, to my eyes, she seemed directly insensible' (184). Heathcliff too reaches death through the exhaustion of his vitality. This exhaustion is brought about by his frantic attempt to reach Cathy's ghost: 'I have to remind myself to breathe – almost to remind my heart to beat! And it is like bending back a stiff spring . . . it is by compulsion, that I do the slightest act, not prompted by one thought, and by compulsion, that I notice anything alive, or dead, which is not associated with one universal idea . . . I have a single wish, and my whole being, and faculties are yearning to attain it. They have yearned towards it so long, and so unwaveringly, that I'm convinced it *will* be reached – and *soon* – because it has devoured my existence – I am swallowed in the anticipation of its fulfilment' (371); '. . . you might as well bid a man struggling in the water, rest within arms-length of the shore! I must reach it first, and then I'll rest' (380).

At the end of *Wuthering Heights* Cathy and Heathcliff have reached the peace of union with one another through God, a God who is at once immanent and transcendent, utterly beyond this world, 'brooding above' it, and within it as what 'pervades' it everywhere, just as the soft breeze breathes over the moors in the last paragraph of the novel. One need not, as Lockwood says, 'imagine unquiet slumbers, for the sleepers in that quiet earth,' and 'under that benign sky' (385). Only in death, the realm of absolute communion, can Heathcliff 'dissolve with' Cathy and 'be happy' at last. The final happiness of Cathy and Heathcliff, like their first union in childhood, can only be spoken of symbolically. The tremendous storm raised by the separation of the two lovers, a storm which has swirled out to engulf all the characters in the novel, has been appeased at last, and calm has returned. Heathcliff has broken through to the still point at the center of the whirlwind, the divine point where all opposites are reconciled and where he can possess Cathy again because he possesses all things in God. The calm he has reached has spread back into the world to be tangible in the soft wind breathing through the grass and blowing through the open windows at Wuthering Heights (350). Emanations from the center of peace have been liberated to flow out to the periphery of the circle, and to irradiate all the world with a benign and pervasive glow. The state of savagery in which Lockwood first found the people at Wuthering Heights has been transcended at last.

[. . .]*

Wuthering Heights is dominated by a sense of immense strain, the effort of longing and will necessary to pierce through to the supernatural world. The storm is greatest near the center. At the center is peace. When Heathcliff finally attains the shore toward which he has been straining, the reconciliation which he finds radiates back into the world he has left behind, and a moderate love is possible for Hareton and the second Cathy. Only through the violence of Heathcliff can calm love be other than the artificiality and self-enclosure of Lockwood or the Lintons.

In *Wuthering Heights* Emily Brontë shows that society, left to itself, gets more and more hollow and artificial, until finally the churches are all empty and God has disappeared. Only a recovery of God will make possible a renewal of society. Communication with the divine realm cannot be established calmly and beneficently. Someone must break religious and moral law and go into the forbidden space between man and God. To enter this space is to go into a region of terror and immorality, to be forced to bring this destructive power into the world, and to be torn to pieces by it. Cathy and Heathcliff have entered this dangerous area by attempting to prolong into adulthood the relation they have had as children.

The happiness of the second generation is made possible by the plunge into the divine storm of Cathy and Heathcliff, followed by its inevitable sequel: suffering and death. Only when the sin of the first lovers has 'spent its last drop of poison,' and they have paid for their pleasure with death – only then can the fierce wind of Wuthering Heights be transformed into the soft breeze which blows on Hareton and the second Cathy and through the open doors and windows at the end of the novel. The replacement of the first lovers by the second pair is the pre-enactment on earth of the transformation of earthly sin and sorrow into the joy of heaven which Emily Brontë speaks of in her essay on the butterfly. The peace of civilization and the irrational violence of Heathcliff's transgressions are not irreconcilable opposites. The destructive love of Heathcliff

---

* The final section of this essay begins with a consideration of the differences and similarities between the stories of the first and second Cathy. [Ed.]

and Cathy is the necessary ground of the benign love of Hareton and the second Cathy.

This relation between the two stories is apparent concretely in the way the second Cathy's purgatorial suffering of the reality of death, as she sits alone by the bedside of her dying husband, is necessary to her growing-up and therefore to her eventual happiness with Hareton. She must suffer death vicariously, and reach the point when she can say, just after the death of Linton Heathcliff: 'You have left me so long to struggle against death, alone, that I feel and see only death! I feel like death!' (335). Only when she has experienced death can she begin the slow process of educating Hareton and initiating the reconstruction of civilization. Her confrontation with death is caused by her unwilling involvement in Heathcliff's scheme to revenge himself on Cathy by destroying the Heights and the Grange. Here again the violence and suffering of the first lovers makes possible the goodness and happiness of the next generation. The individual experience of the second Cathy matches exactly the historical process dramatized in the whole action of the novel: from inauthentic isolation through terror, violence, and death to the establishment of a valid community based on mediated love.

But at the end of *Wuthering Heights*, though a good society has been created, the Chapel of Gimmerton Slough is still without a pastor, and its physical decay has proceeded apace. The dilapidation of the church is insisted upon, and a description of it is given at the very end of the novel, just before the final paragraphs describing the graves of Edgar, Heathcliff, and Catherine, the moths fluttering around the harebells, and the soft wind breathing through the grass. Why is the church not reestablished along with the rest of civilization? The answer to this question will be a final formulation of the meaning of *Wuthering Heights*.

The church is still deserted because it is no longer necessary. God has been transformed from the transcendent deity of extreme Protestantism, enforcing in wrath his irrevocable laws, to an immanent God, pervading everything, like the soft wind blowing over the heath. This new God is an amiable power who can, through human love, be possessed here and now. The breakthrough into God's world of Heathcliff and Cathy has not only made possible the peaceful love of Hareton and the second Cathy; it has also made institutionalized religion unnecessary. The love of Heathcliff and Cathy has served as a new mediator between heaven and earth, and has made any other mediator for the time being superfluous. Their love has brought 'the new heaven and the new earth' into this fallen world as a present reality.

Notes

1. This essay was written by Emily Brontë as a devoir for her teacher M. Héger in Brussels. In its form it is a moralizing or theologizing of natural history in the

manner of the famous *Meditations* of James Hervey, ardent Methodist and friend of John Wesley. But the moral which Emily Brontë derives from her butterfly has no parallel in Hervey's *Meditations*, in Wesley's *Compendium of Natural Philosophy*, or in eighteenth-century natural theology generally – which was dedicated to showing the wisdom and beneficence of God as manifested in the works of the creation. The transformation of the caterpillar into a butterfly is a traditional symbol of resurrection, or of the liberation of the soul. (Harvey makes the silk-worm's change into a butterfly a type of Christ's resurrection and ascent into heaven, and hence of our own attainment of beatitude.) But in her treatment of the butterfly, as in other ways, Emily Brontë pours new allegory into old emblems.

2. Further evidence that Emily Brontë was exposed to this attitude toward children may be found in Charlotte Brontë's portrait of the Evangelical schoolmaster Robert Brocklehurst in *Jane Eyre*. Brocklehurst is modeled on the Reverend William Carus Wilson, the proprietor of the Clergy Daughters' School which Emily Brontë attended with her sisters in 1824 and 1825, when she was seven years old. The real Carus Wilson was scarcely less unpleasant than the fictional Brocklehurst. He was the author of a great many children's books and periodicals, 'spiritual penny dreadfuls,' as Ford K. Brown calls them, all of which attempted to instill in children the fear of God and hell. 'In the business of frightening little children into being Evangelical little children', says Brown, 'he was a prodigious master; his relentless and righteously ferocious hands must have planted a religious terror in the minds of thousands of youthful Englishmen' (Brown 1961, 463). Brown's discussions of Brocklehurst and Wilson are on 451–7, 463–3 of his book.

3. The whole letter (628–44) is a succinct account of the doctrinal differences between Whitefield and Wesley.

4. The classic studies of this process are Max Weber (1904, 1905; English translation: London, 1930) and R. H. Tawney (London, 1926).

5. Surely Ruth M. Adams is wrong when she says the text is Gen. 4: 24. The phrase in Genesis is 'seventy and sevenfold' not 'seventy times seven', as in Mat. 18: 22, and in the title of Jabes' sermon (Adams 1958).

6. I am following the reconstruction in *Gondal's Queen*.

7. See Roger Caillois, 'War and the Sacred' (1959, 163–80) for an interpretation of the religious significance of war which matches Emily Brontë's.

8. 'L'érotisme est,' writes Bataille in his excellent essay on Emily Brontë, '. . . l'approbation de la vie jusque dans la mort' (1957, 12).

6.

The Creation of the Self
in Gerard Manley Hopkins

Seen from one point of view Hopkins' work is some dozen nearly perfect lyrics. Seen from another perspective it is a heterogeneous collection of documents: poems, fragments of poems, letters, notebooks, undergraduate papers, lecture notes, incomplete commentaries, sermons, and so on. But within this seemingly chaotic mass we can detect a certain persistent structure. It is not a structure of abstract thought, nor is it a pattern of concrete images. To create this structure the world of sense perception has been transformed, through its verbalization, into the very substance of thought, and, one may say, into the very substance of Hopkins himself. This paper has as its limited objective the attempt to reveal this pervasive imaginative structure. One of its chief limitations is the necessity of describing discursively and seriatim what is really the non-temporal interior world of Hopkins, the total context in which any single poem exists and has its real meaning.

I

I find myself both as man and as myself something most determined and distinctive, at pitch, more distinctive and higher pitched than anything else I see. (1937, 309)

It would seem that the problem of individuation is solved for Hopkins with his first awareness of himself. No one has had a more intense apprehension of the uniqueness and substantiality of his own identity. Hopkins' version of the Descartean *Cogito* is: 'I taste myself, therefore I exist.' 'My selfbeing,' says Hopkins, 'my consciousness and feeling of myself, that taste of myself, of *I* and *me* above and in all things . . . is more distinctive than the taste of ale or alum, more distinctive than the smell of walnutleaf or camphor, and is incommunicable by any means to another man (as when I was a child I used to ask myself: What must it be to be someone else?)' (1937, 309).

The self for Hopkins, in the very first moment in which it recognizes itself, recognizes itself not as a lack, an appeal, but as a plenitude. It does not need to seek something outside of itself as a source of its life, because that life has already been given. One finds oneself, from the beginning, a 'throng and stack of being, so rich, so distinctive' (1937, 309). Self-awareness for Hopkins does not depend, as it does in the long tradition coming down from Locke, on sense perception of the external world. Much less does it depend on a *relation* to that world. No, Hopkins' *Cogito* is neither a purely intellectual self-consciousness arrived at by putting in doubt and separating from oneself everything which seems to come from the outside, nor is it the Lockean self-awareness which springs out of psychological nothingness in the moment of sensation. It is, like the first, entirely interior, entirely independent of the exterior world, since, for Hopkins, 'when I compare myself, my being myself, with anything else whatever, all things alike, all in the same degree, rebuff me with blank unlikeness; so that my knowledge of it, which is so intense, is from itself alone' (1937, 310).

The first moment of self-awareness is, then, not a thought, but a deeply organic sense experience which permeates the whole being. The self is already fully existent as soon as one is aware of oneself at all, and seems to form an eternally subsisting tasting of oneself which prolongs itself from moment to moment as long as one endures. Since it remains exactly the same through time, it is apparently indestructible. If it extends beyond disembodied consciousness, it is only to include a minimal sense of one's incarnation, minimal because it is a sense of incarnation in a simple, spaceless body which is wholly undifferentiated, wholly made up of a single taste.

The Hopkinsian self is, then, positive and definite, and it is vividly *sensed*, in the same way that objects in the exterior world are sensed. Intrinsic identity is a primary datum for man. He does not need to *do* anything at all to come into existence or to guarantee himself continued existence. And this intense possession of the sensation of self is the occasion of an elated joy at one's interior richness and at one's independence. [. . .] For Hopkins the fact that 'human nature' is 'more highly pitched, selved, and distinctive than anything in the world' is proof that man is 'life's pride and cared-for crown' (1948, 73). Man is, it seems, sufficient unto himself, like God.

But beneath the rejoicing in Hopkins at the uniqueness and self-subsistence of each human individual there is another current of thought, a current of wonder at this uniqueness, a wonder which shades off into a question, one of the fundamental metaphysical questions, a question which reinstates all the problems. If nothing 'explains' or 'resembles' this 'unspeakable stress of pitch,' if I 'taste self but at one tankard, that of my own being,' 'from what then do I with all my being and above all that taste of self, that selfbeing, come?' (1937, 310).

II

The proof of the existence of God for Hopkins is neither from the evidence of the external world, nor from direct intuition. It is a logical deduction from the fact of one's own uniqueness:

Nothing finite then can either begin to exist or eternally have existed of itself, because nothing can in the order of time or even of nature act before it exists or exercise function and determination before it has a nature to 'function' and determine, to selve and instress, with. (1937, 312)[1]

And if this is true for all created things, how much more true for human beings is it that they cannot be self-created and self-existent. In a radical about-face Hopkins sees that his apparently so independent self must, on the evidence of its very nature, depend on something outside of itself, must draw its existence from 'one of finer or higher pitch and determination than itself' (1937, 309). So here, almost in the moment of rejoicing over the distinctiveness of the 'taste of oneself,' strikes the 'terror' of God (1948, 56). For if the Creator could do so much, so can he undo, or do with his creatures as he wishes. For Hopkins, 'a self is an absolute which stands to the absolute of God as the infinitesimal to the infinite' (1937, 331). The question becomes, then, 'What relation do I or should I have to this Being who is so infinitely my superior and so "dangerous" to me?' (1948, 73).

The answer is simple and total: 'Man was created. Like the rest then to praise, reverence, and serve God; to give him glory' (1937, 303). But how do God's creatures 'give him glory'? Merely by being themselves, by *doing* themselves. Selfhood is not a static possession, but an activity:

> Each mortal thing does one thing and the same:
> Deals out that being indoors each one dwells;
> Selves – goes itself; myself it speaks and spells;
> Crying *What I do is me: for that I came.*
>
> (1948, 95)

But it is just here that a radical division among God's creatures appears. Each non-human creature exists in the absolute security of being unable to do other than what it came for. It cannot choose *not* 'to fling out broad its name' (1948, 95) and, in doing so, 'make [God] known,' 'tell of him,' 'give him glory' (1937, 303). 'What they can *they always do*' (1937, 303). But if man can *mean* to give God glory, he can, necessarily, mean *not* to give him glory. His complete fulfillment of his nature, the selving for which he came, is radically contingent. If the full accomplishment of his being puts him 'beyond all visible creatures' (1937, 303), so also he can, because of his free will and its accompanying self-consciousness utterly fail to be, in a way no other of God's creatures can. So then, within the very development of Hopkins' apprehension of the nature of his self-being an amazing transformation takes place. What had seemed so solid and definite turns out to be merely a 'positive infinitesimal' (1937, 322), something that both exists and does not exist, like a point on a line. It is the mere potentiality of being, a self 'intrinsically different from every other self,' but a self to which a 'nature' must be added (1937, 322). What had seemed so self-subsistent is really very much like the Mallarméan 'néant'; it is 'nothing, a zero, in the score or account of existence' (1937, 322): 'For the self before nature is no thing as yet but only possible; with the accession of a nature it becomes properly a self, for instance a person' (1937, 325).

Now we can see how the fearful experience recorded in the 'terrible sonnets,' utter paralysis of the will, and the accompanying spiritual vertigo, is possible, perhaps even necessary, given the premises of Hopkins' universe. Only the self-conscious mind of man can utterly fail to be and plunge downward into the abyss of complete nothingness, and only the mind of man can experience the terror of that plunge:

> O the mind, mind has mountains; cliffs of fall
> Frightful, sheer, no-man-fathomed. Hold them cheap
> May who ne'er hung there. Nor does long our small
> Durance deal with that steep or deep.
>
> (1948, 107)

And if it is only man who can taste himself, can be aware of his own being, it is also only man for whom that self-taste can be a terrifying experience of his isolation from God and from all things, an experience of complete enclosure within the prison of his own self-tormenting self:

> I am gall, I am heartburn. God's most deep decree
> Bitter would have me taste: my taste was me.
>
> (1948, 110)

The self which had seemed so solid, so enduring and self-subsistent discovers not only that it is created, but that it absolutely requires help from outside itself in order to be, since to be necessarily means being able to selve, to *do* one's proper being. Without some relation to something outside oneself, man may remain paralyzed, a mere 'positive infinitesimal,' unable to transform possibility into actuality. Exiled within itself, caged in itself, the self discovers that far from sufficing to itself, it is, in its isolation, entirely impotent, as impotent as a eunuch. It is 'time's eunuch' (1948, 113), that is, it is wholly unable to project into the future an action and then carry that action out. Instead of a growth, change, accomplishment matching the passage of time and filling it, such as we find in non-human creatures, man in his desolation finds that he is plunged into a subterranean darkness where time has lengthened out into an endless succession of empty moments, each one of which, because of its emptiness, seems itself to be lifelong:

> What hours, O what black hoürs we have spent
> This night! what sights you, heart, saw; ways you went!
> And more must, in yet longer light's delay.
> With witness I speak this. But where I say
> Hours I mean years, mean life.
>
> (1948, 109)

In this extremity, any possibility of help will be grasped. Perhaps that non-human world of creatures who 'always do what they can,' even though it rebuffs man with 'blank unlikeness,' may serve in some way to rescue man from his dizzy plunge into the abyss, from the utter cessation of the forward movement of his life. What is the relation of man to nature in Hopkins?

III

There is evident in Hopkins, from the earliest fragmentary notebooks onward, an interest in the exact nature of things in the external world which is extraordinary even in a century to which nature meant so much.

Hopkins' primary relation to nature was what perhaps remains man's most profound reaction to the external world: it was simply the astonished recognition that each perceived object is *there*, exists as a stubborn, irreducible fact. 'But indeed,' says Hopkins, 'I have often felt . . . that nothing is so pregnant and straightforward to the truth as simple *yes* and *is*' (1937, 98). No one has felt more deeply and consciously this wonder at the mere existence of things, and no one has tried more earnestly to cherish that wonder and make it persist throughout as the basic ingredient of his relation to the world.

[. . .]

But what does Hopkins find outside of himself? He discovers that each thing is uniquely itself, that each thing has its own distinct nature, a nature which is never repeated. This individuality is manifested in things by the freshness and sharpness of their outline or pattern. Hopkins' nature is a nature with clearly defined edges. It is a nature without blurring or smudging, a nature in which each thing stands out vividly as though it were surrounded by perfectly translucent air. And air can reach all the surfaces of even the smallest and most intricate object, so abrupt is the frontier between the object and its surroundings:

> Wild air, world-mothering air,
> Nestling me everywhere,
> That each eyelid or hair
> Girdles; goes home betwixt
> The fleeciest, frailest-flixed
> Snowflake
>
> (1948, 99)

Hopkins' word for the design or pattern which is the perceptible sign of the unique individuality of a thing is 'inscape.' I give only one example among a great many: 'Below at a little timber bridge I looked at some delicate fly shafted ashes – there was one especially of single sonnet-like inscape' (1937, 211). But an 'inscape' need not be a single object. It can be a *group* of objects which together form a pattern. Nevertheless, this form of inscape, too, is not a mere extrinsic organization of disparate parts, but is the manifestation of an inner, organic unity. Nor is inscape only discovered through the sense of sight (although that sense certainly predominates in Hopkins). The use of synesthesia in Hopkins' poetry is matched by an explicit analysis in the *Journal* of the way the unitary inscape of a single object may be perceived by all the senses. The passage begins: 'The bluebells in your hand baffle you with their inscape, made to every sense' (1937, 145). 'Inscape,' then, is always used in contexts wherein the oneness, the organic unity, of a single object or group of *composed* objects is seen. And it is always associated with distinctness of outline, with words like 'sharp,' 'wiry' and 'crisp.' Each object in Hopkins' world is distinctly itself, separated starkly from every other object in the universe. And it is not, like the nature of Tennyson and Rilke, seen as suspended statically and mutely in an eternal and fateful present which seems to be in the very act of fading suddenly away into nonexistence. Nature in Hopkins is neither static nor does it hauntingly slip beyond the observer's immediate grasp. It is seen as present to the observer and as acting directly upon him without any intervening distance or vacancy. It does not somehow escape the spectator by withdrawing in upon itself. And even a natural scene which might seem to ask to be treated as static and inanimate is perceived by Hopkins as the center of a vital activity, even of a *personal* activity: 'The mountain ranges, as any series or body of inanimate like things not often seen, have the air of persons and of interrupted activity' (1953, 115).

Natural objects, then, are not dead, but are sustained from within by a vital pressure. They are not static but ceaselessly active, even when they are apparently motionless. It is this inner pressure, permeating all nature, which is the true source of inscape and what is actually manifested by it. The word is *in-scape*, the outer manifestation or 'scape' of an inner principle or activity – not the mere external pattern which things make and which is pleasing to the eye as design: '*All the world is full of inscape* and chance left free to act falls into an order as well as purpose: looking out of my window I caught it in the random clods and broken heaps of snow made by the cast of a broom' (1937, 173, 174). 'There lives the dearest freshness deep down things' (1948, 70). 'Fineness, proportion of feature, comes from a moulding force which succeeds in asserting itself over the resistance of cumbersome or restraining matter' (1938, 159). Some of Hopkins' drawings are startlingly like Chinese paintings: their swirling whirlpool patterns seem to manifest an ubiquitous spiritual force rolling through all nature. Hopkins' nature, as much as Coleridge's or Whitehead's, is the locus of a vital process, the explosive meeting-point of a spiritual elan and the stubborn resistance of matter. It is a nature which is in ceaseless activity and which manifests an extreme tension between the inner energy and the restraining outward form. The inscape is the meeting place of these two.

But for the inner energy itself Hopkins uses another word, a word which suggests not the outer design or pattern of a thing, but that very energy which upholds it from within: 'all things are upheld by instress and are meaningless without it,' wrote Hopkins in an undergraduate essay on Parmenides (1937, 98). Just as the apparently unique and solid 'taste of self' which was discovered in the first moment of awareness turned out to be a mere 'positive infinitesimal,' so nature, apparently so full of sharply defined distinctive objects, turns out to be upheld by a single permeating spirit. This spirit is God himself: 'As we drove home the stars came out thick: I leant back to look at them and my heart opening more than usual praised our Lord to and in whom all that beauty comes home' (1937, 205). Even more striking is a passage from Hopkins' unpublished retreat notes of 1882. In this passage all the solid world is dissolved into expression of God. It is a passage which seems at the furthest possible remove from the naturalism, the humble scientific observation of nature with which Hopkins began: 'God's utterance of Himself in Himself is God the Word, outside Himself in this world. The world then is word, expression, news of God. Therefore its end, its purpose, its purport, its meaning and its life and work is to name and praise him' (cit. Peters 1948, 175). Nature, then, for Hopkins as for the Middle Ages, is the 'book of nature' in which we may read 'news of God.' But there is one crucial difference: the medieval doctrine of analogy has almost disappeared from Hopkins. For the Christian of the Middle Ages each object in the natural world repeated some particular aspect of the supernatural world. It was thus a means of knowing that supernatural world in detail. For Hopkins all the world is 'charged with the grandeur of God,' and we know through the things of this world simply the power and presence of God, not details of the supernatural world.

It is easy to see now why Hopkins was so elated when in 1872 he discovered Duns Scotus's *Commentaries on the Sentences of Peter Lombard*, and why in that year he could write: 'just then when I took in any inscape of the sky or sea I thought of Scotus' (1937, 161). Hopkins found in Scotus confirmation of the theory of nature and of the human self which he already held. Hopkins had always felt that the unique individuality of a thing or person was really a part of it, part of its form and not merely a result of the matter in which the form was actualized as Aristotle and St Thomas maintained. He had always felt that one knows in the act of perception not, by means of the Aristotlean or Thomistic *species intelligibilis*, the mere *quidditas* or 'whatness' of a thing, but its distinctive individuality, its 'thisness.' In the Scotian doctrine of the *haecceitas* or individualizing form, which makes an object not simply a member of a species, a pine tree, for example, but this particular unrepeatable pine tree, Hopkins found his own deepest apprehension of the world systematized. And perhaps even more importantly Hopkins felt that through the immediate sense perception of things in the world he could know God directly as the 'instress' that upheld each thing. He did not want a world of abstract 'ideas' or 'forms' ('pinetreeness,' 'bluebellness' and so on) to intervene between himself and God. Paradoxically, the

Scotian metaphysic, which, from one perspective at least, seems perilously close to nominalism (Landry 1922), was actually a much better basis for Hopkins' view of the universe as 'news of God' than would have been the Aristotlean theory of forms. Only a world in which God himself is directly present without intermediary in each one of his creatures can be 'expression, news of God' in the way Hopkins deeply felt it to be: 'All things', he wrote, 'therefore are charged with love, are charged with God and if we know how to touch them give off sparks and take fire, yield drops and flow, ring and tell of him' (1937, 342).

IV

'*If* we know how to touch them.' The perception of the instress in natural objects, then, is contingent on something in the observer. The true theme of Hopkins' *Journal* and of his nature poems is not nature alone but the man–nature relationship. Hopkins has a striking phrase for the 'bridge,' the dynamic interaction, he felt to exist between subject and object: he called it the 'stem of stress between us and things' (1937, 98). This tension, as between two magnets, is absolutely necessary to 'bear us out and carry the mind over' (1937, 98). Subject and object share one thing at least in common: their possession of the inward energy of instress. This intrinsic spiritual force flashes out from objects; it rays forth from them. Each object is not merely the tense withholding of a spiritual charge. This charge leaps out at the slightest provocation, and all objects are thereby potentially in touch with one another. The world in Hopkins is a vast network of electrical discharges given and received by objects which are an inexhaustible source of the divine energy:

> The world is charged with the grandeur of God.
> It will flame out, like shining from shook foil.
> (1948, 70)

But human beings too are charged with energy: 'Honour is flashed off exploit,' says Hopkins (1948, 112), and 'self flashes off frame and face' (1948, 104). Perception, as in Whitehead, is only a special case of the dynamic interaction between all objects. In the moment of perception a 'stem of stress' is created between subject and object to which the subject contributes as much as does the object: 'What you look hard at seems to look hard at you' (1937, 140). Hopkins' epistemology, like that of the Pre-Socratics (whom he had read), is based ultimately on the 'theory of sensation by like and like' (1937, 102). Only if the beholder is able to return stress for stress will the moment of knowledge, the moment of the coalescence of subject and object, take place.

Hopkins almost always mentions both subject and object in his descriptions of nature. He not only describes the bluebells, he says: 'I caught as well as I could while my companions talked the Greek rightness of their beauty' (1947, 174). 'I caught.' It is an active verb, suggesting the energetic grasp of the mind on things. The phrase echoes through the *Journal* and the poetry; it is Hopkins' special term for the strenuous activity of perception: 'I caught this morning morning's minion, kingdom of daylight's dauphin, dapple-dawn-drawn Falcon' (1948, 73).

Just as Hopkins' self-awareness is an organic taste of himself, not a dry lucidity, so his grasp of the external world in the dynamic moment of instress is as much emotional as intellectual. It is a total possession of the object by the thinking, feeling, sensing subject. The object is internalized by the subject. Hence Hopkins speaks repeatedly of instress as something deeply *felt*, not merely intellectually realized: 'But such a lovely damasking in the sky as today I never felt before' (1937, 143). 'Looking all round but most in looking far up the valley I felt an instress and charm of Wales' (1937, 210). One gathers from the constant use of this word and of the word 'caught' a strong sense of the precariousness of these experiences. They are reported with a tone of elation, as though they were rare occurrences of success among many failures.

And sometimes indeed the instress does fail to come. It depends on just the proper conditions in the perceiver and in what is perceived: in the perceiver a certain freshness of vision and a singleness of concentration on the object perceived: 'Unless you refresh the mind from time to time you cannot always remember or believe how deep the inscape in things is' (1937, 140). For the instress to come it must be as if there were nothing else in the world but the present moment of ecstatic communication with what is directly present to the senses. Hopkins differs from the romantic poets generally in that there is in his writings almost no interest in affective memory, in the linkage to a moment in the past by means of intense perception in the present. Each moment recorded in the *Journal* and in the poems is sufficient unto itself. There is a kind of radical discontinuity in Hopkins' temporal existence. It proceeds by a series of vivid perceptions. Each is distinct from all the others and each fades away almost immediately to be replaced by another or sometimes by mere vacancy and lassitude. If a relation between past and present via memory appears in Hopkins at all it is almost always in the form of a lament for the irretrievable fading away of the ecstacy of instress when it is past: 'Saw a lad burning big bundles of dry honey-suckle: the flame (though it is no longer freshly in my mind) was brown and gold' (1937, 159). The *Journal* entries were often written down long after the event recorded from notes made at the time. In the few cases where the notes themselves exist we can sense a frantic attempt to capture some portion at least of what is known to be fleeting and fragile. And are not the *Journal* and the poems themselves ultimately to be defined as the attempt to give through words some form of permanence to what were actually unique, instantaneous and unrepeatable experiences? There is implicit in the very form of the *Journal* and of the poems a deep anguish at the inevitable passing away of these moments. The loss of these experiences is painful because it is the loss of what the person himself is at that moment. We can detect in the *Journal* both the anxious attempt to give these fleeting moments some permanence in words *and* the obsessive urge to have more and more and more of them. Hopkins can think of no more painful form of self-mortification and penance than to deprive himself of the repetition of one of these experiences (see 1937, 199).

But sometimes even if the precious activity of instressing is permitted and desired it will not come. Not only must one banish the past and future and live wholly in the moment, one must also banish the awareness that any other person exists: 'Even with one companion ecstasy is almost banished: you want to be alone and to feel that, and leisure – all pressure taken off' (1937, 111). One can see clearly and explicitly here what is sometimes obscured in other projects of founding one's self-identity on a direct relationship to nature: such a project is, strictly speaking, amoral. It does not exist in what Kierkegaard called the 'ethical' realm. For Hopkins, as for Keats and Wordsworth, the self is formed not through inter-personal relations but through experiences of non-human nature, experiences which simply ignore the existence of other human beings. Hopkins' *Journal* and his greatest poems are the record of experiences of absolute isolation from other people.

But even to be alone, in the moment, isolated from past and future and from all other human beings, is not always enough. There may be simply a failure of the sensibility, a failure which in some people is total and permanent: 'I thought how sadly beauty of inscape was unknown and buried away from simple people and yet how near at hand it was if they had eyes to see it and it could be called out everywhere again' (1937, 161).

And sometimes it is the *object* which for one reason or another fails to offer itself to perception, fails to flash itself outwards in the stress that can be counterstressed by the poet. This fact is perceived when a change in a natural object makes it possible to detect an inscape that has been present all the time, but hidden: 'This is the time to study inscape in the spraying of trees, for the swelling buds carry them to a pitch which the eye could not else gather' (1937, 141). 'I caught as well as I could [in the bluebells] . . . a notable glare the eye may abstract and sever from the blue colour of light beating up from so many glassy heads, which like water is good to float their deeper instress in upon the mind' (1937, 174). 'Float their deeper instress in upon the mind'! How different this is from the preception, at a *distance*, that each individual thing is its distinct self and has an inscape. Now Hopkins wants to possess that external perception, to internalize it, to 'float it in upon the mind' across the stem of stress between subject and object.

When the communication is total perceiver and perceived come into intimate contact, interpenetrate and coalesce. This experience is the true theme of the early nature poems, of 'Spring,' 'The Starlit Night,' 'The Sea and the Skylark,' and 'Hurrahing in Harvest.' The effect of this experience on the self is, in the etymological sense of the word, 'ecstacy': the self leaps outside of itself and creates a new self by means of a substantial identification with all of perceived nature:

> These things, these things were here and but the beholder
> Wanting; which two when they once meet,
> The heart rears wings bold and bolder
> And hurls for him, O half hurls earth for him off under his feet.
>
> (1948, 75)

V

Another night from the gallery window I saw a brindled heaven, the moon just marked – I *read* a broad careless inscape flowing throughout. (1937, 158; emphasis added)

The [elms'] tops are touched and *worded* with leaf. (1937, 190; emphasis added)

On the one hand, natural objects are intelligible; they can be read by man as though they were not simply objects, but *signs*. On the other hand, they are *mute* signs. They only speak when there is a human being present to read them. Man gives natural objects a voice and a language. In 'reading' them, and in bodying forth that meaning in words man gives nature something it does not possess, self-consciousness and a tongue to speak that awareness:

> And what is Earth's eye, tongue, or heart else, where
> Else, but in dear and dogged man?
>
> (1948, 96)

The true 'stem of stress' between man and nature is the word itself. At the point of fusion, where subject meets object and coalesces with it, is born the word. Words have for Hopkins a magic quality of attaining the object, wresting from it its meaning and making that meaning a permanent possession for man. 'To every word meaning a thing and not a relation,' wrote Hopkins in a brief paper on words dated 1868, 'belongs a passion or prepossession or enthusiasm which it has the power of suggesting or producing, but not always or in everyone' (1937, 95). In one sense, all Hopkins' efforts in his poetry were towards the creation of a continuum of words which would, like a proper name, convey the 'pre-possession,' to use his word, of a unique individual experience. All Hopkins' poetry is based on the fundamental discovery that words can imitate things, re-present them in a different form, rescue them from the ceaselessly moving realm of nature and translate them into the permanent realm of words. Words can, Hopkins discovered, 'catch' things, 'stall' them, as he said,[1] and transform them into spiritual stuff. Metaphors were not, for him, 'poetic lies,' nor were words

arbitrary signs. Hopkins discovered what certain contemporary poets, philosophers and anthropologists are making their central theme: in the word subject
and object merge and we touch the object in a way we never can without
naming it. The word is not an arbitrary label; it carries the object alive into the
heart. Each different word for the 'same thing' transmits to the mind a slightly
(or radically) different aspect of reality. Each new word is a window through
which a new portion of reality is revealed. To name a thing is to perceive it. This
thing is not subjective, not 'imposed' by the mind 'outwards' (1937, 154). It is
'really there', but is only perceived when it is so named. We only truly *see* the
world when we have represented it in words. Metaphor, onomatopoeia,
compound words, inversion, functional shift, and all the other special techniques of verbal representation are only modes of the universal operation of verbal
mimesis. All the seemingly idiosyncratic methods of Hopkins' poetry are, in one
way, directed towards the perfect imitation in words of the object perceived in
all its concreteness and in all its energetic activity.

But if words for Hopkins face outwards towards the object, they also face
inwards towards the mind. Even in the earliest of Hopkins' writings we can see
another fundamental obsession: a fascination for words in themselves, for their
etymology, for their multiplicity of meanings, for their abstract 'prepossession'
without any reference to particular experiences. Hopkins was very sensitive to
the inscape of words in themselves, taken in isolation from their meaning. He
was fascinated by the fact that the same word can in different contexts carry the
'prepossession' of entirely different realities: 'Sky peak'd with tiny flames . . .
Altogether peak is a good word. For sunlight through shutter, locks of hair, rays
in brass knobs etc. Meadows peaked with flowers' (1937, 32). If Hopkins was
the most nature-intoxicated poet of the Victorian period, he was also the poet
most fascinated by words in themselves, by words not as the signs of an external
reality but as the signs of certain definite spiritual states.

Accordingly, alongside the theory and practice of poetry as *mimesis* we can
observe a very different notion, a notion of poetry as a thing to be contemplated
for its own sake and without any reference to the external world: 'But as air,
melody, is what strikes me most of all in music and design in painting, so design,
pattern or what I am in the habit of calling "inscape" is what I above all aim at in
poetry' (1935a, 60). Inscape, said Hopkins, is 'the very soul of art' (1935b, 135).
It is what makes a work of art 'beautiful to individuation,' that is, it gives a poem
or a painting the kind of distinctness, uniqueness, *haecceitas*, possessed by a
natural object. 'Inscape,' then, has two very different meanings. It can refer to
the willed design of a human artifact as well as to the pattern into which natural
objects fall without any human intervention.

Hopkins sought to achieve in his poetry an organic unity in which each part
would be interrelated to all the other parts, and thus transcend its isolation as the
name of an external object: 'Repetition, *oftening, over-and-overing, aftering* of the
inscape must take place in order to detach it to the mind and in this light poetry

is speech which alters and softens its inscape, speech couched in a repeated figure and verse as spoken sound having a repeated figure' (1937, 249). 'Tout le mystère est la,' said Mallarmé, in terms that Hopkins himself might have used, 'établir les identités secrètes par un deux à deux qui ronge et use les objêts, au nom d'une centrale pureté' (All the mystery is there, to establish secret identities by a two by two that gnaws and wears away the objects, in the name of a central purity; cit. Poulet 1952, 343). For Hopkins, as for Mallarmé, the repetition or parallelism which establishes 'secret identities' between one part of a poem and another was for the sake of a 'central purity,' a central purity which Hopkins called the total inscape of the poem. Here we have moved very far indeed from the notion of poetry as the *mimesis* of the external world, as the violent point of contact between subject and object. All the density of texture in Hopkins' verse is as much for the sake of creating its own self-sufficient durée or 'sliding inscape,' as it is to express the packed energy and radiance which some event in nature contains. If the extreme use of various forms of 'over-and-overing' in Hopkins, assonance, alliteration, internal rhyme, Welsh *cynghanedd* and so on, is in one sense all for the purpose of representing nature, it is in another sense wholly indifferent to external nature and all calculated to 'detach the mind' and 'carry' the 'inscape of speech for the inscape's sake.'

Inscape in poetry is 'the essential and only lasting thing' (1938, 225); it is 'species or individually distinctive beauty of style' (1938, 225). But it is only attained via the individuality of the poet himself: 'Every poet,' says Hopkins, 'must be original and originality a condition of poetic genius; so that each poet is like a species in nature (*not an individuum genericum* or *specificum*) and can never recur' (1938, 222). Each poet, then, is very like each inanimate object in that he is a *species*, not a *genus*, a *haecceitas*, not a *quidditas*. 'No doubt my poetry errs on the side of oddness,' wrote Hopkins, '. . . Now it is the virtue of design, pattern, or inscape to be distinctive and it is the vice of distinctiveness to become queer. This vice I cannot have escaped' (1935a, 60). We can see now that when Hopkins said that he aimed above all at 'inscape' in poetry he meant not simply that he aimed at pattern, design, organic unity, but that he aimed at these because only through them could poetry be the affirmation and actualization of his own identity. So in the headnote of the sonnet to Henry Purcell, Purcell is praised for having 'uttered in notes the very make and species of man as created in him and in all men generally' (1948, 84). But in the poem itself the bow to St Thomas is forgotten and Purcell's music is praised not as manifesting 'man generally,' but as the expression of an absolutely unique self, Purcell's own 'arch-especial . . . spirit':

> It is the forgèd feature finds me; it is the rehearsal
> Of own, of abrúpt sélf there so thrusts on, so throngs the ear.
>
> (1948, 85)

But at the center of the project of individuation by means of 'poeting' there lies a double flaw, a flaw which leads to the faltering and ultimate total collapse of the project. In this collapse, Hopkins is left bare again, 'no one, nowhere,' enclosed within the unpierced walls of his own impotent taste of self.

VI

This collapse can be seen from two perspectives. The poet, it is true, however much he may be apparently imitating the external world in his poetry, is actually speaking himself, *doing* himself. The poet poets. But this 'poeting' is accomplished after all through words that have meanings, that remain signs even when they are used for the sake of their own inscapes. A poem is not an act of absolute self-creation. Without the external world it could not exist; however independent it may be it must remain, to be successful, a faithful representation of the external world. The success of this reliance on the external world will depend on the stability and solidity of that world itself.

Hopkins' nature, so densely packed with distinctly singular objects, each sustained by the instress of an inexhaustible energy, would seem perfectly suited to such a dependence on it. Nevertheless, we can see a disastrous transition in Hopkins' apprehension of nature. At first it seems full of solid, static, enduring objects, objects which cannot help but be themselves and which cannot cease to be themselves. But it becomes apparent that these things are in continual movement. Nature is not only full of kinetic energy, it is also a nature in process which is the dynamic expending of that energy. One remembers the clouds in 'Hurrahing in Harvest' which are continually made and unmade, 'moulded ever and melted across skies' (1948, 74). It is only in some kind of movement that things can radiate their inexhaustible energy outwards. But there seems nothing ominous about the discovery that things are not fixed eternally in a single inscape.

Yet in two magnificent poems of Hopkins' maturity, 'Spelt from Sibyl's Leaves' and 'That Nature is a Heraclitean Fire and of the Comfort of the Resurrection,' there is a complete reversal of the earlier feeling of the permanent distinctiveness of things. What had begun as the simple perception that the inscapes of things are in a continual process of change becomes an anguished recognition that the 'forgèd features' of things are ultimately utterly destroyed. Never has the perception of nature as a shifting flux of birth and death been expressed with more intensity. As in Parmenides, 'unmeaning night, thick and wedgèd body' (1937, 102) which inevitably follows day and hides the perceptible forms of things is taken as the symbol of that absolute non-being which will inevitably overtake all created things, all *mortal* beauty:

> Earnest, earthless, equal, attuneable, ' vaulty, voluminous, . . . stupendous
> Evening strains to be time's vást, ' womb-of-all, home-of-all, hearse-of-all night.
> . . . For earth ' her being has unbound, her dapple is at an end, as −

tray or aswarm, all throughther, in throngs; 'self ín self steepèd and páshed – qúite
Disremembering, dísmémbering ' áll now.

(1948, 1948, 104)

Only if we know how much Hopkins cherished the 'original definiteness and
piquant beauty of things' (1938, 72) can we understand fully what violence of
regret, what 'pity and indignation' (1948, 112), there is in the image of 'self ín
self steepèd and páshed.' It is a dynamically experienced image of the return of
all individuated forms to the 'thick and wedgèd body' of primordial chaos. In
that chaos every self will be blurred, smeared, inextricably mixed in the other
selves. Nature will be, in Hopkins' striking coinage, 'all throughther.' The
suggestion that a complete phrase such as 'each interpenetrated through and
through with the others' has been collapsed into 'throughther' makes it a perfect
mimesis of the event described. One feels the forms of the collapsed words
straining to differentiate themselves, just as the identities being crushed into
chaos resist desperately the unbinding of their being.

In the poem called 'That Nature is a Heraclitean Fire' another of the Pre-
Socratic symbols is used, fire, the symbol of the energy of being, 'ethery flame of
fire' as Hopkins calls it in his essay on Parmenides (1937, 102). In this poem all
the thousand forms in which this energy manifests itself are seen to be
impermanent as clouds or as straws in a bonfire, and are continually being
destroyed and replaced by other forms. 'God gave things,' wrote Hopkins, 'a
forward and perpetual motion' (1937, 84). If 'Spelt from Sibyl's Leaves' is the
frightening vision of night as dismembering, the later poem is a hymn to day as
destructive fire, a fire in which 'million-fuèled, nature's bonfire burns on' (1948,
112). The very energy of Being, its fire, what seemed to inhere within things
and to sustain them in selfhood turns out to be itself the source of their undoing.
For that energy drives things on to an activity of selving that eventually
consumes them, unselves them, transforms them out of all resemblance to
their former selves. Only the 'ethery flame of fire' remains constant, that and the
activity of change itself, the ceaseless metamorphosis of one form into another.

How, then, can an identification of oneself with external nature be used to
establish a permanent identity if nature is as unstable as the day which moves every
moment closer towards the tomb of night, as quick to change and as destructive as
fire, and if it is to this universal flux that we must testify in our poems?

VII

The evidence from the other side is equally fatal. If nature fails man, man fails
nature and fails himself even more totally. His relation to nature can be far different
from the reverent and concentrated attention which 'floats its instress in upon the

mind.' If natural objects lack stability and permanence, so even more completely does man. In non-human nature the law is transformation, flux, but the law for man is absolute destruction, since his identity, though incarnated, is too subtle, too spiritual, to retain its distinctness through even so many changes as a tree or flower will endure. The final lesson man learns from nature is that he, too, is part of nature and that this means but one thing for him, death. If all objects are burned in nature's bonfire, man is simply annihilated in that same fire:

> But quench her bonniest, dearest 'to her, her clearest-selvèd spark
> Man, how fast his firedint, 'his mark on mind, is gone!
> Both are in an unfathomable, all is in an enormous dark
> Drowned.
>
> (1948, 112)

Even if a man could achieve through the poetizing of his perception of nature an unwavering and permanent identity, it would be all dismembered and unbound in a moment at his death.

But even within the limits of earthly life the project is bound to fail. As we have seen, the ability to 'instress' nature is intermittent and can be replaced in a moment by the most agonizing spiritual impotence. If the self is unable to selve, as it often is, it will be cut off entirely from the world which can give it such delight. In times of spiritual dryness, of spiritual paralysis, the self is locked entirely within its self-torment and cut off entirely from the outside world:

> I cast for comfort I can no more get
> By groping round my comfortless, than blind
> Eyes in their dark can day or thirst can find
> Thirst's all-in-all in a world of wet.
>
> (1948, 111)

The proper image of spiritual aridity is not of a thirsty man in a desert but of a thirsty man in the midst of water he cannot drink; it is not the image of a man straining to see in the darkness but of a blind man in the midst of light which he cannot see.

There was something ominous in the double orientation of words, and in the split in Hopkins between poetry as *mimesis* and poetry as 'the inscape of speech for the inscape's sake.' Words can become not the point of fusion of subject and object, but the locus of their most absolute and permanent division. Words, instead of reaching out to things, touching them, and *giving* them over to man, can become merely the opaque walls of his interior prison:

> . . . Only what word
> Wisest my heart breeds dark heaven's baffling ban
> Bars or hell's spell thwarts. This to hoard unheard
> Heard unheeded, leaves me a lonely began.
>
> (1948, 109)

Cast outwards by the mind to capture the object, words may fall endlessly through a shadowy void and never touch anything at all, neither things nor the God within things:

> . . . my lament
> Is cries countless cries like dead letters sent
> To dearest him that lives alas! away.
>
> (1948, 109)

The end point of Hopkins' long dialogue with nature is a complete reversal of the ecstatic mood of 'Hurrahing in Harvest.' He is cut off entirely from nature and lives in the utter isolation of his spiritual inertia, 'this tormented mind / With this tormented mind tormenting yet' (1948, 110). His state is very like that of the damned who are also imprisoned in the corrosive contemplation of their own limits. 'Against these acts of its own,' wrote Hopkins, 'the lost spirit dashes itself like a caged beast and is in prison, violently instresses them and burns, stares into them and is the deepest darkened' (Peters 1948, 177).

VIII

If all the positive ways of self-affirmation fail, perhaps there is one final way, a way through the center of the deepest despair and spiritual abnegation: the creation of one's true self by self-sacrifice. The crucifixion, central moment of history, was the act whereby Christ 'annihilated himself' (1935a, 175). Christ was most Christ, the Mediator and Saviour of mankind, when he thus sacrificed himself, just as the windhover is most windhover when it renounces its sovereignty of the air and dives earthward.

Hopkins in his later years planned a treatise on sacrifice. It was never published, but it is clear from texts scattered throughout his work what he would have said. Nonhuman things can praise God simply by being themselves, by 'dealing out that being indoors each one dwells.' Only man in order to praise God and win salvation must cease to be himself. Only through such a total change of his essential being can man escape the damnation of being 'no one, nowhere, / In wide the world's weal,' exiled within himself, separated from all, dwelling in 'the barren wilderness outside of God' (1937, 344), condemned to taste his own self eternally. Only by ceasing to be oneself and becoming Christ can a man avoid an existence which is a continual dizzy falling away in time:

> I am soft sift
> In an hourglass – at the wall
> Fast, but mined with a motion, a drift,
> And it crowds and it combs to the fall.
>
> (1948, 56)

In the subtle and elaborate investigation of free will and grace in the 'Commentary on the Spiritual Exercises of St Ignatius Loyola' Hopkins devises a brilliant metaphor to define this transformation. The actual pitch of self existing at any moment in each person is only one self out of an infinity of possible selves. It is like one cross-section out of all the possible ones of a three-dimensional solid. It is one 'cleave of being' out of the total 'burl of being.' This 'burl of being' is as much really part of a person, though only potential, as his actual self. The transformation of the self when it becomes Christ is the abandonment of one cleave of being and the actualizing of another potential one. For every man, and even Satan himself, has at least one potential cross-section which coincides with Christ.

But how can this transformation be brought about? For man of his own power can do absolutely nothing to move himself from one 'cleave of being' to another. There is only one answer: by God's grace, 'which lifts the receiver from one cleave of being to another and to a vital act in Christ' (1937, 337). Hopkins' concept of grace seems to relate him rather to Post-Reformation theologies than to Thomistic Catholicism. For a Thomist, the initial act of creation gives a man's soul an indestructible permanence. He cannot cease to be himself, even if he veers to one of the extremes of mortal sin or sainthood. Grace, in the Thomistic view, does not exert its power on the permanent identity of a man's being, but only upon the variations of his temporal existence. But grace for Hopkins is precisely a *transubstantiation* of the person's innermost being. It is 'an exchange of one whole for another whole, as they say in the mystery of Transubstantiation, a conversion of the whole substance into another substance, but here it is not a question of substance; it is a lifting him from one self to another self, which is a most marvellous display of divine power' (1937, 337). 'It is not a question of substance,' says Hopkins, but it is difficult to say what else it is, this total transformation from one self to another self, 'through the gulf and void between pitch and pitch of being' (1937, 334, 335).

Where then is free will? It would seem that there is nothing left for God's creature to do but to pray for grace. But in what Hopkins calls the 'least sight of desire,' the 'aspiration' (1937, 333), of man towards God a tiny corner is left for man's free will. 'Correspondence' is the key word in Hopkins' theory of grace. Just as man's salvation is won by achieving a correspondence to Christ, so the only action on man's part that makes this occur is the minute movement of volition whereby he wills to correspond with God's grace: 'and by this infinitesimal act the creature does what in it lies to bridge the gulf fixed between its present actual and worser pitch of will and its future better one' (1937, 333). This 'correspondence with grace and seconding of God's designs' (1937, 344) is man's tiny bit contributed towards the creation of his own best self.

But even when transubstantiated into Christ a man still remains himself, since it is that mere positive infinitesimal which the man is aware of in his first self-consciousness which is so filled with Christ. The proper figure for the achieved transformation is of a hollow shell or vessel which is everywhere inhabited by Christ and brought into positive being by Christ: 'This too,' writes Hopkins, 'but brings out the nature of the man himself, as the lettering on a sail, or the device upon a flag are best seen when it fills' (1937, 343).

However, this metamorphosis of man into Christ remains until his death contingent, in jeopardy. It depends on God's continual gift of fresh grace and on man's continual 'saying Yes' (1937, 333) to God.[2] Only at the Resurrection will man be securely and permanently transformed, soul and body, into Christ: whence the 'comfort of the Resurrection,' the only real comfort for man:

> . . . Flesh fade, and mortal trash
> Fall to the residuary worm: 'world's wildfire, leave but ash:
> In a flash, at a trumpet crash,
> I am all at once what Christ is, 'since he was what I am, and
> This Jack, joke, poor potsherd, 'patch, matchwood, immortal diamond,
> Is immortal diamond.
>
> (1948, 112)

We must leave Hopkins here, at the extreme point of his despair and hope, turned far from nature and from poetry, standing aghast at the sight of a world that is visibly disintegrating and being consumed, as at the last trump. We leave him with nothing but the 'comfort of the Resurrection,' the hope of that miracle of transubstantiation which will change man from the mere impure carbon of matchwood to immortal diamond, change him, that is, from one allotropic form of himself to another so different that if there is any secret continuity between the two it is only in that the same null potentiality of being, is, in each case, actualized by God, actualized by God in ways that are as far apart as the whole distance from hell to heaven.

Notes

1. For a use of this word, see *Notebooks* (127): 'these images . . . once lodged there are stalled by the mind like other images.'
2. See Hopkins' beautiful image for God's continual *sustaining* of man in stanza four of 'The Wreck of the Deutschland' (1948, 56).

7.

Hardy

[. . .]
In my discussion of the linguistic moment in Hardy's poetry, I shall circle around the question of the relation of a sign to the material base on which it is written, carved, or projected. It is generally agreed today that Thomas Hardy is one of the greatest of modern poets writing in English. He is worthy to rank with Yeats or Stevens. Less clearly agreed upon is how to identify that greatness, how to talk intelligently and comprehensively about Hardy's poetry. If the interpreter chooses the road of 'close reading,' the sheer abundance of the poetry is daunting, not to speak of the special difficulties his poems oppose to explication. More than much great lyric poetry, Hardy's poems seem to slip away from commentary. They defy the techniques of analysis or do not seem to need them. [. . .]* Moreover, it is hard to imagine a book consisting of over nine hundred close readings, while all attempts that I know of to reduce Hardy's poetry to manageable size by selection are unsuccessful, including of course my own here discussing only a handful of Hardy's poems. [. . .]†

If individual close readings are unsatisfactory, so are attempts to survey the whole and organize it thematically, or phenomenologically, by noting similarities from poem to poem and generalizing on that basis. One of the themes of Hardy's poetry, as of his fiction, is the uniqueness of each moment of experience, as well as of each record in words of such a moment. Each moment, each text, is incommensurate with all the others. To see an experience or a poem as like others or as repeating them and to begin to make grand interpretative patterns on that basis is to perform just the sort of falsifying simplification that the poems themselves repeatedly warn against.
[. . .]‡
The poems should be read in all the ostentatious disorder of *The Complete Poems*. This ordering in disorder is a matter of radical discord and 'irrelation.' The

---

* Hardy's poetry is situated as a subversion, a 'misreading,' of Romantic pantheism, the transformation being marked by a shift from the Romantics' investment in nature to an interest in the way language and signs mark nature. [Ed.]

† The two passages excised address the problems attendant in any effort to read Hardy's poetry, with reference to critical examples. [Ed.]

‡ Miller offers a *caveat* concerning how to read Hardy's poetry, by considering Hardy's own understanding of the problematic nature of the ordering or unity of the poems. [Ed.]

discord is radical in that it cannot be reduced to concord or unity by going down to the roots. At least that is what Hardy says. The country of 'Hardy's mind,' or of the texts that record the topography of that mind, cannot be charted. It is unmappable.

Several sorts of discord are simultaneously present in a book of Hardy's poems or in the whole collection taken together. One is a discord of time. This is an irrelation resulting from the strange fact that the records of diverse times – for example (but it is only an example), in the form of poems – can be set side by side in a single volume. There they are like contiguous plots of ground on a landscape or on a map of that landscape. Hardy tacitly assumes, in the paragraph quoted above, that 'poems perhaps years apart in the making' will necessarily be 'unrelated, even discordant.' Time, for Hardy, at least in this passage, is the medium of a necessary discontinuity. Space, in the literal sense of a landscape, a map, a book of musical compositions, or of poems on sequential pages in *Late Lyrics and Earlier*, is the realm of 'juxtaposition,' of 'contiguity.' This curious incompatibility of time and space makes possible those 'chance little shocks' produced by the accidental juxtaposition of spatial records of diverse times. The mind of the critic or journalist tries to reconcile them. He tries to make them related in meaning as well as in physical location. It cannot be done. The discord produced by the chance juxtaposition in space of diverse times is a property of texts as such. A text is for Hardy here the physical notation of an 'impression.' It is a strange fact about texts, as of, say, the notations of a piece of music, that they, or any parts of them, can be moved around at will, rearranged. They can be put together in any order. The result is that a collective text like a book of Hardy's poems, organized, so he says, by 'chance,' as a 'miscellany,' is almost certainly going to be cacophonous.

To the discords of time and space and of the fact that a text is an object as well as a meaning must be added a discord of thought and a discord of the self. Hardy always insisted, most overtly in the prefaces to his successive volumes of verse, that it is a mistake to look for 'cohesion of thought' or a coherent philosophy in 'fancies written down in widely differing moods and circumstances, and at various dates' (Hardy 1978, 84). His poems, he says, do not present a single unified 'view of life' but are 'really a series of fugitive impressions which I have never tried to co-ordinate' (1978, 558). Discord of thought follows naturally from the discords of time, space, and accidental textual contiguity. Any conceptual or ideological consistency ascribed to Hardy by a critic is a falsifying construction. It is a product of that irresistible desire to smooth out rough edges. The critic wants to make everything in an author fit so that he can with a clear conscience utter sentences that take the form, 'For Hardy, such and such is the case,' or 'in Hardy's poems, so and so is the regular law.' No such uniformities, the poet tells his readers, exist, except perhaps a law of discrepancy or difference, the regularity of a consistent failure to consist, to hang together, to fit. [. . .]★

★ Hardy's rejection of the unity of the self is considered analogously through a discussion of David Hume's rejection of personal or organic unity. [Ed.]

Hardy's poems are, he says, 'the juxtaposition of unrelated, even discordant, effusions,' and this is so simply because they are 'unadjusted impressions,' 'a series of fugitive impressions which I have never tried to coordinate,' and which were produced by 'humbly recording diverse readings of [life's] phenomena as they are forced upon me by chance and change' (1978, 84). If this is so, the incoherence of the poems presupposes not only the incoherence of the various 'philosophies of life' expressed in the poems, the cacophony of their tunes and tones, but also the disintegration of the self that made the diverse 'readings' of the phenomena of life. If Hardy had gone on being the same person the readings would have been in harmony. The fact that they are not demonstrates that there is no such thing as Thomas Hardy or the mind of Thomas Hardy, if one means by that something continuously identical with itself. Hardy is a null place where diverse impressions happen to have congregated. The value of Hardy's poems lies in their truthful recording of the immediate moment in which a given impression occurred. Their value lies in the fact that each impression remains 'unadjusted,' 'uncoordinated.' All have been thrown together pell-mell in each volume of verse without any attempt to give them a factitious order – not a chronological order, nor a logical order, nor the order of musical 'gradation.' This disorder reflects the way they exist in 'Hardy's mind' (though calling it that falsely unifies the disparate), and in the place where he keeps the physical pieces of paper, in his desk drawer or wherever.

It is in this context that the reader must understand the curious and mostly ignored claim Hardy repeatedly makes that his poems in the first person are dramatic monologues. In the brief preface to the first book of his lyrics, *Wessex Poems* (1898), Hardy affirms that 'the pieces are in a large degree dramatic or personative in conception; and this even where they are not obviously so' (1978, 6). The same phrasing is repeated in the preface to *Poems of the Past and Present* (1902), though with the substitution of 'not explicitly so' for 'not obviously so' (1978, 84), meaning, I suppose, that most of the poems, even where there is no textual indication – for example, in the title or in a certain use of the first person – are to be thought of as spoken by an imaginary person, not by Thomas Hardy himself. In the preface to *Time's Laughingstocks and Other Verses* (1909) the same disclaimer is made, this time with an overt claim that the incoherence of the poems is explained by the fact that they are 'personative': 'the sense of disconnection, particularly in respect of those lyrics penned in the first person will be immaterial when it is borne in mind that they are to be regarded, in the main, as dramatic monologues by different characters' (1978, 190).

[. . .]

For Hardy strict and humble fidelity in lyric poetry to the 'impression' of each passing moment means becoming in turn a whole series of disconnected persons. The result is books of poems that are 'personative,' spoken first by this person, then by that, however much they can also be said to be spoken in the first person by the person Thomas Hardy for the moment is. Hardy does not expand himself by becoming in imagination first this person and then that person from history or from fiction. 'Hardy,' rather, is a sequence of disconnected evanescent persons. Each is called into being by the impression of the moment, then 'recorded' in a poem that personifies the impression. Each person then vanishes, never to return except when the poem is reread, or when the past impression is remembered. 'Thomas Hardy' is not who he is. He is no one, no one but the vacant place, without walls, margins, or location, in which these fugitive persons take shape momentarily and then disappear. They leave behind only their textual silhouettes in the form of those slips of paper with poems on them which Hardy kept, sometimes for forty or fifty years, before he published them.

I have said that the past impression may be remembered. It may be remembered, for Hardy, even without the 'memory aid' of the written text of a poem. Hardy has the worst of both possibilities in the temporal dimension of his existence. On the one hand he cannot remain the same person, have the same thoughts, feel the same feelings, for more than a moment. An irresistible fugacity forces him to be unfaithful to himself however hard he tries to remain the same, as the poem called 'The Wind's Prophecy' brilliantly demonstrates. On the other hand, he cannot, however hard he tries, forget those earlier selves to whom he has been unfaithful, those earlier feelings he no longer feels. They return at intervals, suddenly and unpredictably, mutely reproaching him for his infidelity.
[. . .]*

If all these forms of discontinuity operate to produce discord and irrelation among Hardy's poems, the critic can, in this emergency, best follow Hardy's own advice. He must hope that he has that mental agility 'for right note-catching' Hardy demands in his readers. He must move from poem to poem trying to identify as exactly as possible just what fugitive reading of life's phenomena each one makes. He must resist as much as possible the temptation to link poem with poem in some grand scheme. He must keep as much as possible (it will never be wholly possible) to the close-up view that maps a single field at a time, without ever trying to attain the aerial perspective that sees the whole of the difficult terrain as a single country. As Hardy categorically says, his poems taken together are in principle not to be considered a unified country of the mind or the linguistic notation of such a mind. They are rather a congeries not open to any integration except a falsifying one.

[. . .]†

The constant in Hardy's poems is their inconstancy. Their coherence is their presentation of a peculiar kind of incoherence and of the patient, lifelong, ever

---

* The difference between Hardy and Hume's concepts of memory considered. [Ed.]
† This section of the essay opens with what Miller calls a 'brief recapitulation of a handful of poems,' as they might be encountered in reading through Hardy's *Complete Poems*. [Ed.]

renewed attempt to record this accurately and to account for it. What is peculiar in this case is the combination of fragmentation and a partial hanging together. Poems, moments of experience, states of mind, the self from one time to another, are for Hardy neither wholly disintegrated nor are they wholly integrated. This is the cause of much suffering.

Why is it that for Hardy no unit of life can be either wholly detached or wholly assimilated? The incoherence derives from certain properties of language or of signs generally. All the poems in my list in one way or another explore these features of language. For Hardy, between the intention and the deed, between moment and moment, between the self and itself, between mind and landscape, falls the word. This descent of the word is the linguistic moment in Hardy. All these poems in one way or another have to do with the power of language or of signs to be generated in the first place and to go on functioning. Signs have a coercive effect. They repeat that effect indefinitely or without term, in detachment from any conscious intent either human or divine, in one direction, and in detachment from the material substratum on which they are written, in the other direction. Moreover, these bits of language cannot be made to form a system. Each has meaning in itself, as the kind of detached monad Hardy calls an 'episode' (see 'The End of the Episode' [226–7]), but a given collection of them, for example, the group I have chosen, do not hang together to form a totality, except perhaps as a series of diverse demonstrations of the fact that there can be no rational totality, only discordant conglomerations. One such conglomeration is all Hardy's poems in their disparity going on side by side in the volume of *The Complete Poems*.

Nor do any of these episodes (even if they are detached from those next-door episodes in the book that seem to belong to other life stories) form coherent wholes with their own befores and afters. Each was most often initiated as the betrayal of an earlier commitment. Each in its turn in one way or another betrayed by what comes after. In spite of the fact that the episode in no way forms part of a coherent series, it does not vanish. It goes on happening in the traces of itself it has left behind when it is over. These traces have the power of iteration that cannot be stopped. They have a power to intervene in new contexts where they do not fit, almost certainly with destructive effect. The earlier love affair inscribed on the walls of the room in 'The Re-Enactment' 'leaves no room for later passion anywhere.' It destroys the new liaison that has begun there. The old episode, once it has occurred, can neither be abolished, nor will it, given time, 'obliterate' itself as the inscription on a tombstone is gradually effaced by the weather. The old episode, or rather the mark it makes – its signature, so to speak – goes on repeating itself in new contexts in which it does not fit and to which it can by no effort of trimming or reinterpretation be assimilated (in the root sense of made 'like'). The episode just goes on blindly happening over and over, like a locomotive without a driver plunging down the track.

Let me try to specify the way this works in the not wholly harmonious set of variations on this theme my group of poems constitutes. In a passage in *Tess of the d'Urbervilles* Tess is said to be unusually sensitive to music and never to cease to wonder at the power a composer has, even after his death, to make later generations experience again a series of emotions that he alone had originally felt (chap. 13). A similar idea is expressed in *Jude the Obscure* when Jude goes to visit the composer of a hymn that greatly moves him. The composer tells Jude that he has given up hymn writing because it does not pay and is going into the wine business (part 3, chap. 10). In one case the composer is dead, in the other a changed man, but in both cases the musical notation has the power to go on producing its effect in detachment from any conscious intent on the part of the one who originally put those notes down on paper.

[. . .]

In another variation on this idea, Bathsheba, in *Far From the Madding Crowd*, commits on a whim one of those strange acts that has neither forethought, nor after it is done, afterthought – no expectation of consequences. The act almost passes out of her mind when it is finished. It was hardly in her mind when she did it. Guided in part by what Hardy calls the 'sortes sanctorum' of random prophecy by turning a key on a Bible, in part by pure chance, she sends Farmer Boldwood a valentine: 'Marry Me.' The effect, as readers of the novel will remember, is devastating. Boldwood falls hopelessly in love with Bathsheba, and his life is ultimately destroyed. He becomes the person the valentine invited him to be. He mistakenly assumes that the valentine expresses the deliberate intent of the person who has sent it, though nothing could be further from the case. As the narrator says: 'Since the receipt of the missive in the morning, Boldwood had felt the symmetry of his existence to be slowly getting distorted in the direction of an ideal passion.' The valentine acts autonomously, on its own, in detachment from any conscious mind. It produces deadly effect, just as the pieces of music and the poet's room and poems, in the other examples cited, act to make something happen. In all three instances, signs function to determine the feelings of their fortuitous recipients (see part II, chap. 14).

All my examples from the poems can, with more or less of trimming, be assimilated to this pattern. In 'Beyond the Last Lamp (Near Tooting Common),' for example, a single event thirty years past, two sad lovers slowly pacing back and forth the length of a dreary suburban street on a wet rainy evening, has so marked the spot, at least for the speaker of the poem, that the 'lone lane' has become a permanent sign of the event. The lane has become inextricably connected with what occurred there, as though the event were inscribed on the place. Or rather the existence of the place is dependent on the event, as though the figure brought its background into the open and maintained that merely contiguous scene in being. This does indeed often seem to be the case with the scenes and backgrounds or with inscriptions and the matter on which they are inscribed. In one sense the event and its surroundings have nothing to do with one another, just as an inscription may be transferred from place to place, transcribed, translated, copied, duplicated, and reduplicated. The writing seems to have no necessary relation to the material ground on which it was originally carved. In another sense the two seem indivisibly connected. Each is dependent on the other for its existence, however absurd this may seem. This absurdity and its coercive power over the mind is admirably dramatized in 'Beyond the Last Lamp.' The apparently fortuitous rhyming of the last two words in the last stanza seems to express this contingent and yet implacably operative echoing of scene and event. *Pain, lane, remain*: the chiming of these encapsulates the poem in miniature:

> . . . And yet
> To me, when nights are weird and wet,
> Without those comrades there at tryst
> Creeping slowly, creeping sadly,
> That lone lane does not exist.
> There they seem brooding on their pain,
> And will, while such a lane remain.
>
> (1978, 315)

In one sense 'Beyond the Last Lamp' is a poem supporting the idea that Hardy is a poet of causal rigor. The episode imposes itself on the scene and on the accidental spectator of the scene. It becomes the irresistible cause of its own re-enactment, long after the couple has gone. The re-enactment occurs in the scene, in the mind of the spectator who cannot think of the scene without the two sad lovers, in the poem the spectator-poet is impelled to write, and in the mind of any reader of the poem. In all these places the two lovers pace again as on that rainy night in the dreary lane beyond the last lamp near Tooting Common. The sequence forms a rigorous causal chain, with each link determining the next and determining that the episode will go on happening, in one form or another, indefinitely, again and again, as it is happening now again in the mind of whoever is reading these words.

Various other links of causal connection, however, are decisively broken in this poem. The episode is cut off from what preceded it and from what followed it. The reader is never told why the lovers were so unhappy, what had happened to bring them to this pass, nor what happened afterwards. If determinism in Hardy is supposed to mean stories with beginnings and middles following step by step according to implacable causes toward a predestined end, neither this poem, nor indeed most of Hardy's other poems, would support such generalizations. The episode does not tell a story but a moment in a story. The moment is detached from a before and an after that seem irrecoverable. These were perhaps consistent with the moment, 'caused' in the ordinary sense of a narrative causally connected, perhaps not. There is no way to tell. Moreover, though the episode seems to have the power to cause the scene in which it is enacted to become a sign for the episode, this is without the intent or knowledge of the unhappy pair of lovers. For them the scene is contingent. It is just what happens to be there. It has nothing to do with their plight.

This poem expresses a familiar paradox of Hardy's poetry, present in a different way, for example in, 'In Front of the Landscape.' People are usually so preoccupied with before and after, particularly in moments of crisis or of intense feeling, that they are unable to notice the present moment or the place where they are at that moment. That place is nonetheless becoming so marked by their passion that it will forever after be associated with it. The place will be able to recall the episode even for someone who comes on that place again unawares, as the new lovers do on the place of the old lovemaking in 'The Re-Enactment.' In 'Beyond the Last Lamp' the downcast lovers are so absorbed in 'a misery / At things which had been or might be' that they do not see the present dreary scene at all: 'Some heavy thought constrained each face, / And blinded them to time and place' (1978, 314). Nevertheless, they are unwittingly inscribing the scene with their misery so that their suffering may be read back from it later on. The relationship is that peculiar form of causality or of acausality (it is neither quite one nor the other) always involved in the transformation of an innocent bit of matter, an object, a scene, a sheet of paper, into the bearer of a sign or set of signs, the fragment of a story, a cryptic message: 'Hardy was here.'

The function of the circumstantial subtitle of 'Beyond the Last Lamp,' '(Near Tooting Common),' is, among other things, to invite the reader to try it out for himself or herself. It is as though the subtitle were saying: 'Tooting Common exists. It is a real place to be found on any map of the region. Go there on a rainy night and see for yourself. If you find the right lane and go beyond the last lamp you will find the sad lovers still pacing back and forth there. Or at any rate you will do so if you have read this poem.' And who could say that this would not be the case? Go and see for yourself.

In 'At Castle Boterel,' to turn to another poem, Hardy sees again a long past episode of courtship that had occurred on a certain steep lane in Cornwall. He sees it again when he returns to the spot. Though the episode 'filled but a minute,' and though many other things have occurred in that place, 'to one mind,' at any rate, the mind of the speaker of the poem, the scene records or expresses that event alone. The scene has become like an inscription from which the event can be reread and thereby resurrected, as the scenes and personages in a novel come alive in the mind of its reader when he or she follows the words on the page. The paradox here is that in fact nothing at all is written on the rocks. They are blank but act as if they were inscribed, as if in fact this poem had been carved on them. The rocks act like a text though they are not a text:

> Primaeval rocks form the road's steep border,
> And much have they faced there, first and last,
> Of the transitory in Earth's long order;

But what they record in colour and cast
Is – that we two passed.

(1978, 352)

In the 'same way' – though the placement of Hardy is quite different in each case, in one as passionate participant, in the other as casual and accidental witness – the words of 'Beyond the Last Lamp,' in whatever copy of Hardy's poems they are found and by whatever reader, have the potential of raising again the phantoms of those two lovers and of turning the reader into a duplicate of Hardy. The reader too would now be unable to visit the scene without seeing the lovers 'in his mind's eye' or without reading the shabby lane 'near Tooting Common' as a memorial sign of the long-vanished episode. The elements in question here form a chain, each link of which keeps a certain pattern alive. That pattern is capable of generating itself anew in whatever mind happens to encounter any version of it. Any of these links may be substituted for any of the others. They are interchangeable. From the original episode to the indifferent scene in which the episode happens to occur, to the mind of the participant or casual witness of the scene who is forced to associate the two because they happen to be there side by side, to the poem, words written down on paper, perhaps many years later, by the witness or participant, to the reader who happens to encounter that poem in whatever circumstances and in whatever copy it may have been disseminated, broadcast here and there throughout the world like scattered seed, and who then will see the real scene, if he or she visits it, as the sign of the episode – the pattern proliferates itself.

The reader, in this chain, is the helpless recipient of the pattern. He cannot help but raise the phantoms once again. He cannot help, if he reads the poem, but feel again the emotion Hardy once felt, by a sort of telepathy or feeling at a distance. He cannot help being dispossessed of his own self. He cannot help becoming, in a manner of speaking, the self of Hardy in that aspect or incarnation of it which is invaded at this time or at that time by these particular phantoms, the sad estranged lovers in 'Beyond the Last Lamp,' the happy lovers in 'At Castle Boterel.' This invasion and this reincarnation occur without respect of the situation, intent, or state of mind of the one who is invaded. The possession or dispossession has nothing to do with his own before or after. It may interfere with his life, deflect it, or even destroy it, so that he becomes henceforth malignly inhabited by ghosts who originally belonged to another person. There is great power, but not necessarily power to do good, in an innocent-looking book of poems, as there may be power in a place that happened to be the scene of some passionate encounter, as in 'The Re-Enactment,' or as the unmarked stone that echoed Paul's words in 'In the British Musuem,' in spite of being blank, brings those words back to the mind of someone who encounters the stone centuries later. St. Paul's words were 'in all their intimate accents / Patterned upon / That marble front, and were wide reflected, / And then were gone.' Though they left no traces of themselves on the stone, that stone still can retransmit them again, at least to the mind of the imaginative 'labouring man' who speaks the second half of the poem and who stands with rigid stare looking at the stone in the British Museum, 'as if [he] heard' Paul's words again (1978, 382). Like a sheet of printed paper or like the walls of a room or like a blank stone, any object or set of objects may harbor phantoms, as does for example, the glass in 'Under the Waterfall.' The glass keeps the lovers' picnic in being. In a similar way, the clock, the old viol, and the tinderbox in 'Old Furniture' are inhabited by ghosts of all the generations who have used them, 'hands behind hands, growing paler and paler.'

In 'The Place on the Map,' not words about a place but a conventional representation of that place has power to raise ghosts. The schematic sign of the scene brings back the episode that occurred there. The map perpetuates the scene just as effectively as the place itself or as the poem that recounts the experience of seeing the map: 'So, the map revives her words, the spot, the time, . . . / And its episode comes back in pantomime' (1978, 322). From episode to scene to map of the scene to Hardy's mind to the words of the poem on the page to the mind of the reader of the poem, the pattern is perpetuated, adapting itself with seeming effortlessness to the different substances that must serve as its medium, just as a family face is passed from generation to generation by a genetic code, and just as the ostentatiously complex and artificial rhyme and metrical schemes of so many of Hardy's poems proliferate themselves from stanza to stanza and shape whatever material they express to their own form. The awkward complexity of these stanzaic forms, their individual idiosyncrasy, the great number of different ones, and the fact that many are used only once make the form of the poems the parabolic expression of their content. The uniqueness of each episode or moment of vision, the incommensurability of each with all the others, corresponds to the unique stanzaic pattern used, even if that stanzaic pattern does not seem particularly appropriate to the thematic material it shapes.

'The Obliterate Tomb' may appear to be a poem about one instance in which an inscription is destroyed and with it the pattern it perpetuated. Neither the enemy of the family nor its descendent succeeds in keeping intact the family tombstone that 'records a luminous line whose talents / Told in their day' (1978, 386). The stone, its inscription all but effaced, is broken up, the 'family forgotten,' its 'deeds unknown.' The paradox of the poem (it is not the same paradox as the one in 'Beyond the Last Lamp') is that the poem itself does what neither friend nor foe of the family succeeded in doing. The poem perpetuates the pattern. It substitutes for the obliterate tomb and functions anew to perpetuate the memory of the 'luminous line' every time it is read again. It does this in a characteristically partial and unsatisfactory way. The reader is not told the names of any family members, nor indeed anything about them except that they hated the protagonist of the poem, weighed him falsely and wronged him bitterly. In one sense the family has 'shrunk away into the silence / Like a lost song' (1978, 383), but in another sense the family is maintained still in existence, like fragments of a tune heard at a distance, as if to demonstrate once again that for Hardy no pattern can be wholly obliterated. All find some way to keep themselves in being, in however displaced and partial a form.

'The Wind's Prophecy' differs from the poems so far discussed in orienting toward the future Hardy's interrogation of the power of signs to act at a distance. In this case it is not so much telephony, television, or telepathy, as prevision, foresight, 'forephony,' or 'forepathy,' if there were such words. If, as in 'The Pedigree' or in many others of the poems I have singled out, I, now in the present, can pick up signals transmitted from the past, relayed from one incarnation to another and reaching me finally with a power to determine the way I think, feel, act, even what I am, it would follow that patterns of signs generated now in the present will have a curious power of self-fulfilling prophecy. What the pattern says will come true because the pattern itself will make it come true. In 'I Said and Sang Her Excellence (Fickle Lover's Song),' a poem not so far mentioned here, the fickle lover overpraises his present beloved. His consciously hyperbolic love song is fulfilled, item for unlikely item, with another girl he meets months later:

> Strange, startling, was it then to learn
> I had glanced down unborn time,
> (Have your way, my heart, O!)
> And prophesied, whereby I knew
> That which the years had planned to do
> In warranty of my rhyme.
>
> (1978, 466)

'In warranty of my rhyme' – the phrase is a striking formulation of the idea that time acts to justify or to confirm the most unlikely of conceptual schemes. This is so even if those schemes are conscious fictions or are directed in the present toward persons they do not fit. The heart can confidently expect to 'have its way.' The years are like a company that guarantees a product, in this case a 'rhyme,' to go on working and fixes it up to work if it happens to fail.

'The Wind's Prophecy' is a more subtle and more powerful poem on the same theme, though the tune it sings is not quite in harmony with that of the fickle lover's song. In 'The Wind's Prophecy' the journeying lover affirms and reaffirms his fidelity to the black-haired beloved he leaves behind, but instinctively he personifies the gale winds blowing up from the sea and over the land he traverses. To him the winds seem a loud, hoarse, shrieking voice, or sometimes, in a lull, a low laughing one. That voice foretells that 'Thy love is one thou'st not yet known.' The wind prophesies that the journeyer will betray the black-haired girl and fall in love with a girl with 'tresses flashing fair!' (1978, 494). Prosopopoeia in Hardy is a projection of man's own voice and person, not a response to some personality inhabiting the inanimate. This will be known to careful readers of the famous opening chapter of *The Return of the Native*. There Egdon Heath is personified, but as the reflex of the spectator's person. The phrase at the end of *Tess of the d'Urbervilles* about the 'President of the Immortals,' Hardy said, personifies the impersonal. It is not a name for a conscious deity within or behind nature. The speaker in 'The Wind's Prophecy' projects into the wind his fore-knowledge of his fated infidelity. It is not necessary to relate the poem to Hardy's journey away from Tryphena toward his first meeting with Emma to know that what the speaker projects into the wind, against every conscious wish and intent, will come true, word for word. The ominous tone of the poem indicates this well enough. The prophecy itself breaks the speaker's fidelity to the black-haired girl and prepares for its fulfillment when he meets the fair-haired one.

As was perhaps inevitable, I have come to speak of Hardy as a single person and of his writings as a single unit capable of being marshalled under a single law. This assimilation, however, has been under the law of the inassimilable, the incongruous, the discordant. A strange combination of connection and disconnection characterizes Hardy's work in the various dimensions I have explored. These include the not quite congruous similarity between one poem and another, as well as the presence in those poems of many selves and of many readings of the phenomena of life by the diverse selves. These selves and readings cannot quite be assimilated to one another, and yet they have a family resemblance. In addition there are the not quite harmonious analogies in the poems among the following: the scene or landscape, the episode that takes place there, objects, minds and their contents, and the words of the poem, there on the page as physical marks. Then there is the way an object or a scene that is not strictly speaking a sign and may be as blank as a piece of paper on which nothing is yet written functions as if it were inscribed with language. For Hardy, furthermore, a sign or pattern of signs, a program, is detachable from its material substratum. It may be transmitted from substratum to substratum. It may be written on rocks, rooms, drinking glasses, musical instruments, minds, paper, and yet go on functioning. On the other hand, a given pattern of signs may be inextricably associated with a substratum that remains indifferent to it, unmarked by it. Finally, language or signs have for 'Hardy' a curious power to generate themselves, to proliferate or disseminate themselves according to a self-perpetuating power of iteration. This happens without the direction of any conscious mind or will. Minds intervene only later on as recipients of signs that are already there. All these features of Hardy's poetry are only to be assimilated under the law of the inassimilable. That law can only be expressed anomalously, as I have expressed it here, that is, as a string of not quite parallel anomalies.

I have said that Hardy's abiding topic in his poems is the ability of language or of signs to be generated, to function, and to go on functioning without conscious intent. Another way to put this is to say that Hardy's work constitutes a long, patient, faithful exploration of the consequences for man of the absence of the *logos*, in all the systematically interconnected senses of that word, as mind, voice, ground, word, meaning, reason, message, measure, ratio, logic, concord, gathering. If there is no *logos* in the sense of transcendent conscious directing power, God in short ('I have been looking for God for fifty years,' Hardy wrote, 'and think that if he had existed I should have discovered him'; cit. Duffin 1967, 196), then there is no ontological ground guaranteeing the coherence of beginning, middle, and end, either of collective history or of individual histories. Nor is there a support for the coherence of the mind of the single self – 'Thomas Hardy,' for example – as it persists through time. Nor is there, finally, a support for the coherence of language, neither language taken as a whole, the English language, for example, nor individual language systems within that whole, *The Complete Poems* of Hardy, nor any single poem from that collection, the text of 'The Wind's Prophecy' or of 'The Obliterate Tomb.' The notion of the coherence of language is also a logocentric concept through and through. It vanishes with the vanishing of confidence in the *logos*. For Hardy there is no *logos*, neither in the sense of a conscious transcendent mind, nor in the sense of an immanent reasonable force making for order, nor in the sense of the unified mind of the poet as order-giving perspective, nor in the sense of language itself as a pre-existing order. In place of these forms of unity and coherence only a legion of warring fragments of selves, stories, groups of signs is left. Each of these unsuccessfully attempts to impose itself on the whole in order to become the *logos* of that whole. Each fragmentary urge toward order is neutralized by the force of the others. The whole remains in pieces, like squirming bits of a snake chopped in segments. Hardy's work is an admirable exploration of these various forms of fragmentation, though with many waverings, hesitations, and nostalgias for what is lost. This is appropriate, since when the *logos* is lost, much is lost. It is in this sense that Hardy may be called, in the strictest terms, a poet of 'fierce unreason' (1978, 303).

[. . .]*

One form of unreason in Hardy's work is the co-presence of these two impulses, nostalgia for the old metaphysical way of thinking along with the need to testify that his experience offers no firm support for such thinking – far from it. A book of poems by Hardy presents the 'fierce unreason' of a heterogeneous collection of detached moments, scenes, and episodes all going on side by side, interfering with one another, inhibiting one another, contradicting one another, refusing to form a coherent series. Each moment is an irrevocable cause, but none has the power to organize the whole into a reasonable causal chain.

The 'reason' for this is easy to identify. It is hinted at in my word *irrevocable*.

---

* The missing passage argues that Hardy may be considered a writer of *logos*, reason and cause from certain perspectives. [Ed.]

What functions as cause for Hardy is not mind, force, or deliberate will but voice in the sense of words spoken or written. More broadly, causes for Hardy are almost always signs of some sort. These are generated and go on operating in detachment from any conscious mind, universal or particular. For Hardy, once a sign has been emitted, in however accidental and undeliberate a way, it goes on forcing the meaning that is programmed within it on whatever is around, as a genetic code produces a similar face intermittently. Since these signs are not the product of one cause in the sense of a single designing mind, since they are not the product of any mind at all if one means the deliberate use of words by a single self to communicate a message or to produce a desired effect, they do not form an orderly whole, and their effects are unpredictable, fortuitous. For Hardy, it is not minds that generate signs, but minds that are generated, shaped, and coerced, done and undone, by signs. The Immanent Will for Hardy names the unconscious forces that make things happen as they happen. The phrase expresses a tautology: What happens, happens. The appellation 'President of the Immortals,' Hardy firmly said, was a figure of speech, a prosopopoeia, the personification of the impersonal energies that make things occur as they do happen to occur. Among the most important of these forces are fortuitously generated words or other signs. Among the most important themes of Hardy's work is an exploration of this fact, for example, in the handful of poems I have transmitted to the reader here.

Though Hardy wavered and was inconsistent on this point (as on all the others, as he says himself), it may be that the definition of the universe as a whole that tends to occur more often than the others, is not 'energy,' material or spiritual, nor 'will,' nor any form of 'mind,' conscious or unconscious, but a communication system. The totality of what is, is a web of signs or of language, like that of the postal and telegraph service. Along the fibers of this web messages are constantly transmitted. These make and unmake, willy-nilly, minds that happen to come in the way of one or more of the transmission lines. This may happen, for example, when someone receives a letter, or reads a poem, or sees a map, or finds himself or herself in a place where a certain episode has occurred, even if the place is not visibly marked or inscribed by the story it tells. This immense web of signs is not immaterial or spiritual. It is a result of the strange propensity of matter to be marked by notations and so to turn itself into proliferating signs and ever-extending systems of signs.

In certain forms of mental disorder it seems to a person that he is unwittingly a transmitter of radio or television signals. All he sees and feels, his most secret thought, is being sent out against his will, then picked up and recorded by some sort of 'thought police,' spies from whom nothing can be hidden. This pathological disorder, it may be, is nothing more than an extrapolation from what we all take for granted as objectively the case. We are transfused, pierced, invaded, inundated every moment of the day and night by an unimaginable complexity of various sorts of signals on different wave lengths. Why should we not be transmitters, too? One remembers the story of the man whose teeth-fillings accidentally functioned as a crystal radio receiver, so that, until the doctors figured out what was wrong, he was forced to hear all day and all night the broadcasts from the most powerful local station – music, news, commercials, soap operas, the works. It may be that Jacques Derrida is right, in 'Télépathie' and in *La carte postale*, to see significance in the fact that the evidence Freud uses in his curious essays on telepathy 'is almost always written, literal, not to say solely epistolary (letters, postcards, telegrams, visiting cards).' (1981, 20; my trans.) Derrida sees the Freudian theory of the unconscious, too, as belonging to the age of the modern postal system and of telegraphic communication, impossible without them as models. Modern communication networks are not so much figures of the workings of telepathy and of the unconscious as they are objective incarnations and proofs of them. Telepathy depends on writing. It is an effect of writing. A man happens to get plugged into the network and, behold!, he gets messages at a distance. Radio, television, sonar, radar, information storage, retrieval, and manipulation on tapes, discs, and in ever more compact and more powerful computers are no more than extensions of the human ability to feel, see, hear, and receive messages at a distance. All these are no more than modifications of the 'miraculous' gift of writing, the recording on matter of some kind of sign. The latter has been with us for a long time now, though there has been a quantum leap in its technological powers in the last one hundred and fifty years. Hardy's poetry also belongs to this epoch of telepathy, telephone, television – far-feeling, far-hearing, and far-seeing. The most generalized description of Hardy's universe, it may be, is that it is a vast array of lines along which pass in every direction messages, voices, visions, in incoherent and proliferating multiplicity. These signals are not controlled by an all-powerful, all-knowing 'central.' They are broadcast automatically, un-directed by any comprehensive logical program. They are products of a 'fierce unreason,' an unreason that encompasses the totality of what is.

[. . .]*

A copy of Hardy's *Poems* is receiver and transmitter at once. It is a point of intersection where a large number of the linguistic events making up the universe have happened to come together and take the form of printed words on paper. There they wait to be retransmitted and thereby to take other forms again, most obviously in the mind of someone who reads the words. The reprinting of the book would do this in another way. A reader may become a relay station in his or her turn. He or she may be impelled, for example, to write a critical essay. Such an essay passes the patterns once more on to others. They would go on happening anyhow even if there were no mind anywhere to be aware of them, just as a radio, a television, a telegraph, or a telephone signal does

---

* Following the commentary on Derrida and telepathy, Miller considers the transmission of signals and networks of communication, with specific reference to a scene from *The Dynasts* and 'In the Museum.' [Ed.]

not depend on being received for its existence, and just as a computer silently stores whatever is put in it. That someone becomes conscious of one of the patterns a poem by Hardy records is accidental, contingent, intermittent, in no way essential to its nature.

[. . .]For Hardy nothing dies or can die that has had the good or ill luck to inscribe itself in some way on matter, on someone's heart and brain, on paper or stone, on walls or utensils, on the landscape, or on the mere circumambient air.

I have in this chapter intercepted the signals emitted by a small handful out of the almost one thousand poems stored in Hardy's *Complete Poems*. I have then retransmitted them with more or less, probably with more rather than with less, of static, interference, or, as the French call it, 'parasites,' in the retransmitted signal. Or, to vary the figure, I have acted as a medium. I have resurrected or disinterred a few of the ghosts imprisoned within the covers of that book as within a tomb. I have allowed them to walk again in my mind, on these pages, and in your minds again when you read these pages.

Responses II

The Critic as Orpheus
Pamela K. Gilbert

Progressive loss of the grounds of meaning (God, the logos, the phallus, the epic certainty of home, what-have-you) was, in the late twentieth century, the little black dress of Victorian, and indeed modern, literary criticism more generally. Until recently, it was the unchallenged paradigm for narrating modernity, and remains forceful today. It has such undying appeal because of its undeniable and legitimate explanatory power, not only in regard to the Victorians, but also in regard to us. Perhaps God is always already gone for Hardy, but a hundred-odd years later, he is uncomfortably present in Tehran, Belfast and Washington, DC. Reports of his death, it seems, have been greatly exaggerated. Faith and doubt cohabit in explosive intimacy from Galileo's time to ours, at least. Like the middle class perennially rising, the ground of meaning is always slipping away under our feet, never quite there to begin with, and never quite gone, either. We are haunted – bedeviled – by the ineffectively banished poltergeist of presence.

J. Hillis Miller has cast a long shadow over literary criticism in the second half of the twentieth century. His genius has been not simply to multiply and elaborate the theoretical models we had to understand modern uncertainty, but to attend to its rich formal particularities in individual texts and authors. Indeed, what Miller's work shows us is that if God, the logos, or phallic plenitude have seemed elusive, Victorian authors were spurred by this elusiveness to produce traps of ever greater complexity and ingenuity to catch and hold the luminescent moment in which he, or it, might be grasped. If, as Miller suggests, time and loss – the evanescence of revelation, of experience, of love, of the moment of fulfilled subjectivity – become dominant obsessions, formally reflected in the explosion of narrative's importance, he also shows that Victorian authors used these themes to highlight the preciousness of meaning and truth – whether, as Bronte believed, that truth was objectively real but beyond the veil, or as Dickens did, that it must be cannily created in the very teeth of chaos through a multiplication of partial and conflicting views. Whether the truth was out there, but hard to know, or something created from within, the mechanisms of this creation or apprehension were of paramount interest to post-Enlightenment authors. Literary form and the act of reading used time and repetition to explore these processes. The role of memory and iterability continue to concern Miller, most obviously in *Fiction and Repetition* (1982), *Ariadne's Thread* (1992), and *Topographies* (1995). The authors explored in these texts created the Victorian novel as 'an incomplete self-generating structure' representing a society whose 'incommensurate elements' play off each other to create the society's 'own immanent basis for meaning' (1968, 34). This conception, in place in Miller's work in 1965, has been absolutely fundamental for Victorian narrative criticism from the 1970s to the present.

Miller's analysis of *Wuthering Heights* provides an early (1965) example of his principal concern with the relation of narrative to lack. 'The violent separation of the tree from its root' (xx) is precisely the loss of the ground of meaning. This loss precipitates the fall into language, as we know, and enables narrative, as Miller shows us: only before Heathcliff and Cathy's love was conscious and describable did it exist. 'All storytelling . . . wards off death,' explains Miller (1998, 227). 'The proliferation of incompatible explanations' that is Cathy's storytelling, however, is an attempt to ward off a death foretold, forewent, the very condition of possibility of narrative itself. The sign destroys the signified. Brontë's universe is a Lacanian one in which only 'two extreme situations' are possible: 'the joy of a complete unconscious fusion' and 'the anguish of a complete separation.' Language both marks this loss and attempts to bridge the chasm between past plenitude and present lack. Religion offers us two cruel choices: seek in the present to reclaim that plenitude, and 'reach only a false and damnable image of communion,' or embrace lack in the hope of future mercies. In a universe defined by the absence of the ground of meaning, only narrative's end – death – can provide that meaning once more.

God, logos, is the ground of the self in Miller's analysis of *Wuthering Heights*. Heathcliff and Cathy lose themselves in narrative and regain themselves in death, but they have to undergo the process of loss several times before it 'takes'; this provides the structure of the novel, the frame narrator of which comes in only at the 'real' end. Hopkins, however, sees the self as a permanent function of awareness, which is experienced as a series of moments of self-becoming, of 'plenitude' rather than lack. This selving is fleeting and must be repeatedly and determinedly sought in sense-experience. Human consciousness itself is what fails us, alienates us from being. Being is all around and within us, but perception of that being is elusive. Perception, like language, enables us to be conscious of being and distances us from it: words are the 'stem of stress' between object and perceiver, but also objects in their own right. And in the moment of perception, of grasping the object's uniqueness, we come always smash up against death, lack, loss. In death and in God are meaning's ground, but also the destruction of 'self-being.'

Miller conjures Hardy, a bit like Hopkins, as 'a sequence of disconnected evanescent persons.' However, Hardy is not concerned with perception of objects per se, but with perception though moments created in memory. Here again, signs and inscriptions are significant, but only in relation to event and place, rather than as objects in their own right. Hardy's 'warring fragments' which substitute for order and objective meaning in the universe, are much like Dickens's multiplication of part-objects and points-of-view; however, in Dickens's case, the multiplication of objects serves to build coherence, and in Hardy's, to highlight its impossibilities. Miller finds the common thread of preoccupation with communication as the basis of Hardy's vision. This is Miller's preoccupation, too. Miller offers himself as a 'medium' for Hardy's signs, as the host who is possessed, who transmits the parasitic sign to the reader's own mind.

Miller's approach to these questions is so richly particular in part because it is resolutely textual. Miller once wrote that, 'A theory is all too easy to refute or deny, but a reading can be controverted only by going through the difficult task of rereading the work in question'; further, he admonished that an approach that does not involve close reading is 'a major treason against our profession' (1982, 21). The text, for Miller, is paramount, and carries a great weight of authority and control. Of course, this approach, as countless critics have now observed, favors a particular kind of text. The vast majority of Miller's work has been directed at the undeniably canonical. He has returned to the same authors again and again: Dickens, Eliot, Hardy, Browning, Hopkins, Stevens. *Others* (1991) brings us to the theme of otherness, but through the works of Schlegel, Dickens, Proust, Forster, Trollope, Conrad, Yeats, Derrida, de Man. Yet his work has inspired many other critics whose range of reading is quite other than his; and it has done so by demonstrating a set of reading practices and positing a relation between formal, historical and thematic issues which has provided influential critical tools to a whole generation of readers.

In the *Ethics of Reading*, Miller was most interested in the relation of reader to text; however, for Miller, that relation was always also to an author, and it is authors, finally, who call forth his best effort. In his 1958 study of Dickens, he confidently offered us a glimpse into 'the original unity of a creative mind. For all the works of a single writer form a unity, a unity in which a thousand paths radiate from the same center' (1958, ix). By 1985 (or by Hardy), he is more circumspect: we are warned that any coherence he reads in the poems are imposed upon them. And yet, as readers of Hardy, we become 'in a manner of speaking, the self of Hardy'; Hardy is preoccupied, for Miller, with the enduring and active nature of signifiers which go on acting independent of their creator's will. In an aleatory, fragmented universe, these signifiers are likely to do just about anything. And yet, the anything that they do, for Miller, remains inalienably Hardy's anything. If Hardy's 'heart and brain are part of the totality of the sleeping brain of the universe,' it is not, for Miller, a part that loses its individuality in that totality. If the critic is a host, and the deconstructive reading is contained within the univocal one, it is still a relation between critic and author, and between readings legitimated by the text and that author.

For Miller, then, neither deconstruction nor reader-response criticism threatened the primacy of the author, or the critic's ethical obligation to read for the author's vision. It is nothing less than a recuperation of that individual being from the undifferentiated gulf of death that Hopkins so feared and Bronte so praised and Hardy so bitterly affirmed, back into the realm of lack of selfhood, of language and art. If the author is dead, as Barthes declared, for Miller, that simply redoubles the obligation of the critic. The odd contradictions of his treatment of Hardy, his insistence of the non-generalizeability of Hardy's poems at the same time as he comes to a general conclusion about them, illustrate the dilemma of the Orphic critic. Content with nothing less than the return of the beloved from death entire, he cannot forbear to claim dominion, and in so doing, loses the beloved object itself. In being borne into language, the object itself slips away and is replaced by a new object with its own inscape, its own stress.

Like Orpheus, the deconstructive critic already knows what will happen if he attempts to foreclose the endless play of meaning; like Orpheus, he cannot resist trying to fix it in his gaze. Hillis Miller's vision of criticism is deeply ethical, focusing on the obligation to relate, through the text, to another human being: 'I should agree that "the impossibility of reading should not be taken too lightly" ', he writes, responding to Wayne Booth in 1977: 'It has consequences for life and death, since it is inscribed, incorporated, in the bodies of individual human beings and in the body politic of our cultural life and death together' (1977b). Yet Miller, unlike the critics of a generation previous to his, understands the impossibility of reading, the impossibility that the dead can be led completely out of the underworld, just as he is committed to what is, for him, the inescapable necessity of the attempt. In this tension between love and loss lies the disciplined fertility of his Victorianist work.

Hillis Among the Victorians
James R. Kincaid

J. Hillis Miller came on the Victorian scene with a bomb in one hand and a fan in the other – a modest, reluctant, gracious terrorist. *Charles Dickens: The World of His Novels*[1] launched a series of books that were to revolutionize the field of Victorian scholarship, actually to create that field, certainly to provide it with a new geography and new tools and a new vigor and earnestness. *The Disappearance of God, The Form of Victorian Fiction, Thomas Hardy: Distance and Desire* followed in short order.

Overnight, from a group of apologetic amateurs, Victorian scholars and critics found themselves cohabiting with radical thought and intricate theory. Moldy academics who had been content to maunder on about Ruskin and Carlyle, leaving the heavy stuff to surrounding periods, suddenly found themselves invited to MLA parties, their opinions sought out, their period respected. All because of Hillis.

I think this is the most extraordinary single event in my professional life or memory, by far the most Cinderella-like transformation of a group of people and a field of inquiry I have observed, much less been swept up in. Within weeks, it seemed, old codgers were retooling and new graduate students of an entirely different stripe were pouring in among us, graduate students who, like Maude Gonne (though not like Hillis) were 'high, solitary, and most stern.' Before long, the Victorian period became the most fertile grounds for new work in gender studies, in class and ethnicity, in the new sexuality, in queer theory and studies, in postcolonialism – everything but New Historicism, on which baleful enterprise Hillis kept watch. I well remember his MLA addresses, his use of the power of the Presidency as a bully pulpit to rail against the New Historicism and its assumption that, if you made the past complex enough, you could jolly well read it with comfort, never mind the problems of language, meaning, and time. 'Metaphysical through and through,' thundered Hillis from the podium. We all took notes and took it to heart that the paranoid, crank-turning, predictable return to interpreting texts was something we needn't bother with – Hillis had told us so. Thus, D. A. Miller and Cathy Gallagher could form a backwater populated by two frogs only. Hillis spared the rest of us.

For what, though? What did he tell us to do? Ah, there you see, we have a paradox. Hillis himself often lowered himself to reading texts, almost interpreting them, and does that to this day. As if there were texts, as if there were meanings, as if we could collar them. An amiable weakness, though, and we wink at it; we take no notice; we overlook it.

Hillis's influence was massive, we might say, but not particular – like that of Lady Bracknell or God or climactic changes. I don't think he won a single convert to phenomenology of the mystical woo-woo sort he was advocating, all that stuff about intersubjectivity and finding texts speaking through us. Sounded too much like Shirley MacLaine to most of us, new age twaddle, somewhat embarrassing even. How could anyone peddling that particular non-selling and unsellable item succeed beyond all measure?

I think the answer is simple, really. Hillis brought to the field an intelligence so deft and at the same time generous that he made us all seem smarter. One cannot read a paragraph of these early books without being drawn into a field of play, given a glove, finding the ball coming her way, and, bingo, getting right into the action. Doubtless, all of this had something to do with the introduction of the unfamiliar, the theoretical and the philosophical – a new attention to textual production and, especially, to reading. But it was also, for many of us –

let's say all of us – much more a question of being given permission to stretch, having also been shown how to do it.

Charles Dickens: The World of His Novels (1958) entered into Victorian literary study through the one door that had been opened a trifle prior to Hillis' digging. It was a canny move on his part, as there was some prior readiness, not much, to see Dickens in a new light, thanks to Orwell, Edmund Wilson, Dorothy Van Ghent, and a few others. But certainly no one was prepared for this. 'The hand of Mr. Mould.' I can still remember reading Hillis's staggeringly brilliant riff on that phrase – the hand of Mr. Mould. Mr. Mould, an hilarious but gruesome undertaker in *Martin Chuzzlewit*, makes a good living as a shrewd businessman operating in burying bodies and manipulating grief for profit. He has a hand, Hillis says, in much the same way he has a pocket handkerchief. In an atomized world, we possess things only and all things are merely possessions. It is not Mr. Mould's hand but the hand of Mr. Mould – an odd locution that emphasizes the atomistic disconnectedness everywhere present in the novel. The hand of Mr. Mould – which might go missing at any time or visiting. An eerie absurdist proposition that marked the way Hillis's analysis could also be an artistic rendering, a beckoning into a new way of seeing. Hillis handed us all new glasses.

As a side note, in those days one could easily get research assistants, though it was quite another matter for non-scholars like me to know what to do with them. Struck by the enormous force of the hand of Mr. Mould and Hillis's assertion that this strange locution worked its way under our skin by its proliferation in *Martin Chuzzlewit*, I set this grad student to the tedious job of checking whether, in fact, there was a proliferation of these constructions in *Martin Chuzzlewit* as compared to the surrounding Dickens novels. Predictably, he found the occurrence in *Martin Chuzzlewit* decidedly less frequent, indeed almost non-existent, apart from the one occurrence Hillis had lighted on and assumed was everywhere. 'Ah-ha!' I thought, 'I got you, you careless son of a bitch.' But of course I hadn't got him and didn't want to: Hillis was not talking about texts, much less statistics, but about what kind of equipment you might take with you on a voyage. He was offering so much, so much that was new and risky and exciting. If he sometimes gave us mittens to take to Tahiti, so what!

I would like now to turn to a later book to make exactly the same point.

Some time ago, forty years exactly, Hillis provided students of the Victorian period with the wittiest and most productive metaphor for understanding the period since Walter Houghton told us the Victorians had a 'frame of mind.' What Hillis said, in his justly celebrated book (and title), was that God had disappeared for the Victorians. He said that this disappearance of God was not only a central feature of the Victorian cosmological landscape but *the* central feature we must take into account in understanding how Victorians writers, and other intellectuals especially, saw their world and located their place in it. Without God, how could one understand language or what it did? Suspended in dark uncertainty, how could they locate a geography of the mind? Where could one find structure, continuity, coherence, stability? How did one know how to fashion a plot or a cravat, take council or tea, conduct business or trains, entertain royalty or ideas?

What made the matter all the worse, in every sense, was that God hadn't really died or anything like that, just gone away – on vacation or something. Indisposed, out of the office, nowhere to be located just now. For Miller, then, this God haunted the Victorian world without offering it assurances, left behind traces that could neither be made into solids nor sucked into an exhaust fan. In such a world, everyone was on a melting iceberg – if it indeed was melting, if it indeed was an iceberg. Nothing could be certain, including a certain uncertainty. Miller's finest point is that the Victorians were denied the relatively simple clarity of the modernists, who could declare God and the world he presumably structured vanished, irrelevant; and then make much of their rather gratuitous boldness in saying so. The smug ease and redundancy of modernist pronouncements on their own fragmented and foundationless world were denied the Victorians, not because they could not see that empty world but because they could see so much more, the world that had been there just yesterday, might even, somehow and somewhere, still be there. The layered, anguished complexity of the Victorian vision, Miller argued, rests on precisely their unwillingness to release themselves from a structure of knowledge and vision they also know is not only inadequate but, often, poisonous.

The enormous influence of Miller's idea rests, as I have said, partly on its timing, the feeling afoot that Victorian scholarship in the academy was very genial but a little short on ideas. We needed help in the way of being less soft-headed; especially we needed a better way to speak to what we all had been talking about, 'Victorian doubt.' That soft idea of 'doubt' was the best we could do in the 1960s to compete with the tough-guy strategy used to sell other fields, which were peddling absurdist, radically skeptical, uncompromising darkness. So we were doing what we could, which wasn't much, with doubt. Miller's book was, then, both brilliantly argued and, in a narrow sense, sweetly unoriginal; it took what we all suspected and gave us reason to be proud of it. He also supplied superbly formulated arguments, both historical and philosophical, to use in the presence of scoffers. A now-you-see-it-now-you-don't deity was a convincing inciter of the 'doubt' we had been talking about; and it colored the Victorians dark, somber, and serious. Dark, somber, and serious were good. Still are, unfortunately, but you'll have to wait a bit to get to see me demonstrate that. For now, let's be sure we have straight the influence of this idea of a poof-up-in-smoke God on the business of recent Victorian scholarship.

The illustrations Miller offers of his thesis are well known; I think they include DeQuincey, Browning, Arnold, Emily Bronte, and Hopkins. These are his illustrations, however, and this is not his argument; so we'll use mine. My illustrations of the disappearance of God idea are, as it happens, much better than

Hillis's anyhow, though his are no doubt very good. Mine are drawn from Hardy; but as I've already published them, I will not repeat them here. Well, I will repeat them, actually, but only in a very sketchy form, as I do not remember them well. Hardy, I have argued, bases his world always on what is not there, this what-is-not-there constituting always in Hardy the strongest presence. What is not there is practically everything: reason for hope, justice, kindness, causality, love, and nice weather. It's never there, but Hardy's characters, and clearly Hardy himself, are not about to take their absence lightly. They continue to expect some fairness somewhere. It doesn't come, of course (because nobody comes); but that inevitable failure to show up is treated each time as if it were a tragic shock, justifying suicidal thoughts (or actions), writhing anguish, and (best of all) delicious, self-indulgent resentment. 'A Broken Appointment,' just to cite one instance, is a poem which concerns and also offers the considerable delights that come when one is dumped and the even more exquisite pleasures available in reflecting on the other person's defective character and one's own chin-quivering, self-pitying virtue. If the Appointment (Broken, luckily) were kept, there'd be no poem and no fun. Life, for Hardy (and me), is filled with the tingles of unfulfilled anticipations.

You see the point. Hardy would have nothing to write about and no effects to produce were God safely dead. God ought to be there and isn't: that's the basis of everything he wrote and the basis of the unending pleasure we have in reading him – or so I proclaimed. Not very imaginative of me, you'll be saying, kind of mean-spirited and narrow, bullying and spit-in-the-face/knee-in-the-groin. I agree.

I'm with you entirely that the idea of a disappearing God, like that of a disappearing schoolteacher or prison guard or parent, need not cause anguish. When the teacher leaves the room, trilling, 'Tend to your workbooks. I'll be back in a bit?' who feels paralyzed with horror? 'I've got to run out for a while. Don't break anything!' is not a prompter of tears and torment. A few paranoid Victorians, here and there, may have found God's disappearance alarming, just as some students like workbooks and some of us relish the idea of wardens and keepers. But nearly all Victorians – and it's important that you take this on trust – knew it was time for the fun and the art to begin. They didn't, mind you, feel relief or anything so simple. The teacher might come back at any time, which added a tension to the frolic, a spice of danger: you might get sent to the principal's office or, in the case of God, to Hell. But art thrives on taking risks, especially comic art, which springs into any wedge it can find – Dad's gone to the grocery store! Comedy invents a world independent of wedges, a complete and self-sufficient world.

But that's my own opening into an argument on comedy – and all I can say here is that it is made possible by Hillis. Not that I want to honor Hillis by claiming that he paved the way for me – not exactly – though that would be no mean accomplishment. He paved the way for everything – he is the architect and the groundskeeper of our collective mind.

Just a word on another of his books and then I'll get personal. *The Form of Victorian Fiction*, a series of Notre Dame lectures published in 1968, opened yet more new territory by shifting the ground rules. Now God was dead, decidedly and totally. Having played with the idea of a vacationing God, Hillis decided to see what would happen to a corpse. After all, 'God,' in this sense, is no more than a metaphor for a series of possibilities or constraints, so there's nothing holding us to one center. No one has been so shifty and fast on his feet as Hillis, not Michael Jordan and not Richard Nixon. Hillis works various philosophical centers the way experienced streetwalkers work different corners. The dead God he employs here is not just dead, of course, but 'annihilated,' a 'shocking event' that leaves 'a devouring emptiness and unassauagable hunger.' Yeah sure. These B movie horror effects out of the way, Hillis gets to the tricks he wants to try out: the idea of Victorian fictional experience as play with 'an incomplete self-generating structure.' The readings that follow are demonstrations of a master player, opening up new and malleable rules for that play. Along the way, he deals a crushing blow to what others have called goal-line criticism, criticism that looks to ends, to the completion of formal structures, in order to settle interpretive differences: Emma is rebellious sure, but she gets married. Hillis argues that endings of novels are no more privileged than the endings of symphonies, indeed, that, like the final chords of a symphony, novel endings are likely to be the most conventional and least interesting or captivating. The actual reading experience, he suggests, can fly free of such academic decorum, instructions on how to report our on our reading. Hillis shows us how, and, like a mother bird, pushes us out of the goddam nest.

Two anecdotes and I am finished. Once we lured Hillis to Colorado for what seemed like seven talks, two seminars, and sixteen consultations. But hey, we paid his plane fare. To make matters worse for him, he was snowed in and had to stay with me for many days, several times locking himself into the bathroom and having to climb out windows and clamber over rooftops, a regular Mr. Pickwick. But my story is dignified, on the whole, and I do not wish to distract you by the image of Hillis in his nightshirt, shouting from the rooftops. No – he went with me to several classes and a grad seminar during this period, paralyzing the students with fright and then thawing them with his kindness. Not me, though. Me he made look like an ass, a fool. I recall vividly one nightmare, where, after making a fine point, an original point about George Eliot's *Middlemarch*, I paused for expressions of appreciation – gasps, sighs, applause. I had been going over the passage, seldom noticed except by me, where Eliot's narrator talks about how little reality we can face, how pervasive tragedy is, how knowing the suffering of others would be like hearing the grass grow or the squirrel's heart beat. I had worked myself into tears and would have others too, had not Hillis gently piped in, 'You know, it never seemed to me that awful to hear a squirrel's heartbeat. Isn't there some strange discrepancy between the emptiness presumably evoked and the gentleness of these images, growing grass and the tiny heart of a squirrel?' Then he sat back as if he hadn't just thrown a bucket of shit all over the main performer. What Hillis was doing there was what he has always been absolutely the best at doing: you think you got it? Look over here. Don't ever rest, don't be fooled into thinking that anything, much less a Victorian novel, can be contained or known. Hillis is the sweetest medicine I know for counteracting knowingness.

And also unkindness. Last anecdote. In the early 1970s I found myself on an MLA panel organized by a fledgling Thomas Hardy society. Hillis, it turned out, was assisting some graduate students from, I think, NYU get their society going by helping out with this panel. That meant that he was on it, got me to be on it as filler, and also persuaded a wonderful, dying man, the Victorian scholar William Buckler, to appear as well. After the panel had gone through its usual motions – papers a little bit long, no time for questions – I was gathering my stuff when Hillis collared me. 'You're going to their lunch.' 'No, ' I said; 'I'd love to, but I told them I couldn't make it.' 'They're young kids and Buckler's very sick and you're going.' So – the lunch was held and Hillis, much against his nature, played the genial host, keeping things going and, I feel sure, picking up the check. A very young man himself, Hillis was already opening himself up to others, not just to Hardy but to those just coming on the scene, the young grad students, and those about to leave it, William Buckler. Hillis, like a golden bird, took in what was past and passing and to come.

I wish I could end there – saying that today that Hardy Society is the most vigorous around. Truth is I think it folded – but that says more about Hillis, really, than a roaring success would have. He has never been afraid of lost causes or of lost souls. Beneath the shyness and immense learning there is a kindness that attaches him to one deep core of Victorian being he has never abandoned – a passion for taking risks, intellectual and personal, that will fill other lives. He is the most honorable man I know and the professor and friend I honor most.

Note

1. This essay is chock full or references, some of them doubtless accurate. If you're looking for that sort of scholarship (any sort of scholarship), though, you've come to the wrong shop. My editor, Julian Wolfreys, is good at that and many other things, but I am not. I have learned to accept my deficiencies gracefully, which is more than you can say for most people in our line of work.

Twentieth-Century Occasions

8

Mrs. Dalloway: Repetition as the Raising of the Dead

[. . .] The most important themes of a given novel are likely to lie not in anything which is explicitly affirmed, but in significances generated by the way in which the story is told. Among the most important of those ways is Virginia Woolf's organizing of her novels around various forms of recurrence. Story-telling, for Woolf, is the repetition of the past in memory, both in the memory of the characters and in the memory of the narrator. *Mrs. Dalloway* (1925) is a brilliant exploration of the functioning of memory as a form of repetition.

The novel is especially fitted to investigate not so much the depths of individual minds as the nuances of relationship between mind and mind. [. . .] The manipulation of narrative voice in fiction is closely associated with that theme of human time or of human history which seems intrinsic to the form of the novel. In many novels the use of the past tense establishes the narrator as someone living after the events of the story have taken place, someone who knows all the past perfectly. The narrator tells the story in a present which moves forward toward the future by way of a recapitulation or repetition of the past. This retelling brings that past up to the present as a completed whole, or it moves toward such completion. This form of an incomplete circle, time moving toward a closure which will bring together past, present, and future as a perfected whole, is the temporal form of many novels.

Interpersonal relations as a theme, the use of an omniscient narrator who is a collective mind rising from the co-presence of many individual minds, indirect discourse as the means by which that narrator dwells within the minds of individual characters and registers what goes on there, temporality as a determining principle of theme and technique – these elements are fundamental to Virginia Woolf's work. It would be as true to say that she investigates implications of these traditional conventions of form as to say that she brings something new into fiction. This can be demonstrated especially well in *Mrs Dalloway*. The novel depends on the presence of a narrator who remembers all and who has a power of resurrecting the past in her narration. In *Mrs. Dalloway* narration is repetition as the raising of the dead.

'Nothing exists outside us except a state of mind' (1925, 62) – this seemingly casual and somewhat inscrutable statement is reported from the thoughts of the solitary traveler in Peter Walsh's dream as Peter sits snoring on a bench in Regent's Park. The sentence provides an initial clue to the mode of existence of the narrator of *Mrs. Dalloway*. The narrator is that state of mind which exists outside the characters and of which they can never be directly aware. Though they are not aware of it, it is aware of them. This 'state of mind' surrounds them, encloses them, pervades them, knows them from within. It is present to them all at all the times and places of their lives. It gathers those times and places together in the moment. The narrator is that 'something central which permeate[s],' the 'something warm which [breaks] up surfaces' (1925, 46), a power of union and penetration which Clarissa Dalloway lacks. Or, to vary the metaphor, the narrator possesses the irresistible and subtle energy of the bell of St. Margaret's striking half past eleven. Like that sound, the narrator 'glides into the recesses of the heart and buries itself.' It is 'something alive which wants to confide itself, to disperse itself, to be, with a tremor of delight, at rest' (1925, 74). Expanding to enter into the inmost recesses of each heart, the narrator encloses all in a reconciling embrace.

Though the characters are not aware of this narrating presence, they are at every moment possessed and known, in a sense violated, by an invisible mind, a mind more powerful than their own. This mind registers with infinite delicacy their every thought and steals their every secret. The indirect discourse of this registration, in which the narrator reports in the past tense thoughts which once occurred in the present moments of the characters' minds, is the basic form of narration in *Mrs Dalloway*. This disquieting mode of ventriloquism may be found on any page of the novel. Its distinguishing mark is the conventional 'he thought' or 'she thought,' which punctuates the narrative and reveals the presence of a strange one-way interpersonal relation. The extraordinary quality of this relation is hidden primarily because readers of fiction take it so much for granted. An example is the section of the novel describing Peter Walsh's walk from Clarissa's house toward Regent's Park: 'Clarissa refused me, he thought'; 'like Clarissa herself, thought Peter Walsh'; 'It is Clarissa herself, he thought'; 'Still the future of civilisation lies, he thought'; 'The future lies in the hands of young men like that, he thought' (1925, 74–6) – and so on, page after page. If the reader asks himself where he is placed as he reads any given page of *Mrs. Dalloway,* the answer, most often, is that he is plunged within an individual mind which is being understood from inside by an ubiquitous, all-knowing mind. This mind speaks from some indeterminate later point in time, a point always 'after' anything the characters think or feel. The narrator's mind moves easily from one limited mind to another and knows them all at once. It speaks for them all. This form of language generates the local texture of *Mrs. Dalloway*.

The characters of *Mrs. Dalloway* are therefore in an odd way, though they do not know it, dependent on the narrator. The narrator has preserved their evanescent thoughts, sensations, mental images, and interior speech. She rescues these from time past and presents them again in language to the reader. Narration itself is repetition in *Mrs. Dalloway*. In another way, the narrator's mind is dependent on the characters' minds. It could not exist without them.

Mrs. Dalloway is almost entirely without passages of meditation or description which are exclusively in the narrator's private voice. The reader is rarely given the narrator's own thoughts or shown the way the world looks not through the eyes of a character, but through the narrator's private eyes. The sermon against 'Proportion' and her formidable sister 'Conversion' is one of the rare cases where the narrator speaks for her own view, or even for Woolf's own view, rather than by way of the mind of one of the characters. Even here, the narrator catches herself up and attributes some of her own judgement of Sir William Bradshaw to Rezia: 'This lady too (Rezia Warren Smith divined it) had her dwelling in Sir William's heart' (1925, 151).

In *Mrs. Dalloway* nothing exists for the narrator which does not first exist in the mind of one of the characters, whether it be a thought or a thing. This is implied by those passages in which an external object is used as a means of transition from the mind of one character to the mind of another. Such transitions seem to suggest that the solid existing things of the external world unify the minds of separate persons because, though each person is trapped in his or her own mind and in his or her own private responses to external objects, nevertheless these disparate minds can all have responses, however different they may be, to the same event, for example to an airplane's skywriting. To this extent at least we all dwell in one world.

The deeper meaning of this motif in *Mrs. Dalloway* may be less a recognition of our common dependence on a solidly existing external world than a revelation that things exist for the narrator only when they exist for the characters. The narrator sometimes moves without transition out of the mind of one character and into the mind of another [. . .]. Though she is bound to no single mind, she is dependent for her existence on the minds of the characters. She can think, feel, see only as they thought, felt, and saw. Things exist for her, she exists for herself, only because the others once existed. The omniscient narrator of *Mrs. Dalloway* is a general consciousness or social mind which rises into existence out of the collective mental experience of the individual human beings in the story. The cogito of the narrator of *Mrs. Dalloway* is, 'They thought, therefore I am.'

One implication of this relation between the narrator's mind and the characters' minds is that, though for the most part the characters do not know it, the universal mind is part of their own minds, or rather their minds are part of it. If one descends deeply enough into any individual mind one reaches ultimately the general mind, that is, the mind of the narrator. On the surface the relation between narrator and individual goes only one way. As in the case of those windows which may be seen through in a single direction, the character is transparent to the narrator, but the narrator is opaque to the character. In the depths of each individual mind, this one-way relationship becomes reciprocal. In the end it is no longer a relationship, but a union, an identity. Deep down the general mind and the individual mind become one. Both are on the same side of the glass, and the glass vanishes.

If this is true for all individual minds in relation to the universal mind, then all individual minds are joined to one another far below the surface separateness. The most important evidence for this in *Mrs. Dalloway* is the fact that the same images of unity, of reconciliation, of communion well up spontaneously from the deep levels of the minds of all the major characters. One of the most pervasive of these images is that of a great enshadowing tree which is personified, a great mother who binds all living things together in the manifold embrace of her leaves and branches. This image would justify the use of the feminine pronoun for the narrator, who is the spokeswoman for this mothering presence. No man or woman is limited to himself or herself, but each is joined to others by means of this tree, diffused like a mist among all the people and places he or she has encountered. Each man or woman possesses a kind of immortality, in spite of the abrupt finality of death: 'did it not become consoling,' muses Clarissa to herself as she walks toward Bond Street, 'to believe that death ended absolutely? but that somehow in the streets of London, on the ebb and flow of things, here, there, she survived, Peter survived, lived in each other, she being part, she was positive, of the trees at home; of the house there, ugly, rambling all to bits and pieces as it was; part of people she had never met; being laid out like a mist between the people she knew best, who lifted her on their branches as she had seen the trees lift the mist, but it spread ever so far, her life, herself' (1925, 12; see also 231, 232). [. . .]

This notion of a union of each mind in its depths with all the other minds and with a universal, impersonal mind for which the narrator speaks is confirmed by those notations in *A Writer's Diary* in which, while writing *Mrs. Dalloway*, Woolf speaks of her 'great discovery,' what she calls her 'tunnelling process,' that method whereby, as she says, 'I dig out beautiful caves behind my characters: I think that gives exactly what I want; humanity, humour, depth. The idea is that the caves shall connect' (1954, 59).

[. . .] The fear or attraction of the annihilating fall into nothingness echoes through *Mrs. Dalloway*. The novel seems to be based on an irreconcilable opposition between individuality and universality. By reason of his or her existence as a conscious human being, each man or woman is alienated from the whole of which he or she is actually, though unwittingly or at best half-consciously, a part. That half-consciousness gives each person a sense of incompletion. Each person yearns to be joined in one way or another to the whole from which he or she is separated by the conditions of existence as an individual.

One way to achieve this wholeness might be to build up toward some completeness in the daylight world, rather than to sink down into the dark world of death. 'What a lark! What a plunge!' (1925, 3) – the beginning of the third paragraph of *Mrs. Dalloway* contains in miniature the two contrary movements of the novel. If the fall into death is one pole of the novel, fulfilled in Septimus Smith's suicidal plunge, the other pole is the rising motion of 'building it up,' of constructive action in the moment, fulfilled in Clarissa Dalloway's party. Turning away from the obscure depths within them, the characters may, like Clarissa, embrace the moment with elation and attempt to gather everything together in a diamond point of brightness: 'For Heaven only knows why one loves it so, how one sees it so, making it up, building it round one, tumbling it, creating it every moment afresh'; 'what she loved was this, here, now, in front of her'; 'Clarissa . . . plunged into the very heart of the moment, transfixed it, there – the moment of this June morning on which was the pressure of all the other mornings, . . . collecting the whole of her at one point' (1925, 5, 12, 54). In the same way, Peter Walsh after his sleep on a park bench feels, 'Life itself, every moment of it, every drop of it, here, this instant, now, in the sun, in Regent's Park, was enough' (1925, 119–20). (This echoing from Clarissa to Peter, it is worth noting, is proof that Clarissa is right to think that they 'live in each other.')

'The pressure of all the other mornings' – one way the characters in *Mrs. Dalloway* achieve continuity and wholeness is through the ease with which images from their pasts rise within them to overwhelm them with a sense of immediate presence. If the characters of the novel live according to an abrupt, discontinuous, nervous rhythm, rising one moment to heights of ecstasy only to be dropped again in sudden terror or despondency, nevertheless their experience is marked by profound continuities.

The remarkably immediate access the characters have to their pasts is one such continuity. The present, for them, is the perpetual repetition of the past. In one sense the moment is all that is real. Life in the present instant is a narrow plank reaching over the abyss of death between the nothingness of past and future. Near the end of the novel Clarissa thinks of 'the terror; the overwhelming incapacity, one's parents giving it into one's hands, this life, to be lived to the end, to be walked with serenely; there was in the depths of her heart an awful fear' (1925, 281). In another sense, the weight of all the past moments presses just beneath the surface of the present, ready in an instant to flow into consciousness, overwhelming it with the immediate presence of the past. Nothing could be less like the intermittencies and difficulties of memory in Wordsworth or in Proust than the spontaneity and ease of memory in *Mrs. Dalloway*. Repeatedly during the day of the novel's action the reader finds himself within the mind of a character who has been invaded and engulfed by a memory so vivid that it displaces the present of the novel and becomes the virtual present of the reader's experience. So fluid are the boundaries between past and present that the reader sometimes has great difficulty knowing whether he is encountering an image from the character's past or something part of the character's immediate experience.

An example of this occurs in the opening paragraphs of the novel. *Mrs. Dalloway* begins in the middle of things with the report of something Clarissa says just before she leaves her home in Westminster to walk to the florist on Bond Street: 'Mrs. Dalloway said she would buy the flowers herself' (1925, 3). A few sentences later, after a description of Clarissa's recognition that it is a fine day and just following the first instance of the motif of terror combined with ecstasy ('What a lark! What a plunge!'), the reader is 'plunged' within the closeness of an experience which seems to be part of the present, for he is as yet ignorant of the place names in the novel or of their relation to the times of Clarissa's life. Actually, the experience is from Clarissa's adolescence: 'For so it had always seemed to her, when, with a little squeak of the hinges, which she could hear now, she had burst open the French windows and plunged at Bourton into the open air' (1925, 3).

The word 'plunge,' reiterated here, expresses a pregnant ambiguity. If a 'lark' and a 'plunge' seem at first almost the same thing, rising and falling versions of the same leap of ecstasy, and if Clarissa's plunge into the open air when she bursts open the windows at Bourton seems to confirm this identity, the reader may remember this opening page much later when Septimus leaps from a window to his death. Clarissa, hearing of his suicide at her party, confirms this connection by asking herself, 'But this young man who had killed himself – had he plunged holding his treasure?' (1925, 281). If *Mrs. Dalloway* is organized around the contrary penchants of rising and falling, these motions are not only opposites, but are also ambiguously similar. They change places bewilderingly, so that down and up, falling and rising, death and life, isolation and communication, are mirror images of one another rather than a confrontation of negative and positive orientations of the spirit. Clarissa's plunge at Bourton into the open air is an embrace of life in its richness, promise, and immediacy, but it is when the reader encounters it already an image from the dead past. Moreover, it anticipates Septimus's plunge into death. It is followed in Clarissa's memory of it by her memory that when she stood at the open window she felt 'something awful was about to happen' (1925, 3). The reader is not surprised to find that in this novel which is made up of a stream of subtle variations on a few themes, one of the things Clarissa sees from the window at Bourton is 'the rooks rising, falling' (1925, 3).

The temporal placement of Clarissa's experiences at Bourton is equally ambiguous. The 'now' of the sentence describing Clarissa's plunge ('with a little squeak of the hinges, which she could hear now'), is the narrator's memory of Clarissa's memory of her childhood home brought back so vividly into Clarissa's mind that it becomes the present of her experience and of the reader's experience. The sentence opens the door to a flood of memories which bring that faraway time back to her as a present with the complexity and fullness of immediate experience.

These memories are not simply present. The ambiguity of the temporal location of this past time derives from the narrator's use of the past tense conventional in fiction. Everything that the characters do or think is placed firmly in an indefinite past as something which has always already happened when the reader encounters it. These events are resurrected from the past by the language of the narration and placed before the present moment of the reader's experience as something bearing the ineradicable mark of their pastness. When the characters, within this general pastness of the narration, remember something from their own pasts, and when the narrator reports this in that indirect discourse which is another convention of *Mrs. Dalloway*, she has no other way to place it in the past than some version of the past tense which she has already been using for the 'present' of the characters' experience: 'How fresh, how calm, stiller than this of course, the air was in the early morning' (1925, 3). That 'was' is a past within a past, a double repetition.

The sentence before this one contains the 'had' of the past perfect which places it in a past behind that past which is the 'present' of the novel, the day of Clarissa's party. Still Clarissa can hear the squeak of the hinges 'now,' and the reader is led to believe that she may be comparing an earlier time of opening the windows with a present repetition of that action. The following sentence is in the simple past ('the air was'), and yet it belongs not to the present of the narration, but to the past of Clarissa's girlhood. What has happened to justify this change is one of those subtle dislocations within the narration which are characteristic of indirect discourse as a mode of language. Indirect discourse is always a relationship between two distinguishable minds, but the nuances of this relationship may change, with corresponding changes in the way it is registered in words. 'For so it had always seemed to her' – here the little word 'had' establishes three identifiable times: the no-time or time-out-of-time-for-which-all-times-are-past of the narrator; the time of the single day of the novel's action; and the time of Clarissa's youth. [. . .] The subtly varying tense structure creates a pattern of double repetition in which three times keep moving together and then apart. Narration in indirect discourse, for Woolf, is repetition as distancing and merging at once.

[. . .]* There is no present in a novel, or only a specious, ghostly present which is generated by the narrator's ability to resurrect the past not as reality but as verbal image.

Woolf strategically manipulates in *Mrs. Dalloway* the ambiguities of this aspect of conventional storytelling to justify the power she ascribes to her characters of immediate access to their pasts. If the novel as a whole is recovered from the past in the mind of the narrator, the action of the novel proceeds through one day in the lives of its main characters in which one after another they have a present experience, often one of walking through the city, Clarissa's walk to buy flowers, Peter Walsh's walk through London after visiting Clarissa, Septimus and Rezia's walk to visit Sir William Bradshaw, and so on. As the characters make their ways through London the most important events of their pasts rise

* A comparison is offered between the temporality of cinematic and novelistic narrative. [Ed.]

up within them, so that the day of *Mrs. Dalloway* may be described as a general day of recollection. The revivification of the past performed by the characters becomes in its turn another past revivified, brought back from the dead, by the narrator. [. . .]

Woolf has unostentatiously, even secretly, buried within her novel a clue to the way the day of the action is to be seen as the occasion of a resurrection of ghosts from the past. There are three odd and apparently irrelevant pages in the novel (1925, 122–4) which describe the song of an ancient ragged woman, her hand outstretched for coppers. Peter hears her song as he crosses Marylebone Road by the Regent's Park Tube Station. It seems to rise like 'the voice of an ancient spring' spouting from some primeval swamp. It seems to have been going on as the same inarticulate moan for millions of years and to be likely to persist for ten million years longer:

> ee um fah um so
> foo swee too eem oo

The battered old woman, whose voice seems to come from before, after, or outside time, sings of how she once walked with her lover in May. Though it is possible to associate this with the theme of vanished love in the novel (Peter has just been thinking again of Clarissa and of her coldness, 'as cold as an icicle'; 1925, 121–2), still the connection seems strained, and the episode scarcely seems to justify the space it occupies unless the reader recognizes that Woolf has woven into the old woman's song, partly by paraphrase and variation, partly by direct quotation in an English translation, the words of a song by Richard Strauss, 'Allerseelen,' with words by Hermann von Gilm.[1] The phrases quoted in English from the song do not correspond to any of the three English translations I have located, so Woolf either made her own or used another which I have not found. Here is a translation more literal than any of the three published ones I have seen and also more literal than Woolf's version:

> Place on the table the perfuming heather,
> Bring here the last red asters,
> And let us again speak of love,
> As once in May.

> Give me your hand, that I may secretly press it,
> And if someone sees, it's all the same to me;
> Give me but one of your sweet glances,
> As once in May.

> It is blooming and breathing perfume today on every grave,
> One day in the year is free to the dead,
> Come to my heart that I may have you again,
> As once in May.

Heather, red asters, the meeting with the lover once in May, these are echoed in the passage in *Mrs. Dalloway*, and several phrases are quoted directly: 'look in my eyes with thy sweet eyes intently'; 'give me your hand and let me press it gently'; 'and if some one should see, what matter they?' The old woman, there can be no doubt, is singing Strauss's song. The parts of the song not directly echoed in *Mrs. Dalloway* identify it as a key to the structure of the novel. 'One day in the year' is indeed 'free to the dead,' 'Allerseelen,' the day of a collective resurrection of spirits. On this day the bereaved lover can hope that the beloved will return from the grave. Like Strauss's song, *Mrs. Dalloway* has the form of an All Souls' Day in which Peter Walsh, Sally Seton, and the rest rise from the dead to come to Clarissa's party. As in the song the memory of a dead lover may on one day of the year become a direct confrontation of his or her risen spirit, so in *Mrs. Dalloway* the characters are obsessed all day by memories of the time when Clarissa refused Peter and chose to marry Richard Dalloway, and then the figures in those memories actually come back in a general congregation of persons from Clarissa's past. The power of narrative not just to repeat the past but to resurrect it in another form is figured dramatically in the action of the novel.

Continuity of each character with his own past, continuity in the shared past of all the important characters – these forms of communication are completed by the unusual degree of access the characters have in the present to one another's minds. [. . .] In Woolf's work one person often sees spontaneously into the mind of another and knows with the same sort of knowledge he has of his own subjectivity what is going on there. If the narrator enters silently and unobserved into the mind of each of the characters and understands it with perfect intimacy because it is in fact part of her own mind, the characters often, if not always, may have the same kind of intimate knowledge of one another. This may be partly because they share the same memories and so respond in the same way to the same cues, each knowing what the other must be thinking, but it seems also to be an unreflective openness of one mind to another, a kind of telepathic insight. The mutual understanding of Clarissa and Peter is the most striking example of this intimacy: 'They went in and out of each other's minds without any effort,' thinks Peter, remembering their talks at Bourton (1925, 94). Other characters have something of the same power of communication. Rezia and Septimus, for example, as he helps her make a hat in their brief moments of happiness before Dr. Holmes comes and Septimus throws himself out of the window: 'Not for weeks had they laughed like this together, poking fun privately like married people' (1925, 217). Or there is the intimacy of Clarissa and her servant Lucy: ' "Dear!" said Clarissa, and Lucy shared as she meant her to her disappointment (but not the pang); felt the concord between them' (1925, 43).

In all these cases, there is some slight obstacle between the minds of the characters. Clarissa does after all decide not to marry Peter and is falling in love with Richard Dalloway in spite of the almost perfect communion she can achieve with Peter. The communion of Rezia and Septimus is intermittent, and she has little insight into what is going on in his mind during his periods of madness. Clarissa does not share with Lucy the pang of jealousy she feels toward Lady Bruton. The proper model for the relations among minds in *Mrs. Dalloway* is that of a perfect transparency of the minds of the characters to the mind of the narrator, but only a modified translucency, like glass frosted or fogged, between the mind of one character and the mind of another. Nevertheless, to the continuity between the present and the past within the mind of a given character there must be added a relative continuity from one mind to another in the present.

The characters in *Mrs. Dalloway* are endowed with a desire to take possession of these continuities, to actualize them in the present. The dynamic model for this urge is a movement which gathers together disparate elements, pieces them into a unity, and lifts them up into the daylight world in a gesture of ecstatic delight, sustaining the wholeness so created over the dark abyss of death. The phrase 'building it up' echoes through the novel as an emblem of this combination of spiritual and physical action. Thinking of life, Clarissa, the reader will remember, wonders 'how one sees it so, making it up, building it round one' (1925, 5). Peter Walsh follows a pretty girl from Trafalgar Square to Regent Street across Oxford Street and Great Portland Street until she disappears into her house, making up a personality for her, a new personality for himself, and an adventure for them both together: 'it was half made up, as he knew very well; invented, this escapade with the girl; made up, as one makes up the better part of life, he thought – making oneself up; making her up' (1925, 81). Rezia's power of putting one scrap with another to make a hat or of gathering the small girl who brings the evening paper into a warm circle of intimacy momentarily cures Septimus of his hallucinations and of his horrifying sense that he is condemned to a solitary death: 'For so it always happened. First one thing, then another. So she built it up, first one thing and then another . . . she built it up, sewing' (1925, 219, 221). Even Lady Bruton's luncheon, to which she brings Richard Dalloway and Hugh Whitbread to help her write a letter to the *Times* about emigration, is a parody version of this theme of constructive action.

The most important example of the theme is Clarissa Dalloway's party, her attempt to 'kindle and illuminate' (1925, 6). Though people laugh at her for her parties, feel she too much enjoys imposing herself, nevertheless these parties are her offering to life. They are an offering devoted to the effort to bring together people from their separate lives and combine them into oneness: 'Here was So-and-so in South Kensington; some one up in Bayswater; and somebody else, say, in Mayfair. And she felt quite continuously a sense of their existence; and she felt what a waste; and she felt what a pity; and she felt if only they could be brought together; so she did it. And it was an offering; to combine, to create'

(1925, 184–5). The party which forms the concluding scene of the novel does succeed in bringing people together, a great crowd from poor little Ellie Henderson all the way up to the Prime Minister, and including Sally Seton and Peter Walsh among the rest. Clarissa has the 'gift still; to be; to exist; to sum it all up in the moment' (1925, 264).

Clarissa's party transforms each guest from his usual self into a new social self, a self outside the self of participation in the general presence of others. The magic sign of this transformation is the moment when Ralph Lyon beats back the curtain and goes on talking, so caught up is he in the party. The gathering then becomes 'something now, not nothing' (1925, 259), and Clarissa meditates on the power a successful party has to destroy the usual personality and replace it with another self able to know people with special intimacy and able to speak more freely from the hidden depths of the spirit. These two selves are related to one another as real to unreal, but when one is aware of the contrast, as Clarissa is in the moment just before she loses her self-consciousness and is swept up into her own party, it is impossible to tell which is the real self, which the unreal: 'Every time she gave a party she had this feeling of being something not herself, and that every one was unreal in one way; much more real in another . . . it was possible to say things you couldn't say anyhow else, things that needed an effort; possible to go much deeper' (1925, 259–60).

An impulse to create a social situation which will bring into the open the usually hidden continuities of present with past, of person with person, of person with the depths of himself, is shared by all the principal characters of *Mrs. Dalloway*. This universal desire makes one vector of spiritual forces within the novel a general urge toward lifting up and bringing together.

This effort fails in all its examples, or seems in part to have failed. It seems so implicitly to the narrator and more overtly to some of the characters, including Clarissa. From this point of view, a perspective emphasizing the negative aspect of these characters and episodes, Peter Walsh's adventure with the unknown girl is a fantasy. Lady Bruton is a shallow, domineering busybody, a representative of that upper-class society which Woolf intends to expose in her novel. 'I want to criticise the social system,' she wrote while composing *Mrs. Dalloway*, 'and to show it at work, at its most intense' (1954, 56). Rezia's constructive power and womanly warmth does not prevent her husband from killing himself. And Clarissa? It would be a mistake to exaggerate the degree to which she and the social values she embodies are condemned in the novel. Woolf's attitudes toward upper-class English society of the nineteen-twenties are ambiguous, and to sum up the novel as no more than negative social satire is a distortion. Woolf feared while she was writing the novel that Clarissa would not seem attractive enough to her readers. 'The doubtful point,' she wrote in her diary a year before the novel was finished, 'is, I think, the character of Mrs. Dalloway. It may be too stiff, too glittering and tinselly' (1954, 60). There is in fact a negative side to Clarissa as Woolf presents her. She is a snob, too anxious for social success. Her party is seen in part as the perpetuation of a moribund society, with its hangers on at court like Hugh Whitbread and a Prime Minister who is dull: 'You might have stood him behind a counter and bought biscuits,' thinks Ellie Henderson, '– poor chap, all rigged up in gold lace' (1925, 261).

Even if this negative judgement is suspended and the characters are taken as worth our sympathy, it is still the case that, though Clarissa's party facilitates unusual communication among these people, their communion is only momentary. The party comes to an end; the warmth fades; people return to their normal selves. In retrospect there seems to have been something spurious about the sense of oneness with others the party created. Clarissa's power to bring people together seems paradoxically related to her reticence, her coldness, her preservation of an area of inviolable privacy in herself. Though she believes that each person is not limited to him or herself, but is spread out among other people like mist in the branches of a tree, with another part of her spirit she contracts into herself and resents intensely any invasion of her privacy. It almost seems as if her keeping of a secret private self is reciprocally related to her social power to gather people together and put them in relationship to one another. The motif of Clarissa's frigidity, of her prudery, of her separateness runs all through *Mrs. Dalloway*. 'The death of her soul,' Peter Walsh calls it (1925, 89). Since her illness, she has slept alone, in a narrow bed in an attic room. She cannot 'dispel a virginity preserved through childbirth which [clings] to her like a sheet' (1925, 46). She has 'through some contraction of this cold spirit' (1925, 46) failed her husband again and again. She feels a stronger sexual attraction to other women than to men. A high point of her life was the moment when Sally Seton kissed her. Her decision not to marry Peter Walsh but to marry Richard Dalloway instead was a rejection of intimacy and a grasping at privacy. 'For in marriage a little licence, a little independence there must be between people living together day in day out in the same house; which Richard gave her, and she him . . . But with Peter everything had to be shared; everything gone into. And it was intolerable' (1925, 10). 'And there is a dignity in people; a solitude; even between husband and wife a gulf,' thinks Clarissa much later in the novel (1925, 181). Her hatred of her daughter's friend Miss Kilman, of Sir William Bradshaw, of all the representatives of domineering will, of the instinct to convert others, of 'love and religion' (1925, 191), is based on this respect for isolation and detachment: 'Had she ever tried to convert any one herself? Did she not wish everybody merely to be themselves?' (1925, 191). The old lady whom Clarissa sees so often going upstairs to her room in the neighboring house seems to stand chiefly for this highest value, 'the privacy of the soul' (1925, 192): 'that's the miracle, that's the mystery; that old lady, she meant . . . And the supreme mystery . . . was simply this: here was one room; there another. Did religion solve that, or love?' (1925, 193).

The climax of *Mrs. Dalloway* is not Clarissa's party but the moment when, having heard of the suicide of Septimus, Clarissa leaves her guests behind and goes alone into the little room where Lady Bruton has a few minutes earlier been talking to the Prime Minister about India. There she sees in the next house the old lady once more, this time going quietly to bed. She thinks about Septimus and recognizes how factitious all her attempt to assemble and to connect has been. Her withdrawal from her party suggests that she has even in the midst of her guests kept untouched the privacy of her soul, that still point from which one can recognize the hollowness of the social world and feel the attraction of the death everyone carries within him as his deepest reality. Death is the place of true communion. Clarissa has been attempting the impossible, to bring the values of death into the daylight world of life. Septimus chose the right way. By killing himself he preserved his integrity, 'plunged holding his treasure' (1925, 281), his link to the deep places where each man or woman is connected to every other man or woman. For did he not in his madness hear his dead comrade, Evans, speaking to him from that region where all the dead dwell together? 'Communication is health; communication is happiness' (1925, 141) – Septimus during his madness expresses what is the highest goal for all the characters, but his suicide constitutes a recognition that communication cannot be attained except evanescently in life. The only repetition of the past that successfully repossesses it is the act of suicide.

Clarissa's recognition of this truth, her moment of self-condemnation, is at the same time the moment of her greatest insight:

> She had once thrown a shilling into the Serpentine, never anything more. But he had flung it away. They went on living . . . They (all day she had been thinking of Bourton, of Peter, of Sally), they would grow old. A thing there was that mattered; a thing, wreathed about with chatter, defaced, obscured in her own life, let drop every day in corruption, lies chatter. This he had preserved. Death was defiance. Death was an attempt to communicate; people feeling the impossibility of reaching the centre which, mystically, evaded them; closeness drew apart; rapture faded, one was alone. There was an embrace in death. (1925, 280–1)

From the point of view of the 'thing' at the center that matters most, all speech, all social action, all building it up, all forms of communication, are lies. The more one tries to reach this centre through such means the further away from it one goes. The ultimate lesson of *Mrs. Dalloway* is that by building it up, one destroys. Only by throwing it away can life be preserved. It is preserved by being laid to rest on that underlying reality which Woolf elsewhere describes as 'a thing I see before me: something abstract; but residing in the downs or sky; beside which nothing matters; in which I shall rest and continue to exist. Reality I call it' (1954, 129–30). 'Nothing matters' – compared to this reality, which is only defaced, corrupted, covered over by all the everyday activities of life, everything else is emptiness and vanity: 'there is nothing,' wrote Woolf during one of her periods of depression, ' – nothing for any of us. Work, reading, writing are all disguises; and relations with people' (1954, 141).

[. . .]*

Mrs. Dalloway seems to end in a confrontation of life and death as looking-glass counterparts. Reality, authenticity, and completion are on the death side of the mirror, while life is at best the illusory, insubstantial, and fragmentary image of that dark reality. There is, however, one more structural element in *Mrs. Dalloway*, one final twist which reverses the polarities once more, or rather which holds them poised in their irreconciliation. Investigation of this will permit a final identification of the way Woolf brings into the open latent implications of traditional modes of storytelling in English fiction.

Mrs. Dalloway has a double temporal form. During the day of the action the chief characters resurrect in memory by bits and pieces the central episode of their common past. All these characters then come together again at Clarissa's party. The narrator in her turn embraces both these times in the perspective of a single distance. She moves forward through her own time of narration toward the point when the two times of the characters come together in the completion of the final sentences of the novel, when Peter sees Clarissa returning to her party. Or should one say 'almost come together,' since the temporal gap still exists in the separation between 'is' and 'was'? 'It is Clarissa, he said. For there she was' (1925, 296).

In the life of the characters, this moment of completion passes. The party ends. Sally, Peter, Clarissa, and the rest move on toward death. The victory of the narrator is to rescue from death this moment and all the other moments of the novel in that All Souls' Day at a second power which is literature. Literature for Woolf is repetition as preservation, but preservation of things and persons in their antithetical poise. Time is rescued by this repetition. It is rescued in its perpetually reversing divisions. It is lifted into the region of death with which the mind of the narrator has from the first page been identified. This is a place of absence, where nothing exists but words. These words generate their own reality. Clarissa, Peter, and the rest can be encountered only in the pages of the novel. The reader enters this realm of language when he leaves his own solid world and begins to read *Mrs. Dalloway*. The novel is a double resurrection. The characters exist for themselves as alive in a present which is a resuscitation of their dead pasts. In the all-embracing mind of the narrator the characters exist as dead men and women whose continued existence depends on her words. When the circle of the narration is complete, past joining present, the apparently living characters reveal themselves to be already dwellers among the dead.

Clarissa's vitality, her ability 'to be; to exist,' is expressed in the present-tense statement made by Peter Walsh in the penultimate line of the novel: 'It is Clarissa.' This affirmation of her power to sum it all up in the moment echoes earlier descriptions of her 'extraordinary gift, that woman's gift, of making a

---

* While Clarissa's party seeks to create a unity or centre, Miller argues that Septimus Smith's death, which anticipates Woolf's own, is a defiant attempt to communicate the idea that destruction is the only way to embrace such a centre. [Ed.]

world of her own wherever she happened to be': 'She came into a room; she stood, as he had often seen her, in a doorway with lots of people round her . . . she never said anything specially clever; there she was, however; there she was' (1925, 114–15); 'There she was, mending her dress' (1925, 179). These earlier passages are in the past tense, as is the last line of the novel: 'For there she was.' With this sentence 'is' becomes 'was' in the indirect discourse of the narrator. In that mode of language Clarissa along with all the other characters recedes into an indefinitely distant past. Life becomes death within the impersonal mind of the narrator and within her language, which is the place of communion in death. There the fragmentary is made whole. There all is assembled into one unit. All the connections between one part of the novel and another are known only to the agile and ubiquitous mind of the narrator. They exist only within the embrace of that reconciling spirit and through the power of her words.

Nevertheless, to return once more to the other side of the irony, Clarissa comes back from her solitary confrontation with death during her party. She returns from her recognition of her kinship with Septimus to bring 'terror' and 'ecstasy' to Peter when he sees her (1925, 296). She comes back also into the language of the narration where she may be confronted by the reader in the enduring language of literature.

It is perhaps for this reason that Woolf changed her original plan and introduced Septimus as Clarissa's surrogate in death. To have had a single protagonist who was swallowed up in the darkness would have falsified her conception. She needed two protagonists, one who dies and another who dies with his death. Clarissa vividly lives through Septimus's death as she meditates alone during her party. Then, having died vicariously, she returns to life. She appears before her guests to cause, in Peter Walsh at least, 'extraordinary excitement' (1925, 296). Not only does Clarissa's vitality come from her proximity to death. The novel needs for its structural completeness two opposite but similar movements, Septimus's plunge into death and Clarissa's resurrection from the dead. *Mrs. Dalloway* is both of these at once: the entry into the realm of communication in death and the revelation of that realm in words which may be read by the living.

Though *Mrs. Dalloway* seems almost nihilistically to recommend the embrace of death, nevertheless, like the rest of Woolf's writing, it represents in fact a contrary movement of the spirit. Like Clarissa's party or like the other examples of building it up in *Mrs. Dalloway,* the novel is a constructive action which gathers unconnected elements into a solidly existing object. It is something which belongs to the everyday world of physical things. It is a book with cardboard covers and white pages covered with black marks. This made-up thing, unlike its symbol, Clarissa's party, belongs to both worlds. If it is in one sense no more than a manufactured physical object, it is in another sense made of words which designate not the material presence of the things named but their absence from the everyday world and their existence within the place out of place and time out of time which are the space and time of literature. Woolf's writing has as its aim bringing into the light of day this realm of communication in language. A novel, for Woolf, is the place of death made visible. Writing is the only action which exists simultaneously on both sides of the mirror, within death and within life at once.

Though Woolf deals with extreme spiritual situations, her work would hardly give support to a scheme of literary history which sees twentieth-century literature as more negative, more 'nihilistic,' or more 'ambiguous' than nineteenth-century literature. The 'undecidability' of *Mrs. Dalloway* lies in the impossibility of knowing, from the text, whether the realm of union in death exists, for Woolf, only in the words, or whether the words represent an extralinguistic realm which is 'really there' for the characters, for the narrator, and for Woolf herself. Nevertheless, the possibility that the realm of death, in real life as in fiction, really exists, is more seriously entertained by Woolf than it is, for example, by Eliot, by Thackeray, or by Hardy. The possibility that repetition in narrative is the representation of a transcendent spiritual realm of reconciliation and preservation, a realm of the perpetual resurrection of the dead, is more straightforwardly proposed by Virginia Woolf than by most of her predecessors in English fiction.

Note

1. Opus 10, no. 8. For the score and von Gilm's text see Strauss (1907, 9–11).

9

Franz Kafka and the Metaphysics of Alienation

Had one to name the artist who comes nearest to bearing the same kind of relation to our age that Dante, Shakespeare and Goethe bore to theirs, Kafka is the first we would think of.

W. H. Auden

There is a goal, but no way; what we call the way is only wavering.

Kafka

Franz Kafka, from the very beginning of his life, was chained forever in the place of exile:

It seems to me as if I had not come by myself but had been pushed here as a child and then chained to this spot; the consciousness of my misfortune only gradually dawned on me, my misfortune itself was already complete. (1949, 211)

Outside of the human world, outside of God's law, he felt condemned to wander forever in the wilderness outside of Canaan. This wandering is identical with being chained in one spot, for every place in the desert is identical with every other place, and they are all equally at an infinite distance from the goal:

Why did I want to quit the world? Because 'he' would not let me live in it, in his world. Though indeed I should not judge the matter so precisely, for I am now a citizen of this other world, whose relationship to the ordinary one is the relationship of the wilderness to cultivated land (I have been forty years wandering from Canaan) . . . It is indeed a kind of Wandering in the Wilderness in reverse that I am undergoing. (1949, 213)

Doubtless it is Kafka's acute consciousness of his irrevocable alienation, and the incomparably subtle analysis of it presented in his works, that earn him his place as the most representative figure in twentieth-century literature. For our time is, even more than the time of Hölderlin (it is only an extension of his), the time of distress, the time when the link between God and man is broken, the time when God is no more present and is not yet again present, the time when He can only be experienced negatively, as a terrifying absence.

But the full consciousness of his plight only 'gradually' dawns on the exiled one, and, besides, 'the attraction of the human world is so immense, in an instant it can make one forget everything' (1949, 215). 'I think,' says Kafka, 'that I am continually skirting the wilderness and am full of childish hopes . . . that 'perhaps I shall keep in Canaan after all' (1949, 214). Accordingly, the first act in the Kafkan drama is a frantic attempt to keep within the ordinary human world. At all costs he must believe that he is a perfectly normal person, that he is linked by a thousand ties to the tightly knit circle of the human community, that he has a justified and meaningful existence there, and that, above all, the established human world forms for him an avenue of approach to God. For is not the true way to God through the traditional institutions of the community? And if one does not belong to God, if one is not within the law, one does not exist, one is, literally, nothing: 'The word "*sein*" signifies in German both things: to be and to belong to Him' (1946b, 288).

It is quite clear what Kafka meant by belonging to the human world. It meant, perhaps most of all in Kafka's Jewish tradition, being a good son, and, later, having a wife and children. Thus he writes in his journal: 'The Talmud too says: A man without a woman is no person' (1948, 162). And he expresses again and again his horror of the bachelor's 'ill-luck' and his painful longing for a wife and children. For children are a sign that one is in the right with God, that one has a meaningful part in history, in the temporal fulfillment of God's law on earth.

But belonging to the human world also meant for Kafka having a job and a profession. Only these would give one the strength to act decisively: 'For without a center, without a profession, a love, a family, an income; i.e., without holding one's own against the world in the big things . . . one cannot protect oneself from losses that momentarily destroy one' (1948, 24). Thus the hero of *Amerika*, the shy and diffident Karl Rossmann, becomes aggressive and competent when he thinks he is established in the community, even at its lowest level:

> He marched up to the counter and rapped on it with his knuckles until someone came; . . . he shouted across high walls of human beings; he went up to people without hesitation. . . . He did all this not out of arrogance, not from any lack of respect for difficulties, but because he felt himself in a secure position which gave him certain rights. (1946a, 138)

To possess all these things – a family, a job, and a secured place in the general human family – would be, in other words, to enjoy the sense of wellbeing which K. in *The Castle* momentarily (and falsely) experiences. And it would be to feel, as K. does, that his position allows him an avenue of approach to the divine power, here present in Klamm, the Castle official:

> Yet. I have already a home, a position and real work to do, I have a promised wife who takes her share of my professional duties when I have other business, I'm going to marry her and become a member of the community, and besides my official connection I have also a personal connection with Klamm, although as yet I haven't been able to make use of it. That's surely quite a lot. (1951, 256)

So, then, a number of Kafka's stories, especially the early ones, can be interpreted as continuing that tradition which goes back through Dickens (whom he consciously imitated in *Amerika*) to the eighteenth-century novel. That is, they are stories about people who begin in estrangement from the human community, and who attempt through a series of adventures to find a stable place in society, and through that a meaningful identity. Kafka's most elaborate version of this traditional theme is *Amerika*; no other work expresses more clearly the opposition between the terrible freedom of having no connection with the human world and the longed-for security of a permanent place in the social order. But this same opposition between freedom and status is also central in other stories – in, for example, 'A Report to an Academy,' the disquieting story of an ape who, after being captured, escapes from his cage by finding 'a special way' out, 'the way of humanity':

> With an effort which up till now has never been repeated, [says the ape] I managed to reach the cultural level of an average European . . . There is an excellent idiom: to fight one's way through the thick of things: that is what I have done, I have fought through the thick of things. There was nothing else for me to do, provided always that freedom was not to be my choice. (1952, 179)

It is a choice, then, between 'dreadful freedom' outside the human world and meaningful existence within it. But in Kafka's later writings there is a strange transformation of the value of belonging to the human world. Now, instead of being identified with obedience to God's law, it is opposed to it. The choice now seems to be between fulfilling God's law in isolation and evading its imperatives through self-immersion in the human collective. Thus, in a bitterly ironic journal note of 1917, Kafka asserts that his real aim is not to obey God but to escape into the human world where he can sin with impunity:

> If I closely examine what is my ultimate aim, it turns out that I am not really striving to be good and to fulfill the demands of a Supreme Judgment, but rather very much the contrary: I strive to know the whole human and animal community, to recognize their basic predilections, desires, moral ideals, to reduce these to simple rules and as quickly as possible to trim my behavior to these rules in order that I may find favor in the whole world's eyes: and, indeed (this is the inconsistency), so much favor that in the end I could openly perpetrate the iniquities within me without alienating the universal love in which I am held – the only sinner who won't be roasted. (1949, 187–8)

What has happened to bring about this reversal? The answer is that Kafka has come to recognize that everybody, without exception, is outside the law. The entire human community is in the desert, attempting to build an impious tower of Babel to scale heaven, but really cutting itself off more and more from God and creating a self-enclosed structure of purely human values and institutions. Kafka's judgement of our urban, technological, industrial, bureaucratic world is unequivocal. Once, long ago, as Kafka says in one of his very last stories, the

Word was close to man, and interpenetrated his world, but now it has withdrawn altogether, and all mankind is lost:

> Even in those days wonders did not openly walk the streets for any one to seize; but all the same dogs [for 'dogs' we are, of course, to understand: 'men'] – I cannot put it in any other way – had not yet become so doggish as to-day, the edifice of dogdom was still loosely put together, the true Word could still have intervened, planning or replanning the structure, changing it at will, transforming it into its opposite; the Word was there, was very near at least, on the tip of everybody's tongue, any one might have hit upon it. And what has become of it to-day? To-day one may pluck out one's very heart and not find it. (1946b, 46–7)

To live within the human community is no longer to live in a world which is transparent to God, but is to 'hasten in almost guiltless silence towards death in a world *darkened by others*' (1946, 47). In other words, the true reason Kafka is impelled to reject the way to God that lies through the human world, through a family or a profession or religious observances, is not, it seems, that he is exiled by that community, but that the community is itself no longer a way to God. One *is* lost, but then one *must* be lost. For the entire human community is lost, though this is not generally known. Each of us has taken a wrong turning, and we wander in endless aberration: 'Every person is lost in himself beyond hope of rescue' (1949, 10). The only difference in Kafka's case is that he knows he is lost, and this is his chance. The discovery of alienation is, perhaps, the only remaining possibility of salvation. For the spiritual state of Kafka's heroes is not extraordinary. Rather it is the true state of us all, whether we know it or not. It is not only Kafka who wanders farther and farther into the desert, but all of us, together, and yet separated infinitely by our mutual silence:

> When our first fathers strayed they had doubtless scarcely any notion that their aberration was to be an endless one, they could still literally see the cross-roads, it seemed an easy matter to turn back whenever they pleased, and if they hesitated to turn back it was merely because they wanted to enjoy a dog's life for a little while longer; it was not yet a genuine dog's life, and already it seemed intoxicatingly beautiful to them . . . and so they strayed farther. (1946b, 47–8)

II

The Kafkan man, then, is in exile, and he must *wish* to be in exile, must constantly reaffirm and choose his exile as the only possibility left open to him. Kafka's stories and his personal writings, in spite of the recurrent 'attraction of the human world', and in spite of his momentary feelings that the human world is good and that he belongs to it, are, for the most part, a long, patient, and exhaustive analysis of what it means to be outside of everything, even outside of oneself.

To be outside of everything means, first of all, to be unable to reach and touch anything outside of one's own narrow limits: 'I am divided from all things by a hollow space' (1949, 180), says Kafka, 'I am too far away, am banished.' One remains *here*, and everyone and everything else is *out there*, seen coldly across a gap, as a mere phenomenal spectacle. Moreover, one is also separated from the past and from the future. A really meaningful human life, of course, possesses its past and its future, and they eventually form a full circle, a totality of homogeneous existence supporting one in a fullness of being:

> We . . . are held in our past and future . . . Whatever advantage the future has in size, the past compensates for in weight, and at the end the two are indeed no longer distinguishable, earliest youth later becomes distinct, as the future is, and the end of the future is really already experienced in all our sighs, and thus becomes the past. So this circle along whose rim we move almost closes. (1948, 27)

But the exiled one 'has only the moment, the everlasting moment of torment which is followed by no glimpse of a moment of recovery' (1948, 26). Kafka's stories and journals are perfect expressions of this double isolation in the moment, isolation not only from all past and future moments, but also from what is seen and experienced in the moment itself. His heroes are, like Kafka himself, passive and cold, incapable of the least motion of human warmth which might extend outwards to embrace the world and other people: 'A sad but calm astonishment at my lack of feeling often grips me' (1948, 180); 'It is as if I were made of stone' (1948, 33), 'I have become cold again, and insensible' (1949, 98). And the world seen from the point of view of cold, detached passivity is a long succession of disconnected appearances. One 'isolated momentary observation' (1948, 73) follows another. Each appears suddenly before the field of vision, swells up to fill the whole, and is seen vividly in microscopic detail for a moment: 'observations of the moment, mostly only indoors, where certain people suddenly and hugely bubble up before one's eyes' (1948, 69). Then, what had absorbed all of one's attention dissolves, disappears, to be forgotten and replaced by something else.

To begin to read one of Kafka's stories is to enter a space where one is always *indoors*, where there are always limits to one's vision. Even if one is in the midst of a trackless desert, one's vision is soon stopped by the indeterminate horizon of sand and sky, or by a thick murk of fog, or by the dazzling brilliance of sunlight itself. But most often one finds oneself in a dreamlike interior, a realm of theatrical hallucination. (Kafka was fascinated by the theater, and many of his own dreams took place in a theater.) There is nothing behind the insubstantial backdrops of these stage sets, solid though they seem – nothing but the discarded bric-à-brac of unused props and ropes, or, as it may be, simply another room just like the first. The world of Kafka's stories is a world without depth, a world of sheer surface, a world of continual movement, in which one is condemned to explore, one after another, indefinitely multiplied chambers which replace one another and which are all the equivalents of one another. The scene is always changing, but it never really changes. It is a universe of pure spectacle. And in such a universe all things are traps which fascinate our attention. The people are as depthless as the walls: we see their gestures and expressions with extraordinary distinctness, but the meaning of these gestures and these glances is precisely that they have no meaning. They are simply there before us. They connect with nothing before or after, and they contain no significance hidden in their depths: 'Miserable observation,' says Kafka, 'which again is certainly the result of something artificially constructed whose lower end is swinging in emptiness somewhere' (1948, 310).

The world of *Amerika*, of *The Trial*, and *The Castle*, then, is a *labyrinth*. In this labyrinth, one moves constantly from place to place without ever getting anywhere, or reaching anything conclusive, or even knowing whether there is a goal to be reached:

> The truly terrible paths between freedom and slavery cross each other with no guide to the way ahead and accompanied by an immediate obliterating of the paths already traversed. There are a countless number of such paths, or only one, it cannot be determined, for there is no vantage ground from which to observe. There am I. I cannot leave. (1948, 324)

Thus, not one of Kafka's longer works is really finished. They could not, on principle, reach their end, since the very nature of the experience they describe is to be endless, or, rather, to be the 'eternal recapitulation' (1946b, 293) of the same experience. These novels, at best, can only jump over an infinite number of intermediate stages, and reach, as in the case of *The Trial*, their inevitable end. But, most often, that end is never reached: 'A life like this could last forever and still be nothing but a moment. Moses fails to enter Canaan not because his life is too short but because it is a human life' (1949, 196).

In the end, however, Kafka's universe, for the very reason that it is so completely without depth, comes to seem very deep indeed. For the least gesture or glance from another person, the most insignificant detail observed in an inanimate object, precisely because they can be given no comforting human meaning, seem to put us in touch immediately with some unfathomable meaning from beyond the human world. They seem radiant with an ominous significance which transcends their immediate reality. The most we can hope is that this meaning has nothing directly to do with us; 'The most appropriate situation for me: To listen to a conversation between two people who are discussing a matter that concerns them closely while I have only a remote interest in it which is in addition completely selfless' (1948, 305).

But, alas, such is not the case. The conversation *does* concern me. My guilt is being decided, and the moment of my execution set. All Kafka's stories about persons who wander within the labyrinth of the human world approach closer and closer to the same ending: the death of the hero, which is only the fulfillment of a spiritual death that precedes the beginning of the story. This is the central action of *The Trial*: Joseph K.'s slow recognition that he cannot ignore his trial, that he no longer belongs to the human world, that he is guilty, that his fate is to be executed. To yield onself to the human world, to leave one's safe enclosure, is to put oneself at the mercy of judges who are infinitely powerful and infinitely merciless, and whether one is 'guilty' or 'innocent' (that is, whether one knows or does not know that one is guilty), the end is the same: 'Rossmann and K., the innocent and the guilty, both executed without distinction in the end, the guilty one with a gentler hand, more pushed aside than struck down' (1949, 132).

Only one escape seems to remain: to withdraw altogether from the human world, to surround oneself with impenetrable walls and to live safely in complete isolation within one's own private enclosure: 'I'll shut myself off from everyone to the point of insensibility. Make an enemy of everyone, speak to no one' (1948, 297). 'Two tasks on the threshold of life: To narrow your circle more and more, and constantly to make certain that you have not hidden yourself somewhere outside it' (1946b, 302).

The quality of life within the pure circle of complete isolation is brilliantly dramatized in the story called 'The Burrow.' The interior world too, we discover, is a labyrinth, a labyrinth one has made for oneself. But this labyrinth does not even have the multiplicity and changefulness of the exterior one. Each chamber and each passageway is exactly like all the others, and reflects back only the absolute blandness and indeterminacy of one's own inner life. Where there is nothing but oneself, there is nothing. In isolation, there is a rapid exhaustion of one's forces, an evaporation of the self. In a moment, all thoughts, all emotions, all one's powers, are dissipated, and there is nothing left but a complete void. Kafka's diaries are full of descriptions of the absolute inner emptiness resulting from this disastrous withdrawal into one's own center: 'My inner emptiness, an emptiness that replaces everything else is not even very great' (1948, 323). 'Completely indifferent and apathetic. A well gone dry, water at an unattainable depth and no certainty it is there. Nothing, nothing' (1949, 126). It is as though one had, deliberately or by inadvertence, stepped off the rim of one's circle into a bottomless abyss:

> This circle indeed belongs to us, but belongs to us only so long as we keep to it, if we move to the side just once, in any chance forgetting of self, in some distraction, some fright, some astonishment, some fatigue, we have already lost it into space, until now we had our noses stuck into the tide of the times, now we step back, former swimmers, present walkers, and are lost. (1948, 27)

By enclosing oneself in a narrow circle of isolation, one has indeed stepped into a place of complete nullity. This nullity is not death, it is something worse, it is 'the eternal torment of dying' (1949, 77). Gregor Samsa, for example, in 'The Metamorphosis,' after his horrible transformation into a cockroach, becomes more and more dry and empty within his carapace of solitude, but he is liberated, finally, by death. Gregor's end, however, like the death at the end of 'The Judgment,' or the execution at the end of *The Trial*, is as much wish-fulfillment as a possibility in which Kafka really believes. The true plight of Kafka's heroes is to be unable to die, to remain forever, like the hunter Gracchus, hovering between this world and the world of death, to remain in a prolonged emptiness which is neither death nor life:

> In a certain sense I am alive too. My death ship lost its way; a wrong turn of the wheel, a moment's absence of mind on the pilot's part . . . I am forever . . . on the great stair that leads up to [the other world]. On that infinitely wide and spacious stair I clamber about, sometimes up, sometimes down, sometimes on the right, sometimes on the left, always in motion . . . My ship has no rudder, and it is driven by the wind that blows in the undermost regions of death. (1946b, 210, 214)

The ultimate fate of Kafka's heroes, then, and of Kafka himself, is to reach a frightening state of being neither alive nor dead, in which one can only live by endlessly falling into the void. The Kafkan man is drawn relentlessly toward a supreme moment, a moment as long as eternity itself, a moment in which he is pure negative consciousness speeding with infinite acceleration toward an incomprehensible transcendent power which he can never reach or escape from, however far or fast he goes:

> To die would mean nothing else than to surrender a nothing to the nothing, but that would be impossible to conceive, for how could a person, even only as a nothing, consciously surrender himself to the nothing, and not merely to an empty nothing but rather to a roaring nothing whose nothingness consists only in its incomprehensibility. (1948, 316)

III

> Again encouragement. Again I catch hold of myself, as one catches hold of a ball in its fall. Tomorrow, today, I'll begin an extensive work . . . (1948, 254)

Now one final possibility remains, and it is literature itself, the rescue of oneself through writing. Writing, it may be, is the one action which, depending on nothing outside the self, and deriving from a voluntary and autonomous exercise of the power to transform things into words, can stop the endless fall into the abyss. The self will seize the self, as one catches hold of a ball in mid-air, and give to itself an indestructible solidity. The crucial importance of Kafka for twentieth-century thought lies not only in his extreme experience of the loss of selfhood, but also in his deep exploration of the tangled relations between writing and salvation. For Kafka, as does the thought of our century in general, pursues to its end the attempt, begun by the Romantics, to find in literature itself a means of salvation. Abandoned to utter dereliction by the collapse of every other hope, Kafka turns to writing as the sole possibility remaining. And it was no light burden he put upon words: it was, indeed, a burden no less heavy than the weight of his entire life and destiny: '*I am more and more unable to think, to observe, to determine the truth of things, to remember, to speak, to share an experience; I am turning to stone, this is the truth* . . . If I can't take refuge in some work, I am lost' (1949, 68; emphasis in original). 'But I will write in spite of everything, absolutely; it is my struggle for self-preservation' (1949, 75). 'I am nothing but literature' (1948, 299).

Kafka's notion of the process by which literature would bring him salvation was precise and definite: the words would not merely be put down on the paper to exist independently of their creator. They would be a kind of magical incantation that would replace the inner emptiness with solidity and firmness: they would summon 'life's splendour' which 'forever lies in wait about each of us in all its fulness, but veiled from view, deep down, invisible, far off' (1949, 195). 'The firmness . . . which the most insignificant writing brings about in me is beyond doubt and wonderful' (1949, 314). 'If you summon it by the right word, by its right name, it will come. This is the essence of magic, which does not create but summons' (1949, 195). 'I have now . . . a great yearning to write all my anxiety out of me, write it into the depths of the paper just as it comes out of the depths of me, or write it down in such a way that I could draw what I had written into me completely' (1948, 173).

But at first Kafka's relation to writing remains, precisely, a *striving*, a *yearning*. The transformation of his inner life through writing is something he believes in but has not experienced. For, though all his inner forces rushed toward writing, Kafka was, for long months and years, unable to achieve a definitive experience of the power of words. What he lacked was time, for writing is 'a task that can never succeed except all at once' (1948, 248). His job, his family, all the connections he had with the normal world, left him only the night for writing; and the night was not long enough. Kafka's early diaries are full of laments over his lack of time for writing, and full, too, of fragmentary stories, stories which start off strongly, create their own world in a few powerful sentences, and then suddenly and abruptly stop, like meteors which glow brightly in rarefied air, but are burnt up in a moment by the lower atmosphere and return to darkness. For Kafka cannot remain long enough in the upper air. He must sink back to his quotidian indigence, and leave his story behind to dissipate itself into the inarticulate chaos from which it came. This chaos is within him, and yet painfully separated from him. Only a complete story could bring the two together and give form and expression simultaneously both to the chaos of inner forces and to his consciousness itself: 'I really don't have time for a story, time to expand myself in every direction in the world, as I should have to do' (1948, 61);

> I have too little time to draw out of me all the possibilities of my talent. For that reason it is only disconnected starts that always make an appearance . . . If I were ever able to write something large and whole, well-shaped from beginning to end, then in the end the story would never be able to detach itself from me and it would be possible for me calmly and with open eyes, as a blood relation of a healthy story, to hear it read, but as it is, every little piece of the story runs around homeless and drives me away from it in the opposite direction. (1948, 134)

Far from being able to escape out of his own inner emptiness into the solidity and coherence of a story, Kafka is repulsed by the broken fragments of incomplete ones, and kept outside in the void, hanging on, as it were, with both hands. And, worse yet, within this void, he is conscious of immense unused forces which circle in uncontrollable violence, which permit him no rest or sleep, and, far from holding him together, tear him apart: 'Then, already boiling, I went home, I couldn't withstand one of my ideas, disordered, pregnant, disheveled, swollen, amidst my furniture which was rolling about me; overwhelmed by my pains and worries, taking up as much space as possible' (1948, 101).

'The tremendous world I have in my head. But how to free myself and free it without being torn to pieces' (1948, 288). This is indeed the question: burnt up by 'the unhappy sense of a consuming fire inside [him] that [is] not allowed to break out' (1949, 142), tormented by 'mysterious powers' (1948, 76) which have been unleashed within him and are tearing him to pieces, and prevented by external circumstances from directing them to a single continuous work, Kafka is driven toward a state even worse than those times when his mind is a 'thoughtless vacuum.' Indeed, he is driven, as he often feared, toward madness. In this dangerous condition, he is sustained only by an unproved conviction that this seeming chaos is really a harmony, a harmony which, if it were liberated, would not only fill up all the interior space of his consciousness, but would permit an expansion of that space toward unheard-of limits: 'In the end this uproar is only a suppressed, restrained harmony, which, left free, would fill me completely, which would even widen me and yet still fill me' (1948, 74–5). 'I have . . . experienced states (not many) . . . in which I completely dwelt in every idea, but also filled every idea, and in which I not only felt myself at my boundary, but at the boundary of the human in general' (1948, 58).

It is clear now what form Kafka's stories must take, if they are to be successful. They must be a perfect continuity, sweeping smoothly from beginning to end, with no scission or interstice, and they must be an expression, not of some limited action in the external world, but, precisely, of the *totality* of his inner world. In the words of the story, the emptiness of consciousness and the shapeless storms of unused forces must come together and fuse in the concrete particularity of narrative or image. We can see here why it is incorrect to speak of Kafka's stories as 'symbolic,' as if their mysterious images, descriptions, and actions *stood for* something other than themselves. They are not symbolic, but perfectly literal embodiments of his inner life. They are the very form his consciousness takes when it has any form at all, when it ceases to be a hollow shell filled with indeterminate energies careening in the void.

Kafka's definitive experience of the power of writing came on the night of 22 September 1912, when he wrote, in a single unbroken flow of inspiration, the short story called 'The Judgment.' That night he discovered that his literary powers were real, but he also discovered the true extent of those powers. He discovered that an authentic piece of writing would not simply give cohesion and firmness to his own narrow interior space, but would cause that interior space to expand and grow until it filled the entire universe. Or, rather, he discovered that the interior regions of his consciousness could, through the magic of words, become the entire universe turned inside out. Every person and thing, without exception, everything real or imaginable, could be transformed into words and placed there within himself in an immutable form. Literature was not simply the salvation of his own poor identity; it was also the salvation of the world itself. It was, necessarily, both at once, for so long as any particle or fragment of the world remained unchanged into words, into image, that fragment would remain other than the self and constitute a deadly threat to it. Writing, in other words, he discovered to be ' "an assault, on the last earthly frontier," an assault, moreover, launched from below, from mankind' (1949, 202).

> The strange, mysterious, perhaps dangerous, perhaps saving comfort that there is in writing: it is a leap out of murderer's row; it is a seeing of what is really taking place. This occurs by a higher type of observation, a higher, not a keener type, and the higher it is, and the less within reach of the 'row,' the more independent it becomes, the more obedient to its own laws of motion, the more incalculable, the more joyful, the more ascendant its course. (1949, 212)

Kafka, it seems, has escaped at last, though only by arrogating to himself almost divine powers. If narrowing oneself concentrically to even smaller and smaller dimensions provides no escape from the inexorable power of the world and of God, the other extreme alternative seems to work. By expanding his inner world ever further and further outwards until it includes in a new form everything that is, Kafka liberates himself at last from the annihilating pressures which initially surround him. He makes of his nothing, everything.

IV

[. . .]
Kafka learned by experience that writing is not a smooth continuous movement which changes the world altogether and flies off with it to the free upper air. His

experiences within the literary space were exactly like those he had had in the desert of exile: an endless wavering which rose up only to fall back again, which never reached and possessed the goal. He found writing, like human life itself, to be an interminably prolonged death:

> What will be my fate as a writer is very simple . . . I waver, continually fly to the summit of the mountain, but then fall back in a moment. Others waver too, but in lower regions, with greater strength; if they are in danger of falling, they are caught up by the kinsman who walks beside them for that very purpose. But I waver on the heights; it is not death, alas, but the eternal torments of dying. (1949, 77)

Kafka recognized in the end that the attempt to reach the goal through writing 'is not a task at all, not even an impossible one, it is not even impossibility itself, it is nothing' (1948, 206). This task is even worse than impossible, because the space of literature is, *par excellence*, the place of separation. It is the place of separation, because it is the place where everything is transformed into image. To make an image of something makes that thing at once attainable and unattainable. An image makes what it represents simultaneously present and absent. It makes it available *as image*, therefore unavailable. When we reach out to touch it, it changes again, recedes, and hovers there before us just beyond our grasp. By the very fact that something is described, is turned into image, it becomes illusion, and therefore false, separated from the truth. It becomes the mediate symbol of the goal rather than the goal itself. Far from giving immutable truth to things, Kafka, this 'man with the too great shadow' (1949, 214), destroys all things he approaches. He destroys them by transforming them into the shadows of themselves, by transposing them from the tangibility and closeness of the physical world into the strange inner world where nothing can ever be possessed: 'For all things outside the physical world language can be employed only as a sort of adumbration, but never with even approximate exactitude, since in accordance with the physical world it treats only of possession and its connotations' (1946b, 292).

The realm of literature, then, delivers Kafka over to an endless sterile vacillation between the sin of *impatience* and the sin of *laziness* (see 1946b, 278). On the one hand, Kafka is driven by impatience, by the desire to reach the goal immediately. But to do this means to commit the fatal mistake of taking the mediate for the immediate, of confusing an image of the goal with the goal itself. No, one is condemned to play out the game to the end, without any premature renunciation of method, going with infinite slowness from one stage of the way to the next: 'The road is endless, there is nothing that can be subtracted from it or added to it, and yet everyone insists on applying his own childish measuring yard. "Yes, you will have to go the length of that measuring yard as well; it will not be forgiven you" ' (1946b, 287). But, on the other hand, to become absorbed in the stages of the way is laziness, the negligence which ignores the goal for something less. For each stage is only a delusive mirroring of the goal.

One must go directly toward the goal without intermediary. But this is impossible. Between these two requirements Kafka and all his heroes waver endlessly. He must continuously reject all immanence for the sake of a transcendence. But what is transcendent remains, by definition, out of reach, and Kafka's experience of immanence is not of possession or closeness, but of distance, lack. Belonging to society, an intimate relation to another person, writing, all these forms of life reduce themselves in the end to the same universal mode of existence, and we recognize at last that Kafka can, by no expedient, whether lawful or unlawful, escape from the realm of errancy to which he has been condemned.

The fullest expression of the movement by which every step toward the goal is a step away from it is, however, Kafka's masterpiece, *The Castle*. This novel is Kafka's fullest expression of his sense of human existence, and, at the same time, of his experience as a writer. The two are here identified as the same eternal wandering this side of the goal. K., the hero of *The Castle*, is the most conscious of all Kafka's heroes. True to the lot he has chosen, K. rejects every place or advantage he wins in the village beneath the Castle: Frieda, his room in the inn, his job in the school, and, when at last he has an interview with a secretary from the Castle, he falls asleep! He rejects all things he attains, because, by the very fact that he reaches them, they all become only images of his goal. K. is driven, always, to go beyond whatever he has, to go beyond even Klamm, who belongs to the Castle: 'It was not Klamm's environment in itself that seemed to him worth striving for, but rather that he, K., he only and no one else, should attain to Klamm, and should attain to him not to rest with him, but to go on beyond him, farther yet, into the Castle' (1951, 146). One can see clearly that *The Castle*, like Kafka's other novels, was interminable, or could only end, as Max Brod has told us it was meant to end, with the death, by utter exhaustion, of the hero (though it is significant that Kafka never wrote the ending). The rejection of what one has reached for the sake of a goal which can never be reached can be repeated, must be repeated, again and again, forever.

Kafka remains, then, until the end, within an inner space which may expand indefinitely, or contract to nothing, but always remains the place of solitude, at the same distance from the unattainable paradise of possession. His plight is perpetual dying. It is exile in the desert, without the possibility of ever approaching closer to the goal. His fate might be defined as that of the Protestant who, having pushed to its extreme point the rejection of all mediation as idolatry, goes on to reject even the possibility of a Christ as Mediator: for Kafka believed that the coming of the Messiah would always remain an event to be expected in the future, that Christ would always come a day later than any day which might be named. 'The Messiah will only come when he is no longer necessary, he will only come a day after his arrival, he won't come on the last day, but on the last day of all' (1953a, 90; my trans.). [. . .]

For Kafka, obeying to the end the interdiction against idolatry, against the acceptance of any manifest Mediator, there was no way out of the world of endless wandering and contradiction. For Kafka there was a goal but no way, only endless wavering, and he chose to remain true to the wavering, to his 'deeper, uneasier skepticism': with infinite patience, he pushed on, ever farther and farther into the desert with each work, until, paradoxically, his work became the falsehood which testifies to the truth, the wavering that reveals the goal, even though the goal is never reached. For Kafka God remained '*absconditus*,' yet, in making this testimony, he did, in a way, testify to God's presence. And it is in this testimony to God in a time when he is absent that Kafka fulfills Auden's description of him as the most truly *exemplary* figure of our time.

10

Wallace Stevens's Poetry of Being

[. . .]
'The death of one god is the death of all' (1954, 381; see also Stevens 1957, 165). This evaporation of the gods, leaving a barren man in a barren land, is the basis of all Stevens's thought and poetry. The death of the gods coincides with a radical transformation in the way man sees the world. What had been a warm home takes on a look of hardness and emptiness, like the walls, floors, and banisters of a vacant house. Instead of being intimately possessed by man, things appear to close themselves within themselves. They become mute, static presences:

> To see the gods dispelled in mid-air and dissolve like clouds is one of the great human experiences. It is not as if they had gone over the horizon to disappear for a time; nor as if they had been overcome by other gods of greater power and profounder knowledge. It is simply that they came to nothing. Since we have always shared all things with them and have always had a part of their strength and, certainly, all of their knowledge, we shared likewise this experience of annihilation. It was their annihilation, not ours, and yet it left us feeling that in a measure, we, too, had been annihilated. It left us feeling dispossessed and alone in a solitude, like children without parents, in a home that seemed deserted, in which the amical rooms and halls had taken on a look of hardness and emptiness. What was most extraordinary is that they left no mementoes behind, no thrones, no mystic rings, no texts either of the soil or of the soul. It was as if they had never inhabited the earth. There was no crying out for their return. (1957, 206, 207)

There was no crying out for their return because we knew they would never come back. They would never come back because they had never been there at all.

In this impoverishing of the world when the gods disappear man discovers himself, orphaned and dispossessed, a solitary consciousness. Then are we truly 'natives of poverty, children of malheur' (1954, 322). The moment of self-awareness in Stevens coincides with the moment of the death of the gods. God is dead, therefore I am. But I am nothing. I am nothing because I have nothing, nothing but awareness of the barrenness within and without. When the gods dissolve like clouds they 'come to nothing.' When the gods come to nothing, man is 'nothing himself,' and, since this is so, he 'beholds / Nothing that is not there and the nothing that is' (1954, 10).

After the death of the gods and the discovery of nothingness Stevens is left in a world made of two elements: subject and object, mind and matter, imagination and reality. Imagination is the inner nothingness, while reality is the barren external world with which imagination carries on its endless intercourse. Stevens' problem is to reconcile the two. But such a reconciliation turns out to be impossible. This way and that vibrates his thought, seeking to absorb imagination by reality, to engulf reality in imagination, or to marry them in metaphor. Nothing will suffice, and Stevens is driven to search on tirelessly for some escape from conflict. This endless seeking is the motive and life of his poetry. The human self, for him, is divided against itself. One part is committed to the brute substance of earth, things as they are, and the other just as tenaciously holds to its need for imaginative grandeur. Self-division, contradiction, perpetual oscillation of thought – these are the constants in Stevens' work. Is it possible, as some critics have thought, that he is just confused? Is it from mere absence of mind that he affirms on one page of his *Adagia* that reality is the only genius (1957, 177), only to reverse himself two pages later and declare just as categorically that imagination is the only genius (1957, 179)?

The critic can develop radically different notions of Stevens' aims as a poet, and for each of these it is easy to find apposite passages from the text. It can be shown that Stevens believes poetry is metaphor, and that he believes all metaphors are factitious. At times he is unequivocally committed to bare reality. At other times he repudiates reality and sings the praises of imagination. Nor is it just a question of contradictions in the logical statements of the prose which are reconciled in the poetry. For each position and for its antithesis there are fully elaborated poems or parts of poems. It is impossible to find a single one-dimensional theory of poetry and life in Stevens. His poetry defines a realm in which everything 'is not what it is' (1957, 178). Such poetry is not dialectical, if that means a series of stages which build on one another, each transcending the last and moving on to a higher stage, in some version of the Hegelian sequence of thesis, antithesis, synthesis. At the beginning Stevens is already as far as he ever goes. After the disappearance of the gods the poet finds himself in a place where opposites are simultaneously true. It seems that this situation can be dealt with in poetry only by a succession of wild swings to one extreme or another, giving first one limit of the truth, then the other. To escape such oscillation Stevens must find a way to write poetry which will possess simultaneously both extremes.

The elaboration of such a mode of poetry is Stevens's chief contribution to literature. In the meditative poems of his later years he takes possession of a new domain. The finished unity of his early poems, which makes many of them seem like elaborately wrought pieces of jewelry, is gradually replaced by poems which are open-ended improvisations. Such poems are not a neat enclosure of words forming a complex organic unity. They begin in the middle of a thought, and their ending is arbitrary. 'The Man with the Blue Guitar' has a special place in Stevens's canon. It marks his turning to the new style. The reader has the feeling that the poem has been going on for some time when he hears the first words, and the last verses are not really an ending. The twanging of the strings continues interminably. Such a poem could be endless, and indeed three more 'Stanzas for "The Man with the Blue Guitar" ' are given in *Opus Posthumous* (1957, 72, 73). The man with the guitar is described in 'An Ordinary Evening in New Haven' as a permanent presence, some one always there in the mind's eye, watching the poet, and reminding him of his obligation to a faithful thinking of things as they are (1954, 483).

Life, for Stevens, is a series of states of consciousness with neither start nor finish. If the poem is to be true to life it must be a constant flowing of images which come as they come, and are not distorted by the logical mind in its eagerness for order. 'One's grand flights,' says Stevens, 'one's Sunday baths, / One's tootings at the weddings of the soul / Occur as they occur' (1954, 222). Just as 'The Man with the Blue Guitar' refuses to round itself off formally with beginning, middle, and end, so the parts which are given do not organize themselves into a whole, or even into part of a whole. There is no coherent pattern of symbols and metaphors, each one referring to all the others. One metaphor or symbol is introduced, developed for a while, then dropped. Another motif appears, is developed in its turn, disappears, is replaced by another which has no connection with the other two, and so on. 'The Man with the Blue Guitar' proceeds in a series of disconnected short flights, each persisting for only a brief span of time. Each short flight, while it lasts, is like a 'half-arc hanging in mid-air / Composed, appropriate to the incomplete' (1954, 309).

The same thing is true of Stevens's other long poems, 'Esthétique du Mal,' or 'Notes toward a Supreme Fiction,' or 'An Ordinary Evening in New Haven.' These poems keep close to the quality of life as it is. Such poems, like life, proceed in a series of momentary crystallizations or globulations of thought, followed by dissolution, and then re-conglomeration in another form. 'Thought,' says Stevens, 'tends to collect in pools' (1957, 170). A man's mental energy tends to organize itself momentarily in a certain shape, but life flows on, and a new pattern is called for. The mind has a powerful resistance to doing the same thing twice, and 'originality is an escape from repetition' (1957, 177). 'As a man becomes familiar with his own poetry,' says Stevens, 'it becomes as obsolete for himself as for anyone else. From this it follows that one of the motives in writing is renewal' (1957, 220). Stevens always emphasizes the evanescence of poetry. Poetry is like a snowflake fluttering through the air and dissolving in the sea. It is radically bound to a time experienced as a sequence of present moments, each real and valid only so long as it is present. 'Poetry,' says Stevens, 'is a finikin thing of air / That lives uncertainly and not for long' (1954, 155). In the *Adagia*, 'Poetry is a pheasant disappearing in the brush' (1957, 173). Most succinctly: 'A poem is a meteor' (1957, 158).

This fragmentary quality is evident in Stevens's titles, both those for individual poems and those for books. Each poem by itself, like the whole mass of them together, is a hesitant and uncertain movement toward a goal which is never reached. He calls a poem 'Prelude to Objects,' or 'Asides on the Oboe,' or 'Extracts from Addresses to the Academy of Fine Ideas,' or 'Debris of Life and Mind,' or 'Notes toward a Supreme Fiction,' or 'Prologues to What is Possible,' in each case emphasizing the broken, partial nature of the poem, the way it is a piece of something larger, or is only an indirect and incomplete movement toward its object, something preliminary and unfinished. The titles of his books of poetry suggest the same qualities. The harmonium is a small keyboard organ used in the home. The book of poems called *Harmonium* seems to be a series of improvisations on this amateur's instrument. But Stevens wanted to call his first book 'The Grand Poem: Preliminary Minutiae' (1961, viii). This title would have been a perfect expression of the nature of all his poems. 'Harmonium' too suggests something of this notion of tentative fragments. Stevens may have been remembering this, as well as trying to affirm the unity of his work, when he wanted to call his collected poems *The Whole of Harmonium* (1957, xiv). The titles of his other books are just as tentative: *Ideas of Order, Parts of a World, Transport to Summer* (in which one side of the pun gives the idea of motion in the direction of summer), and *The Auroras of Autumn* (an apt phrase to describe poems which are a flickering continuum of light). Only *The Rock* suggests something final and stable, but that title was affixed after Stevens had attained the ultimate immobility of death. All his poems taken together form a single poem. This poem is a long series of provisional pools of imagery, each drawn toward a goal which can never be named directly or embodied in any poem. Man can never live again in a unified homeland. 'We live in a constellation / Of patches and of pitches, / Not in a single world,' and we are therefore always 'Thinkers without final thoughts / In an always incipient cosmos' (1957, 114, 115).

Within the 'endlessly elaborating poem' (1954, 486) which is life, the same sequence of events is constantly happening over and over again. First something happens which 'decreates,' which destroys an earlier imagination of the world. Then man is left face to face with the bare rock of reality. This happens every year in autumn. When the leaves have all fallen, 'we return / To a plain sense of things,' and 'it is as if / We had come to an end of the imagination' (1954, 502). This clearing away is experienced not as a loss but as a gain. What is removed was a fictive covering of the rock, and what is exposed is the real in all its clarity:

> The barrenness that appears is an exposing.
> It is not part of what is absent, a halt
> For farewells, a sad hanging on for remembrances.

It is a coming on and a coming forth.
The pines that were fans and fragrances emerge,
Staked solidly in a gusty grappling with rocks.

(1954, 487)

The autumnal experience of decreation, as of leaves turning brown and falling, gives man a sense of 'cold and earliness and bright origin' (1954, 481). It is as if the poet were like the first man facing an 'uncreated' world, with everything still to be imagined.

This experience of coldness and earliness is only the start. The poet is not satisfied to confront a bare and unimagined world. He wants to possess it, and it can only be possessed by being imagined well. Man is inhabited by a 'will to change' (1954, 397) which is just as unappeasable as his will to see the rock of reality exposed in all its bareness. The experience of decreation is followed by the reconstruction of a new imagination of the world. Spring follows winter, the rock is covered with leaves which are the icon of the poem, and what had been the simplicity of beginning becomes the ornate complexity of the end. The poet moves from 'naked Alpha,' 'the infant A standing on infant legs' to 'hierophant Omega,' 'twisted, stooping, polymathic Z' (1954, 469). If the beginning is bare and simple, the end is multiple and encrusted with color, like an illuminated manuscript, or like a splendid robe of state, 'adorned with cryptic stones and sliding shines, . . . / With the whole spirit sparkling in its cloth, / Generations of the imagination piled / In the manner of its stitchings, of its thread' (1954, 434).

No sooner has the mind created a new fictive world than this 'recent imagining of reality' (1954, 465) becomes obsolete in its turn, and must be rejected. This rejection is the act of decreation, and returns man once more to unadorned reality. The cycle then begins again: imagining followed by decreation followed by imagining and so on for as long as life lasts. In this rhythmic alternation lies our only hope to possess reality. Each moment is born in newness and freedom, with no connections to the past. Man must match the ever-renewed freedom of time with an equally radical freedom on his own part, a willed disencumbering of himself of all the corpses of the past. This is the sense in which 'all men are murderers' (1957, 168), for 'Freedom is like a man who kills himself / Each night, an incessant butcher, whose knife / Grows sharp in blood' (1954, 292), and 'All things destroy themselves or are destroyed' (1957, 46). So Stevens cries: 'what good were yesterday's devotions?' (1954, 264). This refusal of the past gives him a possession of the present moment in all its instantaneous vitality: 'I affirm and then at midnight the great cat / Leaps quickly from the fireside and is gone' (1954, 264).

The present is the great cat who leaps from the fireside and is gone. It can never be seized or held and it lasts only for the blink of an eye. But if life is a series of such moments, how is it possible to justify even the cycle of decreation followed by a reimagining of reality? This cycle seems to move with a slow and stately turning, like the sequence of the seasons which is so often its image. If the poet pauses long enough to write the poem of winter it will already be part of the dead past long before he has finished it, and so for the poems of the other seasons. It seems that the poet will make sterile vibrations back and forth between one spiritual season and the other, always a little behind the perpetual flowing of reality.

There is one way to escape this impasse, and the discovery of this way gives its special character to all Stevens's later poetry. He can move so fast from one season to another that all the extreme postures of the spirit are present in a single moment. If he can do this he will never pause long enough at any extreme for it to freeze into dead fixity, and he will appease at last his longing to have both imagination and reality at once. An oscillation rapid enough becomes a blur in which opposites are touched simultaneously, as alternating current produces a steady beam of light, and the cycle of decreation and imagining, hopelessly false if the poet goes through it at leisure, becomes true at last to things as they are if he moves through it fast enough. Each tick of the clock is 'the starting point of the human and the end' (1954, 528). In 'this present' there is a 'dizzle-dazzle of being new / And of becoming,' 'an air of freshness, clearness, greenness, blueness, / That which is always beginning because it is part / Of that which is always beginning, over and over' (1954, 530). The present is always beginning over and over because it has no sooner begun than it has gone all the way to the end, and has moved so rapidly that 'this end and this beginning are one' (1954, 506). All the possible elements of experience are always present in every instant of time, and in every season or weather of the mind: consciousness in its emptiness detached from reality and seeking it in bare impoverishment, the imagination covering the rock with leaves, flowers, and fruit, the drying and falling of the leaves in autumn.

Stevens' *Collected Poems* moves in a stately round through the whole cycle of the seasons, from the gaudy, spring-like poems of *Harmonium*, like new buds on the rock, through *Transport to Summer* and *The Auroras of Autumn*, and then back again to winter's bareness with *The Rock*. Every authentic image, from one end of his poetry to the other, recapitulates this sequence in a breath. In 'Notes toward a Supreme Fiction' Stevens says that a true poem allows the reader to share, for a moment, the 'first idea.' This means having a vision of things in the radiance of their presence, without any intervening film between man and the pure sensation of things as they are. To do this, Stevens says, is to see things in 'living changingness' (1954, 380), to go in a moment from the white candor of the beginning in its original freshness to the white candor of the end in its multiplicity of imaginative enhancements. 'We move between these points: / From that ever-early candor to its late plural' (1954, 382).

In 'The Owl in the Sarcophagus' (1954, 431–6) Stevens gives his fullest dramatization of the way time moves from beginning to end in a moment. The poem is about 'the forms of thought,' that is, about the universal limits between which human thought moves, and in terms of which man lives, for 'we live in the mind.' If man lives in the mind he dies there too:

> It is a child that sings itself to sleep,
> The mind, among the creatures that it makes,
> The people, those by which it lives and dies.
>   (1954, 436)

Man dies in the mind because the mind too is bound by time. This means that it is defined by the fact that it will one day die. Life dwells within death, is constantly coming from and returning to death, as its origin, home, and end. The owl, Minerva, the mind, lives in a sarcophagus, and the poem describes 'the mythology of modern death' (1954, 435). It embodies the forces which determine the mind's activity, 'the creatures that it makes.' These forces are 'death's own supremest images, / The pure perfections of parental space, / The children of a desire that is the will, / Even of death, the beings of the mind / In the light-bound space of the mind, the floreate flare . . .' (1954, 436).

Since the figures of the poem live in the perpetual present of mental space, they live 'in an element not the heaviness of time' (1954, 432), that is, in 'a time / That of itself [stands] still, perennial' (1954, 432). The moment is 'less time than place' (1954, 433) because it is outside of time, though it is the only living part of time.

The figures of the mythology of modern death are three: sleep, peace, and 'she that says / Good-by in the darkness' (1954, 431). Sleep is the beginning, the radiant candor of pure mind without any content, mind as it is when it faces a bare unimagined reality, or mind as it is when it has completed the work of decreation, and is ready 'in an ever-changing, calmest unity' (1954, 433) to begin imagining again: 'Sleep realized / Was the whiteness that is the ultimate intellect, / A diamond jubilance beyond the fire' (1954, 433).

If sleep is the beginning, peace is the end, 'the brother of sleep,' 'the prince of shither-shade and tinsel lights' (1954, 434). 'Peace after death' is the end in the sense that it represents a fulfillment of imagination. Sleep is prior to life, since ultimate intellect cannot even be called consciousness, or is consciousness with no content. Peace is the death at the end of life, the death of a consummation of the imagination. Peace, like sleep, is that death man touches in every moment as he moves all the way from the immaculate beginning to its late plural. Peace is 'that figure stationed at our end, / Always, in brilliance, fatal, final, formed / Out of our lives to keep us in our death' (1954, 434).

What of the third figure, 'she that says good-by,' who is she? She broods over the moment of life, the infinitesimally brief flash between start and finish which is living reality, surrounded on all sides by death. She dwells in what Stevens calls in another poem 'the mobile and the immobile flickering / In the area between is and was' (1954, 474). This moment, evanescent as it is, is the only reality, and it is only in the moment, a moment which changes and evaporates with the utmost rapidity, that man can glimpse things as they are. Things exist only in the time they are moving from is to was, and the third figure is the embodiment of this presence of the present, a presence which is like that of a glow in molten iron, such a glow as fades even as we watch it.

How is it possible to write poetry which will match the mobility of the moment? It would seem that any image or form of words would be too fixed to move with a time which changes so instantaneously. A poem of any length would be far too long to be a meteor. It would transform the living flow of reality into a clumsy machine wholly unable to keep up with time. Such a poem would be a dead relic of the past long before the reader had reached the last line.

Stevens gradually develops, as his poetry progresses, a way of matching the fluidity of time. He comes to write a poetry of flickering mobility, a poetry in which each phrase moves so rapidly it has beginning and ending at once. Instead of being fixed and unyielding, a solid piece of language interacting with other words, each image recapitulates within itself the coming into being of the moment and its disappearance. The fluctuation between beginning and ending has become so rapid that it takes place in a single phrase, or in a 'syllable between life / And death' (1954, 432). Each image in a poem of such phrases is a meteor. 'An Ordinary Evening in New Haven,' for example, constantly generates itself out of its own annihilation, ending and beginning again indefatigably. It expresses, in its 'flickings from finikin to fine finkin,' 'the endings and inchings of final form, / The swarming activities of the formulae / Of statement, directly and indirectly getting at' (1954, 488).

At first, after the dissolution of the gods, it seemed that Stevens was left, like post-Cartesian man in general, in a world riven in two, split irreparably into subject and object, imagination and reality. All his work seems based on this dualism. Any attempt to escape it by affirming the priority of one or the other power leads to falsehood. But as his work progresses, Stevens comes more and more to discover that there is after all only one realm, always and everywhere the realm of some new conjunction of imagination and reality. Imagination is still present in the most absolute commitment of the mind to reality, and reality is still there in the wildest imaginary fiction. The later Stevens is beyond metaphysical dualism, and beyond representational thinking. In his late poems it is no longer a question of some reality which already exists out there in the world, and of which the poet then makes an image. The image is inextricably part of the thing, and the most extreme imaginative 'distortion' is still based on reality. There is only one ever-present existence: consciousness of some reality. Imagination is reality, or, as Stevens says: 'poetry and reality are one' (Stevens 1951, 81). In another formulation: 'the structure of poetry and the structure of reality are one' (1951, 81). If this is the case, then there is no real thing which is transformed into various imaginary aspects. The real thing is already imagined, and 'imaginative transcripts' are as much a part of reality as anything else is.

'What our eyes behold,' says Stevens, 'may well be the text of life but one's meditations on the text and the disclosures of these meditations are no less a part of the structure of reality' (1951, 76). As he puts it in the title of a very late poem: 'Reality Is an Activity of the Most August Imagination' (1957, 110).

This discovery of the identity of all the elements of life means a redefinition of poetry. Words are not pictures of reality. They are part of the thing, tangled inextricably with the event they describe. 'The poem is the cry of its occasion, / Part of the res itself and not about it' (1954, 473), and therefore 'description is revelation' (1954, 344). Words are the vortex of the whirlpool, where imagination and reality merge, for 'words of the world are the life of the world' (1954, 474).

This seems to be Stevens's ultimate position: a resolution of imagination and reality in a theory of the identity of poetry and life, and the development of a poetry of flickering mobility to sustain this identity. But there is one more aspect of his thought, and this is the most difficult to see or to say.

It begins with an increasing movement toward nothingness in Stevens's later poetry. Along with the phrases expressing the swarming plenitude of the moment there is something different. At the same time as its tensions are resolved, Stevens's poetry gets more and more disembodied, more and more a matter of 'the spirit's alchemicana,' and less and less a matter of the solid and tangible, the pears on their dish, the round peaches with their fuzz and juice. It seems as if the poetry becomes more and more intangible as the oscillations between imagination and reality get more and more rapid, until, at the limit, the poem evaporates altogether. At the extreme of speed all solidity disappears. It is as if the same speed which allows beginning and ending to merge also releases something else: a glimpse of the nothingness which underlies all existence.

The word or the idea of nothingness comes back more and more often. Nothingness appears as early as *Harmonium*, but there it is associated with the bareness of winter. Only the snow man, the man who is 'nothing himself,' is free of imagination's fictions and can behold 'nothing that is not there and the nothing that is.' Stevens's later poetry is continuous with this early intuition of nothing, but the theme of nothingness gradually becomes more dominant. In the later poetry nothingness appears to be the source and end of everything, and to underlie everything as its present reality. Imagination is nothing. Reality is nothing. The mind is nothing. Words are nothing. God is nothing. Perhaps it is the fact that all these things are equivalent to nothing which makes them all equivalents of one another. All things come together in the nothing. Stevens speaks of 'the priest of nothingness who intones' on the rock of reality (1957, 88). In another poem the wind 'intones its single emptiness' (1954, 294). He tells of a room 'emptier than nothingness' (1954, 286) or of a moon which is 'a lustred nothingness' (1954, 320). He asks for a 'god in the house' who will be so insubstantial that he will be 'a coolness, / A vermilioned nothingness' (1954, 328), and speaks of metaphysical presences which are like 'beasts that one never sees, / Moving so that the foot-falls are slight and almost nothing' (1954, 337). Again and again he says that all things, 'seen and unseen,' are 'created from nothingness' (1954, 486; 1957, 100), or 'forced up from nothing' (1954, 363). The growth of leaves on the rock of reality comes from nothing, 'as if,' says Stevens, 'nothingness contained a metier' (1954, 526). In another poem, the first breath of spring 'creates a fresh universe out of nothingness' (1954, 517).

The rock of reality seems not to be a substantial reality, material and present before the poet's eyes. It seems to have come from nothingness. If it has come from nothingness, its source still defines it, and all things dwell in the 'stale grandeur of annihilation' (1954, 505). As Stevens says in a striking phrase: 'Reality is a vacuum' (1957, 168).

A number of his poems attempt to express the way reality is a vacuum. In such poems 'we breathe / An odor evoking nothing, absolute' (1954, 394, 395). 'A Clear Day and No Memories' (1957, 113) describes a weather in which 'the air is clear of everything,' 'has no knowledge except of nothingness,' and 'flows over us without meanings' in an 'invisible activity.' 'Chocorua to Its Neighbor' (1954, 296–302) is an extraordinarily disembodied poem, the subject of which is a strange shadow, 'an eminence, / But of nothing' (1954, 300). In *The Auroras of Autumn* a serpent is present everywhere in the landscape, and yet present as form disappearing into formlessness:

> This is where the serpent lives, the bodiless.
> His head is air . . .
> ★   ★   ★
> This is where the serpent lives. This is his nest,
> These fields, these hills, these tinted distances,
> And the pines above and along and beside the sea.
> This is form gulping after formlessness,
> Skin flashing to wished-for disappearances
> And the serpent body flashing without the skin.
>   (1954, 411)

Such poems accomplish a hollowing out or subtilizing of reality. They give the reader the feeling of what it is like to see reality not as a solid substance, but as something less tangible than the finest mist. They attempt to make visible something which is 'always too heavy for the sense / To seize, the obscurest as, the distant was' (1954, 441). They are based on the presupposition that the center of reality is a nothingness which is 'a nakedness, a point, / Beyond which fact could not progress as fact. / . . . Beyond which thought could not progress as thought' (1954, 402, 403). If it is true that the underlying substance of reality is a vacuum, 'the dominant blank, the unapproachable' (1954, 477), then we must give up the idea that reality is a solid rock, and see it as a nameless, evanescent flowing, something hovering on the edge of oblivion. 'It is not in the premise that reality / Is a solid,' says Stevens in the last words of 'An

Ordinary Evening in New Haven.' 'It may be a shade that traverses / A dust, a force that traverses a shade' (1954, 489).

If reality is a vacuum, imagination is no less empty. It is the 'nothing' of 'Imago' (1954, 439), which lifts all things. Man in a world where reality is nonentity 'has his poverty and nothing more' (1954, 427). Such a man is defined as 'desire,' and is 'always in emptiness that would be filled' (1954, 467).

It seemed that Stevens was moving closer and closer to a full possession of the plenitude of things, but as the tension between imagination and reality diminishes there is an unperceived emptying out of both, until, at the moment they touch, in the brevity of a poem which includes beginning and ending in a breath, the poet finds himself face to face with a universal nothing.

Nevertheless, this apparent defeat is the supreme victory, for the nothing is not nothing. It is. It is being. Being is the universal power, visible nowhere in itself, and yet visible everywhere in all things. It is what all things share through the fact that they are. Being is not a thing like other things, and therefore can appear to man only as nothing, yet it is what all things participate in if they are to exist at all. All Stevens' later poetry has as its goal the releasing of the evanescent glimpse of being which is as close as man can come to a possession of the ground of things. The paradoxical appearance to man of being in the form of nothing is the true cause of the ambiguity of his poetry. Man's inability to see being as being causes the poet to say of it: 'It is and it / Is not and, therefore, is' (1954, 440), and yet in the supreme moments of insight he can speak directly of it, in lines which are a cry of ecstatic discovery:

> It is like a thing of ether that exists
> Almost as predicate. But it exists,
> It exists, it is visible, it is, it is.
> (1954, 418)

The nothing is, but it is not merely the nothingness of consciousness. Human nature participates in being, but so do all other existences. Wherever the poet thinks to catch it, it disappears, melting into the landscape and leaving just the pines and rock and water which are there, or being absorbed into the mind and taking the mind's own shape: 'If in the mind, he vanished, taking there / The mind's own limits, like a tragic thing / Without existence, existing everywhere' (1954, 298). Being is released in the flash of time from is to was, just as it is released in the expansion of perception to occupy space. Being is the presentness of things present, the radiance of things as they are, and is therefore 'physical if the eye is quick enough' (1954, 301).

In two late poems, 'Metaphor as Degeneration' (1954, 444) and 'The River of Rivers in Connecticut' (1954, 533) Stevens sees being as a river, hidden behind all the appearances that tell of it, and yet flowing everywhere, through all space and time, and through all the contents of space and time. In these two poems he gives his most succinct expression of his apprehension of being:

It is certain that the river

Is not Swatara. The swarthy water
That flows round the earth and through the skies,
Twisting among the universal spaces,

Is not Swatara. It is being.

(1954, 444)

It is not to be seen beneath the appearances
That tell of it. The steeple at Farmington
Stands glistening and Haddam shines and sways.

It is the third commonness with light and air,
A curriculum, a vigor, a local abstraction . . .
Call it, once more, a river, an unnamed flowing,

Space-filled, reflecting the seasons, the folk-lore
Of each of the senses; call it, again and again,
The river that flows nowhere, like a sea.

(1954, 533)

At the heart of Stevens's poetry there is a precise metaphysical experience. Or, rather, this experience is beyond metaphysics, since the tradition of metaphysics is based on a dualism putting ultimate being in some transcendent realm, above and beyond what man can see. Being, for Stevens, is within things as they are, here and now, revealed in the glistening of the steeple at Farmington, in the flowing of time, in the presentness of things present, in the interior fons of man.

Stevens' experience of being is 'a difficult apperception,' 'disposed and re-disposed / By such slight genii in such pale air' (1954, 440). To speak directly of this apperception, to analyze it, is almost inevitably to falsify it, to fix it in some abstraction, and therefore to kill it. Though man participates in being, he does not confront it directly. It is the center of which each man is an eccentric particle, for he is always 'helplessly at the edge' (1954, 430). When he tries to grasp it, it disappears. Man can never possess 'the bouquet of being' (1957, 109), that fugitive aroma. The best we can do is 'to realize / That the sense of being changes as we talk' (1957, 109), and go on talking in the hope that if we are careful to see that 'nothing [is] fixed by a single word' (1957, 114), nothing will be, in another sense, fixed momentarily in a word, and we shall have another evanescent insight into being.

The only passage in Stevens's prose which speaks directly of his perception of being, 'that nobility which is our spiritual height and depth' (1951, 33, 34), is curiously evasive. It is evasive because its subject is evasive. There is *something* there, Stevens says, but it can only be described negatively, for to define it is to fix it, and it must not be fixed:

I mean that nobility which is our spiritual height and depth; and while I know how difficult it is to express it, nevertheless I am bound to give a sense of it. Nothing could be more evasive and inaccessible. Nothing distorts itself and seeks disguise more quickly. There is a shame of disclosing it and in its definite presentations a horror of it. But there it is. The fact that it is there is what makes it possible to invite to the reading and writing of poetry men of intelligence and desire for life. I am not thinking of the ethical or the sonorous or at all of the manner of it. The manner of it is, in fact, its difficulty, which each man must feel each day differently, for himself. I am not thinking of the solemn, the portentous or demoded. On the other hand, I am evading a definition. If it is defined, it will be fixed and it must not be fixed. As in the case of an external thing, nobility resolves itself into an enormous number of vibrations, movements, changes. To fix it is to put an end to it. (1951, 33, 34)

To fix it is to put an end to it, but in poetry it can be caught unfixed. The mobile, flickering poetry of Stevens's later style, poetry which fears stillness beyond anything, is more than a revelation of the impossibility of escaping the war of the mind and sky. It is a revelation of being. The poem names being, the human-like figure which the mind is always confronting at every extreme, but which it is never able to catch and immobilize in words. The nothing which makes it impossible ever to rest, which makes nonsense of any attempt to express things rationally, and which always drives the poet on to another effort to seize the nothing by marrying imagination and reality – this nothing turns out to be being. The poetry of flittering metamorphosis is the only poetry which is simultaneously true to both imagination and reality, and it is the only poetry which will catch being. Being is 'the dominant blank, the unapproachable,' but it is nevertheless the source of everything, all man sees and all he is. The ultimate tragedy is that being is transformed instantaneously into nothing, and therefore though the poet has it he has it as an absence. Only a poetry of iridescent frettings will remain in touch with it, for 'life / Itself is like a poverty in the space of life, / So that the flapping of wind . . . / Is something in tatters that [man] cannot hold' (1954, 298, 299). Being is inherent in human nature, but it is inherent as a center which can never be embraced. In the process of going in a moment through the whole cycle from A to Z something is released, glimpsed, and annihilated, like those atomic particles which live only a millionth of a second. This something is being. As soon as it is named, it disappears, takes the limits of the mind, or melts into the limited existence of the object. But for a moment it is seen. 'It is and it / Is not and, therefore, is.'

The motive for rapid motion in Stevens's poetry is not only that speed reconciles imagination and reality. Speed also makes possible a vision of being – in the moment of its disappearance. After reading one of Stevens's poems the reader has the feeling that, after all, nothing has happened, no change of the world such as science or technology can perform: 'And yet nothing has been changed except what is / Unreal, as if nothing had been changed at all' (1957, 117). At the end it *was* there. It is already part of the past. Poetry is a pheasant disappearing in the brush, So Santayana, in 'To an Old Philosopher in Rome,' lives 'on the threshold of heaven,' and sees things double, things and the presence of being in things, 'The extreme of the known in the presence of the extreme / Of the unknown' (1954, 508). To see things transfigured in this way is still to see them just as they are, in all their barrenness and poverty. This world and the other are 'two alike in the make of the mind' (1954, 508), and the old philosopher's ultimate insight, like Stevens' own, is not at all a vision of things beyond this world:

> It is a kind of total grandeur at the end,
> With every visible thing enlarged and yet
> No more than a bed, a chair and moving nuns,
> The immensest theatre, the pillared porch,
> The book and candle in your ambered room . . .
>
> (1954, 510)

But merely to see being in things is not enough. Being must be spoken. The speaking of poetry liberates being in the presence of things. Through words man participates in being, for words of the world are the life of the world, and 'the word is the making of the world, / The buzzing world and lisping firmament' (1954, 345). Poetry does not name something which has already been perceived, or put in words a pre-existent mental conception. The act of naming brings things together, gathers them into one, and makes present the things which are present. Speaking belongs to being, and in naming things in their presence poetry releases a glimpse of being.

From De Quincey through Arnold and Browning to Hopkins, Yeats, and Stevens the absence of God is starting point and basis. Various poets, Browning or Yeats for example, beginning in this situation are able to make a recovery of immanence. Perhaps it is Stevens's way, the movement from the dissolution of the gods to the difficult apperception of being, which represents the next step forward in the spiritual history of man. Stevens may be in the vanguard of a movement 'toward the end of ontology,' as Jean Wahl calls it (1956). Central in this movement is the idea that all our spiritual height and depth is available here and now or nowhere. The last stanza of 'A Primitive like an Orb' is one of Stevens's most eloquent statements of his belief that all the words and all the experiences of man are part of being, eccentric particles of the giant 'at the centre on the horizon,' the giant who can never be fully possessed or spoken in any words, but who is shared by all. If this is the case, then the simplest phrase, in all its limitation, is indeed 'the human end in the spirit's greatest reach' (1954, 508):

> That's it. The lover writes, the believer hears,
> The poet mumbles and the painter sees,
> Each one, his fated eccentricity,
> As a part, but part, but tenacious particle,

Of the skeleton of the ether, the total
Of letters, prophecies, perceptions, clods
Of color, the giant of nothingness, each one
And the giant ever changing, living in change.

(1954, 443)

Responses III

'Poised in their irreconciliation: Loss and Recovery in J. Hillis Miller's Twentieth-Century Occasions
Thomas Albrecht

> If *Mrs. Dalloway* is organized around the contrary penchants of rising and falling, these motions are not only opposites, but are also ambiguously similar. They change places bewilderingly, so that down and up, falling and rising, death and life, isolation and communication, are mirror images of one another rather than a confrontation of negative and positive orientations of the spirit.
>
> '*Mrs. Dalloway*: Repetition as the Raising of the Dead'

The three essays by J. Hillis Miller collected here under the rubric 'Twentieth-Century Occasions' offer no unifying claims about twentieth-century literature, though they do share an attention to figures of unity in the specific texts they examine. They put forth no master or trope that would decisively link the writings of Woolf, Kafka, and Stevens to one another or to some totalized conception of twentieth-century thought. They are not connected by means of any obvious thread. Like the characters in *Mrs. Dalloway*, each must be taken in terms of its separateness, its *singular* occasion. Yet as much as these essays are irreducibly different from one another, each traces a similar movement in the texts it considers: a movement between the recognition of an existential threat, and the (attempted and partially successful) overcoming of that threat by means of writing. Following these parallel movements in Miller's essays, as Miller follows them in the texts he reads, ultimately leads to a questioning, rather than a confirmation, of received ideas from literary history about the characteristic 'negativity' and 'nihilism' of exemplary twentieth-century writers like Woolf, Stevens, and Kafka. It also leads to a questioning of received ideas about Miller's own writings.

In all three essays, Hillis Miller is interested in the association of literature with rescue or salvation; this salvation takes the form of a joining or rejoining of things that are apart or have been severed. For Miller, figures of separation and disconnection indicate a shared predicament in the texts of Woolf, Kafka, and Stevens. Both the Kafka essay and the Stevens essay begin with a rupture between the human community and God. The rupture then extends to a broader isolation of the self from anyone and anything that is in some way outside of itself: the minds of other people, external reality, the law, the community, the past, the future, the present moment. Kafka's writings open up 'a long, patient, and exhaustive analysis of what it means to be outside of everything, even outside of oneself.' In Stevens's poetry, the divided self, 'orphaned and dispossessed, a solitary consciousness,' finds itself unable to reconcile subject and object, mind and matter, imagination and reality. And Woolf's novel *Mrs. Dalloway*, Miller writes, 'seems to be based on an irreconcilable opposition between individuality and universality,' on irreconcilable divisions that separate the minds of the individual characters not only from the larger whole of which they are a tenuous part, but from one another.

The work of literature, it seems, provides the possibility of an antidote against these separations. For Kafka, literature offers the conviction that his sense of inner chaos and emptiness might reveal itself as an inner harmony and totality, one which could be liberated and externalized into an outer totality, the perfect literary work. This conviction not only revives but reconnects Kafka's inner and outer worlds: 'Literature was not simply the salvation of his own poor identity; it was also the salvation of the world itself,' because the world has through the power of literary language assumed the immutable form of words and images. Similarly, Stevens's late poetry achieves a reconciliation of the inner and outer worlds through its recognition that imagination and reality are not mutually opposed, but necessarily co-present at any instant. This recognition moves the later Stevens 'beyond metaphysical dualism, and beyond representational thinking,' towards a conception of poetry as performative utterance. For such a conception, words and things are not in a broken mimetic relation, but fundamentally inextricable: 'This seems to be Stevens's ultimate position: a resolution of imagination and reality in a theory of the identity of poetry and life, and the development of a poetry of flickering mobility to sustain this identity.' For Virginia Woolf, meanwhile, it is the conceit of the ubiquitous omniscient narrator ('something central which permeated') that is able to guarantee reassuring connections and continuities between past and present, between the narrator's universal consciousness and the individual consciousnesses of the characters, and between one character's mind and another's.

A telling metaphor in Miller's essays for the connecting and illuminating power of literature is the recurring figure of a meteor. Tracing Wallace Stevens's elaboration of a poetry that would join together reality and imagination, Miller quotes the line 'A poem is a meteor,' and goes on to extend this metaphor in his discussion of what he calls Stevens's 'poetry of flickering mobility.' It is by the light of this kind of poetry (and by the light of this image of poetry) that subject and object will be rejoined. The meteor designates the intense speed, the brief flashes of imagery, and the flickering luminosity that would allow Stevens's poetry to unite imagination and reality in rapid oscillations between imagining, creation, dissolution, reimagining, recreation, dissolution, and so on. But even as Miller associates it on the one hand with the reconciliation of a seemingly irreconcilable division, the meteor is a fundamentally ambiguous image. It evokes at once powerful illumination and evanescence, so any lasting reconciliation by means of poetry is put into doubt. In the section on literature as potential salvation in 'Franz Kafka and the Metaphysics of Alienation,' Miller writes, 'Kafka's early diaries are full of . . . stories which start off strongly, create their own world in a few powerful sentences, and then suddenly and abruptly stop, like meteors which glow brightly in rarefied air, but are burnt up in a moment by the lower atmosphere and return to darkness.' The image of a momentary light and a subsequent return to darkness appears as well in slightly modified form in *Mrs. Dalloway*, in a passage in which the narrator articulates Rezia Smith's painful consciousness of her own solitude:

> There was nobody. Her words faded. So a rocket fades. Its sparks, having grazed their way into the night, surrender to it, dark descends, pours over the outlines of houses and towers; bleak hillsides soften and fall in. But though they are gone, the night is full of them; robbed of colour, blank of windows, they exist more ponderously, give out what frank daylight fails to transmit – the trouble of things conglomerated there in the darkness; huddled together in the darkness; reft of the relief which dawn brings when, washing the walls white and grey, spotting each windowpane, lifting the mist from the fields, showing the red-brown cows peacefully grazing, all is once more decked out to the eye; exists again. I am alone; I am alone! she cried, by the fountain in Regent's Park . . . such was her darkness. (23–4)

Although Miller does not refer to this moment in his essay on *Mrs. Dalloway*, Rezia's predicament here mirrors that of the writer in the Stevens and Kafka essays. Utterance is like a rocket or meteor that briefly illuminates, then surrenders to the darkness. What Woolf's passage adds to the above versions of the trope is the association of the subsequent darkness with a renewed feeling of solitude and disconnection: Rezia's sense of being alone even on a beautiful midmorning in a busy park, the 'trouble of things' given out by the neighboring houses and towers that are isolated from one another by the night's darkness. It seems that the brief and reassuring illumination by means of words only reinforces and intensifies a subsequent feeling of being in darkness.

    The figure of the meteor's sudden and temporary brilliance already implies the destruction of the very saving power of literature it designates. In all three of Miller's essays, there is a strong counter-movement which follows and undoes the initial movement towards literature as salvation or union. In the Stevens's essay, Miller calls this counter-movement 'an increasing movement towards nothingness.' He describes it as the gradual disintegration of a solid body, or (somewhat differently) as the revelation that what had *seemed* a solid body is in actuality an aggregate cluster of incandescent, insubstantial particles:

> At the same time that its tensions are resolved, Stevens' poetry gets more and more disembodied . . . and less and less of a matter of the solid and the tangible . . . It seems as if the poetry becomes more and more intangible as the oscillations between imagination and reality get more and more rapid, until, at the limit, the poem evaporates altogether. At the extreme of speed all solidity disappears. It is as if the same speed which allows beginning and ending to merge also releases something else: a glimpse of the nothingness which underlies all existence.

For Stevens, Miller writes, this process of evaporation culminates in what would seem to be a complete defeat of literature as antidote against nothingness, a complete emptying out of both imagination and reality. Miller's essay on Kafka introduces the figure of disintegration in a similar context, and similarly relates it to 'the collapse of the attempt to identify literature and salvation.' The following lines ostensibly refer to the execution machine in 'The Penal Colony,' but they also evoke once again the evaporating meteor: 'the world of words in Kafka undergoes a hideous process of disintegration in which piece after piece, driven by some irresistible internal compulsion, bursts out of its place, and rolls senselessly away, until finally the entire structure is reduced to dispersed and meaningless fragments.' For Miller's reading of Kafka, the disintegration of the literary work designates the return within literature itself of an irreconcilable separation, specifically the separation of image and reality. The images we create of things only reinforce and remind us of our separation from the things themselves. They make things attainable and also unattainable, present and also absent. In this sense, literature is for Kafka as much a form of death or destruction as a giving of immutable form to things.

In the essay '*Mrs. Dalloway*: Repetition as the Raising of the Dead,' the counter-movement against literature as salvation is implicit in the failure of the characters to 'build up,' in the temporariness and spuriousness of their attempts to assemble and to connect. It is implicit in Clarissa's final recognition of death as the only place of true communion, reality, and authenticity. The novel implicates not only the actions and words of the individual characters, but the unifying embrace of the omniscient narrator, in its indictment of 'all speech, all social action, all building it up, all forms of communication' as lies, as forms of destruction or obscuring. Like Kafka's writings that culminate in a death for which literature is responsible, Woolf's novel seems to end with an awareness of a death of which literature is at best a defacing or compromise. The Stevens essay, by contrast, concludes on an ostensibly more affirmative note, when poetry's 'apparent defeat' becomes its 'supreme victory,' when the perception of nothing is redeemed into a poetry of being, a poetry beyond metaphysics and ontology, 'the next step in the spiritual history of man.' But *Mrs. Dalloway* seems to end up decisively privileging death over life, isolation over communion, falling over rising. Kafka's texts seem to end up privileging separation over union, endless wandering over arrival, God's absence over his presence, exile over home, wavering over the way. These conclusions, however negative, are also fundamentally reassuring since they confirm received ideas about the characteristic nihilism of Woolf and Kafka.

But Miller's readings of Woolf and Kafka do not simply culminate in an abyss of isolation and death. In both essays, there is another turn, another movement, one that is perhaps easier to overlook than the prior movement back towards the negative. This final move is both a positive recuperation of the negative insight, and a placing of the negative and positive movements into a state of mutual suspension. In 'Mrs. Dalloway: Repetition as the Raising of the Dead,' Miller signals this step only briefly and discreetly: 'There is, however, one more structural element in Mrs. Dalloway, one final twist which reverses the polarities once more, or rather which holds them poised in their irreconciliation.' He proposes that while the novel 'seems almost nihilistically to recommend the embrace of death,' it also performs through death a kind of rescue or preservation from death. This preservation takes the form of words on the page, words that generate their own reality. As Kafka recognized and as Miller points out, the preservation of people and things in words depends on the absence or death of those people and things in the everyday world. In Mrs. Dalloway, Septimus has to die and Clarissa has to die vicariously through him, so that she can figuratively be reborn and return to the living. To Miller, this crossing, in which the living must die so that the dead can be resurrected, is the condition of literary preservation, of Clarissa's entry into the realm of communication in death, and of the revelation of that realm in language. Literature designates at once the existence of the things it names in words, and their absence from the everyday world. Thus 'writing is the only action which exists simultaneously on both sides of the mirror, within death and within life at once.' Life and death cannot be opposed or synthesized in Mrs. Dalloway, as two contrary movements of the spirit. Rather, as Miller puts it, they are poised in their irreconciliation, like two sides of an irony, like Septimus's plunge into death and Clarissa's simultaneous resurrection from death.

Miller's reading of Mrs. Dalloway is irreducible to demonstrating either a predominantly affirmative or nihilistic vision on Woolf's part; it is rather suspended in a place between life and death, presence and absence, resurrection and plunging, a place in which the constitutive terms of those oppositions are themselves radically refigured. Its conclusions about literature as a form of absence generating the material presence of what it names are structurally analogous to the paradoxical conclusions about Kafka's work in 'Franz Kafka and the Metaphysics of Alienation,' where the falsehood of literature testifies to truth, wavering indicates a way, and the revelation of God's absence testifies to his presence. They are also not unlike the endpoint of 'Wallace Stevens's Poetry of Being,' where poetic utterance reveals being, but only as an absence, as being glimpsed and then annihilated instantaneously into nothing. So even if Miller's final remarks about *Mrs. Dalloway* are not the kind of positive recuperation that could be meaningfully opposed to or synthesized with a negative counterpart, they give an affirmation of literary narrative as potential resurrection: 'The possibility that repetition in narrative is the representation of a transcendent spiritual realm of reconciliation and preservation, a realm of the perpetual resurrection of the dead, is more straightforwardly proposed by Virginia Woolf than by most of her predecessors in English literature,' that is to say by her seemingly less nihilistic and ambiguous predecessors like George Eliot, Thackeray, and Hardy. At the beginning of the essay Miller claims that 'It would be as true to say that [Woolf] investigates implications of . . . traditional conventions of form as to say that she brings something new into fiction.' His conclusion locates the transformative and transcendent possibility of literature in the former, in Woolf's often overlooked investigations of traditional novelistic conventions, especially in her omniscient and all-remembering narrator. What Miller takes away from received notions about Woolf as nihilistic advocate of death and as stylistic innovator he makes up for by the strangely reconciling Virginia Woolf encountered in his text.

The essay on Kafka begins with a citation from W. H. Auden: 'Had one to name the artist who comes nearest to bearing the same kind of relation to our age that Dante, Shakespeare, and Goethe bore to theirs, Kafka is the first we would think of.' While Auden does not specify the relation between the artist and the age, Miller takes it as exemplarity: 'it is in this testimony to God in a time when he is absent that Kafka fulfills Auden's description of him as the most truly *exemplary* figure of our time.' In qualifying Kafka's exemplarity, Miller ultimately stresses his testimony to God's presence, not to God's absence. This is easy to miss, especially since Miller has claimed earlier about Kafka (as he does about Stevens) that it is the emphasis on the disappearance of God that makes Kafka so representative of our time: 'Doubtless it is Kafka's acute consciousness of his irrevocable alienation . . . that earns him his place as the most representative figure in twentieth-century literature. For our time is . . . the time of distress, the time when the link between God and man is broken.' By the end of the essay, Miller has placed the doubtlessness of his statement into doubt. This turn is significant not only for his understanding of Kafka, but for our understanding of Miller's own works.

The essays on Kafka (1957, published under the name J. Hillis Miller, Jr.!) and Stevens (1964) can be classified as examples of Miller's early phenomenological criticism, a kind of analysis commonly associated with affirmation, with revealing the consistency of an authorial consciousness, 'the original unity of a creative mind' (1958, ix). The Woolf essay (from 1982's *Fiction and Repetition*), on the other hand, can be identified with Miller's later move into deconstruction, a kind of criticism commonly associated with an emphasis on 'nihilism,' an emphasis on revealing disconnections and separations. Yet any reading of the actual essays does not sustain these categories and definitions. Not unlike the way Woolf's, Kafka's, and Stevens's texts defy our expectations about their characteristic negativity, Hillis Miller's work (as exemplified by the three essays discussed here) would hardly give support to a scheme of the history of literary criticism, or to a narrative scheme of Miller's career, which sees the later deconstructive writings as more negative, more nihilistic, or more ambiguous than the earlier phenomenological writings.

'When the Gods Dissolve like Clouds': Modernism, Modernity, and the Space of Literature
Arkady Plotnitsky

The nature of the literary works and the phenomenon of literary modernism discussed in the essays of J. Hillis Miller – and how they are discussed or, better, *read* there – further complicate an already difficult task of responding to these essays, the task that would be difficult even within much larger limits than those of these brief remarks. Indeed, in a certain sense, this task is impossible within any limits. For, we are now compelled to view the space of literature and the space of reading themselves thus opened as structurally, irreducibly nonsimple, insofar as their complexity cannot be reduced to the ultimate set of simple elements from which it is built. Any attempt to reach such elementary building blocks always arrives at the complexity at least as great as the one with which we begin. There could, accordingly, be no single map or even a containable set of maps or an atlas that would allow one to ultimately map the space(s) of this literature or the space(s) of these readings, ultimately defeating the very conception of spatiality or indeed any possible conception or figure in figuring (out) the nature of such spaces. This view itself is in part shaped by J. Hillis Miller's work and the work of such authors, to name those arguably closest to Miller, as Maurice Blanchot, Jacques Derrida, and Paul de Man, and their key precursors, and by certain literary authors, at least in a certain type of reading, such as that offered by Miller here. The space of literature is Blanchot's famous phrase, which J. Hillis Miller promptly invokes in his reading of Franz Kafka (a key figure for Blanchot in this context) in 'Franz Kafka and the Metaphysics of Alienation.' One might, however, equally speak of the space of reading, which this literature demands and which Miller's readings inhabit. The thought and practice of these authors (again, literary authors included) gives both expressions, the space of literature and the space of reading, a radical meaning, beginning with the irreducible complexity and un-mapping-ness – the unavoidable residue of any mapping –

that defines these spaces and extending to their ultimate un-figurability as spaces, including in terms of space itself. Blanchot (who, it may be noted, is also a writer of fiction, discussed by other figures here mentioned) relates the question of literature to the possibility of a certain 'unfigurable Universe' (the term, he also notes, 'henceforth deceptive'), which is also the universe or un-universe of the unfigurable (Blanchot 1993, 350). For, the irreducible residue of all mapping just invoked tells us that it may not be possible to see the topology of this 'space' or, at least, a certain residual (it is actually more primordial than residual) a-topology in it as spatial or as anything we can conceive of. Nor, by the same token, can one call this 'literature' literature – unless one uses the term to designate this impossibility of ultimately mapping or naming this space, including literature.

Both literature and reading could of course be, and have been, conceived of and practiced otherwise, including bordering but not quite reaching the radical sense in which both terms are understood here. In particular, the present sense of literature and reading, and of their relationships (also as both relating and, ultimately, failing to relate to each other) precludes the possibility of giving the ultimate 'beyond-ness' at stake a certain implied architecture, even if not a name, however unknown or unknowable, or *beyond* any human conception, this architecture may be. It is this possibility of reaching this 'beyond' that would make literature possible and would define it in accordance with the idea and ideology (aesthetic ideology?), introduced, as 'divine madness,' in Plato's *Ion*, which has shaped the practice of (most) literature and reading ever since. In the spaces of literature and reading here in question, this possibility or even hope for it is abandoned. Nothing appears to be immortal anymore: neither light nor poetry; neither the body nor spirit; neither gods we can conceive of nor gods whom we can postulate as beyond any conception. Nor can the 'beyond' itself in question be conceived of as anything, nothingness included. Although felt throughout these essays and, I would argue, governing them throughout, this disappearance and dissolution of gods as Miller himself would describe it, is stated perhaps most powerfully in his elaboration on Wallace Stevens in 'Wallace Stevens's Poetry of Being:'

> The moment of self-awareness in Stevens coincides with the moment of the death of the gods. God is dead, therefore I am. But I am nothing. I am nothing because I have nothing, nothing but awareness of the barrenness within and without. When the gods dissolve like clouds they 'come to nothing.' When the gods come to nothing, man is 'nothing himself,' and, since this is so, he 'beholds / Nothing that is not there and the nothing that is'. (*CP*, 10)

At the same time at stake in Stevens's poetry, or Kafka's and Virginia Woolf's work, or in literature in the present sense in general, is not a nihilistic abandonment of knowledge and meaning (which may be that of 'the snow-man' of Stevens's poem itself). It is instead an affirmative abandonment of the ultimate knowledge concerning what makes possible the knowledge and meaning that we can have. As such, it is akin to Nietzschean affirmation, the affirmation of life and knowledge even and especially in their most tragic aspects or, in Stevens's words Miller cites elsewhere in his essay, 'the human end in the spirit's greatest reach.' It may be added that, rather than merely or, again, nihilistically, abandon ethical practices, in view of the impossibility of classically grounding them, this tragic view of the world also makes one reconsider ethics, especially in relation to literature, a subject of Miller's important and influential reflections. If I could choose one way to describe the ultimate message of these works or this type of literature in general and of these essays, it would be this affirmative pathos of tragedy, defined by literary imagination, by 'the spirit's greatest reach.'

There are, however, many trajectories leading to this point of (or in) reading, still only an intermediate point of an ultimately a-topological (non-spatial) labyrinth, an image invoked by Miller in his essay on Kafka and elsewhere as one of the images or allegories of the space or un-space of literature. Beyond the stage of discovering that each point in this labyrinth is only another labyrinth in an endlessly expanding (quasi-fractal) space, to be lost in this labyrinth is also to lose the spatiality of space (or temporality of time) itself, something that Kafka, Miller reminds us, discovers as literature. I would like to sketch one such trajectory, which appears to me especially significant in addressing twentieth-century occasions in Miller's work.

I would argue that *literary modernism* is essentially (although, it follows from the preceding discussion, not uniquely) defined by a particular type of engagement with and critique of (the culture of) *modernity* – the type of engagement essentially defined by the epistemological a-topology of the space of literature, as just outlined. *Modernism*, thus, is to be used here primarily as an aesthetic category. As such it could be extended to other arts, mostly those of the twentieth century, along with the earlier instances of the traits defining modernism. I shall, however, only be concerned with *literary modernism*, given Miller's work as my subject and a special significance of literary modernism in the engagement here in question with the culture of modernity. *Modernity*, then, will be used here as a broad cultural, including political and politico-economic, category. The emergence of modernity could be traced both to the Renaissance (or what we used to so call, naively) and the Enlightenment (the same parenthesis applies), and the relationships between them defined by scientific, industrial, and political revolutions. In his earlier influential essay, 'Literary History and Literary Modernity,' published in 1969, de Man spoke in a related number of contexts of 'literary modernity,' rather than modernism, although the latter term occurs in the essay as well (de Man 1981, 142–65). De Man (rightly) links literary modernity most essentially to Charles Baudelaire and Friedrich Nietzsche, both of whom are also crucial precursors for de Man's epistemology of allegory or irony, analogous to the epistemology of the space of literature, as here considered. Nietzsche is arguably the single most dominant philosophical presence in Miller's essays here discussed as well, in part for the same set of reasons. De Man's essay does not address the twentieth-century literature. It traces the epistemology in question from Rousseau, through Romanticism and Idealism, on, which trajectories are also found in Miller's essays discussed here, or elsewhere in his work, especially (but not exclusively) on his Romantic occasions. But then, Baudelaire and Nietzsche, or indeed this Romanticism and this Idealism, could hardly be seen as any less radical or any less modern and modernist than anything in the twentieth or, by now, the twenty-first century.

Now, I would argue that, beginning with its physics (known as classical physics), modernity, as the way of thinking and cultural practice, defined itself, in part but essentially, by the following idea and the ideology (mathematical-scientific, philosophical, historical, or aesthetic) based on it, both of which extend to and still often govern our own culture. The idea is that of the possibility, *at least in principle*, of the unity of spatial-temporal coordination of events and the causality of the relationships between them, the unity and indeed (this, as will be seen presently, is significant) each of the two parts forming it further grounded in the idea of continuity. 'In principle' is a crucial qualification here and is part of the ideology of modernity. For, in practice, as modernity has always recognized, this unity or indeed either spatial-temporal coordination of events or their causal relationships in their own right would be difficult to maintain – or, rather, to properly track epistemologically by human means, for example, my means of (deterministic) predictions of what could happen or where. The nature of the claim in question is, thus, ontological, in principle, at a deeper or the deepest level, rather than epistemological, as relating to our actual or even possible knowledge concerning the ultimate nature of things responsible for what is manifest on the surface or near the surface.

By contrast, beginning with its physics, the twentieth-century tells us that this unity of spatial-temporal coordination and causality, may be impossible – impossible in principle, ontologically, as concerns the ultimate, *deep* or *deepest*, nature of the existence of things, rather than only in terms of epistemological practice, as concerns our *surface* knowledge of things. As must be apparent from the preceding discussion and as will be seen in more detail presently, ultimately this is only a step towards a more radical view of Blanchot's unfigurable (un)universe, as the (un)universe of the unfigurable. For the moment, the very relationships between the surface and the depth of things, between the deeper ontology and the surface epistemology, or between the surface and the depth within each, and a certain *modernist* and then postmodernist conception of the world without depth are essentially linked to this situation. If 'the world of Kafka's stories is a world without depth,' as Miller argues, it is also because this world that does not hide a deeper, more fundamental, ontology (causal or a-causal), not even that of the Heideggerian ontology of Being (*Sein*), as Derrida famously argued, in introducing *writing* (in his radical sense) and its a-topology in *Of Grammatology* (1976, 19–20). As such, is it indeed closest to the world of Nietzsche, in which God is dead for the same reason, and Derrida's argument just referred to proceeds via Nietzsche as well. (Accordingly, by 'ontology' I mean a particular, if possibly unknowable or even unconceivable, mode of existence rather than the fact of the existence of something, the point to which I shall return below.) These themes permeate the essays here considered, from the subtle interactions of the depth and the surface in Virginia Woolf's *Mrs. Dalloway*, to Kafka's 'world without depth,' to Stevens's 'end of ontology,' with which Miller closes his essay in Stevens. This passage could, again, be linked to the question of Platonism and literature, as discussed earlier. Miller writes:

> Stevens may be in the vanguard of a movement 'toward the end of ontology,' as Jean Wahl calls it. Central in this movement is the idea that all our spiritual height and depth is available here and now or nowhere. The last stanza of 'A Primitive like an Orb' is one of Stevens' most eloquent statements of his belief that all the words and all the experiences of man are part of being, eccentric particles of the giant 'at the centre on the horizon,' the giant who can never be fully possessed or spoken in any words, but who is shared by all. If this is the case, then the simplest phrase, in all its limitation, is indeed 'the human end in the spirit's greatest reach' (*CP*, 508):
>
> > That's it. The lover writes, the believer hears,
> > The poet mumbles and the painter sees,
> > Each one, his fated eccentricity,
> > As a part, but part, but tenacious particle,
> > Of the skeleton of the ether, the total
> > Of letters, prophecies, perceptions, clods
> > Of color, the giant of nothingness, each one
> > And the giant ever changing, living in change.
> >   (*CP*, 443)

One would not want to take too far Stevens's use of the language of physics here – particle and the ether (the latter abandoned by physics with Einstein's relativity). It is difficult, however, to bypass this use either, for one thing, given the significance of the relationships, inescapable in Stevens's poem, between Platonism, specifically mathematical Platonism, and Democritean (materialist) atomism for all physics, from Aristotle to Einstein and beyond. Indeed, one might want to take this invocation of physics as far as possible epistemologically, as perhaps Stevens does in the end, at least in the (meta)-physics of his poetry and in the a-topology of its space as the space of literature. For, beginning with its physics, the twentieth-century and its modernism told us something more than we can no longer causally link events in space and time. They told us that such concepts as location in space and time, or space and time (especially if defined by a continuous topology), or causality (conceptually, a form of continuity as well) are themselves ultimately inapplicable at least to certain things we are dealing with. Nor, as I said, are any other concepts, such as 'things' or 'concept,' the concept of concept. There is a certain irony that the concept of space-time, a topological (and ultimately a-topological) concept, which emerged in relativity, was one of the initial points of this dislocation of the ideology of *modernity* in physics (classical physics). It was, however, the modernism of quantum theory that, along with literary and philosophical modernism, brought us to the radical limits here in question.

In philosophical and literary-critical terms, we are in regimes such as those of Blanchot's space of literature, Derrida's *différance* (and related operators, such as supplements, traces, writing, etc.), or of the radical discontinuity of de Man's allegory or irony, and the philosophical and critical practices (such as deconstruction) these regimes entail. Miller's essays, I argue, operate in this type of regime as well, and, in particular, engage the question of continuity and discontinuity, and of the relationships between them throughout. These relationships are, I would argue, ultimately governed by a certain discontinuity and the resulting irreducible randomness, modelled in part on the event of death, where, I think, Miller is close to de Man. It is crucial that, although, as in quantum physics, often made apparent through discontinuous or (correlatively) random phenomena, the discontinuity here in question is fundamentally epistemological in nature. It designates the irreducible impossibility of any ultimate underlying ontology, especially of causal and continuous type, of the events considered. The very concept of 'event' may, and is in Miller, Derrida, and de Man, defined accordingly in terms of 'effects' ('effects' without, it follows, 'causes') of a certain dynamics, which cannot be conceived by means of any spatio-temporal, causal, or, again, any other means available to use (the concept of effect is accordingly provisional as well). Hence, as I said, it cannot any longer be seen in terms of a deeper ontology. It is not that nothing exists except what is found on this surface, but these other things cannot be assigned 'depth' any more than anything else, such as 'thing-ness' or 'otherness' for example. We can of course and must use such terms and concepts, since we can only have terms and concepts that we can have, which creates a certain linguistic and conceptual (or, to begin with, perceptual) enclosure of our language and thought, sometimes invoked by Derrida. They can, however, only apply at the level of effects, at the surface level, while we are prohibited from thinking in terms of the ultimate depth, the deepest depth, to which we can ascribe anything of which we can conceive.

The problematics just outlined are often linked to what we came to call the 'postmodern' (leaving aside the terminological qualifications this term and its avatars require). Here, I relate them to literary *modernism* and related trends in visual arts and elsewhere, including in philosophy and mathematics and science, in the twentieth century. But then, the emergence of the key epistemological features of postmodernity is often linked to these trends (which inhabit and inhibit modernity as well, but in a different way) by founding theorists of postmodernity, such as Jean-François Lyotard. It is also true that this type of modernism, literary or other, but perhaps especially literary, has its history, which extends in particular, to the Romantics, such as Hölderlin and Kleist, or Shelley and Keats, all considered by de Man or, on his Romantic occasions, Miller in this set of contexts. (See especially 'The Critic as Host,' the first essay in this reader. The epistemology itself in question, or at least certain aspects of it, can be traced to a much earlier history, beginning with the pre-Socratics.) Given my limit here, I put a *discussion* of the history of this problematic in German Idealism or elsewhere in philosophy aside here – a discussion, but not this history itself, since it is pervasive in the essays in question and throughout Miller's work. For, if the literature and, hence, Miller's essays are engagements with modernity, they are also engagements with modern philosophy, including the philosophy of modernity, which, in its various aspects (scientific, literary, cultural, ethical, or political), is reciprocally shaped by its engagement with philosophy. Miller's readings in these essays are also framed by the history of *modern* philosophy, from Descartes's cogito to Nietzsche's death of god, both invoked most implicitly, with some remarkable variations on both themes, and their combination.

Thus, Miller writes in '*Mrs. Dalloway*: Repetition and the Raising of the Dead,' 'The cogito of the narrator of *Mrs. Dalloway* is, "They thought, therefore I am" Or, as he says, bringing Descartes and Nietzsche together, in the elaboration on Stevens that I cited earlier: 'God is dead, therefore I am.' If often more implicitly, however, these readings are engagements with a great many key junctures in the history of philosophy, from (and before) Kant and Hegel on. The essay on *Mrs. Dalloway*, specifically Miller's discussion of the relationships between 'the general mind' and 'individual minds' or, again, continuity and discontinuity, there, could also be read as an engagement, on both Woolf's and Miller's part, with Hegel, and the history of philosophy leading to and extending from Hegel to Nietzsche and then Heidegger and Derrida, among others. The novel thus also becomes an allegory (also in de Man's sense) of the history of philosophy and of reading philosophy, and as such gives the space of philosophy the a-topology of the space of literature. This same is also true for Miller's readings of Kafka and Stevens. I single out the essay on Woolf primarily because this way of reading the novel, a philosophical reading in the best sense of the phrase, may appear to be more unexpected but should not, as Miller's essay indeed tells us. But the essay and all three essays together also tell us that, as part of their engagement with modernity itself, literary modernism is also an engagement and a continuous reengagement with the history of modern philosophy, again, also as the philosophy of modernity.

J. Hillis Miller is a subtle reader of this engagement of literary modernism with philosophy and, in part through philosophy, with modernity. One might indeed define modernism as this literature, whenever it is written, and this practice of reading. It is this modernism that led us to a discovery that we live in the unfigurable (un)universe, the un-universe of the unfigurable, invoked by Blanchot, who also asks:

> But will [man] ever be ready to receive such a thought [of this universe], a thought that, freeing him from the fascination with unity, for the first time risks summoning him to take the measure of an exteriority that is not divine, of space entirely in question, and even excluding the possibility of an answer, since every response would necessarily fall anew under the jurisdiction of the figure of figures? This amounts perhaps to asking ourselves: is man capable of a radical interrogation? That is, finally, is he capable of literature, if literature turns aside and towards the absence of the book? (*The Infinite Conversation*, 350)

Perhaps no other literature deserves the name. But this a-topology of literature also demands and is indeed discovered in a practice of reading, a form of radical interrogation, of which, Miller's work of reading shows us, we, at least some of us, appear to be capable. And no other reading may deserve the name either.

Ghostly Preoccupations: Response to J. Hillis Miller, 'The Ethics of Topography: Stevens'
Nicholas Royle

The case of Wallace Stevens is compelling. Stevens is difficult, as everyone knows or is supposed to know. 'Case' is perhaps especially apt. Hillis Miller has been on the case from at least 1964, with the essay 'Wallace Stevens's Poetry of Being' (1991b, 33–49). His essays perform an immeasurably valuable task in expounding and elucidating difficult cases – not only the critical and philosophical writings of Paul de Man or Jacques Derrida, for example, but also the poetry of Stevens. Miller's writing is resolutely straightforward, clear, patient, guided by a powerful if also unspoken ethical imperative of its own, namely the demand to describe, clarify and explain in ways that, at least in principle, everyone who can read an essay in English might be able to understand. Stevens says, in one of his 'Adagia': 'The fundamental difficulty in any art is the problem of the normal' (1957, 169). There is in Miller, we might say, a commitment to the 'normal,' together with a shrewd sense of its difficulty. Linked to this is a sense of the political as well as ethical dimensions of Miller's work. One of the striking if understated details of his reading of Stevens in 'The Ethics of Topography' has to do with his designation of this poetry as 'democratic' (1995, 281).

Through these essays on Stevens one can follow Miller's critical development, the shifts and transformations in the unfolding topography of his oeuvre.

It might appear that the most obvious changes in the Millerian landscape have to do with a shift from a phenomenological to a deconstructive mode. This is something that becomes especially visible in the second half of the 1970s and can be traced in the essays on Stevens written or published in this period, in particular 'Stevens's Rock and Criticism as Cure' (1976) and 'Theoretical and Atheoretical in Stevens' (1980). Actually of course this shift is less a landslip than a refining of vision (even to the point of black holes). Miller's phenomenological preoccupations do not disappear, any more indeed than Derrida's have disappeared in the course of the past forty years or so. Conversely, through the wonders of a Stevensian glass (at once mirror, telescope, and 'microscope of potency' (1954, 367–8)), we can see deconstructive shades shifting in Miller's writing in the 1960s. The title of the 1964 essay, 'Wallace Stevens's Poetry of Being,' indicates the sort of phenomenological, Heideggerian, and of course Stevensian character of Miller's approach at this point. Towards the end of this essay he writes:

> The speaking of poetry liberates being in the presence of things. Through words man participates in being, for words of the world are the life of the world, and 'the word is the making of the world, / The buzzing world and lisping firmament.' Poetry does not name something which has already been perceived, or put in words a pre-existent mental conception. The act of naming brings things together, gathers them into one, and makes present the things which are present. Speaking belongs to being, and in naming things in their presence poetry releases a glimpse of being. (48–9)

The somewhat effusively Heideggerian language of gathering, being, and making present is not characteristic of Miller's later writings, but the way in which he draws on Stevens here points to a remarkable consistency in the trajectory of Miller's work. He is one of the few critics to have drawn in productive ways on what is, I think, one of Stevens's richest and most underrated longer poems, 'Description without Place' (1945; 1954, 339–46). He quotes from it here: 'the word is the making of the world, / The buzzing world and lisping firmament' (1954, 345). In acknowledging the Stevensian notion of poetry as 'act of naming' Miller is already gesturing towards everything that he will later write about speech acts in literature: 'Poetry does not name something which has already been perceived, or put in words a pre-existent mental conception.'

Among the various meanings of 'case' there is 'that which happens,' what occurs or befalls (the word 'case' coming from the Latin verb *cadere*, 'to fall'); 'state or condition'; 'subject of question, investigation or inquiry'; and (in a different case, from the Latin *capere*, 'to take') 'case' as 'a covering, box or sheath containing something.' To quote from the dictionary (here from *Chambers*) might serve to recall Miller's love of dictionaries, the way he can pick up on a definition from, say, *The American Heritage Dictionary* or *Webster's New Collegiate Dictionary*, and in doing so sharpen and alter our understanding of a word and, in effect, the world (see, for example, Miller's 'Deconstruction and a Poem,' 2000b, 179; also 1995, 265, 282). Miller's sense of the relations between word and world is intimately bound up with his reading of Stevens's poetry. To recall another of Stevens's 'Adagia': 'In poetry, you must love the words, the ideas and the images and rhythms with all your capacity to love anything at all' (1957, 161). The 'ethics of reading' is at issue here. As Miller describes his encounter with Stevens's 'The Idea of Order at Key West,' the poem on which he focuses in 'The Ethics of Topography': 'when I read the poem I have the sense that the poem needs my care, demands my care' (289). Miller loves words, loves to take a word, or let it fall, let its force and signification spread, and see what happens. This is also a way of construing 'deconstruction.' Deconstruction is the case: it is what happens, as Derrida likes to say. One can see this 'seeing what happens' at work in the titles of Miller's books, such as *Illustration* or *Black Holes*. 'Topography' (or 'topographies') would be another good example. Miller lets this rather old-fashioned, beautiful word happen all over again, and over and over again, throughout the pages of the book entitled *Topographies*. Seeing what happens involves an engagement with the unforeseeable and unprogrammable. As he declares at the end of the chapter on Stevens: 'I did not know where [this chapter] was going to go when I began writing it . . . Things have happened through the act of writing that no amount of simple thinking or silent reading could have achieved. Writing this chapter . . . has taken me to a place I did not even know existed, much less intend to reach, before I started writing' (290). There is a sense here again then of a Stevensian conception: the poem is an (unforeseeable) act, writing is discovery or, in the phrasing of 'Description without Place,' 'description is revelation' (1954, 345).

One of the most remarkable things that happens to the word and concept of 'topography' in the course of Miller's book has to do with the logic of the crypt that he reads through the work of Abraham and Torok, and above all through Derrida's essay 'Fors' (1986b, xi–xlviii). This happens, or appears to happen, in 'Derrida's Topographies,' the chapter that comes after the essay on Stevens. 'Topography' is literally description of, or writing about, place (from the ancient Greek *topos*, place, and *graphein*, to write). In its normal sense, 'topography' depends on 'the law of non-contradiction,' notes Miller: 'A place is either there in a given place or not there, and no thing, a building, for example, can be in more than one place at once.' But the notion of the crypt, he goes on to suggest, 'upsets all the logic of this mapping.' A crypt 'is there and not there, neither inside nor outside, or both inside and outside at once. It cannot be located on any map' (303). There is, Miller argues, an intimate relation between the notion of the crypt and literature. As he remarks: 'the crypt can only be named in language that suspends and is suspended from the referential dimension of language' (312). Stevens's 'Description without Place' is description without place: there is a strange quasi-tautology here. In this 'description without place' that is there and not there, an upsetting of what is in or outside ('on' or 'about') the poem, we read: 'It is a world of words to the end of it, / In which nothing solid is its solid self' (DWP, 344).

'Topography' becomes a cryptic *case*, already to be located in the chapter on Stevens.[1] Miller comments: 'Description without place is *graphein* without *topos*, a strange kind of atopical topography' (258). Miller recognizes in Stevens's poems sites of cryptic atopography: if, as Derrida says, 'It is the place that speaks orders to me' (quoted in *Topographies*, 284), it is not necessarily clear who or what is being ordered. Miller reads 'The Idea of Order at Key West' as 'a poem about the performative power of poetic language,' about the way in which 'words and other signs can make something happen' (276). But it is a crucial element of this 'performative power' that it retain a certain unreadability, that it remain cryptic and 'indecipherable' (313), undecidable, elusive and chancy, linked to the future as unprogrammable. As Stevens's poem of 1945 has it: 'The future is description without place' (DWP, 344). Miller is wary of generalizing about Stevens or any other writer: he stresses that 'his work is heterogeneous'; it 'says now one thing and now another' (257). He seeks, in other words, to be attentive to detail, to the singularity and specificity of a certain poem, a certain line or word or even piece of punctuation and, at the same time, to a sense of what in an earlier essay he calls 'the vast shifting panoramic linguistic theater of Stevens's work' (1991b, 215). Miller analyzes the effects of syntactical structures (grammatical order and disorder) and rhetorical figures (such as metaphor, catachresis, and prosopopoeia) that show up as, in more than one sense, ghostly preoccupations in Stevens's poetry.[2] It is at this apparently rather dry and abstract level that he situates the stakes of Stevens's work. It is in details of grammar, syntax, and rhetoric that we encounter the urgency of the double-life-sentence at once announced and encrypted in the title of the Stevens poem with which Miller opens his discussion of the 'ethics of topography': 'How to Live. What to Do' (1954, 126–7). A preoccupation with this double-question (or double affirmation), says Miller, 'runs all through Stevens's poetry' (255). In the remarkable range of Miller's writings it is perhaps easy to overlook the singularity and importance of this rhetorical, deconstructive, and ethico-political engagement with Stevens. It signals one of the ways in which the case of Miller, like that of Stevens, remains ahead of us, still to come.

Notes

1. Miller's *Topographies* explores some of the innumerable places where writers write about place or places. The privileged 'place' of the chapter on Stevens in this respect is suggested by the fact that the cover (or 'outside') of the book shows a map of Key

West, the setting of Stevens's 'The Idea of Order at Key West,' the poem on which Miller chiefly focuses in 'The Ethics of Topography.'

2. Besides those essays already mentioned, Miller's writings on Stevens include 'When is a Primitive like an Orb?' (1986) and 'Prosopopoeia in Hardy and Stevens' (1989) (both collected in *Tropes, Parables, Performatives*). *The Linguistic Moment: From Wordsworth to Stevens* (1985) contains material on Stevens based on (in some respects significantly reworked) versions of 'Stevens's Rock and Criticism as Cure' and 'Theoretical and Atheoretical in Stevens.'

IV

Practice and Theory

11

Line

Line is the thread of Ariadne, which leads us through the labyrinth of millions of natural objects. Without line we should be lost.

George Grosz

Ich bin dein Labyrinth.

Friedrich Nietzsche, 'Klage der Ariadne,' Dionysos-Dithyramben

Now, in the pictures of this imaginary maze, you are to note that both the Cretan and Lucchese designs agree in being composed of a single path or track, coiled, and recoiled, on itself. Take a piece of flexible chain and lay it down, considering the chain itself as the path: and, without an interruption, it will trace any of the three figures . . . And recollect, upon this, that the word 'Labyrinth' properly means 'rope-walk,' or 'coil-of-rope-walk,' its first syllable being probably also the same as our English name 'Laura,' 'the path,' and its method perfectly given by Chaucer in the single line – 'And, for the house is crenkled to and fro.' And on this note, farther, first, that *had* the walls been real, instead of ghostly, there would have been no difficulty whatever in getting either out or in, for you could go no other way. But if the walls were spectral, and yet the transgression of them made your final entrance or return impossible, Ariadne's clue was needful indeed.

Note, secondly, that the question seems not at all to have been about getting in; but getting *out* again. The clue, at all events, could be helpful only after you had carried it in; and if the spider, or other monster in midweb, are you, the help in your clue, for return, would be insignificant. So that this thread of Ariadne's implied that even victory over the monster would be vain, unless you could disentangle yourself from his web also.

John Ruskin, Fors Clavigera

String is my foible. My pockets get full of little hanks of it, picked up and twisted together, ready for uses that never come. I am seriously annoyed if anyone cuts the string of a parcel instead of patiently and faithfully undoing it fold by fold. How people can bring themselves to use india-rubber rings, which are a sort of deification of string, as lightly as they do, I cannot imagine. To me an india-rubber ring is a precious treasure. I have one which is not new – one that I picked up off the floor, nearly six years ago. I have really tried to use it, but my heart failed me, and I could not commit the extravagance.

Elizabeth Gaskell, Cranford

Devilry, devil's work: – traces of such you might fancy to be found in a certain manuscript volume taken from an old monastic library in France at the Revolution. It presented a strange example of a cold and very reasonable spirit disturbed suddenly, thrown off its balance, as by a violent beam, a blaze, of new light, revealing, as it glanced here and there, a hundred truths unguessed at before, yet a curse, as it turned out, to its receiver, in dividing hopelessly against itself the well-ordered kingdom of his thought. Twelfth volume of a dry enough treatise on mathematics, applied, still with no relaxation of strict method, to astronomy and music, it should have concluded that work, and therewith the second period of the life of its author, by drawing tight together the threads of a long and intricate argument. In effect, however, it began, or, in perturbed manner, and as with throes of childbirth, seemed the preparation for, an argument of an entirely new and disparate species, such as would demand a new period of life also, if it might be, for its due expansion.

But with what confusion, what baffling inequalities! How afflicting to the mind's eye! It was a veritable 'solar storm' – this illumination, which had burst at the last moment upon the strenuous, self-possessed, much-honoured monastic student, as he sat down peacefully to write the last formal chapters of his work ere he betook himself to its well-earned practical reward as superior, with lordship and mitre and ring, of the abbey whose music and calendar his mathematical knowledge had qualified him to reform. The very shape of Volume Twelve, pieced together of quite irregularly formed pages, was a solecism. It could never be bound. In truth, the man himself, and what passed with him in one particular space of time, had invaded a matter, which is nothing if not entirely abstract and impersonal. Indirectly the volume was the record of an episode, an interlude, an interpolated page of life. And whereas in the earlier volumes you found by way of illustration no more than the simplest indispensable diagrams, the scribe's hand had strayed here into mazy borders, long spaces of hieroglyph, and as it were veritable pictures of the theoretic elements of his subject. Soft wintry auroras seemed to play behind whole pages of crabbed textual writing, line and figure bending, breathing, flaming, into lovely 'arrange-ments' that were like music made visible; till writing and writer changed suddenly, 'to one thing constant never,' after the known manner of madmen in such work. Finally, the whole matter broke off with an unfinished word, as a later hand testified, adding the date of the author's death, '*deliquio animi.*'

Walter Pater, 'Apollo in Picardy'

What line should the critic follow in explicating, unfolding, or unknotting these passages? How should the critic thread her or his way into the labyrinthine problems of narrative form, and in particular into the problem of repetition in fiction? The line of the line itself? The motif, image, concept, or formal model of the line, however, far from being a 'clue' to the labyrinth, turns out, as the passage from Ruskin suggests, to be itself the labyrinth. To follow the motif of the line will not be to simplify the knotted problems of narrative form but to retrace the whole tangle from the starting place of a certain point of entry.

This overlapping of the part, even a 'marginal' part, with the whole is characteristic of all such theoretical investigations. The same thing would happen, in a different way, if the problems of narrative form were entered by way of character in the novel, or of interpersonal relations, or of the narrator, or of temporal structure, or of figurative language and mythological references, or of irony as the basic trope of fiction, or of realism, or of multiple plots, and so on. The motif of the line may have the advantage of being a less used point of entry and of being at once a local motif, microscopic, and an overall formal model, macroscopic. The image of the line, it might be noted, has, by an unavoidable recrossing, already contaminated this topological placing of the image of the line. Since this line is more figure than concept (but is there any concept without figure?), the line can lead easily to all other conceptual problems in narrative: character, intersubjectivity, narrator, time, mimesis, and so on. Perhaps it begs the questions less from the start, or begs the questions in a different way.

To begin at the beginning with the physical aspects of the book, the novel as book, its conditions of production and use. The linearity of the written or printed book is a puissant support of logocentrism. The writer, Walter Pater or Elizabeth Gaskell, George Eliot or Charles Dickens, sits at a desk and spins out on the page a long thread or filament of ink. Word follows word from the beginning to the end. The manuscript is set for printing in the same way, whether letter by letter, by linotype, or from tape by computer. The reader follows, or is supposed to follow, the text in the same way, reading word by word and line by line from the beginning to the end. This linearity is broken, in the Victorian novel for example, only by the engravings that juxtapose 'illustrations' in another medium to the continuous flow of printed words, or by anything in the words on the page which in one way or another says, see page so and so. An example of this is the repetition from one place to another of the same word, phrase, or image. The physical, social, and economic conditions of the printing and distribution of Victorian books, that is, the breaking of the text into numbered or titled parts, books, or chapters, and publication in parts either separately or with other material in a periodical, interrupts this linearity but does not transform it into something else. The text of a Victorian novel, to remain with that as prime example for the moment, with its divisions into chapters and parts, is like bits of string laid end to end in series. Its publication in parts over a period of time that, in the case of Dickens's big novels, was almost two years in length, only emphasizes this linearity. Publication in parts gives that linearity an explicitly temporal dimension, a dimension already present in the time it takes to follow a novel word by word, line by line, page by page. Victorian readers had to read one part of *Bleak House* and then, after an interval, the next part, and so on. The spurious instantaneous unity or simultaneity of the single volume held in one's hand was further broken by the fact that Victorian novels, even when their scattered parts were gathered in volume form, were often printed in two, three, or even four volumes. The linearity of a novel is always temporal. It is an image of time as a line. Martin Heidegger, in *Sein und Zeit* and elsewhere, has shown how all the language of temporality is contaminated by spatial terms. From Aristotle on, according to Heidegger, this spatializing of time has reinforced the systematic assumptions of logocentric metaphysics. More recently, Paul Ricoeur, in *Temps et récit*, has explored the relation between notions of time in Aristotle and St. Augustine and forms of narrative coherence in our tradition (see Ricoeur 1983, 19–84; 1984, 5–51). One must distinguish sharply, however, between effects of discontinuity, spaces or hiatuses between segments of a narrative line, and true disturbances of the line that make it curve back on itself, recross itself, tie itself in knots. Those spaces may have a powerful effect, in one way or another, on the meaning, but they are not in themselves forms of repetition breaking linearity.

The image of the line and the contrary possibility for the line to return on itself have entered deeply into the terminology used to describe written or printed documents. The root of the word *script* itself, as in manuscript, superscript, and so on, is *skeri*, to cut, separate, sift. The Latin *scribere* meant scratch, incise, write. The words *scrabble, crisis, critic,* and *criminal* have the same root. Writing is the scratching of a line, as when one says 'drop me a line.' In the eighteenth and early nineteenth centuries, when paper was precious, letters were 'crossed,' that is, written both ways on the paper, one script superimposed at right angles to the other. A text cited by critic or scholar is a 'passage,' a narrow defile or *detroit*, a way to get from one place to another in the argument. If writing is a form of dividing, sieving, sifting, or discrimination, a book is made of 'gatherings' or 'folds' bringing the divided back together. The pages are in order, with a margin framing the lines in a white border, 'justified,' as we say, suggesting some vague ethical or judicial responsibility to keep neat and straight the frontiers between meaningful sign and unmeaning blank. A justified margin is well policed. It does not straggle. A whole book is a collection of gatherings 'bound,' given a distinct edge or boundary line. In Pater's 'Apollo in Picardy' the physical manifestation that the Prior Saint-Jean's lamentable twelfth volume is a 'solecism,' evidence that the line of logic is irremediably broken, deviated, or distorted, is the irregularity of its pages: 'It could never be bound.'

If writing is initially a form of scratching or engraving, the cutting of a line, penetration of some hard substance with a marking tool, it may also, after the invention of pencils and pens, be thought of as the pouring out on a flat surface of a long line or filament, lead or ink making a cursive line of characters stamping, cutting, contaminating, or deflowering the virgin paper, according to a not very 'submerged' sexual metaphor. What is a metaphorical transfer in this case? Which is the metaphor of which? Is the pleasure of scribbling the 'sublimated' or 'displaced' pleasure of sex or is the pleasure of sex the pleasure of writing, the pleasure (male?) of penetrating, furrowing, or marking a blank page, the pleasure of extending the genetic line and of making a copy of oneself, saving the seed from fruitless scattering. On the other hand, is the pleasure or function of sex the pleasure of writing in the sense (female?) of texturing or weaving a text, making a pattern? Is the womb a typewriter or is it a sewing machine? Feminist critics have in recent years taken up these traditional 'phallogocentric' figures and challenged them (see, for example, Gubar 1981, 243–63). They have had great currency and power. Gerard Manley Hopkins, for example, describes the 'mind . . . mother of immortal song' as a gestating weaver: 'Nine months she then, nay years, nine years she long/Within her wears, bears, cares and combs the same' (Hopkins 1987, 108). The other sexual figure for writing is brought to the surface, for example, not only in a crucial passage in Hardy's *Tess of the d'Urbervilles* but also in a well-known text in Freud's *Problem of Anxiety*:

> Why it was that upon this beautiful feminine tissue, sensitive as gossamer, and practically blank as snow as yet, there should have been traced such a coarse pattern as it was doomed to receive. (Hardy 1974, 107)

> If writing – which consists in allowing a fluid to flow out from a tube upon a piece of white paper – has acquired the symbolic meaning of coitus, or if walking has become a symbolic substitute for stamping upon the body of Mother Earth, then both writing and walking will be abstained from because it is as though forbidden sexual behavior were thereby being indulged in. The ego renounces these functions proper to it in order not to have to undertake a fresh effort of repression, *in order to avoid a conflict with the id*. (Freud 1936, 15)

The paradox here is that the paper is already thought of as a tissue, a woven surface of crisscross lines or filaments. The word *line* comes from a root *lino* meaning linen, flax. The text is scratched, cut, stamped, poured out, imprinted, or embroidered on a blank integument that is itself already a woven fabric. *Text* comes from *texere*, to weave. Writing lays fabric on fabric in a hymeneal stitching, joining, or breaking, transgressing a line or frontier, tracing on the woven pattern another pattern, coarse or fine.

If letters in the epistolary sense are 'lines,' written documents that may be copied or cited, in whole or in part, strung together with more or less commentary, frame, or interpolation to make that strange kind of text, the novel in letters, the basis of a written or printed narrative is letters in another sense. Letters in the alphabetic sense are made of lines carved, stamped, or inscribed which turn back on themselves in one way or another to make a knot, a glyph, a character, or sign. The intelligibility of writing depends on this twisting and breaking of the line that interrupts or confounds its linearity and opens up the possibility of repeating that segment, while at the same time preventing any closure of its meaning.

A straight line conveys no information beyond the fact that the line is there, like a continuous dial tone on the telephone, a single monotonous tone on the radio, or the straight line on an oscilloscope when it is not monitoring any changes. Such a straight line may both be cited exactly and may not be cited. It may be cited because every straight line is like every other straight line in its featureless perfection. It may not be cited because for that very reason it is impossible to tell which line is being cited. The model remains unidentifiable, and so the perfectly straight line conveys no information beyond itself.

Only the curved, crossed, or knotted line can be a sign making the line simultaneously something intelligible, conveying meaning, standing for something else, and at the same time repeatable, already a repetition, so imposing on the sign the aporias of repetition, the blind alleys in thought to which repetition leads. No repetition is exact, but the meaning of a sign depends on taking it as the exact repetition of some other sign. Nonetheless, the meaning of a sign, as linguists have told us, lies not in its exact contours but in the possibility of differentiating it from other signs, adjacent or nearby, in the possibility of recognizing that an 'a,' however made, is an 'a' and not a 'b' or a 'z.' In any sign something is always left over that is not sublimated in its meaning but remains stubbornly heterogeneous, unique, material. This remainder, which links a text to its means of production, repetition, and consumption, its physical base, makes it possible for there to be texts, something other than the nonexistent phantasm of pure spiritualized, immaterial meaning. There is no meaning without some textual base, even if it is only modulated air. At the same time this exigency makes all texts undecidable in meaning. They are undecidable because the role of that physical substratum either as determining meaning or as being safely excludable from the determination of meaning, as trivial or accidental, can never finally be decided for sure. Does it matter, for example, that blue, black, or red ink is used to inscribe a given written document? It might or it might not. No convention or code can ever fully circumscribe these alternatives. Each letter, mark, or sign, as Jacques Derrida has more than once said, must have an ideal iterability in order to be identifiable and have meaning. At the same time each mark is divisible, marked by the possibility of being used, in whole or in part, in different contexts and therefore with different meanings. Derrida names this propensity to wander away from itself, intrinsic to any sign, 'destinerrance.' The meaning of any sign is always, each time it is used, posited performatively. This positing is an act for which the one who acts must take responsibility. The meaning is not fixed a priori in the sign itself. (See Derrida 1984a, 16.)

The terms for letters or written signs 'characteristically' go back to some physical act, some gesture of marking, incising, or stamping, with some suggestion of the possibility of repetition. The word *write* itself comes from Old English *writan*, from Germanic *writan* (unattested), meaning to tear, scratch. All the *graph* words – graph itself, paragraph, paraph, epigraph, graffito, and graft, in both the botanical and economic senses – go back to words meaning pencil, to inscribe, or the inscription itself: Latin *graphium*, pencil, from Greek *graphion*, pencil, stylus, from *graphein*, to write, derived from the root *gerebh-*, scratch. Grammar, diagram, epigram, and so forth belong to the same family. 'Sign' is from Latin *signum*, distinctive mark or feature, seal. 'Glyph' is from Greek *gluphein*, to carve, from the root *gleubh-*, to cut, cleave. 'Mark' comes from Old English *mearc*, boundary, hence landmark, sign, trace. The root is *merg-*, meaning boundary or border, that is, a line traced around the edges of a region. 'Character,' as in my word 'characteristically' above, is from Latin *character*, character, mark, instrument for branding, from Greek *kharakter*, engraved mark, brand, from *kharassein*, to brand, sharpen, by synecdoche or metonymy, or by exchange of result for cause, from *kharax*, pointed stake, from the root *gher-*, to scrape, scratch. 'Letter' comes from Latin *littera*, letter, possibly borrowed from Greek *diphthera*, tablet, leather used to write on, by synecdoche or metonymy again, a transfer from the act to what is acted upon, though with a different structure, from the root *deph-*, to stamp.

From the pointed stake to the incised brand, from the act of stamping to the material on which the writing is stamped to the stamped figure, from act to material cause to effect – what sort of transfers are these? Metonymy of accidental contiguity or the more intrinsic participation of synecdoche? Active or passive, something done or something suffered, a performative act producing something new or a supposition copying something already there? In any case, in any writing somewhere there is an act of violence, a blow, a cut, cleaving, or stamping, perhaps even a division between the cause and its effect. In writing the effect is not commensurate with its cause. The way writing is a troubling or twisting of the logocentric line is inscribed in the terminology which must be used to write or speak of the act or the paraphernalia of writing. *Signum, gleubh-, gher-, gerebh-, gno-* (the root of 'narration') – is it only an accident that these words or roots not only 'originally' mean the act of cutting, scratching, or pointing but express that act with a strangulated 'guh,' the throat's closure, plus some consonant? Writing is named by the involuntary sound in the throat caused by the bodily effort required to do it. This sound is primitive or inarticulate speech. Derrida, in *Glas*, has glossed at length this guh – gn, gl, gh, gr.

Ariadne's thread is a line that traces out the corridors of a labyrinth that is already a kind of writing, as Ruskin, in the passage cited above, suggests. Dionysus's 'I am your labyrinth,' said to Ariadne, marks the moment of the happy ending of her story, the moment of Dionysus and Ariadne's marriage and apotheoisis. [. . .]*

---

* In the elided passages, Miller traces the fortunes of key moments in the narrative of Dionysus and Ariadne /Ariachne, from classical and Renaissance versions of the myth, to more recent interpretations of Strauss and Nietzsche, examining the relation between line, narrative, and labyrinth, as these converge in the marriage of Dionysus and Ariadne. [Ed.]

When Dionysus speaks, he offers himself in turn as a maze for her to penetrate and retrace with her thread . . . This is the wisdom of a doubling interpersonal relation between the sexes. It is a relation of simultaneous love and hate that is at the same time the narcissistic mirroring of an androgynous self by itself in self-hate and self-love. The line of Ariadne's thread is at once the means of retracing a labyrinth that is already there and is itself the labyrinth. The line, Ariadne's thread, is both the labyrinth and a means of safely retracing the labyrinth. The thread and the maze are each the origin of which the other is a copy, or each is a copy that makes the other, already there, an origin: Ich bin dein Labyrinth.

The tangles of love and hate and the question of who penetrates whom, in a love that, in its intensity of self-abnegation, is a fatal labyrinthine betrayal, is expressed at a crucial moment of *The Golden Bowl* in a reference to Ariadne's thread. It will be remembered that the biblical source of James's title contains the image of a broken or united line: 'Also when they shall be afraid of that which is high, and fear shall be in the way, and the almond tree shall flourish, and the grasshopper shall be a burden, and desire shall fail: because man goeth to his long home, and the mourners go about the streets: Or ever the silver cord be loosed, or the golden bowl be broken, or the pitcher be broken at the fountain, or the wheel broken at the cistern' (*Ecclesiastes* 12:5–6). Desire and the failing of desire in death, broken containers of the bounty of life, interrupted lines for holding or drawing those vessels – the biblical passage 'contains' already elements of the Ariadne story. James's reference to Ariadne comes just after Mrs. Assingham, one of James's most brilliant 'ficelles,' or auxiliary characters, has smashed the bowl and has left Maggie to confront her adulterous husband and to offer him the 'help' of a delay. She sets the outrageous price he must pay for her complicity in her own betrayal. He must allow her penetration into the winding corridors of his inmost self. He must be her labyrinth: 'It had operated within her now to the last intensity, her glimpse of the precious truth that by her helping him, helping him to help himself, as it were, she should help him to help *her*. Hadn't she fairly got into his labyrinth with him? – wasn't she indeed in the very act of placing herself there for him at its centre and core, whence, on that definite orientation and by an instinct all her own, she might securely guide him out of it?' (James v.24, 187)[1] Maggie, like Ariadne/Arachne, is both the source of the thread that will make it possible for her husband to escape his labyrinth and at the same time a central energy spinning a web to entangle him. His labyrinth is both his own and the one she has made inescapable for him by penetrating it and retracing it.

The image of the line cannot be detached from the problem of repetition. Repetition might be defined as anything that happens to the line to trouble its straightforward linearity: returnings, knottings, recrossings, crinklings to and fro, suspensions, interruptions. As Ruskin says in *Fors Clavigera*, the Daedalian labyrinth, made from a single thread or path curved and recurved, may serve as a model for everything 'linear and complex' since. The phrase is an oxymoron. It names a line that is not simply linear, not a straightforward movement from beginning to middle to end. In what follows, I shall explore the way linear terminology and linear form used to discuss realistic fiction subverts itself by becoming 'complex' – knotted, repetitive, doubled, broken, phantasmal.

To put down first, pell-mell, like the twisted bits of string in the pockets of the narrator of *Cranford*, some line images as they are associated with narrative form or with the everyday terminology of storytelling: narrative line, life line, by-line, main line, drop me a line, 'break up their lines to weep,' linotype, what's my line?, genealogical line, genetic strain, affiliation, defile, thread of the story, ficelle, lineaments, crossroads, impasse, dénouement, cornered, loose thread, marginal, trope, chiasmus, hyperbole, crisis, double bind, tie that binds, circulation, recoup, engraving, beyond the pale, trespass, crossing the bar, missing link, marriage tie, couple, coupling, copulation, plot, double plot, subplot, spin a yarn, get an angle on, the end of the line.

It may be possible gradually to untwist these banks, to lay them end to end in a neat series, to make an orderly chain of them, knot added to knot in macramé, or to crochet them into a fabric making a visible figure, a figure in the carpet, initially to be emphasized is how rich and complex is the family of terms involving the line image – figures of speech, idioms, slang, conceptual words, or narrative motifs like Hercules at the crossroads. Dozens of examples spring to mind in proliferating abundance, like a tangled skein of yarn bits. This is especially the case if the line is extended slightly to include the adjacent figures of cutting, weaving, and setting limits, drawing boundary lines. How can one find the law of this tangled multitude or set limits to it? The notions of legislation (imposed from without or found within) and of boundary are themselves already images of the line. (*Lex* is from the root *lege*, to collect. It is the same root as that for *logic* and *coil*.) The thing to be defined enters into and contaminates the definer, according to a recurrent aporia.

One can see that the line image, in whatever region of narrative terms it is used, tends to be logocentric, monological. The model of the line is a powerful part of the traditional metaphysical terminology. It cannot easily be detached from these implications or from the functions it has within that system. Narrative event follows narrative event in a purely metonymic line, but the series tends to organize itself or to be organized into a causal chain. The chase has a beast in view. The end of the story is the retrospective revelation of the law of the whole. That law is an underlying 'truth' that ties all together in an inevitable sequence revealing a hitherto hidden figure in the carpet. The image of the line tends always to imply the norm of a single continuous unified structure determined by one external organizing principle. This principle holds the whole line together, gives it its law, controls its progressive extension, curving or straight, with some *arché, telos,* or ground. Origin, goal, or base: all three come together in the gathering movement of the logos. *Logos* in Greek meant transcendent word, speech, reason, proportion, substance, or ground. The word comes from *legein,* to gather, as in English collect, legislate, legend, or coil.

What is the status of these etymologies? Identification of the true meaning of the word? Some original presence rooted in the ground of immediate experience, physical or metaphysical? By no means. They serve rather to indicate the lack of enclosure of a given word. Each word inheres in a labyrinth of branching interverbal relationships going back not to a referential source but to something already, at the beginning, a figurative transfer, according to the Rousseauistic or Condillacian law that all words were originally metaphors. The searcher through the labyrinth of words, moreover, often encounters for a given word not a single root, but rather forks in the etymological line leading to bifurcated or trifurcated roots or to that philologist's confession of archeological ignorance: 'Origin unknown.' No reason (that I can see) prevents there being bends or absolute breaks in the etymological line. The realm of words is a free country. Or is it? No reason (that I can see) forbids deploying a given sound or sign to uses entirely without affiliation to its figurative roots. Or is this impossible? What coercion does the word itself, as a material base, exert over the range of meanings one can give it? Can one bend, but not break, the etymological line? In any case, the effect of etymological retracing is not to ground the word solidly but to render it unstable, equivocal, wavering, groundless. All etymology is false etymology, in the sense that some bend or discontinuity always breaks up the etymological line. If the line suggests always the gatherings of the word, at the same time, in all the places of its use, the line contains the possibility of turning back on itself. In this turning it subverts its own linearity and becomes repetition. Without the line there is no repetition, but repetition is what disturbs, suspends, or destroys the line's linearity, like a soft wintry aurora playing behind its straightforward logic.

Linear terminology describing narrative tends to organize itself into links, chains, strands, figures, configurations, each covering one of the topographical regions I have identified as basic to the problematic of realist fiction: time, character, the narrator, and so on. To identify line terminology used for stories, bit of string by bit of string, will be to cover the whole ground, according to the paradox of Ariadne's thread. That thread maps the whole labyrinth, rather than providing a single track to its center and back out. The thread is the labyrinth, and at the same time it is a repetition of the labyrinth.

The bits of string I have gathered may be organized in nine areas of linear terminology.

First come the physical aspects of writing or of printed books: letters, signs, hieroglyphs, folds, bindings, and margins, as well as letters in the sense indicated in the phrase 'drop me a line.'

A second region of linear terminology involves all the words for narrative line or diegesis: dénouement, curve of the action, turn of events, broken or dropped thread, line of argument, story line, figure in the carpet – all the terms, in short, assuming that narration is the retracing of a story that has already happened. Note that these lines are all figurative. They do not describe the actual physical linearity of lines of type or of writing. Nor do most of them even describe the sequence of chapters or episodes in a novel. Most name rather the imagined sequence of the events narrated.

A third topic is the use of linear terms to describe character, as in the phrases 'life line,' or 'what's my line?' Physiognomy is the reading of character from facial lineaments. The word *character* itself is a figure meaning the outward signs in the lines on a person's face of his inward nature. A character is a sign, as in the phrase 'Chinese written character.'

A fourth place is all the terminology of interpersonal relations: filiation, affiliation, marriage tie, liaison, genetic or ancestral line, and so on. One cannot talk about relations among persons without using the line images.

Another region is that of economic terminology. The language of inter-personal relations borrows heavily from economic words, as in 'expense of spirit in a waste of shame,' or when one says 'pay him back' or 'repay him with interest' or speaks of someone as 'out of circulation.' Many, if not all, economic terms involve linear imagery: circulation, binding promise or contract, recoup, coupon, margin, cutback, line your pockets, on the line (which means ready for immediate expenditure), currency, current, and pass current.

Another area of narrative terminology involves topography: roads, crossroads, paths, frontiers, gates, windows, doors, turnings, journeys, narrative motifs like Oedipus murdering Laius at the place where three roads cross or Hercules at the crossroads.

Another topic for investigation is illustrations for novels. Most nineteenth-century novels were of course illustrated by etchings or engravings, that is, by pictures printed from plates incised with lines.

Another region for investigation is figurative language in the text of a novel. The terminology for figures of speech is strongly linear, as when one speaks of tropes, of topoi, of chiasmus, of ellipsis, of hyperbole, and so on.

A final topos in the criticism of fiction is the question of realistic representa-tion. Mimesis in a 'realistic' novel is a detour from the real world that mirrors that world and in one way or another, in the cultural or psychic economy of production and consumption, leads the reader back to it.

Each of these topological areas invites separate discussion. The image, figure, or concept of the line threads its way through all the traditional terms for storywriting or storytelling. Line images make the dominant figure in this particular carpet. The peculiarity of all these regions of criticism is that there are no terms but figurative ones to speak of any of them. The term *narrative line*, for example, is a catachresis. It is the violent, forced, or abusive importation of a term from another realm to name something which has no proper name. The relationship of meaning among all these areas of terminology is not from sign to thing but a displacement from one sign to another sign that in its turn draws its meaning from another figurative sign, in a constant displacement. The name for this displacement is allegory. Storytelling, usually thought of as the putting into language of someone's experience of life, is in its writing or reading a hiatus in that experience. Narrative is the allegorizing along a temporal line of this perpetual displacement from immediacy. Allegory in this sense, however, expresses the impossibility of expressing unequivocally, and so dominating, what is meant by experience or by writing. My exploration of the labyrinth of narrative terms is in its turn to be defined as a perhaps impossible search for the center of the maze, the Minotaur or spider that has created and so commands it all.

The reasons for this impossibility may be variously formulated. Perhaps it might be better to say, since what is in question here is the failure of reason, that the inability of the mind to reach the center of narrative's maze and so dominate it may be encountered from various directions. One way is in the blind alley reached when any term or family of terms is followed as far as it will go as a means of talking about objective aspects of specific novels. No one thread (character, realism, interpersonal relation, or whatever) can be followed to a central point where it provides a means of overseeing, controlling, and under-standing the whole. Instead it reaches, sooner or later, a crossroad, a blunt fork, where either path leads manifestly to a blank wall. This double blind is at once the failure to reach the center of the labyrinth and at the same time the reaching of a false center, everywhere and nowhere, attainable by any thread or path. These empty corridors are vacant of any presiding Minotaur. The Minotaur, as Ruskin saw, is a spider, Arachne-arachnid who devours her mate, weaver of a web that is herself. This ubiquitous figure both hides and reveals an absence, an abyss.

The impasse in the exploration of a given novel or of a given term in narrative criticism occurs differently in each case, yet in each case it is experienced as something irrational, alogical. The critic suffers a breakdown of distinctions – for example, that between figurative and literal language, or between the text and that extratextual reality the text mirrors, or between the notion that the novel copies something and the notion that it makes something happen. The critic may be unable to decide, of two repeating elements, which is the original of which, which the 'illustration' of the other, or whether in fact they repeat or are rather heterogeneous, inassimilable to a single pattern, whether they are centered, double-centered, or acentric. The critic may be unable to tell whether a given textual knot is 'purely verbal' or has to do with 'life.' The reader may experience the impossibility of deciding, in a given passage, who is speaking, the author, the narrator, or the character, where or when, and to whom. Such a passage in its undecidability bears the indelible traces of being a written document, not something that could ever be spoken by a single voice and so returned to a single *logos*. Always, in such passages, something is left over or missing, something is too much or too little. This forbids imputing the language back to a single mind, imagined or real. In one way or another the monological becomes dialogical, the unitary thread of language something like a Möbius strip, with two sides and yet only one side. An alternative metaphor would be that of a complex knot of many crossings. Such a knot may be in one region untied, made unperplexed, but only at the expense of making a tangle of knotted crossings at some other point on the loop. The number of crossings remains stubbornly the same.

The critic, in a further frustration, may experience the impossibility of detaching a part of narrative form from the whole knot of problems and so understanding that. He cannot separate one piece and explore it in isolation. The part/whole, inside/outside division breaks down. The part turns out to be indistinguishable from the whole. The outside is already inside. Character in the novel, for example, may not be defined without talking about inter-personal relations, about time, about figures of speech, about mimesis, and so on.

The critic may also experience the impossibility of getting outside the maze and seeing it from without, giving it its law or finding its law, as opposed to trying to reach a commanding center by exploration from within. Any terminology of explication is already folded into the text the critic is attempting to see from without. This is related to the impossibility of distinguishing analytical terminology, the terms the critic needs to interpret novels, from terminology used inside the novels themselves. Any novel already interprets itself. It uses within itself the same kind of language, encounters the same impasses, as are used and encountered by the critic. The critic may fancy himself safely and rationally outside the contradictory language of the text, but he is already entangled in its web. Similar blind forks or double binds are encountered in the attempt to develop a general 'theoretical' terminology for reading prose fiction and, on the other hand, in the attempt to eschew theory, to go to the text itself and, without theoretical presuppositions, to explicate its meaning.

Criticism of a given novel or body of novels should therefore be the following of one or another track until it reaches, in the text, one or another of these double blinds, rather than the attempt to find a presupposed unity. Such a unity always turns out to be spurious, imposed rather than intrinsic. This can be experienced, however, only through the patient work of following some thread as far, deep into the labyrinth of the text, as it will go. Such an effort to read is not the 'deconstruction' of a given novel. It is rather a discovery of the way the novel deconstructs itself in the process of constructing its web of storytelling. These blind alleys in the analysis of narrative may not by any means be avoided. They may only be veiled by some credulity making a standing place where there is an abyss – for example, in taking consciousness as a solid ground. The thinly veiled chasm may be avoided only by stopping short, by taking something for granted in the terminology one is using rather than interrogating it, or by not pushing the analysis of the text in question far enough so that the impossibility of a single definitive reading emerges.

The impasse of narrative analysis is a genuine double blind alley. It results first from the fact that there is in no region of narrative or of its analysis a literal ground – in history, consciousness, society, the physical world, or whatever – for which the other regions are figures. The terminology of narrative is therefore universally catachresis. Each is a trope breaking down the reassuring distinction between figure and ground, base of so much theoretical seeing.

The other fork of this double blind is the fact that the terminology of narrative may by no effort be compartmentalized, divided into hanks of different colored thread. The same terms must be used in all regions. All the topoi overlap. Neither the critic nor the novelist can, for example, talk about sexual relations without at the same time using economic terminology (getting, spending, and so on), or without talking about mimetic representation (re-production), or about topography (crossings), and in fact about all the other topics of narrative. The language of narrative is always displaced, borrowed. Therefore any single thread leads everywhere, like a labyrinth made of a single line or corridor crinkled to and fro.

[. . .]*

I shall come full circle, to conclude this chapter, to one of the texts with which I began, *Cranford*. *Cranford* is about a village in danger of becoming entirely populated by old maids and fastidious bachelors. The village is in danger of dying out through a failure of family lines to continue. This will happen through a failure of sexual doubling or genealogical crossing. The masculine power of capitalization seems to have been lost in an effeminate or effeminizing doubling, as in Freud's recognition that the multiplying of the images of the phallus means its loss: 'As Miss Pole observed, "As most of the ladies of good family in Cranford were elderly spinsters, or widows without children, if we did not relax a little, and become less exclusive, by-and-by we should have no society at all" ' (Gaskell 1906, 2: 77). The passage in question in *Cranford* has to do with generation and with the passing on of names from generation to generation in family crossings. It has to do with the letter f, in fact with a double f. F is genealogically derived from G, gamma in Greek, which is another kind of crossing, the fork in the road, a truncated X, like Y. The f is a doubling of that turn, a *digamma* or 'double gamma,' as it was called in Greek. The cursive or

---

* Miller illustrates the foregoing point concerning the dispersal of the narrative line with an analysis of the letter X. [Ed.]

minuscule gamma is y-shaped: γ, while the capital gamma is like a right-angled turn: Γ. In the passage in *Cranford* the f or double g is further doubled in an effete purity of family names and family bloodlines that almost, but not quite, makes further genealogical crossings impossible. It is as though the double f or quadruple g were the true double blind or end of the line, as it ends my line of argument in this chapter.

The passage, in its admirably quiet but devastating irony, speaks for itself, thought it should be noted that it is doubled, dialogical. It is alogical, not only in its irony, but in its use of that Möbius strip form of language called indirect discourse. The passage has quotation marks around it. It is presented as spoken by Mrs. Forrester at the convocation of Cranford ladies brought together to decide whether to call upon the parvenue Mrs. Fitz-Adam, née Mary Hoggins, a farmer's daughter. Mrs. Forrester's words are not presented directly, however. They are expressed in the third person past tense of indirect discourse as if what she says were, absurdly, printed in a newspaper as reported from a parliamentary debate. The words on the page, the tenses and the pronouns, are neither the narrator's nor Mrs. Forrester's. The language belongs properly to no one. It is a double diegesis, that kind of narration Plato so deplored in *The Republic*. In fact the passage is a double double diegesis, if the reader thinks, as she should, of the narrator of *Cranford* as an invented character not identical to Elizabeth Gaskell. The words on the page could be spoken, in the real world of person to person dialogue, by no man or woman. They are a pure invention of writing, like the double f in the names ffaringdon or ffoulkes. The passage is not so much dialogical, with two originating voices, like an ellipse with two foci, as alogical, parabolical, hyperbolical,[2] thrown permanently off-base. It has no conceivable ground in any logos, not even in a double one:

> 'She had always understood that Fitz meant something aristocratic; there was Fitz-Roy – she thought that some of the King's children had been called Fitz-Roy; and there was Fitz-Clarence now – they were the children of dear good King William the Fourth. Fitz-Adam! – it was a pretty name; and she thought it very probably meant 'Child of Adam.' No one, who had not some good blood in their veins, would dare to be called Fitz; there was a deal in a name – she had had a cousin who spelt his name with two little ffs – ffoulkes – and he always looked down upon capital letters, and said they belonged to lately-invented families. She had been afraid he would die a bachelor, he was so very choice. When he met with a Mrs. ffaringdon, at a watering-place, he took to her immediately and a very pretty genteel woman she was – a widow, with a very good fortune; and "my cousin," Mr. ffoulkes, married her; and it was all owing to her two little ffs.' (1906 2: 77)

Notes

1. Another explicit reference to Ariadne is made later. Maggie, betrayed by her husband, feels herself to be like 'Ariadne roaming the lone sea-strand' (24: 307).
2. Both these geometrical figures have one focus at infinity.

12

How to Read Literature

Teaching How to Read is a Mug's Game

Telling someone who knows how to read how to read is a mug's game, as T. S. Eliot said of poetry writing. He presumably meant poetry writing requires a lot of swotting up. According to the *Oxford English Dictionary*, 'mug' is, or was, a slang term at Oxford for a student who studies a lot, a 'grind.' 'To mug' is 'to get up (a subject) by hard study.' Eliot may also have meant that a poet is like a 'mug' in the sense of being criminal, another (United States) meaning of the word. He notoriously said meaning in a poem is like the piece of meat the burglar gives to the watchdog so he can get inside the house. Teaching reading is a mug's game in both senses. You have to know a lot, all about tropes, for example, not to speak of history and literary history. Moreover, what you are teaching is by no means an innocent skill.

Teaching reading also seems unnecessary. If you can read, you can read. Who needs any more help? Just how someone gets from illiteracy to literacy or from basic literacy to being a 'good reader' remains something of a mystery. A talent for irony, for example, is a requisite for good reading. Sensitivity to irony seems to be unevenly distributed in the population. A sense for irony is by no means identical to intelligence. You get it or you don't get it. Dickens in *Bleak House* in what he says about Jo the crossing sweeper has movingly imagined, for us readers, what it must be like not to be able to read:

> It must be a strange state to be like Jo! To shuffle through the streets, unfamiliar with the shapes and in utter darkness as to the meaning, of those mysterious symbols, so abundant over the shops, and the corner of streets, and on the doors, and in the windows! To see people read, and to see people write, and to see the postman deliver letters, and not to have the least idea of all that language – to be, to every scrap of it, stone blind and dumb!

A blindness to irony, even in someone who can 'read' perfectly well, is not altogether unlike Jo's blank incomprehension.

Probably what actually happens within a given person's mind and feelings when he or she has 'learned to read,' and reads a given page, differs more than one might wish, or expect, from person to person. Teachers, those incurable optimists in a discouraging situation, often want to assume that the same thing happens to all their students when they follow directions to 'Read *Bleak House* by next Tuesday,' or 'Read the following poems by Yeats for Friday's class.' In my experience, dismayingly diverse things happen when students do that. Or, alternatively, one might rejoice at the way students resist being poured into a mold. Getting hard data about what actually happens when students read an 'assignment' is not all that easy. It is as hard to ascertain this as it is to learn other important things about the interiority of another person, for example just what he or she means when saying 'I love you,' or just how colors look to another person.

Still instructive are the wild divergences and 'misreadings' I. A. Richards found, and reported in *Practical Criticism*, when he asked students to respond to poems he circulated as 'hand outs.' These students were relatively homogeneous Cambridge undergraduates. They had more or less the same class backgrounds and the same earlier educations. Nevertheless, they not only 'got the poems wrong,' by most educated people's standards, misunderstanding them, as well as judging the good ones bad and the bad ones good. They also got the poems wrong in diverse and not easily classifiable ways.

Almost universal literacy has been a major component of print culture and the concomitant rise of the democratic nation-state. As Patricia Crain has shown in *The Story of A*, teaching the alphabet to children through 'alphabet books' was, within print culture, a major way of indoctrinating them into the reigning ideologies of an increasingly capitalist and consumerist culture. 'A is for Apple Pie,' for example, invites the child to think of learning the alphabet as connected to eating, and what could be more American than apple pie? After the child learns to read, children's books, for example *The Swiss Family Robinson*, then continue the work of making children model citizens. Nowadays, literacy is perhaps less and less necessary for that work. Television and cinema do the same job of interpellation by way of visual and aural images. The children's television show *Sesame Street* teaches the alphabet and phonics. Its real teaching power, however, is in the skits and puppet shows that powerfully indoctrinate even those who cannot read. That is not necessarily a bad thing. It seems a feature of language possession that human beings should join together in 'communities' of people who see and judge things in similar ways, though no conceivable society is without its prejudices and injustices. That is one reason why democracy is always 'to come.' It is a far-off horizon of justice toward which all should work.

Well, then, assuming one still wants to read literature, how should one do it? I make two contradictory and not easily reconcilable prescriptions. I call these, taken together, the aporia of reading.

Reading as Schwärmerei

If it is really the case, as I have argued, that each literary work opens up a singular world, attainable in no other way than by reading that work, then reading should be a matter of giving one's whole mind, heart, feelings, and imagination, without reservation, to recreating that world within oneself, on the basis of the words. This would be a species of that fanaticism, or rapture, or even revelry that Immanuel Kant calls 'Schwärmerei.' The work comes alive as a kind of internal theater that seems in a strange way independent of the words on the page. That was what happened to me when I first read *The Swiss Family Robinson*. The ability to do that is probably more or less universal, once you have learned to read, once you have learned, that is, to turn those mute and objectively meaningless shapes into letters, words, and sentences that correspond to spoken language.

I suspect that my interior theater or revelry is not by any means the same as another person's. Even so, each reader's imaginary world, generated by a given work, seems to that reader to have unquestionable authority. One empirical test of this is the reaction many people have when they see a film made from a novel they have read: 'No, No! It's not at all like that! They've got it all wrong.'

The illustrations, particularly of children's books, play an important role in shaping that imaginary theater. The original Sir John Tenniel (1820–1914) illustrations for the Alice books told me how to imagine Alice, the White Rabbit, Tweedledum and Tweedledee, and the rest. Still, my imaginary world behind the looking-glass exceeded even the Tenniel pictures. Henry James, in *A Small Boy and Others*, paid homage to the power of George Cruikshank's (1792–1878) illustrations for *Oliver Twist* to determine the way that imaginary world seemed to him:

> It perhaps even seemed to me more Cruikshank's than Dickens's; it was a thing of such vividly terrible images, and all marked with that peculiarity of Cruikshank that the offered flowers or goodnesses, the scenes and figures intended to comfort and cheer, present themselves under his hand as but more subtly sinister, or more suggestively queer, than the frank badnesses and horrors.

What reader, who has happened to see them, to give two other examples, has not had his or her imagination shaped by the wonderful photographs by Coburn that are used as frontispieces for the New York Edition of James's works or by the frontispiece photographs for the Wessex or Anniversary Editions of Thomas Hardy's work?

I am advocating, as the first side of the aporia of reading, an innocent, childlike abandonment to the act of reading, without suspicion, reservation, or interrogation. Such a reading makes a willing suspension of disbelief, in

Coleridge's famous phrase. It is a suspension, however, that does not even know anymore that disbelief might be possible. The suspension then becomes no longer the result of a conscious effort of will. It becomes spontaneous, without forethought. My analogy with reciprocal assertions of 'I love you' by two persons is more than casual. As Michel Deguy says, 'La poésie comme l'amour risque tout sur des signes. (Poetry, like love, risks everything on signs.)' The relation between reader and story read is like a love affair. In both cases, it is a matter of giving yourself without reservation to the other. A book in my hands or on the shelf utters a powerful command: 'Read me!' To do so is as risky, precarious, or even dangerous as to respond to another person's 'I love you' with an 'I love you too.' You never know where saying that might lead you, just as you never know where reading a given book might lead you. In my own case, reading certain books has been decisive for my life. Each such book has been a turning point, the marker of a new epoch.

Reading, like being in love, is by no means a passive act. It takes much mental, emotional, and even physical energy. Reading requires a positive effort. One must give all one's faculties to re-creating the work's imaginary world as fully and as vividly as possible within oneself. For those who are no longer children, or childlike, a different kind of effort is necessary too. This is the attempt, an attempt that may well not succeed, to suspend ingrained habits of 'critical' or suspicious reading.

If this double effort, a positive one and a negative one, is not successful, it is not even possible to know what might be dangerous about submission to the magic power of the words on the page. In a similar way, you can hardly hear a piece of music as music if all your attention is taken up in identifying technical details of the score or in thinking about echoes of earlier music. You must become as a little child if you are to read literature rightly.

A certain speed in reading is necessary to accomplish this actualization, just as is the case with music. If you linger too long over the words, they lose their power as windows on the hitherto unknown. If you play a Mozart piano sonata or one of Bach's *Goldberg Variations* too slowly it does not sound like music. A proper tempo is required. The same thing is true for reading considered as the generation of a virtual reality. One must read rapidly, *allegro*, in a dance of the eyes across the page.

Not all readers are able to read all literary works in this way. I much prefer Emily Brontë's (1818–48) *Wuthering Heights* to Charlotte Brontë's (1816–55) *Jane Eyre*. I feel I ought to admire the latter more than I do, since so many good readers like it. *Jane Eyre* seems to me a sentimental wish-fulfillment, in its grand climax of Jane's marriage to a blinded and maimed Rochester, symbolically castrated: 'Reader, I married him.' I have the same resistance to D. H. Lawrence (1885–1930). The climactic scene in *Women in Love*, in which Ursula and Birkin finally make love, seems to me laughable, not in itself, but in Lawrence's overblown language for it: 'She had her desire fulfilled. He had his desire fulfilled. For she was to him what he was to her, the immemorial magnificence of mystic, palpable, real otherness.' Wow! This seems to me simply silly. Seeing something as silly deprives it of the power to open a new world. It becomes dead letters on the page. Other readers will have other candidates. I find Anthony Trollope's novels consistently enchanting, both in their recreation of Victorian middle-class ideology and in their implicit critique of that ideology. I know someone who finds Trollope's work annoying in what she sees as its false presentation of female psychology.

Good Reading is Slow Reading

Good reading, however, also demands slow reading, not just the dancing *allegro*. A good reader is someone on whom nothing in a text is lost, as James said a good writer is in relation to life. 'Try to be one of those on whom nothing is lost.' That means just the opposite of a willing suspension of disbelief that no longer even remembers the disbelief that was willingly suspended. It means the reading *lento* that Friedrich Nietzsche advocates. Such a reader pauses over every key word or phrase, looking circumspectly before and after, walking rather than dancing, anxious not to let the text put anything over on him or her. 'When I picture to myself a perfect reader,' says Nietzsche, 'I always picture a monster of courage and curiosity, also something supple, cunning, cautious, a born adventurer and discoverer.' Slow reading, critical reading, means being suspicious at every turn, interrogating every detail of the work, trying to figure out by just what means the magic is wrought. This means attending not to the new world that is opened up by the work, but to the means by which that opening is brought about. The difference between the two ways of reading might be compared to the difference between being taken in by the dazzling show of the wizard in *The Wizard of Oz* and, on the contrary, seeing the shabby showman behind the facade, pulling levers and operating the machinery, creating a factitious illusion.

This demystification has taken two forms throughout our tangled tradition. These two forms are still dominant today. One is what might be called 'rhetorical reading.' Such reading means a close attention to the linguistic devices by which the magic is wrought: observations of how figurative language is used, of shifts in point of view, of that all-important irony. Irony is present, for example, in discrepancies between what the narrator in a novel knows and what the narrator solemnly reports the characters as knowing, thinking, and feeling. A rhetorical reader is adept in all the habits of 'close reading.'

The other form of critical reading is interrogation of the way a literary work inculcates beliefs about class, race, or gender relations. These are seen as modes of vision, judgement, and action presented as objectively true but actually ideological. They are linguistic fictions masking as referential verities. This mode of demystification goes these days by the name of 'cultural studies' or, sometimes, of 'postcolonial studies.'

Literary works, it should be remembered, have always had a powerful critical function. They challenge hegemonic ideologies, as well as reinforcing them. Literature in the modern Western sense, as a concomitant of print culture, has taken full advantage of the right to free speech. Proust's depiction of Marcel's infatuation with Albertine in *À la recherche du temps perdu* presents his mystification so powerfully that the reader shares in it. The reader finds the imaginary Albertine irresistibly attractive, charming liar though she is. Proust also remorselessly deconstructs that infatuation. He shows it to be based on misreadings, illusions. Cultural criticism continues and makes more obvious a critical penchant of literature itself within Western print culture. Nevertheless, both these forms of critique – rhetorical reading and cultural criticism – have as one of their effects depriving literary works, for given readers, of the sovereign power they have when they are read *allegro*.

The Aporia of Reading

The two ways of reading I am advocating, the innocent way and the demystified way, go counter to one another. Each prevents the other from working – hence the aporia of reading. Combining these two modes of reading in one act of reading is difficult, perhaps impossible, since each inhibits and forbids the other. How can you give yourself wholeheartedly to a literary work, let the work do its work, and at the same time distance yourself from it, regard it with suspicion, and take it apart to see what makes it tick? How can one read *allegro* and at the same time *lento*, combining the two tempos in an impossible dance of reading that is fast and slow at once?

Why, in any case, would anyone want to deprive literature of its amazing power to open alternative worlds, innumerable virtual realities? It seems like a nasty and destructive thing to do. This chapter you are now reading, alas, is an exemplification of this destructiveness. Even in its celebration of literature's magic, it suspends that magic by bringing it into the open.

Two motives may be identified for this effort of demystification. One is the way literary study, for the most part institutionalized in schools and universities, to a lesser degree in journalism, is part of the general penchant of our culture toward getting knowledge for its own sake. Western universities are dedicated to finding out the truth about everything, as in the motto of Harvard University: 'Veritas.' This includes the truth about literature. In my own case, a vocation for literary study was a displacement of a vocation for science. I shifted from physics to literature in the middle of my undergraduate study. My motive was a quasi-scientific curiosity about what seemed to me at that point (and still does) the radical strangeness of literary works, their difference from one another and from ordinary everyday uses of language. What in the world, I asked myself, could have led Tennyson, presumably a sane man, to use language in such an exceedingly peculiar way? Why did he do that? What conceivable use did such language use have when it was written, or could it have today? I wanted, and still want, to account for literature in the same way as physicists want to account for anomalous 'signals' coming from around a black hole or from a quasar. I am still trying, and still puzzled.

The other motive is apotropaic. This is a noble or ignoble motive, depending on how you look at it. People have a healthy fear of the power literary works have to instill what may be dangerous or unjust assumptions about race, gender, or class. Both cultural studies and rhetorical reading, the latter especially in its 'deconstructive' mode, have this hygienic or defensive purpose. By the time a rhetorical reading, or a 'slow reading,' has shown the mechanism by which literary magic works, that magic no longer works. It is seen as a kind of hocus-pocus. By the time a feminist reading of *Paradise Lost* has been performed. Milton's sexist assumptions ('Hee for God only, shee for God in him') have been shown for what they are. The poem, however, has also lost its marvelous ability to present to the reader an imaginary Eden inhabited by two beautiful and eroticized people: 'So hand in hand they passed, the lovliest pair / That ever since in loves embraces met.' The demystified reader may also have been reminded by the implacable critic that this Edenic vision is presented through the eyes of a resentful and envious witness, Satan. 'O Hell!,' says Satan, 'what doe mine eyes with grief behold.'

Milton's Satan might be called the prototypical demystifier, or suspicious reader, the critic as sceptic or disbeliever. Or the prototype of the modern critical reader might be Friedrich Nietzsche. Nietzsche was trained as a professor of ancient rhetoric. His *The Genealogy of Morals*, along with much other writing by him, is a work of cultural criticism before the fact. In a famous statement in 'On Truth and Lie in an Extra-Moral Sense,' Nietzsche defines truth, 'veritas,' not as a statement or representation of things as they are, but as a tropological fabrication, in short, as literature. 'Truth,' says Nietzsche, 'is a mobile army of metaphors, metonymies, and anthropo-morphisms.' The reader will note that Nietzsche sees cultural forms, including literature, as warlike, aggressive, a 'mobile army' that must be resisted by equally warlike weapons wielded by the critic. The reader will also note that Nietzsche gives an example of this by using an anthropo-morphism of his own in calling truth a mobile army. He turns truth's own weapon against itself.

No doubt about it, these two forms of critical reading, theoretical reading and cultural studies, have contributed to the death of literature. It is no accident that critical reading as demystification arose in exacerbated forms at just the time literature's sovereign power for cultural indoctrination was beginning to fade. We no longer so much want, or are willing, to be bamboozled by literature.

13

The Problematic of Ending in Narrative

It is no accident that the notion of ending in narrative is difficult to pin down, whether 'theoretically,' or for a given novel, or for the novels of a given period. The notion of ending in narrative is inherently 'undecidable.'

The impasses of closure in narrative are present already in the terms most commonly used to describe endings. An example is the tradition, going all the way back to Aristotle's *Poetics*, of the use of the image of the knotted and unknotted thread to describe the narrative line. 'To every tragedy,' says Aristotle, 'there pertain (1) a Complication and (2) an Unravelling, or *Dénouement*. The incidents lying outside of the drama proper, and often certain of the incidents within it, form the Complication; the rest of the play constitutes the *Dénouement*' (1947, 58–9). Where does the complication, folding up, or tying together end and the untying start? Aristotle suggests the possibility of a narrative which would be all unraveling or denouement, in which the 'turning-point' from tying to untying would be the beginning of the narrative proper and all the complication would lie prior to the action as its presupposition. 'More specifically,' he says, 'by Complication is meant everything from the beginning of the story up to the critical point, the last in a series of incidents, out of which comes the change of fortune; by *Dénouement*, everything from the beginning of the change of fortune to the end of the play. In the *Lynceus* of Theodectes, for example, the Complication embraces the incidents anterior to the drama proper, the seizure of the child Abas, and then the seizure of the parents: the *Dénouement* extends from the indictment for murder to the end' (1947, 59). By a strange but entirely necessary paradox, the problem of the ending here becomes displaced to the problem of the beginning. The whole drama is ending and beginning at once, a beginning ending which must always presuppose something outside of itself, something anterior or ulterior, in order either to begin or to end, in order to begin ending. The moment of reversal, when tying becomes untying, can never be shown as such or identified as such because the two motions are inextricably the same, as in the double antithetical word 'articulate,' which means simultaneously putting together and taking apart. The tying/untying, the turning point, is diffused throughout the whole action. Any point the spectator focuses on is a turning which both ties and unties. This is another way of saying that no narrative can show either its beginning or its ending. It always begins and ends still *in medias res*, presupposing as a future anterior some part of itself outside itself.

These aporias of closure underlie disagreements among critics about whether a given novel or the novels of a given period exhibit closure or are 'open-ended.' These puzzles are present also in the way a given apparently closed novel can, it seems, always be reopened. Virginia Woolf's evidently definitive treatment of the Dalloways in *The Voyage Out* is reopened much later to produce *Mrs. Dalloway*. Anthony Trollope, a novelist of closure if there ever was one, in the cases of the Barset series and the parliamentary series reintroduces in later novels characters whose lives have seemingly been entirely closed in earlier novels. The apparently triumphant closure of Elizabeth Gaskell's *Cranford* has its unity quietly shattered ten years later by the publication of the continuation story, 'The Cage at Cranford.' 'The Cage at Cranford' is in fact a story about the impossibility of closure, of 'caging.'

'Our tale is now done,' says Trollope at the beginning of the last chapter of *The Warden*, 'and it only remains to us to collect the scattered threads of our little story, and to tie them into a seemly knot' (1963, 259). On the other hand, the ending of a narrative or dramatic action is still today spoken of as its resolution or denouement: that is, of course, its untying. The vogue in the seventeenth century of that story of a Byzantine complexity by Heliodorus, the *Aetheopica*, was the pleasure of an untying, the sudden pleasure felt by one caught in a labyrinthine entanglement of mistaken identity and inextricably knotted narrative lines when suddenly he escapes into the full light of day. It is like the explosive release felt when one sees the point of a joke, or the pleasure of the final *éclaircissement*, the 'he done it' at the end of a detective story. The contrary pleasure, however, no less intense, is that of closure, the neat folding together of elaborate narrative materials in a single resolution leaving every story line tucked in. Solve, dissolve, resolve – why this blank contradiction in our images of closure in narrative? Why cannot we describe unambiguously the moment of coming full circle in a final revelation at an end point toward which the whole story has been moving, fixing the characters in a new relation, their final destiny? This tying/untying would provide the sense of an ending, casting a retrospective unity over the whole. It is most commonly marriage or death. This ending must, however, it seems, simultaneously be thought of as a tying up, a neat knotting leaving no loose threads hanging out, no characters unaccounted for, and at the same time as an untying, as the combing out of the tangled narrative threads so that they may be clearly seen, shining side by side, all mystery or complexity revealed.

The aporia of ending arises from the fact that it is impossible ever to tell whether a given narrative is complete. If the ending is thought of as a tying up in a careful knot, this knot could always be untied again by the narrator or by further events, disentangled or explicated again. If the ending is thought of as an unraveling, a straightening of threads, this act clearly leaves not one loose thread but a multitude, side by side, all capable of being knotted once more. If marriage, the tying of the marriage bond, is a cessation of the story, it is also the beginning of another cycle in the endless sequence of generations. 'Every limit is a beginning as well as an ending,' says George Eliot in *Middlemarch* (2003, 832). Death, seemingly a definitive end, always leaves behind some musing or bewildered survivor, reader of the inscription on a gravestone, as in Words-worth's 'The Boy of Winander,' or in Emily Brontë's *Wuthering Heights*, or in that mute contemplation of a distant black flag, sign of Tess's execution, by Angel Clare and 'Liza-Lu at the end of *Tess of the d'Urbervilles*. Death is the most enigmatic, the most open-ended ending of all. It is the best dramatization of the way an ending, in the sense of a clarifying *telos*, law or ground of the whole story, always recedes, escapes, vanishes. The best one can have, writer or reader, is what Frank Kermode, in his admirable phrase, calls 'the *sense* of an ending.'

Knotted, unknotted – there is no way to decide between these images. The novelist and the critic of novels needs them both and needs them both at once, in an indeterminable oscillation. Trollope, for example, goes on after his neat image of tying up in *The Warden* to open up his story once more in the figure of a speculative or indefinite closure left to the free imagination of the reader: 'we have not to deal with many personages, or with stirring events, and were it not for the custom of the thing, we might leave it to the imagination of all concerned to conceive how affairs at Barchester arranged themselves' (1963, 259). Trollope both ties his novel neatly up and opens it to the free imagination of the reader. He leaves it open even to his own imagination, so that the whole sequence of Barset novels can follow over the years. The apparently closed story of Eleanor Bold, for example, is reopened again with the death of John Bold and her courtship by Arabin in *Barchester Towers*.

All this problem of endings is neatly tied within another double antithetical word: ravel. The word ravel already means unravel. The 'un' adds nothing not already there. To ravel up a story or to unravel it comes to the same thing. The word cannot be given a closure by however extravagant a series of doubling negatives attempting to make the initial opening into closure: ravel, unravel, un-unravel, un-un-unravel, and so on. In a similar way, no novel can be unequivocally finished, or for that matter unequivocally unfinished. Attempts to characterize the fiction of a given period by its commitment to closure or to open-endedness are blocked from the beginning by the impossibility of ever demonstrating whether a given narrative is closed or open. Analysis of endings leads always, if carried far enough, to the paralysis of this inability to decide.

14.

The Function of Literary Theory at the Present Time

Not long ago Paul de Man could cheerfully say, with how much or how little of irony is impossible to know, that *the* task of criticism in the coming years would be a kind of imperialistic appropriation of all of literature by the method of rhetorical reading often called 'deconstruction.' 'But there is absolutely no reason why analyses of the kind suggested here for Proust,' said de Man, 'would not be applicable, with proper modifications of technique, to Milton or to Dante or to Hölderlin. This will in fact be the test of literary criticism in the coming years' (1979, 16–17).[1] It can hardly be said that this task has been carried out in the years since 1979 with much systematic rigor. This is true in spite of the widespread influence of 'deconstruction,' in spite of the many books and essays written about it, and in spite of the brilliant work of younger critics influenced by de Man. But there has been more talk about deconstruction, as a 'theory' or as a 'method,' attempts to applaud it or to deplore it, than there has been an attempt to do it, to show that it is 'applicable' to Milton or to Dante or to Hölderlin, or to Anthony Trollope and to Virginia Woolf.

In fact there has been a massive shift of focus in literary study since 1979 away from the 'intrinsic,' rhetorical study of literature toward study of the 'extrinsic' relations of literature, its placement within psychological, historical, or socio-logical contexts.

All honor to the motivations which underlie this shift, the noble desire for social justice, for the improvement of the situation of women and minorities, for a clear understanding of the ideological presuppositions which invisibly manip-ulate us, of which the shift in commitment I am describing is surely a conspicuous example. And all honor to the impatience with the actual hard work of reading, the nagging sense that reading may be cut off from the real obligations of life, the desire to make the study of literature somehow count, have effects of power in society and in history. It is hard to imagine whole-heartedly admiring the man or woman who does not have some kind of passion for social justice and is willing to work for it.

The question is what this has to do with the study of literature. It is in defining that liaison that the difficulties and disagreements begin. My contention is that the study of literature has a great deal to do with history, society, the self, but that this relation is not a matter of thematic reflection within literature of these extra-linguistic forces and facts, but rather a matter of the way the study of literature offers perhaps the best opportunities to identify the nature of language as it may have effects on what de Man calls 'the materiality of history.' Here 'reading,' in the sense of a rhetorical analysis of the most vigilant and patient sort, is indispensable. How else are we going to know just what a given text is and says, what it can do? This can never be taken for granted beforehand, not even after that text has been overlaid by generations of commentary.

Since 'reading' in this sense is indispensable to any responsible concern for the relations of literature to what is outside it, it would be a catastrophe for the study of literature if the insights of deconstruction, along with those of the New Criticism and of such critics as William Empson and Kenneth Burke, were to be forgotten or were to be relegated to an overpassed stage in some imagined historical 'development,' so that they no longer need to be taken seriously in the actual, present-day work of literary study. I should go so far as to say that, to paraphrase de Man, 'the task of literary criticism in the coming years' will be mediation between the rhetorical study of literature, of which 'deconstruction' is by far the most rigorous in recent times, and the now so irresistibly attractive study of the extrinsic relations of literature. Or rather, since, as Thomas Keenan reminds me, the word *mediation* is part of the vocabulary of dialectical thinking and suggests always the possibility of some synthesis or *Aufhebung*, usually at the expense of one or the other parties, it would be better to say 'confrontation' or 'encounter' or 'negotiation of the non-negotiable,' since, it may be, the rhetorical study of literature or of the 'literariness' in any piece of language as soon as it is taken as a text is the encounter with that thing articulated within language which is altogether irreducible or explicable by historical, sociological, or psychological methods of interpretation. Even 'encounter' or 'confrontation' is misleading, since that thing of which I speak can never be seen face-to-face, only indirectly, as in those traces or tracks of the passage of a cosmic particle in a bubble chamber. In any case, without the rhetorical study of literature, focused on language, its laws, what it is, and what it can do, particularly on the role of figurative language in interfering with the straightforward working of grammar and logic, as the parasitical virus interferes with the working of the host cell, we can have no hope of understanding just what the role of literature might be in society, in history, and in individual human life.

In our anxiety to make the study of literature count we are always in danger of misplacing that role, of claiming too much for literature, for example, as a political or historical force, or of thinking of the teaching of literature as too explicitly political. No one can doubt that literature is performative, that it makes things happen, that it is a way of doing things with words, and no one can doubt that the teaching of literature always has a political component, perhaps most when I am most silent about its political implications, ignorant of them or indifferent to them. It is not so much that the performative effects of literature, for better or for worse, are overestimated, as that they are often located in the wrong place. Sociological theories of literature which reduce it to being a mere 'reflection' of dominant ideologies in fact tend to limit its role to that of passive mirroring, a kind of unconscious anamorphosis of the real currents of power. Study of literature would then tell readers something they could probably learn better elsewhere, by direct study of historical documents, for example. De Man, on the other hand, goes so far as to say that 'textual allegories on this level of rhetorical complexity [he is speaking of Jean-Jacques Rousseau's *Social Contract*] generate history' (1979, 277). In order to understand how it might be the case that a certain kind of language would make what we call history happen it is necessary first to understand what it means, in the case of a given text, to speak of it as a textual allegory with a high level of rhetorical complexity. It is necessary, that is, to *read* the *Social Contract* or whatever other text is our concern, no easy matter, nor one that happens as often as one would like, before going on to studying with confidence those extrinsic relations. To put this another way, those extrinsic relations themselves are intrinsic to the text. The distinction between intrinsic and extrinsic, like most such binary oppositions, turns out to be false and misleading. Those apparently 'extrinsic' relations themselves require a rhetorical analysis, for example a clear understanding of the various figures of speech always necessary in one form or another to talk about the relation of a work of literature to its 'context': 'reflection,' which is metaphor; 'context,' which is metonymy; 'ideology,' which is anamorphosis, and so on.

It is in fact not the case that the work of de Man or Derrida is entirely 'intrinsic,' entirely concerned with language as such, limited to language in rarefied isolation from the extralinguistic. There is a fully elaborated theory of the historical, psychological, and ethical relations of literature already present, for example, in de Man's *Allegories of Reading*. Work he was doing in the last two or three years of his life was increasingly focused on such questions, no doubt as one more example of that almost universal shift to politics, history, and society which marks the specificity of the current moment in literary study. No doubt this present essay is yet another example of that. In an essay entitled 'The Resistance to Theory,' for example, de Man has this to say about the contribution of a rhetorical study of literature to social, political, and historical understanding:

> It would be unfortunate, for example, to confuse the materiality of the signifier with the materiality of what it signifies. This may seem obvious enough on the level of sight and sound, but is less so with regard to the more general phenomenality of space, time or especially of the self: no one in his right mind will try to grow grapes by the luminosity of the word 'day,' but it is very difficult not to conceive the pattern of one's past and future existence as in accordance with temporal and spatial schemes that belong to fictional narratives and not to the world. This does not mean that fictional narratives are not part of the world and of reality; their impact upon the world may well be all too strong for comfort. What we call ideology is precisely the confusion of linguistic with natural reality, of reference with phenomenalism. It follows that, more than any other mode of inquiry, including economics, the

linguistics of literariness is a powerful and indispensable tool in the unmasking of ideological aberrations, as well as a determining factor in accounting for their occurrence. Those who reproach literary theory for being oblivious to social and historical (that is to say ideological) reality are merely stating their fear at having their own ideological mystifications exposed by the tool they are trying to discredit. They are, in short, very poor readers of Marx's *German Ideology*. (1979, 11)

One may wish to argue with this or to say that de Man has got the relation of the study of language and literature to politics all wrong, but only in bad faith could one say he does not explicitly account for the political and historical implications of his theory of language and his theory of what he calls 'literariness.' Or rather it would be better to speak of what he has written not as abstract theory but as praxis, since almost all of his work centers on the reading of some text or other, for example the series of essays on different works by Rousseau in *Allegories of Reading*. Or rather, to refine still further, what he has written, like all good literary study, is neither pure theory nor pure praxis, 'practical criticism,' nor yet a mixture of the two or something between the two, but a mode of interpretive language which is beyond this false and misleading opposition. One might call it 'exemplification,' but that would leave open the question, 'exemplification of just what?' The answer must be that each good example of reading is an exemplification of other examples, according to a strange logic of synecdoche in a situation like literary study in which there exists no possibility of totalization or the establishment, once and for all, of an all-encompassing general theory. If, in any case, one of the simultaneously practical and theoretical dimensions of Paul de Man's work is a scrupulous accounting for the referential, historical, social, and political effects of literature, the same thing can just as decisively be demonstrated for Jacques Derrida, who has all along included consideration of the institutional, political, and social implications of his work, for example in *Positions*, or, more recently, in an interview entitled 'Deconstruction in America' (1985a, 1–33).

That the opponents of the rhetorical study of literature from both sides of the political spectrum continue to misrepresent it as ahistorical and apolitical may indicate the importance of what is in question here. The stakes, one can see, are enormous, both for literary study as such and for the function of literary study in society as it is now and as it is likely to be in the coming years. The stakes are enormous, that is, in continuing to think out the implications of a rhetorical study of literature for our political and ethical life.

The consensus on the function of the humanities in American life lasted until about the time I went to college in 1944. That consensus was largely the product of the humanism of Matthew Arnold as it was embodied in the curriculum of American colleges and universities. That curriculum was oriented primarily toward preparing white Anglo-Saxon middle-class males for professions: law, medicine, teaching, public service, business, the protestant ministry, and toward preparing white Anglo-Saxon middle-class women to be better wives, mothers, hostesses, and community servants. The idea was that you went off for four years to a protected and sequestered place, often protected and sequestered from the 'opposite sex,' and there assimilated the humanistic values by reading Plato, Shakespeare, Robert Browning, and so on, in preparation for entering society. The consensus about humanistic study saw it as primarily thematic and stylistic. Courses in the humanities were in aid of the assimilation of the best that has been thought and said in our Western tradition from the Bible and the Greeks on down. Such courses also provided models of style mostly taken from Victorian prose. In the required Freshman course I had at Oberlin College in 1944 we read Arnold, Newman, Mill, Huxley, and the Lang, Leaf, and Meyers translation of the Iliad. There was a general consensus on the canon a student of literature should read. It was primarily English: Chaucer, Shakespeare, Milton, Pope, Wordsworth, Tennyson, Arnold, T. S. Eliot, not a woman among them, and foreign works were usually read in translation, as is still the case in innumerable courses in 'masterpieces of Western literature' across the United States today. This meant a general assumption of the translatability of works in that canon that happen to have been written in Latin, Greek, or Italian. In spite of lip service paid to 'language requirements' and to the desirability of being able to read French, German, or Latin, the consensus I am describing depended fundamentally on the assumption that the great masterpieces in any language can and have been translated without significant loss into English. It is no wonder that those 'language requirements' gradually eroded, since the necessity of reading Homer or Dante or Dostoevsky or Baudelaire or Nietzsche 'in the original' was by no means generally recognized.

At that very moment, though I certainly did not know it, this consensus was breaking down. *Understanding Poetry* was already being tried out in a gingerly fashion in certain advanced classes in English at Oberlin, and the same thing was happening all across the country. The New Criticism was, as Walter Jackson Bate astutely recognizes (1982, 46–53), a major blow at the consensus. As soon as you start assuming that anyone can read a poem, that no special knowledge or membership in a particular class with a particular education is necessary, and as soon as you shift, however benignly, from attention to *what* is said, the thematic content, to *how* it is said, to tone, style, figures of speech, devices of presentation, it is the beginning of the end for that consensus. Sooner or later some teachers or students will see that the how contaminates and undermines the what. The long-term effect of the New Criticism, that is, was far different from, perhaps exactly the opposite of, the conservative intentions of its founders. The birth of American deconstruction out of Paul de Man's participation in Reuben Brower's 'Hum 6' course at Harvard might be taken as an allegory of that process (1982, 1355–6).

A second blow at the consensus was struck by the introduction of the discipline of comparative literature into the curriculum of American colleges and universities. However benignly intended and conservative in its intent, this move led ultimately to a recognition of an essential untranslatability from one language to another. This means, as Bate sees clearly, a breaking of the authority and domination of Departments of English, a gradual recognition of why it is one must study foreign languages: not to come back from them into English but to stay in them, to go native, one might say. From the point of view of that old Arnoldian consensus about the humanities both the New Criticism and the development of comparative literature were subversive. They were ultimately lethal invasions, destructive parasites within the host organism, generated by the organism itself.

To these two internal self-generated attacks on the old consensus about the humanities may be added social changes outside the university: the new assumption that all Americans ought to have a higher education; the rise of great public universities; the shift to a notion that women too should be educated for professional work (a change of incalculable importance); the gradual realization that the United States is a multilingual not a monolingual country; technological developments like television; jet planes that bring European scholars here in a few hours; extremely rapid translation of European 'theoretical' works, so that they often appear in English first – in short, the general internationalization of humanistic study.

The result of all this crossing of borders has been a breakdown or dissolution of that old consensus. I do not think it can be reconstructed by fiat. At most, or at worst, a beguiling but ultimately repressive simulacrum can be reimposed in its place, as is in some quarters being attempted now. This is in fact perhaps the greatest danger to the humanities at the moment. By 'repressive' I mean for example forcing a Latino or Thai in Los Angeles, a Puerto Rican in New York, an inner-city African-American in either city to read only *King Lear*, *Great Expectations*, and other works from the old canon, and to read them for a 'content' and according to theological assumptions that are prescribed beforehand. This is what Joseph Conrad called 'The Suppression of Savage Customs,' which, as you remember, turned into 'Exterminate all the brutes.' The Latino, Thai, African-American, or Puerto Rican is assumed to be a 'brute' until she or he can be turned as much as possible into that white middle-class male for whom the canon was intended. The dissolution of the consensus about humanistic study, a dissolution in which both internal and external factors have, as I have said, cooperated, has meant an irrevocable breakdown of the canon, a breakdown of the assumption of translatability, and, finally, a breakdown of the assumption that humanistic education is primarily aesthetic (has to do with pleasure) and thematic (has to do with values).

What I mean by the shaking of the canon should not be misunderstood. I do not mean we should no longer read Sophocles, Dante, Shakespeare, Milton, Wordsworth, and the rest. Surely it is good that they still be read. But they are read differently now, partly as a result of new ways of reading which have shown that they are far more problematic than perhaps they once seemed, far less the secure and stable repositories of the values and ideas of our cultural tradition than some defenders of the canon still seem to think they are. Canonical works now can be seen as especially concentrated forms of universal features of language, the tendency of figurative language, for example, to subvert straight-forward grammatical or logical meaning. In addition, canonical works are read differently now because they are read in a different context, by students brought up on television, cinema, and popular music, for example, or in courses in which they are set side by side with noncanonical works. The ideology of the traditional canon involves both the exclusion of noncanonical works and strong presuppositions about how the canonical works are to be read. The shaking of the canon is accomplished by the rejection of both these forms of delimitation.

What rationale for the study of the humanities should be put in the place of the old consensus? I think there can be only one answer. Preservation, conservation, the keeping of the archives, the whole work of memory, remembering, and memorialization: yes, this remains an indispensable task of humanistic study. But our past is remembered differently now and some different things are now recalled into memory, for example, African-American literature and history or the history of women and writing by women. Memory and the storing and interpretation of what is remembered is not a passive but a vital and passionate act, an act each generation does anew and differently as it appropriates history for its own purposes. One of the important effects of the new modes of literary theory has been to redefine what it is that is worth remembering and what procedures of recovery and reinterpretation should be followed to make sure we remember what we want to remember.

Along with that perennial task of humanistic study, however, study of the humanities, in the present context of our multilingual, multiracial society, a society whose cultural traditions, for better or worse, are primarily shaped by the mass media, must become again focused on another traditional task, the teaching of *reading*. Courses in the literature departments should become primarily training in reading and writing, the reading of great works of literature, yes, but with a much broader notion of the canon, and along with that training in reading all the signs: paintings, movies, television, the news-paper, historical data, the data of material culture. An educated people these days, an informed electorate, is a people who can read, who can read all the signs, no easy thing to learn.[2]

Our fundamental task, the new rationale for the humanities, is to teach reading and the effective writing that can only come from or accompany a sophisticated ability to read. This transformation of the task of teachers in the humanities has come partly from radical changes in our society itself, and therefore from changes in the role of the universities and colleges that are a major institution within that society, and partly from accompanying internal changes in the disciplines themselves. The most conspicuous of the latter, especially in literary study, is the new centrality of theory. The future of literary theory is immense (to paraphrase Matthew Arnold) because it is the fundamental tool of both the tasks of humanistic study in the coming years as I have defined them: the work of archival remembering and the work of the teaching of critical reading as the primary means of combating that disastrous confusion of linguistic with material reality, one name for which is 'ideology.'

Notes

1. This essay was written before the discovery of the wartime writings of Paul de Man, and the subsequent flood of essays in the mass media and elsewhere, about them. I have written elsewhere about de Man's early writings, but will say here that I remain as convinced as when I wrote this essay that de Man's later writings are indispensable to present-day study of literature.

2. Though Jonathan Culler and I might conceivably disagree a bit about exactly what it means to teach good reading, I take heart from his substantial agreement with what I am saying here. Here are some sentences from an essay by him entitled 'The Future of Criticism,' which I have just encountered as I have been typing up my own essay:

   But when one thinks about the future of our multi-lingual, multi-racial society, one finds it hard seriously to imagine the establishment of a common culture based on the Greeks or other classics. Such common culture as we have will inevitably be based on the mass media – especially films and television. Schools will not counter this culture effectively by requiring the study of particular historical artifacts, seeking to impose a canon. The struggle against the debilitating effects of mass culture must take place on a different front: by teaching critical thinking, perhaps by analyzing the ideological stakes and structures of mass media productions and exposing the interests at work in their functioning. Argument about what literary works and what historical knowledge to require will only distract attention from the pressing problem of how to insure that schools encourage intellectual activity, teach critical thinking, close reading, analysis of narrative structures and semiotic mechanisms. (Culler 1988)

15

What is Iterability?

Jacques Derrida includes a new concept and practice of performative utterances that emerges as a critique of the models of speech act theory of J. L. Austin and John Searle as a fundamental part of all his work, especially his later writing and teaching. The new concept and practice are associated with new notions of ethical and political decision, action, and responsibility. Derrida's recent seminars and books have almost all centred on particular examples of performative utterances and gestures: the gift, the secret, testimony, hospitality, responsibility, pardon and perjury (*pardon* and *parjure* in French, words whose prefixes echo one another). The distinction between law and right, ethical decision, political declaration, capital punishment, and so on. This prolonged meditation about speech acts has been closely intertwined with a continued interrogation of the relation of speech acts to literature and with an interrogation of literature itself.[1]

The three essays in *Limited Inc*[2] taken together make up an extended treatise on iterability and its implications. As Derrida indicates more than once, iterability, which is neither a concept nor not a concept, is a new name for what is given many different names in the course of Derrida's work: *différance*, hymen, *supplément*, *pharmakon*, dissemination, writing, margin, parergon, the gift, the secret, and so on. Each name works differently. Each is part of a different semantic or tropological system. Derrida says just this in a footnote to the 'Afterword.' The footnote also indicates what is peculiar about the word 'iterability' within this series. It is both a member of the series and at the same time also a feature of each member of the series. They all are marked by iterability or all are iterable or all name a form of iterability:

> The list of these words is not closed, by definition, and it is far from limiting itself (currently) to those that I cite here or see often cited (*pharmakon, supplement, hymen, parergon*) . . . If the list remains indeed open, there are already many others at work [*au travail*]. They share a certain functional analogy but remain singular and irreducible to one another, as are the textual chains from which they are inseparable. They are all marked by iterability, which however seems to belong to their series. (1988, 155; 1990, 211–12)

That there are so many of these words, potentially a limitless number, indicates that no one of them is proper. What these words name has no proper name, only deferred, displaced, figurative, or improper names, that is, catachrestic labels.

What Derrida means by iterability seems straightforward enough and easy enough to understand. The reader, nevertheless, should be wary, since it turns out to be 'difficult,' almost unfathomably so, to understand iterability. Iterability is nothing more, as a passage already cited indicates, than the possibility for every mark to be repeated and still to function as a meaningful mark in new contexts that are cut off entirely from the original context, the 'intention to communicate' of the original maker of the mark. That originator may be absent or dead, but the mark still functions, just as it goes on functioning after the death of its intended recipient. I must repeat again here the passage already cited, so the reader can be sure that Derrida says what I say he says.[3] The passage can never be repeated too often. My repetition is an example of iterability: the first time, I made the citation to exemplify Derrida's 'logical' style; and this time, I make it to highlight the way the passage defines 'iterability.' The same words in a new context are altered, which, as I shall show, is one of Derrida's chief points about iterability. Here is the passage again:

> I repeat, therefore, since it can never be repeated too often: if one admits that writing (and the mark in general) *must be able* to function in the absence of the sender, the receiver, the context of production, etc., that implies that this power, this *being able*, this *possibility is always* inscribed, hence *necessarily* inscribed *as possibility* in the functioning or the functional structure of the mark. (1988, 48)

'Mark' is Derrida's general name for any sign or trace, including a word, but it also includes, for example, a deictic gesture, a gesture that has meaning and is therefore more than itself.

To say 'mark' rather than 'word' or even 'sign' has important implications, as Derrida indicates. It allows him, for example, to challenge the age-old notion, going back to Aristotle, that man is the only animal with language and therefore radically distinct from the other animals. Cats, for example, make and use marks of many sorts. They must therefore, it might appear, be included in the human family; or rather, the border between human and animal in this case breaks down. Nevertheless, what Derrida means by iterability seems simple and clear enough: A mark can be iterated. Who could dispute it? The consequences of this are far-reaching.

The first consequence is radically to disqualify the basic strategy of Austin's theory of speech acts, that is, the exclusion from analysis and definition of the marginal, the etiolated, the nonstandard, the nonserious, the fictional, the parasitic, the impure. [. . .] Speech acts, for Austin, conventionally depend on an assumed subordination of the nonserious to the serious, the impure to the pure. First, for example, comes the standard promise made by an 'I,' ego, or subject, a person, ideally male, in full possession of his senses, speaking in the present with deliberate intention, and uttering 'I promise so and so.' Then come all the impure promises as deviations from that, for example promises imitated in a novel, or acted on the stage, or said with intent not to keep them, or under coercion, or by someone who is insane or drugged, or by someone from a culture that does not share our assumptions about promises. Since all these are secondary, impure, etiolated, fictive deformations of real promises they can be safely set aside so the standard, serious promise can be analyzed. This sounds reasonable enough. Such subordination of the fictive to the real is reason itself, from Plato and Aristotle on.

Derrida, in a characteristic gesture, reverses this hierarchy. For him, the pure promise is a 'fictional' phantasm derived from the impure one. Why is that? Because what exists 'originally' are speech acts marked, from the beginning or even before the beginning, by iterability, that is, by impurity. The impure is the original. The pure, normal, standard speech act, if there were such a thing, would be derived from that. Since impurity is always possible, that possibility cannot be set aside. It must always be considered in the analysis of any speech act or other utterance, even the apparently most verifiable constative ones.
[. . .]

When a sentence or other mark is reused in a different context, it does not remain the same. It is altered. Derrida recalls that the Latin root *iter* in 'iterability' probably comes from a Sanskrit word meaning 'other.' Derrida here quotes in a new context in 'Limited Inc a b c . . .' a passage from 'Signature Event Context':

> Limiting the very thing it authorizes, transgressing the code or the law it constitutes, the graphics of iterability inscribes alteration irreducibly in repetition (or in identi-fication): a priori, always and already, without delay, *at once* [*toujours déjà, sans attendre, aussi sec*]: 'Such iterability – (*iter*, again, probably comes from *itara*, *other* in Sanskrit, and everything that follows can be read as the working out of the logic that ties repetition to alterity) structures the mark of writing itself, no matter what particular type of writing is involved' (*Sec* [as reprinted in 1988], 7). (1988, 62; 1990, 120)

These sentences already involve a further feature of iterability, the most counterintuitive, enigmatic, and difficult to grasp of all the aspects of Derrida's concept/nonconcept of iterability. It is easy enough to accept the fact that a given sentence can function differently in many different contexts, though perhaps not so easy to accept the fact that this means the impure is the original, the putative pure is the derived and secondary. Even more difficult to under-stand and accept (perhaps it is the un-understandable and unacceptable as such) is Derrida's assertion that even a sentence or other collection of marks that appears only once never to appear or be used again, never to be iterated or altered by being inserted in a new context, is already, from the beginning, divided within itself. There is no such thing as a pure, standard, nonfictive, self-identical utterance. Such marks are divided within 'a priori, always and already, without delay, *at once, aussi sec*.' (The play here is between the French idiom *aussi sec*, meaning at once, and the acronym *Sec*, meaning 'dry,' that Derrida has chosen for 'Signature Event Context.' The same play governs Derrida's admission at the end of *Sec* that it has been a 'very *dry* discussion [*propos très sec*].') Here is Derrida's way of saying this:

> But let's go a bit further. Does this kind of *fact* [a pure utterance that exists only once and is tied to a single sender and a single receiver] really exist? Where can we find it? How can we recognize it? Here we reach another type of analysis and of necessity. Isn't the (apparent) *fact* of the sender's or receiver's presence complicated, divided, contaminated, parasited by the *possibility of an absence* inasmuch as this possibility is necessarily inscribed in the functioning of the mark? This is the 'logic,' or, rather, the 'graphics' to which *Sec* seeks to do justice: As soon as [*aussi sec*] a possibility is essential and necessary, *qua possibility* (and even if it is the possibility of what is named, *negatively*, absence, 'infelicity,' parasitism, the non-serious, non-'standard,' fictional, citational, ironical, etc.), it can no longer, either de facto or de jure, be bracketed, excluded, shunted aside [*laisser de côté*], even temporarily, on allegedly methodological grounds. [This is what Austin does when he says he won't trench on the nonserious. – JHM] Inasmuch as it is essential and structural, this possibility is always at work [*cette possibilité travaille*] marking *all the facts*, all the events, even those which appear to disguise it. Just as itera*bility*, which is not iteration, can be recognized even in a mark which *in fact* seems to have occurred only once. I say *seems*, because this one time is in itself divided or multiplied in advance by its structure of repeatability. This obtains *in fact*, at once [*aussi sec*], from its inception on [*dans l'unique fois*: this means rather 'in the singular occurrence']; and it is here that the graphics of iterability undercuts [*brouille*] the classical opposition of fact and principle [*le droit*], the factual and the possible (or the virtual), necessity and possibility. In undercutting these classical oppositions, however, it introduces [*contraint à*] a more powerful 'logic.' (1988, 48; 1990, 97)

The hardest part of iterability to understand is the way it 'broaches and breeches' (Samuel Weber's translation of the difficult French word *entame*) the utterance even the first and perhaps only time it is spoken. Iterability is *différance*, that is, an opening within the utterance itself that makes it differ from itself, within itself. Iterability opens a gap within the utterance, but also makes it defer itself, opening up abysses of temporality before and after, in a kind of future anterior. This temporality makes the present never present because it always reaches toward a past that was never present and a future that will never be reached as present, as in what Derrida says about the way the democracy to come [*à venir*] is always future. Iterability, because of its gapping or gaping, is dehiscent, disseminative.

The word 'dehiscent' is a botanical word meaning 'opening at pores or by splitting to release seeds within a fruit or pollen from ananther.' 'Indehiscent' means not splitting open at maturity. 'Dehisce' means to burst or split open along a line or slit, as do the ripe capsules or pods of some plants. These words come from Latin *dehiscere: de*, off + *hiscere*, to open, split, inceptive of *hiare*, to be open, to gape, from *ghei* to yawn, gape, suffixed variant form of Greek *khasma*, yawning gulf, related to modern English 'chasm,' 'gap,' 'gape,' 'gasp.' Related English words are 'gill,' meaning ravine, chasm; 'gyrfalcon,' meaning voracious or yawning bird. The connection to 'chasm' is provocative. It stresses the yawning gap from which the seeds are cast forth, as from a mysterious, in a certain sense empty, and in any case not wholly intelligible or masterable, source. Iterability comes from the iter, the alter, what Derrida has more recently called *le tout autre*, the wholly other.

One can see the connection, nevertheless, of dehiscence and dissemination. It is because both the coded message of the speech act and the intention of the one who speaks or writes it is dehiscent, breached, divided, with a yawning gap, that it is not so much polysemic (Derrida firmly dismisses that) as disseminated, like seed broadcast by a bursting seed pod. As a result, consciousness, intentionality, meaning, and intention unequivocally identifiable by the hearers, or promisees, are effects of iterability, rather than the other way around. As Austin well recognized, and as Derrida also knows, the whole traditional juridico-political system depends on believing the opposite, on having the opposite fully institutionalized and operative. Otherwise, how could you hold someone responsible for a promise or for a signature to a contract and then put them in jail if he or she failed to live up to the commitment?

An example of dehiscence might be my own discourse here. It is a feature of iterability that I am able to cite Derrida's words, repeat them exactly. That citation would seem to deprive Derrida's words of force. If, for example, I quote him as saying, 'Through these difficulties, another language and other thoughts seek to make their way. This language and these thoughts, which are also new responsibilities, arouse in me a respect which, whatever the cost, I neither can nor will compromise [*transiger*]' (1988, 153; 1990, 282), no one is likely to think that I am myself affirming that something arouses in me a respect that I neither can nor will compromise. Nevertheless, the demand on me to 'teach Derrida,' or write about his work, whatever exactly that means, comes not from my institution but from the texts of Derrida's work and to some degree against the institution, since there are some features of the institution that would *not* want Derrida to be repeated in the classroom or written about. This demand on me to teach Derrida and to write about him, imposed on me by the texts he has written, means that when I do so my own words have or may have an independent performative force, even when I am citing and commenting on what Derrida wrote.

Derrida, in his recent seminars on witnessing, has repeatedly cited Celan's striking phrase, 'Nobody bears witness for the witness':

Niemand

zeugt für den
Zeugen. (1995, 178)

One sees the force of what this means. The witness I bear, the testimony I give, can be given only by me alone. I alone can bear witness for what I witnessed. Witnessing is absolutely individual, sui generis, unique, private, singular. Derrida draws an extreme conclusion from this, namely that no act of testimony can be verified. It is Derrida alone who knows what demand is being made on him by that other law, the demand that arouses his respect and that he cannot and will not compromise. Nevertheless, as Derrida also reminds us, the word 'testimony' comes from *testis*, from *terstis*, meaning the third. The witness testifies as a third to some transaction between at least two others. In this case I bear witness to the transaction between Derrida and that other law that arouses in him an infinitely exigent respect. As a witness or third to Derrida's witnessing, I come to testify to my respect for what Derrida has said. This respect leads me to wish to bear witness in my turn in an act of teaching or writing that wants to be as faithful as possible to just what Derrida said. I want to pass it along to my own auditors or readers in a repetition with difference, a dissemination, a dehiscence that will have incalculable effects, or perhaps no effects. Who can know beforehand? How would you confirm even afterwards the effect of teaching or writing? Another way to put this is to say that even the most exact repetition of Derrida's words on my part does not exonerate me from responsibility. Far from it. That act of repetition or manifestation of iterability is a speech act that puts a heavy burden, debt, responsibility, or obligation on my shoulders. I am responsible for what I say even if what I say stems from an attempt to say again as exactly as I can just what Derrida says, with abundant citation to prove he said just that.

Notes

1. This opening paragraph is taken, slightly amended, from the beginning of the extensive reading of Jacques Derrida's work on the notion of speech acts, particularly the performative dimension of them, in the chapter, 'Jacques Derrida' from *Speech Acts in Literature*, from which the present chapter, 'What is Iterability?,' and the following, 'Je T'aime,' are taken. The paragraph appears here as a means of providing an open-ended frame, both a frame and an opening of the frame to which we conventionally refer as 'context,' for this chapter and that which follows. Miller's chapter on Derrida offers, I would suggest, the most scintillating, thorough, and attentive single introduction to the writing of Derrida outside of Derrida's own writing in its patient and rigorous consideration of Derrida's rereading of the speech act theory of Austin and his critique of John Searle. Rather than attempt to edit the entire chapter, I have chosen two short sections, which remain more or less intact. [Ed.]
2. The translation of 'Signature Event Context' (henceforth, following Derrida's usage, *Sec*) in *Limited Inc* is by Jeffrey Mehlman and Samuel Weber. The other two translations – 'Limited Inc a b c . . .' and 'Afterword: Toward an Ethic of

Discussion' – are entirely by Weber. The French original of these essays, paradoxically gathered in a single volume only after the publication in English of *Limited Inc*, is translated by Elisabeth Weber (1990). Weber 'presents' what was originally written in French, though 'Limited Inc a b c . . .' and 'Afterword: Toward an Ethic of Discussion' had never before been published in the French original. She translates into French the citations from Searle and others that Derrida left in English (since 'Limited Inc a b c . . .' and 'Afterword' were written in French but intended for translation into English).

3. The passage referred to is first cited in the uncut version of this essay (75). [Ed.]

16

'Je t'aime'

Derrida explores the phrase 'Je t'aime' ('I love you') as an exemplification of the speech-act theory he wants to put in place of Austin's or Searle's. Derrida originally presented his analysis of this phrase in two seminars given in December 1992 at the École des Hautes Études in Paris. He presented it again as one seminar in spring 1993 at the University of California at Irvine, in an English translation that he improvised on the spot. It has yet to be published.

The center of Derrida's argument is the claim that 'Je t'aime' is a performative, not a constative, utterance. This is true even though the locution seems to be set up as an assertion of fact: 'It is the fact that I love you. Make what you will of that fact.' 'Je t'aime' is a performative locution in part because the one to whom it is spoken has absolutely no way to verify that what I claim is a fact. You must take it on faith that I am telling you the truth. Another way to put this is to say that my locution 'Je t'aime' is always implicitly, even sometimes explicitly, accompanied by something like 'I swear to you that what I say is true.' The swearing is an explicit performative. Derrida goes so far as to assert that all performative language is testimony, bearing witness, and vice versa. Testifying is exemplary of performative speech acts. It is a way of doing things with words. Uttering 'Je t'aime' is in turn an exemplary case of bearing witness. Why is this? Derrida's thought about this question depends on several basic presuppositions, which I will enumerate here.

First presupposition: Though I have direct access to what I am thinking and feeling (however much I may be fooling myself or however much my self-awareness may be distorted by primary masochism or by my unconscious motivations), no one else does. The presumption of the isolation of the separate ego is fundamental here. Derrida refers to Husserl's fifth Cartesian Meditation as the crucial text for this. Derrida states:

> This act of faith is required by love, just as by all witnessing insofar as witnessing is a question of what takes place or is experienced within someone, some singular existence (*ego* or *Dasein*) there where the other cannot in any way have a direct, intuitive, and original [*originaire*] access. The other will never be on my side and will never have an intuitive, original access, in person, to the phenomenality for which I am origin of the world. In order to describe this zone which remains basically that of the secret and of absolute singularity, the secret and singularity of what is absolutely proper to me and of which I cannot expropriate myself, one of the best routes to

follow would be that of the Fifth of Husserl's *Cartesian Meditations*. Husserl recalls
there what is at once an axiom and an absolute evidence, that is to say, that the ego
which has an intuitive, immediate, and original phenomenological access, in person,
to the present phenomenality of its own experiences and of all that is proper to it can
never have access other than an indirect one, appresentative and analogical [*appré-
sentatif ou analogique*], to the experiences of the other, of the alter ego, which will
never themselves, in person, appear to the ego, and of which the constitution within
me requires such embarrassing procedures for transcendental phenomenology . . .
The irreducible alterity [*L'irréductible altérité*], which is also the irreducible singularity
and therefore the irreducible secret, is the condition of love and of the declaration of
love as witness and not as proof [*comme témoignage et non comme preuve*].[1]

The second presupposition is this: the fact that you have absolutely no way to
find out or to be certain one way or the other about my state of mind, though
nothing could be more important, both makes 'Je t'aime' possible and at the
same time always undermines it with the possibility that I may be lying, or
joking, or citing someone else. Its possibility depends on its impossibility,
according to an aporia encountered in my discussion of the more general theory
of iterability in *Limited Inc* [in the previous chapter. Ed.]. In the following
passage, Derrida expresses how in this new context the impossibility of knowing
is both a catastrophe for knowledge and at the same time absolutely essential, a
piece of good luck for it. The possibility that saying 'Je t'aime' might be a
felicitous performative, a successful way to do things with words, depends on
this lucky catastrophe:

> As I often do, I insist on the fact that here menace and chance [*chance*] are
> indissociable, and on the fact that what makes possible is also what puts in danger.
> I retain here the word 'chance,' which well testifies at once to good and to evil, to the
> condition of possibility that allows testimony to happen, which makes the event of
> witnessing possible but at the same time makes it risk losing itself or degenerating into
> non-singularity and into truth of the constative type of the 'what,' of the pointer, of
> the proof, of the sign, of the archive, etc. The word 'chance' testifies admirably to
> this; it is good luck [*il tombe bien*], since it expresses a happy chance, a possibility, a
> good probability in order to allow testimony to follow [*pour que le témoignage
> survienne*], in order that there is such a thing [*pour qu'il y en ait*], and also what
> brings about a fall, descent, decadence, or a falling due as forfeiture, fall, or decay [*et
> aussi ce qui fait tomber, la chute, la décadence ou l'échéance comme déchéance*]. There is a
> falling-due of testimony that renders indissociable in the body of the event this
> condition of possibility and this corruptibility.

Third presupposition: 'Je t'aime' creates the event it names. What Derrida
means here sounds scandalous: You do not fall in love until you say 'Je t'aime.'
The question of the relation of language to passion, affect, or pain has an
important place in twentieth-century thought, even in Anglo-American philosophy. The question is seen as in one way or another exemplary of the
opposition between constative and performative language. When I express one

passion or another, love or anger, or articulate my pain, do my words do no more than name something that already exists, or do my words create what they name, performatively? Wittgenstein's interminable reflections about the impossibility of a private language and about the problems of expressing my private pain, a pain that only I can feel or know; Austin's essay 'Pretending,' which takes off from the claim, made by another philosopher, that you are not angry until you express anger; and Proust's claim that lies, for example his lie to Albertine that he no longer loves her and wants to break with her, have a way of coming true just because we have said them out loud – here are three examples of the problematic that Derrida takes up in his own way in his claim, based explicitly on the human wisdom of Proust and of other great French novelists, that you are not in love until you say 'Je t'aime.' Saying 'Je t'aime' is therefore for Derrida an exemplary case of his special kind of performative utterance, the kind that is ungrounded but creates its own grounds in the act of being proffered:

> 'Je t'aime' is not a description; it is the production of an event by means of which, claiming not to lie, claiming to speak the truth (the 'Je t'aime' is always true, deemed to be true, immediately true, and . . . [it has an] extraordinary allure of indubitability . . .), I tend to affect the other, to touch the other, literally or not, to give the other or to promise the other the love that I speak to him or her . . . This performative declaration creates an event in manifesting, in attesting to that of which it speaks, in bearing witness to it; and that to which it testifies is not elsewhere, but here and now, nearly merging [*se confondant*] with the act that consists in saying it, which had caused more than one to say [*ce qui a pu faire dire à plus d'un*], from Stendhal to Gide or to Proust (I can't remember), that one begins truly to love after or at the earliest from the moment when love is declared and not before that [*qu'on commence veritablement à aimer après que ou au plus tôt au moment où l'amour est déclaré et non plus tôt*].

Fourth presupposition: A felicitous utterance of 'Je t'aime,' even if it is written in a letter, or spoken over the telephone, or sent by fax or e-mail, requires something more than words. It requires a breath, a gesture, a touch or the insinuation of a touch, something bodily that incarnates it in the here and now:

> I tend to affect the other, to touch the other, literally or not, to give the other or to promise him or her the love that I speak to him or her. In touching the other, by a certain caress in the words, even by a body to body engagement, of the body given or promised, even if this were beyond all present contact, in a letter, or on the telephone or in the facsimile of a fax . . . This also implies that the enunciation is not effective [*ne s'en puise pas*] in what is strictly speaking the enunciation, in a purely discursive manifestation, I mean verbal (lexical or syntactic); the body, intonation, and gesture are necessary, were it a breath, a look, not necessarily a caress, but in any case something singular and singularly sensible which makes it the case that the verbal speech alone does not suffice to a testimony, which signifies that the act or the gesture of witnessing, in a declaration of love, does not reduce itself to language, or to that in language which belongs to lexico-grammatical verbality.

This particular seminar contained a final insinuating ironic joke. It is impossible to be sure that Derrida, in merely citing 'Je t'aime' in his seminar, as he repeats the phrase over and over, more or less acting it out, is not also using it to seduce each member of his large audience. The uncertainty goes both ways:

> This also means, other ineffaceable face of the same truth, that the citation of 'Je t'aime,' a citation whose possibility remains implicit in the iterability itself that is the condition of every 'Je t'aime,' can, in certain conditions, to be sure, far from turning away from the 'Je t'aime,' therefore have certain seductive effects, certain seductive bonuses [*certains effets de séduction, certaines primes de séduction*], which it is also perhaps necessary to guard oneself against.

It is necessary to guard oneself from this danger, the danger of committing a strange case of sexual harassment with a whole lecture hall full of seventy or eighty students and faculty of all ages and both sexes, but Derrida cannot, by his own analysis, or even by Austin's, guard himself from doing this, since all mention is to some degree use and even the most deliberately constative statement has an element of the performative, and vice versa. I cannot say or write 'Je t'aime' without to some degree using it.

I have allowed myself to quote abundantly here partly because this admirable seminar has not yet been published, much less translated, and partly to guard myself, of course, from doing anything more than mentioning by citation what Derrida says. Citing the phrase in French is another protection. Surely I am not really saying 'I love you' to my readers when I cite Derrida's French phrase, which he used, by the way, even in the English version of the seminar in order to call attention to what is idiomatic and untranslatable in the French phrase. You can say 'Je t'aime' only in French, the true language of love. This is most obvious in the way, in French, the object of the declaration is given in the second-person singular, an impossibility in English, unless you say something archaic like 'I love thee,' which is not likely to be too effective these days. Nevertheless, by appropriating Derrida's words to my own purposes, I too have not eluded turning mention into use. By taking 'Je t'aime' as paradigmatic for the ethical situation in general, I have committed an ethical act of my own and have solicited my readers to understand in a certain way the new ethics and politics Derrida proposes.

Note

1. Jacques Derrida, seminar of 2 December 1992, given at École des Hautes Éludes, Paris, France, my translation, used by permission of the author, from a computer file in my possession. Further citations will be from this text. I thank Barbara Cohen and Peggy Kamuf for help with the translation. Since a computer file does not have

fixed page numbers (because its format may be altered), I do not give page references. The discussion of 'Je t'aime' continued in the seminar of 9 December 1992, but I make no citations from this continuation. Both seminars may be consulted in the Derrida Collection at the Critical Theory Archive in the library of the University of California at Irvine.

17

A Profession of Faith

A decisive moment in my life was my first encounter with Jacques Derrida. I first met him at the famous Johns Hopkins University International Colloquium on 'Critical Languages and the Sciences of Man' in October 1966. I missed his lecture on 'Structure, Sign, and Play in the Discourse of the Human Sciences' (Derrida 1978), because I had a class to teach at that hour. I did hear, however, his interventions in the discussions of other papers. I met my colleague and friend Georges Poulet in the Hopkins quadrangle just after Derrida's own lecture. He told me that Derrida's lecture was opposed to everything to which his own work (that is, Poulet's) was committed. Poulet at that time was writing on circles and centers, whereas Derrida's talk was about decentering. Nevertheless, said Poulet, it was the most important lecture of the conference by far, even though Jacques Lacan and many other worthies were also giving papers. I have always remembered Poulet's intellectual insight and generosity in saying that. He was right. Derrida's lecture marked the moment of the entry of so-called deconstruction into United States intellectual life. I had already, however, begun to read Derrida: the long two-part essay published in *Critique* in December 1965 and January 1966 that was developed into the first part of *De la grammatologie*.

When Derrida came a couple of years later as a visiting professor to Hopkins I went to his first seminar. I went just to see whether I could understand his spoken French. It was the seminar contrasting Plato on mimesis and Mallarmé's 'Mimique,' part of 'La double séance,' in *La dissémination* (Derrida 1972). I thought, and still think, it was an absolutely brilliant seminar. I still have somewhere the sheet he passed out juxtaposing 'Mimique' and a passage from Plato's Philebus. I have been faithfully attending Derrida's seminars ever since, first at Hopkins, then at Yale, and now at the University of California at Irvine. We began to have lunch together at Hopkins and have continued that practice ever since, for over forty years of unclouded friendship. Derrida and his writings have been major intellectual influences on me.

One of the strongest Derridean influences on my thinking has been his notion of the 'wholly other.' This has become more and more a salient motif in Derrida's work. Just what he means by 'the wholly other,' 'le tout autre,' is not all that easy to grasp. For many people, it is even more difficult to accept or to endorse with a profession of faith or a pledge of allegiance. One way to approach the Derridean wholly other is by way of his distinction between sovereignty and unconditionality. Unconditionality is, for Derrida, a name for the research university's hypothetical freedom from outside interference. Derrida defines the university's unconditionality as the privilege without penalty to put everything in question, even to put in question the right to put everything in question. In the interview with Derek Attridge that forms the first essay in the volume of Derrida's essays on literature that Attridge gathered and called *Acts of Literature* (Derrida 1992), Derrida defines literature in much the same way as he defines the university in more recent lectures, for example in *L'Université sans condition* (originally a President's Lecture at Stanford, Derrida 2001), and in a related essay, the speech he gave on receiving an honorary degree from the University of Pantion in Athens in 1999 (Derrida 2001b). That essay is entitled 'Inconditionnalité ou souveraineté: L'Université aux frontiers de l'Europe.' Both lectures are based on a fundamental distinction between sovereignty and what Derrida calls (the word is a neologism in English) 'unconditionality.' What is the difference? Sovereignty, says Derrida, is a theologically based 'phantasm.' It is something that looks like it is there but is not there. Sovereignty has three features: 1) The sovereign is above the law. He or she is free to subvert the law, as in the act of pardon. 2) The concept of sovereignty cannot be dissociated from the idea of the nation–state. 3) The sovereign is God's vicar, appointed by God, authorized by God. Even in a country like the United States, a country that was founded on the principle of the separation of church and state, the Pledge of Allegiance to the flag now defines the United States as 'one nation, under God.' All United States citizens were exhorted to sing 'God Bless America' after the Trade Center destruction of 9/11. George W. Bush apparently thinks of himself as appointed by God to preserve the United States from the 'threat of terrorism.' Such assumptions are a 'phantasm,' a ghost in broad daylight, since no verifiable data exists on which to base an assumption that God is on the United States' side any more than any data exists supporting the 'terrorists'' assumption that Allah was on their side when they blew up the World Trade Center towers or when they kill another American soldier in Iraq. Being told that sovereignty is a phantasm by no means cures one of faith in it. Far from it. The ghost of sovereignty always returns, as a 'revenant.'

Unconditionality has, apparently, no such fraudulent theological basis. Literature is dependent in its modern form on the rise of constitutional democracies in the West from the seventeenth century on and on the unconditional democratic freedom to say anything, that is to put everything in question. Such a democracy is of course never wholly established in fact. It is always 'to come':

'What is literature?' [asks Derrida]; literature as historical institution with its conventions, rules, etc., but also this institution of fiction which gives *in principle* the power to say everything, to break free of the rules, to displace them, and thereby to institute, to invent and even to suspect the traditional difference between nature and institution, nature and conventional law, nature and history. Here we should ask juridical and political questions. The institution of literature in the West, in its relatively modern form, is linked to the authorization to say everything, and doubtless too to the coming about of the modern idea of democracy. Not that it depends on a democracy in place, but it seems inseparable to me from what calls forth a democracy, in the most open (and doubtless itself to come) sense of democracy. (Derrida 1992a, 37)

Such a definition of literature allows us to understand better the role of the 'comme si' or 'as if' in *L'Université sans conditon.* Literature, or what Derrida here calls 'fiction,' can always respond (or refuse to respond) by saying, that was not me speaking as myself, but as an imaginary personage speaking in a work of fiction, by way of a 'comme si.' You cannot hold me responsible for my 'as ifs.' Derrida says just this in passages that follow the one just quoted:

What we call literature (not belles-lettres or poetry) implies that licence is given to the writer to say everything he wants or everything he can, while remaining shielded, safe from all censorship, be it religious or political . . . This duty of irresponsibility, of refusing to reply for one's thought or writing to constituted powers, is perhaps the highest form of responsibility. To whom, to what? That's the whole question of the future or the event promised by or to such an experience, what I was just calling the democracy to come. Not the democracy of tomorrow, not a future democracy which will be present tomorrow but one whose concept is linked to the to-come [*à-venir,* cf. *avenir,* future], to the experience of a promise engaged, that is always an endless promise. (Derrida 1992a, 37, 38)

Crucial in the passage just cited is the 'To whom, to what?' How can a refusal to take responsibility, a refusal addressed to sovereign state powers, be defined as 'perhaps the highest form of responsibility'? To whom or to what else can it have a higher obligation? Derrida's answer to this question goes by way of the new concept of performative language he proposes in 'Psyché: l'invention de l'autre' and again as the climax of *L'Université sans condition.* It might seem that literature, conceived by Derrida as an 'as if,' a free, unconditioned fiction, would correspond to a concept of literature as unconditioned performative speech acts, speech acts based neither on previously existing institutionalized sanctions nor on the authority of the 'I' who utters the speech act. The title of the honorary degree lecture in Athens is 'Inconditionalité ou souveraineté' and *L'Université sans condition* distinguishes sharply between the phantasm of theologically based state sovereignty and the unfettered, 'unconditioned,' liberty to put everything in question in the ideal university, the university without condition. Such a university, like a truly democratic state, is always 'to come.' Derrida seems to pledge allegiance to, or, to use his own expression, make a 'profession of faith in,' a stark either/or. His word 'profession' alludes of course to the academic title of 'professor.' A professor professes faith in the validity of what he or she teaches or writes. The 'ou' or 'or' in Derrida's title opposes always-illegitimate sovereignty to unconditional freedom.

This unconditionality, it might seem, is especially manifested in literary study. Literature, as institutionalized in the West in the last three centuries, is, according to Derrida, itself unconditioned, irresponsible, free to say anything. Literature is an extreme expression of the right to free speech. To study literature is to profess faith in literature's unconditionality.

Matters are, however, not quite so simple. In the last section of *L'Université sans condition*, in the seventh summarizing proposition, Derrida makes one further move that undoes all he has said so far about the university's unconditionality. He poses a 'hypothesis' that he admits may not be 'intelligible' (Derrida 2001a, 79) to his Stanford audience. (This audience may have included Condoleezza Rice, then Provost of that university. Would that she had listened, understood, and given her allegiance.) Derrida admits, in a quite unusual confession, that what he asserts is not easy to understand. It is 'extrêmement difficile et presque im-probable, inaccessible à une preuve' (Derrida 2001a, 76). What he says is based on a hypothesis that is extremely difficult, almost improbable, prima facie highly unlikely, and almost impossible to prove. What he proposes, that is, is contrary to a true scientific hypothesis. A bona fide hypothesis can be proved to be false, if it is false.

What is this strange hypothesis? It is the presupposition that the unconditional independence of thinking in the university depends on a strange and anomalous speech act that brings about what Derrida calls an 'event' or 'the eventful (l'éventuel)' (Derrida 2001a, 76). Such a speech act is anomalous both because it does not depend on pre-existing rules, authorities, and contexts, as a felicitous Austinian speech act does, and because it also does not posit freely, autonomously, lawlessly, outside all such pre-existing contexts, as, for example, de Manian speech acts seem to do, or as judges do in Austin's surprising and even scandalous formula: 'As official acts, the judge's ruling makes law' (Austin 1980, 154).

No, the performative speech act Derrida has in mind, is a response to the call of what Derrida calls 'le tout autre,' the wholly other. Such a response is to some degree passive or submissive. It obeys a call or command. All we can do is profess faith in the call or pledge allegiance to it. Only such a speech act constitutes a genuine 'event' that breaks the predetermined course of history. Such an event is 'impossible.' It is always an uncertain matter of what, Derrida recalls, Nietzsche calls 'this dangerous perhaps' (2001, 75). Nevertheless, says Derrida, 'seul l'impossible peut arriver' (2001, 74), only the impossible is able to arrive. That is why Derrida speaks of 'le possible événement de l'inconditionnel impossible, le tout autre' (2001, 76), 'the possible happening of the impossible unconditional, the wholly other.' Derrida is playing here on the root sense of 'event' as something that comes, that arrives. It appears of its own accord and in its own good time. We can only say, 'yes' or, perhaps, 'no,' to it. We cannot call it. It calls us.

What is 'the wholly other'? Derrida works out in detail, in 'Psyché, ou l'invention de l'autre,' what he means by 'invention' as discovery, as uncovering rather than making up, and what he means by 'the wholly other.' For my purposes here, however, the crucial text is *Donner la mort*, translated, in part, as *The Gift of Death*. There Derrida makes spectacular readings of the story of Abraham and Isaac in Genesis, of Kierkegaard's *Fear and Trembling*, and of Melville's *Bartleby the Scrivener*. In extended sections of this book Derrida defines the wholly other in ways that identify it with a certain conception of God, as 'absent, hidden and silent, separate, secret' (1995, 57), with the secret in general, and with death, the gift of death, death as always my own solitary death, and as wholly other to my knowledge. 'Without knowing from whence the thing comes,' says Derrida, 'and what awaits us, we are given over to absolute solitude. No one can speak with us and no one can speak for us; we must take it upon ourselves, each of us must take it upon himself (*auf sich nehmen* as Heidegger says concerning death, our death, concerning what is always "my death," and which no one can take on in place of me)' (ibid.). The wholly other is also manifested, without manifesting itself, in the total inaccessibility of the secrets in the hearts of other people.

> *Every other [one] is every [bit] other [tout autre est tout autre]*, [says Derrida], every one else is completely or wholly other. The simple concepts of alterity and of singularity constitute the concept of duty as much as that of responsibility. As a result, the concepts of responsibility, of decision, or of duty, are condemned a priori to paradox, scandal, and aporia . . . As soon as I enter into a relation with the other, with the gaze, look, request, love, command, or call of the other, I know that I can respond only by sacrificing ethics, that is, by sacrificing whatever obliges me to also respond, in the same way, in the same instant, to all the others. I offer a gift of death, I betray, I don't need to raise my knife over my son on Mount Moriah for that. Day and night, at every instant, on all the Mount Moriahs of this world, I am doing that, raising my knife over what I love and must love, over those to whom I owe absolute fidelity, incommensurably. (1995, 68)

Included in this concept of the wholly other is literature. Literature too hides impenetrable secrets. A work of literature too is a response to a wholly other that strongly recalls the relation of literature to death in Blanchot's 'Literature and the Right to Death' (Blanchot 1981). This is made explicit in Derrida's reading of 'Bartleby the Scrivener,' but also in the second, untranslated, part of *Donner la mort*, entitled 'La literature au secret: Une filiation impossible.' In this section, by way of further discussion of Abraham and Isaac, of Kierkegaard, and of Kafka, Derrida reaches the surprising conclusions not only that literature hides secrets that cannot be revealed, but also that literature is both irresponsible and at the same time works by 'aggravant d'autant, jusqu'à l'infini sa responsabilité pour l'événement singulier que constitue chaque oeuvre (responsabilité nulle et infinie, comme celle de Abraham) (by aggravating, moreover, even to infinity its responsibility for the singular event that constitutes each work (responsibility null and infinite, like Abraham's))' (1999, 206). Literature, so defined, is the unfaithful inheritor of a theological legacy without which it could not exist:

> . . . la literature hérite, certes, d'une histoire sainte dont le moment abrahamique reste le secret essentiel (et qui niera que la literature reste une reste de religion, un lien et un relais de sacro-sainteté dans une société sans Dieu?), mais elle renie aussi cette histoire, cette appartenance, cet heritage. Elle renie cette filiation. Elle la trahit au double sens du mot: elle lui est infidèle, elle rompt avec elle au moment même d'en manifester la 'vérité' et d'en dévoiler le secret. À savoir sa proper filiation: possible impossible.

> (. . . literature inherits, certainly, a sacred history of which the Abrahamic moment remains the essential secret (and who will deny that literature remains a remainder of religion, a connection and a relay of sacrosanctity in a society without God?), but it also denies that history, that belonging, that heritage. It denies that filiation. It betrays it in the double sense of the word: it is unfaithful to it, it breaks with it in the moment of manifesting its 'truth' and of unveiling its secret. That is to say its own filiation: possible impossible.)

> (1999, 208)

It is only necessary to add to what Derrida says here that literary study, as institutionalized in the university, is especially the place where the responsibility / irresponsibility of literature, its unconditionality, is received or 'professed' by professors and passed on to students. One small example: the dissident notions of state sovereignty in Forster's *Howards End* (Forster 1989).

I have now professed, in the sense of specifying and transmitting, Derrida's notions of sovereignty and unconditionality. I have done this, however, apparently at the cost of blurring the distinction between theologically based state sovereignty and the unconditional freedom of the university and of literary study within the university. Both, in the end, seem to be theological or quasi-theological concepts. What's the difference? That difference is easy to see, but perhaps not all that easy to accept. The distinction is 'improbable' and 'not provable,' though it is essential to Derrida's thinking. For Derrida, and for me too, all claims by earthly sovereigns, such as those made implicitly by George W. Bush, to wield power by mandate from God, are phantasms. They claim to see and to respond to something that is not there. A work of literature, on the other hand, and therefore the teaching of that work in a 'university without condition,' if there ever were to be such a thing, are responses to a call or command from the wholly other that is both impossible and yet may perhaps arrive. Each work is entirely singular, 'counter, original, spare, strange' as Gerard Manley Hopkins puts it ('Pied Beauty,' l. 7, Hopkins 1948, 74). Each work is as different from every other work as each person differs from all others, or as each leaf differs from all others. When I as reader or teacher respond to the wholly other as embodied in a literary work and try to mediate it to my students or to readers of what I write, I am, perhaps, just 'perhaps,' fulfilling my professional duty to put everything in question, and to help make or keep my university 'without condition.'

Whether or not I have 'got Derrida right' in my profession of faith in what he says I must leave to Derrida himself to tell me. Probably, however, he will not tell me one way or the other. According to Derrida's own testimony and according to his profession of faith, I will be left on my own, as professors always are, to respond as best I can to the demand made on me by his notion of the wholly other.

Responses IV

'How About a Game of Tennis?'[1]
Megan Becker-Leckrone

'I am still trying, and still puzzled.'
J. Hillis Miller

When I began teaching a newly-required theory course for English majors at my university, I did something that testified to Hillis Miller's indelible influence on the way I understand theory – reading it, teaching it, and 'doing' it. I changed the title of the course, inherited from the university catalog and from the tenuous consensus established by (I'm told) heated faculty meetings that preceded my hire. 'Introduction to Literary Theories and Practices' became, according to my syllabus at least, 'Introduction to Literary Theory.' After reading and listening to Hillis Miller for years, it had become impossible for me to accept the mandate implied by that name. According to the catalog description, introducing students to 'theories and practices' meant exposing them to 'a variety of literary theories,' after which or through which '[l]iterary texts' would be 'examined from a variety of perspectives.' The practical contours of such a course are clear: an if-it's-Tuesday-it must-be-Marxism survey of -isms (which rarely involve reading Marx) thereafter seen at work in a sampling of 'practical' applications to *Hamlet*, or *Heart of Darkness*, or any literary text.

The problematic premise of the 'theories and practices' approach is that, no matter the literary work, you can find a Marxist, feminist, structuralist, psycho-analyst, deconstructionist, new historicist, queer theorist, postcolonialist who has interpreted it through one among this great 'variety' of theoretical lenses. Constatively, that may indeed be an historical fact. Performatively, however, the prismatic survey of how theorists do things with, say, *Hamlet* does something in itself and makes other things happen in turn, many of which we might dub 'infelicitous.'

For just what kinds of things get done in such a course? And what do those doings teach about the relation between 'practice' and 'theory'? Is theory merely something that can be 'done' in a value-neutral 'variety' of ways, as the few exemplary pieces of theory in action show us in those ironically named 'Critical

Readers' on *Hamlet*, and so on? Is it something students, in turn, simply 'do' according to the dictates of a syllabus or at the invitation of a homework assignment? According to Miller, literary theory makes a demand, imposes a responsibility, upon every reader. The stakes are always high, the conditions always fairly treacherous. Despite the fluent approachability of his essays, the evident joy he takes in reading literature and writing about it, the generous encouragement he gives to his students, Miller never promises readerly success, not his own or anyone else's. Instead, the countless pithy, laconic statements of 'advice' tend to carry with them an undertone of threat. 'Reading is extraordinarily hard work,' he warns in *The Ethics of Reading*. 'It hardly ever happens.' Good reading is slow reading. But there is no way to do it but to do it, for ourselves. The tools and moves the 'variety' of theories offer us ultimately come down, in every case, to a reader and a text. Indeed, given the perils of reading and its demands, 'It might be better not to read.' Ethically, however, 'the most responsible way' to proceed 'is to do something . . . I must read something' (20). Doing something is better than nothing, it seems.

Miller's admonitions about good theory, good practice, tend to be carefully implicating speech acts in themselves, the very opposite of the casual invitation implied by the 'Critical Reader'/ 'Theories and Practices' model. Miller speaks of *teaching* reading as a similarly fraught, similarly unpredictable, event that precipitates other unpredictable things in turn, in such good natured, plainspoken terms that it is possible for the casual reader to overlook the profound implications of this act as well. '[D]ismayingly different things happen,' for instance, when teachers tell students to 'Read *Bleak House* by next Tuesday' – especially given the fact that, as Miller notes with characteristically exquisite irony, '[s]ensitivity to irony seems to be unevenly distributed in the population.'

When a very earnest student enrolled in just such a 'theory and practice' course long ago complained to me that she had so many 'things to do' that weekend – she had a tennis tournament *and* had to 'deconstruct a poem' – I understood the full ideological force behind such course designs. 'Theory,' so understood, becomes nothing more than a series of utterly practical training exercises. Or at least this student understood them as such. This week's deconstructionist would be compelled next week to practice the swing of the new historicist. Both moves get the ball across the net. Except that maybe sometimes they don't. For Miller, of course, 'doing things' with theory has always been a more nuanced, complex, precarious endeavor, at once much harder work, always freighted with the burden of deep responsibility, with the specter of failure, but also with the promise of something happening – *reading* – altogether more transformative than any casebook survey of -isms ever could be.

We can see Miller's vision of this transformation on the institutional level in 'The Function of Literary Theory at the Present Time.' He begins with a wistful remembrance of past time, namely the ambitious vision of a critical future Paul de Man momentarily imagines in the midst of a meticulous reading of Proust. 'Not that long ago,' he recalls, de Man 'could cheerfully say, with how much or how little of irony is impossible to know, that *the* task of criticism in the coming years would be a kind of imperialistic appropriation of all literature by the method of rhetorical reading often called "deconstruction" '. In the 'Present Time' of Miller's essay, he tempers such cheer with the observation that the task de Man assigns to future critics has not been carried out 'with much systematic rigor.' There seems to have been, in the intervening years, more talk *about* deconstruction 'as a "theory" or as a "method"' than there has been doing it, or showing how it is done.

A massive mobilization of 'extrinsic' literary studies – interpretive methods that consider literature within 'psychological, historical, or sociological contexts' – is a key factor in the uneven distribution of critical labor that leaves so much of de Man's 'intrinsic' rhetorical work still to be done. But also instrumental is the ideological staying power of the false and misleading binary assumption that kinds of readings can indeed be organized according to interests 'intrinsic' or 'extrinsic' to the text in question. Miller's invocation of these terms, ultimately to reject them, refutes the tired but apparently tireless charge that the 'intrinsic' focus of rhetorical or deconstructive criticism ignores the real world outside the text. But it does so by subtly turning the tables on those who righteously deplore the supposed nihilistic bad faith and insular, apolitical indifference of decon-struction. Instead, what becomes unethical by Miller's reckoning is unselfcon-scious criticism not actively devoted to 'understanding just what the role of literature might be in society, in history, and in individual human life.' Too often, 'extrinsic' criticism takes that relation (literature *in* . . .) for granted, or worries too little about the persistent 'danger of misplacing that role, of claiming too much for literature . . . as a political or historical force, or of thinking of the teaching of literature as too explicitly political.'

As in so many of Miller's eloquent meditations on theory and literature, what effectively undoes the intrinsic/extrinsic opposition on which such accusations depend, what reminds such accusers of their own critical responsibilities, is the disarming yet devastating way in which he defines 'reading.' For surely no kind of literary criticism, no matter how ambitiously it seeks to account for forces 'outside' the text, would deny that the real work of criticism is *reading*, especially given Miller's eminently practical, common-sense definition of this labor. 'Reading,' in this sense, names the humble effort 'to know just what a given text is and says, what it can do.' It would be hard to disagree with Miller's assertion that such work is 'indispensable' for 'intrinsic' and 'extrinsic' critics alike. But if reading is an obvious task, it is nevertheless also unpredictable. For what a text is and says and does 'can never be taken for granted beforehand.' Reading, so defined, may be an obvious practical necessity, but it also poses a radical theoretical challenge to critics who too easily assume that literature ever offers a stable thematic or mimetic 'reflection' of some reality external to it.

What becomes an act of critical bad faith in Miller's reckoning, thus, is the mimetic assumption itself, and with it, the neglect or willful forgetting of deconstruction's insights about the figurative language's interference 'with the straightforward working of grammar and logic,' as if those insights were but a stage in some developmental history of criticism which we have absorbed, or worse, moved beyond.[2]

Miller's definitions of reading tend to appear in two different modes: those that follow the cadences of plain-spoken common sense ('to know just what a given text is and says') and those that point polemically, though still with measure and grace, at a fairly ferocious intellectual battle whose stakes could not be higher. In the latter mode, Miller calls reading 'indispensable to any responsible concern for the relations of literature to what is outside it,' warning of the 'catastrophe' that would ensue from merely relegating the 'rhetorical study of literature' to the past. Indeed, without this rhetorical focus – sharpened not just by deconstruction, but before it by the New Criticism and Empson and Burke – 'we can have no hope of understanding just what the role of literature might be in society, in history, and in individual human life.' Seemingly invoking the pieties of traditional humanistic studies, those modeled on an Arnoldian vision of the liberal arts as the torch-bearer of moral and aesthetic values, the purveyor of the Western tradition's 'best' intellectual products, Miller's polemical high alert in fact aligns deconstruction with critical methods more avowedly devoted to consensus-busting 'social justice.' New Criticism itself, perhaps in spite of its own conservative motivations, was 'a major blow at the consensus' because 'as soon as you shift, however benignly, from attention to *what* is said, the thematic content, to *how* it is said,' the humanistic consensus – about what is read and what it means – can no longer hold. 'Sooner or later,' Miller mildly portends, 'some teachers or students will see that the how contaminates and undermines the what.'

Any careful reader of Miller's title could foresee this turn, from defending rhetorical reading against charges of obsolescence or political quietism to more broadly reflecting on the ways the theoretically-informed humanities of the future utterly transforms the humanities of the past. For it not only reworks the name of Arnold's famous essay on the subject – 'The Function of Criticism at the Present Time' – it also fully adopts its form, and in a sense its argument, though with a crucial difference. Arnold advocates a 'criticism' that aims 'to see the object as in itself it really is' in an emphatically disinterested manner, 'aloof' from 'what is called "the practical view of things".' It may do so by 'steadily refusing to lend itself to any of those ulterior, political, practical considerations about ideas . . . which criticism has really nothing to do with' (Arnold 1993, 1397). Miller's reworking of Arnold's title through the opposition between an 'intrinsic' rhetorical criticism and 'extrinsic' criticisms privileging historical, political, or sociological contexts reanimates Arnold's own opposition between a supposedly pure, disinterested criticism of the text as 'object' and those with 'ulterior' concerns. But at the same time, he pits Arnold's own words, his own binaries and boundaries, against themselves. 'The Function of Criticism at the Present Time,' 'The Function of Literary Theory at the Present Time': Miller's parasitic title indeed performatively illustrates the precise 'function' of rhetorical criticism within 'literary theory' as such. The unassuming shift in terminology marks the more cataclysmic shift Miller describes 'at the Present Time' and calls for in the future. The shift from a criticism of *what* (Arnold's 'best that is thought and said') to a criticism of *how* (the formal contours of form, style, figure, and voice) dealt insurmountable blows to Arnoldian humanism. But what is truly remarkable about this transformation, Miller argues, is that Arnold's vision may have set the conditions for its own demise: 'From the point of view of that old Arnoldian consensus about the humanities both the New Criticism and the development of comparative literature were subversive. They were ultimately lethal invasions, destructive parasites within the host organism, generated by the organism itself.'

What Miller demonstrates as much as argues here is the genuinely subversive power of 'rhetoric' itself, or rather the extent to which the *performativity* of language outpaces, in unpredictable ways, any stable critical effort to account for 'the object as in itself it really is,' whether through intrinsic or extrinsic methods of analysis. Again, 'reading' is the name Miller gives to the literary theory, any literary theory, that might responsibly endeavor to describe the unique, variable ways in which a given text 'makes things happen,' how each text 'is a way of doing things with words.' Miller's ideal model of such a rigorous reader is de Man. In much of 'what he has written' (a phrase Miller highlights by stating twice), we can see at work 'neither pure theory nor pure praxis . . . but a mode of interpretive language which is beyond this false and misleading opposition.' We can look to de Man's work, which almost always center 'on the reading of some text or other' as exemplary in a certain sense, but not simply as examples. Like de Man's, Miller's work similarly exemplary yet inimitable, showing us the slow, hard, risk work of good reading. His texts are always complex performances of 'how deconstruction works' that are nevertheless never simply 'how to' guides to master in a weekend, in between tennis matches. They represent far more than one -ism among many, as ill-suited to a 'theories and practices' version of theory as J. L. Austin's *How to Do Things with Words* would be to the do-it-yourself aisle at Barnes and Noble.

Notes

1. In *Speech Acts in Literature* (7), Miller uses this phrase as an example of an utterance, an invitation, that demonstrates the complicated performative and constative dimensions of 'How' phrases, such as J. L. Austin's *How to Do Things with Words*.

2. One of Miller's most trenchant critiques of this mode of thinking, a 'handy bit of ideological storytelling' that characterizes deconstruction as an important but flawed moment in the development of a more fully realized, more politically sensitive literary theory, can be found in 'Derrida's Topographies,' *Topographies* (1995). Miller marshals Tom Cohen's analysis of this gesture that 'abjects' deconstruction's most powerful, but also most uncomfortable, implications for reading and interpretation.

Response to J. Hillis Miller, 'A Profession of Faith'
Rachel Bowlby

'Tout autre est tout autre.' Derrida's sentence, the focus of Hillis Miller's commentary in this piece, is untranslatable into English. Its snap depends on the repetition of 'tout autre,' but no English expression will do the job of meaning both 'every other' and 'quite other.' David Mills, as quoted above by Miller, does the best he can: 'Every other [one] is every [bit] other.' 'Every other is quite different.' 'And yet, 'every other is every other.' The sentence can also be read or heard in this tautological form, literally so, even without a translation, since the same two words appear on either side of the central 'is.' The visible circularity of 'tout autre est tout autre' is present alongside, or against, the 'quite different' meaning of the sentence, which says almost the opposite.

Miller begins with a scene in which a passage takes place from circularity to something like the contrary. '[Georges Poulet] told me that Derrida's lecture was opposed to everything to which his own work (that is, Poulet's) was committed. Poulet at that time was writing on circles and centers, whereas Derrida's talk was about decentering.' Poulet, however, generously acknowledges the quality of Derrida's thinking and it is a moment that implicitly gives Miller permission to make the move himself from centers to decentering, or from Poulet to Derrida. He speaks of this occasion, in the opening sentence of this piece, as a 'decisive moment in my life,' his 'first encounter with Jacques Derrida.' In the story he tells, it is also a humorously missed encounter. Miller didn't go to the lecture because 'I had a class to teach at that hour.' He was there and not there – present on the campus at Hopkins at the moment of the epoch-making lecture, but not present at the actual 'event.' Or not until subsequently. For Miller's brilliantly understated narrative also lets us see how the other encounter, with Poulet, marked the lecture as being, as having come to be, an event in the Derridean sense which Miller goes on to explicate. Something had happened, someone had 'arrived'; 'this marked the moment of the entry of so-called deconstruction into United States intellectual life.'

Through this engaging, seemingly incidental opening Miller introduces most of the themes and tensions that will occupy his 'profession of faith.' The presence and uniqueness of the person – Derrida, Poulet, in this place, on this occasion – is vividly evoked at the same time as the question of the professor's professional obligations – the class to teach. These ostensibly divergent concerns are intertwined throughout Miller's essay. What the professor professes, to students in a seminar, or in writing, cannot be separated from a form of belief, a calling from 'le tout autre,' 'the wholly other.' That calling enjoins upon the professor to try, faithfully, to transmit its significance to others, in a work that is bound to be incomplete – the other remains other, there is a remainder of otherness – but may and must nonetheless be attempted. This calling comes from an individual thinker or from individual works of literature; Miller's own avowed response to Derrida joins and extends what Derrida says, in the passages Miller quotes, of the singularity of literary works. Responsibility, as Miller elucidates it here, encompasses both professional duty and something that may appear as quite the opposite, an obligation to follow the thought in its questioning of everything and a call for the utmost commitment, for a faith that must go against and exceed the general requirements of everyday 'respon- sibilities.'

Miller begins by following Derrida's critique of the notion of sovereignty as a kind of theological delusion, 'a ghost in broad daylight' that proffers itself as a phantasm falsely compelling belief. He sets this, with Derrida, against the ideal of unconditionality, associated with democracy and with literary freedom as the right to say anything, to put everything in question. This is the right embodied in the ideal of the research university, hypothetically free from all outside interference, whether from government or from religion. But then, still following Derrida, Miller beautifully shows, step by step, how theology returns to, or is never absent from that apparently quite secular, quite faithless democratic right. Literature denies this legacy or 'filiation.' But it is there, in connection with the singularity of every work, every work as uniquely itself, as 'wholly other' because it does not give up all its secrets to the notional daylight of lucid exposition or transparency to understanding.

The attempt to clarify or explain is nonetheless inescapable and essential. It is the professor's vocation, his or her duty to (try to) transmit a way of thinking or the distinctiveness of a literary work. Miller deliberately stresses this for his own part: 'It is only necessary to add to what Derrida says here that literary study, as institutionalized in the university, is especially the place where the responsible/ irresponsibility of literature, its unconditionality, is received or "professed" by professors and passed on to students.' And Miller then goes on to make the point clear in relation to the present accomplishment: 'I have now professed, in the sense of specifying and transmitting, Derrida's notions of sovereignty and unconditionality.'

But this is not the end. Miller's final move is to separate out again the two concepts whose unexpected imbrication he had previously drawn out. Sover- eignty and unconditionality can be differentiated after all, as George W. Bush's parade of divine right is evidently distinguishable from the kind of faith called forth by what is wholly other in a literary work and from the unconditionality of the university, where it may be conceivable for some sense of that literary singularity to be conveyed by the professor's own teaching or example: 'When I as reader or teacher respond to the wholly other as embodied in a literary work and try to mediate it to my students or to readers of what I write, I am, perhaps, just "perhaps," fulfilling my professional duty to put everything in question, and to help make or keep my university "without condition."'

In this piece, as in everything he has written, Miller writes with a disarming and wholly appealing lucidity. He presents himself as a pedagogical mediator, here of Derrida's thinking and elsewhere of particular literary texts. Always there is a shining modesty. 'Whether or not I have "got Derrida right" in my profession of faith in what he says I must leave Derrida to tell me.' Always the stress on a singularity, of text or person, that no amount of exegesis will ever exhaust. No reading can ever fully explain, which would be to return to the circularity of 'tout autre est tout autre,' x is x (is x is x) abolishing or disregarding what makes the other uniquely what it (or he or she) 'is,' as utterly distinct from all (other) others. The interpretation and the transmission are necessarily partial in relation to something that can never be simply or wholly made manifest. But by the same token they are also something else, if not wholly other, and perhaps not knowingly different at all (which might seem like a breach of faith or a failure of the professor's duty). Here Miller's professedly faithful endeavor is happily marked by the difference his writing and teaching do make – a difference that has the effect of positive addition and amplification of possibility. Enabling lucidity is one facet of that. Miller traverses the stages of a process of understanding and so passes on to his readers (and listeners) the means of following him as he follows the text or the thinker in question.

'A Profession of Faith' reminds me of what I have learned from Hillis Miller over the years – from his teaching and his professional example and his friendship. From his writing above all. A decisive moment in my life occurred one day in 1978 when, as an undergraduate, I came across Miller's 1971 article on Wordsworth's 'Westminster Bridge' sonnet (1971, 297–310). The previous year, I had heard Derrida talk on the parasite when he visited Oxford, but I had no idea of how to put together the dimly perceived new perspectives of deconstruction with the kind of reading, critical and literary, that I was doing for my courses. Miller's article was a breath of fresh air, at once inspiring and refreshingly comprehensible. Looking back at it now, you can see the historical signs of the conversion or revolution of thinking, from centers to decentering, a few years before this article, that Miller describes in 'A Profession': 'Most concepts of form presuppose covertly or overtly the existence of a center outside the play of elements in the poem. This centre is at once the origin of meaning and at the same time the control over meaning' (309–10). As Miller argues, it is one of the achievements of Wordsworth's 'Sonnet' to have put that centre in question, and the Derrida text to which he refers his readers is none other than the lecture from the Hopkins conference, 'Structure, Sign and Play.' With this as one of his frames, Miller builds a reading of Wordsworth that is wholly original. It is Derridean but *sui generis tout autre*. By his own confession and profession, Miller has thus been transmitting Derrida's thinking for more than thirty years, a period encompassed by the 'forty years of unclouded friendship' he has enjoyed with him. But this is not a process that passes only in one direction. From the same year as the *New Literary History* piece, Derrida closes his book *Dissemination* with a dedication to four interlocutors who, he says, 'will perhaps recognise what intervenes of their reading here.' One of the four (the others are Rodolphe Gasché, Jean-Joseph Goux and Jean-Claude Lebensztein) is Hillis Miller (Derrida 1972).[1]

Note

1. The dedication is dated December, 1971.

Hillis Miller – Flâneur of the Archive
Tom Cohen

there has been more talk about deconstruction, as a 'theory' or as a 'method,' attempts to applaud it or to deplore it, than there has been an attempt to do it.

J. Hillis Miller

The thread is the labyrinth, and at the same time it is a repetition of the labyrinth.

J. Hillis Miller

The editor's quiet inversion of the classic order of 'theory and practice' into 'practice and theory' in the above section points to a counter-strophe in Hiller Miller's work. It suggests more than the appearance of working from the singular example (close reading) as if back to performative implications rather than, typically, how theoretical ideas are as if applied or how a literal practice generates theoretical insights. It anticipates a more central objection to the two terms being joined as such *at all*. When speaking of an exemplary critic – Hillis will recurrently formulate the notion of 'the critic' in this way – the latter rather dismisses the famous *binary* tout court and points instead to 'a mode of interpretive language which is beyond this false and misleading opposition':

what he has written, like all good literary study, is neither pure theory nor pure praxis, 'practical criticism,' nor yet a mixture of the two or something between the two, but a mode of interpretive language which is beyond this false and misleading opposition.

We are forced to ask a different question: what is this practice that is 'beyond' practice and theory, and what might it be called, aim at, mark itself as however discretely, if it cannot simply return to either term?

To examine what is meant we might review how Hillis sketches the task of what he sometimes simply calls 'the critic.' The 'critic' is Miller's Zarathustran hypothesis and alter-ego, spectral and at times lost in labyrinthine calibrations – continually altering archival premises and concealed switchboards of thought in what seems an irreversible or irrevocable direction: 'The dissolution of the consensus about humanistic study, a dissolution in which both internal and external factors have, as I have said, cooperated, has meant an irrevocable breakdown of the canon, a breakdown of the assumption of translatability, and, finally, a breakdown of the assumption that humanistic education is primarily aesthetic (has to do with pleasure) and thematic (has to do with values).' This critic's movement is not always promising, since the direction he takes irreversibly leads to recurrent aporia – that is, toward impasses within logical templates that would be effaced yet invisibly control the latter's transit routes. For instance, when he takes note of the complex way in which the critic alters and is altered (or produced) by the logics he engages, agent and subject can not be segregated out: 'The thing to be defined enters into and contaminates the definer, according to a recurrent aporia.' Having evacuated received assumptions the critic cannot get back to routine logics of representation, subjects, and historical data. In fact, the prefigural zone under scrutiny enters and begins to recast familiar fields governed by metaphor: 'Many, if not all, economic terms involve linear imagery: circulation, binding promise or contract, recoup, coupon, margin, cutback, line your pockets, on the line (which means ready for immediate expenditure), currency, current, and pass current.' Hillis implies, if one pays attention, that something has altered and that the recasting of an entire epistemological chart is underway or has already occurred – and he is examining its aftermath. I cite from the essay 'Line' opening this section, which speaks of a labyrinth that the reader enters:

> What line should the critic follow in explicating, unfolding, or unknotting these passages? How should the critic thread her or his way into the labyrinthine problems of narrative form, and in particular into the problem of repetition in fiction? The line of the line itself? The motif, image, concept, or formal model of the line, however, far from being a 'clue' to the labyrinth, turns out . . . to be itself the labyrinth.

The critic here has pursued a certain direction, sauntering through archival riddles from which he might not return – at least not to any familiar hermeneutic. The labyrinth lies in the structure of the medium (motif, image, concept) rather than in a content ('clue'): that is to say, in the graphematic orders which the archive is programmed by yet outwardly effaces. Nietzsche asked after the freedom of human thought as long as man required grammar; Miller asks the same question with reference to prefigural inscriptions which determine or define what is received as meaning, performance, the political, the aesthetic, 'literature,' reading, the 'wholly other.' This is quite a network for 'the critic' to be asked to patrol, if he had any choice in the matter, but it reminds us again of a dimension of Hillis that may be insufficiently noted: not only that he finds himself linked to transitional critical figures such as Walter Benjamin, but that the *task* of Miller's 'critic,' like that of the former's translator, seems preparatory to a coming shift, more or less everywhere implied, in the epistemo-political template. With this in mind, one might suggest that Miller returns again and again to a site or non-site in collective post-Enlightenment programs where all of these histories intertwine, arrive, and depart again. It is at such a site that certain interventions may seem possible.

The bracketing of 'practice and theory' as residue of an old conceptual disorder occurs with the question of *performativity*. The 'materiality' that de Man sought, at a point where the word abandons its referential pretext, lies in archival orders that mutatingly program or forecast historial experience – in the non-anthropomorphic domain of what he chose to call *inscriptions*.[1]

Hillis does not merely shuttle, as in the selections offered here, between a graphic effect and institutional politics like the definition and place of 'the Humanities.' He finds these questions themselves linked to two premises: that *events* – such as canonized texts attest to – operate from within historical and political archives, under cover yet with incremental power and diverse roles, and that seeking those sites or nodes represents a virtual site of rewiring. But how does the critic yoke something like an analytic of the 'line' or the *zero* (as in a recent essay by Miller) to institutional politics affecting the futures not only of the Humanities but 'humanity'? Miller here evokes an *other* model of what is called materiality and history:

> My contention is that the study of literature has a great deal to do with history, society, the self, but that this relation is not a matter of thematic reflection within literature of these extra-linguistic forces and facts, but rather a matter of the way the study of literature offers perhaps the best opportunities to identify the nature of language as it may have effects on what de Man calls 'the materiality of history.'

This intervention occurs as if where theorization turns back upon itself in the practice of a writing that is transformed by what it, transformatively, tracks ('the thing to be defined enters into and contaminates the definer'). Miller's 'critic' is a transitional figure, a figure of and in transit. He suggests the itinerary of a Benjaminian *flâneur* working within the archiving archive: stop here, in this poet's phrase or this mark, in this institutional impasse or aporia, and a ganglia of trace-chains rise for inspection upon which different histories gather and are determined – as if the closely read *fractal* incident functioned as a Benjaminian *monad*, an irreducible singularity in whose rewriting alternative pasts and futures lay dormant or legible: 'Each word inheres in a labyrinth of branching interverbal relationships going back not to a referential source but to something already, at the beginning, a figurative transfer.' The parallel is not gratuitous, since it is from Benjamin's performative redefinition of allegory, which is by no means simply 'modernist,' that a core aspect of Miller's project departs. Benjamin turned the traditional figure of *allegory* inside out and then rewired it: instead of naming a representational fixity outside of language, or 'modernist' reflexivity cleverly pointing to a work's own formal logics, he redirects it toward the instant not just when a system turns upon (or against) its own premises but does so as an active if virtual displacement and what it calls *negation* of what it names. It ingests representation and enters the intricate calculus of the act, which is the zone 'beyond' binarized catalogues which Hillis gestured to.

De Man spoke of this movement as the shift from a language of tropes to an 'other' model of language he allied to the performative, adding that once this shift is made, something drops away, and one finds oneself in an 'irreversible' position. It would be an impossible experience or, as Derrida might say, an experience of the impossible – yet also the only definition of experience possible, if the latter implies the rupture of a prerecorded program. This phantom instant which on one level Benjamin allied to 'shock' or caesurae would encounter a suspension of trace-chains in which different programs of memory vie for reinscription or disinscription: 'the whole work of memory, remembering, and memorialization.'

Allegory is the sometime name for where such a writing or reading act occurs – essentially, a recasting of the template and pre-recordings. For Benjamin, this spectral model of intervention would be renamed many times over in his work – here as that of a certain 'translation,' there as 'cinema,' and finally as what he calls '*materialistic* historiography.' The materiality in question, like the phrase 'materiality of *inscription*' in de Man, is without a *referential* correlative among familiar realisms (the empirical, pragmatic, materialist redactions de Man termed idealisms). What Benjamin called 'materialistic historiography' in the *Theses on the Philosophy of History* would access a 'materiality' that is without correspondence and essentially spectral. Occurring within the facticity of archival inscriptions, it does not subscribe to any familiar materialist model – indeed, referential premises would be forgetfully generated from such a phantom site.[2] I reference Benjamin not only to add to Miller's family tree a notable precursor but to reframe, for an instant, how Miller connects to the legacy of a project which posed, most notably, the question of how the aesthetic shapes and intervenes in the political – and how both terms are redistributed. At this juncture, as de Man refines the problem, the *aesthetic* as term covers the site at which inscriptions are, deformingly, phenomenalized – how the very topos of perception is not a passive receipt of sense data but programmed, in advance, through installed models and tropological systems. Miller's 'critic' is not the traditional model of the *literary* critic: he is not an adjudicator of aesthetic value;

he is not the specialist refining archival lore; he is not the formalist reader; and he is not the historicizing allegorist. Miller's 'critic' seeks nothing less in the labyrinthine forces released by active reading than the site or non-site from which the representations of world, and its regimes of consumption, are generated – and there are different entries to this nonsite.

The idea of 'materiality' here includes graphematic and spectral traces – which structure hermeneutic reflexes, define anthropomorphic borders and commodify others. This returns us to Miller's immersion in literature as the framed use of performative language most wired to diverse historical engines – and allowed to be, as long as that was held to be merely 'play,' merely aesthetic. Miller's investment is not that different from Aristotle's defense of poetry as more true than history – if read a certain way. It also reminds us that, among other variants, what de Man meant by 'language' implied all tele-technic systems that traverse and comprise communities and knowledge bases on a virtually planetary and chronographic basis. When Benjamin invokes the figure of the *pre*historial, or natural history (neither 'natural' nor 'historical'), he indicates that the politics which drives his thought involves bracketing an entire history of 'man' – the several thousand years of scriptive 'culture' that has set anthropomorphic programs of cognition and definitions of history accordingly. This is why Benjamin, when he attacks the 'fascist' enemy that the practice of 'materialistic historiography' would assault, equates it not with the Nazi war machine, which would have been easy enough, but an epistemic style of archivization: 'historicism.' *Historicism* partakes of an aesthetic ideology passing as archival fact, producing dead time and passive, displaced faith in the archive as such. Miller thus views the task of the critic as involved in intrinsic and perpetual combat of sorts: 'the primary means of combating that disastrous confusion of linguistic with material reality, one name for which is "ideology".' De Man revisits this same motif – a battle with historicist or mimetic agendas which more or less rule the academy as elsewhere–when referring to the '*nihilistic* allegories of historicism.' The inversion is clear, and one perhaps cannot fully grasp the 'ethics' of this moment without accounting for it: deconstruction, argued against as nihilistic, is instead a model of active intervention or transformation; historicism, guardian of archival accumulations, is in fact nihilistic in its deferral of responsibility for its production of 'facts' in a generally co-opted and passive faith. *Historicism*, like any version of model and copy, or archival indexing, re-enforces a faux or post-Enlightenment episteme that had become a historical trap – one more totalized today than in Benjamin's time perhaps. From a certain perspective, for Benjamin liberal democracy may have been merely at the other extreme pole of the *same* spectrum from the fascist, both driven by capital and the façades of transparency, with the victor absorbing – rather than vanquishing – its defeated other. The residue of Enlightenment tropes inform liberal democracy and fascism differently. Benjamin surmised that performative interventions which might prove decisive would have to precede this program or access the non-site where inscriptions are set or retooled, the sensorium crafted, memory regimes installed or allowed to enter zones of translation. When Miller speculates on the 'line' or its many forms, he seems to be enjoying the aurora-like displays that occur as one approaches this zone: 'Without the line there is no repetition, but repetition is what disturbs, suspends, or destroys the line's linearity, like a soft wintry aurora playing behind its straight-forward logic.' Numerous avenues seem possible to generate here:

> The image of the line, it might be noted, has, by an unavoidable recrossing, already contaminated this topological placing of the image of the line. Since this line is more figure than concept (but is there any concept without figure?), the line can lead easily to all other conceptual problems in narrative: character, intersubjectivity, narrator, time, mimesis, and so on.

I have undertaken this detour to highlight an enigma in Hillis Miller's writing, where several implications seem almost modestly to escape note.[3] I have already noted that in raising the question of practice and theory, Miller immediately points to a site *beyond* which this binary cannot re-establish itself. One will have moved a step *beyond*, one knows because one cannot get back, but where to is not provided. De Man, in writing of Benjamin, speaks of this as a site of *translation* preparatory to the possibility of the event – which can always be called an event of disinscription and reinscription. To alter the 'world' is, from this position, to alter its archival programs, what can be posited not by yet another *descriptive* poetics but by entering mnemonic orders and other legibilities than those apparent. If one has stepped out of the humanist machines fabricating aura, and viewed their mechanisms as tropological evasions, one cannot go back and inhabit them again. One simply cannot get back to the anthropocentric and auratic model, one must proceed or stand in arrest or, as we noted, invoke prehistorial time and natural history when addressing things as irreducible as graphic lines, metric *caesurae*, the zero.

Does this mean that behind what Miller calls his 'critic' lies a gambit involving historical redefinition, which the separation of 'theory' and 'practice' had been meant to stop or police?

Where Benjamin's writing orients itself toward an instance of reconfiguration and *where* de Man's does toward the apotropaic impasses and logical aporia which guard that, Hillis recurs quietly in the example above to an examination of the 'line' or of the 'zero.' Hillis warns us not to confuse the Minotaur in this labyrinth with a center or end to the wandering maze or that center's absence. When Miller leads us into the labyrinth of the 'line' he plays Minotaur – since what is examined is a graphematic force that defines horizons, borders, chronographics, economics, and so on, though without content or perhaps even existing *as such*. Picking up from his precursors in the project of 'materialistic historiography,' Hillis moves toward the site or non-site from which aesthetic ideologies are shaped – and he plays with it like a shoe lace, twisting it in different forms in an unthreatening if not outright entertaining gallery display. What may not be apparent to the reader is that this performance already testifies to being in or near a site that is 'irreversible' in its epistemo-political implications, in or near a site from which the definition of the aesthetic or the hermeneutics of the senses are designed. The 'line' assents to or underwrites none of these. It is too proximate, too much everywhere, like the zero figure. It curls up and retreats, as if into the discrete 'J' which stands before and introduces Hillis Miller's autograph.[4]

The 'line' Miller analyzes leads into a labyrinth without outside that threads diverse histories and coming impasses 'we' are embedded in and shaped by. This prefigural zone leads to mnemonic orders from which the 'present' is defined. In fact, getting to this site may constitute a paradoxical sort of ethics – since one would not orient oneself toward the human other but to a 'wholly other' (in the phrase of Derrida) that is nonetheless accessed only through teletechnic and graphematic channels. When one attempts to speak, today, of something like the 'planetary' one pretends to leave behind the totalizing metaphor of the global – yet one cannot quite identify the conceptual terrain attested to by astronomical metaphor. One names, without naming it, teletechnic orders of 'life' and chemical processes as well. Miller resorts, not infrequently, to mathematical or scientific figures not as casual metaphors but as active interfaces between linguistic laws and nonanthropomorphic systems.

Which may be why Miller, in pursuing and executing a self-altering itinerary which is 'irreversible,' adopts a term of astrophysics to negotiate a site at which aporia are approached not as logical impasses but as active force fields redefining the textures and agency. Everything in Miller seems to gesture toward a translation still to come. Scouring the aporetic sentences that lace de Man's work, Miller begins to see constellations and patterns that operate as if in the gravity fields of black holes of space – into which nonsites galaxies and configurations of time-space resolve. The black holes of conceptual matrices are without personification or aura. The black hole absorbs even 'light' – which is exposed as a semiotic effect rather than a natural trope of illumination. But in Miller's use the term takes a proactive role. For Hillis the term black hole does not suggest cognitive desperation, like some nihilist plunge, so much as aporetic sites that elude the application of conceptual order yet shape and mutate – if only as a mode of relapse before them – ever-altering archival and logic programs. Miller's project presupposes, here, a sort of remapping – implied by his earlier title *Topographies*. The persistent if underlying trajectory at this point can be seen when we track the program Miller advances for his 'critic' through this terrain.

The 'J' which is another version of the 'line' finds one of its origins in the early hieroglyph for *hand* – and this association with digits or fingers persists in Roman and Greek variants, before the medieval spur was added by scribes no doubt wary of its proximity to number. The *hand* has always been the emblem for sheer technicity and the advent of the human with the acquisition of scriptive technologies – going back to the cave paintings. It is in touch with the digital and the 'global,' with techno-weaponry and mnemonics, with the special nonplace of 'literature' and with media politics, and we can perhaps name this order more broadly that of tele-technics. Miller is aware that this thinking persists through the era of the 'Book' as well as that of the electronic archive, through mnemotechnics generally and historial events, through habits of reading and the politics of institutions. Miller's championing of close reading has been sometimes misread as a championing of 'literature,' yet in fact he ceaselessly relinquishes any such privileging, dissolving these models before a mutating historical motherboard of epistemic forces and tele-technic implications. If anything, his *fractalization* of literary study opens the supposed field to a remapping of the historial event and mnemonics, a labor, so far as the archive is concerned, that draws near to the famed black holes of disinscription and reinscription. The very span of Miller's work suggests that this shuttle traverses pan-historial, pan-generic, prehistorial and post-contemporary terrain at once. The task of *J* – that is, Miller's 'critic' – can appear a translational undertaking that is preparatory to and, at moments, a Rosetta stone for critical tasks and horizons to come. For instance, in what we may call, with a certain assurance – for this is what is implied by the blind of a 'global' war on *terror* – coming wars of terrestrial *reinscription*. During these a key outpost, one must assume, will involve 'combating that disastrous confusion of linguistic with material reality' – at a site, that is, as if where aura and personification, anthropomorphism and spectral chases, are drawn back.

Notes

1. For de Man, the rhetorical claims to possess a material praxis and prosecute worldly action or claim various forms of realism mistake for facts or perceptions the manner in which the imprint of the senses and interpretive programs are preset then naturalized. One does not enter the zone of Miller's deconstructive labor from an already centered position that stands to be reminded of the powers of the marginal or decentered. One arrives amid mnemonic programming that is, in advance, inscribed as a blind or relapse – what de Man elsewhere terms *aesthetic ideology*. The rhetoric of truth, subjectivity, mimetic reference, and historicism have been implicitly aestheticized, as the prefigural event is given back aura and organic semblance – is, implicitly, personified.

2. It is not incidental, here, that Benjamin's *Theses* appears the work which Derrida's *Specters of Marx* seems most in covert dialogue when elaborating to political import of the spectral.

3. The term *allegory* which de Man recirculated and Miller takes as a point of depature, therefore, is one which deflates the phantom binary of practice and theory or

renders it unrecognizable *as such* – which explains Miller's simply setting it aside, as I cited at the opening. In the process, it reconfigures how the 'aesthetic' would be defined. One could inadequately say, at this point, that for de Man but implicitly Benjamin as well, at issue is *epistemo-political* (which is also to say biopolitical) programs. De Man insists that an 'epistemological critique of tropes' precedes any possible intervention, and Benjamin in his work on allegory, in the *Trauerspiel*, indirectly calls the shift that is accomplished 'epistemo-critical.' The epistemological, in this mode, includes how sense and the senses are programmed through tropological systems. The *aesthetic* is encountered as the perceptual and political field which archival orders control. Benjamin would speak of the historial models of the senses as a *sensorium*, the way the senses are programmed as and through hermeneutic channels and mnemonics. Rather than the "aesthetic" being traditionally cast out as a neutralized field, in 'play,' the term attests to a preoriginary inversion within the term's spectrum of meanings, a sort of relapse – even as it effaced in the process the origins of the word in the Greek *aisthanumai*, referencing perception or the sensorial as such. For de Man what would be 'material' is the order of inscriptions that govern perceptual narratives and judgement, from which the world appears *phenomenalized* – like a projector screening celluloid.

4. This one letter anchors itself where it is barely visible – yet as a 'line' inhabits any other letteral form, such as the tendency in the letters of Miller's autograph to stutteringly recur to it (H-I-l-l, M-I-l-l).

V

Pedagogical and Political Commitments

18

Paul de Man's Wartime Writings

The new statement is always hated by the old, and, to those dwelling in the old, comes like an abyss of scepticism. But the eye soon gets wonted to it, for the eye and it are effects of one cause: then its innocency and benefit appear . . .

Ralph Waldo Emerson, 'Circles'

The violence of the reaction in the United States and in Europe to the discovery of Paul de Man's writings of 1941–2 marks a new moment in the collaboration between the university and the mass media. This is so at least in the United States, where literary theory and literary theorists have hardly been of much interest to the newspapers. It is an extremely instructive moment, one worth much sober reflection.

For the most part, so far at least, it has been a question of journalism all the way. It has also been a question of reading, a question of how one reads what de Man wrote both early and late, a question of what would constitute an accurate and adequate reading of the facts in the case. These facts are almost all written documents. The wartime writings of Paul de Man were published in a student journal, *Les Cahiers du libre examen*, and in two Belgian newspapers, *Het Vlaamsche Land* and *Le Soir*. The outpouring of denunciations of de Man and of so-called 'deconstruction' has been, so far, primarily in newspapers, in the *New York Times*, the *Nation*, *Newsweek*, and the *Los Angeles Times*, along with some student newspapers, in the United States, and, most recently, the *Village Voice*, in an article full of resentment, malice, and undisguised xenophobia; in *La Quinzaine littéraire*, the *Frankfurter Allgemeine Zeitung*, and the *Manchester Guardian* in Europe. Most, though not all, of these attacks have been written by academics who also write journalism. It is as though these professors had somewhat abruptly discovered the power of the press in this area, just as the young de Man discovered the power of the press in wartime Belgium, long before he began the advanced university study of literature as a Junior Fellow at Harvard in the mid-1950s.

Why was the finding of de Man's wartime writings so 'newsworthy'? And why has the reporting of them in the mass media given rise to such extraordinary falsifications, misreadings, distortions, and selective slanting of quotations, both of what de Man actually said in those writings and of 'deconstruction,' the mode of interpretation of philosophy, literature, and culture with which he came to be associated thirty years later? And why have the falsehoods and distortions taken just the forms they have taken, with just the same errors being repeated from newspaper to newspaper? One of the most scandalous aspects of the whole affair, at least to an outsider to the way journalism apparently works, is that the same errors, the same quotations out of context, the same false characterizations of 'deconstruction,' are repeated from newspaper to newspaper in the United States, France, Germany, and Great Britain, apparently without any attempt to verify the facts or to read de Man's writings, early or late. One would have thought that in a case of such gravity a little checking of facts and re-reading of the evidence would have been in order, especially on the part of those journalists who are also professors, professionally committed to a sober truth-telling. Liberal newspapers and conservative newspapers have rushed to condemn what they see as a common enemy and they have said almost the same things – the *Nation*, on the one hand, and *Newsweek* and the *Frankfurter Allgemeine Zeitung*, on the other.

No doubt the reasons for this are multiple. They include a suspicion of any new and difficult mode of thought, especially (in the United States) when imported from the Continent; a general hostility to critical theory (but that in itself takes some explaining); the fact that at this moment in history there is widespread concern to identify the last remnants of the Nazi regime and to purify ourselves of them, to cut ourselves off from that period of history and to deny that anything like that could happen again. (False analogies of de Man's 'case' with those of Waldheim and Heidegger have of course been made.)

But the strongest motivation for the irresponsible errors and insinuations in these newspaper articles is clear enough. The real target is not de Man himself. He is dead, beyond the reach of attack. The real aim is to discredit that form of interpretation called 'deconstruction,' to obliterate it, as far as possible, from the curriculum, to dissuade students of literature, philosophy, and culture from reading de Man's work or that of his associates, to put a stop to the 'influence' of 'deconstruction.' Beyond that, as the article in *Newsweek* and a later one in the *Wall Street Journal* attacking the English Department at Duke University made clear, the target is literary theory or critical theory generally, for example the so-called 'new historicists,' or feminist theorists, or students of popular culture, or practitioners of so-called 'cultural criticism.' The rapid widening of the targets of hostility has been a conspicuous fact.

The argument, implied or overt, goes as follows, in a crescendo of distortions. First error: it is asserted that de Man's wartime writings are fascist, collaborationist, antisemitic through and through, and that he was himself a fascist, collaborator, and antisemite. Second error: de Man's later writings, after 1953, when he became a famous professor, theorist, and teacher in the United States – at Cornell, Johns Hopkins, and Yale – are asserted to be continuous with the early writings, whether by being a disguised autobiographical apology for them or by continuing to affirm in new and more sophisticated forms the same ideas and commitments. Third error: de Man was a 'deconstructionist.' All deconstruction must be all of a piece. De Man was a Fascist. Now we know what we have suspected all along: Deconstruction is Fascist. Therefore get rid of it.

All these propositions are false. The facts are otherwise. What is most terrifying in this argument is the way it repeats the well-known totalitarian procedures of vilification it pretends to deplore. It repeats the crime it would condemn.

I have said the facts are far otherwise. Let me try to state them as succinctly and exactly as possible, with a strong recommendation to all who read this and who interest themselves in these questions to read all of de Man's wartime writings (they will soon be published *in toto*), to read de Man's later writings too and those of other 'deconstructionists' – and then judge for yourselves. In this matter as in all such matters, there is no substitute for hard reading and for making up one's own mind. This is not a matter where you would want to let the newspapers do your reading and thinking for you.

First fact: de Man was by no means in these early writings totally fascist, antisemitic, and collaborationist. The facts are much more complex. De Man was first editor of a student journal of the University of Brussels called *Les Cahiers du libre examen*. This journal defined itself as 'democratic, anti-clerical, anti-dogmatic and anti-fascist.' Like most newspapers and periodicals in Belgium, it was shut down by the Germans after they occupied Belgium in 1940. De Man then obtained a position as cultural correspondent with a prominent Brussels evening newspaper that had been taken over by collaborationists, *Le Soir*. The job was perhaps obtained through the influence of Paul de Man's uncle Henri de Man, though there is no hard evidence for this that I have seen. Henri de Man was a prominent Belgian socialist who deluded himself into brief collaboration with the Germans. He remained behind to advise the monarchy after the Belgian government fled into exile. After a few months Henri de Man left Belgium for France in November, 1941 and then went into permanent exile in Switzerland in the closing days of the war. He was condemned in absentia by the Belgian authorities after the war. In the general review by the authorities after the war, Paul de Man, on the other hand, was not included among collaborators. He was allowed freely to leave the country when he chose to do so.

Paul de Man wrote some 169 articles for *Le Soir* from December 1940 to November 1942, when he was twenty-one and twenty-two years old. He also published during the same period ten articles for a Flemish journal, *Het Vlaamsche Land*, also under the control of the Germans. These articles are all book reviews, concert notes, and general statements about literature and culture. They are a strangely heterogeneous mixture, the work of a brilliant and widely read young man with little formal literary education who clearly enjoys passing judgements pro and con on a wide variety of authors, composers and musicians, and who is prepared to make general pronouncements about the specific character of the different national literatures and about the development of literature in the past and in the future. There is one inexcusable and unforgettable article, 'The Jews in Contemporary Literature' (*Le Soir*, 4 March 1941) written for a special antisemitic section of *Le Soir*, and there is one sentence echoing antisemitic rhetoric in one of the essays in Flemish (*Het Vlaamsche Land*, 20 August 1942). The essay in *Le Soir* uses the language of antisemitism to argue that the Jews have not corrupted modern European literature, but that European literature has remained fundamentally healthy. European literature, the essay argues, would hardly be weakened at all if all European Jews were put in a separate colony. This is an appalling idea, in itself and in view of what happened so soon thereafter, and it is an appalling untruth, but it must be recognized that this is not the same thing as saying that the Jews are a pollution of Western culture. This latter idea *is* expressed in the articles by other authors published adjacent to de Man's, and this idea is explicitly condemned by de Man as 'vulgar antisemitism.' 'The reality,' he says, is 'different.'

This is an example of a *leitmotif* of all de Man's essays for *Le Soir*, namely a putting in question of received ideas and opinions. Moreover, the same essay, strangely, mentions Kafka along with Hemingway and Lawrence as three great and exemplary modern authors. Other essays (in *Le Soir*, 27 May 1941; in *Het Vlaamsche Land*, 17–18 May, 1942; and 26–27 July 1942) praise Proust as a major writer. Did de Man not know Kafka was a Jew, or could the mention of Kafka here be an example of the kind of double-talk one learns to practise under a totalitarian regime? In an essay written at the end of his life de Man, in one of the two references to Leo Strauss in his writings, praises Strauss for having under-stood 'double-talk, the necessary obliqueness of any persecuted speech that cannot, at risk of survival, openly say what it means to say' (1986, 107). To suggest that this may explain the oddnesses of de Man's essay on the Jews in no way exonerates him from responsibility for whatever support his essay may have given to the then developing German policy that led seventeen months later to the first deportations of Jews from Belgium to the death camps. But it is important to note that the essay itself is by no means straight party-line antisemitism such as is represented in the attacks on Freud and Picasso in adjacent articles in the same issue of *Le Soir*.

Moreover, it is also important to put the now notorious article on the Jews in Western literature in the context of the other 168 articles in *Le Soir* and to recognize that antisemitism does not recur in them, nor does de Man, as has been asserted in the newspaper accounts, by any means consistently praise collaborationist authors or collaborationist ideas. One article on Charles Péguy, for example (*Le Soir*, 5 June 1941), praises Péguy's support for the cause of Dreyfus. An antisemite would not have so unequivocally praised a Dreyfusard. Another article attacks with more than a little insolence as ignorant and mistaken a political book by the collaborationist writer Montherlant (*Le Soir*, 11

November 1941). Just because Montherlant is a polished writer, says de Man, does not mean he knows anything about politics or history. In fact, says de Man, his book is very bad. In another much later article (*Le Soir*, 1 September 1942), written after the deportations of Jews from Belgium had begun, de Man's discussion of a poem by Hubert Dubois called 'Le Massacre des Innocents' seems a clear outcry against those deportations as evidence of 'the guilt that has led humanity to the frightful state in which it finds itself at this moment.'

These early writings must also be put in the context of the testimony of three people who knew de Man at the time, a colleague at *Les Cahiers du libre examen*, Charles Dosogne; a man linked to the Belgian resistance, Georges Goriély; and another man associated with the Resistance, Georges Lambrichs, later editor of *La Nouvelle revue française*. All testify that Paul de Man was not antisemitic, that he was 'anything but a collaborator,' that he was neither fascist nor pro-Nazi. In the absence of personal testimony on the other side, from those who knew de Man in Belgium during the war, the assertions of these witnesses should carry much weight. I might add here my own testimony that in all the years I knew de Man (from 1966 until his death in 1983) I never heard him utter a single antisemitic word. The evidence suggests that he stupidly wrote the deplorable essay in order to please his employers and keep his job, putting in as much 'double-talk' as he dared. According to the letter he wrote to Renato Poggioli when he was a Junior Fellow at Harvard and had been anonymously denounced, he quit writing for *Le Soir* in November of 1942 when 'Nazi thought control' made it impossible for him any longer to express himself freely. This seems to have been the moment when Nazi propaganda control was extended from the political to the cultural parts of *Le Soir*, for which of course de Man wrote and which had until then been free of direct censorship.

Nevertheless, what *is* a crucial fact about the articles for *Le Soir* and *Het Vlaamsche Land*, taken as a whole, and with all proper recognition of their truly heterogeneous character, is the way they allow an understanding of the implicit connection between the article on the Jews and certain nationalist ideas about literature which are present there and which recur in many of the essays that are in no way antisemitic or even explicitly political, just book reviews or concert notes. These are ideas about the specificity of national character and of the literature of each nation, ideas about the power of literature to express directly transcendent truth, and, beyond that, certain ideas about the individual organic development of the literature of each country according to intrinsic laws of its own. The article on 'The Jews in Contemporary Literature' depends on the absurd and extremely dangerous notion that there is a specific national and racial character in French literature, a different one in German literature, and that the Jews have yet another specific identity. These ideas about the specificity of the German, French, Spanish, Flemish, Walloon, and Dutch national characters recur in essay after essay in which there is nothing at all antisemitic or even explicitly political, for example in reviews that praise now-forgotten Belgian novelists or composers for having roots in Belgian folklore or folk music and in the constant concern for the differences in culture between French-speaking and Flemish-speaking Belgium. (De Man himself came from a Flemish-speaking family.)

Now then, what about de Man's later writings and what about 'deconstruction' generally? Like his wartime writings, the writings of Paul de Man after he came to the United States and began publishing again in 1953, are heterogeneous. The heterogeneity of the later writings, however, is more a matter of a series of three discernible phases. There is an initial 'phenomenological' phase in which the main categories of his criticism are consciousness, intentionality (in the Husserlian sense), and temporality. This phase culminates in *Blindness and Insight* (1971). Far from being a 'deconstructionist' in this work, de Man opposes Derrida's reading of Rousseau in a long essay in *Blindness and Insight*. The second phase can be conveniently thought of as initiated by the transitional essay of 1969, 'The Rhetoric of Temporality.' The work of this period is gathered in *Allegories of Reading* (1979). In this phase the major categories of criticism are linguistic and rhetorical: metaphor, irony, symbol, allegory, the distinction between constative and performative uses of language. In the final phase, initiated with 'The Resistance to Theory' (1982), there is a more overt turn to history, ideology, and politics, though a concern for all three is there all along in de Man's post-1953 work. As he asserted in the interview of 4 March 1983 with Stefano Rosso: 'I don't think I ever was away from these problems, they were always uppermost in my mind' (1986, 121).

In spite of this developmental diversity, the connection between all de Man's later work and his early wartime writings – for there is a connection, though it is not at all the one the journalists have attempted to find – can best be defined by saying that the special and most urgent targets of all his later work are just those ideas about national character, the independent and organic evolution of each national literature, and so on, that are presupposed in his writings for *Le Soir, Het Vlaamsche Land*, and even in what he wrote for *Les Cahiers du libre examen*. De Man later called this whole cluster of ideas 'aesthetic ideology.' It was the main object of his systematic attack in essay after essay of his writings after 1953, especially but by no means exclusively in the essays of his last years, for example in an important seminar on 'Kant and Schiller' (1983). But already in 1955, for example, in an essay published in *Monde nouveau* entitled 'Tentation de la permanence,' de Man sharply criticizes the Heidegger of the later essays on Hölderlin for being tempted by the lure of an ahistorical permanence attained through poetic language.

What is significant and instructive about the presence of this 'aesthetic ideology' in de Man's early writings is the confirmation it gives to one of his basic later insights about literature, namely his recognition of the potentially disastrous political implications of apparently innocuous and purely 'aesthetic' mistakes in assumptions about the nature of literature and of literary history.

This may help to explain the urgency with which he always contested those ideas – in his writing, in his teaching and in his interventions in discussions of papers presented at conferences and symposia. The reading of the early writings *will* help to clarify the importance and the political import of de Man's writings after 1953.

As my account of his early writings has, I hope, made absolutely clear, the phrase 'innocency and benefit' in my epigraph from Emerson is by no means meant to apply to de Man's early writings. Both the phrase and the whole citation from Emerson do describe, however, the indispensable usefulness of his later writings and of the work of 'deconstruction' generally. For 'aesthetic ideology' and the nationalism associated with it have by no means disappeared. They are extremely widespread and powerful in Europe and America today, for example in the xenophobia in the United States that resists literary theory because it is a foreign import. What de Man called 'aesthetic ideology' forms an important part of the contemporary tissue of received opinion about literature, national identity, and culture, both in the mass media and in the university. It was what I was taught at college and university, and it is what we are all likely to say or think on these topics if we are not vigilant. Which of us can say he or she is free of it? And yet de Man's work and his historical placement shows it is both false and can lead to hideous political and historical consequences.

What I have said about de Man's later work can also be said of 'deconstruction' generally. Like his work, 'deconstruction' is not one single thing. It is diverse and heterogeneous, with many active aspects, facets, and functions, for example in religious studies, in architecture, and in legal theory, as well as in philosophical and literary studies. Of 'deconstruction' generally the same thing can be said that de Man said of his own work in the 'Preface' to the posthumously published *The Rhetoric of Romanticism* (1984): it does not 'evolve in a manner that easily allows for dialectical progression or, ultimately, for historical totalization.' Nevertheless it can be said of 'deconstruction,' first, that the negative clichés that have been repeated over and over about it are false. 'Deconstruction' is not nihilistic, nor anti-historical, nor mere play of language in the void, nor does it view literature or language generally as free play of language, nor is it committed to the notion that readers and critics are free to make texts mean anything they like. 'Deconstruction,' in all its diversity, is a certain kind of 'critique of ideology,' namely a kind that presupposes, as de Man put it in the interview with Rosso, that 'one could approach the problems of ideology and by extension the problems of politics only on the basis of critical-linguistic analysis, which had to be done in its own terms, in the medium of language' (1986, 121). This approach goes by way of identifying the linguistic constructions that are the basis of ideologies. Ideology is defined by de Man as 'the confusion of linguistic with natural reality' (1986, 11). Of special importance are those linguistic constructions that depend on thinking in terms of oppositions, literal versus metaphorical language, man against woman, inside against outside, and so on. An example would be the way the nationalism that is so important a part of 'aesthetic ideology' leads to defining one group in opposition to another. This can lead, as in the case of Nazi Germany, to the horror of the slaughter of the Jews in the attempt to create an Aryan nation purified of all 'polluting' elements.

Far from being without an interest in history or being without political import, 'deconstruction,' as de Man said in a crucial late essay, 'The Resistance to Theory,' is 'more than any other mode of inquiry, including economics . . . a powerful and indispensable tool in the unmasking of ideological aberrations, as well as a determining factor in accounting for their occurrence. Those who reproach literary theory for being oblivious to social and historical (that is to say ideological) reality are merely stating their fear at having their own ideological mystifications exposed by the tool they are trying to discredit' (1986, 11). It is fear of this power in 'deconstruction' and in contemporary critical theory as a whole, in all its diversity, that accounts better than any other explanation for the unreasoning hostility, the abandoning of the canons of journalistic and academic responsibility, in the recent attacks on de Man, on 'deconstruction,' and on theory generally.

19

President's Column

(i) Responsibility and the Joy of Reading

My first responsibility as president of the MLA [Modern Language Association; Ed.] is the task of writing this little essay for the *Newsletter*. I start with a question about responsibility: To whom or to what am I responsible as a teacher of literature? After that I'll get to joy, the joy of reading.

No doubt the MLA has responsibility primarily for what might be called the institutional side of our profession. So a new president might well choose, among things of importance that have happened at the MLA during the last year, to write about the choice of a new executive director, Phyllis Franklin, or about the MLA's role in challenging the nomination of Edward Curran as director of the National Endowment for the Humanities, or about the move of MLA headquarters to 10 Astor Place. Or I might celebrate all the things the MLA does for the institutional side of our professional lives: the annual convention, or the *Job Information List* and the services of the annual convention to job seekers, or the annual *Bibliography*, or our activities to improve the conditions of teachers of composition, languages, and literature on part-time or one-year appointments, or the conference being planned for summer 1987 by the English Coalition, of which the MLA is a part, to reconsider the English curriculum from grade school to the graduate level. Or I might reiterate the continuing commitment of the MLA to affirmative action and to a strong role for the interests of all our members, through such bodies as the Committee on Academic Freedom, the Commission on the Status of Women in the Profession, the Commission on Foreign Languages, Literatures, and Linguistics, or the Commission on the Literatures and Languages of America. Or I might take note of a major change in *PMLA* [*Publications of the Modern Language Association*; Ed.], the appointment of John Kronik of Cornell as the first editor of *PMLA* who is not also the executive director of the association.

I might indeed do all that, But after the last paper has been read at the convention, the last vacancy filled, the last item listed in the *Bibliography*, the last essay published in a given year of *PMLA*, a question still remains: Exactly what is all this vast institutional and professional activity supposed to aid or 'facilitate'? I suggest that one answer to that question, perhaps the bottom-line answer, is that it is all for nothing unless it supports the activity of reading. I mean, initially, the reading of the teacher, not the reading of the student. How can we teach reading if we are not readers ourselves? And I suggest that real reading, when it occurs, which may not be all that often, is outside the institution, allergic to institutionalization, private, solitary. I suggest, finally, that real reading, when it occurs, is characterized primarily by *joy*, the joy of reading.

What do I mean by the joy of reading? The *OED* defines *joy* as 'a vivid emotion of pleasure arising from a sense of well-being or satisfaction; the feeling or state of being highly pleased or delighted; exultation of spirit; gladness, delight.' The word of course has sensual and erotic overtones, as in 'the joy of cooking,' or 'I wish you all joy of the worm.' It is associated with cognate words like *delight, pleasure, ecstasy, exultation*. To speak of the joy of reading will remind some of Roland Barthes' *plaisir du texte*.

But I have in mind more specifically the powerful uses of the word in the Romantic period, not only Schiller's 'Ode to Joy' but Coleridge's 'Dejection: An Ode,' where the 'shaping spirit of Imagination' gives that 'Joy' which is 'Life, and Life's effluence, cloud at once and shower,' 'the spirit and the power / Which wedding Nature gives to us in dower / A new Earth and new Heaven.' And I have in mind Wordsworth's 'Surprised by joy – impatient as the wind,' where a sudden inrush of joy can make the poet forget even the sorrow of his daughter's death and turn instinctively to 'share the transport' of his joy with her, forgetting that she is 'deep buried in the silent tomb.' For me, the joy of reading, when it comes, is something like Wordsworth's sudden joy: surprising, unpredictable both in its nature and in its possible effects, a break in time, in that sense anarchic, a dissolution of pre-existing orders, the opening of a sense of freedom that is like a new earth and a new heaven, an influx of power. The joy of reading is in this sense apocalyptic. It has to do with transfiguration and the end but also has to do with a momentary lapse of the fear of death.

I open, for example, a volume of Francis Ponge I have at hand. Ponge is an author I have no responsibility to write about or teach. What I read by Ponge, those strange poems that 'take the side of *things*,' gives me that joy of reading. No doubt this is partly because of my freedom from obligation toward Ponge or to teach Ponge. 'Puisque tu me lis, cher lecteur,' says Ponge, 'donc je suis; puisque tu nous lis / (mon livre et moi), cher lecteur, / donc nous sommes (toi, lui et moi).' I am, at least in part, because I read, and that is the widest import of the joy of reading.

Our professional vocation, with all its responsibilities, begins and ends in that joy of reading. It is a joy that is only with difficulty institutionalized, if it can be institutionalized at all. All our meetings, commissions, publications, and so on are for the sake of that. Our primary responsibility is to that. I would alter Yeats's 'in dreams begins responsibility' to say, 'in reading begins responsibility.' Now I am not so naive as to think that reading is ever altogether solitary, that the reader is ever cut off from all his or her context of familial, community, departmental, institutional, even national or historical responsibility. If writing, for Henry James in the preface to *The Golden Bowl*, is part of the 'conduct of life,' and if he defines the conduct of life as 'things done, which do other things in their turn,' reading too, I claim, is part of the conduct of life in this sense. It is a thing done that does other things in its turn. Institutional and professional responsibility, the responsibility to teach and to write, to read all those manuscripts and to serve on all those committees, begins when the act of reading turns outward and does other things in its turn.

About those other forms of responsibility I may say something in a future *Newsletter*, but here and now I want to affirm that our primary professional and vocational responsibility is to the impatience, transport, and surprise of the joy of reading.

(ii) Responsibility and the Joy (?) of Teaching

In the last president's column, in the Spring 1986 *Newsletter*, I raised the question of the responsibilities of the teacher of language and literature. To whom or to what are we primarily responsible when we write about, read, or teach literature? I concluded that our professional vocation, with all its responsibilities, to students, to colleagues, to our institutions, to the various communities to which we belong, begins and ends with what I called the joy of reading. The joy of reading is a sense of insight, freedom, and power that comes, when it comes, always as a somewhat surprising and unpredictable effect of reading. We can never know just what is going to happen when we read. That act of reading, I said, then turns outward and does other things in its turn. In that sense it is part of what Henry James, echoing Emerson and speaking of writing rather than of reading, called 'the conduct of life.'

This column takes up the most immediate and direct of those doings resulting from reading: teaching. The first thing that reading 'does in its turn' is bring about another act of language. Those new words may be no more than the silent and almost inarticulate commentary we add as marginal response when we read. This commentary first enters the realm of efficacious conduct, for most of us, when we teach what we have read.

But is there a joy of teaching? The truth is that, for me at least, teaching is by no means always an unmitigated joy. Joy of reading, yes. But teaching is often a hazardous and unsatisfactory activity. Whether we are prepared or unprepared the class may go well or ill, for reasons that are not always easy to understand or to explain to oneself. Nothing is more disheartening than a class that inexplicably 'bombs.' It can ruin your whole day, and decades of teaching experience are no guarantee against that happening.

But the joy of teaching, when it comes, is exhilarating. A student makes a comment or asks a question that leads the teacher to see something new in the poem, novel, or whatever it is she or he is teaching. Some unexpected insight comes to the teacher in the midst of the class hour. In either case teaching suddenly becomes no longer the presentation of something the teacher already knew when the class began. It becomes rather an active process of invention or discovery. Such teaching is an inaugural event in itself, like the original reading on which the teaching is based. Teaching too brings something new into the world.

It will be seen that I do not think of teaching as simply the transmission to the students of knowledge already fully possessed by the teacher. The teacher is not a colorless medium or relay station by means of which a message is carried over from here (the library or the archives or 'the tradition') to there (the students' minds). This is true even though one of the primary duties of the teacher is to make manifest 'historical and philological facts as the preparatory condition for understanding,' to borrow Paul de Man's phrasing in his already classic essay 'The Resistance to Theory.' Teaching, in fact, is not oriented entirely toward the students, responsible exclusively to them. Teaching, as de Man says, is not a species of therapy or counseling, nor is it, according to an even more venerable figure, a species of midwifery, a maieutic procedure that elicits the birth in the students of something they obscurely knew already but did not know they knew. Teaching is rather primarily responsible to the texts being 'read in class' or to the 'material' or the 'things' presented.

Another way to put this is to say that teaching is a prolongation, extension, or modulation of that first, virtually solitary act of reading that I celebrated in my earlier column. Even that solitary and mute reading, as I have said, is already accompanied by an at least rudimentary ground bass of commentary, an implicit scribbling in the margin. The chief thing, along with the indispensable scholarly and philological information, that the teacher displays to her or his students is a method of reading in action. This formulation must not be misunderstood. The phrase 'in action' emphasizes the way neither 'method' nor 'theory' amounts to much when it is taught as such, detached from the activity of reading this or that particular text. Theory and method arise from reading, if they are to have force. The act of reading, when it occurs, which may not be as often as we would like to think, is more often the severe modification or even disconfirmation of presupposed theory and method than their peaceful ratification. The new theory that comes out of reading, moreover, may by no means be altogether compatible with that philological and scholarly knowledge, received from the tradition, the teacher began by accepting the responsibility to pass on to his or her students. This would follow as an inevitable consequence if reading has those qualities of surprise and inaugural novelty I claim it has. The reader rarely finds in those venerable poems, novels, or plays just what he or she has been led to expect to find there.

This fact has important consequences for teaching. It means that, contrary to what is often assumed, teaching is not primarily an interpersonal transaction oriented toward an interchange between teacher and students. The teacher is, rather, oriented primarily toward the text, primarily responsible to that, obligated in what he or she says to that, responsive to that. Though there can be no doubt that the successful teacher has an obligation not only to tell it like it is but to make that telling as clear as possible to the particular group of students in that particular class, nevertheless students are not so much partners in an intersubjective relation as the witnesses or overhearers of an activity of reading that is the teacher's interaction with the text at hand taking place before their eyes and ears, so to speak. I have at any rate learned most from those teachers in whom that responsibility to the text was displayed as a current event.

It also follows from what I have been saying, finally, that the teacher's authority by no means comes from her or his 'personality' or from the possession of some unique method of reading that is validated by the personal 'I' or by the authority of some 'community of readers' to which she or he belongs, along with its attendant methods of interpretation. The teacher's authority, when she or he has it, comes from an impersonal response to the work being read, a response that transcends the 'I.' It is not the subjectivity of the teacher that is obligated to the work but an impersonal power of reading that he or she shares, to some extent, with all other readers of the same work. Hence the possibility of teaching literature, if it is possible. Teaching is an interlinguistic transaction, not an intersubjective one. It is a reaction necessitated by an implacable demand made by the language of the work on its reader and manifested in its turn by the teacher to his or her students. The joy of teaching, when it occurs, arises from the teacher's formation of new insights into the work on the spot, through the act of trying to explain it to students.

(iii) The Obligation to Write

In two previous *Newsletters*, I wrote brief essays entitled 'The Joy of Reading' and 'The Joy (?) of Teaching.' (The question mark in the second title indicates that the idea that teaching is always or even primarily joyful is problematic.) In those essays I claimed that reading and teaching are not imposed from without, as social, professional, or institutional responsibilities. They are, rather, the consequences of an interior and linguistic imperative. The obligations to read and to teach come from language, from the poems, novels, and plays we read and teach. They come as almost irresistible compulsions, in the form of 'Thou must.'

The third and last topic completing the repertoire of our professional responsibilities is, of course, writing. As I did with the other two obligations of our profession, I want to argue that writing is only apparently a merely institutional or conventional responsibility, imposed on us from the outside by chairpersons and administrators or by an absurd tradition that says 'publish or perish.' Writing, I claim, is in fact intrinsic to the vocation that begins with the more or less private joy of reading. Writing too remains rooted in that solitary transaction with the words on the page. The insistence on measuring our professional worth by our bibliographies, the demand that we write and publish to get tenure and 'advance in the profession,' is only the extrinsic and in a certain sense contingent institutionalization of an intrinsic compulsion to write. That compulsion remains private and obscure because it comes from reading.

It seems at first difficult to argue persuasively that writing scholarship or criticism is an intrinsic obligation in the same way that reading and even teaching are. Surely reading and teaching do not demand to be completed by writing! We all know, or think that we know, strong and original readers, brilliant teachers, who have never, or hardly ever, lifted pen to paper or fingers to the word processor's keyboard. The need to write seems another matter or métier entirely. It seems to be something present sporadically here and there in some readers and teachers but by no means present as a genuine vocation in all of them. Nevertheless, I claim that reading and teaching are completed only by writing. The obligation to write is as strong as the obligations to read and to teach, for those who have a vocation for reading and teaching.

In fact, strange as it may seem, the most difficult thing for the reader and teacher is, paradoxically, not to write, as Maurice Blanchot argues in *L'écriture du désastre* [*The Writing of the Disaster*; ed.]: 'Que d'efforts pour ne pas écrire, pour que, écrivant, je n'écrive pas, malgré tout – et finalement je cesse d'écrire, dans le moment ultime de la concession . . .' (How many efforts in order not to write, in order that, writing, I should not write, in spite of everything – and finally I cease to write, in the ultimate moment of concession . . .) Strange words! No doubt they have a different meaning within the intricate fragmentary argumentation by aphorism of *L'écriture du désastre*, and a different meaning for a 'primary' writer like Blanchot from the meaning I give to them in relation to the more humble métier of 'secondary' writing as you or I might be obligated to practice it. Nevertheless, what writer could have demonstrated more strikingly than Blanchot has, in all those hundreds of review essays written over the past decades, the necessary connection between reading and writing about what we read? And what writer could have made more problematic that distinction between 'primary' and 'secondary' writing, without in any way denying that *La folie du jour* is a 'récit' and *L'écriture du désastre* is something else, perhaps 'criticism' or 'literary theory'?

It is a commonplace these days to observe that the act of reading is always accompanied by secondary acts of language. As we read we compose, without thinking about it, a kind of running commentary or marginal jotting that adds more words to the words on the page. There is always already writing as the accompaniment to reading. The actual writing down of that involuntary ground bass of commentary in a form that is readable by others, publishable, assimilable by one or another of the professional communities to which we belong, may be said to be accidental. It may happen or it may not happen. What we cannot prevent, what *must* happen, is the first writing that is inseparable from reading. Blanchot might call this 'writing without writing.'

This 'first writing' is fundamentally heterogeneous and problematic. On the one hand it is a rudimentary assimilation of what we are reading to what we already know. We make what we read accord with the assumptions, norms, and codes of the 'community of readers' to which we happen to belong. The 'first writing' of this sort is an assertion of mastery over what is strange, idiomatic, unfamiliar, unassimilable in what we are reading. Writing about what we read in this mode is apotropaic. It wards off the threat in what we are reading by turning it into what we have already read and already know. When this kind of 'first writing' is actually written down, published as an essay in a journal, as a review, as a chapter in a book, it becomes part of that vast enterprise of rationalizing appropriation, of making regular, comprehensible, usable, familiar, ready for the archives that is the essence of the modern research university.

On the other hand, however, that 'first writing,' that involuntary accompaniment of reading, is not so much a response to what is unfamiliar and eccentric in the work as a response to what the strange and eccentric in the work itself responded to. Henry James, in the preface to *The Golden Bowl*, speaks of that splendid effort of critical or 'secondary' writing, the prefaces to the New York edition of his work, not as a response to his novels and stories themselves, when he reread them, but as the result of renewed access to what called them into being. This he calls the 'thing' the story is about, the 'matter' of the story. He figures this 'matter' or 'thing' as a blank wall on which a shadow is cast or as limitless 'fields of light' or as a shining expanse of untrodden snow.

Mixed with the apotropaic act of covering over in the 'first writing,' scribbled so to speak in invisible ink in the margin of the book we read, there is something else, a submission to what the work itself submitted to. This submission dispossesses the reader, appropriates him or her, rather than yielding itself to rationalizing appropriation. This too carries over into the essay, chapter, or review, in spite of our best efforts to conceal it. Such carrying over gives, perhaps, the chief interest and value to what we write.

On the other hand (again), it would no doubt be a piece of foolishness to imagine that either what is eccentric, idiomatic, and unassimilable in what we read or what is eccentric, idiomatic, and unassimilable in what we write about what we read is adequate to the 'matter' or 'thing' to which both respond, adequate in the sense, to use another of James's metaphors, that a silhouette matches a shadow on the wall. This perpetual inadequacy tends to blur the distinctions not only between 'primary' and 'secondary' writing but also between the two kinds of secondary writing, the one that covers over and wards off and the one that seems faithful to the strangeness in primary writing.

Moreover, in spite of the implications of my metaphors (or James's), the 'matter' of either the 'primary' or the 'secondary' text is not something outside language, extrinsic to it. As I began by saying, the obligation to write is intrinsic to language, part of our transaction with it and of its transaction with us.

To succeed in ceasing to write, as Blanchot would wish to do, would be the only way to escape from the double bind of a categorical obligation to write what always turns out to be an inadequate response to that demand. As Blanchot recognizes, however, we cannot achieve not writing by a simple refraining or by a simple act of will. The obligation to write remains a fundamental part of our everyday practice of our profession, intrinsic to it, not accidentally imposed from without. It coexists with the joy of reading and with the more intermittent joy of teaching as the third and by no means least of the main features of our vocation.

(iv) The Future for the Study of Languages and Literatures

In earlier columns I have written about the intrinsic activities of our vocation: reading, teaching, and writing. The other things we do, serving on committees or as administrators, advising students, writing letters of recommendation for students and colleagues, and so on, seem to me, important as they are, ancillary to those main activities. They are ways, for the most part, we help others get on with our common business. In this last of my presidential columns I shall say something about our future as I see it. I mean by this the context in which reading, teaching, and writing about languages and literatures will be carried on in the United States in the coming years. Prophecy is perilous, but I see the present moment and the next couple of decades as a time of special hope, opportunity, and challenge for us.

Most of us know through immediate experience how the placement of what we do within colleges and universities and within society has changed in recent years. Several factors seem to me of special importance. Demographic and actuarial facts presage increased numbers of students in the 1990s and an unusually rapid turnover in teaching staff. A large number of senior professors will retire in the mid-nineties. Their departure will provide a great opportunity for renewal and change, for taking new directions. It will also require courage and foresight on the part of those making all those appointments and tenure decisions. If we, do not figure out what we want to do with our profession, someone else will figure it out for us.

The courage and foresight I have mentioned will require seeing clearly what is new about our situation. Among the most important of these novelties are the following: (1) The United States is becoming a multilingual and multiracial country, a country in which, for increasing numbers of our citizens, English is a second language. We are becoming in new ways a country of many overlapping cultural heritages. Making decisions about how to deal with this pluralism in our culture will be a major responsibility for public policy in the coming years; it will be our responsibility, as teachers of the modern languages, to make sure our voice is heard by those making these decisions. (2) The United States is more and more becoming a country in which, for better or for worse (and it is not necessarily all for the worse), our common culture is primarily determined not by the reading of books, canonical or otherwise, but by the domination of the mass media: television, cinema, popular music. There is no use simply deploring this trend. We must think through its implications and take advantage of it. (3) The function of colleges and universities as institutions within our society is changing with unusual rapidity. It is changing especially, for example, by way of the rapid increase in cooperative research sponsored not by governmental agencies but by industries, especially high-tech industries like computer technology and biotechnology. This situation may seem far from the teaching of languages and literatures, but is going to have decisive effects on what we do. (4) The women's movement is having incalculable effects on our society. Among these are major changes in the curriculum, the canon, and procedures in the study of languages and literatures.

Exactly what differences ought these changes to make in *what* we read, teach, and write about and in *how* we do those things? I see two clear differences. The first is a major alteration in the canon of what we read, teach, and write about and in how these texts are organized in curricula, in class reading lists, and in the contents of books and articles. The second is a new centrality of literary theory to our enterprise. This interest is not merely fashionable. It responds to a deep intellectual need. Literary theory is the indispensable bridge allowing movement back and forth among the various canons and curricula and allowing also for the use of many different sorts of texts to accomplish that primary responsibility of teaching good reading, critical thinking, and accurate, forceful writing. Our main business in the coming years will be to teach people to read – to read all the signs, including those of the newspaper and of the mass culture surrounding us, as well as those signs inscribed on the pages of the old canonical books. In the coming years an informed citizenry in our democracy will be one that can read and think clearly about all the signs that at every moment bombard us through eye and ear. Figuring out the best ways to ensure the existence of this citizenry will be a great responsibility but also an exhilarating opportunity.

20.

The Imperative to Teach

The questions ask: Who or what (today) calls on us to teach? Does that demand lay out a clear road for us to follow? Is that road, if there is one, 'under construction,' that is, I take it, is it in the midst of a social or historical process into which we as teachers or students might intervene, taking a hand in the work of construction? Is that road, if there is one, a one-way street, an *Einbahnstrasse*, presumably in that case going straight from the teachers to the students, with 'Do Not Enter' marked at the other end, to keep the students from driving the wrong way, in defiance of the authority of the teacher?

The questions can be extrapolated a little, perhaps down the one-way street that waits to be traversed, showing me the way to go: Is teaching a contingent addition to 'literary study,' or to 'humanistic study' generally? Or, to put it more simply, does reading, the reading of a poem, a novel, or a philosophical text, for example, require teaching it or lead inevitably to teaching it?

It would seem not. It would seem that the teaching of literature or philosophy is a contingent and somewhat artificial addition to reading. It is something added on by the accidental requirements of the institutions some readers happen to be hired by. We are hired to teach and so we teach. The circumstances of that teaching are open to all sorts of empirical, sociological, and historical investigations, for example, study of the development of higher education in the United States, the place of the humanities within that, difference in demands made on teachers by public and private institutions, differences between the demands on teachers of literature *today* and those made in one or another *yesterday*, differences between the role of teaching in the humanities and the role of teaching in the social sciences and sciences, and so on. It might be shown, for example, that literary study in the university, at least in this country, is much more difficult to imagine *without* teaching than is, for example, the study of economics or astrophysics. Our society in general seems to have an uneasy conscience about supporting people or supporting them for long to do humanistic study entirely detached from teaching, whereas a postdoctoral researcher within the university in physics or biology may be more or less free of teaching for relatively prolonged periods.

At the same time one feels, or one may feel, that this demand for teaching made on humanists in the university does not have anything intrinsic or essential to do with reading. It may be because reading as such is so detached from 'the real world,' as opposed to research in science, with its presumed 'applied' usefulness, that our society feels reading literature or philosophy can only be justified if it is firmly attached to the social and socializing activity of teaching, the passing on and reinforcing of the 'values' of that society through the teaching of canonical interpretations of canonical works. This need to justify reading through teaching of a socially useful kind may explain why there is so much resistance or hostility to modes of reading and teaching in the humanities which conspicuously do not fulfill that demand.

All this, as I said, is open to empirical study by historians and sociologists of our institutions and professions. Such study would take it for granted that the demand or call for teaching, *l'appel à l'enseignement*, comes 'today' from our technological, industrial, or 'post-industrial,' 'post-modern' society. It comes relayed by way of one of the most powerful institutions of such a society, the modern 'research university,' now in the midst of a major shift. This is the shift from support primarily by government agencies to support increasingly by industry, by pharmaceutical companies, for example, or by bio-genetic laboratories, or by computer corporations.

Such an answer to the question of who or what gives the call to teaching would itself be a mode of sociological, even 'scientific,' research. It can and should be accomplished, as part of that general program of rationalizing appropriation, even of its own procedures, protocols, and assumptions, that fundamentally characterizes the modern university and gives it its reason for being.

The problem with doing this is that it would be barking up the wrong tree, like all attempts to assimilate the study and teaching of literature and the other humanities to the demands of sciences, in the sense that we might think of the humanities as part of 'the human sciences.' The irresistible call to teach literature comes not from the institution within which the teaching takes place but from reading itself. I mean by this that the command to teach is a purely linguistic call inscribed within works of literature or philosophy (or indeed within any other texts when they are taken as 'texts'). This call comes neither from any transcendent source, nor from any subject or subjectivity, for example that of the author or reader, nor from society and its institutions – universities, departments, curricula, programs, courses – however compelling or even coercive those may be. The call, the imperative to teach, does not come from anywhere but from within the text itself.

The text demands that the reader go outside the text to attempt to verify its referential and performative validity, that is, to find out whether it tells the truth and whether it can be efficacious in helping us and our students in living our lives, in making judgements and decisions 'in the real world.' As Werner Hamacher has observed, it is not one's mother or grandmother, as representatives of social and institutional authority, who beseech the reader to go outside,

328   *Pedagogical and Political Commitments*

as Marcel's grandmother, in Proust's novel, begged him to do. It is the text itself that exhorts the reader to stop reading.

Teaching is one of the most important ways to respond to that imperative to go outside the text. Contrary to what is often assumed, it is rhetorical reading, or, to give it another name, 'deconstructive reading,' which, more than hermeneutic, semiological, or sociological ways of reading, most urgently and consistently recognizes and responds to this intrinsic demand of works of literature or philosophy not only to be read but to be tested for their referential verity and their functional efficacy. This demand can in no way be resisted by trying to sequester the text in one way or another from that 'real world,' for example, by trying to see it as a free play of signifiers detached from all questions of reference. Teaching, as one response to that demand, would and does take place even where there is no institution to sanction it.

Teaching, it follows, is not primarily communication or dialogue or group therapy. It is the public expression or allegory (in the etymological sense of saying something other than itself out where people can hear, in the *agora*) of the act of reading. Further problems begin, however, to put it mildly, when the act of teaching brings into the open the impossibility of verifying either the referential validity of the text or being certain of what it makes happen or whether what it makes happen is what one would or should want to happen (though one can be sure, or almost sure, that reading makes *something* happen). The impossibility of distinguishing for certain between literal and figurative language in the text, that is to say, the interference of rhetoric in grammar and logic, does not mean that no text is truthfully referential but that neither reader, nor teacher, nor student, whatever his or her location along that one-way or two-way street, can ever be certain whether or not the text is truthfully referential. The celebrated 'unreadability' of literary or philosophical texts, of texts in general, does not mean that the reader or teacher can have absolutely certain negative knowledge of the text's lack of referential and performative validity. It means that the reader or teacher can never be sure whether or not the text is truthfully referential and vividly performative or not. It may be or it may not be. There is no way to tell for sure, and the reader-teacher is suspended in the extreme discomfort of responding to an imperative call which at the same time he or she is altogether unable to fulfill.

That intolerable discomfort, 'worse than madness,' is one reason the attraction of an achieved negativity is perhaps the most dangerous temptation of literary study today, or at any time, since it seems to promise escape from a painful uncertainty and in addition because the thematic assertions of canonical literary works seem so strongly to present a negative knowledge, the demystification of every illusion through the reading of Wordsworth, or Dickens, or Melville, or Wallace Stevens, Proust, Rilke, or Homer, Sophocles, or Virgil, for that matter.

No, all we can learn to know as readers is that we do not yet know for sure one way or the other, and that we are unable to devise rules whereby validity could be certainly tested. It is this unfortunate and dismaying lack of methods of valid testing in literary study which forbids assimilating it into that general enterprise of rationalizing and validating which, as I said, defines the modern university. The teaching of literature is therefore at once the response to a demand made by literature itself and at the same time the demonstration, again and again, in public, before the students, of the impossibility of responding adequately to that demand. Though the teaching of literature is not dialogue but the making public of acts and procedures of reading, there is no reason why remarks made by students in class or papers presented by them should not be teaching too, or do exactly the same thing the teacher's discourse does. Teaching is, in that sense at least, a two-way street. The teaching of literature (and other 'humanistic texts') is, nevertheless, as many people are uneasily aware, an anomaly or odd man out in the modern university. This may explain the urgency of various attempts to assimilate it. The teaching of literature, in fact, is neither a one-way street nor a two-way street, but a permanent impasse, or a road impassable for an indefinite time while it is 'under construction.' It might always have, at the beginning of the way it lays out, that sign one sees in England where roads are under construction: 'Road Up!' Or, the sign might say, 'You can't get there from here.' This unbuilt and perhaps unbuildable construction project might have as motto Kafka's aphorism: 'There is a goal but no way. What we call the way is only wandering.'

This does not mean that the teaching of literature and other humanistic texts does not and cannot occur. Far from it. Teaching happens all the time, I am happy to say. But it happens as the patient, iterated, and reiterated demonstration, out there in the open, whatever the teacher may think he or she is doing, of the impasse I have tried to define.

21

Politicizing Art – What are Cultural Studies?

Walter Benjamin, in a celebrated aphorism at the end of his essay on 'The Work of Art in the Age of Mechanical Reproduction,' asserted that if the aestheticization of politics was being brought about by Fascism (*die Ästhetisierung der Politik, welche der Faschismus betreibt*), 'Communism responds by politicizing art' (*Der Kommunismus antwortet ihm mit der Politisierung der Kunst*) (1969, 242).[1] The problem with such symmetrical reversals is that they may, in the end, come to the same thing, as Jean-Joseph Goux argues about this particular reversal (Goux 1989, 21). To see the state as a work of art is to presume, as the Nazis did, not only that the state is a work of art, the creation of the Führer, but that, as a consequence, art should be in the direct service of the nation-state, the calculated instrument of state ideology. To politicize art, on the other hand, as happened in the Soviet Union, may be to presume that art should be in the direct service of the nation-state, the calculated instrument of state ideology. In both cases art and politics are seen as so intimately related that what happens in one happens in the other. Both tend to presuppose that art is so closely associated with some people or nation-state that it cannot be understood without understanding its roots in a specific language, nation, moment in history, class and gender structure, ideological formation and technological level of production, distribution and consumption.

A little reflection, however, will show that Benjamin's chiasmus is asymmetrical and irreversible. The elements in the two statements not only change places but also change their natures when they are displaced. 'Aestheticization' is not the same thing as 'art.' 'Politicization' is not the same thing as 'politics.' In each case, a tropological transformation replaces a conceptual name. To aestheticize politics is to treat the state as though it were a work of art and therefore to treat human beings as though they were the raw materials of a work of art, able to be manipulated and shaped to fit some rigid scheme, just as dancers are swept into a dance and must obey its pattern, according to a figure used by both Schiller and Yeats. This, says Benjamin, is Fascism. The politicizing of art, on the other hand, the context of Benjamin's essay suggests, means affirming the political value and force of art. Politicizing art means demystifying concepts like genius and eternal value, but also demystifying the idea – present, for example, in Heidegger – that art expresses the essential nature of some nation or race. These are replaced with the assumption that art of a given time is deeply embedded in history, in a particular language and class structure, in specific modes of production, distribution and consumption, particular states of technology, a particular subject-position in the maker. Benjamin attempts to politicize art in this way in his essay. Communism, at least in principle, takes art seriously not just as cultural product but as cultural force.[2]

To 'politicize' art is one project of cultural criticism as it has rapidly developed into a leading way of organizing teaching and research in the United States and in Europe. At the same time, the actual development of twentieth-century art has been toward an internationalization that makes considerations of local provenance perhaps less and less pertinent. This development of international styles in high art has accompanied technological developments that have collaborated in the uprooting of art and popular culture from their local origins. A worldwide culture of blue jeans and tee-shirts, film, television, video-cassettes, popular music on radio and CD is irreversibly displacing, or at least transforming, local cultures everywhere. The local deeper differences remain, but the surface culture is remarkably the same around the world. The power of this culture to erode local differences is so great that it makes one extremely anxious about the possibility of enhancing or developing those regional specificities that seem the normal and proper human condition. To do so, however, to give those fragile, marginalized ways of living a vital power of self-determination, is one main goal of cultural studies.

One anecdotal example will indicate what I mean. One Sunday a couple of years ago I was in Kathmandu, Nepal, in the house of an extended upper-caste family of Brahmins. This was about as far away from my own, American, culture as I had ever been. How did they spend the Sunday afternoon? By watching on VCR a movie in Hindi. Much can be said about these films. They are the product of a complex indigenous film tradition, but to an American eye they look, in part, something like American films and television shows of urban violence, for example *L.A. Law* or *Miami Vice*. The latter is shown on Nepali state television.

A similar uprooting and internationalizing has happened to the university. Rather than being, as was the case in the nineteenth century, in the direct service of a specific nation state and its aspirations, each university is now more and more truly universal, transnational. The university, for example, works in the service of multinational pharmaceutical or computer industries. In the case of the humanities, a given university shares in a collective research and teaching effort that knows few national boundaries and limitations. Young scholars from all over the world attend the Dartmouth School of Criticism and Theory. Moreover, technological developments associated with copying machines, fax machines, and computers are transforming the conditions of research and teaching in the humanities, just as mechanical reproduction transformed the conditions of the making and using of art in the nineteenth and early twentieth centuries, as Benjamin argues in 'The Work of Art in the Age of Mechanical

Reproduction.' What is the place of cultural studies in this age not of mechanical but of digital reproduction? What are the manifest and latent presuppositions of cultural studies and their place in the university and in society at this moment in history? What do you find, I am asking, if you make culture studies the object of cultural study?

Cultural studies of various sorts are no doubt overdetermined. They have many, and to some degree contradictory, sources, or perhaps it would be better to say concomitant factors, to avoid begging a question that ought to be at the heart of any interrogation of the significance of cultural studies. This is the question of what causes cultural changes. One thing is certain: it would be a gross error to assume that the reorientation from language to history, politics, and society as the focal points of humanistic study is merely another shift in the winds of critical fashion. The shift is a response to profound motivations in the multitude of (mostly younger) scholars who now see such studies as their vocation. Among these motivations are ideological ones that may not be readily apparent to those caught up in the changes.

In saying this I am aware that just as persons undergoing psychoanalysis resist having their neuroses identified and brought to light, so all of us resist having our ideological presuppositions identified and brought to light. If ideology is the confusion of linguistic with material reality, it also depends, as Althusser said, on functioning unconsciously, on being unthought out, 'impensée.' To think it out, to reflect theoretically about it, may be to risk disabling it. This is one of the things that is meant when theory is falsely accused of being nihilistic. On the other hand, even if insight and effective action always pivot on an area of blindness necessary to their functioning, that blindness may damage both the insight and the effective action. Such blindness is not necessarily the benign and productive center of a radiant light. The insight may be no more than another form of disastrous blindness. The action may be effective but have dismayingly different results from those intended. It is probably best to try to see as clearly as possible, even though clear-seeing or theory is always at least one step behind a blindness that always reforms itself and that is the condition of seeing. The term 'ideological' may itself not be appropriate if it is implicitly or explicitly set against the idea of real material conditions, since the latter is itself an ideological concept requiring critical scrutiny.

What are Cultural Studies?

Cultural studies take a number of different institutional forms, forms not entirely congruent with one another either in theory or in practical, political, and institutional orientation. Ethnic studies do not have quite the same presuppositions as women's studies, nor are either of those the same as the transformation of what used to be called American studies into a multimedia, multilinguistic form of cultural studies. Different from all these are 'new historical' studies as applied to Renaissance or Victorian English literature. Still different are British Birmingham School cultural studies, with their strongly institutionalized pedagogical programs and their particular political agenda within a Britain governed by the Conservative Party. By comparison, cultural studies in the United States or in Australia are diffuse, heterogeneous, and not yet firmly institutionalized.[3] Nevertheless, certain presuppositions tend to persist throughout all these different forms of cultural studies. I shall focus to some degree on minority discourses.

(1) Cultural studies tend to assume that a work of art, popular culture, literature, or philosophy can best be understood if accompanied by an attempt to understand the work's historical context, including the political elements of that history: the material, social, class, economic, technological, and gender circumstances in which the work was produced and consumed. If you want to understand Henry James, study the conditions of the publishing industry during the period in which James wrote. These conditions are essential to the meaning of James's work, not adventitious to it. The work, whether of high art or of popular culture, can only be fully understood by way of an understanding of the subject position of the maker, the place in society where the maker stood. 'Subject' here is, of course, a pun. It means both subjectivity and subjected to, or subject to, as when we say 'Queen Victoria's subjects.'

(2) Cultural studies are cross-disciplinary and multimedia in orientation. They presuppose a crossing or breaking down of traditional disciplinary separations. They study films, novels, poems, television soap operas, advertising, painting, popular music, photography, dress, and culinary practices side by side as concomitant evidence of a given culture's state at a given time. They use procedures developed in the social sciences as well as in the humanities. Cultural studies owe much to the procedures of anthropology and ethnography, though they are also critical of these disciplines. The interdisciplinarity of cultural studies would appear to put in question in various ways earlier language-oriented theory, for example its concentration on literary or philosophical texts. Nevertheless, though the focus on popular culture displaces scholarly attention from language to signs of all sorts, a reading of these signs is still necessary. The question is what changes in procedure are involved when we read an advertisement or a soap opera rather than a poem, a novel, or a philosophical treatise.

(3) Cultural studies deliberately attempt to break down the assumption that there is an agreed-upon canon of works that ought to be the center of humanistic studies. Partly, as in ethnic studies and women's studies, this assault on the canon is motivated by the desire to include in the curriculum hitherto neglected works by women and minorities. Partly, as in the new American studies, it is motivated by the presupposition that if your focus is culture, not literature or art according to some assumption that there is a timeless pantheon

of classics, then popular culture is as important or even more important than highbrow works produced for an élite of connoisseurs.

(4) Cultural studies tend to assume that a work of art, popular culture, literature or philosophy not only can best be understood in its historical context, but also has its best value or purchase on the world if it remains understood in relation to some specific and local people, a people defined by language, place, history, and tradition, the experience of African-American or Chicano/a people, for example, or those who wrote for the theater or attended it in Shakespeare's England. This does not mean that a work does not have value when it is transferred to a new context, but that it had best not be detached in that displacement from an understanding of the subject position of its maker. To do so is to be in danger of sentimentalizing or aestheticizing the work. The work, for example, may be uprooted and made into a quaint aesthetic toy for the hegemonic class of consumers, as 'Anglos' may admire reproductions of Chicano/a murals, whereas each cultural artefact is best seen, to borrow phrases from Abdul JanMohamed, as 'a performative utterance/event as opposed to its existence as an aesthetic object.'[4]

Cultural studies do not see the context of a cultural artefact as a passive, stable, and timeless background of ethnicity. The work is not just embedded in its context, as a rock is embedded in the earth or a precious stone in a ring. That context is a dynamic, heterogeneous field, constantly changing, in part through the performative effects on it of newly made cultural artefacts. Nor is the ethnic culture safely sequestered from the dominant culture. In an important un-published paper, in part a response to an earlier version of this book's first part, David Lloyd distinguishes between individual ethnic cultures and minority discourse. An ethnic culture, says Lloyd, 'can be conceived as turned, so to speak, towards its internal differences, complexities and debates, as well as to its own traditions or histories, projects and imaginings.' An ethnic culture

> is transformed into a minority culture only along the lines of its confrontation with a dominant state formation which threatens to destroy it by direct violence or by assimilation. Minority discourse is articulated along this line, and at once registers the loss, actual and potential, and offers the means to a critique of dominant culture precisely in terms of its own internal logic.[5]

The context to which a given artefact is related by cultural studies is not a homogeneous ethnic culture, but that culture both as differentiated within itself and as threatened, damaged, and displaced by the dominant culture. The situations of Native American and Chicano/a cultures within the United States are good examples of that damage and displacement.[6]

(5) Cultural studies tend to define themselves through a set of oppositions that may appear to be reductively binary: élite versus popular, hegemonic as against marginal, theory as against praxis, cultural artefact as reflection of culture as against art as the maker of culture, and so on. Such thinking has its dangers, as

the example of the apparent reversibility of the politicizing of art into the aestheticizing of politics suggests. Some hierarchy and possibility of dialectical sublation tend to be assumed. It is difficult to get thought and practice to move outside the presuppositions that are being contested.

Many cultural critics are fully aware of this problem, both in its theoretical form and as a practical problem, to use one of these oppositions. Abdul JanMohamed, for example, disinguishes between 'binary negation' and 'negation as analogue.' He may be punning on the terms 'analogue' and analog,' thereby alluding to two different forms of calculation possible in computer systems, binary and analog.[7] Binary negation is dialectical, subject to hierarchical ordering and to he kind of recuperation I have named as a danger. Mystifying presuppositions about grounding origin and pre-existing goal are almost inevitably implied. Negation by analogue sees each element as part of a differential series without hierarchial priority, without fixed original or end.[8] I see this distinction as a crucial theoretical point. It is crucial because cultural studies must hold on to it firmly if they are to resist being recuperated by the thinking of the dominant culture they would contest. It is also a good example of the debt of cultural studies to previous theoretical work developed in other contexts. The distinction is, for example, something like the distinction between two kinds of representation or repetition, repetition as copy and repetition as simulacrum, as developed in different ways by Derrida, Foucault, or Deleuze (see Derrida 1972, 199–317; Foucault 1973; Deleuze 1969, 292–307).

(6) Cultural studies have an uneasy relation to theory, particularly to the deconstructive or post-structuralist theory that preceded them and without which they would have been impossible in the form they have taken. On the one hand, cultural studies are theoretical through and through, so much so that 'critical theory' is almost a synonym for 'cultural studies.' On the other hand, they are sometimes deeply suspicious of theory, sometimes define themselves as resolutely anti theoretical, and would stress their practical orientation as against the 'sterile' ratiocinations and élite institutional placement of 'pure theory.' The fear is that since theory was developed by the élite dominant culture it cannot be appropriated by cultural studies without disabling the latter in some form of recuperation. David Lloyd, in the unpublished paper cited above, has argued forcefully against this assumption. For Lloyd, theory is an essential part of minority discourse, essential to its practical political goals of changing the university and gaining self-determination for minority individuals and groups.

(7) This uneasy relation to theory goes with an attitude towards reading that is somewhat different from either that of the New Criticism or of so-called deconstruction. If reading, for deconstruction, or rhetorical criticism, is the center of a humanistic study that is oriented towards the understanding of language or other signs and that presupposes some element of the unique and unaccountable in each work, cultural studies may sometimes be primarily thematic, paraphrastic, and diagnostic in their way of reading. Just as a physician

or psychoanalyst must go rapidly through the details of a physical or psychological illness to diagnose it as a case of measles or of schizophrenia, in order to get on with the urgently needed treatment, so the practitioner of cultural studies sometimes goes as rapidly as possible through the evident features of the work to diagnose it as another case of the particular culture it manifests. The orientation is more toward the culture and less toward the work in itself, even though the heterogeneity of each culture is in principle recognized. Rhetorical reading, or so-called deconstruction, presupposes that only an active and interventionist reading of texts and other cultural artefacts can be socially and politically effective. A merely thematic reading will remain caught in the ideology that is being contested, whatever its overt theoretical or political assertions. In the realm of words, which are the medium of cultural criticism, only an active reading wrestling with the excess of language or other signs over transparent meaning, a wrestling with what might be called the material dimension of signs, will *work*, that is, effect changes in the real institutional and social worlds. This is an important point in my argument, to which I shall return.

(8) Cultural studies, finally, are explicitly political. They stress the performative over the merely theoretical in what they do. Their goal is the transformation of the university by aligning present departments and disciplines and establishing new ones. Through the refashioning of the university they want to dismantle the present dominant culture and empower ones that are at present peripheral – minorities, women, gays and lesbians, all those disadvantaged, silenced, without power. This empowering means not just preserving the minority cultures as they are or have been, but giving members of those minority cultures the ability to transform their own cultural forms and to repair the damage done to them by the dominant culture in new self-determined and self-determining creations.

The political aspect of cultural studies is the noblest and most attractive. Who could oppose the righting of injustice and the enfranchising of the disenfranchised? Who would not be attracted by the idea that he or she is not just reading this or that work, but furthering the cause of universal justice? The problem is to know you are really doing that, or at least know as much as can be known about why you cannot know. Theoretical reflection may be essential to this – or perhaps may keep it from happening. That is the question. Since what cultural studies produce is discourse, whatever effect they have will, properly speaking, be performative, that is, a way of doing things with words. That effect will, therefore, be subject to linguistic constraints on the relation between power and knowledge in discourse.

The overtly political aspect of cultural studies is disquieting from the point of view of the traditional self-definition of the university as the place of disinterested pursuit of knowledge. The modern Western university has defined itself as the place where the principle of reason reigns. Everything can and should be rationalized, its grounding principle identified, and results of this research stored in the vast archives of what has been made reasonable. That self-definition has no doubt been a blinded cover for the perpetuation of the dominant white, male Eurocentric ideology. The university is not disinterested at all, it is an instrument of power. It is not a matter of politicizing an apolitical university. The university is already political through and through. Nevertheless, the overt definition of a component of the university as oriented toward revolutionary transformation not only of the university but of the society whose instrument the university is, rocks the boat quite a bit. It may be that there has been so little resistance to this assertion of the goal of cultural studies just because those hegemonic custodians of the old university cannot bring themselves to take cultural studies seriously, though that is now beginning to change. Many of those running the university are scientists, secure in the knowledge of their power to remake the world. They are probably wrong in taking the goals of cultural studies so lightly, though the university's powers of recuperation are immense, as proponents of cultural studies recognize.[9]

A further danger is the appropriation of cultural studies by the dominant culture. This is already happening. Cultural critics are, for example, enlisted for the work of the United States Information Service or for the British Council. One cultural critic, for example, was asked recently to provide the British Council with the twenty-five best records by British rock groups for diffusion abroad as examples of the vitality of British culture. The celebration and transformative liberation of cultural diversity by cultural studies can, with dismaying ease, be transformed into a promulgation by the dominant culture of a liberal pluralism that falsifies and covers over the actual power and property relations between the dominant and marginal cultures within a given nation.

Notes

1. Several versions of this essay exist. I have used the one canonized by standard German editions and by the English translation. Philippe Lacoue-Labarthe has developed in detail the catastrophic effects of seeing the state as a work of art in a description of Nazi Germany as a case of 'national aestheticism' (1987, 92–113). See also de Man (1996, 129–62).
2. I have been helped in thinking this through by Philip Leider.
3. For information about cultural studies in Australia and a lively essay about cultural studies generally, see Morris (1988, 15–26).
4. In a letter of 5 March 1991 from JanMohammed to me.
5. David Lloyd, 'Ethnic Cultures, Minority Discourse and the State,' unpublished ms, 8. The fact that Lloyd should have responded to my paper and I in turn to his through the exchange of computer-produced and laser-printed mss before either of the papers has been published is an example of those changed conditions of scholarship in the humanities. The humanities are in this merely catching up with

the sciences, where such pre-publication exchange has been normal for the last two decades at least. Electronic mail has already made such interactions even easier and faster. It will, no doubt, come to be used more and more by humanists.

6. David Lloyd describes this eloquently: 'What is perhaps most immediately striking about the historical experience of minorities in general . . . is its determination by processes of dislocation rather than enracination. That continuing dislocation has taken many forms, materially and culturally, including the internal colonization of an already hybrid Chicana/o population and its continuing patterns of labour migration and acculturation; the enslavement and diaspora of African-Americans and their continuing economic dispersion; the genocide and displacement of Native Americans in an effort precisely to loosen their claim to 'local' land rights; the immigration and exploitation of Chinese and Filipino workers; and so forth' (13).

7. The fact that JanMohammed takes a term from computer language is significant. It is an example of the way the language of technology can be appropriated for theoretical reflection. It also raises the question of whether digital computers, almost exclusively used these days for research and writing in cultural studies, for example, may not have built into them an inclination toward binary negation rather than negation by what he calls 'analogue.' Analog computers have have already shown themselves to be better for certain industrial uses where approximations rather than stark either/or oppositions are more effective.

8. Abdul JanMohamed, in the letter to me of 5 March 1991, characterizes this opposition as follows: 'In my book on Wright I intend to make the distinction by characterizing the first negation (practised by the dominant culture) as *digital*, which is binary, and the second negation (practised by minority cultures in various forms – from "signifying" to the kind of violent negation that Wright explored) as *analogue*, which 'negates' by invoking a whole set of differences, which can be thought of as "sublation," the "blues," or what Kojève calls 'dialectical overcoming."' JanMohamed's quotation marks around 'negation,' 'sublation,' and 'dialectical overcoming' are important here, since the words belong to the vocabulary of 'digital negation.' They must be twisted to a new use to apply to 'negation by analogue.' JanMohamed may be alluding by word-play to analog computing. In any case, the two kinds of computers are called 'digital' and 'analog.' Digital computers express input and output only in numbers (base 2 in the case of our familiar desktops), while analog computers express input and output in a continuous 'language,' like a clock with hands moving around a dial, in a way something like the differential series JanMohamed calls 'negation by analogue.'

9. Of all these features of cultural studies the admirable essay by Abdul JanMohamed and David Lloyd (1990) is an excellent example, as is the whole volume, previously published as numbers 6 and 7 of *Cultural Critique*. Though no one work can characterize adequately a discourse as diverse, controversial and heterogeneous as cultural studies, I have had the essay by JanMohamed and Lloyd in mind as a salient expression of the assumptions of cultural studies. I am grateful for their comments on my discussion of cultural studies. These comments have led to revisions.

22

Literary Study in the Transnational University

The Fractal Mosaic

Something drastic is happening in the university. Something drastic is happening *to* the university. The university is losing its idea, the guiding mission that has sustained it since the early nineteenth century.[1] It was then, in Germany, that the modern research university was invented. John Henry Newman's *The Idea of a University* (1852, 1859, 1873) expounded for English readers both this concept of the university and, among other things, the place of literary study in it.[2] Idea – the word has a Platonic resonance. It names a transcendent form – presiding, generative, paternal – on which particular material embodiments are modeled. The university governed by an idea is rapidly being replaced by what Bill Readings calls the university of 'excellence.' Whatever a given discipline defines at the moment as important work is 'excellent.' Excellence does not refer to an ahistorical transcendent model operating above the university to determine what it should be and do, giving it a mission and a goal. Excellence is, as Readings observes, a tautological self-definition.

What is the use of literary study now, in this new university without idea? Should, ought, or must we still study literature? What is the source now of the obligation to study literature? Who or what addresses to us a call to do so? Why should we do it? To what purpose? Can literary study still be defended as a socially useful part of university research and teaching or is it just a vestigial remnant that will vanish as other media become more dominant in the new global society that is rapidly taking shape?

[. . .]*

If a work of literature may be assumed to be like a human individual, if it is the fractal image of its author, as Proust repeatedly and eloquently argues in *À la recherche*, then the study of literature, it would follow, should be organized as the separate study of each national literature's most important works. These would

---

* The excised passage considers the question *why literature?* at a point in the history of the university when the study of literature appears unjustifiable. It does so through consideration of a passage from Proust and, to a lesser extent, a passage from *Middlemarch*, in order to show how characters belong to a fractal mosaic; each is a singular allegory, or, in Eliot's words, a parable of every other. Thus each character, and, by extension, each literary work, is a singular figure indirectly figuring ideology, history, politics, the nation, and so on. [Ed.]

be the works that most directly embody that culture's self-understanding of its tradition. Each major national author is a little polygon mirroring in a special way the whole nation. The work of each author, will echo in fractal self-similarity the unity and specificity of the national culture – what makes France France, Germany Germany, the United States the United States. Moreover, the law of fractal self-similarity means that study of a limited number of carefully chosen representative works from different historical periods will allow the reader to understand the unified culture of a whole nation.

A further support for the current applicability of the mosaic figure comes from the way this image is often proposed these days by scholars of United States multiculturalism. It is used as an appropriate replacement for the traditional figure of the United States as a melting pot transforming immigrants from many lands, cultures, and languages into homogeneous, monolingual 'Americans' (as by metonymy we habitually call them, forgetting that the United States is only one part of America). The United States, in the now outmoded figures, is filled, after the melting pot has done its work, with millions of little polygons repeating with a difference the national culture's unified shape. In a multicultural nation, on the contrary, the tesserae remain distinct, the side by side juxtaposition of elements that are never assimilated to universal sameness. Nevertheless, the notion of ethnic groups repeats in a different way the nationalist assumptions of Proust's fractal polygon. The implication is that all African Americans or Native Americans or Chicanos and Chicanas are essentially defined by their participation in their ethnic group. Each group is a nation within the nation. The term 'mosaic' is a focus for the battle between differing notions of what United States culture is or ought to be.

'Mosaic,' in addition, is the name of a once widely used browser program for navigating the World Wide Web of the Internet. The figure invites us to think of the Internet as a spatial array of contiguous fields that may be explored by multiple hypertext links, since each tessera in the mosaic is adjacent to many others. A user can advance through such an array in many different ways to reach the same goal. 'Mosaic' functions as a program for finding things in the World Wide Web. It does this by allowing its user to move efficiently by a series of choices out of many possible routes from link to link to reach the desired goal.

'Get "Geist"': *The Crisis in Representation*

United States universities characteristically have a number of discrete departments, each devoted to the separate study of a single national literature. The dominant department is the one representing our nation's language and literary tradition. Does this well-established paradigm still hold? Can we accept the figure of the fractal mosaic both as a true description and as a heuristic pattern indicating not only how the study of literature ought to be organized in the university but also what use such study is? What is happening today with the study of national literatures? By 'today' I mean not only the time when new communication technologies – computers, e-mail, faxes, VCRs, videos, CD-ROMs, hypertexts, and 'surfing on the Internet' – are fundamentally changing the ways humanistic scholars interact and do their work. I mean also the time when the Cold War has ended, when the power and integrity of nation-states are weakening, when economic and cultural systems are being globalized, and when as a consequence the university's mission is being transformed.[3]

[. . .]*

Many curious signs abound of the way globalization is changing our cultural and practical life. The Public Broadcasting System in the United States, until recently still to such a degree funded by Federal money that it seemed almost an arm of the government, one of the state apparatuses under the rubric of 'media,' has now changed its name, no doubt for good commercial and ideological reasons, to 'Public Radio International.' Presumably this means they sell some of their programs abroad. A shop in Camden, Maine, advertises that it 'unconditionally guarantees everything it sells to be "Made on Earth." ' This is a globalizing joke, of course, a play on 'Made in the USA' or 'Made in Japan.' Our shops are full of things that are 'Made on Earth,' that is, designed in one country, their parts manufactured in many different countries, assembled in another, and sold in many more.

Analogous changes are occurring in our universities. Though some of these are being imposed from the outside, most obviously in the reduction of funding, the changes are also happening from the inside, with the conscious or unconscious complicity of university teachers and administrators. The traditional word 'crisis' is not appropriate for this change. That word suggests the possibility of going beyond the crisis and returning to a new form of the previous condition, as a sick person weathers a crisis and gets well. The change in the university going on now is irreversible. It affects all branches and departments of the research university, but in different ways. Its effect on the teaching of national literatures is especially strong. Those who teach and do research in departments of national literatures have hardly begun to be aware of the way these changes alter their work. They have only begun to develop the conceptual figurations necessary to grasp the changes.

I want here to identify what these changes are and how they alter the vocation of literary study. When something traumatic is happening, the academic's response is to try to understand it. In this case, it may be, knowledge is not enough. By the time we are aware of it, the change has already occurred and it is too late, as a parallel with trauma suggests. Apparently we have walked

---

* Following an article by Vincent Cable, Miller addresses the ways in which new technologies have globalized business, and the consequent transformation of literature as cultural artefact. [Ed.]

away unharmed from what has been done to the university. The old departments are still there, seemingly doing what they have always done. We have
survived unscathed. Only later do the symptoms of post-traumatic stress
syndrome begin. They often take the form of a painful repetition of the events
whose traumatic power we did not notice at the time. They were events that in
a sense did not take place when they took place, since they were not
experienced as traumatic. They take place as traumatic only now, in retrospect,
after the fact, when it is already too late and the old university we thought we
were still inhabiting is in ruins. Far from liberating us, moreover, in this case
trying to take stock of what is happening to the university, for example my
effort here, may only accelerate the process of globalization and denationaliza-
tion it describes.

I take the study of English literature in the United States as my example, since
it is my field. It should be recognized from the start, however, that the choice is
hardly innocent. English literature is not just one national literature among
others. A main feature of globalization is that the English language, primarily by
way of the United States, is gradually becoming, for better or for worse, a
universal language. English is already spoken everywhere in the world as the
second language of millions and millions of people for whom it is not the
mother tongue. With the study of the English language goes the study of its
literature, as one of the most potent instruments of the spread of capitalist
ideologies. Or at least we used to be confident that this is the case. It is not quite
clear, when you think of it, how the study of Shakespeare or Hardy will aid the
economic imperialism of the United States.

What is happening, as a result of these societal changes, to the study of English
literature in the United States? For one thing, it is gradually being swallowed up
by increased offerings in American, that is, United States literature. Most United
States universities now have departments of English and American literature,
whatever they may be called. United States literature has become more and
more dominant within such agglomerations. Moreover, a 'crisis in representation,' as Brook Thomas terms it (1994, 79), exists for writing, teaching, and
curricular design in departments of the national literatures. Most teachers in
American colleges and universities used to believe in the validity of a part for
whole relation in literary study. A good literary work was presumed to be an
organic whole, so the study of a part could be a means of understanding or
teaching the whole. Teachers could use with a clear conscience the detailed
study of a passage. Such a procedure was brilliantly exploited as a method of
reading by Erich Auerbach in *Mimesis* (1953). The whole work, carefully chosen
and explicated on the assumption that each part of it mirrored its totality and also
the totality of the culture around it, could then be used as a way of understanding what was assumed to be a homogeneous surrounding culture. For
Auerbach, one citation from Virginia Woolf's *To the Lighthouse* could illustrate
the entire modernist practice of realistic representation. It was possible for other

scholars to imply that study of *Moby-Dick* and a few other canonical works would give readers something approaching a full understanding of mid-nineteenth-century American culture. Of course, such claims were often made with careful qualification, but some version of the synecdochal assumption operated widely as an unquestioned ideologeme. An ideological element is by definition unquestioned, since it is an unconscious assumption, a cultural artefact taken as a fact of nature. This particular ideologeme may have had all the more power for being an unspoken presupposition that guided the choice of the canon and the devising of curricula.

Few people have any longer an unshaken confidence in this paradigm, even those who most stridently assert it. We recognize that the United States is a multicultural and multilingual nation. A given work or canon represents only one part of a complex, nontotalizable whole. To choose to teach *Moby-Dick* rather than *Uncle Tom's Cabin* or even to choose to teach both of them together, is not the result of a proof that either work is objectively representative of its culture. The choice is motivated and unjustifiable – which does not mean that it is necessarily bad. It means that those who devise syllabi and curricula must take responsibility for their choices, not defend them by pointing to universal criteria of exemplarity. Nor do we any longer have recourse to some standard of intrinsic superiority allowing us to say that *Moby-Dick* is a better work than *Uncle Tom's Cabin*, or vice versa. That standard too is the result of ideological bias. This loss of confidence in the possibility of justifying a syllabus on the basis of its verifiable representative status is almost as much of a disaster for those trained in the old ways of teaching literature (me for example) as would be, for citizens of the United States, a loss of confidence in the power of their elected representatives to represent them.

The 'crisis' of representation in the humanities leads to enormous problems in establishing curricula, in the practical work of teaching and writing about literature, in making decisions about appointments and programs. One reason that so much time is spent these days in theoretical speculation is that we have no consensus about just how we should proceed. Many feel they must reinvent the whole institution of teaching literature from the ground (or lack of ground) up.

For literature departments the so-called crisis of representation accompanies a larger crisis of representation for the humanities as an element in a new kind of university in a different world. This change accompanies a recognition, in the United States at least, that we are not and never have been a nation-state with a unified culture, as least not as that concept has supervised the European sense of citizenship since the Renaissance or, in its more modern form, since the eighteenth century.

The loss of a special role for the study of English literature puts English departments especially under stress in the new university that is developing. Professors of English have been deprived of their traditional role as preservers and transmitters of a nation-state's unified culture. There was always something of an anomaly in basing the cultural ideals of the United States on the study of English literature, that is, on the study of a foreign literature that happens to be written in a version of our dominant language. English literature has had a role in United States education parallel to that of Greek and Latin literature in eighteenth- and nineteenth-century English education, before the university study of English literature had been formally institutionalized. A British citizen and a United States citizen, whatever their class, gender, or race, are likely to read Shakespeare, Milton, or Dickens in quite different ways. These authors do not belong to United States citizens or express our national values or even the values of our hegemonic class in the same ways that they belong to or express such values for British citizens. This does not mean that English literature is not of great importance as an influence on the developing United States literature. Reading Shakespeare in order to understand *Moby-Dick* better is not the same thing, however, as reading it as a primary expression of your own native heritage. A parallel might be made between the function *Oedipus the King* had for Athenians and the importance knowing it and other Greek tragedies has for understanding A. C. Swinburne's *Atalanta in Calydon*. Shakespeare's ringing affirmation of England's island unity and his patriotic depiction of victory at Agincourt have a hollow sound in a country that established itself in a revolutionary war by defeating the British. The names 'Lexington,' 'Bunker Hill,' 'Yorktown,' and 'Valley Forge' have more resonance for us than 'Agincourt.' Nevertheless, English literature was the basis of a literary education in the United States when I got my undergraduate and graduate degrees not all that many decades ago. My graduate qualifying examination for the PhD in English stopped with Thomas Hardy and included no United States literature at all, much less any theory.

   The study of English literature in the United States is in one major way like its study in Korea, Norway, Taiwan, Germany, or Italy. In another major way it is unlike. To study English literature in the United States, Korea, Spain, or Norway, to take it seriously as a source of values and humanistic understanding, is to study the literature of a foreign country, a small island nation off the west coast of Europe. The difference of course is that a version of English also happens to be the dominant, one might even say 'official,' language of the United States, whereas it is a second language in Korea, Norway, Taiwan, Spain, Germany, and the rest. The dominance of the American version of the English language in the United States, however, perhaps only makes it harder for us to see what is problematic about basing United States training in humanistic values on a literature that is not native to our soil. United States literature and British literature are by no means parts of one homogeneous whole, even though United States literature has traditionally been taught as a subordinate part of English literature, as at my own university now and at the other two universities at which I have taught: Johns Hopkins and Yale . . .

Training in British literature is still the basis of literary education in the United States. At the University of California at Irvine, where I now teach, there are between six and seven hundred English majors. It is the most obvious choice for undergraduates who want to concentrate on literature, even though almost half of the students at Irvine are Asian Americans, many of whom have English as a second language. Chaucer, Shakespeare, Milton, Wordsworth, Dickens, Woolf – these still play a large role in determining the way citizens of the United States with a higher education think and behave.

These days, however, radical changes in society, in the university's relation to society, and in the study of literature are putting in question the traditional English major. By traditional English major I mean the more or less sequestered study of major canonical works by British authors from '*Beowulf* to Virginia Woolf,' organized in courses devoted to historical 'periods': Medieval literature, the Renaissance, the eighteenth century, Romanticism, the Victorian period, modernism, and postmodernism. Such a division makes many problematic assumptions about the canon, about the unity of works and periods, about the linear continuity of literary history, and so on. Just what changes are dismantling those assumptions, and just why have they occurred?

The Western research university in its modern form originated with the founding in the early nineteenth century of the University of Berlin, established according to a plan devised by Wilhelm von Humboldt. Such universities had as their primary role service to the nation-state, still nascent at that time in Germany. The nation-state was conceived as an organically unified culture with a single set of ideals and values enshrined in a unified philosophical tradition and national literature (or in a certain way of appropriating Greek and Latin literature). The university was to serve the nation-state in two ways: (1) as the place of critical thinking and research, of finding out the truth about everything, of giving everything its rationality, according to the Leibnizian formula that says nothing is without its reason; (2) as the place of education, formation, or *Bildung*, where male citizens (they were all male then in the university) are inculcated, one might almost say 'inoculated,' with the basic values of a unified national culture. It was the business of the university to produce subjects of the state, in both senses of the word *subject*: as subjectivities and as citizens accountable to state power and capable of promulgating it. For Humboldt and his colleagues, following Kant, the basis of *Bildung* was the study of philosophy. People with a higher degree are still, for the most part, called 'doctors of philosophy,' whatever the discipline in which they received the degree. This practice is something of an absurdity these days, since philosophy proper does not, to say the least, still have the role it did in German universities in the days of Kant, Fichte, and Hegel, while most PhD's in other fields know little or nothing about philosophy.

With some support from Schiller's *Letters on Aesthetic Education*, Anglo-Saxon countries in the mid-nineteenth century, first England and then the United

States, deflected this paradigm in an important way by substituting literature for philosophy as the center of cultural indoctrination. Grounds for this shift already existed in the centrality granted to literary education by many German theorists: the Schlegels, Schelling, and Hegel, for example. The shift occurred in England and in the United States to a considerable degree under the aegis of Matthew Arnold's formulations about culture and anarchy, about the study of poetry, and about the function of criticism. The modern United States research university has inherited the double mission of Humboldt's university. This continuity was evident in the founding of the Johns Hopkins University in Baltimore in 1876. The Hopkins was based explicitly and self-consciously on the German university rather than on the English university. An admirable proliferation of both public and private research universities in the United States followed soon after or was already under way.

The combination of gathering scientific knowledge (which includes knowledge of history, cultural history, and literary history, as well as knowledge of anthropology, physics, biology, and other social and physical sciences) while at the same time teaching a nation's unifying values seems coherent enough. Nevertheless, a tension has always existed between these two goals as charges to the department responsible for doing research and teaching in a country's national literature. On the one hand, the charge is to teach students by way of literature the central ideas and values of a national culture. These are presumed to be enshrined in the nation's canonical works – in *Beowulf*, Chaucer, Shakespeare, and the rest. On the other hand, scientific research is supposed to be critical and 'disinterested' (in a way different from Arnold's use of the word), a search for truth independent of subjective bias. Research is value free, *wertfrei*. It is organized according to a universal methodology of verifiable research applicable mutatis mutandis to the human sciences as well as to the physical, social, and life sciences.

A touching confidence that these two enterprises would achieve the same results for a long time made it possible for those in departments of national literatures to believe they were fulfilling both missions and reconciling the two contradictory charges the university had given them. A professor of English could simultaneously pursue research of the most positivistic kind into the minutiae of an author's life, or do the most mind-numbing bibliographical or editorial work, and at the same time teach undergraduate classes extolling the ethical virtues contained in works by Milton, Johnson, Browning, Arnold, and the rest. The first activity made him (they were almost all male) feel he was doing something useful to support his university's scientific devotion to truth seeking. He was adding to the archives of achieved knowledge. The second made him feel he was fulfilling his responsibility to *Bildung*.

The Culture Evermore About To Be

The use of a foreign country's literature in the formation of United States citizens is a symptom of a fundamental change in the Humboldtian research university that took place when the model was adopted in the United States. Bill Readings is right when he says that the concept of a unified national culture in the United States has always been a promise or hope for the future. It is something always yet to be created by contractual agreement among the free citizens of a republic rather than something inherited as an inescapable tradition from the nation's historical past.[4] It always remains up for grabs. English literature was co-opted by American schools and universities as the basic tool for the creation of a national culture that remains about to be, rather than something that is. [. . .]

Some might argue that over the past fifty years United States citizens have come to recognize that they have an indigenous national literature which unifies them and makes them all Americans, little polygons all like the big polygon of the whole United States. But the rise of 'American literature' and 'American studies' as separate disciplines in universities and colleges demonstrates just the opposite. The important books on United States literature, from those by F. O. Matthiessen, Charles Feidelson, Jr, R. W. B. Lewis, and Perry Miller down to more recent work by Roy Harvey Pearce, Sacvan Bercovitch, and Harold Bloom,[5] have been devoted not so much to describing as to attempting to create the unified national culture we do not have. They characteristically do this by a complex, performative scholarly ritual that masquerades as objective scholarship. They appeal to such general concepts as the frontier ('Go west, young man'), the American Renaissance, the American Adam, a certain use of symbolism, a certain use of romance, the Puritan ideal, the unity of a canonical poetic tradition from Emerson, Dickinson, and Whitman through Crane and Stevens to Ammons and Ashbery, and so on, in incoherent multiplicity. Different figurative paradigms for totalizing American literature appear and disappear like shadows in the mist. Each scholar makes up his or her own idea about the unity of American literature, and each idea is incompatible with the others. [. . .] If one has a canon that can be taken for granted, as to a considerable degree the educated classes do in England, one does not need to worry about it or theorize about it. [. . .]

[. . .] Any attempt to unify United States literature, however, will be biased and political – in short, ideological. I mean by 'ideology' here the mistaking of a linguistic reality for a phenomenal one. Recent work, for example by Carolyn Porter, calls for a disunified and multilingual American Studies, a discipline more reflective of the actual state of things (Porter 1994, 469–526),[6] and recognizes that these claims of unity were all along ideological, not real, or rather that they were performative, not constative. Their aim was to create by a speech act the unified culture we do not yet have. Such claims do this by appealing to a certain selective way of reading the past as though it were a tradition we all in the United States share in the way Germany, France, or England each might appear to have a unified national culture participated in by all its citizens. Or at any rate Germany, France, and England have sometimes thought they have a unified culture, while we are uneasily uncertain.

Of course the cultural oneness of Germany, France, or England was built on the exclusion of minority cultures, on the subordination of women, and on many other unjust acts of power. England achieved cultural unity through savage violence toward the Scots and Irish, through the suppression of Cornish, Gaelic, Scots, and Welsh languages, and so on. German cultural unity was to a considerable degree a fabrication of poets and philosophers: from Kant, Hegel, Fichte, Schiller, Goethe, the Schlegels, Hölderlin, and others on down to Heidegger and the poets of the Stefan George school. This German culture was built on two weird ideas, or ideas that at any rate seem weird to anyone outside the German tradition. One was Fichte's assertion that anyone anywhere can think philosophically – as long as he or she does it in the German language, though of course not all Germans think philosophically.[7] The other was the notion of a continuity between Greek and German culture, leaving Latin and Latinate or romance cultures out of the loop, so to speak, of cultural transmission. Both these strange but immensely productive notions are still fundamental in Martin Heidegger's thinking (see Derrida 1987, 112–16).[8] Linguistic nationalism has great power to determine national sentiment generally. It is as important as race or blood, as crucial as attachment to a single territory with sharp borders, the one-colored patch on the map. Nationalist sentiment in European countries has depended on extremely problematic and dangerous assumptions, and therefore has contained its own vulnerability within it. Yet it has been even harder to sustain the idea of cultural unity in the United States.

'The University in Ruins'

Humboldt's concept of literary study within the university lasted until quite recently, at least as an ideal, in the United States. It is now rapidly losing its force. We are entering an era in which new paradigms for the university, as well as new justifications for literary study, will need to be found. The changes are occurring simultaneously outside and inside the university.

On the outside, many forces are weakening the unity and borders of the nation-state. The end of the Cold War, along with economic and technological globalization, are, as I have said, more and more replacing separate nations with transnational corporations as centers of power. The European Union and the North American Free Trade Agreement are striking examples of the blurring of national borders and concurrent weakening of individual countries' self-de-termining autonomy. The development of 'the Pacific Rim' is another example. This means that California belongs both to the United States and to an economic entity that includes companies in Japan, Korea, Taiwan, Singapore, Hong Kong, Australia, and New Zealand, and will more and more include mainland China as well, especially now that it has repossessed Hong Kong. These changes by no means make nationalist sentiment vanish. In fact they often exacerbate it. An example is England's resistance to using the Euro, in part because it would mean giving up coins engraved with the queen's effigy, though there are also deeper economic reasons. Other examples are the return to isolationist policies in the United States, nationalist wars in Eastern Europe after the collapse of the Soviet Union, similar civil wars in postcolonial Africa, and nationalist imperialism in Iraq and North Korea. Such forms of nationalism more and more appear inappropriate to present economic realities. The way to prosperity, to put it ironically, is to learn English and to get as many inter-national corporations as possible to set up factories in one's area and make capital investments there. As the nation-state's existence as a unified entity weakens through one form or another of globalization and the consequent eroding of national boundaries, it will be harder and harder to tell where France ends and Germany begins, even where the United States ends and Mexico begins. We shall all come to feel ourselves living on some margin, fringe, or borderland, at the periphery.

At the same time the integrity of the nation-state is weakening in another way. The United States is a striking example. In spite of energetic attempts by conservative politicians and educationists to impose a single language and a single literary curriculum, United States cultural life is made up of diverse, interpenetrating cultural communities speaking and writing in many different languages. These communities cannot easily be reconciled. Their sites are the loci of mutually incompatible goods. These values would be impossible to unify by some overarching idea of universal human 'culture.' Nor does any individual belong unequivocally to any one of these communities. In a few years more than half the citizens of California will have English as a second language. A poll taken recently of kindergarten classes in Irvine, California, an upper-middle-class and homogeneous-looking city (though not really a city in the traditional sense, since it has no center), found that over twenty different languages were spoken in the homes of these children. [. . .] The traditional single set of values transmitted by aesthetic education is now seen as what it always was: an ideological fabrication made to serve primarily the power of educated white middle- or upper-class heterosexual males.

What possible role can literary study have in the new technological, transnational university? In the United States and, in one degree or another, in many other Western nations those responsible for funding higher education no longer believe that their nation needs the university in the same way as it once did. The primary evidence has been the cutting off of funds, almost always justified by budget constraints, as has happened in the past few years at the University of California. That university was until recently arguably the greatest research university in the world. Now it has been weakened by budget cuts and through early retirements made irresistibly attractive for many professors by 'golden handshake' offers of retirement benefits. About two thousand professors have taken early retirement. This procedure is borrowed from the corporate world. Those who pay for the university no longer have the same confidence they once had in the need for basic research as something directly funded by the nation (that is, the federal government) or by its subdivisions, the separate states of the United States. Basic research was in any case always largely supported as ancillary to the military buildup. With the end of the Cold War came the end of the apparent need for many kinds of basic research. It is difficult for most humanities professors to accept the fact that their prosperity in the 1960s, 1970s, and 1980s was as much a result of the Cold War as was the prosperity of aircraft and weapons manufacturers, or as was the space race that put men on the moon. Nevertheless, we were part of the military-industrial complex. The expensive development of humanities programs was an ancillary part of our need to be best at everything, including the humanities, in order to defeat the Soviet Union in the Cold War. This goal was made explicit in the legislation establishing the National Endowment for the Humanities. Now that the Cold War is over, humanities programs are being 'downsized' along with scientific parts of university research and teaching. The NEH survives today with greatly reduced funding and is threatened with extinction. The job situation for new PhD's in English it is extremely bad. What those in charge (legislators, trustees, granting agencies, university administrators, foundation officers, and corporate executives) need, or think they need, and therefore demand, is immediately applicable technology. Much applied research can be done just as well or better by computer or pharmaceutical companies and the like. These have been increasingly funding applied research inside the university, co-opting the university's scientific skills and laboratory facilities (often originally paid for by federal money) for research oriented toward the discovery of patentable procedures that will make the companies rich. In response to these radical changes, the university is becoming more and more like a bureaucratic corporation itself, for example by being run by a corps of proliferating administrators whose bottom-line business, as in any bureaucracy, is to perpetuate themselves efficiently, even if this sometimes means large-scale 'administrative cutbacks.' The analogy between a university and a corporation is imperfect, however, since universities do not need to show a profit to shareholders. The university's primary 'product,' in addition to applicable research, is students who have earned degrees.

The lack of a unified national culture in the United States has made it especially easy for educators to shift with the global decline in the nation-state's importance to a university modeled to some degree on the bureaucratic corporation. The answer to the question 'Who now governs our universities?' is that universities are more and more coming to be governed, however invisibly or indirectly, by corporations. This major change will have incalculable effects on university teaching and research. Money is power, in this area as in others. As federal and state sources of funding are greatly reduced, both public and private universities are turning to corporations for funding. At my own university, the University of California at Irvine, corporate support means seeking money from pharmaceutical companies, computer companies, medical technology companies, parts of the so-called financial industry, media companies, and the like. These companies may be owned by Japanese, English, French, German, Korean, or Taiwanese corporations, or they may do much of their manufacturing or much of their sales outside the United States. In any case, they do not owe primary allegiance to a single nation-state. Moreover, they are not just any kind of corporation. They are participating in the worldwide transformation we call the coming of the information age or, more negatively, the age when everything is turned into spectacle.

[. . .]* Giorgio Agamben, in a terrifying passage in *The Coming Community*, describes the way the new 'society of spectacle' is transforming humankind everywhere and putting an end to the old securely founded and authorized nation-state:

> In this extreme nullifying unveiling, however, language (the linguistic nature of humans) remains once again hidden and separated, and thus, one last time, in its unspoken power, it dooms humans to a historical era and a State: the era of the spectacle, or of accomplished nihilism. This is why today power founded on a presupposed foundation is tottering all over the globe and the kingdoms of the earth set course, one after another, for the democratic-spectacular regime that constitutes the completion of the State-form. Even more than economic necessity and technological development, what drives the nations of the earth toward a single common destiny is the alienation from linguistic being, the uprooting of all peoples from their vital dwelling in language . . . Contemporary politics is this devastating *experimentum linguae* that all over the planet unhinges and empties traditions and beliefs, ideologies and religions, identities and communities. (1993, 81–2)

So what's the difference? As long as we get funding, can we in the humanities not go on about our business of teaching and research in more or less the same old way? Do the faculty and the administration not still govern the university, determining its curricula and its research priorities? Are we not skilled in taking the money and doing more or less what we want with it? Have not humanists always benefited from the affluence of scientific colleagues? To some degree the answer to all these questions is yes. Nevertheless, the shift from state and

---

* The passage considers the relationship between developments in teletechnologies and global economics. [Ed.]

federal funding to transnational corporate funding is altering the research university and its governance more radically than many people yet recognize. Agamben does not mention the university, but it is easy to see that as the state loses its foundation so does the university that served the state. The university is transformed from being an educational state apparatus, in Althusser's term (1972, 127–86), or, to put it more benignly, a place of critical and innovative thinking, into being one site among many others, perhaps an increasingly less important site, for the production and transfer of globally exchanged information.

If the secrecy demanded by university military research during the Cold War was deplorable, a new kind of secrecy is invading our universities, the secrecy demanded by corporations as a quid pro quo for their support of research. Two senior scientists in a department of biology, for example, each with his or her team of junior faculty, postdoctoral researchers, graduate students, and technicians, may each be funded by a different pharmaceutical company. Each scientist is accountable to the funding company. This means a subtle shift from basic research toward doing research that will result in marketable products, even though the companies probably tell the scientists to go on doing what they have been doing but to promise them first development rights if anything patentable happens to be discovered. It is also in the interest of the funding company to keep the results of research secret as long as possible, at least until the results are patented. This may delay the publication of research results, whereas research funded by the National Science Foundation or the National Institutes of Health has as a condition timely publication and universal access to the results of research. In the new situation two graduate students or two post-docs in the same department may be inhibited from discussing with one another or from using in teaching what they are doing in their research work, in fundamental violation of basic assumptions about academic freedom. The measure of research accomplishment will be more and more not the acquisition of new knowledge but productivity as defined by the companies to whom the university is accountable. [. . .]

Individual professors in this new kind of university belong as much to international communities of those working in the same areas as they do to local research communities within their own universities. I shall discuss later the role of new communications technologies in creating these transnational research 'teams.' These technologies mean you can stay put in your own university and still be working on a research project with colleagues from many countries thousands of miles away. Another globalizing factor is the constant migration of professors and students from one country to another. This migration is a small-scale version of the unprecedented migration these days of large groups from one country to another, as work patterns change. [. . .]

In a concomitant change, 'society' also no longer needs the university in the old way to transmit national cultural values. This is true however much such authorities may still pay lip service to this traditional role of humanities departments. The work of ideological indoctrination and training in consumerism, it is tacitly understood, can be done much more effectively by the media, by newspapers and magazines, by television and cinema. Moreover, these academic bureaucrats and legislators are not stupid. After what has happened in humanities departments from the 1960s on, they now no longer trust professors of literature to do what they used to do or even, the bureaucrats might claim, what they are hired to do. The cat is out of the bag. Whatever may be the protestations of those running the universities about the eternal values embodied in the Western canon, the news has got through to them that the actual culture of the United States is multifarious and multilingual. Moreover, they know now that you can no longer trust professors to teach Chaucer, Shakespeare, Milton, and the rest in the old ways. New ways of reading them have shown that these authors, read from a certain angle, as professors seem inclined to do and to teach their students to do, are what some governing the university consider to be dynamite that might blow up the social edifice. So the more or less unconscious strategy is to welcome the transformations of traditional literature departments as they shift to cultural studies and then perhaps gradually cut off the money. In public universities this deed is done in the name of financial stringency and the need to build more prisons and fund welfare programs. In private universities the attempt to control what is taught in the humanities is sometimes more direct and blatant. An example is the twenty-million-dollar gift to the humanities at Yale by Lee Bass, a member of a wealthy United States oil family. He thought his gift would entail the right to choose the professors his money would endow and the curriculum they would teach. What is most sinister about this dark episode, from which Yale admirably extricated itself by ultimately returning the gift, is the possibility that Bass's naïveté was not in assuming that his money would give him some right to govern the university but in being so up-front about it. Most such control is exercised in more tactful, subtle, and indirect ways. In a related change, professors have less and less importance as public affairs experts, no doubt because the media that allow those authorities to speak no longer have confidence that the experts from within the university will say what they want to hear, just as Bass did not trust Yale to make appointments of which he would approve. The experts on public television panels, for example, are often drawn from conservatively funded think tanks rather than from universities.

Robert Atwell, president of the American Council on Education, asserted in 1992 that American colleges and universities will be leaner and meaner by the year 2000: 'Higher education is in its most dire financial condition since World War II' (1992, Sec. B, 5B). This 'slenderizing' is happening not because universities want to be smaller and dumber, but because the money supply is being cut off. The articles discussing this bleak future recognize that many valuable programs are being eliminated. During the recession in the early 1990s, faculty at the University of California were told that state funding would never rise again to the levels of the 1980s. This could not have been because the state would never again have enough money to return to those levels. In 1995 California was out of its recession and becoming prosperous again, with surplus tax revenues. The annual state budget of the University of California now has regained the level it had before the recession. This increase in funding must not, however, be misunderstood as a return to the prosperity of the 1980s. The increase is necessary to support salaries and student aid in the new downsized university. Funding for individual divisions is still sharply down from historical levels.[9] Less than one quarter of the total revenue of the University of California at Irvine in 1994–95 came from the State of California, whereas 52 percent was from state funding in 1984–85 (*UCI News* 1996, 3). In the latest information I have (1998), it is 24 percent. The assertion that funding will never rise to the old levels can have only one meaning. It means that the State of California, in the form of its governor and legislature, will not promise to give quite the old level of funding to the University of California even when the money again becomes available. They do not need the old university enough to pay for it. They do not need its basic research in the same way. It is not yet clear whether or not they even need the university for the primary, stated purpose of giving a higher liberal education to all young citizens of California who have grade averages in high school above a certain level. The latter commitment was to some degree a cover for another mission of the university, namely, to do Cold War research. It remains to be seen whether that commitment will be maintained in the new circumstances.

The return of funding now is based on a new image of the university's mission: to aid the economic prosperity of the State of California as it becomes a big player on the global stage. It took those in charge only five years to figure out a new use for the university. This change is strikingly clear in statements by Pete Wilson, governor of California, and Richard C. Atkinson, University of California president. In presenting his proposals for the California 1996–97 budget, Wilson said, 'California universities and colleges have long been revered as the finest institutions in the world. Like the pioneers, entrepreneurs, and innovators who made California a land where any dream is possible, our institutions of higher learning are carrying on that tradition by preparing our students to compete and win in the global marketplace.' Atkinson echoed Wilson almost word for word: 'I applaud the governor's recognition of the important role higher education plays in preparing a skilled workforce for competition in the global marketplace and the important role UC plays in a healthy California economy.' Atkinson again stressed this new orientation in a more recent policy statement issued in January 1997. 'We must have substantial economic growth,' he said. 'This requires investments in university-based research and a highly educated workforce.' Atkinson mentions the humanities only once in his six-page statement: 'Lyric poetry and magnetic resonance imagery may be very different, but both are ways of giving us access to information that would be otherwise inaccessible.'[10] 'Information' here is the key word, as in the term 'Informatics' used to name new required under-graduate courses at my university designed to make all the students computer literate. Lyric poetry is, for Atkinson, valuable if, like magnetic resonance imagery, it gives us information available in no other way. It is kind of President Atkinson to include lyric poetry along with magnetic resonance imaging. I suppose there is a sense in which lyric poetry gives 'information,' but that is hardly the right way to name the most important thing it does. To say Tennyson's 'The Lady of Shallott' gives information about England's canals in the 1830s or about Tennyson's state of mind when he wrote it is true, but trivial. 'The Lady of Shallott' gives knowledge, of an exceedingly peculiar kind, but that is not the same thing as information. That poem is also a speech act, a way of doing things with words, something not allowed for in the reigning paradigm of 'information.' We should probably capitalize on such generous analogies in defending the humanities. Nevertheless, the analogy is clearly a false one.

The question that haunts me, that has haunted me ever since I first read Bill Readings's *The University in Ruins*, but haunts me even more when I read statements like President Atkinson's, is this: what is now the function of literary study, if any, in the new technologized, globalized, postcolonial research university, the university whose mission is to produce an educated workforce to make the region where it is located 'competitive in the global economy'? I do not think that question is at all easy to answer, particularly if we try to follow Readings in not fooling ourselves into thinking that the old ways and old justifications can continue. Handwringing will accomplish little. Some other justifications for the humanities and for literary study within the humanities must be found.

[. . .]

How We Got from There to Here

So far I have discussed some of the external forces that are changing the study of English literature in the United States. How, looked at from the inside, did departments of English evolve from a relatively coherent program into the not easily defensible mixture that now characterizes many of them? The changes began just after the Second World War. The evolution occurred in a number of distinct phases: from the triumph of the New Criticism in the 1950s and 1960s, to the dominance of language-based theory in the 1970s and early 1980s, to the inclusion of cultural studies in the 1980s and in the 1990s. Each of these has been a stage in the dismantling of the old idea that the humanities should teach the values of a unified culture.

Current accounts of the rise of literary theory over the last half century tend to be organized around a certain narrative. The story about literary theory's rise and fall, however, is so taken for granted that it is hard to see how it is in part an ideologically motivated fabrication. Ideology is by definition unconscious. It is therefore difficult or impossible to eradicate it by demonstration that it is erroneous. Ideology arises as a phantasmal reflex of our real material conditions of existence in the world, including the institutions within which we live and work. It would be a mistake to hope to change that ideology merely by exposing it. Ideology critique does not change ideologies. That requires a different kind of work. Nevertheless, an ideological story, however ghostly, is by no means without its effects on our collective life and behavior. Far from it. Being infatuated by an ideology is like being in love as Proust describes it. You can fall out of love, just as you can lose an ideological mystification, but that does not happen because someone has patiently explained how wrong you are about your beloved or how mystified your understanding of institutional changes is. Why have we needed to tell ourselves just this story about our recent disciplinary history? I think I can specify at least part of the answer.

Once upon a time, so the story goes, were those primitive days before the Second World War when a single canon was firmly in place. Professors did biography, philology, literary and intellectual history, character description, and impressionistic evaluation without any conscious need for theory. They had little awareness of the implicit theoretical presuppositions of their work. What they did was a naive form of extrinsic criticism. It was also the United States version of Humboldtian *Bildung*, the Arnoldian study of the best that has been thought and said in the world. When I entered Oberlin College in 1944, just before the end of the Second World War and just before the introduction of the New Criticism, the required freshman course in English was a composition class. The textbook was a series of readings about the ideals of a liberal education by nineteenth-century English authors: Newman, Arnold, Huxley, and others. This book had first been published in 1914, but was still being used as a required text for all students at Oberlin in 1944 (see Aydelotte 1914).[11] The writings of Arnold, Newman, and the rest were not only presented as models of good prose. Reading them also provided the inculcation in basic cultural ideas that was still considered a primary function of higher education. I doubt if many such courses are taught anywhere in the United States today as a requirement for all undergraduates.

Then came the epoch of the New Criticism. The New Criticism was in part a response to the need to teach literature to veterans of World War II. They could now go to college because of the 'GI Bill,' but many were almost wholly ignorant of the Western tradition. The New Criticism did not respond to this, as might have been expected, by devising crash courses in that tradition. Quite the contrary. In a politically and pedagogically brilliant move, the New Criticism presumed that it is not necessary to have any special knowledge of literary or intellectual history in order to read a poem. One could be a good reader and a good citizen without ever learning that history. The poems in Cleanth Brooks and Robert Penn Warren's *Understanding Poetry*, the bible of the New Criticism, are detached from their original cultural contexts. They are given dates and authors, but that is about all. A good dictionary is the only required tool of explication. Each poem is found by accident, so to speak, written on a loose sheet of paper blown by the wind. The poem is then given the powerful context of *Understanding Poetry* itself. The New Criticism, according to the usual story, was an extreme form of atheoretical intrinsic criticism. It claimed to be so commonsensical as not to need theoretical presuppositions. At the same time it insinuated into students' minds a set of theoretical presuppositions about the superiority of lyric poetry, the autonomy of the literary work, the organic unity of good works, the importance of metaphor over other figures, and so on. The New Criticism, as its critics have observed, also smuggled in a good many conservative political and ethical ideas by way of an apparent formalist objectivity. The New Criticism was a mode of what has recently been called 'aesthetic ideology.' In the New Criticism version aesthetic ideology also meant asserting a large degree of self-enclosed autonomy for literature. The 'organic unity' of the good literary work justified cutting it off from its biographical and historical contexts. The work could be studied as a self-enclosed formal monad that could be 'analyzed' and appreciated in isolation. Such a work is its own end. It should be appreciated as such, in detachment from any vulgar instrumental use, and largely in detachment from its historical conditions. [. . .]

Such an account of the New Criticism fails to see that attention to how meaning is generated by words as opposed to discussion of thematic meaning is already a more than rudimentary theoretical move. Such a move has far-reaching consequences. The move subverts the conservative agenda many New Critics had. The political effect of the New Criticism can by no means be summed up by identifying the politics of its founders. Whatever those founders intended, the New Criticism in its attention to textual details endangered the traditional idea that literary study transmits a single culture's permanent values. In place of that, the New Criticism put, more or less in spite of itself, technical training in the skills of 'close reading.' Such skills were detached from any fixed cultural values. They could be applied to any text of any time. The New Critics asserted certain universal cultural values while at the same time teaching an ahistorical, technologized form of reading antipathetic to those values.

The New Criticism, the story continues, was superseded in the 1960s, 1970s, and early 1980s by the heyday of theory – theory structuralist, semiological, phenomenological, reader response, Marxist, Lacanian, or Foucauldian, but especially and quintessentially deconstructionist theory. Deconstruction was the model of exigent and rigorous theory. Like the New Criticism, so the story goes (but in this case the story lies, just as it to some degree falsifies the New Criticism), deconstruction was a form of intrinsic criticism, but an intrinsic criticism supported by subtle theoretical reflection. Deconstruction, so this false story goes, is apolitical, ahistorical, turns everything into language, suspends reference, and so on, according to a familiar apotropaic litany. Most educated people have encountered this story not only in journalism but also in academic discourse of both the right and the left.

Everything in this widely accepted account of deconstruction is distorted, often by asserting the exact opposite of what is actually the case. Jacques Derrida, not only in the manifest orientation of his work, but also in patient argument in many interviews, has demonstrated repeatedly the error of these false characterizations. 'Deconstruction,' he says in 'Mochlos,' 'is also, and at the least, the taking of a position [*une prise de position*], in the work itself [*dans le travail même*], toward the politico-institutional structures that constitute and regulate our practice, our competences, and our performances' (1992, 22–3). The important words here are 'work' and 'position taking.' Deconstruction is work. It works. It works by taking a position, by an active intervention in the university and in the political field within which the university is situated . . . Similarly, it can easily be demonstrated that this is the case with the work of Paul de Man. De Man's work is always concerned with ideology, politics, and history, with the social effect of literary study's institutionalized ideological errors, and with developing alternative forms of active intervention in history.

These forms of intervention, however, were no more compatible with transmitting the fixed values of a national culture than was the New Criticism. The rise of theory was the next stage after the New Criticism in undoing the traditional role of national literature departments as the place where citizens are imbued with a national culture. Those who have seen theory as inimical to this traditional role of the humanities are right. It needs to be added, however, that this model was in the United States and in the West generally already much weakened at the time theory became dominant. The rise of theory was more a symptom than a cause. It arose, as I have suggested, out of the necessity of understanding rapid historical and ideological change. The error has been to see theory as causing what it registered and attempted to confront. It responded in part by fulfilling with a clear conscience that other half of the university's mission: to comprehend everything rationally. Literary theory is conceptual reflection on how meaning is generated by words. Theory is intrinsically transnational. It is no accident that European theory, especially as transformed and extended within the United States university, is being appropriated by universities all over the world. This diffusion parallels the global spread of Western technology and capitalist economic organization. That does not mean it is the same thing.

Today, as so-called cultural studies becomes more and more important, in some universities and colleges at least, theory of the 1960s, 1970s, and 1980s goes on being carefully read, appropriated, and used in ever-new and diverse ways. Moreover it is constantly being extended in new theoretical work. By the new importance of 'cultural studies' I mean the shift in the 1980s and 1990s within literature departments in United States colleges and universities, as well as in other countries around the world, to a new interest in the social contexts of literature. This has meant, among other things, a turn to the study of popular culture, minority discourses, non-Western literatures and cultures, hitherto marginalized literature by women, gays, and lesbians, as well as attention to media like film, television, and video. What was once the Department of Comparative Literature at the University of Minnesota has been renamed to include the phrase 'Cultural Studies.' The Critical Theory Institute at the University of California at Irvine, originally founded to study such topics as mimesis and representation, spent three years during the early 1990s attempting, not with complete success, to define and understand what is meant by cultural studies. The Institute then shifted to the topic of 'globalization.'

[. . .]

In many, but by no means all, cases the reorientation to cultural studies has meant a return to mimetic, representationalist assumptions about the relation of a work to its context. Though the modern concept of culture has nationalist origins, the new cultural studies tends to recognize the existence of an indefinitely large number of subcultures within a given dominant culture. An individual is likely to be 'hybrid' or to belong to several different cultures simultaneously. The United States, for example, is seen as multicultural, multilingual, multiracial, and multiethnic. The new cultural studies is by no means homogeneous in its presuppositions and practices, nor has the shift to doing cultural studies taken place at the same rhythm or to the same degree in all departments, institutions, or countries. It is different in England, Australia, South Africa, or the People's Republic of China from what it is in the United States. Lively debates among those doing such work in all those countries indicate not only cultural studies' heterogeneity, the way it is a site of dissensus, but also the way something serious is at stake. People in general do not fight so hard about something that is trivial. Scarcely a literature department, in the United States at least, has not been marked in one way or another by what we call cultural studies. Such orientations have been around for a long time in literature departments. They are to some degree a return to practices and attitudes that prevailed before the advent of the New Criticism and subsequent language-oriented theory. In many ways, however, contemporary cultural studies is different from its predecessors, for example, in the sharp attention to gender, race, and ethnicity. Moreover, cultural studies comes after the New Criticism and theory. Its historical position as post-poststructuralist marks and distinguishes it – for example, its assimilation of previous theory or resistance to it.

Rey Chow expresses the connection between theory and cultural studies elegantly and succinctly: 'One of the strongest justifications for studying the non-West has to do precisely with the fundamental questioning of the limits of Western discourse which is characteristic of deconstruction and poststructuralist theory. The question of the sign as such leads logically to the opening up of the study of other signs and other systems of significations, other disciplines, other sexualities, other ethnicities, other cultures. Thus, against the arguments of many, I would say that deconstruction and poststructuralist theory have very close ties with cultural studies, gender studies, gay and lesbian studies, and ethnic studies, in that the investigations of disciplines, class, race, gender, ethnicity, and so forth, however empirical, must always already contain within them the implicit *theoretical* understanding of the need to critique hegemonic signs and sign systems from without as well as from within' (Chow 1995, 12). Wherever cultural studies is effective both in getting new knowledge and in making institutional or political change it will have done this by appropriating or reinventing, whether consciously or not, the theory it sometimes denigrates.

Nevertheless, as Rey Chow recognizes when she says that what she asserts is 'against the arguments of many,' the mistaken characterization of deconstruction, as a synecdoche for 'theory' generally, along with its energetic repudiation, has seemed to some scholars necessary to clear a space for cultural studies. Since 'high theory' was done primarily by white males in elite institutions, it must, such scholars assume, be complicit with the status quo that cultural studies wants to contest. Even to read it might be to be contaminated by the conservative ideology it presumably supports. Theory bashing is an intrinsic part of cultural studies. This is especially true wherever such studies are an antitheoretical return to extrinsic criticism.

It was in reaction to the supposed dead end of formalist criticism in deconstruction, so the story goes, that in the mid-1980's, or even earlier, there was a swing back to extrinsic criticism, to a new desire to politicize and rehistoricize the study of literature, to make such study socially useful, to make it an instrument of the liberation and intellectual enfranchisement of women, minorities, and the once-colonized in a postcolonial, posttheoretical epoch. 'Culture,' 'history,' 'context,' and 'media'; 'gender,' 'class,' and 'race'; 'the self' and 'moral agency'; 'multilingualism,' 'multiculturalism,' and 'globalization' – all have now become in different mixes watchwords of the new historicism, of neo-pragmatism, of cultural studies, of popular culture study, of film and media studies, of women's studies and gender studies, of gay studies, of studies of various 'minority discourses,' and of studies in 'postcolonialism.'[12] The list is by no means homogeneous. What we call 'cultural studies' today, as I have said, is a heterogeneous and somewhat amorphous space of diverse institutional practices. These practices can hardly be said to have a common methodology, goal, or institutional site. In spite of their diversity, however, all these new projects have an interest in the historical and social contexts of cultural artefacts. They tend to presume the context is explanatory or determining. The author is back in. His or her death was prematurely announced. The subject, subjectivity, the self is back in, along with personal agency, identity politics, responsibility, dialogue, intersubjectivity, and community. A new or renewed interest has developed in biography and autobiography, in popular literature, in film, television, advertising, in visual culture as opposed to linguistic culture, and in the nature and role of 'minority discourses' within the hegemonic discourse.

For cultural studies literature is no longer the privileged expression of culture, as it was, say, for Matthew Arnold, or for the United States university until recently. Literature is just one symptom or product of culture among others, to be studied side by side not only with film, video, television, advertising, magazines, and so on, but also with the myriad habits of everyday life that ethnographers investigate in non-Western cultures or in our own. [. . .]

Though people in this new field tend to be defensive about the relation of cultural studies to the social sciences, it seems evident that if cultural studies becomes more dominant in the humanities, the humanities will approach closer to a merger with the social sciences, especially with anthropology. Just as anthropologists have learned much from colleagues in the humanities, so training at the graduate level in protocols of anthropology and sociology would be helpful for those going into cultural studies, for example training in statistical analysis, in the relation between data and generalization, in the university's obligations when human subjects are used, in the need to learn by hook or by crook the languages necessary for the work undertaken, and so on. A traditional Eurocentric literary education is not much help for many of the projects of cultural studies.

Those in cultural studies will be quick to point out that the social sciences in the United States are complicit in many ways with American imperialism, just as Rey Chow observes that the study of non-Western languages and cultures is already institutionalized in the university as another part of that imperialist project (1995, 110–11).[13] This is true, but anthropology has been struggling to confront this problem since at least Lévi-Strauss's *Tristes Tropiques.* Cultural studies has much to learn from anthropology's procedures and strategies, including those devised to deal with its ingrained Eurocentrism. Moreover, the fact that the social sciences have done cultural studies in the wrong way does not make cultural studies any the less in many of its features a social science. There is no reason to be scandalized by this. The present standard division of the disciplines in United States universities is just one arrangement among others. It could be different.

[. . .]*

---

* The section that has been removed, 'Comparing Everything,' considers, through a reading of the 1993 Bernheimer Report of the American Comparative Literature Association, the changing fortunes in the study of literature, and the rise of cultural studies in relation to comparative literary study. [Ed.]

Abjecting Theory

Though 'theory' continues to play a subsidiary role in cultural studies, as in the disciplinary names 'film theory' or 'queer theory,' it has sometimes been superseded, in the Bernheimer report and in many other places, by a return to precritical or pretheoretical assumptions about the way literature, along with other arts, mirrors its historical and social contexts. The rejection of language-based theory on the basis of the false characterization of it I sketched above has, for some scholars, been an essential part of this shift to a new form of extrinsic criticism. Why is this the case? Just why has it seemed necessary to some to 'abject' theory, as Tom Cohen puts it (1994, 1–8),[14] to tell a false story about it in order to clear a space for these new developments? How does this mistake about theory vitiate some work in cultural studies? Deconstruction never rejected the referentiality of language. Far from it. But it saw the inescapable referential vector of language as a problem to be interrogated, not a solution that can be taken for granted. Insofar as cultural studies still depends on the traditional idea of culture as the production in a subject or subjectivity of an identity produced through indoctrination by a nation-state or by a subculture such as an ethnic or gender community, for example, the presumed community of African Americans, Chicanos and Chicanas, gays, or lesbians, it was necessary to resist the questioning by deconstruction of all the key concepts necessary to this idea of culture. These include identity, agency, the homogeneity of a given culture, whether hegemonic or minority, the definition of the individual by his or her participation in a nation or community, the unbreakable tie of a text or any other assemblage of signs to its context. The questioning by theory of these concepts often needed to be sidestepped in order for the project of cultural studies and related new disciplines to get going. These key concepts are glued together by a reinstalled referentiality that can no longer afford to be put in question and remain a question. An example is the presumed specular relation between a culture as a whole and any subject identity within it, in another version of the fractal polygon. Hence the need to abject 'theory,' among some, at least, of those in cultural studies.

The term 'cultural studies' itself suggests the degree to which this new discipline has in its own self-definition accepted one side of the traditional mission of the nation-state university that it would transform. That mission, you will remember, was double: (1) to amass and archive critical knowledge, knowledge both of physical or biological nature and of culture, including literary history as a key form of culture, and (2) to form subjects of the state by inculcating in them the national culture through the process the Germans call *Bildung* and we in the United States have traditionally called a 'liberal educa-tion.' Cultural studies has tended to repudiate the second mission. To fulfill it would be to fall into the hands of the conservatives who want a single canon and the values of a single national culture taught in schools and universities. Those in cultural studies have, however, embraced a form of the first mission by making culture itself an object of study, understanding, and archival storage. The second word in the term 'cultural *studies*' expresses this. Rather than being what determines the subject as who he or she is, after a lengthy process of education by the educational state apparatus, culture in all its diversity is now an object of study like any other, like astrophysics and the human genome. It may be less an eagerness to give minority cultures representation in the university than a recognition that cultural studies can easily be co-opted that explains the suspicious ease with which it has been institutionalized in American universities. Turning minority cultures into objects of university study like elemental particles and genomes may be a way of destroying those cultures, not preserving their vitality.

Opposition to cultural studies might be stronger if it were understood that all these diverse cultures are going to be inculcated in students, not just studied. Most celebrations of cultural studies, such as the Bernheimer report and other essays in that volume, carefully avoid defining the new project as performative or activist. On the contrary, cultural studies is characteristically defined as the gathering of new knowledge, as 'studies.' This is necessary to gain legitimacy within the research university. Whenever the shift from *Wissenschaft* to *Bildung* has overtly happened for minority or subordinate cultures, the university has tended to respond with violence, by calling in the police, as in the late 1960s. In any case the project of *Bildung* by the university depended on the notion of a nation-state with a single unified culture. It does not seem to make sense to interpellate students to be subjects of many cultures simultaneously. Or it makes sense only through a radical redefinition of culture along the lines of the global consumerist economy that is reshaping the university these days. Culture then becomes a surface matter of fashion and dress. This is just the way the new global capitalism may want it – a whole world full of people in vestigial native costumes wearing blue jeans underneath and listening to transistor radios. This is sometimes called 'glocalization.' The question is how to live within a multicultural situation without succumbing to this superficiality.

The goals of the new developments are laudable. Who could oppose giving a voice to the heretofore voiceless, to women and minorities, to those defined as gays and lesbians, to the economically disadvantaged? Who could oppose giving a place in the university to all the ethnic varieties that characterize both our national society and the new global society that is more omnipresent every day?[15] Who could oppose using such transformation of the university to help create the democracy to come, that horizon of all our political and intellectual effort? Who could oppose the careful study of popular culture and of the media – television, video, cinema – that shape our minds and behavior far more than books do these days? A fundamental part of scholarship in cultural studies has been descriptive and archival. Works in different media and from different cultures, works by women and minorities, need to be identified, categorized, edited, republished, brought into the open, made available in the university and to the general public so they can be effective there. This work is essential and necessary. This present chapter is, in its own small way, in part an effort in cultural studies, since historical investigation of literary study's institutionalization has been an important aspect of cultural studies, as in books and articles already mentioned above. I am fearful, however, that the efforts of cultural studies, the desire of those in that field to change the university and through that to help create a more just society, may be thwarted by features in what they do that will allow cultural studies to be recuperated by conservative forces within the university.

Putting neglected works in the classroom, in the curriculum, in books, articles, conferences, and study groups is only the beginning of the work. Knowledge is not enough. These works must be put to work. Only what might be called a materialist reading will accomplish that. 'Materialist' here does not mean displacing attention from the work to its historical context, but attention to the materiality of the work's inscription in its original language. Archiving multiculturalism, expanding the curriculum to include works from all over the world hitherto little read in United States universities, may even, as I have suggested, negate the power such works have to effect cultural change. The university has a formidable power of neutralization.

Literature in Cyberspace

Why did the shift to cultural studies from language-based theory begin when it did, around 1980? The reorientation was no doubt overdetermined and even contradictory. Many factors contributed to it, such as the Vietnam War, the student movement in the 1960s, and the civil rights movement. Those creating cultural studies had been decisively marked by those events. Moreover, literature in the old-fashioned sense of canonical master works, the evidence suggests, plays a smaller and smaller role in the emerging global multiculture. It is natural that young scholars should not wish to spend their time on something that seems increasingly marginal. The large numbers of women and minority scholars who now do graduate work in the humanities or have joined humanities faculties have certainly contributed much to the change. Such people are unable or unwilling to draw their sense of themselves from works in the old white male canon read in the old way. It is natural that they should look elsewhere to find works that will help them establish a sense of cultural identity, just as it is natural that sooner or later American citizens in general will come to recognize that English literature is the literature of a foreign country, a literature no doubt deeply linked to our own self-development, but foreign nevertheless.

As Wallace Stevens puts this in the 'Adagia': 'Nothing could be more inappropriate to American literature than its English source since the Americans are not British in sensibility' (1957, 176).

[. . .]*

Cultural studies is intertwined in the immense network of economic, ideological, and political forces within which the university is embedded today. Moreover, cultural studies itself, as I have said, cannot be justly summarized under a single set of conceptual presuppositions. Its relation to the language-oriented theory that preceded it is particularly complex and diverse. One major force, however, leading to the rise of a cultural studies that tends to marginalize literature has been the growing impact of new communication technologies. Technology has been changing society throughout the nineteenth and twentieth centuries. No one doubts that. The rate of change, however, has much accelerated in recent years with the advent of the electronic age. The younger United States scholars who have turned to cultural studies are the first generation of university teachers and critics brought up with television and with new forms of commercialized popular music. Many of them as children and teenagers spent as much time watching television or listening to popular music as they did reading books. I do not say these activities are bad. They are just different. Reading books can be bad for you, as Flaubert's Emma Bovary and Conrad's Lord Jim show. The critics of this new generation have been to a considerable degree formed by a new visual and aural culture. 'Culture' has a somewhat new meaning now. It names in part the media component of a global consumerist economy. The new media include of course some counter-hegemonic elements. This new electronic culture is fast replacing the culture of the book. It is not surprising that these young scholars should wish to study what has largely made them what they are, in spite of their participation in the culture of the book. Clear evidence of literature's weakening force in the United States is the way many young scholars trained in literary study should now feel so great a call to study popular culture that they more or less abandon canonical literature or even literature in toto.

However we might wish it were not the case, the sad fact is that literature in the old-fashioned sense is playing a smaller and smaller role worldwide in the new globalized cultures . . . All the statistics show that more and more people are spending more and more time watching television and cinema. Now there has been a rapid shift even from those to the computer screen. The cultural function once served, for example in nineteenth-century England, by novels is now being served by movies, by popular music, and by computer games. There may be nothing intrinsically wrong with this, unless you happen to have, as I do, a big investment in the old printed-book culture. Though many works of

---

* Here consideration is given to the unsettling force of literature and the inability of the critic to control its communications, and the threat this might pose to particular practitioners and advocates of cultural studies. [Ed.]

literature are available on line, ready to be downloaded into anyone's computer, I believe relatively few people are using that wonderful new resource. Certainly the new 'digital young' Jon Katz describes, in an essay in *Wired*, are not using the Internet to get access to Shakespeare. One strong point made by Katz about the citizens or 'netizens' of the new Digital Nation is their commitment to popular culture and their disdain for those who still live outside it and want to lecture them about the shallowness of popular music, cinema, etc.

'The digital young,' says Katz, 'share a passion for popular culture – perhaps their most common shared value, and the one most misperceived and mishandled by politicians and journalists. On Monday mornings when they saunter into work, they are much more likely to be talking about the movies they saw over the weekend than about Washington's issue of the week [or, I might add, about what a wonderful poem Milton's *Paradise Lost* is]. Music, movies, magazines, some television shows, and some books are elementally important to them – not merely forms of entertainment but means of identity' (Katz 1997, 184).[16] Poems and novels used to be means of identity. Now it is the latest rap group. 'As much as anything else,' Katz continues, 'the reflexive contempt for popular culture shared by so many elders of journalism and politics has alienated this group, causing its members to view the world in two basic categories: those who get it, and those who don't. For much of their lives these young people have been branded as ignorant, their culture malignant. The political leaders and pundits [one might add: the educators] who malign them haven't begun to grasp how destructive these perpetual assaults have been, how huge a cultural gap they've created' (ibid.). The colophon page of *Wired* not only lists the 'Zines [that is, magazines] of Choice,' but also 'music that helped get this magazine out.' The April 1997 issue of the latter lists, among others, Matthew Sweet, *100% Fun*; Arvo Pärt, *De Profundis Clamavi, Psalm 130*; Melvins, *Interstellar Overdrive*; Steven Jesse Bernstein, *Prison*; *Miami Vice*; Mari Boine, *Radiant Warmth*. What does this have to do with globalization? This popular culture is disseminated all over the world as films, tapes, CDs, radio broadcasts, and now through the Internet as the latter becomes more and more a multimedia operation. This media culture has immense power to drown out the quiet voice of the fading book culture and also to drown out the specificities of local cultures everywhere, though these are often deliberately appealed to and encouraged by global media corporations in their search for 'niche' local markets. This is one thing meant by 'glocalization.'

At the same time the new communication technologies are rapidly transforming the way research and teaching are carried on in the humanities. These transformations have accompanied and to some degree brought about the replacement of the Humboldtian university by the new technologized, transnational university that serves the global economy. This new kind of university is an important feature of the weakening of the nation-state. Some of the claims for the revolutionary effect of computers and the Internet on the humanities have been exaggerated or wrongly formulated. Seen from a certain perspective, a computer, even one connected by modem or Ethernet to the World Wide Web, is, as many people would claim, no more than a glorified typewriter. One should not, however, underestimate the changes this glorification makes, for example, the new ease of revision, the facility with which things can be added, deleted, or moved from one place to another in a computer file as opposed to a typed manuscript. Such ease gradually encourages the adept in computer composition to think of what he or she writes as never being in quite finished form. Whatever is printed is always just one stage in a potentially endless process of revision, deletion, addition, and rearrangement. [. . .]

Nothing, however, prevents using the computer and the Internet for quite conventional work in humanities research or teaching. Certain programs, 'hypertext' and multimedia though they may be, encourage traditional notions about the relation of a work to its author and to its historical and cultural contexts. [. . .] The apparent freedom for the student to 'browse' among various 'links' may hide the imposition of predetermined connections. These may reinforce powerful ideological assumptions about the causal force of historical context on literary works. It depends on what links have been set up or on the user's inventiveness in creating new ones. Hypertext can also be a powerful way to deploy what Kenneth Burke called 'perspective by incon-gruity,' that is, a way to break up conventional assumptions about explanatory context.

Hypertexts of whatever sort, moreover, are powerful solvents of the assump-tion that proper meaning fits into the traditional printed book's linear con-tinuity. On the one hand, the significance of the computer, as of the typewriter, the linotype machine, or any other technological device, depends on what use is made of it. On the other hand, neither the computer nor the typewriter nor the linotype machine is just one technological device among others. Each belongs to the special class of prostheses to the hand, voice, ears, and eyes in the generation, projection, reception, and exchange of signs. As one such device, the computer is quite different from the typewriter. It imposes its own new matrix on the process of sign generation, reception, and exchange. It would be a mistake to minimize the changes this will make in the way humanists do research and teaching and in the intellectual space within which they are rapidly coming to live. Just what are these changes? They are hard to define and understand, partly because we are in the midst of them. The digital revolution now going on, however, is clearly as radical and as irreversible as the move from a manuscript to a print culture. E-mail, faxes, computerized library catalogues, composition on the computer rather than in longhand or on the typewriter, the increasing use of computers and networks in instruction, often as a commercial venture, the availability online of more and more material, the move from linear print media to multimedia hypertext, online publishing of articles and monographs that is altering the way research results are disseminated – all these are rapidly and irrevocably transforming the way teachers and students of literature (and of other disciplines) do their work.

The most dramatic and spectral effect, however, is the hardest to see, understand, and gauge. This is the change effected in the objects of our study by their digitizing. What is the difference between reading Henry James's *The Golden Bowl* in a printed copy and as a cybertext downloaded into my desktop or laptop? At first there might seem to be little difference beyond the not unimportant one of the ability to 'search,' extract from, and otherwise manipulate the cybertext version. I claim, on the contrary, that the difference is radical and profound, no less than a transformation of the literary object's mode of existence. Understanding, even in a preliminary way, this change may help to see why the information model does not apply to all those literary works that are circulating through cyberspace at the speed of light, located everywhere and nowhere as so many black holes in the presumed transparency of information networks. Much is made these days of problems of security on the Internet and of the need for strong cryptography as against the government's desire to have the keys to all encrypting programs. Literary works continue to hide their secrets, however, secrets as dark as death, even if they are totally exposed and made public, universally available all over the world to anyone with a computer, a modem, and a service provider. Paradoxically, the new digitized existence only makes more evident, if we have eyes to see it, eyes to see what cannot be seen, what was perhaps more hidden in print versions, that is, the way literary works hide what I call black holes.

Walter Benjamin recognized that new media are radically transformative. He applied this insight to the analysis of photography and cinema under the name 'the age of technical reproducibility.' Print, too, as we perhaps tend to forget, is also a form of technical reproducibility, but the effects of reproducibility are, it may be, more evident in the instantaneous flash of the camera shutter that produces a negative, giving a spectral, endlessly repeatable life to what is already dead in the instant it is preserved. What is photographed is killed and given an indefinite afterlife of survival in the act of clicking that camera shutter. [. . .] Our time of computers, of an unimaginable chaos of digitized images and texts accessible on the Internet, is the age of technological reproducibility with a vengeance, that age squared or cubed, hyperbolically or exponentially expanded and so transformed, taken beyond a threshold or limit of *technischen Reproduzierbarkeit*. Digitizing, which melts down the distinction between image and text, produces image/texts that are much more fleeting and ubiquitous than a photograph. They bring even more into the open the other side of Benjamin's sense of the photograph as instantaneous: its way of giving a ghostly and spectral persistence, everywhere and nowhere, a life after death to what has been 'shot.' Literature has always had a strange connection to ghosts, to death, and to survival after death, but this has tended to be sidestepped in much literary study. To read *The Golden Bowl* is to encounter the traces of James's dictating voice, a little like Tennyson's voice or Browning's on one of those primitive phonograph records, voices that truly sound as if they were coming from the grave, voices of the shuttle weaving a shroud. The new digitized mode of existence for literary works in databases and on the Internet turns those works into an innumerable, murmurous swarm of ghosts that return and can return again at our command, like the shades from the underworld that rise for Ulysses in Book Eleven of *The Odyssey*, or like the recorded sounds of Glenn Gould playing Bach's *The Well-Tempered Clavier* back in the 1960s, which I am listening to on my computer at this moment. (I leave it to you to establish the referent of 'at this moment' and 'I' in that sentence.)

My claim is that this new digitized existence will change literature and literary study in manifold and as yet unforeseen ways. I would go so far as to say that it will transform, is already transforming, the concept of literature or of literarity, killing literature and giving it a new existence as the survivor of itself. Students of literature will and should remain as the guardians and surviving witnesses of previous historical epochs, just as classicists bear witness to what was the nature and function of Greek tragedy within a vanished classical culture. Literature as we know it, as Derrida has argued, is inextricably associated with democracy, that is, with freedom of speech, the freedom to say or to write anything and everything (never completely obtained, of course). Even the concept of free speech, I would add, is being changed by the electronic revolution. 'Literature' is also, I further claim, concomitant with industrialization prior to the electronic revolution, with the age, now coming to an end, of the printed book, and with Cartesian and post-Cartesian conceptions of selfhood, along with associated notions of representation and of 'reality.' All these are intertwined and mutually self-sustaining factors. Literature as a distinctive way to use language arises not from any special way of speaking or writing, but from the possibility of taking any piece of language whatsoever as fictional or, on the other hand, as possibly truthtelling, as referential in the ordinary sense. This 'taking' happens according to complex historically determined conventions, codes, and protocols. That neat opposition between fiction and truth telling is a feature of print culture. In the digitized world of the Internet the distinction breaks down or is transformed, just as it has already been transformed by television.

[. . .]*

---

* Miller considers the effects on the act of reading and the ramifications for research as a result of the transformation of texts from conventional printed media to hypertextual form. In particular, he addresses the electronic version of Trollope's *Ayala's Angel*, extending the discussion to the contexts of such transformed reading acts. The consideration of hypertextual transformation is extended at the beginning of the section that follows. [Ed.]

The Ethics of Hypertext

[. . .]

Hypertexts are commonly multimedia assemblies of signs. Hypertext expansion can turn a linear verbal text into a vast indeterminate assemblage that mixes sounds and pictures with words. These can be navigated in innumerable different ways, as each link leads to further links, and as you choose or do not choose to click on a given marked element or on some object in a hypertext graphic that will open up to a new world.

[. . .]*

It could be argued that hypertext does no more (though that is quite a lot) than make more easily available through a new technological mechanism what has always been the case about linguistic assemblages and perhaps about the 'life' with which they are intertwined. In a passage almost at the end of Proust's *À la recherche du temps perdu*, Marcel, meditating on the form the great work he is about to write will have to take, describes the way any of his encounters with a person involves everything else in his life and can lead to it. Therefore, says Marcel, he realizes he needs a new technique of narration, a three-dimensional technique not all that different from what we would now call hypertext:

> I have said that it would be impossible to depict our relationship with anyone whom we have even slightly known without passing in review, one after another, the most different settings of our life. Each individual therefore – and I was myself one of these individuals – was a measure of duration for me, in virtue of the revolutions which like some heavenly body he had accomplished not only on his own axis but also around other persons, in virtue, above all, of the successive positions which he had occupied in relation to myself. And surely the awareness of all these different planes within which, since in this last hour, at this party, I had recaptured it, Time seemed to dispose the different elements of my life, had, by making me reflect that in the book which tried to tell the story of a life it would be necessary to use not the two-dimensional psychology [*la psychologie plane*] which we normally use but a quite different sort of three-dimensional psychology [*une sorte de psychologie dans l'espace*], added a new beauty to those resurrections of the past which my memory had effected while I was following my thoughts alone in the library, since memory by itself, when it introduces the past, unmodified, into the present – the past just as it was at the moment when it was itself the present – suppresses the mighty dimension of Time which is the dimension in which life is lived [*cette grande dimension du Temps suivans laquelle la vie se réalise*]. (Proust 1989/1982, 608/1087; trans. slightly altered)

Marcel treats his memories as though he had a hypertext program for moving around within them. Anywhere he begins will lead ultimately by a series of links

---

* The discussion of hypertext is extended to consider the virtual reality of a game world, such as that of *Myst*, and the way that such a game has within its narrative structure an open-endedness not present in a hypertextual form of a Trollope novel. [Ed.]

everywhere else in that vast storage disk of recollections, but not according to any predetermined pathways. We readers must do the same. We are constantly coached into doing the same by the narrator's intricate system of cross-references. These are not entirely unlike hypertext links, though the reader must have stored the whole enormous text in his memory and do the work a hypertext does for its user. The good reader will connect whatever passage he or she is reading with similar earlier passages. The reader will create a virtual hypertext without the aid of any machine other than the printed pages and his or her own memory.

Nevertheless, in the period now coming to an end, when the printed book dominated as the chief means of storing and retrieving information, it was still possible to be beguiled into thinking of a work like *À la recherche du temps perdu* as a stable and unmoving organic unity, on the model of a spatial array. Northrop Frye, for example, habitually spatialized literature in this way. Joseph Frank's 'Spatial Form in Modern Literature' was an influential codification of this presupposition. T. S. Eliot's 'Tradition and the Individual Talent' invited a generation of literature students to think of all Western literature as such a spatial array (see Frye 1963, esp. 21–38 and 69–87).[17] A fixed, spatialized text imposed on its readers a single unified meaning generated by a linear reading from the first word through to the end, in Proust's case more than three thousand pages later. The reader who accepted this model could think of the act of reading as a purely cognitive matter. I as reader do not create a meaning that did not exist before I engaged myself, 'interactively,' in the text. The meaning was there, waiting to be generated in me in an experience of passive reception. A hypertext that is overtly organized as such, on the contrary, offers the reader the necessity of deciding which path to follow through the text, or of letting chance choose for him or her. Nor is there any 'right' choice, that is, one justified objectively, by a pre-existing meaning. A hypertext demands that we choose at every turn and take responsibility for our choices. This is the ethics of hypertext. Hypertext brings into the open the way the generation of meaning in the act of reading is a speech act, not a passive cognitive reception. As a doing things with words it is not fully authorized or justified by the text. The text makes a demand on me to read it. My reading is a response to that demand. It is a response to an irresistible obligation to read all the books, and now all those texts on the Internet too. Whether or not I have fulfilled this obligation in a given case can never be confirmed. I am, in the end, responsible for what I make of a text.

Hypertexts on computers expose this uneasy situation. They teach us to see earlier works of literature in a different way. We come to see them as already proto-hypertexts that invite or allow many different pathways of reading. All reading, even the most linear, involves the constant to and fro of cross-referencing memory inside the text and out that Proust describes as the structure of human time. For this mobile, ungrounded, and unmasterable vibration fixed visual spatial images like 'Internet' or even 'fractal mosaic' are not adequate.

They do not do justice to the semiotic structure that is possessed by novels from the age of the printed book like *À la recherche du temps perdu*. Works of literature are black holes in the Internet Galaxy. The presence of literature and the literary on the Internet forbids thinking of the Internet as a transparent electronic highway system on which 'information' passes back and forth freely, without interruption, as an open secret. Concerning this blocking of information transfer by what might be called the 'literary' or 'rhetorical' element in any sign system, even the most transparently 'scientific,' there would be much more to say.

Cultural Studies and the Ontopolitopological

One effect of globalization and the new telecommunications technologies is the way they are leading to many new forms of constructive and potentially powerful social organization, new kinds of communities. These include research and university communities. An example is the sense of lively and often contentious solidarity among those who interact with one or another website or chatgroup, those, for example, devoted to a theorist like Derrida, or to canonical writers like Shakespeare, Henry James, or Proust, or to special interest groups like feminists or those in minority studies.

The new forms of transnational organization by way of the Web are going beyond that, however, to new forms of political groupings. A recent essay by Jon Katz in *Wired*, cited already, describes and celebrates what is going on, in the United States at least, as not only 'the slow death of the current political system' but also 'the rise of postpolitics and the birth of the Digital Nation.' Surfing the Net during the recent presidential election, Katz claims that he 'saw the primordial stirrings of a new kind of nation – the Digital nation – and the formation of a new postpolitical philosophy. This nascent ideology,' he continues, 'fuzzy and difficult to define, suggests a blend of some of the best values rescued from the tired old dogmas – the humanism of liberalism, the economic opportunity of conservatism, plus a strong sense of personal responsibility and a passion for freedom.' Whether this new, postpolitical community will come to anything remains to be seen. I think Katz is right, however, to say that a new form of dynamic change or even a disquieting fluidity characterizes interaction on the Web. 'Ideas,' says Katz, 'almost never remain static on the Web. They are launched like children into the world, where they are altered by the many different environments they pass through, almost never coming home in the same form in which they left.' Katz is hopeful that these postpolitical communities can lead to a better world, if those belonging to them choose to use their power in the right way. 'The ascending young citizens of the Digital nation can, if they wish,' he says, 'construct a more civil society, a new politics based on rationalism, shared information, the pursuit of truth, and new kinds of community' (Katz 1997, 184). We shall see about that. It might go the other way. It all depends – on many unpredictable factors. Certainly tremendous efforts of various sorts are now being made in the United States both to control or censor the Web and to commercialize it.

Another effect of globalization is even more problematic and also closer to accounting for the radical changes in literary study and humanistic study generally that are currently occurring, at least in the United States. Walter Benjamin long ago argued that new technologies, new modes of production and consumption, all the changes made by nineteenth-century industrialization, had already created a radically new human sensibility and therefore a new way of living in the world. 'As the entire way of being changes for human collectives over large historical periods so also change their modes of sensual perception [*die Art und Weise ihrer Sinneswahrnehmung*]' (1974–89, I: 478). All the changes brought about by industrialization, the rise of great cities, and the development of new communications technologies like photography and cinema produced, according to Benjamin, a new way of being human, the nervous, solitary Baudelairean man of the crowd, hungry for immediate experience while at the same time obsessed with the sense of a faraway, unattainable horizon that undermines every immediacy. Benjamin's most often cited essay on this topic is 'The Work of Art in the Age of Technical Reproducibility' (1955/1969, 148–84/217–51). One would do well to be skeptical about such claims for a mutation in sensory experience. These claims are associated, in Benjamin's formulations, with the rise of new collectivities. We still have the same five senses that our ancestors had. Evolutionary mutations usually take thousands and thousands of years, not a mere two centuries. Nevertheless, the human sensory, emotional, and cognitive apparatus is unusually flexible among those possessed by different life forms. It may be that a man or woman today sitting before a computer screen or watching a film on a VCR or watching television has a radically different sense of being in the world from that once possessed by the inhabitant of an eighteenth-century village. Reading works of literature from the past is one way to find out about that. This is one strong defense of reading literature. The evidence, I must say, is ambiguous. Shakespeare's people, or even Chaucer's, seem in many ways more like us than they seem radically different, in spite of the fact that they had no television. Nevertheless, the differences are important too. They need to be studied carefully in order to be identified accurately.

Jacques Derrida, in an eloquent passage in a recent seminar, stresses the strange combination of solitude and a new kind of being with others of the person using a computer to reach the World Wide Web, as well as the breakdown of traditional boundaries between inside and outside brought about by new telecommunications. As this epochal cultural displacement from the book age to the hypertext age has accelerated, we have been ushered ever more rapidly into a threatening living space. This new electronic space – the space of television, cinema, telephone, videos, fax, e-mail, hypertext, and Internet – has profoundly altered the economies of the self, the home, the workplace, the university, and the nation-state's politics. These were traditionally ordered around the firm boundaries of an inside-outside dichotomy, whether those boundaries were the walls between the home's privacy and all the world outside or the borders between the nation-state and its neighbors. The new technologies invade the home and confound all these inside/outside divisions. On the one hand, no one is so alone as when watching television, talking on the telephone, or sitting before a computer screen reading e-mail or searching an Internet database. On the other hand, that private space has been invaded and permeated by a vast, simultaneous crowd of verbal, aural, and visual images existing in cyberspace's simulacrum of presence. Those images cross national and ethnic boundaries. They come from all over the world with a spurious immediacy that makes them all seem equally close and equally distant. The global village is not out there, but in here, or a clear distinction between inside and out no longer operates. The new technologies bring the *unheimlich* 'other' into the privacy of the home. They are a frightening threat to traditional ideas of the self as unified and as properly living rooted in one dear, particular culture-bound place, participating in a single national culture, firmly protected from any alien otherness. They are threatening also to our assumption that political action is based in a single topographical location, a given nation-state with its firm boundaries, its ethnic and cultural unity. Derrida calls this set of assumptions the *ontopolitopologique*. It is not surprising that there should be strong reactions to what Derrida calls 'a new and powerful advance in the technological prosthesis that, in a thousand ways, ex-propriates, de-localizes, de-territorializes, *extirpates*, that is to say, in the etymological and therefore radical sense of this word, uproots, therefore *de-etymologizes*, dissociates the political from the topological, separates from itself what has always been the very concept of the political, that is, what links the political to the topical, to the city, to the territory, to the ethno-national frontier.'[18]

One reaction to this uprooting, dislocation, and blurring of borders, also discussed by Derrida, is the violent return to the nationalisms, ethnic purities, and fanatical, militarized religions that are leading to such horrible bloodshed around the world these days. Another reaction is the hysterical return to isolationism in the United States. Yet another very different response, it may be, is the rapid switch in university humanities departments, beginning around 1980, from literary study, organized primarily around the separate study of national literatures, to cultural studies. Though nothing could be more different from ethnic cleansing in Rwanda or Bosnia than a program in cultural studies, the development of such studies may to some degree be another very different reaction to the transformations in daily life new communications technologies bring about. Cultural studies can function as a way to contain and tame the threat of the invasive otherness the new technologies bring across the thresholds of our homes and workplaces.

This containing and taming takes a double, contradictory form. On the one hand, it tends to reestablish firm boundaries between one nation and another, one ethnic group and another, one gender or sexual orientation and another. It may sometimes assume that a given individual can be defined by his or her participation in an ethnic group, and can therefore be understood by understanding the ethos of that ethnicity. The tradition of dividing university disciplines along national, linguistic, generic, or ethnic lines remains to a considerable degree intact after the introduction of cultural studies, in spite of much talk about interdisciplinarity and much recognition of what is problematic about defining identity through membership in a given group or community. Often the traditional divisions are now simply expanded to include separate programs in women's studies, gay and lesbian studies, Native American studies, African American studies, Chicano and Chicana studies, Asian American studies, film studies, visual culture studies, and so on. All these 'others' are now given a place in the university, but they are fenced off in a firm reestablishment of the inside/outside dichotomy that the new technologies threaten. The 'others' are still kept safely outside. Interdisciplinarity still presupposes the separate integrity of the disciplines that interact, just as 'hybridity' presupposes the fixed nature of the two genetic strains that are hybridized. Joint appointments (say in English and African American studies) may cause scholars to lead a double, hybrid life, subject to the presuppositions and protocols of two different disciplines. One should not, however, underestimate the long-term transformative effect on national literature departments the presence of such scholars within those departments will cause.

On the other hand, the return, wherever it happens, to a mimetic, representational, descriptive methodology tends to turn those threatening others into something that in theory (for this is a theory too) can be easily understood, 'translated,' and appropriated. This happens, or is presumed to happen, along the lines proposed for intercultural translation in the Bernheimer report. The universalizing idea of culture in cultural studies, just because it is a term so all-inclusive as to be virtually empty, may be a place of exchange, of turning the other back into the same. This might be the case even though all cultures and all individuals may be seen as to some degree hybrid, not as fixed, univocal essences. Individual works may be seen as unproblematically representative of the culture they reflect. A few carefully chosen examples can stand for a whole culture and give us a means of understanding it and taking it in. This procedure depends on a thematic way of interpretation that sees texts or other cultural artefacts as directly reflective of a historical or social context that is open to understanding by way of the work, though of course separate study of the context is also necessary. This form of study also sometimes depends on uncritical acceptance of the extremely dubious trope of synecdoche, part for whole, just as does taking 'deconstruction' as standing for the whole of theory. The historical context can then by way of the representative work be easily transposed into the terms of the university discipline assigned to assimilate it. That translation can occur without essential loss is the key presupposition here. Such forms of archival appropriation have been in place in the university since the Humboldtian research university was first established. They are part of the foundational heritage of the university, which says that everything has its reason, can be brought to light, known, understood, and appropriated. This double, contradictory gesture says at once that the other is really other and may be kept safely outside the traditional literary disciplines and that the other is not really other and may be made a *heimlich* member of the family.

[. . .]

The acceptance by the university of cultural studies has been relatively rapid and easy, though no doubt it has not seemed that way, for example, to those who have had to fight for years for the institutionalizing of women's studies. The firm establishment of cultural studies in the university has nevertheless taken only fifteen years or so, a relatively short time for such a genuinely revolutionary change. This may be because cultural studies is unconsciously assumed by those in charge to be non-threatening, to leave the old institutional structures more or less intact. If so, I think university administrators may have misjudged cultural studies' power to transform the university. Nevertheless, the university may even think of cultural studies as a way of policing minority groups. Once these new disciplines have been set up, at least the authorities will know where to find members of those groups.

The rise of cultural studies has accompanied the technologizing and globalizing turn in the university and, where it is an antitheoretical return to mimetism, is a concomitant of that turn. Why does this antitheoretical turn, when it occurs, disable cultural studies? For one thing it is a regression to just the conservative hegemonic ideology cultural studies would contest. The right and certain components of the left are sometimes similar in their basic presuppositions about cultural forms. Both sometimes accept, for example, the notion that cultural artefacts unproblematically reflect their cultural contexts. You cannot use the ideology of those you would displace to displace their ideology. Wherever cultural studies deploys precritical notions of the self and its agency, of referentiality, of cultural artefacts' transparency, or wherever it assumes that history can be narrativized unproblematically or that cultural artefacts can be exhaustively described by a repertoire of themes, its work will be politically ineffective.

Fortunately much work in cultural studies has great theoretical sophistication and is able, through interventionist acts of 'reading,' to pass on the dislocating energy of the cultural artefacts it discusses. 'Reading' here names a transaction not just with literary or exclusively verbal texts but 'readings' of works in other media: visual or aural media like film, television, popular music, or advertising.

'Reading,' however, must be distinguished from 'theory.' Though theory may facilitate reading and should ideally have arisen from acts of reading, the two are not the same thing, nor are they by any means always in harmony. Genuine acts of reading are always to some degree sui generis, inaugural. They always to some extent disable or disqualify the theory that may have been the motivating presupposition of the reader. It is easy enough to sprinkle a text in cultural studies with cogent, correct, and forceful appeals to 'theory' – for example, references to Foucault, Benedict Anderson, Bhabha, Fanon, Said, or Irigaray – while performing acts of reading that are precritical, pretheoretical, and predominantly thematic. Simple tests make possible a distinction between the two kinds of reading. A thematic reading summarizes plots, describes characters as if they were real people, and, where the work is in a language other than the language of the reader, can cite a translation without needing to go back to the original language. What I am calling a 'genuine reading' always must have recourse to the original language of the work, however awkward and time-consuming this may be, and however much it may go against the powerful ideology of journals and both university and commercial presses. This ideology assumes that everything can be translated without loss into English. This recourse to the original language is necessary because the force of the original work, its happening as a cultural event that to some extent exceeded the social context from which it arose, lies in its unique use of its own vernacular idiom.

I call this unique use the irreducible otherness of the work, even its otherness to the culture that apparently 'generated' it. Use of a translation uproots the work, denatures it, transforms it into a *hortus siccus* or dried, specimen flower ready to be stored in the bottomless archives of a transnational university system that is more and more dominated by the English language as a global language. This argument for return to the original languages in acts of reading is, however, only the most visible version of a need, even in studying works in the same language as that of the critic, to get behind thematic reading and pay attention to what might be called the materiality of the work. The work's force as an event bringing cultural value or meaning into existence depends on a certain performative use of language or other signs. Such a reading must attend to what is internally heterogeneous, contradictory, odd, anomalous about the work, rather than presupposing some monolithic unity that directly reflects a cultural context. Only such a reading can hope to transmit or preserve some of the force as an event the original work had or can still have. This might even make the reading, as recorded in an essay or lecture, a new event helping to bring about social change.

[. . .]

The Other Other

The concept of otherness has great importance both in recent theoretical thinking and as an indispensable term in cultural studies, women's studies, African American studies, and so on. A single hegemonic culture, cultural studies tends to presume, needs to define all other cultures as 'other' in order to establish its own integrity and power. The word or the concept of 'the other' is used, however, in many different, incompatible ways in current humanistic discourse.

[. . .]*

Despite the obvious incommensurability between the usages of 'otherness' in the humanities, in these different notions of otherness a single problematic may be observed. On the one hand, the other is seen as part of a dialectical dyad either allowing for an *Aufhebung* or presupposing some 'one' of which the two are derivatives, as all particular cultures may be seen as examples of culture in general. Such an alterity does not lead to aporias. If the other is really another form of the same, powerful machines of thinking, saying, and doing are not impeded in their working. Understanding and reconciliation are possible. The various sides can talk, perhaps reach a consensus. The concept of multiculturalism, for example, often, though by no means always, presupposes a notion of culture that is common to all the cultures juxtaposed in rainbow bands. However strange the other culture is, however different is the minority culture within the hegemonic culture, it is still a culture. 'Culture' can be a universal concept making possible a horizon of reconciling coexistence, which the terms 'pluralism' and 'multiculturalism' name. This universalism means I may assume I can understand the alien culture, put myself within it, negotiate with it, in one way or another assimilate it, absorb it within sameness, as the Bernheimer report suggests those in comparative literature should do. I do not need to be a Native American in order to understand and teach Native American literature and culture, just as I do not need to be a British citizen to teach English literature. The institutionalization of the humanities in the United States (and in many other countries too) depends on such assumptions. These are the basic presuppositions, for example, of comparative literature as a discipline, the older kinds as well as the new project that will make comparative literature a branch of cultural studies. New programs in cultural studies or in 'multiculturalism' do not consistently put that presupposition in question, in spite of their respect for the singularity of cultures.

---

* What follows considers specific examples and discussions of the other, otherness, alterity, along with other non-synomyous quasi-cognates such as the differend, haunting, dissensus, the dialogical, and materiality in the work of Levinas, Lacan, Derrida, Abraham and Torok, Fanon, Said, Lyotard, Blanchot, Nancy, Bakhtin, and de Man. [Ed.]

On the other hand, the other may be entirely other, the *tout autre* Derrida names. In the dialogue with Richard Kearney, Derrida defines deconstruction as a response to this wholly other: 'I do not mean that the deconstructing *subject* or *self* affirms. I mean that deconstruction is, in itself, a positive response to an alterity which necessarily calls, summons, or motivates it. Deconstruction is therefore vocation – a response to a call' (1984b, 118). If the other is wholly other, then no negotiation will reach consensus. All that can occur is some speech act inventing, inaugurating, or instituting what might be called a fiction of the other. This alternative possibility is intertwined, necessarily, with the first. If the other is the wholly other, that does not mean there is nothing there. The nonconcept of the wholly other is as far as can be from any nihilism. In fact it may be a prejudice or habit that leads us to speak of the other in the singular. Perhaps it might be better to speak of the 'wholly others,' I call the wholly others a 'nonconcept' because a concept forms part of a thought system open to logical or dialectical synthesis, whereas the wholly others cannot be assimilated into any such system. The evidence that something inassimilable is making a demand on me is the way the wholly others perturb every speech-act-instituted fiction, for example, the fiction of personal, group, or national identity. The wholly others divide such unities within themselves, make them nontotalizable.

A parallel, though it is only a figurative one, a juxtaposition of incommensurables, may be drawn between the wholly others and the black holes astronomers hypothesize. A black hole does not, strictly speaking, exist, if existence depends on being observable and measurable. Black holes cannot be observed because their gravity is so great no light emanates from them. That is why astronomers are so careful to remind us that no black hole has ever been observed. Black holes remain an unproved and perhaps unprovable hypothesis that explains certain observed celestial phenomena. Nevertheless, though it cannot be verified directly, a black hole may be inferred from matter's violent perturbation in its vicinity and the consequent emission of signals at various frequencies. Like black holes, the wholly others never manifest themselves directly. They give evidence of themselves in a variety of perturbations that can be registered.[19]

Perhaps my inner self, my conscience, presumed ground of my decisions and commitments, of all the speech acts I enunciate, may be 'encountered' (though it is not really an encounter) as wholly other. Perhaps the wholly other might be an incomprehensible and unknowable otherness glimpsed when I come face to face with another person. Then perhaps the wholly other may be a power transcending cultural and personal difference, for example, the inscrutability of Apollo and the other divinities in *Oedipus the King* or the inassimilable irrational in Aristotle's *Poetics* and *Rhetoric*. Such others come, as they say, 'from beyond the world.' Death, finally (what could be more final than death?), may be wrestled with as something wholly other, as in Henry James's *The Wings of the Dove* and Wallace Stevens's 'The Owl in the Sarcophagus.' Death as other by no means necessarily presupposes the existence of some transcendence, the gods or God, nor does it presume some heaven or hell, some other place to which we go when we are dead. Death leaves those questions permanently open, since death is that bourn from which no traveler returns. The strength of Socrates's irony in the face of death in *The Apology* was his resolute insistence that since he knew nothing of death, he could not be afraid of it. Death, my death, the death that most matters to me and that I would most like to know, cannot be experienced. Death is not the object of any 'I's' experience. It is wholly other.

Perhaps the wholly other may be a racial, national, class, or gendered other that is truly other and cannot be comprehended by analogy with my own knowledge of myself and therefore negotiated with. As I have said, today's 'cultural studies,' like the discipline of anthropology, often, though not always, presupposes that the cultural other can be understood and accommodated in some coalition subsumed under a common concept of culture. Suppose it was wrong about that? What would follow? Could there be a cultural studies of the wholly others? The critic treads on dangerous ground here, since this assumption about the wholly others may excuse much violence and injustice. The human instinct when confronted with an inassimilable other is to obliterate it, as the Europeans who colonized the New World did their best to kill Native Americans and destroy their cultures. Kurtz's idealism, in Conrad's *Heart of Darkness*, his desire to bring the light of civilization to darkest Africa, turns into what it has covertly been all along, a desire to 'Exterminate all the brutes!'[20] Could there be a cultural studies of the wholly others that would avoid this, that would respect the others' otherness? If so, this would generate an organization of the university radically different from one that presupposes transparency, reconciliation, or consensus as goal.

The University of Dissensus

It follows from the more radical presumption about otherness that we should have a university of dissensus.[21] Such a university would institutionalize in its programs the various forms of unknowable otherness I have named. Two distinct notions of dissensus, corresponding to the two forms of otherness, may be identified. The word dissensus is a neologism. It sounds like a negative double of consensus, as 'deconstruction' sounds like a negative double of 'construction,' though in neither case is this true. To assume that dissensus is the negative of consensus would lead one to believe that consensus is a horizon of total agreement to be reached beyond dissensus through a perhaps interminable dialogue, the rational give and take of conversation. Dissensus in this case is no more than a stage along the way toward agreement. For a time we disagree, but if we just go on talking long enough we shall come to agree. This notion of dissensus assumes that disagreement is posited on a ground of fundamental sameness. We are all rational human beings together. That sameness ultimately transcends differences of gender, sexual orientation, class, race, language, nation, ethnic culture, personal singularity, and so on. Though it is not quite the case – we are likely to think – that one culture is as good as another, at any rate they are all cultures. The one that happens to dominate, or the one to which I belong, has a plausible right to believe that those from other cultures, however much they are to be respected, should eventually come to be subsumed in the dominant one. It will make things so much simpler if we all come to share the same language, customs, and assumptions. American English, such a line of argument suggests, should be the official language of the United States. Dissensus is a momentary perturbation within a potential collective sameness guaranteed by a universal rationality that defines what it is to be human, defines 'man' (and woman too) as the rational animal.

On the other hand, dissensus might be based on an otherness that goes all the way down. Perhaps this may be the radical otherness of another culture or its artefacts, perhaps the radical otherness of another person, possibly the result of a different gender or sexual orientation, but possibly also an otherness in other persons, of whatever gender or sexual orientation, that is the relay for an absolute otherness that speaks through them and makes demands on me for ethical commitment, decision, and action. If any of these possibilities were the case, then the imposition of consensus, even by a long process of rational discussion and compromise, would always be an unjustified coercion, violating something of infinite value in the other person or culture. If it were the case that otherness goes all the way down, then justice would demand a culture of dissensus made up of persons with irreconcilable values and goals.

Just what form would the humanistic side of the university take if cultural studies were to be based on the second notion of dissensus? It would mean, for one thing, a fuller shift from constative to performative models of cultural artefacts and of what happens in teaching and writing about them. It would also mean confronting the difficult task of creating a university of dissensus as a way of resisting the drift toward technologizing levelling.[22] A university of dissensus would be the locus of irreconcilable and to some degree mutually opaque goods. We should acquire as much understanding of other cultures as possible. We should do that, however, with an uneasy recognition that just as translation may be ultimately impossible, though we go on doing it, so the otherness of other cultures, like the otherness of other persons, may be ultimately unknowable, though we must go on trying to know it. That 'must,' however, should be accompanied by the realization that knowledge, too, can be a form of violence against other cultures. The demand made on us by other cultures is not just for understanding but, as Kwame Anthony Appiah has forcefully argued, for respect.[23] Respect is not a statement of knowledge, a constative, assertion. It is a speech act, a pledge, an attestation: 'Yes, I respect that. I respect its otherness.

I want that otherness to persist.' In this attestation, however, the 'I' as a pre-existing ethical agent is disarticulated. It becomes other to itself. The pledge is not made by a pre-existing 'I' that remains the same after the affirmation of respect. The affirmation, as it responds to a call made by the other, dislocates, displaces, and recreates the self that utters it. Nor should the university of dissensus be thought of as made of pre-existing interest groups or communities that are unchanged by the teaching or writing performed by members of those groups: for example, those in women's studies, or in the different ethnic studies, or in gay and lesbian studies. It is a fallacy to think of each person as wholly defined by his or her participation in a given class, culture, or group. Each act of dissensus recreates the self of the one who makes it, for example, in teaching a given passage from John Milton or Toni Morrison. Moreover, each such act also implicitly recreates or alters the university.[24]

Institutionalizing dissensus in the university would be difficult but by no means impossible. The word 'university' names not only the totalizing goal of the university, its aim to rationalize everything, but also the singleness of the university, 'turning everything into one,' as its etymology suggests. The university has always claimed to be the place of rational investigation, teaching, and discussion in different fields with consensus as horizon, even though that claim may have always masked an actual heterogeneity. Nevertheless, every time a work of literature is read or taught, this event may break the continuity and wholeness of the university community. Though such an event may not occur as often or as easily as Derrida suggests, when it does happen it cannot be assimilated into what was already there as a pregiven set of assumptions and methodologies. In literary study, each act of reading or teaching of this sort is an encounter with the irreducible strangeness of works of literature. We have told ourselves that in teaching literature we are fulfilling our contract to provide more knowledge and to inculcate humanistic values in our students. That, however, is just the idea of the university that is being widely questioned now. Our task is to imagine and to bring into existence a university that will be a *communauté désoeuvrée*, in Jean-Luc Nancy's phrase (1986). Such an 'unworked' or dismantled community will be an assemblage of groups, each other to the others and each working within a horizon of goals and purposes that cannot be reconciled with the others in some overarching principle of reason or idea of universal culture. Such a university would be decentered. It would be made up, to borrow Agamben's phrase again, of 'peripheral singularities,' not of people who have been educated by some universalizing *Bildung* fulfilling the idea of a given nation's cultivated citizen. Nor, as I have said, would those singularities be defined by their participation in some pre-existing community, even some borderland community for whose predetermined good they are active.

Agamben, in a remarkable section of *The Coming Community* entitled 'Tiananmen,' shows how difficult it is to imagine a university of dissensus. Agamben, at least in this English translation, uses the phrase 'whatever

singularities' rather than 'peripheral singularities.' The word 'whatever' translates the Latin *quodlibet* and the Italian *qualunque*. 'Whatever singularities,'
Agamben explains, cannot be defined 'by any condition of belonging (being
red, being Italian, being communist) nor by the simple absence of conditions (a
negative community, such as that recently proposed in France by Maurice
Blanchot), but by belonging itself' (1993, 84; Agamben is referring to Blanchot,
Communauté inavouable). Though Agamben sees that all persons in the new
globalized culture are turning into 'whatever singularities' and that such
singularities will join together to form 'the coming community,' he argues
that such singularities and the communities they will form are 'a threat the State
cannot come to terms with'; 'What the State cannot tolerate in any way,
however, is that the singularities form a community without affirming an
identity, that humans co-belong without any representable condition of
belonging' (87). The demonstrations in Tiananmen Square were an example
of such a co-belonging: 'Wherever these singularities peacefully demonstrate
their being in common there will be a Tiananmen, and, sooner or later, the
tanks will appear' (86). Though the State in one of its apparatuses, the university,
is easily able to tolerate those identities that it can label as African American,
Chicano or Chicana, and so on, the university of dissensus for which I am calling
would be more like the co-belonging of 'whatever singularities' Agamben
describes. That makes the phrase 'university of dissensus' an oxymoron.
Institutionalized dissensus is profoundly alien to the traditional 'idea of a
university.' Like the 'democracy to come' the university of dissensus is a
horizon, always something 'to come.'

That such a redefinition of the university would happen without resistance I
am not so naive as to believe. More attainable might be a university of
identifiable dissensual groups such as the one cultural studies may conceivably
be bringing about, with here and there, now and then, some inaugural act of
reading or teaching that could not be encompassed within the new boundaries.
Such an event might pass unnoticed. It might not appear to be something for
which it is worth bringing in the tanks. But it might nevertheless be effective in
bringing about change, at least in some minute degree. In number 216 of the
Atheneum Fragments, Friedrich Schlegel asserts that 'The French Revolution,
Fichte's philosophy, and Goethe's *Meister* are the greatest tendencies of the age
[*die größten Tendenzen des Zeitalters*].' *Tendenzen* here names an intervention that
is materially effective in deflecting the course of history. In an admirably witty
formulation Schlegel goes on to say: 'Even in our shabby histories of civilization
[*unserm dürftigen Kulturgeschichten*], which usually resemble a collection of variants
accompanied by a running commentary for which the original classical text has
been lost; even there many a little book, almost unnoticed by the noisy rabble
[*die lärmende Menge*] at the time, plays a greater role than anything they did [*als
alles, was diese trieb*]' (Schlegel 1964, 48; 1991, 46).

The initiatory acts of reading, writing, or teaching I have described will have a performative as well as constative function. Only academic discourse that is a speech act as opposed to being just descriptive will make anything happen in the work toward fulfilling our unfulfillable obligation to the democracy to come. Only teaching or writing that is performatively effective will make anything happen institutionally and politically, as opposed to inadvertently supporting the status quo. One limitation of many descriptions of cultural studies, as well as of expressions of opposition to them – for example, those in the Bernheimer volume – is that they tend to be couched according to the traditional notion that the university is a place exclusively of *Wissenschaft*, a place where new facts are found as a result of 'study,' rather than a place where teaching and writing are to some degree also speech acts.

Even though the discourse of cultural studies may include graphic and even aural material, the basic medium will continue to be language. Whatever political effectiveness cultural studies has will come at least to a considerable degree through language, though pictures and music can also have powerful performative effects. Accounting for the latter calls for a radical revision of speech act theory. I have used the terminology of speech act theory to describe the work of dissensus within the new university. Such terminology, however, needs to be twisted, anasemically, as Abraham and Torok would say (1978; 1979, 19–28), in order to name the use of language or other signs to bring about an event that will make a break in history rather than perpetuating what is already there. A performative use of language, in J. L. Austin's classic analysis in *How to Do Things with Words*, depends for its efficacy on an elaborate context of protocols, rules, institutions, roles, laws, and established formulae. These need to be in place before the performative utterance is made. They remain in place just as they were after that utterance. The performative neither creates them nor alters them. It depends on their unaltered continuity. It is in itself a repetition of perhaps innumerable other utterances of the same speech act that also depend on the same context. The minister's or justice of the peace's utterance of the phrase 'I pronounce you man and wife' is a classic example. It depends on the prior existence of the marriage ceremony, on ecclesiastical or civil sanctions that empower the minister or justice of the peace to marry people, and so on. These are operative before any given utterance of 'I pronounce you man and wife.' They remain operative and unchanged afterwards. The Austinian performative also presupposes the pre-existence of the perdurable self as agent, the ego or 'I' who can say, 'I promise,' or 'I decide,' or 'I pronounce.'

The alternative kind of performative creates the norms and laws that validate it. Each such performative is unique and unrepeatable because it leaves everything different thereafter, in however small a way. It constitutes a happening that changes decisively the surrounding context. It responds to a call or demand from an 'other' that can never be institutionalized or rationalized. Such a performative creates the 'I' that utters it. As Derrida puts it, such a speech act is a catachresis that 'while continuing to work through tradition emerges at a given moment as a *monster*, a monstrous mutation without tradition or normative precedent' (1984b, 123).[25] A university of dissensus should be the locus of a continual series of such mutations. The archiving of knowledge, however, also has its performative aspect, while those performative 'mutations' also bring knowledge. The difficulty (in fact impossibility) of either sharply distinguishing or happily reconciling performative and cognitive language should not be underestimated, nor the resistance in the university to any performative goal, especially when that goal is stated overtly.

What should teachers and students do in this new situation? First, they should take stock of the changes in the university I have described and try to understand them. Second, they must begin to think out ways to justify what they do in the humanities to their various constituencies. This task will not be at all easy, especially since corporation executives and officials have probably had their ideas about the humanities formed by the attacks in the media on theory, 'political correctness,' women's studies, and multiculturalism. Academics often start out with two strikes against them. Moreover, many of these funding sources as well as the university bureaucrats who govern for them may have a predisposition to think that the humanities are primarily of use to teach communication skills. In the new research university rapidly coming into being it will be extremely difficult to justify what is done in the old way, that is, as the production of new knowledge, the *Wissenschaft* appropriate in the humanities, as new knowledge about living things is appropriate in biology. New 'information' about *Beowulf*, Shakespeare, Racine, Goethe, Hugo, or even Emerson, William Carlos Williams, and Toni Morrison is not useful in the same way new knowledge about genes is when it leads to the making of a marketable medicine. Those corporation officers who will more and more control the university, along with legislators and administrators drawn from the sciences, are likely to say they admire the production of new knowledge in the humanities. Their reluctance to give money to support such research indicates that they may not really mean it. Most professors in the humanities these days know many brilliant, highly trained, and dedicated young humanists who have failed to find tenure-track positions, or sometimes any position at all. Most of a recent issue of the *ADE Bulletin* (Spring 1998, no. 119) is devoted to presenting the grim facts about current professional employment in English and other modern languages. The articles stress the rapid increase in part-time and adjunct faculty and report that only half of new PhD's in English and other modern languages can expect to get tenure-track jobs in the first year after receiving the PhD.

The product of value humanities professors and students make is discourse of a particular kind: new readings, new ideas. Nicholas Negroponte argues this forcefully for the research university in general in a recent essay in *Wired* (1996, 204).[26] Such ideas inaugurate something new, something unheard of before. Another way to put this is to say that the university is the place where what really counts is the ungoverned, the ungovernable. The ungovernable does not occur all that often. Most of what goes on in the university is all too easily governed. In fact it is self-governing, as when we say a machine has a 'governor' that keeps it from running too fast. It just turns round at a moderate speed and keeps repeating the same. Nevertheless, the university ought to have as its primary goal working to establish conditions propitious to the creation of the ungovernable. Only if we can persuade the new corporate governors of the university that such work has indispensable utility are we likely to flourish in the new conditions. Doing that will take much patient thought and rhetorical skill.

Notes

1. The best discussion of this is by Bill Readings (1996). I have learned much from this important book, the best of many current books about the transformation of the Western university. Readings' death in a commuter plane crash in the fall of 1994 was a major loss to humanistic study. My dedication of this book [*Black Holes*, from which the present chapter is taken; Ed.] to him indicates a little my own debt to him, both as a friend and as a colleague.

2. See Young (1993, 99–116), for a discussion of Newman's book as a stage in the development of the British university from the eighteenth century to the present.

3. The advice '*Get "Geist"* ' is given to the English people by Arminius, Matthew Arnold's imaginary German philosopher, in the first letter of *Friendship's Garland* (1871; see Arnold 1965, 5: 42). '[I]n Berlin,' Arminius explains to Arnold, 'we oppose "Geist," – *intelligence*, as you or the French might say, – to "Ungeist" . . . We North-Germans have worked for "Geist" in our way, by loving knowledge, by having the best-educated middle and lower class in the world . . . France has "Geist" in her democracy, and Prussia in her education. Where have you got it? – got it as a force, I mean, not only in a few scattered individuals. Your common people is barbarous; in your middle class "Ungeist" is rampant; and as for your aristocracy, you know "Geist" is forbidden by nature to flourish in an aristocracy' (40–1). See Derrida's discussion of Arnold's ironic '*Get "Geist"* ' (1987, 114–16).

4. As Readings puts this in a comment on Judy's *(Dis)Forming the American Canon*: 'I am concerned to introduce a transitional step into the passage from the modern German University of national culture to the bureaucratic University of excellence, one which positions the American University as the University of a national culture that is contentless' (1996, 201).

5. Matthiessen (1941); Fiedelson (1953); Lewis (1955); Perry Miller (1953); Pearce (1961); Bercovitch (1975); Bloom (1976).

6. Important work in this area includes: Lauter (1983); Ruoff and Ward (1990); Yans-McLaughlin (1990); Pease (1990); Fisher (1991); Pérez Firmat (1990); Kaplan and Pease (1993); Pease (1994); Lauter (1991); the new *Cambridge History of American Literature*, ed. Bercovitch and Patell (1994, 1995 [at the time of writing, two of the eight volumes planned had been published]). John Carlos Rowe helped me with

this list. In the fall of 1996, Rowe convened a residential research group on postnational American studies at the Humanities Research Institute of the University of California. The goal was to work toward institutionalizing the new American studies in the University of California and other universities. See Liu, *The Future Literary*, for a brilliant and fascinating discussion of the influence of computer technology and its graphic layouts on the presentation of new multicultural American literary histories or anthologies such as Lauter (1994), and Rico and Mano (1991). Lauter's essay in the 'Teacher's Manual' (1994) is a good description of the changes now taking place in American literature and American studies.

7. This is a schematic summary of the complex argument made in the seventh of Fichte's *Reden an die Deutsche Nation*, 'Noch tiefere Erfassung der Ursprünglichkeit, und Deutschheit eines Volkes' (1955, 106–24) and, for a translation, *Addresses to the German Nation* (1968, 92–110).

8. For Heidegger, German is even better than Greek for speaking of the highest spiritual things. As Derrida paraphrases this: 'German is therefore the only language, in the final analysis, that can name the highest or superlative excellence (*geistigeste*), which it does not share in the end except to a certain point with Greek' (1987, 113; my trans.).

9. The division of humanities at the University of California at Irvine, for example, suffered $1,215,035 in budget cuts in the years 1992–95. No one seems to expect that support to return. A recent memorandum from the Dean of Humanities at Irvine quotes two recent statements by experts on American higher education in the 1990s. Donald Kennedy, former president of Stanford University, says: 'It is inconceivable that our societal commitment to the support of knowledge acquisition will be maintained at historical levels. That circumstance alone signifies that university leaders are facing a period of resource restraint unlike any they – or their faculties – have ever experienced' (1993, 130). David Breneman, an economist and specialist on higher education, declares: 'Higher education is moving into a new era of permanently diminished financial support . . . The 'comprehensive college or university' may be an educational luxury that can no longer be supported in a meaningful way.' 'Having lost ground in the jockeying for state revenue, colleges and universities will find it hard to increase their share of appropriations . . . [California's] budgetary prospects continue to be bleak, particularly for higher education . . . My conclusion is that higher education in California is in a state of emergency.' (The first two sentences come from Breneman (AGB no. 22 n.d.), the second two, Breneman (1995).) The Irvine dean's response to this is to begin discussions of 'Possible Academic and/or Administrative Reconfiguration of the School of Humanities.' The reconfiguration is driven not just by the budget crisis but also by changing priorities resulting from a new definition of the university's mission. That mission will no longer be 'knowledge acquisition' but service to the global economy. The study of European languages and literatures, for example, will be likely to have a lower value in the new university, especially one situated strategically on the Pacific Rim.

10. Press release of January 3, 1996, and policy statement of January 1997.

11. Significantly, Aydelotte was a Rhodes Scholar and wrote a history of the Rhodes Scholarships in the United States (1946). The Rhodes Scholarships were originally

endowed for the purpose of spreading British culture and British values to British colonies or former colonies.

12. A specific example is the addition in the 1995 edition of Lentricchia and McLaughlin, eds, *Critical Terms for Literary Study*, of new entries for: 'Imperialism/Nationalism'; 'Desire'; 'Ethics'; 'Diversity'; 'Popular Culture'; and 'Class.' In the first edition of 1990, these were not yet 'critical terms for literary study.' Now they are important enough to warrant doing the book over. The tendency to thinking by appeal to a list of slogan words or 'buzz words' is characteristic of these new developments.[. . .]

13. '[A]lready, in myriad forms for an extended period of time, the very disciplinary structures that we seek to challenge have been firmly established in the pedagogical practices related to non-Western languages and literatures . . . "qualifications" and "expertise" in so-called other cultures have been used as the means to legitimate entirely conservative institutional practices in hiring, tenuring, promotion, reviewing, and publishing, as well as in teaching.'

14. Cohen uses the phrase 'ferocious abjection' (4) to describe the repudiation of Paul de Man's work after the wartime writings were discovered. This particular abjection has been an essential moment in the story I have been following, for example, in Charles Bernheimer's version in the introductory essay 'The Anxieties of Comparison' (1995, 1–17). Bernheimer does me the honor of citing an essay of mine as an example of the sort of thing the revolt against theory revolted against (5–6). A little later he says: 'History, culture, politics, location, gender, sexual orientation, class, race – a reading in the new mode has to try to take as many of these factors as possible into account. The trick is to do so without becoming subject to Miller's criticism, without, that is, suggesting that a literary work can be explained as an unmediated reflection of these factors' (8). That is the trick all right.

15. I speak of the United States and from my 'subject position' in the here and now of 1998.

16. The essay is also available online at www.wired.com/5.04/netizen/. A more recent essay by Jon Katz modifies somewhat, on the basis of a Merrill Lynch Forum and *Wired* poll, some of his generalizations about the 'digital young' (1997, 68–82, 274–75). 'Where I had described [the digital citizen] as deeply estranged from mainstream politics,' says Katz, 'the poll revealed that they are actually highly participatory and view our existing political system positively, even patriotically' (71).

17. See also Frank (1963, 3–62) and T. S. Eliot (1932, 3–11).

18. From a recent, unpublished seminar on witnessing and questions of responsibility, my trans.

19. For an authoritative account of black holes by a distinguished physicist, see Thorne (1994). Astrophysicists have recently become more willing to assert the indubitable existence of black holes, but they still often hedge what they assert by saying something like 'A massive black hole *may* lie at the center of the galaxy.' Recent work in quantum mechanics even suggests that the information in matter sucked into a black hole may not be wholly lost. See Susskind (1997, 52–57).

20. This terrifying admonition is scrawled at the bottom of Kurtz's idealistic essay on 'The Suppression of Savage Customs.'

21. What is said here about a university of dissensus develops ideas I proposed in a brief

essay published in *The Times Literary Supplement* in the summer of 1994. A funny thing happened to that essay on the way of the printer. It was cut and elegantly revised by the *TLS* editor, Alan Jenkins. I was given the opportunity to read and approve this new version. At some later point, however, the word 'dissensus,' still present in the final version I approved, was changed to 'dissent.' The word 'dissenter' was then used in the title invented by someone at the *TLS*: 'Return Dissenter.' This change made my essay the exact opposite of what I intended to say. 'Dissent' names a resistance to some hegemonic orthodoxy, as the dissenters in England resisted the established Church of England, or as Matthew Arnold makes fun of what he calls the 'dissidence of dissent.' 'Dissensus,' on the other hand, presupposes a situation in which no dominant orthodoxy esists from which to dissent, only decentered and non-hierarchical communities made of 'peripheral singularities,' as Bill Readings called them, borrowing the phrase from Giorgio Agamben. I do not suppose that the change from 'dissensus' to 'dissent' was the result of a conspiracy by the *TLS* to subvert what I was trying to say. Some copy editor or perhaps even some computer programme was probably offended by the word 'dissensus' and replaced it with a word in the *TLS*'s vocabulary. The subversion of my meaning was a striking example of the massive power of ideological assumptions as they work in the apparently neutral form of a journalistic 'house style.' It is apparently just not possible within the *TLS*'s style to say what I was trying to say. The present book attempts to get it said.

22. The final chapter of Bill Readings' *The University in Ruins* is entitled 'The Community of Dissensus' (18–193). That chapter has much aided my thinking about this topic. See also Diane Elam, *Feminism and Deconstruction*, especially the last two chapters, on what Elam calls 'groundless solidarity.'

23. In a lecture given in New York on 4 March 1994.

24. Jacques Derrida, in 'Mochlos,' speaks eloquently of this transformative power in teaching (1992c, 21–2).

25. According to Derrida, 'the found concepts of metaphysics – *logos, eidos, theoria*, etc. – are instances of *catachresis* rather than metaphors . . . In a work such as *Glas*, or other recent ones like it, I am trying to produce new forms of catachresis, another kind of writing, a violent writing which stakes out the faults [*failles*] and deviations of language, so that the text produces a language of its own, in itself' (1984b, 123). Tom Cohen's *Anti-Mimesis* brilliantly builds on de Man and Derrida but goes beyond them in its focus on United States literature and film and in its demonstrations of what materialist, interventionist writing and reading are. Another theoretically exigent example is Walter Benjamin's materialist historiography. In his essay on Eduard Fuchs, Benjamin says, 'cultural history only seems to represent a deepening of insight; it does not present even the appearance of progress in dialectics.' Benjamin means by 'dialectics' the active work of materialist historiography. He describes in the seventeenth of the 'Theses on the Philosophy of History' the way a 'historical materialist' sees 'a revolutionary chance in the fight for the oppressed past' when he (or she) finds a way 'to blast [*herauszusprengen*] a specific era out of the homogeneous course of history – blasting a specific life out of the era or a specific work out of the lifework' (1969, 263). In order to change the future we must change our grasp of the past. Only something like Benjamin's *Herauszospren-*

gen will make cultural studies an effective intervention. Benjamin spent the last part of his life developing a method of criticism that would be materialist in this way. The use of theory, in such thinkers as these, turns out paradoxically not to be its contribution to knowledge but its power to facilitate politically and institutionally transformative praxis, and moreover, to exemplify it.

26. Negroponte claims that research universities will have a crucial role in the new situation, where companies rather than governmental agencies increasingly support universities. The companies will need the universities as the place where new ideas in all fields are developed. Quite correctly he sees the process as expensive, given that not all new ideas pan out. According to him, however, the pedagogical mission of the university (producing educated students) will support that crucial innovative role: 'companies have realized that they cannot afford to do basic research. What better place to outsource that research than to a qualified university and its mix of different people? This is a wake-up call to companies that have ignored universities – sometimes in their own backyards – as assets. Don't just look for "well-managed" programs. Look for those populated with young people, preferably from different backgrounds, who love to spin off crazy ideas – of which only one or two out of a hundred may be winners. A university can afford such a ridiculous ratio of failure to success, since it has another more important product: its graduates' (1996, 204). What Negroponte says is as true for the humanities as for the sciences. The challenge is to persuade those in charge that new ideas in the humanities are also valuable.

Responses V

Envoy 1 *titles*

(c)(s)i(gh)ting the ungovernable translation
The Ascuity of Terminal Readings

Envoy 2 *author*

John Leavey

Envoy 3 *epigraphs*

'I dream of immense cosmologies, sagas, and epics all reduced to the dimensions of an epigram. In the even more congested times that await us, literature must aim at the maximum concentration of poetry and of thought.'

Italo Calvino

' "If a book truly interests me, I cannot follow it for more than a few lines. . .".
' ". . . Reading is a discontinuous and fragmentary operation. Or, rather, the object of reading is a punctiform and pulviscular material. . . . I must not be distracted if I do not wish to miss some valuable clue. . .".
' ". . . I too feel the need to reread. . . . The conclusion I have reached is that reading is an operation without object; or that its true object is itself. The book is an accessory aid, or even a pretext".
' ". . . For years I have been coming to this library, and I explore it volume by volume, shelf by shelf, but I could demonstrate to you that I have done nothing but continue the reading of a single book. . .".
' ". . . In my reading I do nothing but seek that book read in my childhood. . .".
' ". . . The moment that counts most for me is the one that precedes reading. At times a title is enough to kindle in me the desire for a book that perhaps does not exist. . . . the promise of reading is enough".
' ". . . I also seek openings in reading . . . but my gaze digs between the words to try to discern what is outlined in the distance, in the spaces that extend beyond the words 'the end' ".'

Italo Calvino

Envoy 4 methodology

I will begin with the ending of the memo on quickness, which is the second of five memos completed (six were projected, only five completed before his death) for this millennium. Calvino ends with a story that will guide my responses here.

> I began this lecture by telling a story. Let me end it with another story, this time Chinese: Among Chuang-tzu's many skills, he was an expert draftsman. The king asked him to draw a crab. Chuang-tzu replied that he needed five years, a country house, and twelve servants. Five years later the drawing was still not begun. 'I need another five years,' said Chuang-tzu. The king granted them. At the end of these ten years, Chuang-tzu took up his brush and, in an instant, with a single stroke, he drew a crab, the most perfect crab ever seen. (54)

I am attracted to this story as the end of the end, of the end that seemed without much relation to the previous ten years. Chuang-tzu needed ten years to draw a line. My response here then falls under the category of quickness and respects the formality of the end that marks this story. The story occurs at the end of the memo, and it is about the end, finally, the drawing in an instant, and that instant perhaps without relation to what happened before.

I am also attracted to place my response under the rubric of the bad reader. In the 'Envois' of *The Post Card*, Derrida writes:

> Because I still like him, I can foresee the impatience of the *bad* reader: this is the way I name or accuse the fearful reader, the reader in a hurry to be determined, decided upon deciding (in order to annul, in other words to bring back to one self, one has to wish to know in advance what to expect, one wishes to expect what has happened, one wishes to expect (oneself)). Now, it is bad, and I know no other definition of the bad, it is bad to predestine one's reading, it is always bad to foretell. It is bad, reader, no longer to like retracing one's steps. (1987c, 4)

I must predestine my reading, and my impatience is the impatience of the press and its calendar. I am the last respondent to the last section of the reader, and so I rush headlong to the end, to the ends each time of the pieces, the books, the glimpses of the eye, and quasi-concepts, on translation. This also might be designated as a terminal reading without the time for the patient exposition of all that earns the concentration. Perhaps I am also a bad writer, as impatient as the bad reader.

So my reading response is concentrated, terminal, and contracted, according to the terms of the contract of this volume (a request, of course, that binds).

Envoy 5 gloss on ascuity

I might be able to demonstrate, if that were my task, how each of Calvino's readers and the Reader of *If on a Winter's Night a Traveler* find some moment of support in the texts of the reader (of) J. Hillis Miller. So too would the problem of translation and translators, intimates to Calvino's writing, from story to story. I might be able to demonstrate, if that were my task, how Miller's theory of reading, criticism, theory, and the like, never escapes reading, either in the sense of being read in a reading or in the sense of never escaping from acts of readings that reading is. But my task here is a response, a response to a section of a reader of selections from Miller's immense *oeuvre*. I cannot take responsibility for the *oeuvre*, for all that might be implicated and implied in that word, or for its immensity, for lack of time and space, for the difference of the contract and the contact at hand, but more importantly because such a desire betrays an ascuity (the being-askew-and-acute jointly, separately) that characterizes reading and writing. The canons of integrity and priority that define an *oeuvre*, perhaps more akin to an earlier Miller, do not suit my terminally bad reading. The integrity of a body of work, or some assumed priority of either author or context for establishing the limits of such a body and integrity – these two canons forget the technological condition and attempt to ground the technology of reading as without technology. Discussion of technological innovations often succumb to one or the other of these canons in order to narrate. The ascuity of reading starts from the technological condition, even in a terminally bad reading.

Envoy 6 further delimitations of ascuity, but as a proleptic reference to another end passage in Miller

I cannot be responsible for the influences of the readings either, not only of what or who is read, but also of those that also made them possible and probable. I am to respond, to respond to a small, even if it overflows its divisions, section. And perhaps only to one passage or even one word. An impossible task to get it right.

But no passage or word is simple. Much of Miller's work of reading is in the situation of siting, of a theory of context, of the specific and general that crisscrosses any passage or word (heterogeneity, heteroglossia, hetero . . . dissensus). The act of such citing indicates the immediate recognition and the failure of siting, with many of the fault lines coming along with the insight of the word or passage, of the word or passage being in sight of . . . something else: pure language, lost original, translation as mistranslation.

Envoy 7 gloss on inaugurative responsibility

'Inaugurative Responsibility' are his words, his word about the ascuity of reading, its in(c)(s)i(gh)ting. Miller writes that we are responsible for reading as a doing without precedent or blame for the work. The reading then exceeds the work, for the work cannot serve as precedent. Hence reading's inaugurative responsibility and power lie, as we shall see, in translation.

'Our' freedom comes back again in the end to the responsibility to read, to read all
sorts of signs and to criticize them or make them effective again in the present. This
responsibility is both political and ethical. It can justify itself by no appeal to
precedent, no established procedures of reading, nor can it blame the text or work
for what we do with it, even though what happens in reading happens. (1992b, 59)

Miller points to the change that cultural criticism can effect in the faculty's
relation, for good or bad, to the institution that pays for its service, but
'responding' to the responsibility and the freedom is the first obligation in
cultural criticism. The truism that Miller points to is the marginalization of the
humanities in the corporate university, often a self-marginalization in the
exercise of this freedom and this responsibility.

Envoy 8 thesis

My response then requires a concentration and a formalisation. Too new critical
perhaps, and I can only hope that new criticism was always an impossible task,
even if it is really a 'bad' cousin of 'close' reading. The section on Pedagogical
and Political Commitments would seem to eschew relations to reading, and my
title would seem to be some kind of parenthetical miswriting, perhaps concentration, of a longer title on the relations of siting and sighting and citing, of
the line of sight that establishes the site of reading, its situations, and the
possibility and impossibility of citing those situations. Everything leads to the
simple definition of the ungovernable and, in this section perhaps, Miller's
ascuity in the use of translation.

   In brief, Miller often uses a notion of translation founded on original texts and
a love of literature for that 'original' site that becomes an original citing and so its
necessary translation. Hence translation founds and founders on those very
insights for the ungovernable that Miller wants for the university. My responsibility for an argument is predestined. The argument of commitments turns on
translation.

Envoy 9 terminal reading i: the ends of Topographies and of Speech Acts in Literature

A first commitment: the translation of the original. Miller has read Benjamin and
Jacobs and Derrida on translation. He knows the argument that Benjamin
advances regarding the translation of the original as its afterlife and ultimately its
status as literature under the auspices of the interlinear bible. The original is
slightly askew only in pure language, which is the translating tool giving afterlife
to any original. The original can be original only in sight of pure language, i.e. in
translation. Translation in–cites the original to its position within pure language.
In the last piece of *Topographies*, in a piece entitled 'Border Crossings, Translat-

ing Theory: Ruth,' Miller writes: 'A work is, in a sense, "translated," that is, displaced, transported, carried across, even when it is read in its original language by someone who belongs to another country and another culture or to another discipline' (1995, 316). Yes, to be sure. And so American or USese is not English. And English literature is a translated literature in the American contexts. But what of American literature, perhaps more properly US literature for a US citizen, native speaker of what we have no name for? Other languages do, French, for instance: *l'américain*. Is American literature translated? And is literature then always translated unless one is of that culture? Miller is quite aware of these questions, as he is expanding the notion of translation regarding the sites of theory versus the sites of the pedagogical, which are site specific ('the latter are tied to particular sites and situations' [1995, 318]). He reiterates Benjamin regarding the translation of theory (the 'promiscuity' of theory for translation):

> Another way to put this is to say that the theoretical formulation in its original language is already a translation or mistranslation of a lost original. This original can never be recovered because it never existed as anything articulate or able to be articulated in any langauge. Translations of theory are therefore mistranslations of mistranslations, not mistranslations of some authoritative and perspicuous original. (336–7)

But if one never escapes reading, only has acts of reading as reading, which citing de Man are the allegories of reading, never reading itself, then the sites and situations of readings are less site specific than site misspecific (see 'Coda: Allegory as Speech Act' in *Speech Acts in Literature*; 2001b, 214–15). And then '"Getting it right" no longer has the same urgency when it is seen to be impossible, though that by no means means we should not try our utmost to do so' (1995, 337). I am not sure what could constitute our utmost in this situation, but it is perhaps the utmost of ascuity – an always out of skew desire for acuity.

And so, getting it right in reading is less urgent but more acute. The ascuity of my trying is the holding of the impossibility of reading in sight, hence our allegory, its reading of reading, now our theorization, improper, mistranslated, from one allegory to another. Acutely askew. Askew in a specific angle. And with a keenness of sight on the moving target.

Here come the others. And they just won't seem to leave the scene. In the name of a process of truth, Badiou rightly points out in *Ethics* the lack of the other in the ethics of the other (he cites Levinas and Lacan). His ethics points out the situation of the situation (no god, situated truth or truth process, the failure to recognize the other except as the same other) in order to rethink ethics. Truth to be situated must have one moment of opinion that cannot be named, and evil is the attempt to name that unnameable, he states. The situation of truth is always n-1, singular but not the one.

Envoy 10 terminal reading ii: the end of Others

Miller ends this volume with 'Derrida's Others,' which recalls the envoy of the title piece of a collection of Derrida on the invention of the other. It ends with a dialogue of two voices:

> 'Psyché: Invention de l'autre' itself ends with two unidentifiable voices speaking in a question-and-answer sequence in which the final voice denies that 'l'autre' can ever be invented and says that rather the other calls (something) to come, or calls forth, names, the future. This other calling on us to respond, this future that comes into being by way of the response, can only get here, arrive on this shore, speaking in tongues, in a multitude of overlapping and contradictory voices . . .

> L'autre appelle à venir et cela n'arrive qu'à plusieurs voix. (2001a, 273–4)

Envoy 11 terminal reading iii: the end of Illustration

A 'citation' 'into the current cultural situation.' The critic is responsible for what the inaugural reading does. The performative must differentiate and translate. The translation ('rhetorical reading') is current, responsible, and without the ability or desire to lay blame. Doing is doing askew.

> I have exemplified, finally, what follows from this, namely the necessity of vigilant and detailed rhetorical reading of works of art in any medium in order to identify what is different in each. By this identification the force of the work can be passed on in a new form, through the reading, into the current cultural situation. For that new form the reader-critic must take responsibility. It cannot be blamed on the work, in spite of the critic's obligation to a faithful representation of the work. The critic must be held accountable for whatever inaugural power the reading has. This is an accountability not so much for the knowledge the reading gives as for what the reading *does* when it is re-read. (1992b, 151)

Envoy 12 terminal reading response: the end of the section, and the last words

The situation of the university requires reading. And the last section wants desperately to place that situation in sight, the university 'without idea' (an allusion to the changes from Newman's *The Idea of a University*). For Miller, the changes are numerous. Technology and the sites of literature must be deciphered in this new pedagogy and this new politics. The political import is 'indirect,' always after a 'laborious process of reading and deciphering' (31). And Miller provides that reading. The two functions of the Western research university, new knowledge according to reason and the formation of good citizens, no longer go hand in hand in the transnational university. Politics and pedagogy were considered related, and such relation contributed to the situation of the nation-state. Literature departments, contributing knowledge of the language and culture, inculcated a national culture. The study of English, of course, in the United States then becomes a story of translation. The use of English literature and its accessory American literature ran up against this function of formation, of formation in the nation's 'unified' culture. English literature is translated to the United States, and the difficulty of this transfer is acute in its lack of decipherment. A global vector was already assumed in this translation, much as in a comparative literature lacking the desire or need for comparison or translation. We do not make the simple statement that we speak American or United States. We speak English. And yet, in that statement, we might say, comparison falls, translation founders for lack of difference, and pedagogy fails. And so, in the most abbreviated and concentrated history, so the story goes, cultural studies answers to both universities, with and without the idea. (I leave out the intervention of theory only to quicken my response.) Cultural studies answers to the idea of failed translation through the situatedness of the object of study, both the particular object and the notion of 'culture' itself, which is more portable than language. 'Lively debates among those doing such work in all those countries indicate not only cultural studies' heterogeneity, the way it is a site of dissensus, but also the way something serious is at stake' (52). Ultimately, for Miller, at stake is a materialist reading, which he notes is also a rereading of materiality. Miller concentrates on the contextualization of cultural studies, and he argues against their reduction of explanation to that context, one might say, before reading. Or before recognizing the labor of reading and the materiality of its inscription 'in its original language' (57). Materialist reading refuses the neutralization of the university and (of) contextualism.

> Putting neglected works in the classroom, in the curriculum, in books, articles, conferences, and study groups is only the beginning of the work. Knowledge is not enough. These works must be put to work. Only what might be called a materialist reading will accomplish that. 'Materialist' here does not mean displacing attention from the work to its historical context, but attention to the materiality of the work's inscription in its original language. Archiving multiculturalism, expanding the curriculum to include works from all over the world hitherto little read in United States universities, may even, as I have suggested, negate the power such works have to effect cultural change. The university has a formidable power of neutralization. (57)

Along with the original language and against the university's power of neutralization, Miller calls for 'genuine acts of reading' in cultural studies. The genuine reading is inaugural, again without precedent, without – in a sense, a very limited, but real, sense – theory, or with a disabled theory. Genuine reading must go back to the original language, to the material inscription. A translation of a theory gives you nothing but the dried flower for the universal herbarium.

But Miller does not stop there. Reversion to the original applies not just to works in another language, but to works even in a common language, one's own language. Genuine reading, in other words, returns to a more embedded notion of translation, to a notion of the original as translated, to the reading itself as the act of translation that should ground the new university because it makes the recognition and reinscription of the anomalous possible. The materiality of the inscription is singular, an event, for Miller. And only translation brings about its inauguration. Miller writes:

> Genuine acts of reading are always to some degree sui generis, inaugural. They always to some extent disable or disqualify the theory that may have been the motivating presupposition of the reader . . . What I am calling a 'genuine reading' always must have recourse to the original language of the work, however awkward and time-consuming this may be, and however much it may go against the powerful ideology of journals and both university and commercial presses. This ideology assumes that everything can be translated without loss into English. This recourse to the original language is necessary because the force of the original work, its happening as a cultural event that to some extent exceeded the social context from which it arose, lies in its unique use of its own vernacular idiom. (73)

Miller sees the excess and access of the site of inscription as the excess and access of citing the singular ('its own vernacular idiom'). This excess and this access are the excess of and the access to both the loss and the gain that are translation. Translation gives way to translation. Reliance on monolithic translation (for example, on the translation of theory, according to a different level of abstraction and reading, or even simply on that of a work to be read) gives way to another translation, a more fundamental translation that is 'the materiality of the work,' such that the reading of the translation can itself become 'a new event' of possible political import. Genuine acts of reading are translations of translations with a force of possible change.

> I call this unique use the irreducible otherness of the work, even its otherness to the culture that apparently 'generated' it. Use of a translation uproots the work, denatures it, transforms it into a *hortus siccus* or dried, specimen flower ready to be stored in the bottomless archives of a transnational university system that is more and more dominated by the English language as a global language. This argument for return to the original languages in acts of reading is, however, only the most visible version of a need, even in studying works in the same language as that of the critic, to get behind thematic reading and pay attention to what might be called the materiality of the work. The work's force as an event bringing cultural value or meaning into existence depends on a certain performative use of language or other signs. Such a reading must attend to what is internally heterogeneous, contradictory, odd, anomalous about the work, rather than presupposing some monolithic unity that directly reflects a cultural context. Only such a reading can hope to transmit or preserve some of the force as an event the original work had or can still have. This might even make the reading, as recorded in an essay or lecture, a new event helping to bring about social change. (74)

In my responsive reading, slightly askew, Miller brings forth translation as an ungovernable governor, as the ascuity that takes the indirect import of pedagogy and politics in the transformation of the transnational university to account for the value of the inaugural reading. The very problem of the status of the humanities, of their unrelatedness to the idea of the university, would now translate the humanities to the site and citation of the ungovernable, would now make the humanities the site and citation of the ungovernable, which must become the site of the transnational university. He, patiently, and I (impatiently) end:

> The product of value humanities professors and students make is discourse of a particular kind: new readings, new ideas. Nicholas Negroponte argues this forcefully for the research university in general in a recent essay in *Wired*. Such ideas inaugurate something new, something unheard of before. Another way to put this is to say that the university is the place where what really counts is the ungoverned, the ungovernable. The ungovernable does not occur all that often. Most of what goes on in the university is all too easily governed. In fact it is self-governing, as when we say a machine has a 'governor' that keeps it from running too fast. It just turns round at a moderate speed and keeps repeating the same. Nevertheless, the university ought to have as its primary goal working to establish conditions propitious to the creation of the ungovernable. Only if we can persuade the new corporate governors of the university that such work has indispensable utility are we likely to flourish in the new conditions. Doing that will take much patient thought and rhetorical skill. (183)

Committed to wait, the genuine reading is patient to the end. The ungovernable translation arrives infrequently; the university is to become the site of its creation – a translation without precedent, hence always as terminal as inaugural, rushing to the end, like the bad reader who reads only the end, the end bits, the bits and pieces (often run through the mill) that have been ungovernable and ungoverned, and are without precedent from what precedes. Always a response, without original, the translation, in the end, reads that end, and it does so with an impatient patience that knows no blame or fealty. Such is a Miller's ascuity.

J. Hillis Miller: In Print and On-line
Barbara Cohen

> This new digitized existence will change literature and literary study in manifold and as yet unforeseen ways.
>
> J. Hillis Miller

Since his early days as literary theorist and teacher, Hillis Miller has taken the opportunity to write extensively, and with remarkable insight, on the state of literary study and the teaching of it within the university. That work is represented in this chapter by a group of essays that I use here as a trajectory to address one of Miller's thought streams on changes in literary study and pedagogy, that is those brought about by the evolution from a print to a digital culture.

In the series of essays reprinted here that Miller wrote in 1986 during his tenure as President of the MLA, he expresses his thinking about what he sees as the performative acts of literary scholarship, that is reading, teaching, and writing. There exists for him a duality of calling and 'joy'[1] along with the obligation and the responsibility of these acts, with reading as the beginning and end to the others. For Miller, reading starts as a wonder filled and solitary act where one experiences a sense of magic, a first taste of virtual reality, just as he experienced as a young boy reading *The Swiss Family Robinson*. Yet reading is solitary only up to a point, and once it turns outward, Miller asserts that it goes beyond itself by bringing about other language acts, including teaching and writing. Teaching for Miller 'is a prolongation, extension, or modulation of that first, virtually solitary act of reading . . . .' And writing literary scholarship is as strong an obligation and inextricably interwoven with reading and teaching for those in the field: 'The obligation to write remains a fundamental part of the everyday practice of our profession, intrinsic to it, not accidentally imposed from without. It coexists with the joy of reading and with the more intermittent joy of teaching as the third and by no means least of the main features of our vocation.' In these essays, and with much more complexity than a short article as this can address, Miller underscores his theories of literary study and teaching to which he has remained steadfast, expounding on and appending them through-out his career.

However, Miller has also foreseen many changes in literary study. It is notably in 'Literary Study in the Transnational University,' published relatively recently in 1999, where he projects beyond the then present state of literary study to predict stunning changes brought about by the digitization of texts and by the Internet. Those changes have now occurred. For one, the very act of reading itself in electronic form diverges from the print version, in relation both to the sense of fragility of a book on screen – the seeming 'disappearance' of pages as the next screen comes up and potential ability for alteration – and, even more significant, to the power of hypertext. But my primary interest here is in another aspect of Miller's thinking about changes in literary study in this digital area, summarized in the following comment:

> My claim is that this new digitized existence will change literature and literary study in manifold and as yet unforeseen ways. I would go so far as to say it will transform, is already transforming the concept of literature or of literarity, killing literature and giving it a new existence as the survivor of itself. Students of literature will and should remain as the guardians and surviving witnesses of previous historical epochs, just as

classicists bear witness to what was the nature and function of Greek tragedy within a vanished classical culture. Literature as we know it, as Derrida has argued, is inextricably associated with democracy, that is, with freedom of speech, the freedom to say or write anything and everything (never completely obtained, of course). Even the concept of free speech, I would add, is being changed by the electronic revolution.

In two essays Miller has written within the past year,[2] he once again takes up the discussion of changes in literary study in this age of digitization and multimedia, but he now transcends prediction through his own observations and participation as a teacher of literary studies. According to Miller, literature, specifically the field of literary studies, is indeed disappearing, not in the sense of becoming extinct, but of changing so drastically as to be unrecognizable from what it was before. Just as manuscript culture has survived a long time in the era of print, so will the print culture survive the digital era. And not that this disappearance is necessarily a bad thing, or as Miller has cited in several instances, a cause for hand-wringing, but that it requires recognition and new ways of thinking about literary study. 'For those still interested in literary study, a chief issue now is, as Alan Liu has said, the role of literature in the age of new media. Literature, or rather what might be called "literarity" will survive in new forms that will incorporate visual and sound media as well as words.'[3] Reading, teaching, and writing remain key to literary study, but the shapes they take and the questions they raise will respond to literature not as we have known it and not as we know it yet.

Miller sees other positive signs for literary study emerging in this new multimedia age, namely the rise of collaborative communities among literary scholars and the potential of increased accessibility to literature in its new multimedia forms. In the first, the rise of literary scholarly communities, Miller notes a great advantage over the past isolated study of literature, particularly in his view of these communities as proponents of dissensus[4] where there is strong potential for the nurture of independent political thinking. In the second, the potential of increased accessibility to literature in its new multimedia forms, Miller notes, along with its obvious promise for literary scholars and teachers, the parallel emergence of a serious dilemma. That is, while exciting new forms of multimedia provide the *potential* for greater accessibility to works of literature, the resistance – often arising from fear – to these new means of access and disseminations, in reality has been impeding access. As an example, most university presses, and many scholars as well, have been reluctant to take the predictable step of publishing new literary scholarship on-line, using as justification a litany of obstacles including financial costs, peer review issues, and copyright concerns. Yet on-line literary scholarship could provide an opportunity for the previously mentioned recognition of a new literarity. It is indeed part of the new literarity itself. Further, on-line, peer-reviewed publication would give literary scholars, especially younger scholars just coming into the field, new venues for publication, and, in turn, greater accessibility to their work by peers in their scholarly communities, especially in light of the present financial crisis in academic publishing. This crisis has produced a significant decline in traditional scholarly book publication, most prevalent in literary study. However, at present, this step is being taken only rarely and with much trepidation of the possible obstacles.

Let me address one of those so-called obstacles: copyright. As Miller has pointed out, the fear of academic presses of forfeiting copyright control with online publishing is parallel to the record industry's opposition to the dissemination of popular music on the web. The interests of the publisher are not necessarily the same as the interests of the literary scholar, again, just as those of record company producers aren't the same as those of composers and musicians. This returns us to Miller's earlier thinking that the very right of free speech is being challenged by the electronic revolution. Recent trends in US copyright law expanding copyright to an average of seventy years after the life of a creator, and thus creating increasingly limited access to creative works – often referred to as a shrinking or diminishing public domain – bear out Miller's concerns. This situation has led to a viable and growing grassroots movement within the academic and creative communities, spearheaded by Lawrence Lessig, Professor of Law at Stanford, who advocates limitations on present long-term copyrights on the basis of several important arguments including the infringement on free speech. Toward this end, he has founded the Creative Commons,[5] which gives both writers and scholars in all fields the opportunity to have their work disseminated and used by others with new licensing arrangements that still protect creative works, yet reduce the limitations and restraints of present US copyright law. Minimizing these restraints would widen accessibility to creative and scholarly work, and if applied to academic online publication, would deflate copyright as an obstacle to publishing venues for literary studies online. As Miller has both predicted in his earlier writings and confirmed in later ones, it is essential for the survival of literary studies to be incorporated into the digital media.

> I also conclude that if scholarship in the humanities is to survive and flourish in the age of the networked computer, exploitation of digital technology by humanistic scholars must become universal and fully institutionalized . . . I realize it is utopian to think of going around the print publishing convention for scholarly publishing in the humanities. It will be a long time before this happens, but I believe it should, and ultimately will, happen, as digital forms gradually replace print or analogue forms . . . I want to get what I write read by as many people as possible, by whatever means possible . . . Insofar as the literature of the fast vanishing print age depends on the university for its preservation, interpretation and circulation, digitizing both primary and secondary works . . . is an urgent necessity.[6]

In the earlier mentioned MLA columns on reading, teaching, and writing, Miller asserts that the act of writing completes those of reading and teaching. It follows then that the above stated wish to have his written work read by as wide an audience as possible is an extension of the responsibility to teach. The fulfillment of any promise of wide dissemination of work in literary study for the present and future relies ultimately on its prospects for digitization.

Notes

1. Miller's definition of the 'joy' of reading (in 'Responsibility and the Joy of Reading'): 'For me, the joy of reading, when it comes, is something like Wordsworth's sudden joy: surprising, unpredictable both in its nature and in its possible effects, a break in time, in that sense anarchic, a dissolution of pre-existing orders, the opening of a sense of freedom that is like a new earth and a new heaven, an influx of power. The joy of reading is in this sense apocalyptic. It has to do with transfiguration and the end but also has to do with a momentary lapse of the fear of death.'
2. Both are unpublished. One is titled, 'Get a Life! The Way We Live (Now and Then),' the other 'The Disappearance of Literature?'
3. 'The Disappearance of Literature?' 2.
4. Miller discusses 'dissensus' in depth in 'Literary Study in a Transnational University.'
5. See the Creative Commons website (*http://www.creativecommons.org*) for its full background, mission, and players.
6. 'The Disappearance of Literature,' 7–8.

Why Literature? A Profession:
An interview with J. Hillis Miller

JW: Why literature?

JHM: Like all such decisions, my choice of literary study as a vocation was overdetermined. I always liked reading, but I thought of reading literature as more or less a private avocation. I wanted to be a scientist. I went to college intending to be a physics major. In the middle of my sophomore year at Oberlin College I had a vocational experience; you might call it a 'calling.' I realized that what I really wanted to do was to spend the rest of my life studying literature and teaching it. I was aided in this by my wife-to-be, Dorothy. We were what in those days was called 'going together' already. We used to have long conversations about poverty, about accepting poverty together so I could study literature. Dorothy said, 'Yes, I'll live in a cottage with you.' My father was also helpful in encouraging me.

So I turned to literature from science. That shift defined to some degree the form my interest in literature took. That interest has always been double. On the one hand, I have an immense pleasure and investment in reading literature. A literary work is for me the magic entry into an imaginary world or, as I would call it now and as other people also might, a virtual reality. Entering the imaginary, for some reason, gives me great pleasure, as it also no doubt does for others. On the other hand, I have always been fascinated by the question of how that magic is concocted, how it works, what makes it happen. I think that was as important a motive as the slightly hedonistic one of saying this is what I really want to do. I like reading Dickens. Why shouldn't I spend the rest of my life doing that, rather than doing physics experiments? But the other side was equally important. It was a desire to account for literature and to understand it, in a quasi-scientific way.

It has always seemed to me that literature is, in one way or another in different cases, anomalous or strange in its use of language. This is a distinguishing feature of literature: the weird way in which language is used in it. I can remember still the specific example that I had in my mind. This was Tennyson. Tennyson's language seemed to me clearly contrary to fact and strange: 'Tears from the depth of some divine despair.' What in the world could that mean? No wonder Tennyson's speaker, or singer, says of those tears, 'I know not what they mean'! My basic question was: how could somebody come to use the English language in this strange way.

Let me give you another example. I have noticed recently, in teaching *Light in August*, that the Reverend Hightower reads Tennyson. Hightower is obsessed with the Civil War, and, more particularly, with the moment when his grandfather, who was in the Confederate cavalry, was killed by a shotgun blast when he and his comrades were robbing a hen-house. It's a serio-comic moment. They'd been heroically blowing up a northern supply depot. On the way back, they were very hungry, so they stopped to steal some hens or eggs from a farmer's hen-house. A woman, no doubt the farm-wife who has been left behind because her husband is away fighting in the Confederate Army, shoots Hightower's grandfather. Every night Hightower relives the sound of the galloping horses, and the shotgun blast. Another thing he does at one point in the novel, as an escape from a painful reality, is to read Tennyson. Faulkner describes Tennyson's language as empty and gutless: 'the fine galloping language, the gutless swooning full of sapless trees and dehydrated lusts.' It wasn't Tennyson's emptiness that fascinated me, but what I thought of as his strange use of words. I was, and am, willing to give Tennyson the benefit of the doubt. He's supposed to be a great poet, so he must have known what he was doing. Finding out what Tennyson and the rest of that ilk are doing with words has remained a strong motivation for me.

Faulkner, by the way, uses language in strange ways too. Who but he would have thought of calling the succession of mule-drawn farm wagons in which Lena Grove rides in *Light in August*, 'creakwheeled and limpeared avatars'? That's pure Faulknerese.

So it's the linguistic peculiarity in works of literature that interests me most. That's a quasi-scientific impulse. What scientists are supposed to do, good ones at least, is to notice anomalies, things that don't quite fit the received paradigm, and to account for them. Scientific advances are generally made in that way. I have a big resistance, and always have, to what you might call the received opinions about literary works, for example, the opinions that come to be enshrined in prefaces of modern editions. I'm suspicious of such introductions, though I've written some myself. Of course, I have great admiration and respect for many of those prefaces written by other scholars, but I would read them last, in order not to have my reading of the novel, or book of poems, or whatever, distorted by them. I want to read for myself. I don't want possibly to be misled by what is always, to some degree, an expression of what everybody is supposed to know about a given work. I have found this abstinence really works. If you have an eye out for contradictions, inconsistencies, oddnesses, things that are not quite explicable by thematic descriptions of the work's features, things not highlighted by previous critics, you may see something of importance.

As you can see, I value most the idiosyncrasy of literary works, the way a given work cannot be entirely encompassed by the ideological assumptions of the period in which it was written. You can't easily fit it into history. The best works are other to their times. I no longer think of this idiosyncrasy as reflecting the idiosyncrasy of the author's mind, though those two forms of otherness may be analogous. Literature is made of language, not of bits of consciousness. That the work reflects the author's mind is an unprovable assumption. What we have is the words on the page. Though no doubt the author wrote them down, we cannot fully reconstruct the relays by which they got there on the page. Nor, for dead authors at least, do we any longer have direct access to the authors' minds. Do we even have direct access to the minds of living authors or just the people around us? I doubt it. One of the pleasures of literature is that it gives the reader the illusion of such direct access, for instance to the minds of characters in novels or to the narrator's mind.

In Hardy's *The Return of the Native* – I've just been teaching that too – why is there so much spying on other people? It is a bit strange. It is not evidently necessary to the story, but it happens over and over again. A grotesque embodiment of this is the way Eustacia Vye in that novel wanders around the heath with her father's spyglass. It seems unlikely, implausible, and yet she is always looking through the spyglass. So, you say, OK here's a feature that recurs. It doesn't seem to fit the story or be necessary to the story. Why is it there? It's that *why* that interests me as much as the general role that literature has played in my life and in so many people's lives – the unreflective plunge into the work as an alternative world.

The same thing goes for Faulkner. *Light in August* is a spectacular and powerful novel, a double plotted novel. One story comes out happily. Lena Grove substitutes for Lucas Burch, who has made her pregnant and then run away, Byron Bunch, whom she accepts. She replaces Burch with Bunch! She keeps moving on through the whole novel. She keeps saying things like, 'I have come from Alabama: a fur piece. All the way from Alabama a-walking. A fur piece, ' or 'My, my, . . . here I aint been on the road but four weeks, and now I am in Jefferson already. My, my. A body does get around.' Eventually, at the end of the novel, she ends up in Tennessee, about to be married to Byron Bunch and presumably to live happily ever after, whereas Joe Christmas ends up committing a murder and getting lynched. The same figure of life as a journey is used for him, but for him it is a figure for inescapable repetition. In a climactic passage, when he's being hunted after the murder of Joanna Burden, Christmas says to himself, 'I have been further in these seven days than in all the thirty years . . . But I have never got outside that circle. I have never broken out of the ring of what I have already done and cannot ever undo.' He has travelled in a circle, whereas Lena Grove has travelled in a progressing line.

The obvious question about *Light in August* is why these two stories come out so differently. There are various answers to that question. One answer is suggested by looking at one of those anomalies of the sort I've mentioned and by asking, why is there so much attention to food and to eating in the novel? It doesn't seem necessary, though I suppose you might say it serves as realistic information. There's not much eating in *The Return of the Native*, however, but it is a major topic in *Light in August*. Realism doesn't require it. Lena not only accepts rides. She also politely accepts food. When she's taken in for the night by a farmer, Armstid, his wife is very harsh on her. Here is a young woman who is clearly not married and yet is visibly pregnant. For one night the Armstids give Lena a bed to sleep in. They offer her food. She accepts it, but she doesn't really eat as much as she wants. Later she says, 'Like a lady I et,' meaning that she didn't eat much at breakfast, only a piece of cornbread and a cup of coffee. Mrs. Armstid, by the way, though she looks at Lena with cold contempt for being so dumb as not only to have got herself pregnant, but also then to believe that her seducer is actually going to marry her. In spite of her contempt, Mrs. Armstid gets out her piggybank, with her egg money in it. She breaks the piggybank because she can't shake the money out fast enough. She gives Lena all her egg money. The egg money is hers. I know this from my own grandparents in Virginia. The farm husband would work in the fields, grow the corn, take care of the cattle, milk the cows, and so on, but the farm wife would have care of the chickens. That was certainly true of my grandmother. She had to feed the chickens, collect the eggs, and so on. Faulkner, I am sure, is right on the mark about this. Mrs. Armstid would have had charge of the chickens. She would have sold the eggs, and little by little, she would have gradually have collected quarters, nickels, dimes, and pennies. When her husband asks if she's going to give Lena all the money, Mrs. Armstid replies that it's her own money to do with as she pleases. She earned it and he didn't have anything to do with it. Armstid agrees. He says, "Sho . . . I reckon it ain't any human in this country is going to dispute them hens with you, lessen it's the possums and the snakes.' Lena accepts the money.

So Lena accepts food and money, not only from the Armstids but also from others along the way. She uses Mrs. Armstid's egg money to buy food. She goes into a country store and orders crackers and a nickel can of what she calls 'sour-deens.' The storekeeper says, 'we ain't got no nickel sardines.' She asks how much do they cost, and he says fifteen cents. A struggle has gone on in her mind between her "providential caution" and her desire to eat for her unborn baby's sake. Faulkner says finally she wins out over caution. She buys the crackers and sardines. She says yes to the kindness of other people. 'Folks have been kind,' she says. 'They have been right kind.'

Christmas, on the contrary, always says no. In a number of scenes he repeats the word 'no.' For example, when Miss Burden wants him to get down on his knees and pray and admit that he's a terrible sinner, he says 'no,' 'no,' 'no,' three times in response to her repeated demand. That's one example. More interesting, and a bit more surprising, is his refusal of food from other people. He can steal food but cannot bring himself to take it as a gift. Sharing food as a kind of communion. One sign of being graceful, of being inside a community, is the ability to accept hospitality. Christmas can't do that. Several important scenes show this. When he's a child in an orphanage, he has got into the habit of stealing and eating the toothpaste that belongs to the orphanage dietician. He sneaks into her room to get some more toothpaste. The dietician comes into her room with the orphanage doctor, who is her lover. Christmas hides in the closet while they're making love on the bed outside. He eats too much toothpaste, so he throws up and is caught. He eats the toothpaste, but it's stolen toothpaste, a transgression, not a sharing. Eating is here associated with sex.

In another scene with Mrs. McEachern, his foster mother, whose husband is trying to make him a Christian, he refuses food again. McEachern has adopted him, teaches him to work on the farm, and beats him senseless when he refuses to learn the Presbyterian catechism. Mrs. McEachern brings him food when he awakens in his room. He won't eat it. He says, 'I ain't hungry.' Finally, he is so hungry that he gets down on his hands and knees like an animal, eating the food with his hands that he has earlier thrown on the floor. Much later in his story, Miss Burden leaves food for him in the kitchen of her big house. It's African-American food, as he thinks to himself: '*Set out for the nigger. For the nigger.*' He takes each of the dishes up one by one, identifying each (e.g. 'Ham,' 'Beans'), throws it against the wall, and smashes it. Earlier in the novel, when he first gets a job in the planing mill in Jefferson, he hasn't eaten for a good while. He won't have any money until he's paid. When Byron Bunch realizes that, he offers to share his lunch food. Christmas says, 'I ain't hungry. Keep your muck.'

All this attention to eating or the refusal to eat is a significant, strange detail in *Light in August*. You wouldn't assume ahead of time it was going to be there, even if you knew the outlines of the story. When you begin to look at this motif and ask why is it here, it turns out to be a useful clue as to what is important at the deepest level of the novel's meaning.

This interest in literature's strangeness has kept me going now for well over fifty years. I continue to read and teach literature because I expect that I am going to find something that I hadn't seen before, even with a book that I know well and have taught often before. I used to teach *Light in August* at night school at Johns Hopkins. Since this year is my last seminar at UC Irvine, I wanted to end with Faulkner and Stevens, both of whom I read when I was a graduate student, though American literature was not my 'field.' I don't know whether that makes me like Lena or like Joe Christmas, saying no to received opinion, or saying yes to what's there in the book. Christmas's saying no to the impossible position his surrounding society puts him in, as someone neither black nor white, is his only way of maintaining integrity and a measure of freedom, though it leads him straight to his lynching. When he is tempted by the ease Joanna Burden offers him, he says to himself, 'No. If I give in now, I will deny all the thirty years that I have lived to make me what I chose to be.' Lena has an easier time saying yes because her situation allows that as a way to live productively within her community. No doubt there is some condescension as well as affection for Lena on the part of the narrator. Nevertheless she shows that by 'an inwardlighted quality of tranquil and calm unreason,' you can triumph even in such a shrewd situation as she is in, whereas Christmas's more rigorous integrity and even worse situation, as neither black nor white, means that he can only triumph by saying no to every effort McEachern, Joanna Burden, and others make to get him to accept the subject position Southern racism and Southern Protestantism would determine for him.

What I hadn't noticed when I used to teach *Light in August* – this is a long time ago; I left Hopkins in 1972 – was the way in which Faulkner carefully and deliberately associates three ideological features of southern post Civil War culture. He sees these three features as inextricably intertwined. One is the sexism that puts women on a pedestal, while at the same time oppressing them, and being more or less unforgiving if they have sex with somebody to whom they're not married, as Lena does. That's one part of the ideology. The second part is the racism. Christmas's problem is that he is neither black nor white. He thinks he's part African American, though he is never certain. In one passage near the end, the narrator says that what really got to the people in the community is that Christmas doesn't act either like a white man or like a black man. 'That was it. That was what made folks so mad.' His situation is certainly worse than Lena's because he doesn't know just who or what he is, whereas Lena and the people around her know just what and who Lena is. At one point when Christmas is still a child in that orphanage, he asks an African American working in the yard, 'How come you are a nigger? . . . I ain't a nigger.' The man answers him, 'You are worse than that. You don't know what you are. And more than that, you won't never know. You'll live and you'll die and you won't never know.' When Miss Burden asks Christmas if he knows for sure he is part African American, he admits, 'I don't know it,' and then he adds, 'If I'm not, damned if I haven't wasted a lot of time.' Lena knows who she is. She is a white woman who has borne a child out of wedlock whose father is a white man. Since Christmas doesn't know who he is and will never know, whatever "who" he becomes will be the result of his own choices and actions, as he several times says of himself.

The third feature of southern ideology is Protestant Christianity. Faulkner sees racism as inextricably linked to that form of Christianity. In a passage that I had never before seen as so important, Hightower expresses this, or the narrator reports his thinking it. Hightower has been thrown out of his position as minister in his Jefferson church, partly because he keeps preaching wild sermons about the Civil War. His grandfather riding his cavalry horse and getting shot in the chicken house keeps getting into his sermons. He is also evicted from his pulpit because his wife periodically runs off to Memphis, the wicked city, and sleeps with strange men. She finally kills herself by jumping out of a hotel window. Hightower's parishioners can't stand the fact that their minister's wife is living this other life. So they drive him out of his pulpit, but he continues to live nearby. He listens especially to the organ music and to the hymn singing of

Sunday night prayer services. In those southern Protestant churches, as the narrator specifies, evening prayer service differs from the Sunday morning service because there is no sermon, no fire and brimstone, simply prayer and hymns. This is much more peaceful. Hightower thinks of those small town people and the country people, the families, once his congregation, coming to church. They greet one another and talk quietly to one another before the service begins. This signals their community belonging, their togetherness and peacefulness. Peace is a key word here, not only because it's repeated here, but also because it echoes through the novel. One of the things Christmas thinks to himself when he's running away after the murder and becomes aware of the quiet gray dawn and the 'air, inbreathed, [that] is like spring water,' is 'That was all I wanted . . . That was all, for thirty years. That didn't seem like a whole lot to ask in thirty years.' Earlier he says to himself, *'All I wanted was peace.'* In the Hightower passage about the evening prayer service, there's a modulation to a description of the hymn that the congregation sings, and the organ music. These seem to Hightower a celebration of crucifixion, self-crucifixion and worship of Christ, the crucified. Then in a further modulation, Hightower thinks to himself that these are the same people, these good people, who in the coming week will joyfully participate in Christmas's lynching. They will kill him gladly because, Hightower thinks, if they pitied him they would have to admit that they might need pity themselves, so they crucify somebody else: 'Since to pity him would be to admit selfdoubt and to hope for and need pity themselves. They will do it gladly, gladly.' I hadn't before seen the relation between southern Protestantism and the lynching so clearly, partly perhaps because I was brought up in such a community. I was born in Virgina, but have lived all my life in the north, unless you count Baltimore as south, which I suppose you might do. My father was a southern Baptist minister, my mother a southern Presbyterian. My Virginia forbears were good people. They read the Bible and went church every Sunday, and I went to church and attended Baptist Sunday school until I was twelve or thirteen. Nevertheless, I think Faulkner is right to see a deep connection between southern racism, lynch law, and southern Protestantism. I have probably had some resistance to facing up to what Faulkner is saying. What he's saying is that you can't have this particular kind of racism without this particular kind of religion. How do you explain those thousands and thousands of lynchings, some still going on now and then in the south? The lynchings are a concomitant, Faulkner wants to demonstrate, of this particular form of Protestantism. He doesn't see this as particularly a feature of conservative Protestantism, the Christian right. It's a component of a much more traditional form of southern Protestant Christianity. All of the characters in *Light in August* are in one way or another determined in their judgement and behavior by that triple-faceted ideology.

I think I wasn't, forty years ago, as good a reader of *Light in August* as I am now, though no doubt my reading of the novel will change yet again in the future. That's one way of saying that you can teach the same book over and over, and always see something in it that you haven't seen before.

Good reading is more or less inexplicable. It just happens, or doesn't happen. Marcel Proust's dramatization of the protagonist's discovery of Charlus's homosexuality, in *À la recherche du temps perdu*, describes a closed hermeneutical circle, a circle impossible, logically, to break into. You can read signs right only because you happen to know how to read them. How do you happen to know how to read them? It's because you read the signs right. If you don't read the signs right, it's not logically explicable how you can get from not reading the signs right to reading them correctly. It's not something you can explain or tell someone how to do. You must make a lucky leap, just as, for Wittrgenstein, you can only learn to play a language game by playing it, not by being taught the game's rules. You learn to read by reading.

The various forms of literary criticism that I have found interesting over the years, and useful, have all been, in one way or another, valuable for me in helping me account for literature's strangeness. These critical methodologies have little to do with my preliminary immersion in a given work. They presuppose it. I don't think you learn that immersion. You either like a given work or don't like it; you get it or don't get it. But I have found other critics' procedures useful in helping me account in teaching and writing for the results of reading. I'm not going to be so naïve or disingenuous as to say that I've never done any theory, nor written any theoretical essays. This Reader includes some. Nor do I deny that I'm interested in theoretical formulations. Nevertheless, my primary interest in theory has been in the way it can come to the aid of reading. In this I differ from some people, those whose interest in theory is for its own sake. Some people seem to feel that they have to know all the theoretical approaches. They feel an obligation to read all of Foucault, Lacan, Baudrillard, Lyotard, Bourdieu, and so on. I don't feel that obligation. I read the theorists that I find intrinsically interesting in themselves, and I read them as if they were literature – Levinas, de Man, Derrida, yes; Lyotard, less; Foucault, very little. I feel somewhat ashamed of that. I have read a good bit of Foucault, but I don't find his work very useful for my own work, except his readings of Raymond Roussel or Nietzsche, for example. Foucault was, among other things, a good reader and critic.

I'm now asking, not so much why literature, as why literary criticism? Why was I initially interested in literary criticism? Because it gave me ways of reading, models of reading, but also because I found it fun to read, though in those far off days it was never assigned in courses, not even in my graduate courses at Harvard. Maybe that is in part why I liked it. Doing so was slightly illicit. The New Critics I found most interesting, however, were the slightly odd ones, especially Burke and Empson, also G. Wilson Knight, if you can call him a New Critic. I greatly admired Empson's work, not only *Seven Types of Ambiguity*, but also *Some Versions of Pastoral*, especially the latter. I thought that a wonderful book, and still do. Of course I read the other New Critics, Brooks, Tate, Ransom, from all of whom I benefited, but I gained most from Burke and Empson. Both Burke and Empson are slightly wild and wacky. Their wildness is to some degree commensurate with the wildness of literature. Empson's chapter on *Alice's Adventures in Wonderland* is superb, as is his notion – he was on to something that I wouldn't have thought of – that Shakespeare's *As You Like It* is a dramatic working out in the different plots of the contradiction between lust and love. As Empson says, you have different versions of this in the different plots. As Empson also avers, you cannot logically reconcile lust and love. What you can do is get married, and live within the contradiction. This is why, Empson argues, *As You Like It* ends with so many marriages. Marriages don't solve the contradiction. They provide a quasi-solution to the problem through life not through theory. Not that you can have both love and lust at once. You can't, but you can, in a productive way, deal with the problem if you are married or if you are living more or less permanently with a partner.

Kenneth Burke's notion that the work of literature is for the writer a strategy for encompassing a situation relates literature back to life in an unexpected way, unexpected at least for me when I was a graduate student. A literary work, Burke claims, is motivated by some kind of problem the writer has, perhaps an Empsonian contradiction, though of course not necessarily the love/lust one. Writing the work is a way of working through the problem. I found Burke's paradigm productive. My dissertation on Dickens is strongly influenced by Burke. It tries to read Dickens's novels according to Burke's conception of literature.

Then, somewhat later, when I was at The Johns Hopkins University and had Georges Poulet as a colleague, I quite accidentally started reading the first of Poulet's essays that had been translated, the introduction to *Studies in Human Time*. It had appeared in a little magazine called *The Hopkins Review*. I can still remember my excitement and intellectual elation. At that time I really couldn't read French, though I had passed the graduate school French exam. I taught myself French in order to read Sartre, Valéry, Poulet, Levinas, Merleau-Ponty, Marcel Raymond, Gaston Bachelard, Jean-Pierre Richard, and others. A lot of Sartre, for example, was not yet translated, for example the Genet book. What I found fascinating about Poulet's work was that he had a solution for what was for me at that point a big problem. I had many ideas and aperçus about Dickens's novels. These had accumulated as notes, 200 pages of these on a given novel. I considered them, no doubt fatuously, to be brilliant insights, really great ideas, but I couldn't see how to put them together to make a chapter. I was trying to write a book on Dickens, and did eventually publish as my first book *Charles Dickens: The World of His Novels*. What Poulet taught me was modes of economy. He's marvellous at this. He can put all the works of Victor Hugo in a 25-page essay, while my tendency is to go on and on. I remember Poulet telling me that my essays were like a *fleuve*, a great river that disperses itself in a delta at the end. Poulet achieves economy by strategic use of a few short citations to represent a certain feature of a writer's habitual consciousness. That presumes that the writer's consciousness is homogeneous and constant through time. These assumptions would seem extremely problematic to me now. Poulet also uses in his essays what you might call, to use an oversimplified term for it, a dialectical sequence. He starts with one originary motif in the author in question, often a moment of waking to self-consciousness, and then moves on to a related motif that is antithetical to the first one. The essay then moves on rapidly through such stages until it reaches its conclusion. Those two strategies of criticism are marvellous modes of economy.

I learned a lot from studying how Poulet puts an essay together. It was a very practical problem that I had: how to write critical essays that would encompass the whole work of some leading Victorian and modernist poets: Arnold, Browning, Hopkins, Yeats, Stevens, Williams. I was working on what were to become my second and third books: *The Disappearance of God* and *Poets of Reality*. Poulet held that the literary works by a given author, including letters, essays, etc. represent a specific, unique consciousness, an interior space. One of Poulet's books is called *The Interior Distance, La distance intérieur*. Poulet thinks of the complete works of Victor Hugo as forming a singular space, an interior space, the space of Hugo's special consciousness, and he believed the same thing was true for all other writers, Rousseau or Proust or Balzac or Pascal.

When I talk these days about the way a literary work allows entry into an imaginary world or a virtual reality, I am still thinking in somewhat the same way. A critical essay then would be generated by moving around within that interior space. It would be a topographical exploration. I found that notion helpful to me as a specialist in Victorian literature. I was, for example, much interested in Matthew Arnold. He was one of the people I was supposed to teach. I found both his poetry and his prose powerful, but the New Critical approach doesn't work very well for Arnold. If you're a true New Critic, and you try to read one of Arnold's poems, you find there isn't very much you can do with it. You might be likely to say, as Harold Bloom has said, that it's not good poetry. It doesn't amount to anything because it isn't like Keats; or, as Bloom has said, it's a shallow pastiche of Keats. Yet Arnold's poetry seemed to me more interesting than that. Poulet's criticism of consciousness was a help to me in articulating what I saw in Arnold.

Today, however, I would say that Poulet, to some degree, bypasses the specificities of language in the authors about whom he writes essays. Poulet tends to look upon the passages that he cites as transparent expressions of the author's consciousness. It's not quite so simple as that with Poulet, however, as Paul de Man long ago argued in his essay on Poulet in *Blindness and Insight*. Poulet is a very great critic. He is attentive to language almost in spite of himself. One might make a law out of that, 'Miller's Law': 'The greatest critics are those whose readings exceed their theoretical presuppositions.' Poulet's critical procedure, nevertheless, leads him away from attention to those anomalies that are not thematic or reducible to being seen as features of consciousness. His procedure leads him away also from rhetorical or tropological aspects of literature. Those aspects for Poulet are more or less taken for granted.

When I began to read Derrida, I found someone who does pay attention to language, to put it mildly. I found articulated in his early work a presupposition opposed to presumed New Critical dogma that assumed a good work will be organically unified. Neither Empson nor Burke make that assumption, but other New Critics tend to do so. Derrida liberated me to recognize that a work can be a great work and nevertheless be contradictory. It need not hang together and the not-hanging-together is perhaps the most important part about it, its value, or virtue, or integrity. My reading of *De la grammatologie* and of Derrida's other early work was a turning point for me. Derrida's work combines in a quite singular way the two traditions that had influenced me until then, the New Criticism and so-called phenomenological criticism. Derrida's allowed me to understand better my resistance to my closest colleague at Johns Hopkins, Earl Wasserman. He was an organic unity man through and through. If he couldn't show that a work of literature was an organic unity, it must not be a good work. Wasserman would never have written on Shelley's *The Triumph of Life* because it's not finished. He would say, 'Well, who knows how it was going to come out?' Therefore we can't write about that work, but we can write about Keats's odes and even about *Prometheus Unbound*. His goal, Wasserman assumed, was to show that a given work all hangs together. What interested me instinctively, on the contrary, were those places where you can't make a work hang together, parts that seem important but that don't fit the general pattern. Both of those are useful heuristic attitudes. Wasserman had a sharp eye for details. His desire to show that they fitted was useful in his work. It led him to say, 'I've got to work this in somehow.' That is very different from an assumption that there may be something there that can't be fitted in, not at least in any rational scheme, but that is nevertheless important. Wasserman and I were close colleagues for nineteen years. We used to argue about these issues endlessly, often with Georges Poulet as a third in the discussion, and usually apropos of some work Wasserman was writing about.

Hopkins was my real formation, more than Oberlin or Harvard. It was a wonderful place at that time. Poulet was there. Leo Spitzer was there, along with other very distinguished scholars like Don Cameron Allen, A. O. Lovejoy, and William Albright. The Humanities Group was small enough so that even a non-tenured member, as I was at first, knew all these people. Wasserman, Poulet, and I used to have lunch together all the time, at least once a week, with me as an assistant professor listening to these two distinguished people arguing about, say, Shelley's *Mont Blanc*, and never coming to agreement. I remember one time when I thought I had a good interpretation of *Wuthering Heights*, a novel Wasserman knew very well. I went to Wasserman, and I said, 'Earl, I've really got it.' I then presented Wasserman with my reading. He said, 'Well, what about this passage on page so and so?' I had to admit that it didn't fit with my little reading, so my reading was disqualified. He was saying: 'Unless you can incorporate this passage in your reading somehow, it is not a satisfactory reading.' That claim, however, was based on the assumption that you have to make everything fit into a presumed organic unity.

Derrida helped me defend my insights by not assuming a good work is necessarily unified. It was not – and still isn't – Derrida's theoretical formulations, *la différance* and so on, that have interested me most in his work. I admire Derrida most as a reader, as an absolutely spectacular literary critic and reader of philosophical texts. He is among the best literary critics in the twentieth century. I feel the same way about Paul de Man. I'm interested, for example, in de Man's theory of allegory, of course, but what I find really interesting about de Man's work and what kept me coming to his seminars at Yale is that his readings were always surprising, at least to me. I tip my hat to anyone who sees something new to me in a work that I know quite well, something that I hadn't seen, but that seems right to me when it is pointed out. Both Derrida and de Man can do that. With de Man, I would know that he was going to talk about some text or other, often one I had already read carefully. I would try to anticipate what he would be likely to say, and I always got it wrong. He'd always seen something that I hadn't thought of. It's the same with Derrida's seminars. There are two cases I remember, both fairly recent. In one seminar he talked about Melville's *Bartleby the Scrivener*, on which I had written a long essay, so I knew the novel really well. Derrida talked about the very end of the story, which is a reference to Job ('He's with kings and counsellors now'). His brief reading was wonderfully perceptive and original. It was certainly not something I had thought of. The other seminar was on Proust. Derrida discussed a small section of the *Recherche* on the death of Bergotte. Derrida noticed that Proust uses a whole series of words that are forms of *prendre* – *comprendre*, *apprendre*, etc. Derrida made that small detail really work to support his reading. Proust, he showed, plays on the strength of those French words, with their latent image of grasping, as in German *Begriff*, the word for 'notion.' Derrida implied that you can't really see this in the standard English translation of Proust. The translation is correct enough, but it necessarily misses the implicit play in the echoing French words. It was a splendid reading of this one episode. The reading was not overtly theoretical. It arose from a close attention to details of language, from Derrida's possession of what one might call an 'ear.' That's what I most value about Derrida. Think about just his work on English literature: essays on Shelley, Shakespeare, Joyce, Melville, etc. These are magnificent essays, not to speak of the ones on continental literature, on Mallarmé or Proust or Celan.

Now I take up once more your question, 'Why literature?' I take the question now to refer to literature's use, its role in human life. In a sense, literature is its own end. It may be a mistake to worry too much about literature's social or psychological utility. When you read a novel or poem you don't ordinarily say to yourself, 'Am I doing something useful? Is there some further end? Is what I am doing good for something, good for me, or am I wasting my time?' The other day I thought of that phrase whose source I can't identify: *la rose est sans pourquoi*, the rose doesn't have any why, it's just beautiful. Perhaps you can find the source.[1] I don't think this is aestheticism in the bad sense of that word. I think that literature has had a function *sans pourquoi*, without any why. Cinema is nowadays replacing this old function of literature. If you go to a movie, you don't usually go because it's good for you, but because it's intensely pleasurable. It is an end in itself. I think that would be an initial answer to the question, 'Why literature?'

Literature – in the sense in which we use the word in the West – is a relatively recent and historically conditioned institution. It began in the Renaissance. We tend to assume that *Beowulf* is literature, but it verges on being myth or an aid to nation-building or support of a specific religion. It does not have an identifiable author, as most post-Renaissance literature in the West does. It is the somewhat accidental writing down of an oral poem, whereas literature is tied to the printed word. Greek tragedy, to take another example, had a very specific ritual function, a function you wouldn't expect Tennyson to have had in his time. Modern secular literature is detached from any necessary religious function, and this change is quite recent. I think Derrida is right, literature in our culture is associated with the rise of Western-style democracies, with the spread of literacy, with the development of printing, and with freedom of speech, theoretical freedom of speech at least, the right in a democracy to write anything you want. That freedom is never complete, of course, but it is more nearly complete in modern Western democracies, than, for example, in Renaissance monarchies. So Western literature belongs to the epoch of the Enlightenment, that is, the last three centuries. Clearly it has had an important social function during this period, even if you say, well I'm not thinking about social utility when I am reading George Eliot's *Middlemarch*, or *Alice in Wonderland*, or *The Swiss Family Robinson*, or Shakespeare.

This new answer to the *why* is double. First, literature reinforces and to some degree creates reigning ideologies. How, for example, did people learn in nineteenth-century England how courtship and marriage ought to take place? Certainly in part through family and social conditioning, but also by reading Trollope. Trollope tells you how young marriageable women ought to behave, and how young men ought to behave, and how their parents ought to behave. No doubt Trollope's representations of courtship and marriage bear some relation to the way things really were, but their function was also performative. Trollope's novels coached people into behaving in ways similar to the behavior of Trollope's good characters. No doubt literature functions in this way. It has functioned that way for me from the beginning without my being aware of it. *Alice in Wonderland*, for example, had a big influence on me. I taught myself to read at age five so I could read it for myself and not be dependent on my mother to read it to me. The *Alice* books taught me all kinds of things that have to do with gender relations, with word play, and with the ways in which people are idiosyncratic. There are a lot of mad hatters in the world! There are lots of rabbits with watches in their waistcoat pockets.

A second social function of literature exists, another answer to the question, 'Why literature?' The *Alice* books are a good example of that. Even as a naive, childish reader, I probably was already at least implicitly aware of this other function. Literature functions as a critique of ideology, not just as a reinforcement of it, as in the political satire in the *Alice* books, or the many subversive jokes about the way girls were brought up in those days. If you were to ask me what is the purest expression of Victorian middle-class ideology, I would say Trollope's novels. Nevertheless, Trollope's novels also put into question the Victorian middle-class assumptions he dramatizes.

This side of literature is, I think, sometimes underestimated by cultural studies specialists. They may see a given work as a pure expression of, let's say, imperialist ideology. Most literary works are not that simple. Usually questions are raised about the ideological assumptions that are dramatized in the work, if only in an ironic treatment of some of these assumptions. Faulkner's treatment of Southern post-Civil War ideology is a good example of such irony. That is one reason why Empson interested me so much. He was the first important theorist of irony I read.

I can give you another example, this one from Trollope. You might plausibly claim that Trollope's novels depend absolutely on the assumption that being in love is an ontological reality. Henry James says that Trollope made the British maiden his especial subject; he wrote about her over and over again; he turned her inside out and every which way. One of Trollope's assumptions concerning these young women is that falling in love changes a person's being. If you are really in love then you will be faithful to that love even if it is against the advice of all your aunts and uncles, your parents, siblings, and friends. Often in Trollope's novels this is the situation. Usually in Trollope it works out that the young woman can marry the man she loves and live happily ever after. In Henry James's novels you have the same subject but it usually leads to disaster, for example in the marriage of Isabel Archer to Gilbert Osmond in *The Portrait of a Lady*. In a wonderful novel by Trollope about which I have written elsewhere, *Ayala's Angel*, the reigning Victorian assumptions about falling in love are put in question. What is tricky about falling in love is that there was a time when you were not in love and then a time when you are in love. Once you really are in love, for Trollope, it's for life. If you stand back from that and think a little about it, you can see that this assumption is somewhat absurd; it is an ideologeme. The idea that being in love is an unalterable change of the person is of course still current. It is very hard to do without it. Nevertheless, it is a problematic idea, even though it is useful for keeping people married. It's good for families and family values. It makes for arguments against divorce. It lies perhaps somewhere in the background as part of the current hostility to same-sex marriage. Some people find it threatening to think that being in love could take place between members of the same sex. Two women, two men, cannot love one another in the way I love my wife or love my husband, such people think. Such people are clearly wrong.

Ayala's Angel is a novel in which the heroine, Ayala, a charming, intelligent young woman, thinks that the only person worth her loving would be an angel come down from heaven. She remembers the passage from the Old Testament in which the angels came down from heaven to marry the daughters of men. So she's waiting around for an angel. Nobody matches up to her ideal, in particular a red-haired, awkward young man named Jonathan Stubbs who dances with her early on in the novel. She says to herself, 'This is not my angel.' (I'm quoting from memory.) Jonathan Stubbs keeps on proposing to her, and she keeps turning him down. Finally she accepts him. He asks an obvious question: 'When did you begin loving me?' Ayala says, "I think I was in love with you the first time I met you.' You say to yourself, or I did anyway, I must have missed something. So you go back to the scene when they first meet, and look again at all of the scenes of their meetings in-between. In no one of these does Trollope represent a transition from harsh rejection of Stubbs to being in love with him. It must have happened without happening, so to speak, or it must not be possible to represent it, since Ayala was not aware of its happening. For Trollope only what the characters are aware of can be represented. This suggests that there's something extremely peculiar and even dubious about the ideology of being in love. *Ayala's Angel* end with a glorification of happy marriage, like most Trollope novels. Ayala is really in love with Stubbs, and everybody approves of her marriage choice. Nevertheless, several people ask her, Ayala's aunt for example, 'When did you begin loving him? You said he was not at all to your taste.' She gives the same answer: 'I think I've always loved him.' What this shows is that Trollope cannot show the transition from not being in love to being in love. This hints at the possibility that being in love is a subjective fantasy, or an ungrounded performative commitment, not an ontological reality.

I think the function of literature as a critique of ideology is just as important as its role in the reinforcement and or even creation of ideological assumptions.

Literature, I conclude, is an end in itself. It doesn't have any *why*, and yet it does have a *why*. That second *why* is in my view historically conditioned. Literature in the modern sense had a beginning in the West and it could have an end. That would not be the end of civilization. Other cultural forms could take literature's place, or are even now taking its place. I've written elsewhere about the end of literature. Literature is going to be around for a long time yet. Nevertheless, we're in the midst of a radical and fairly rapid transition to other media, as what I would call the literary or literariness is transferred into media like film, but also like computer games. A lot of literary invention goes into computer games. I have no problem with that. Many new forms of "the literary" will be around, alongside printed literature. Literature in the old-fashioned sense of novels, poems, and plays, however, clearly already has a smaller role in the cultural life of ordinary citizens, at least in the United States and probably in Europe too. The evidence for this is that the average American spends about five hours a day watching television. You can't watch television or play a computer game and read Shakespeare at the same time, though some students claim they can. Although a lot of books are no doubt still read, this takes place in combination with going to the movies, watching television, and using the internet. The nineteenth century didn't have those other quasi-literary media. Even when I was a child, we didn't have the second two of those. That is bound to make a difference to the social function of literature. It is already doing so. That doesn't mean that literature isn't going to be around for a long time, being studied and being read. What it does mean is that literature, particularly in the United States the study of British literature, will have a different role, a different *why*. It will become gradually more a matter of historical interest than of current concern.

Literature, British literature, not American literature, used to be a primary means by which American ideological assumptions were instilled into people. When I began to reflect on this some years ago, it struck me as strange, and still does, that we made the basis of the American ethos the literature of a foreign country, much more than our own literature. It was, moreover, the literature of a foreign country that we had defeated in a war of revolution. In this respect, we went right on acting like a colony. Most people still, today, especially educators, say that every American should read Shakespeare. I agree that reading Shakespeare is a good thing. Nevertheless, Shakespeare doesn't belong to us as he does to a British citizen, not to speak of the way Samuel Johnson, Chaucer, Beowulf, Matthew Arnold, Virgina Woolf, Yeats belong especially to the British. Everybody ought to read them. I understand, however, why many young Americans find knowing the whole range of British literature less obviously necessary than knowing modernist literature in a global context, and why non-British literature, whether it's Anglophone or in translation, begins to have a larger and larger function among the American people, so many of whom are now not European in origin. I can see various reasons why you might say, 'To assimilate them they'd better read Shake-speare,' but it might be better to say, 'To assimilate them they'd better read

Walt Whitman or Wallace Stevens,' which is not the same thing. American literature has a different tradition.

For many American readers, certainly for me, non-English literature in translation, had, even when I could not read any of them in the original languages, a special appeal, for example Kafka, Tolstoy, Proust, or Dostoyevsky. In some ways those writers were more important for me in my adolescence than some works in British literature. I have elsewhere told the story about how when I was a sophomore in college I read, more or less by accident, Dostoyevsky's *Notes from the Underground*. I remember saying to myself, 'This is me; at last I have found somebody like me!' It begins, 'I'm a sick man, I'm a spiteful man, I think my liver is diseased.' As a sophomore in college, this came home to me in a way that I have never felt about, say, *Rasselas,* or, to tell the truth, about Shakespeare's characters, much as I admire and delight in Shakespeare. They do not invite, for me, identification, immersion, in the same way that Dostoyevsky, or that Conrad, who was after all 'not English,' but Polish, did. For Dickens I have much more affinity. I think that such a selective response to British literature and an affinity for non-English literature may happen for many Americans. One has to explain why so many Americans today read with such enthusiasm Salman Rushdie or African or Indian Anglophone literatures. Their engagement is not simply political, 'politically correct.' Something in these works rings a bell because the stories they tell are somehow more like our own experience than is much in canonical English literature.

Well, our time is up, and I've only answered your first question.

JW: I had only one question: Why literature?

Irvine, CA, 27 April 2004

Note

1. The phrase, *la rose est sans pourquoi*, first appears, as far as I have been able to ascertain, originally in German, and is from Angelus Silesius (born Johannes Scheffer b. 1624, d. 1677), *Der Cherubinische Wandersmann* (1657), a collection of over 1600 rhyming couplets. The phrase is a fragment of one of Silesius' epigrammatic couplets intended to render the ineffability of God somehow apprehensible. It articulates and anticipates the notion of analogical apperception proposed by Edmund Husserl in his *Cartesian Meditations: An Introduction to Phenomenology*, (1950) trans. Dorion Cairns (Dordrecht: Kluwer Academic Publishers, 1995). Jacques Lacan paraphrases the line in an article in *Ornicar?* No. 140 (1977) when he remarks: 'la rose en somme est la parce qu'elle est la, elle est sans pourquoi . . .' The idea that natural beauty is

without a *why* is echoed in Kant's *Critique of Judgement* (1790), trans. James Creed Meredith (Oxford: Oxford University Press, 1952). A possible French source comes from a letter from Martin Heidegger to Luc Benoit, in a response to remarks concerning Heraclitus. Heidegger cites Silesius' aphorism as the expression of apophatic theology. Heidegger also discusses the Silesian fragment in *The Principle of Reason*, (1957) trans. Reginald Lilly (Bloomington: Indiana University Press, 1996), 41. [JW]

Works Cited

The following bibliography contains works cited throughout the various essays of this reader, both those by J. Hillis Miller and the contributors to the reader.

Abraham, Nicolas. 'The Shell and the Kernel.' Trans. Nicholas Rand. *diacritics*, 9: 1 (Spring 1979).

Abraham, Nicolas, and Maria Torok. *Cryptonymie: Le verbier de l'homme aux loups*. Int. Jacques Derrida. Paris, 1976. *The Wolf Man's Magic Word*. Foreword Jacques Derrida. Trans. Richard Rand. Minneapolis, 1986.

Abraham, Nicolas, and Maria Torok. *L'écorce et le noyau*. Paris, 1978. *The Shell and the Kernel*. Vol. I. Ed., trans. and int. Nicholas T. Rand. Chicago, 1994.

Abrams, M. H. 'Rationality and Imagination in Cultural History.' *Critical Inquiry*, II: 3 (Spring 1976).

Adams, Ruth M. 'Wuthering Heights: The Land East of Eden.' *Nineteenth-Century Fiction*, XIII (1958).

Agacinski, Sylviane. *Aparté: Conceptions and Deaths of Søren Kierkegaard*. Trans. Kevin Newmark. Tallahassee, 1988.

Agamben, Giorgio. *The Coming Community*. Trans. Michael Hardt. Minneapolis, 1993.

Althusser, Louis. *Lenin and Philosophy and Other Essays*. Trans. Ben Brewster. New York, 1972.

Aristotle. *Aristotle on the Art of Poetry*. Trans. Lane Cooper. Ithaca, 1947.

Armstrong, Isobel. *Victorian Poetry: Poetry, Poetics and Politics*. London, 1993.

Arnold, Matthew. *The Complete Prose Works*. Ed. R. H. Super. Ann Arbor, 1965a.

Arnold, Matthew. *The Poems of Matthew Arnold*. Ed. Kenneth Allott. London, 1965b.

Arnold, Matthew. 'The Function of Criticism at the Present Time.' *The Norton Anthology of English Literature*, Vol. 2, 6th edn. Ed. M. H. Abrams. New York, 1993.

Attridge, Derek. *The Singularity of Literature*. London, 2004.

Atwell, Robert H. 'Financial Prospects for Higher Education.' *Policy Perspectives*. The Pew Higher Education Research Program 4: 3 (September 1992).

Auerbach, Erich. *Mimesis*. Trans. Willard R. Trask. Princeton, 1953.

Austin, J. L. *How to Do Things with Words*. 2nd edn. Ed. J. O. Urmson and Marina Sbisà. Oxford, 1980.

Aydelotte, Frank. *Materials for the Study of English Literature and Composition: Selections from Newman, Arnold, Huxley, Ruskin, and Carlyle*. New York, 1914.

Aydelotte, Frank. *The American Rhodes Scholarships: A Review of the First Forty Years*. Princeton, 1946.

Bailey, J. O. *The Poetry of Thomas Hardy: A Handbook and Commentary*. Chapel Hill, 1970.

Bal, Mieke. 'Literary Canon and Religious Identity.' Religious Canon and Literary Identity (Plenary Lecture at 10th Conference for Society for Literature and Religion, University of Nijmegen, 7–9 Sept. 2000). *European Electronic Journal for Feminist Exegesis*, 2/2000 (no page nos.).

Bal, Mieke. *Travelling Concepts in the Humanities: a Rough Guide.* Toronto, 2002.

Bal, Mieke. 'Visual Essentialism and the Object of Visual Culture.' *Journal of Visual Culture*, 2.1 (2003).

Bataille, Georges. *La littérature et le mal.* Paris, 1957.

Bate, Walter Jackson. "The Crisis in English Studies." *Harvard Magazine.* 85: 12 (1982).

Battersby, Christine. *The Phenomenal Woman: Feminist Metaphysics and the Pattern of Identity.* Cambridge, 1998.

Benjamin, Walter. *Illuminationen.* Frankfurt am Main, 1955. *Illuminations.* Trans. Harry Zohn. New York, 1969.

Benjamin, Walter. *Gesammelte Schriften,* 7 vols. Eds. Rolf Tiedemann and Hermann Schweppenhäuser. Frankfurt am Main, 1974–1989.

Bercovitch, Sacvan. *The Puritan Origins of the American Self.* New Haven, 1975.

Bercovitch, Sacvan, and Cyrus Patell, eds. *Cambridge History of American Literature.* Cambridge, 1994, 1995.

Bernheimer, Charles. 'The Anxieties of Comparison.' *Comparative Literature in the Age of Multiculturalism.* Ed. Charles Bernheimer. Baltimore, 1995.

Bérubé, Michael. 'Standard Deviation: Skyrocketing Job Requirements Inflame Political Tensions.' *Academe,* 81: 6 (November-December, 1995).

Blanchot, Maurice. 'Literature and the Right to Death.' *The Gaze of Orpheus.* Trans. Lydia Davis. Barrytown, 1981.

Blanchot, Maurice. *La communauté unavouable.* Paris, 1983.

Blanchot, Maurice. *The Infinite Conversation.* Trans. Susan Hanson. Minneapolis, 1993.

Bloom, Harold. *Figures of Capable Imagination.* New York, 1976.

Breneman, David W. 'Higher Education: On a Collision Course with New Realities.' *Association of Governing Boards of Universities and Colleges.* AGB Occasional Paper 22, n.d.

Breneman, David W. 'Sweeping, Painful Changes.' *The Chronicle of Higher Education.* Section 2 (8 September 1995).

Brill, Arthur S., and Daniel J. Larson. 'Are We Training Our Students for Real Jobs?' *Academe,* 81: 6 (November-December, 1995).

Brontë, Emily. *Wuthering Heights.* 'The Shakespeare Head Brontë.' Boston and New York, 1931.

Brontë, Emily. 'The Butterfly.' *Five Essays Written in French.* Trans. Lorine White Nagel. Int. Fannie E. Ratchford. Austin, 1948.

Brown, Ford K. *Fathers of the Victorians: The Age of Wilberforce.* Cambridge, 1961.

Burke, Kenneth. 'Paradox of Substance.' *A Grammar of Motives.* New York, 1945.

Butcher, S. H. *Aristotle's Theory of Poetry and Fine Art; With a Critical Text and Translation of The Poetics.* New York, 1951.

Butler, Judith P. *Gender Trouble: Feminism and the Subversion of Identity.* New York, 1990.

Butler, Judith P. *Bodies that Matter: On the Discursive Limits of "Sex'.'* New York, 1993.

Caillois, Roger. *Man and the Sacred.* Trans. Meyer Barash. Glencoe, 1959.

Calvino, Italo. *Six Memos for the Next Millennium.* Trans. Patrick Creagh. Cambridge, 1988.

Celan, Paul. *Breathturn (Atemwende).* Bilingual edn., trans. Pierre Joris. Los Angeles, 1995.

Chaucer, Geoffrey. *The Legend of Good Women. Works,* 2nd edn. Ed. F. N. Robinson. Boston, 1961.

Chow, Rey. 'In the Name of Comparative Literature.' *Comparative Literature in the Age of Multiculturalism.* Ed. Charles Bernheimer. Baltimore, 1995.

Cohen, Tom. ' "Well!": Voloshinov's Double-Talk'. *SubStance,* 21: 2 (1992).

Cohen, Tom. *Anti-Mimesis: From Plato to Hitchcock.* Cambridge, 1994.

Cohen, Tom. *Ideology and Inscription: 'Cultural Studies' after Benjamin, de Man, and Bakhtin.* Cambridge, 1998.

Crabbe, George. *The Poetical Works.* Eds. A. J. Carlyle and R. M. Carlyle. London, 1932.

Culler, A. Dwight. 'Monodrama and the Dramatic Monologue.' *PMLA* 90 (May 1975).

Culler, Jonathan. *Framing the Sign: Criticism and Its Institutions.* Norman, 1988.

Damisch, Hubert. 'La Danse de Thesée.' *Tel Quel,* 26 (1966).

de Man, Paul. Foreword. Carol Jacobs, *The Dissimulating Harmony.* Baltimore, 1978.

de Man, Paul. *Allegories of Reading: Figural Language in Rousseau, Nietzsche, Rilke and Proust.* New Haven, 1979.

de Man, Paul. *Blindness and Insight: Essay in the Rhetoric of Contemporary Criticism.* Minneapolis, 1981.

de Man, Paul. 'The Return to Philology.' *The Times Literary Supplement.* 4,158 (Friday, 10 December 1982).

de Man, Paul. *The Resistance to Theory.* Foreword Wlad Godzich. Minneapolis, 1986.

de Man, Paul. *Aesthetic Ideology.* Ed. and int. Andrzej Warminski. Minneapolis, 1996.

Deleuze, Gilles. *Logique du sens.* Paris, 1969.

Derrida, Jacques. *Of Grammatology.* Trans. Gayatri Chakravorty Spivak. Baltimore, 1976.

Derrida, Jacques. *Writing and Difference.* Trans. Alan Bass. Chicago, 1978b.

Derrida, Jacques. *"Télépathie,"* *Furor,* 2 (February 1981).

Derrida, Jacques. *"My Chances/Mes Chances*: A Rendezvous with Some Epicurean Stereophonies.' Trans. Irene Harvey and Avital Ronell. *Taking Chances: Derrida, Psychoanalysis, and Literature.* Eds. Joseph H. Smith and William Kerrigan. Baltimore, 1984a.

Derrida, Jacques. 'Deconstruction and the Other.' *Dialogues with Contemporary Continental Thinkers: The Phenomenological Heritage.* Manchester, 1984b.

Derrida Jacques. 'Deconstruction in America.' *Critical Exchange,* 17 (Winter, 1985a).

Derrida, Jacques. 'Préjugés, *devant la loi.' La faculté de juger.* Paris, 1985b.

Derrida, Jacques. *Glas.* Paris, 1974. Trans. John P. Leavey, Jr, and Richard Rand. Lincoln, 1986a.

Derrida, Jacques. 'Fors: The Anglish Words of Nicolas Abraham and Maria Torok.' Trans. Barbara Johnson. *The Wolf Man's Magic Word: A Cryptonymy.* Nicolas Abraham and Maria Torok. Trans. Nicholas Rand. Minneapolis, 1986b.

Derrida, Jacques. *Psyché: Inventions de l'autre.* Paris, 1987a.

Derrida, Jacques. *La vérité in peinture.* Paris, 1978a. *The Truth in Painting.* Trans. Geoff Bennington and Ian McLeod. Chicago, 1987b.

Derrida, Jacques. *La carte postale.* Paris, 1980. Trans. Alan Bass. The Post Card: From Socrates to Freud and Beyond. Chicago, 1987c.

Derrida, Jacques. *De l'esprit: Heidegger et la question.* Paris, 1987. *Of Spirit: Heidegger and the Question.* Trans. Geoffrey Bennington and Rachel Bowlby. Chicago, 1989.

Derrida, Jacques. *Limited Inc.* Trans. Samuel Weber and Jeffrey Mehlman. Evanston, 1988. *Limited Inc.* Presentation and trans. Elisabeth Weber. Paris, 1990.

Derrida, Jacques. *Acts of Literature.* Ed. Derek Attridge. New York, 1992a.

Derrida, Jacques. 'Tout autre est tout autre.' *L'éthique du don: Jacques Derrida et la pensée du don.* Eds. Jean-Michel Rabaté and Michael Wetzel. Paris, 1992b.

Derrida, Jacques. 'Mochlos ou le conflit des facultés.' *Du droit à la philosophie.* Paris, 1990b. Trans. Richard Rand and Amy Wygant as 'Mochlos; or, the Conflict of the Faculties.' *Logomachia: The Conflict of the Faculties.* Ed. Richard Rand. Lincoln, 1992c.

Derrida, Jacques. 'Apories: Mourir − s'attendre aux "limites de la verité'." Rpt. as *Apories.* Paris, 1996. *Aporias.* Trans. Thomas Dutoit. Stanford, 1993.

Derrida, Jacques. *Points de suspension: Entretiens.* Ed. Elisabeth Weber. Paris, 1992. *Points . . . : Interviews, 1974–1994.* Trans. Peggy Kamuf et al. Stanford, 1995a.

Derrida, Jacques. *The Gift of Death.* Trans. David Wills. Chicago, 1995b.

Derrida, Jacques. *Résistances de la psychanalyse.* Paris, 1996.

Derrida, Jacques. *Adieu à Emmanuel Levinas.* Paris, 1997.

Derrida, Jacques. *Donner la mort.* Paris, 1999.

Derrida, Jacques. *La Dissémination.* Paris, 1972. Rpt. 2001a.

Derrida, Jacques. *L'Université sans condition.* Paris, 2001b.

Derrida, Jacques. *Inconditionality ou souveraineté: L'Université aux frontières de l'Europe.* Bilingual edition in French and Greek. Allocutions by Dimitris Dimiroulis and Georges Veltsos. Annotations by Vanghelis Bitsoris. Athens, 2001c.

Derrida, Jacques. ' "Justices".' *Justices: for J Hillis Miller.* Eds Barbara L. Cohen and Dragan Kujundzic. New York, 2005.

Duffin, H. C. *Thomas Hardy.* Manchester, 1967.

Easthope, Antony. *Literary into Cultural Studies.* London, 1991.

Elam, Diane. *Feminism and Deconstruction: Ms. en Abyme.* London, 1994.

Elam, Diane. 'Waiting in the Wings.' *Acts of Narrative.* Eds. Carol Jacobs and Henry Sussman. Stanford, 2003.

Eliot, George. *Middlemarch.* Ed. Rosemary Ashton. London, 2003.

Eliot, T. S. *Selected Essays: 1917–1932.* New York, 1932.

Fanon. Frantz. *The Wretched of the Earth.* Trans. Constance Farrington. New York, 1991.

Fichte, Johann Gottlieb. *Reden an die Deutsche Nation* (1808). Hamburg, 1955. *Addresses to the German Nation.* Ed. George Armstrong Kelley. New York, 1968.

Fiedelson, Charles. *Symbolism and American Literature.* Chicago, 1953.

Firmat, Gustavo Pérez, ed. *Do the Americas Have a Common Literature?* Durham, 1990.

Fisher, Philip, ed. *The New American Studies.* Berkeley, CA, 1991.

Forster, E. M. *Howards End.* New York, 1989.

Foucault, Michel. *Ceci n'est pas une pipe.* Montpellier, 1973.

Frank, Joseph. *The Widening Gyre.* New Brunswick, 1963.

Freud, Sigmund. *The Problem of Anxiety.* Trans. Henry Alden Bunke. New York, 1936.

Frye, Northrop. *Fables of Identity: Studies in Poetic Mythology.* New York, 1963.

Gaskell, Elizabeth. *The Life of Charlotte Brontë.* London, 1879.

Gaskell, Elizabeth. *Works,* Knutsford edition, vol. 2. London, 1906.

Geertz, Clifford. *Local Knowledge: Further Essays in Interpretive Anthropology.* New York, 1983.

Goux, Jean-Joseph. 'Politics and Modern Art – Heidegger's Dilemma.' *diacritics,* xix/3–4 (1989).

Greenblatt, Stephen. *Shakespearean Negotiations: The Circulation of Social Energy in Renaissance England.* Berkeley, 1988.

Gubar, Susan. ' "The Blank Page" and the Issues of Female Creativity.' *Critical Inquiry,* 8 (Winter 1981).

Habermas, Jürgen. *Knowledge and Human Interests.* Trans. Jeremy J. Shapiro. London, 1972.

Hamacher, Werner. 'To Leave the Word to Someone Else.' *Thinking Difference: Critics in Conversation.* Ed. Julian Wolfreys. New York, 2004.

Hardy, Florence Emily. *The Life of Thomas Hardy: 1840–1928.* London, 1965.

Hardy, Thomas. *Tess of the d'Urbervilles.* New Wessex edition. London, 1974.

Hardy, Thomas. *The Complete Poems.* Ed. James Gibson. New York, 1978.

Hatfield, C. W., ed. *The Complete Poems of Emily Jane Brontë.* New York, 1941.

Hopkins, Gerard Manley. *Letters of Gerard Manley Hopkins to Robert Bridges.* Ed. C. C. Abbott. London, 1935a.

Hopkins, Gerard Manley. *Letters of Gerard Manley Hopkins and Richard Watson Dixon.* Ed. C. C. Abbott. London, 1935b.

Hopkins, Gerard Manley. *The Notebooks and Papers of Gerard Manley Hopkins.* Ed. Humphrey House. London, 1937.

Hopkins, Gerard Manley. *Further Letters of Gerard Manley Hopkins.* Ed. C. C. Abbott. London, 1938.

Hopkins, Gerard Manley. *Poems of Gerard Manley Hopkins,* 3rd ed. Ed. W. H. Gardner. New York, 1948.

Hopkins, Gerard Manley. *Poems and Prose of Gerard Manley Hopkins.* Ed. W. H. Gardner. London, 1953.

Hopkins, Gerard Manley. *Poems.* 4th edn. Eds W. H. Gardner and N. H. Mackenzie. London, 1987.

Huber, Bettina J. 'The MLA's 1993–94 Survey of Ph.D. Placement: The Latest English Findings and Trends through Time.' *ADE Bulletin* 112 (Winter 1995).

Irigaray, Luce. *This Sex Which Is Not One*. Trans. Catherine Porter and Carolyn Burke. Ithaca, 1977.

James, Henry. *The Golden Bowl*. Vol. 24, New York Edition of *The Novels and Tales of Henry James*. New York, 1907–17.

JanMohamed, Abdul, and David Lloyd. *The Nature and Context of Minority Discourse*. Oxford, 1990.

Joyce, James. *Ulysses* (1922). Ed. Hans Walter Gabler et al. London, 1986.

Kafka, Franz. *Amerika*. Trans. Edwin Muir. New York, 1946a.

Kafka, Franz. *The Great Wall of China*. Trans. Willa and Edwin Muir. New York, 1946b.

Kafka, Franz. *Diaries: 1910–1913*. Ed. Max Brod. Trans. Joseph Kresh. New York, 1948.

Kafka, Franz. *Diaries: 1914–1923*. Ed. Max Brod. Trans. Martin Greenberg and Hannah Arendt. New York, 1949.

Kafka, Franz. *The Castle*. Trans. Edwin and Willa Muir. New York, 1951.

Kafka, Franz. *Selected Short Stories*. Trans. Willa and Edwin Muir. New York, 1952.

Kafka, Franz. *Hochzeitsvorbereitungen auf dem Lande*. New York, 1953a.

Kafka, Franz. *The Trial*. Trans. Willa and Edwin Muir. Harmondsworth, 1953b.

Kant, Immanuel. *The Critique of Judgment*. Trans. J. H. Bernard. New York, 1951.

Kant, Immanuel. *Grundlegung zur Metaphysik der Sitten. Werkausgabe*. Frankfurt am Main, 1982. *Foundations of the Metaphysics of Morals*. Trans. Lewis White Beck. Indianapolis, 1978.

Kaplan, Amy, and Donald Pease, eds. *National Identities and Post-Americanist Narratives*. Durham, 1994.

Katz, Jon. 'Birth of a Digital Nation.' *Wired*, 5: 04 (April 1997). www.wired.com/5.04/netizen/.

Katz, Jon. 'The Digital Citizen.' *Wired*, 5: 12 (December 1997).

Kennedy, Donald. 'Making Choices in the Research University.' *Daedalus* (Fall, 1993).

Lacan, Jacques. *Écrits*. Paris, 1966.

Lacan, Jacques. 'Seminar on "The Purloined Poe." *The Purloined Poe: Lacan, Derrida, and Psychoanalytic Reading*. Eds John P. Miller and William J. Richardson. Baltimore, 1988.

Lacoue-Labarthe, Philippe. *La fiction du politique*. Paris, 1987.

Landry, Bernard. *La Philosophie de Duns Scot*. Paris, 1922.

Lauter, Paul, ed. *Reconstructing American Literature: Courses, Syllabi, Issues*. New York, 1983.

Lauter, Paul. *Canons and Contexts*. New York, 1991.

Lauter, Paul, gen. ed. *Heath Anthology of American Literature*, 2nd edn. Lexington, 1994.

Lentricchia, Frank, and Thomas McLaughlin, eds. *Critical Terms for Literary Study*. Chicago, 1995.

Levinas, Emmanuel. *Humanisme de l'autre homme*. Montpellier, 1972.

Levinas, Emmanuel. *Autrement qu'être ou au-delà de l'essence*. The Hague, 1974.

Levinas, Emmanuel. *Otherwise than Being, or Beyond Essence*. Trans. Alphonso Lingis. The Hague, 1981.

Levinas, Emmanuel. 'La trace de l'autre.' *Tijdschrift voor Philosophie* (September, 1963). Trans. Alphonso Lingis. *Deconstruction in Context: Literature and Philosophy*. Ed. Mark C. Taylor. Chicago, 1986.

Levinas, Emmanuel. *Hors sujet*. Montpellier, 1987.

Levinas, Emmanuel. *Outside the Subject*. Trans. Michael B. Smith. Stanford, 1994.

Lewis, R. W. B. *The American Adam: Innocence, Tragedy, and Tradition in the Nineteenth Century*. Chicago, 1955.

Lyotard, Jean-François, and Jean-Loup Thébaud. *Au juste*. Paris, 1979.

Lyotard, Jean-François. *Peregrinations: Law, Form, Event*. New York, 1988a.

Lyotard, Jean-François. *The Differend: Phrases in Dispute*. Trans. Georges van den Abeele. Minneapolis, 1988b.

Matthiessen, F. O. *American Renaissance: Act and Expression in the Age of Emerson and Whitman.* London, 1941.

Miller, J. Hillis. *Charles Dickens: The World of His Fiction.* Cambridge, 1958.

Miller, J. Hillis. *The Form of Victorian Fiction: Thackeray, Dickens, Trollope, George Eliot, Meredith, and Hardy.* Notre Dame, 1968.

Miller, J. Hillis. *Thomas Hardy: Distance and Desire.* Cambridge, 1970.

Miller, J. Hillis. 'The Still Heart: Poetic Form in Wordsworth.' *New Literary History,* II: 2 (Winter 1971).

Miller, J. Hillis. 'History as Repetition in Thomas Hardy's Poetry: The Example of "Wessex Heights".' *Victorian Poetry,* Stratford-upon-Avon Studies, 15. Eds. M. Bradbury and D. Palmer. London, 1972.

Miller, J. Hillis. 'Stevens's Rock and Criticism as Cure,' *Georgia Review,* 30: 1 & 2 (1976).

Miller, J. Hillis. 'Ariachne's Broken Woof.' *Georgia Review,* 31 (1977a).

Miller, J. Hillis. 'The Critic as Host.' *Critical Inquiry,* 3 (1977b). Rpt. in Harold Bloom et al., *Deconstruction and Criticism.* New York, 1979.

Miller, J. Hillis. 'Theoretical and Atheoretical in Stevens.' *Wallace Stevens: A Celebration.* Eds. Frank Doggett and Robert Buttel. Princeton, 1980.

Miller, J. Hillis. *Fiction and Repetition: Seven English Novels.* Cambridge, 1982.

Miller, J. Hillis. 'Topography and Tropography in Thomas Hardy's In Front of the Landscape.' *Identity of the Literary Text.* Eds. Mario J. Valdes and Owen Miller. Int. Jonathan Culler. Toronto, 1985a.

Miller, J. Hillis. *The Linguistic Moment from Wordsworth to Stevens.* Princeton, 1985b.

Miller, J. Hillis. *The Ethics of Reading: Kant, De Man, Eliot, Trollope, James, and Benjamin.* New York, 1987.

Miller, J. Hillis. *Hawthorne and History: Defacing it.* Oxford, 1991a.

Miller, J. Hillis. *Tropes, Parables, Performatives: Essays on Twentieth-Century Literature.* Durham, 1991b.

Miller, J. Hillis. *Ariadne's Thread: Story Lines.* New Haven, 1992a.

Miller, J. Hillis. *Illustration.* London, 1992b.

Miller, J. Hillis. *Topographies.* Stanford, 1995.

Miller, J. Hillis. 'Derrida's Others.' *Applying: to Derrida.* Eds. Julian Wolfreys et al. London, 1996.

Miller, J. Hillis. *Reading Narrative.* Norman, 1998.

Miller, J. Hillis. *The Disappearance of God: Five Nineteenth-Century Writers.* Urbana, 2000a.

Miller, J. Hillis. 'Deconstruction and a Poem.' *Deconstructions: A User's Guide.* Ed. Nicholas Royle. Basingstoke, 2000b.

Miller, J. Hillis. *Others.* Princeton, 2001a.

Miller, J. Hillis. *Speech Acts in Literature.* Stanford, 2001b.

Miller, J. Hillis. 'Derrida and Literature.' *Derrida and the Humanities: A Critical Reader.* Ed. Tom Cohen. Cambridge, 2001c.

Miller, J. Hillis. 'Lying Against Death: Out of the Loop.' *Acts of Narrative.* Eds. Carol Jacobs and Henry Sussman. Stanford, 2003.

Miller, J. Hillis. 'Zero.' *Zero and Literature.* Special issue of *Journal of Cultural Research.* Ed. Rolland Munro. Forthcoming.

Miller, Perry. *The New England Mind: From Colony to Province.* Cambridge, 1953.

Morris, Meaghan. 'Banality in Cultural Studies.' *Block 14* (1988).

Morris, William, ed. *The American Heritage Dictionary of the English Language.* Boston, 1969.

Muller, John P., and William J. Richardson, eds. *The Purloined Poe: Lacan, Derrida, and Psychoanalytic Reading.* Baltimore, 1988.

Nancy, Jean-Luc. *La communauté désœuvrée.* Paris, 1986.

Negroponte, Nicholas. 'Where Do New Ideas Come From?' *Wired,* 4: 1 (January, 1996).

Nell, Onora. *Acting on Principle: An Essay on Kantian Ethics.* New York, 1975.

Nelson, Cary. 'Lessons from the Job Wars: Late Capitalism Arrives on Campus.' *Social Text*, 13: 3 (Fall/Winter 1995a).

Nelson, Cary. 'Lessons from the Job Wars: What is to Be Done.' *Academe*, 81: 6 (November-December 1995b).

Nietzsche, Friedrich. *The Portable Nietzsche*. Trans. Walter Kaufmann. New York, 1954.

Nietzsche, Friedrich. *Also Sprach Zarathustra. Werke in Drei Bänden*. Vol. 2. Ed. Karl Schlechta. Munich, 1966.

Nietzsche, Friedrich. *On the Genealogy of Morals*. Trans. Waller Kaufmann and R. J. Hollingdale. New York, 1967.

Pater, Walter. 'A Study of Dionysus.' *Greek Studies*. London, 1895.

Pearce, Roy Harvey. *The Continuity of American Poetry*. Princeton, 1961.

Pease, Donald, ed. *Revisionary Interventions into the Americanist Canon*. Durham, 1990.

Peirce, Charles Sanders. 'Logic as Semiotic: The Theory of Signs.' *Semiotics: An Introductory Anthology*. Ed. and int. Robert E. Innis. Bloomington, 1984.

Porter, Carolyn. 'What We Know That We Don't Know: Remapping American Literary Studies.' *American Literary History*, 6: 3 (Fall 1994).

Poulet, Georges. *La Distance Intérieure*. Paris, 1952.

Proust, Marcel. *A la recherche du temps perdu*. Ed. Jean-Yves Tadié. Paris, 1989. Trans. C. K. Scott Moncrieff. New York, 1982.

Ratchford, Fannie E., ed. *Gondal's Queen: A Novel in Verse by Emily Jane Brontë*. Austin, 1955.

Rawls, John. *A Theory of Justice*. Cambridge, 1971.

Readings, Bill. *The University in Ruins*. Cambridge, 1996.

Reiman, Donald H., ed. *Shelley's' 'The Triumph of Life': A Critical Study*. Urbana, 1965.

Richards, I. A. *Speculative Instruments*. London, 1955.

Rico, Barbara Roche, and Sandra Mano, comp. *American Mosaic: Multicultural Readings in Context*. Boston, 1991.

Ricoeur, Paul. *Temps et récit*. Vol. 1. Paris, 1983. *Time and Narrative*, Vol. 1. Trans. Kathleen McLaughlin and David Pellauer. Chicago, 1984.

Ruoff, A. LaVonne Brown, and Jerry W. Ward, eds. *Redefining American Literary History*. New York, 1990.

Said, Edward. *Culture and Imperialism*. New York, 1994.

Schlegel, Friedrich. *Kritische Schriften*. Munich, 1964. Trans. Peter Firchow. *Philosophical Fragments*. Minneapolis, 1991.

Schorer, Mark. Introduction. *Wuthering Heights*. New York, 1950.

Shelley, Percy Bysshe. *Poetical Works*. Ed. Thomas Hutchinson. Corrections, G. M. Matthews. Oxford, 1973.

Simpson, David. *Romanticism, Nationalism, and the Revolt Against Theory*. Chicago, 1993.

Sophocles. *Oedipus the King*. Trans. Thomas Gould. Englewood Cliffs, 1970.

Spivak, Gayatri Chakravorty. *In Other Worlds: Essays in Cultural Politics*. New York, 1987.

Spivak, Gayatri Chakravorty. *A Critique of Postcolonial Reason: Toward a History of the Vanishing Present*. Cambridge, 1999.

Spivak, Gayatri Chakravorty. *Death of a Discipline*. New York, 2003.

Sprinker, Michael. 'We Lost It at the Movies.' *MLN*, 112 (1997).

Stevens, Wallace. *The Necessary Angel: Essays on Reality and the Imagination*. New York, 1951.

Stevens, Wallace. *The Collected Poems of Wallace Stevens*. New York, 1954.

Stevens, Wallace. *Opus Posthumous: Poems, Plays, Prose by Wallace Stevens*. Ed. Samuel French Morse. New York, 1957.

Stevens, Wallace. *Poems by Wallace Stevens*. Selected and int. Samuel French Morse. New York, 1961.

Strauss, Richard. *Lieder für Mittlere Stimme mit Klavierbegleitung*. Universal Edition, III. Leipzig, 1907.

Susskind, Leonard. 'Black Holes and the Information Paradox.' *Scientific American* (April 1997).

Tawney, R. H. *Religion and the Rise of Capitalism*. London, 1926.

Thomas, Brook. 'Parts Related to Wholes and the Nature of Subaltern Opposition.' *Modern Language Quarterly*. 55:1 (1994).

Thorne, Kip. S. *Black Holes and Time Warps: Einstein's Outrageous Legacy*. New York, 1994.

Trollope, Anthony. *The Warden*. Oxford, 1963.

Trollope, Anthony. *He Knew He Was Right*. New York, 1983.

UCI News (24 January 1996).

Volosinov, V. N. *Freudianism: A Marxist Critique*. Trans. I. R. Titunik. New York, 1976.

Wahl, Jean. *Vers la Fin de L'Ontologie*. Paris, 1956.

Watt, Stephen. 'The Human Costs of Graduate Education; or, The Need to Get Practical.' *Academe,* 81:6 (November-December, 1995).

Weber, Max. 'Die protestantische Ethik und der Geist des Kapitalismus.' *Archiv für Sozialwissenschaft und Sozialpolitik*. XX. XXI. (1904, 1905). English translation: London, 1930.

Wesley, John. *Works*. New York, 1826.

Whitefield, George. 'A Letter from the Rev. George Whitefield to the Rev. John Wesley.' John Gillies, *Memoirs of Rev. George Whitefield*. New Haven, 1834.

Williams, Raymond. *Problems in Materialism and Culture*. London, 1980.

Woolf, Virginia. *Mrs. Dalloway*. London, 1925. New York, 1981.

Woolf, Virginia. *A Writer's Diary*. New York, 1954.

Yans-McLaughlin, Virginia, ed. *Immigration Reconsidered: History, Sociology, and Politics*. New York, 1990.

Young, Robert. 'The Idea of a Chrestomathic University.' *Logomachia*. Ed. Richard Rand. Lincoln, 1993.

Bibliography of Works by J. Hillis Miller

The following bibliography includes all principal publications, including books, essays, articles, reports and reviews in English, including reprints and reissues, as well as English-language contributions to collections published in non-English speaking countries. Translations are not included. The order in each year is as follows (and where applicable): self-authored volume; co-authored volume; edited volume; co-edited volume; contribution to book; essay or article in journal or other periodical; review.

2004

'Moving *Critical Inquiry* On.' *Critical Inquiry.* 30 (2004 Winter): 414–20.

2003

Zero Plus One. Valencia, 2003.
'Lying Against Death: Out of the Loop.' *Acts of Narrative.* Ed. Carol Jacobs and Henry Sussman. Stanford, 2003: 15–30.
' "World Literature" in the Age of Telecommunications.' *Twayne Companion to Contemporary World Literature.* Ed. Pamela A. Genova. New York, 2003: 55–8.
'My Fifty Years in the Profession.' *ADE Bulletin* 133 (2003 Winter): 63–6.
'Time in Literature.' *Dædalus*, 132: 2 (2003 Spring): 86–97.

2002

On Literature. London, 2002.
With Gary A. Olson and Stanley Fish. *Justifying Belief: Stanley Fish and the Work of Rhetoric.* Albany, 2002.
'Should We Read *Heart of Darkness*?' *Conrad in Africa: New Essays on Heart of Darkness.* Eds. Attie De Lange, Gail Fincham, Wieslaw Krajka. Lublin, 2002: 21–40.
'The Two Rhetorics: George Eliot's Bestiary.' *The Mill on the Floss and Silas Marner.* Eds. Nahem Yousaf and Andrew Maunder. New York, 2002: 57–72.
'Promises, Promises: Speech Act Theory, Literary Theory and Politico-Economic Theory in Marx and de Man.' *NLH*, 33: 1 (2002 Winter): 1–20.

2001

Speech Acts in Literature. Stanford, 2001.
Others. Princeton, 2001.

Ed., with Tom Cohen, Barbara Cohen, and Andrzej Warminski. *Material Events: Paul de Man and the Afterlife of Theory.* Minneapolis, 2001.

'Paul de Man as Allergen.' *Material Events: Paul de Man and the Afterlife of Theory.* Eds. Tom Cohen, Barbara Cohen, J. Hillis Miller, and Andrzej Warminski. Minneapolis, 2001. 183–204.

'How to Be "in Tune with the Right" in The Golden Bowl.' *Mapping the Ethical Turn: A Reader in Ethics, Culture, and Literary Theory.* Eds. Todd F. Davis and Kenneth Womack. Charlottesville, 2001: 271–85.

'Moments of Decision in Bleak House.' *The Cambridge Companion to Charles Dickens.* Ed. John O. Jordan. Cambridge, 2001: 49–63.

'Derrida and Literature.' *Jacques Derrida and the Humanities: A Critical Reader.* Ed. Tom Cohen. Cambridge, 2001: 58–81.

'Will Literary Study Survive the Globalisation of the University and the New Regime of Telecommunications?' *REAL,* 17 (2001): 373–86.

'Questionnaire.' With Claude Imbert, James Clifford, Caren Kaplan, Peggy Kamuf, Verena Conley, Richard Terdiman, Fredric Jameson, and Dean MacCannell. *Sites,* 5: 1 (2001 Spring): 221–6.

2000

'The Mayor of Casterbridge, the Persistence of the Past, and the Dance of Desire.' *The Mayor of Casterbridge.* Ed. Julian Wolfreys. New York, 2000: 21–30.

'Friedrich Schlegel and the Anti-Ekphrastic Tradition.' *Revenge of the Aesthetic: The Place of Literature in Theory Today.* Michael P. Clark. Berkeley, 2000: 58–75.

' "World Literature" in the Age of Telecommunications.' *World Literature Today,* 74: 3 (2000 Summer): 559–61.

'Whistler/Swinburne: "Before the Mirror".' *Journal of Pre-Raphaelite Studies,* 9 (2000 Spring): 13–24.

'Passions Performatives Proust.' *REAL* 16 (2000): 31–42.

'Reference in *The Wings of the Dove*: Literature as Speech Act.' *Publication des Groupes de Recherches Anglo-Américaines de l'Université François Rabelais de Tours,* 20 (1999): 165–77.

1999

Black Holes. Stanford, 1999.

1998

Reading Narrative. Norman, 1998.

1997

'The Roar on the Other Side of Silence: Otherness in *Middlemarch.'* *Rereading Texts, Rethinking Critical Presuppositions: Essays in Honour of H. M. Daleski.* Ed. Shlomith Rimon-Kenan, Leona Toker, and Shuli Barzilai. Frankfurt, 1997.

'Cultural Studies and Reading.' *ADE Bulletin,* 117 (Fall 1997): 15–18.

1996

'Border Crossings, Translating Theory: Ruth.' *The Translatability of Cultures: Figurations of the Space Between.* Eds. Sanford Budick and Wolfgang Iser. Stanford, 1996: 207–23.

'Derrida's Others.' *Applying: to Derrida.* Eds. John Brannigan, Ruth Robbins, and Julian Wolfreys. London, 1996: 153–170.

'Heart of Darkness Revisited.' Joseph Conrad. *Heart of Darkness.* Boston, 1996. 206–20.

'Just Reading *Howards End.*' *Howards End.* Ed. Alistair M. Duckworth. Boston, 1996.

'Literary Study in the Age of Electronic Reproduction.' *Why Literature Matters: Theories and Functions of Literature.* Eds. Rudiger Ahrens and Laurenz Volkmann. Heidelberg, 1996: 297–310.

' "Le Mensonge, le Mensonge Parfait": Theories of Lying in Proust and Derrida.' *Passions de la Littérature.* Ed. Michel Lisse. Paris, 1996.

'Reading and Periodization: Wallace Stevens' "The Idea of Order at Key West".' *The Challenge of Periodization: Old Paradigms and New Perspectives.* Ed. Lawrence Besserman. New York, 1996.

'Literary Study in the University without Idea.' *ADE Bulletin* 113 (Spring 1996): 30–3.

'The Other's Other: Jealousy and Art in Proust.' *Skrift* 16 (January 1996): 52–67.

'Picture This: Review of W. J. T. Mitchell's *Picture Theory*'. *Artforum* 34: 5 (January 1996): 18, 99.

1995

Topographies. Stanford, 1995.

'Ideology and Topography in Faulkner's Absalom, Absalom!' *Faulkner and Ideology: Faulkner and Yoknapatawpha 1992.* Eds. Donald M. Kartiganer and Ann J. Abadie. Jackson, 1995: 253–76.

'Narrative.' *Critical Terms for Literary Study,* 2nd edn. Eds. Frank Lentricchia and Thomas Laughlin. Chicago, 1995: 66–79.

'Parabolic Exemplarity: The Example of Nietzsche's *Thus Spoke Zarathustra.*' *Unruly Examples: On the Rhetoric of Exemplarity.* Ed. Alexander Gelley. Stanford, 1995: 162–74.

'The Disputed Ground: Deconstruction and Literary Studies.' *Deconstruction is/in America.* Ed. Anselm Haverkamp. New York, 1995: 79–86.

'Foreword.' *The Critical Double: Figurative Meaning in Aesthetic Discourse.* Ed. Paul Gordon. Tuscaloosa, 1995: ix–xviii.

'The "Grafted" Image: James on Illustration.' *Henry James's New York Edition: The Construction of Authorship.* Ed. David McWhirter. Foreword James Carlos Rowe. Stanford, 1995: 138–41.

'Sam Weller's Valentine.' *Literature in the Marketplace: Nineteenth-Century British Publishing and Reading Practices.* Eds. John O. Jordan and Robert Patten. Cambridge, 1995: 93–122.

'William Carlos Williams.' *Critical Essays on William Carlos Williams.* Eds. Steven Gould Axelrod and Helen Deese. New York, 1995: 92–102.

'The Ethics of Hypertext.' *Diacritics* 25: 3 (Fall 1995): 27–39.

'Governing the Ungovernable: Literary Study in the Transnational University.' *Between the Lines,* 2: 2 (Winter 1995): 2–3.

'History, Narrative and Responsibility: Speech Acts in Henry James's *The Aspern Papers.*' *Textual Practice,* 9: 2 (Summer 1995): 243–67.

'The University of Dissensus'. *Oxford Literary Review* 17: 1–2 (1995): 121–43.

'Reply to Hans Hauge'. *Edda,* 4 (1995): 355–7.

'The Roar on the Other Side of Silence: Otherness in *Middlemarch.*' *Edda,* 3 (March 1995): 237–45.

'What is the Future of the Print Record?' *Profession* (1995): 33.

1994

'Beginning from the Ground Up.' *Critical Architecture and Contemporary Culture.* Eds. William J. Lillyman, Marilyn F. Moriarty, and David J. Neuman. Oxford, 1994: 13–19.

'Nietzsche in Basel: Writing Reading.' *Composition Theory for the Postmodern Classroom.* Eds. Gary A. Olson and Sidney I. Dobrin. Albany, 1994: 277–94.

'The Role of Theory in the Development of Literary Studies in the United States.' *Divided Knowledge.* Beijing, 1994: 85–107.

'Pater, Walter.' *The Johns Hopkins Guide to Literary Theory and Criticism.* Eds. Michael Groden and Martin Kreiswirth. Baltimore, 1994: 556–8.

'Border Crossings.' *Contemporary Criticism and Theory,* 8 (1994): 252–79.

'Derrida's Topographies.' *South Atlantic Review* 59: 1 (January 1994): 1–25.

'Literary Study in the University Without Idea.' *Proceedings of the 1994 ELLAK International Symposium, English Studies in Korea: Retrospect and Prospect.* The English Language and Literature Association of Korea, 1994: 283–302.

'Return, Dissenter.' *TLS* 4763 (15 July 1994): 10.

'Humanistic Discourse and the Others.' *Surfaces,* 4: 304 (1994): 1–18.

1993

'Shelley's "The Triumph of Life".' *Shelley.* Ed. Michael O'Neill. London, 1993: 218–40.

'Thinking Like Other People.' *Wild Orchids and Trotsky: Messages from American Universities.* Ed. Mark Edmundson. New York, 1993: 289–305.

'Border Crossings: Translating Theory.' *Selected Essays of the Third Conference on American Literature and Thought: The Literary Section.* Ed. Shan Te-hsing. Taipei, 1993: 1–27.

'Image and Word in Turner.' *Word & Image Interactions: A Selection of Papers given at the Second International Conference on Word and Image, Universität Zurich, August 19–31, 1990.* Eds. Martin Heusser, Max Nanny, Peter de Voogd, and Hans A. Luthy. Basel, 1993: 173–89.

'Is Literary Theory a Science?' *Realism and Representation: Essays on the Problem of Realism in Relation to Science, Literature, and Culture.* Ed. George Levine. Madison, 1993: 155–68.

'The Search for Grounds in Literary Study.' *Contemporary Literary Criticism.* Ed. Robert Con Davis and Ronald Schleifer. New York, 1993: 109–21.

'*Mrs. Dalloway*: Repetition as Raising of the Dead.' *'Mrs. Dalloway' and 'To the Lighthouse.'* Ed. Sue Reid. London, 1993: 45–56.

'The Genres of A Christmas Carol.' *The Dickensian,* 89: 431 (Winter 1993): 193–206.

'Is Deconstruction an Aestheticism?' *Nineteenth-Century Prose* 202 (Fall 1993): 23–41.

'Nietzsche in Basel: Writing Reading.' *Journal of Advanced Composition,* 13: 2 (Fall 1993): 311–28.

'A Response to Jonathan Loesberg.' *Victorian Studies.* 37: 1 (Autumn 1993): 123–8.

'Border Crossings: Translating Theory.' *Haritham,* 1: 2 (1993): 105–25.

1992

Ariadne's Thread: Story Lines. New Haven, 1992.

Illustration. London, 1992.

'Deconstruction Now? The States of Deconstruction: Or, Thinking without Synecdoche.' *Afterwords.* Ed. Nicholas Royle. Tampere, 1992: 7–18.

'Laying Down the Law.' *Deconstruction and the Possibility of Justice.* Ed. Drucilla Cornell, Michel Rosenfeld, and David Gray Carlson. New York, 1992: 305–29.

'Theory and Translation in Comparative Literature.' *Bologna, la cultura italiana e le letterature straniere moderne.* Vol. II. Ed. Vita Fortunati. Ravenna, 1992: 31–41.

'Translation as the Double Production of Texts.' *Text and Context: Cross Disciplinary Perspectives on Language Study.* Eds. Claire Kramsch and Sally McConnell. Lexington, 1992: 124–34.

'*Wuthering Heights*: Repetition and the Uncanny.' *Wuthering Heights.* Ed. Linda Peterson. Boston, 1992: 371–84.

'Introduction' to Thomas Hardy's *Jude the Obscure*. New York, 1992: vii–xxi.
'Interlude as Anastomosis in "Die Wahlverwandtschaften".' *Goethe Yearbook* 6 (1992): 115–22.
'Literature and Value: American and Soviet Views.' *Profession* 92 (1992): 21–7.
'Responses.' *Yale Journal of Criticism*, 5: 2 (Spring 1992): 82–7.
'Temporal Topographies, Tennyson's Tears.' *Victorian Poetry*, 30: 3–4 (Fall-Winter 1992): 277–89.

1991

Hawthorne & History: Defacing It. Cambridge, 1991.
Theory Now and Then. Durham, 1991.
Victorian Subjects. Durham, 1991.
'The Role of Theory in the Development of Literary Studies in the United States.' *Divided Knowledge Across Disciplines, Across Cultures*. Eds. David Easton and Corinne Schelling. Newbury Park, 1991: 118–38.
'Literary Theory, Telecommunications, and the Making of History.' *Scholarship and Technology in the Humanities*. Ed. May Katzen. London, 1991: 11–20.
'Cultural Criticism in the Age of Digital Reproduction.' *Genre*, 24: 4 (Winter 1991): 435–59.
'Deconstruction and Cultural Criticism.' *Cardozo Law Review*, 13: 4 (December 1991): 1255–61.
'The Mirror's Secret: Dante Gabriel Rossetti's Double Work of Art.' *Victorian Poetry* 29:4 (Winter 1991): 333–49.
'Preserving the Literary Heritage.' *Commission on Preservation & Access Report* (July 1991): 1–7.

1990

Tropes, Parables, Performatives: Essays on Twentieth-Century Literature. London, 1990.
Versions of Pygmalion. Cambridge, 1990.
Victorian Subjects. New York, 1990.
'Face to Face: Plato's Protagoras as a Model for Collective Research in the Humanities.' *The States of 'Theory': History, Art, and Critical Discourse*. Ed. David Carroll. New York, 1990. 281–95.
'Laying Down the Law in Literature: The Example of Kleist.' *Cardozo Law Review*, 11: 5–6 (July-August 1990): 1491–538.
'Naming and Doing: Speech Acts in Hopkins's Poems.' *Religion & Literature*, 22: 2–3 (Summer-Fall 1990): 173–91.
'Review Essay: Translating the Untranslatable.' *Goethe Yearbook*, 5 (1990): 269–78.

1989

The Ethics of Reading: Kant, de Man, Eliot, Trollope, James, and Benjamin. New York, 1989.
'Anthony Trollope: General.' *The Critical Perspective, Volume 8: Mid-Victorian*. Ed. Harold Bloom. New York, 1989: 5002–9.
'The Function of Literary Theory at the Present Time.' *The Future of Literary Theory*. Ed. Ralph Cohen. New York, 1989: 102–11.
'Heart of Darkness Revisited.' *Joseph Conrad, The Heart of Darkness: A Case Study in Contemporary Criticism*. Ed. Ross C. Murfin. New York, 1989: 209–24.
'"Hieroglyphical Truth" in *Sartor Resartus*: Carlyle and the Language of Parable.' *Victorian Perspectives: Six Esssays*. Eds. John Clubbe and Jerome Meckier. Newark, 1989: 1–20.

'An Open Letter to Professor Jon Wiener.' *Responses on Paul de Man's Wartime Journalism*. Eds. Werner Hamacher, Neil Hertz, and Thomas Keenan. Lincoln, 1989: 334–42.

'Praeterita and the Pathetic Fallacy.' *Victorian Connections*. Ed. Jerome J. McGann. Charlottesville, 1989: 172–8.

'Prosopopoeia and Praeterita.' *Nineteenth Century Lives: Essays Presented to Jerome Hamilton Buckley*. Eds. Laurence S. Lockridge, John Maynard, and Donald D. Stone. Cambridge, 1989: 125–39.

'Prosopopoeia in Hardy and Stevens.' *Alternative Hardy*. Ed. Lance St John Butler. New York, 1989. 110–27.

'Robert Browning: "The Englishman in Italy".' *The Critical Perspective, Volume 9: Late Victorian*. Ed. Harold Bloom. New York, 1989: 5259–67.

'The Search for Grounds in Literary Study.' *Contemporary Literary Criticism: Literary and Cultural Studies,* 2nd edn. Eds. Robert Con Davis and Ronald Schleifer. New York, 1989: 566–78.

'The Search for Grounds in Literary Study.' *Literary Criticism and Theory: The Greeks to the Present*. Eds. Robert Con Davis and Laurie Finke. New York, 1989: 814–27.

'Is There an Ethics of Reading?' *Reading Narrative: Form, Ethics, Ideology*. Ed. James Phelan. Columbus, 1989: 79–101.

1988

'The Critic as Host.' *Modern American Critics Since 1955*. Ed. Gregory S. Jay. Detroit, 1988: 327–32.

'The Critic as Host.' *Modern Criticism and Theory: A Reader*. Ed. David Lodge. London, 1988: 278–85.

'The Function of Rhetorical Study at the Present Time.' *Teaching Literature: What is Needed Now*. Eds. James Engell and David Perkins. Cambridge, 1988: 87–109.

' "Reading" Part of a Paragraph in *Allegories of Reading*.' *Reading de Man Reading*. Eds. Lindsay Waters and Wlad Godzich. Minneapolis, 1988: 155–70.

'Wallace Stevens.' *Critical Essays on Wallace Stevens*. Eds. Steven Gould Axelrod and Helen Deese. Boston, 1988: 77–83.

'William Carlos Williams and Wallace Stevens.' *Columbia Literary History of the United States*. Ed. Emory Elliott. New York, 1988: 972–92.

'Literature and History: The Example of Hawthorne's "The Minister's Black Veil".' *Bulletin of the American Academy of Arts and Sciences,* 41 (February 1988): 15–31.

'NB.' *TLS.* 4446 (17, 23, June 1988): 676–85.

'Reply to Eugene Goodheart.' *PMLA* 103: 5 (October 1988): 820–1.

'Humanistic Research.' *ACLS Occasional Paper,* 6 (15 April 1988): 25–30.

1987

The Ethics of Reading: Kant, de Man, Eliot, Trollope, James, and Benjamin. New York, 1987.

'But Are Things as We Think They Are?' Review of Paul Ricoeur's *Temps et récit. Tome III: Le Temps raconté* and *Time and Narrative, Vol. 2. TLS*, 4410 (9–15 October 1987): 1104–5.

'The Dark World of Oliver Twist.' *Charles Dickens*. Ed. Harold Bloom. New York, 1987: 29–69.

'J. Hillis Miller.' *Criticism in Society: Interviews with Jacques Derrida, Northrop Frye, Harold Bloom, Geoffrey Hartman, Frank Kermode, Edward Said, Barbara Johnson, Frank Lentricchia, J. Hillis Miller*. Ed. Imre Salusinszky. London, 1987: 208–40.

'Topography and Tropography in Thomas Hardy's "In Front of the Landscape".' *Post-Structuralist Readings of English Poetry*. Eds. Richard Machin and Christopher Norris. Cambridge, 1987: 332–48.

'Theory-Example-Reading-History.' *ADE Bulletin* 88 (Winter 1987): 42–8.

'The Ethics of Reading.' *Style,* 21: 2 (Summer 1987): 181–91.

'Figure in Borges's "Death and the Compass": Red Scharlach as Hermeneut.' *Dieciocho,* 10: 1 (Spring 1987): 53–62.

'The Triumph of Theory, the Resistance to Reading, and the Question of the Material Base.' *PMLA: Publications of the Modern Language Association* 102: 3 (May 1987): 281–91.

'The Imperative to Teach.' *Qui Parle?* 1: 2 (Spring 1987): 1–7.

'Hillis Miller Interview.' *Magazine,* 3 (Summer 1987): 46–7.

1986

Ed., with Peter Brooks and Shoshana Felman. *The Lessons of Paul de Man.* London, 1986.

'Catachresis, Prosopopoeia, and the Pathetic Fallacy: The Rhetoric of Ruskin.' *Poetry and Epistemology: Turning Points in the History of Poetic Knowledge.* Eds. Roland Hagenbuchle and Laura Skandera. Regensburg, 1986: 398–407.

'The Critic as Host.' *Critical Theory Since 1965.* Eds. Hazard Adams and Leroy Searle. Tallahassee, 1986: 452–68.

'George Eliot.' *Nineteenth-Century Literature Criticism.* Vol. 13. Detroit, 1986: 340–2.

'Hopkins: The Linguistic Moment.' *Gerard Manley Hopkins.* Ed. Harold Bloom. New York, 1986: 147–62.

'Impossible Metaphor: Stevens's "The Red Fern" as Example.' *The Lessons of Paul de Man.* Eds. J. Hillis Miller, Peter Brooks and Shoshana Felman. London, 1986: 150–62.

'In Memoriam.' *The Lessons of Paul de Man.* Eds. J. Hillis Miller, Peter Brooks, and Shoshana Felman. London, 1986: 3–4

'*Troilus and Cressida.'* *Shakespearean Criticism.* Vol. 3. Detroit, 1986: 635–8.

'When Is a Primitive like an Orb?' *Textual Analysis: Some Readers Reading.* Ed. Mary Ann Caws. New York, 1986: 167–81.

'William Shakespeare: Tragedies: *Troilus and Cressida.'* *The Critical Perspective, Volume 2: Spenser and Shakespeare.* Ed. Harold Bloom. New York, 1986: 1081–6

'Yeats: The Linguistic Moment.' *William Butler Yeats.* Ed. Harold Bloom. New York, 1986: 189–210.

'J. Hillis Miller.' *A Recent Imagining: Interviews with Harold Bloom, Geoffrey Hartman, J. Hillis Miller, Paul de Man.* Ed. Robert Moynihan. Hamden, 1986: 97–131.

'On Edge: The Crossways of Contemporary Criticism.' With 'Postscript 1984.' With 'Questions and Answers.' *Romanticism and Contemporary Criticism.* Eds. Morris Eaves and Michael Fischer. Ithaca, 1986: 96–126.

'[Point of View].' *Thomas Hardy.* **Far from the Maddening Crowd**: An Authoritative Text, Backgrounds, Criticism. Ed. Robert C. Schweik. New York, 1986: 393–400.

'An Explanation and an Example of a Deconstructionist Reading.' *Orange County Register* (22 February 1986): A20.

'Is There an Ethics of Reading?' *English Literary Society* [Tokyo] (1986): 2–25.

'President's Column: The Future for the Study of Languages and Literatures.' *MLA Newsletter* (Winter 1986): 3–4.

'President's Column: Responsibility and the Joy of Reading.' *MLA Newsletter,* 18: 1 (Spring 1986): 2.

'President's Column: Responsibility and the Joy of Teaching.' *MLA Newsletter,* 18: 2 (Summer 1986): 2.

'President's Column: The Obligation to Write.' *MLA Newsletter* 18: 3 (Fall 1986): 4–5.

'The Future for the Study of Languages and Literatures.' *MLA Newsletter* 18: 4 (Winter 1986): 3–4.

'How Deconstruction Works.' *New York Times Magazine* (9 February 1986): 25.

1985

The Linguistic Moment: From Wordsworth to Stevens. Princeton, 1985.

Ed., with Peter Brooks and Shoshana Felman. *The Lessons of Paul de Man*. New Haven, 1985.

'Charles Dickens.' *Nineteenth-Century Literature Criticism*. Vol. 8. Detroit, 1985, 200–1.

'Dismembering and Disremembering in Nietzsche's "On Truth and Lies in a Non-Moral Sense".' *Why Nietzsche Now?* Ed. Daniel O'Hara. Bloomington, 1985: 41–54.

'Friedrich (Wilhelm) Nietzsche.' *Twentieth-Century Literature Criticism*. Vol. 18. Detroit, 1985: 346–9.

'Heart of Darkness Revisited.' Ed. Ross C. Murfin. *Conrad Revisited: Essays for the Eighties.* Tuscaloosa, 1985: 31–50.

'Impossible Metaphor: Stevens's "The Red Fern" as Example.' *The Lessons of Paul de Man*. Eds. J. Hillis Miller, Peter Brooks, and Shoshana Felman. New Haven, 1985: 150–62.

'In Memoriam.' *The Lessons of Paul de Man*. Eds. J. Hillis Miller, Peter Brooks, and Shoshana Felman. New Haven, 1985: 3–4.

'Joseph Conrad: Lord Jim.' *Twentieth-Century British Literature*. Vol. 1. Ed. Harold Bloom. New York, 1985: 386–7.

Panelist, with Barbara Johnson and Louis Mackey. 'Marxism and Deconstruction: Symposium at the Conference of Contemporary Genre Theory and the Yale School 1 June 1984.' *Rhetoric and Form: Deconstruction at Yale*. Eds. Robert Con Davis and Ronald Schleifer. Norman, 1985: 75–97.

'The Search for Grounds in Literary Study.' *Rhetoric and Form: Deconstruction at Yale*. Eds. Robert Con Davis and Ronald Schliefer. Norman, 1985: 19–36.

'Stevens' Rock and Criticism as Cure.' *Wallace Stevens*. Ed. Harold Bloom. New York, 1985: 75–95.

'Topography and Tropography in Thomas Hardy's "In Front of the Landscape".' *Identity of the Literary Text*. Eds. Mario J. Valdes and Owen Miller. Int. Jonathan Culler. Toronto, 1985: 73–91.

'The Two Rhetorics: George Eliot's Bestiary.' *Writing and Reading Differently: Deconstruction and the Teaching of Composition and Literature*. Eds. G. Douglas Atkins and Michael L. Johnson. Lawrence, 1985: 101–14.

'Walter Pater: A Partial Portrait.' *Walter Pater*. Ed. Harold Bloom. New York, 1985: 75–95.

'Impossible Metaphor: Stevens's "The Red Fern" as Example.' *Yale French Studies*, 69 (1985): 150–62.

'Gleichnis in Nietzsche's "Also Sprach Zarathustra".' *International Studies in Philosophy*, 17: 2 (1985): 3–15.

'In Memoriam.' *Yale French Studies*, 69 (1985): 3–4.

1984

'Theology and Logology in Victorian Literature.' *American Critics at Work: Examinations of Contemporary Literary Theories*. Ed. Victor A. Kramer. Troy, 1984: 193–209.

'Thomas Hardy, Jacques Derrida, and the "Dislocation of Souls".' *Taking Chances: Derrida, Psychoanalysis and Literature*. Eds. Joseph H. Smith and William Kerrigan. Baltimore, 1984: 135–45

'Constructions in Criticism.' *Boundary, 2* 12: 3 & 13: 1 (Spring-Fall 1984): 157–72.

'Introduction' to 'Interview with Paul de Man' by Robert Moynihan. *Yale Review*, 73: 4 (Summer 1984): 576–602.

Panelist, with Barbara Johnson and Louis Mackey. 'Marxism and Deconstruction: Symposium at the Conference of Contemporary Genre Theory at the Yale School June 1984.' *Genre*, 17: 1–2 (Spring-Summer, 1984): 75–97.

'The Search for Grounds in Literary Study.' *Genre*, 17: 1–2 (Spring-Summer, 1984): 19–36.

1983

'Composition and Decomposition: Deconstruction and the Teaching of Writing.' *Composition and Literature*. Ed. Winifred B. Horner. Chicago, 1983: 38–56.

' "Herself against Herself": The Clarification of Clara Middleton.' *The Representation of Women in Fiction*. Eds. Carolyn G. Heilbrun and Margaret R. Higonnet. Baltimore, 1983: 98–123.

'Mr. Carmichael and Lily Briscoe: The Rhythm of Creativity in *To the Lighthouse.*' Eds. Robert Kiely and John Hildebidle. *Modernism Reconsidered*. Cambridge, 1983: 167–89.

'Thomas De Quincey.' *Nineteenth-Century Literature Criticism*. Vol. 4, Detroit, 1983: 82–4.

'The Two Relativisms: Point of View and Indeterminacy in the Novel: *Absalom, Absalom!*' *Relativism in the Arts*. Ed. Betty Jean Craige. Athens, 1983: 148–70.

'Interview with J. Hillis Miller.' *PN Review*, 9: 6 (1983): 32–4.

1982

Fiction and Repetition: Seven English Novels. Cambridge, 1982.

'From Narrative Theory to Joyce: From Joyce to Narrative Theory.' *The Seventh of Joyce*. Ed. Bernard Benstock. Bloomington, 1982: 3–4.

'Parable and Performative in the Gospels and in Modern Literature.' *Humanizing America's Iconic Book*. Eds. Gene M. Tucker and Douglas A. Knight. Chico, 1982: 57–71.

'The Interpretation of Otherness.' Review of Giles Gunn's *The Interpretation of Otherness: Literature, Religion, and the American Imagination. Journal of Religion*, 62: 3 (July 1982): 299–304.

'Interview with J. Hillis Miller, Yale, Fall 1979.' *Criticism* 24: 2 (Spring 1982): 99–125.

'Hommage à Georges Poulet.' *MLN*, 97: 5 (December 1982): viii–ix.

'Trollope's Thackeray.' *Nineteenth-Century Fiction*, 37: 3 (December 1982): 350–7.

1981

'Character in the Novel: A Real Illusion.' *From Smollett to James: Studies in the Novel and Other Essays Presented to Edgar Johnson*. Eds. Samuel I. Mintz, Alice Chandler, and Christopher Mulvey. Charlottesville, 1981: 277–85.

'The Ethics of Reading: Vast Gaps and Parting Hours.' *American Criticism in the Poststructuralist Age*. Ed. Ira Konigsberg. Ann Arbor, 1981: 19–41.

'The Two Allegories.' *Allegory, Myth, and Symbol*. Ed. Morton W. Bloomfield. Cambridge, 1981: 355–70.

'Introduction' to Anthony Trollope's *Cousin Henry*. Ed. John H. Hall. New York, 1981: v–xiii.

'Thomas Hardy.' *Twentieth-Century Literature Criticism*, Vol. 4. Detroit, 1981: 174.

'Introduction' to Anthony Trollope's *Lady Anna*. Ed. John H. Hall. New York, 1981: v–xiv.

'A Plenitude of Genuine Poetry.' Review of Justus George Lawler's *Celestial Pantomine: Poetic Structures of Transcendence. Commonweal* 108: 19 (23 October 1981): 601–4.

'Topography in *The Return of the Native.*' *Essays in Literature*, 8: 2 (Fall 1981): 119–34.

'The Disarticulation of the Self in Nietzsche.' *Monist* 64: 2 (April 1981): 247–61.

'Dismembering and Disremembering in Nietzsche's "On Truth and Lies in a Nonmoral Sense" .' *Boundary 2*, 9: 3 & 10: 1 (Spring-Fall 1981): 41–54.

1980

'Wallace Stevens.' *Twentieth-Century Literature Criticism*, Vol. 3. Detroit, 1980: 468–9.

'The Rewording Shell: Natural Image and Symbolic Emblem in Yeats's Early Poetry.' *Poetic*

Knowledge: Circumference and Centre. Eds. Roland Hagenbuechle and Joseph T. Swann. Bonn, 1980: 75–86.

'Theoretical and Atheoretical in Stevens.' *Wallace Stevens: A Celebration.* Eds. Frank A. Doggett and Robert Buttell. Princeton, 1980: 274–85.

'Theory and Practice: Response to Vincent Leitch.' *Critical Inquiry,* 6: 4 (Summer 1980): 609–14.

Response to Vincent B. Leitch's 'The Lateral Dance: The Deconstructive Criticism of J. Hillis Miller.' *Critical Inquiry,* 6: 4 (Summer 1980): 593–608.

'*Wuthering Heights* and the Ellipses of Interpretation.' *Notre Dame English Journal,* 12: 2 (April 1980): 85–100.

'The Figure in the Carpet.' *Poetics Today,* 1: 3 (Spring 1980): 107–18.

'A Guest in the House: Reply to Shlomith Rimmon-Kenan's Reply.' *Poetics Today,* 2: 1b (Winter 1980–81): 189–91.

'On Shlomith Rimmon-Kenan's "Deconstructive Reflections on Deconstruction: in Reply to Hillis Miller".' *Poetics Today,* 2: 1b (Winter 1980–81): 185–8.

'Master Mariner of the Imagination.' Review of Ian Watt's *Conrad in the Nineteenth Century. Washington Post* Book World 10: 14 (6 April, 1980): 1–8.

'*Middlemarch.* Chapter 85: Three Commentaries.' *Nineteenth-Century Fiction,* 35: 3 (December 1980): 432–53.

1979

Reprint with a new preface of *The Form of Victorian Fiction: Thackeray, Dickens, Trollope, George Eliot, Meredith and Hardy.* Cleveland, 1979.

'Burke, Kenneth.' *International Encyclopedia of the Social Sciences.* Biographical Supplement Vol. 18. New York, 1979: 78–81.

'The Critic as Host.' *Deconstruction and Criticism.* Eds. Harold Bloom et al. New York, 1979: 217–53.

'A "Buchstabliches" Reading of The Elective Affinities.' *Glyph #6: Johns Hopkins Textual Studies.* Eds. Rodolphe Gasché, Carole Jacobs, and Henry Sussman. Baltimore, 1979: 1–23.

'The Function of Rhetorical Study at the Present Time.' *ADE Bulletin,* 62 (September–November 1979): 10–18.

'On Edge: The Crossways of Contemporary Criticism.' *Bulletin of the American Academy of Arts and Sciences,* 32: 4 (January 1979): 13–32.

Review of Felicia Bonaparte's *The Triptych and the Cross: The Central Myths of George Eliot's Poetic Imagination. Notre Dame English Journal* 12: 1 (October 1979): 78–80.

'Theology and Logology in Victorian Literature.' *Journal of the American Academy of Religion,* 47: 2 (1979): 345–61.

1978

'Ariadne's Thread: Repetition and the Narrative Line.' *Interpretation of Narrative: Papers.* Eds. Mario J. Valdes and Owen J. Miller. Toronto, 1978: 148–66.

'Dylan Thomas.' *Twentieth-Century Literature Criticism.* Vol. 1. Detroit, 1978: 474–5.

'Joseph Conrad.' *Twentieth-Century Literature Criticism.* Vol. 1. Detroit, 1978: 213–14.

'William Butler Yeats.' *Twentieth-Century Literature Criticism.* Vol 1. Detroit, 1978: 575–8.

'Narrative Middles: A Preliminary Outline.' *Genre,* 11: 3 (Fall 1978): 375–87.

'The Problematic of Ending in Narrative.' *Nineteenth-Century Fiction,* 33: 1 (June 1978): 3–7.

Review of James R. Kincaid's *The Novels of Anthony Trollope. Yale Review,* 67: 2 (Winter 1978) [December 1979]: 276–9.

1977

'Nature and the Linguistic Moment.' *Nature and the Victorian Imagination*. Eds. U. C. Knoepflmacher and G. B. Tennyson. Berkeley, 1977: 440–51.

'[A Nightmare of Frustrated Desire].' *Thomas Hardy*. **The Mayor of Casterbridge**: An Authoritative Text, Backgrounds, Criticism. Ed. James K. Robinson. New York, 1977: 413–15.

'Optic and Semiotic in *Middlemarch*.' *The Worlds of Victorian Fiction*. Ed. Jerome H. Buckley. Cambridge, 1977: 125–45.

'Ariachne's Broken Woof.' *Georgia Review* 31: 1 (Spring 1977): 44–60.

'The Critic as Host.' *Critical Inquiry*, 3: 3 (Spring 1977): 439–47.

1976

'The Linguistic Moment in "The Wreck of the Deutschland".' *The New Criticism and After*. Ed. Thomas D. Young. Charlottesville, 1976: 47–60.

'Ariadne's Thread: Repetition and the Narrative Line.' *Critical Inquiry*, 3: 1 (Autumn 1976): 57–77.

'Beginning with a Text.' Review of Edward W. Said's *Beginnings*. *Diacritics*, 6: 3 (Fall 1976): 2–7.

'Stevens' Rock and Criticism as Cure (Part I).' *Georgia Review*, 30: 1 (Spring 1976): 5–31.

'Stevens' Rock and Criticism as Cure (Part II).' *Georgia Review*, 30: 2 (Summer 1976): 330–48.

'The Truth about Trollope.' Review of C .P. Snow's *Trollope: His Life and Art*. *Yale Review*, 65: 3 (March 1976): 450–5.

'Walter Pater: A Partial Portrait.' *Daedalus*, 105: 1 (Winter 1976): 97–113.

1975

Reissue with new preface. *The Disappearance of God: Five Nineteenth-Century Writers*. Cambridge, 1975.

'Fiction and Repetition: *Tess of the d'Urbervilles*.' *Forms of Modern British Fiction*. Ed. Alan Warren Friedman. Austin, 1975: 43–71.

With James Cowan, James Gindin, Charles Rossman, Avrom Fleishman and John Unterecker. 'Panel Discussion.' *Forms of Modern British Fiction*. Ed. Alan Warren Friedman. Austin, 1975: 201–32

'Introduction' to Thomas Hardy's *The Well-Beloved: A Sketch of Temperament*. London, 1975: 11–21.

'Optic and Semiotic in *Middlemarch*.' *The Worlds of Victorian Fiction*. Ed. Jerome H. Buckley. Cambridge, 1975: 125–45.

'Literature and Religion.' *Religion and Modern Literature: Essays in Theory and Criticism*. Eds. G. B. Tennyson and Edward E. Ericson, Jr. Grand Rapids, 1975: 31–45.

'Books Considered.' Review of Reed Whittemore's *William Carlos Williams: Poet from Jersey*. *New Republic*, 173: 16 [3171] (18 October 1975): 23–5.

'Deconstructing the Deconstructors.' Review of Joseph N. Riddel's *The Inverted Bell*. *Diacritics*, 5: 2 (Summer 1975): 24–31.

'Myth as "Hieroglyph" in Ruskin.' *Studies in the Literary Imagination* 8: 2 (Fall 1975): 15–18.

'The Year's Books: On Literary Criticism.' *New Republic*, 173: 22 (November 29, 1975): 30–3.

1974

'Narrative and History.' *ELH: A Journal of English Literary History*, 41: 3 (Fall 1974): 455–73.

1972

'History as Repetition in Thomas Hardy's Poetry: The Example of "Wessex Heights".' *Victorian Poetry*. Eds. Malcolm Bradbury and David Palmer. London, 1972: 222–53.

'The Stone and the Shell: The Problem of Poetic Form in Wordsworth's "Dream of the Arab".' *Mouvements premiers: Études critiques offertes à Georges Poulet*. Paris, 1972: 125–47.

'Tradition and Difference.' Review of M. H. Abrams' *Natural Supernaturalism*. *Diacritics*, 2: 4 (Winter 1972): 6–13.

1971

Ed., and foreword. *Aspects of Narrative: Selected Papers from the English Institute*. New York, 1971: Foreword, v–vii.

Ed., with David Borowitz. *Charles Dickens and George Cruikshank*. Los Angeles, 1971.

'The Fiction of Realism: *Sketches by Boz, Oliver Twist*, and Cruikshank's Illustrations.' Ed., with David Borowitz. *Charles Dickens and George Cruikshank*. Los Angeles, 1971: 1–69.

'The Fiction of Realism: *Sketches by Boz, Oliver Twist*, and Cruikshank's Illustrations.' *Dickens Centennial Essays*. Eds. Ada Nisbet and Blake Nevius. Berkeley, 1971: 85–113

'Georges Poulet's "Criticism of Identification".' *The Quest for Imagination: Essays in Twentieth-Century Aesthetic Criticism*. Ed. O. B. Hardison, Jr. Cleveland, 1971: 191–224.

'*Our Mutual Friend*.' *The Victorian Novel: Modern Essays in Criticism*. Ed. Ian Watt. New York, 1971: 123–32.

'Introduction' to Charles Dickens' *Bleak House*. Ed. by Norman Page. Harmondsworth, 1971: 11–34.

'The Still Heart: Poetic Form in Wordsworth.' *New Literary History*, 2: 2 (Winter 1971): 297–310.

1970

Thomas Hardy: Distance and Desire. Cambridge, 1970.

'Virginia Woolf's All Souls' Day: The Omniscient Narrator in *Mrs. Dalloway*.' *The Shaken Realist: Essays in Modern Literature in Honor of Frederick J. Hoffman*. Eds. Melvin J. Friedman and John B. Vickery. Baton Rouge, 1970: 100–27.

'The Geneva School: The Criticism of Marcel Raymond, Albert Béguin, Georges Poulet, Jean Rousset, Jean-Pierre Richard, and Jean Starobinski.' *Modern French Criticism: From Proust and Valery to Structuralism*. Ed. John K. Simon. Chicago, 1970: 277–310.

'The Interpretation of Lord Jim.' *The Interpretation of Narrative: Theory and Practice*. Ed. Morton W. Bloomfield. Cambridge, 1970: 211–28.

'Recent Studies in the Nineteenth Century. Part II.' *Studies in English Literature 1500–1900*, 10: 1 (Winter 1970): 183–214.

'The Sources of Dickens's Comic Art: From *American Notes* to *Martin Chuzzlewit*.' *Nineteenth-Century Fiction*, 24: 4 (March 1970): 467–76.

'Williams' "Spring and All" and the Progress of Poetry.' *Daedalus*, 99: 2 (Winter 1970): 405–34.

'Geneva or Paris? The Recent Work of Georges Poulet.' *University of Toronto Quarterly*, 39: 3 (April 1970): 212–28.

1969

Poets of Reality: Six Twentieth-Century Writers. New York, 1969.

Charles Dickens: The World of His Novels. Bloomington, 1969.

'An Exercise in Discrimination.' Review of Helen Hennessy's *On Extended Wings: Wallace Stevens' Longer Poems. Yale Review* 59: 2 (Winter 1970) [December 1969]: 281–9

'Howe on Hardy's Art.' Review of Irving Howe's *Thomas Hardy. Novel,* 2: 3 (Spring 1969): 272–7.

'Recent Studies in the Nineteenth Century.' *Studies in English Literature 1500–1900,* 9: 4 (Autumn 1969): 737–53.

1968

The Form of Victorian Fiction: Thackeray, Dickens, Trollope, George Eliot, Meredith and Hardy. Notre Dame, 1968.

'Three Problems of Fictional Form: First Person Narration in *David Copperfield* and *Huckleberry Finn.' Experience in the Novel.* Ed. Roy Harvey Pearce. New York, 1968: 21–48.

' "Wessex Heights": The Persistence of the Past in Hardy's Poetry.' *Critical Quarterly,* 10: 4 (Winter 1968): 339–59.

'William Carlos Williams: The Doctor as Poet.' *Plexus,* 3: 4 (June 1968): 19–20.

1967

'Dickens, Charles John Huffam.' *The New Catholic Encyclopedia.* Vol. 4. New York, 1967: 856–7.

'The Geneva School: The Criticism of Marcel Raymond, Albert Béguin, Georges Poulet, Jean Rousset, Jean-Pierre Richard, and Jean Starobinski.' *Virginia Quarterly Review,* 43: 3 (Summer 1967): 465–88.

'Literature and Religion.' *Relations of Literary Study: Essays on Interdisciplinary Contributions.* Ed. James Thorpe. New York, 1967: 111–26.

'Some Implications of Form in Victorian Fiction.' *Mansions of the Spirit: Essays in Religion and Literature.* Ed. George Panichas. New York, 1967: 200–12.

'Thomas Hardy: A Sketch for a Portrait.' *De Ronsard à Breton: Recueil d'essais, hommages à Marcel Raymond.* Paris, 1967: 195–206.

'Recent Work on Hardy.' *Victorian Studies,* 10: 3 (March 1967): 278–82.

1966

Poets of Reality: Six Twentieth-Century Writers. London, 1966.

Ed., and Introduction. *William Carlos Williams: A Collection of Critical Essays.* Englewood Cliffs, 1966: 1–14.

'Action on the Inner Stage.' Review of Louis L. Martz's *The Poem of the Mind: Essays on Poetry English and American.Virginia Quarterly Review,* 42: 4 (Autumn 1966): 653–6.

'The Antitheses of Criticism: Reflections on the Yale Colloquium.' *MLN,* 81: 5 (December 1966): 557–71.

'The Geneva School: The Criticism of Marcel Raymond, Albert Béguin, Georges Poulet, Jean Rousset, Jean-Pierre Richard, and Jean Starobinski.' *Critical Quarterly,* 8: 4 (Winter 1966): 305–21.

Review of Nathan A. Scott Jr.'s *Forms of Extremity in the Modern Novel. Journal of Religion,* 46: 3 (July 1966): 422.

'Some Implications of Form in Victorian Fiction.' *Comparative Literature Studies*, 3: 2 (1966): 109–18.

1965

The Disappearance of God: Five Nineteenth-Century Writers. New York, 1965.
Poets of Reality: Six Twentieth-Century Writers. Cambridge, 1965.
Ed., with Roy Harvey Pearce. *The Act of the Mind: Essays on the Poetry of Wallace Stevens*. Baltimore, 1965.

1964

'Afterword' to Charles Dickens' *Our Mutual Friend*. New York, 1964: 901–11.
'Mark Spilka, *Dickens and Kafka*.' Review of Mark Spilka's *Dickens and Kafka: A Mutual Interpretation*. *Nineteenth-Century Fiction*, 18: 4 (March 1964): 404–7.
Review of Earle Davis' *The Flint and the Flame: The Artistry of Charles Dickens*. *JEGP*, 63: 3 (July 1964): 534–6
'Some Implications of Form in Victorian Fiction.' *Mansions of the Spirit: Essays in Religion and Literature*. Ed. G. A. Panichas. New York, 1964: 200–12.
'Wallace Stevens' Poetry of Being.' *ELH*, 31: 1 (March 1964): 86–105.

1963

The Disappearance of God: Five Nineteenth-Century Writers. London, 1963.
Review of Samuel Hynes. *The Pattern of Hardy's Poetry*. *Sewanee Review*, 71: 1 (Winter 1963): 107–9.
'The Theme of the Disappearance of God in Victorian Poetry.' *Victorian Studies*, 6: 3 (March 1963): 207–27.
'The Literary Criticism of Georges Poulet.' *MLN*, 78: 5 (December 1963): 471–88.

1962

'Introduction' to Charles Dickens' *Oliver Twist*. New York, 1962.
With others. *Dickens Criticism: Past, Present, and Future Directions*. Charles Dickens Research Center, 1962.
Review of D.G. James. *Matthew Arnold and the Decline of English Romanticism*. *College English* 24:1 (October 1962): 71.

1961

'"Orion" in "The Wreck of the Deutschland".' *MLN* 76:6 (June 1961): 509–14.
Review of A. O. J. Cockshut. *The Imagination of Charles Dickens*. *Victorian Studies* 5:2 (September 1961): 174–176.

1960

'The Anonymous Walkers.' *Nation* 190:17 (April 23, 1960): 351–4.

1959

'K. J. Fielding's *Charles Dickens.*' Review of K. J. Fielding. *Charles Dickens: A Critical Introduction Nineteenth-Century Fiction,* 14: 2 (September 1959): 178–82.

1958

Charles Dickens: The World of His Novels. Cambridge, 1958.
Review of Kenneth A. Lohf and Eugene P. Sheehy. *Conrad at Mid-Century: Editions and Studies, 1895–1955. MLN,* 73:1 (February 1958): 131–2.

1957

'Franz Kafka and the Metaphysics of Alienation.' *The Tragic Vision and the Christian Faith.* Ed. Nathan A. Scott. New York, 1957: 281–305.

1956

'Baird's *Ishmael.*' Review of James Baird's *Ishmael. Journal of the History of Ideas,* 17: 4 (October 1956): 555–60.

1955

'The Creation of the Self in Gerard Manley Hopkins.' *ELH,* 22: 1 (March 1955): 293–319.

1952

'D. H. Lawrence: The Fox and the Perspective Glass.' *Harvard Advocate,* 137 (December 1952): 14–16, 26–8.

J. Hillis Miller: a Brief Professional Chronology

Education

Oberlin College, BA Summa Cum Laude 1948
Harvard University, MA 1949, PhD 1952

Principal Teaching Positions

Teaching Fellow in English, Harvard University, 1950–52
Instructor in English, Williams College, 1952–53
Assistant Professor of English, The Johns Hopkins University, 1953–59
Associate Professor of English, The Johns Hopkins University, 1959–63
Professor of English, The Johns Hopkins University, 1963–67
Professor of English and Humanistic Studies, The Johns Hopkins University, 1967–72
Chairman, Department of English, The Johns Hopkins University, 1964–67
Chairman, Humanities Group, The Johns Hopkins University, 1963–67
Academic Council, The Johns Hopkins University, 1964–65; 1966–72
Ward-Phillips Lecturer, Notre Dame University, 1967
Professor of English, Yale University, 1972–75
Director of the Literature Major, Yale University, 1973–74; 1980–83
Gray Professor of Rhetoric, Yale University, 1975–76
Frederick W. Hilles Professor of English, Yale University, 1976–79
Frederick W. Hilles Professor of English and Comparative Literature, Yale University, 1979–86
UCI Distinguished Professor, University of California at Irvine, 1986–

Fellowships, Awards, and Honors

Phi Beta Kappa, 1948
Fellow of Society for Religion in Higher Education (Kent Fellow), 1949
Research grant, American Philosophical Society, 1964
Guggenheim Fellowships, 1959–60; 1965–66
E. Harris Harbison Award for Distinguished Teaching (The Danforth Foundation), 1968
Member of Modern Language Association (Research Committee, 1968–69; Executive Council, 1970–73; PMLA Editorial Board, 1975–77; 2nd Vice-President, 1984; 1st Vice-President, 1985; President, 1986)
English Institute (Supervising Committee, 1968–70; Chairman, 1970)
Fellow of American Academy of Arts and Sciences, 1970
Fellow of Center for the Humanities, Wesleyan University, 1971
Trustee, Keuka College, 1971–80
National Endowment for the Humanities Senior Fellow, 1975, 1986

New England College English Association, President 1975–76
College English Association, Board of Directors, 1977–80
Phi Beta Kappa Lecturer, 1977–78
Honorary Degree, Doctor of Letters, University of Florida, Gainesville, 1980
Carnegie Fellow, University of Edinburgh, January-June, 1981
Visiting Professor of English, Emory University, Spring Term, 1982
Honorary Degree, Doctor of Humane Letters, Bucknell University, 1983
Regional Director, Mellon Graduate Fellowships
Fellow, Whitney Humanities Center, Yale University 1983–86
Honorary Fellow, Stanford Humanities Center
Fulbright Fellow, Autonomous University of Barcelona, March, 1990
University of California Distinguished Faculty Lectureship, 1991–92
University of Washington Walker-Ames Visiting Professorship, 1992
Doctor Honoris Causa of the University of Zaragoza, 1993
Harry Levin Prize of the American Comparative Literature, Association for Illustration, 1993
Honorary Professor of Peking University, 1994
Member, American Philosophical Society, 2004

Contributors

Thomas Albrecht is Assistant Professor of English at Tulane University. He studied with J. Hillis Miller in the Comparative Literature Program at the University of California, Irvine.

Derek Attridge is Professor of English at the University of York. His books include *Peculiar Language: Literature as Difference from the Renaissance to James Joyce* (1988; reissued, 2004); *Joyce Effects: On Language, Theory, and History* (2000); *The Singularity of Literature* (2004); and *J. M. Coetzee and the Ethics of Reading: Literature in the Event* (2004). He edited *Acts of Literature*, a selection of Jacques Derrida's writing (1992).

Mieke Bal is Professor of Theory and Literature at the University of Amsterdam. She has written and edited more than twenty books. Among her most recent publications are *Louise Bourgeois' Spider: The Architecture of Art-Writing* (2001) and *Travelling Concepts in the Humanities: A Rough Guide* (2002), which was awarded the Amsterdam School for Cultural Analysis Book Award (2003).

Megan Becker-Leckrone is Assistant Professor of English at the University of Nevada, Las Vegas, where she teaches literary theory and nineteenth- and twentieth-century British Literature. She is the author of *Julia Kristeva and Literary Theory* (2004). Her essays on Wordsworth, Wilde, Pater, psychoanalytic and feminist theory have appeared in *NLH*, *MLN*, and elsewhere.

Rachel Bowlby was supervised by Hillis Miller for her PhD in Comparative Literature at Yale University. She is Northcliffe Chair of Modern English Literature at University College London. Her books include *Just Looking: Consumer Culture in Dreiser, Gissing and Zola*, *Still Crazy After All These Years*, *Shopping with Freud*, *Feminist Destinations and Further Essays on Virginia Woolf*, and *Carried Away: The Invention of Modern Shopping*.

Barbara L. Cohen is Director of HumaniTech in the School of Humanities at the University of California, Irvine. She is the author of a number of articles on the intersection of humanities and technology and co-editor of *Material Events* with

Tom Cohen, J. Hillis Miller, and Andrzej Warminski. She was formerly a senior editor and French instructor and translator.

Tom Cohen, Professor of Literary and Media Studies in the English Department at the University at Albany, SUNY, is author of *Anti-Mimesis* (1994), *Ideology and Inscription: 'Cultural Studies' after Benjamin, Bakhtin, and de Man* (1998), and two forthcoming volumes on the aesthetic politics of cinema, *Hitchcock's Cryptonymies–Volume 1: Secret Agents* and *Volume 2: War Machines* (2004). He also co-edited *Material Events – Paul de Man and the Afterlife of Theory* (2001) and edited *Jacques Derrida and the Humanities* (2002).

Pamela K. Gilbert is Associate Professor of English at the University of Florida and editor of the series, Studies in the Long Nineteenth Century (SUNY Press). Her publications include, *Disease, Desire and the Body in Victorian Women's Popular Novels* (1997) and *Visible at a Glance* (2004), a book tracing the mapping of the social body and cholera epidemics in London and India in the mid-nineteenth century. She has co-edited, with Marlene Tromp and Aeron Haynie, *Beyond Sensation, Mary Elizabeth Braddon in Context* (2000). She has also edited the collection *Imagined Londons* (2002).

James R. Kincaid, sometime fashion model (see GQ 1943–47, *passim*) and professional jockey, is now temporarily Aerol Arnold Professor at the University of Southern California, where he has settled in happy and undetected.

John P. Leavey, Jr. is Professor and Chair of the Department of English at the University of Florida. He is the author of *Glassary* and has translated several texts of Derrida. He is currently at work on a book on occasionality within translation theory.

Juliet Flower MacCannell is Professor Emerita of English and Comparative Literature at the University of California, Irvine. She is the author of a number of critical books, including *Figuring Lacan* (1986), *The Regime of the Brother* (1991), and *The Hysteric's Guide to the Future Female Subject* (2000). In addition, she has edited or co-edited several critical collections, including *Thinking Bodies* (1994), *Feminism and Psychoanalysis: A Critical Dictionary* (1992) and *The Other Perspective in Gender and Culture* (1990). She is currently at work on critical reflections on space in art, film, and literature.

Arkady Plotnitsky is Professor of English and Director of the Theory and Cultural Studies Program at Purdue University. His most recent books are *The Knowable and the Unknowable: Modern Science, Nonclassical Thought, the 'Two Cultures'* (2002) and a collection of essays, *Idealism Without Absolute: Philosophy and Romantic Culture,* co-edited with Tilottama Rajan (2003). His book *Reading*

Bohr: Physics and Philosophy is scheduled to appear in 2004–5. He is currently completing a book-length project on British Romanticism, *Minute Particulars: Romanticism, Science, and Epistemology.*

Nicholas Royle is Professor of English at the University of Sussex. His books include *Telepathy and Literature: Essays on the Reading Mind* (1991), *After Derrida* (1995), *The Uncanny* (2003), *Jacques Derrida* (2003), and (with Andrew Bennett) *An Introduction to Literature, Criticism and Theory* (3rd edn, 2004). He is editor of *Deconstructions: A User's Guide* (2000) and joint editor of the *Oxford Literary Review.*

Julian Wolfreys is Professor of English at the University of Florida. His books include *Occasional Deconstructions* (2004), *Writing London Vol. II: Memory, Spectrality, Materiality* (2004), and *Thinking Difference: Critics in Conversation* (2004). He is the editor of an edition of Richard Marsh's novel, *The Beetle* (2004), and *Glossalalia* (2003).

Index